Sport and Exercise Psychology

BPS Textbooks in Psychology

BPS Wiley presents a comprehensive and authoritative series covering everything a student needs in order to complete an undergraduate degree in psychology. Refreshingly written to consider more than North American research, this series is the first to give a truly international perspective. Written by the very best names in the field, the series offers an extensive range of titles from introductory level through to final year optional modules, and every text fully complies with the BPS syllabus in the topic. No other series bears the BPS seal of approval!

Many of the books are supported by a companion website, featuring additional resource materials for both instructors and students, designed to encourage critical thinking, and providing for all your course lecturing and testing needs.

For other titles in this series, please go to http://psychsource.bps.org.uk

Sport and Exercise Psychology

PRACTITIONER CASE STUDIES

EDITED BY

STEWART COTTERILL
University of Winchester

NEIL WESTON
University of Portsmouth

GAVIN BRESLIN
Ulster University

WILEY

This edition first published 2017 by the British Psychological Society and John Wiley & Sons, Ltd.

Registered Office
John Wiley & Sons Ltd, The Atrium, Southern Gate, Chichester, West Sussex, PO19 8SQ, UK

Editorial Offices
350 Main Street, Malden, MA 02148-5020, USA
9600 Garsington Road, Oxford, OX4 2DQ, UK
The Atrium, Southern Gate, Chichester, West Sussex, PO19 8SQ, UK

For details of our global editorial offices, for customer services, and for information about how to apply for permission to reuse the copyright material in this book please see our website at www.wiley.com/wiley-blackwell.

Library of Congress Cataloging-in-Publication Data

Names: Cotterill, Stewart, editor. | Breslin, Gavin, editor.
Title: Sport and Exercise Psychology : practitioner case studies/edited by Stewart Cotterill, University of Winchester, Neil Weston, University of Portsmouth, Gavin Breslin, University of Ulster.
Description: Hoboken : John Wiley & Sons, Inc., 2017. | Series: BPS Textbooks in Psychology | Includes bibliographical references and index.
Identifiers: LCCN 2016006535 (print) | LCCN 2016012849 (ebook) | ISBN 9781118686522 (cloth) | ISBN 9781118686546 (paper) | ISBN 9781118686508 (pdf) | ISBN 9781118686515 (epub)
Subjects: LCSH: Sports—Psychological aspects—Case studies. | Exercise—Psychological aspects—Case studies.
Classification: LCC GV706.4 .S646 2017 (print) | LCC GV706.4 (ebook) | DDC 796.01/9—dc23
LC record available at http://lccn.loc.gov/2016006535

A catalogue record for this book is available from the British Library.

Cover image: Getty/©stefanschurr

Set in Dante MT Std 10/12 by Aptara
Printed and bound in Malaysia by Vivar Printing Sdn Bhd

1 2017

Contents

About the Contributors

Peter Aitken is the Manager of the Bristol Rovers Community Trust. He is a Welsh footballer who played nearly 300 games in the Football League. Peter is a former Gas Head, having played for Bristol Rovers for over eight years and also saw time with Bristol City, York City, Bath City, Bournemouth, Gloucester City, Trowbridge Town, and Forest Green Rovers. In his free time he is a keen golfer.

Colin Baker is a Research Fellow in the School of Sport and Exercise at the University of Gloucestershire. He has extensive applied experience of research and consultancy projects for local government, the NHS, and national sport organizations. His current research interests include sports clubs as health promotion settings, new forms of commissioning in health and factors determining partnership success in sport and physical activity.

Sian Barris is a Biomechanist with the South Australian Sports Institute, having completed her doctorate with the Australian Institute of Sport Diving Programme at the Queensland University of Technology in Brisbane. She has published research studies in biomechanics, performance analysis, and skill acquisition, and presented at national and international conferences on these topics. She currently works with multiple Olympic sports and is interested in the application of skill acquisition and biomechanics concepts in representative training environments.

Joanne Batey is a Senior Lecturer in Sport Psychology at the University of Winchester, UK. She is also a BASES Accredited Chartered Scientist. She has worked in a variety of sports with athletes of varying ages and abilities. Much of her recent applied work has been focused on working with military teams.

Abbe Brady is a Senior Lecturer in Sport and Exercise Psychology at the University of Gloucestershire. She is also a HCPC registered sport and exercise psychologist, and a BASES accredited sport and exercise scientist. She has worked with a range of amateur and professional coaches, teams and individual athletes, and parents to design and provide educational sports programmea, and/or intervention programmes and support through sport psychology. This support has transcended all levels of performance from grassroots to Paralympic/Olympic standards.

Deirdre Brennan is Professor of Physical Education and Sport at Ulster University and Director of Ulster Sports Outreach. She has extensive experience in public and community engagement using sport and physical activity. She has designed award-winning physical activity and sport interventions for a range of populations from primary-school aged children to hard-to-reach youth at risk. Her current interests are in university knowledge transfer and engaging in research designed for impact.

Gavin Breslin is a Senior Lecturer in Sport and Exercise Psychology in the Sport and Exercise Science Research Institute at Ulster University, Northern Ireland a Registered Sport and Exercise Psychologist (Health Care Professions Council) and a Chartered Psychologist (British Psychological Society).

He has extensive applied research and teaching experience in a wide range of sports at a national and international level. His current research interests include the psychology of human performance, motor learning, health behaviour change, and, physical activity and psychological wellbeing.

Anna Campbell is Reader in Clinical Exercise Science at Edinburgh Napier University. Anna is also Physical Activity Advisor to the charity Macmillan Cancer Support and Director of CanRehab which provides training courses to move research into practice with allied health professionals and fitness instructors. Her research interests include examining the physiological, functional, and psychological impact of physical activity interventions on cancer survivorship.

Fiona Chambers is the Director for Sports Studies and Physical Education in the School of Education at University College Cork. She is a Senior Lecturer in Education (Sports Studies and Physical Education). Prior to this role, she worked in the banking sector for six years and then, for 12 years taught physical education, biology, and science at secondary-school level. Fiona's main research interest is in initial and career-long professional learning for PE teachers and its impact on young people's learning in PE and sport. Fiona has a particular interest in the role of mentor education in developing the pedagogies that PE teachers need to use sport effectively to promote the health and wellbeing of pupils.

Stewart Cotterill is Head of Department for Sport and Exercise at the University of Winchester, a Registered Sport and Exercise Psychologist (HCPC), a Chartered Psychologist, and BASES accredited Sport and Exercise Scientist. He has extensive applied experience in a wide range of sports at a national and international level. Stewart is also Reader in Sport and Performance Psychology at the University of Winchester. His current research interests include the psychology of performance, leadership in sport, factors determining team performance and professional practice in sport and exercise psychology. He is also author of *Team Psychology in Sports: Theory and Practice* (2013).

Diane Crone is Professor of Exercise Science at the University of Gloucestershire. She has considerable applied experience in the design, delivery, and evaluation of health-promoting interventions in primary care and in the community. Her current research interests include the use of purposeful activity for health improvement (arts and physical activity), the role of exercise in the treatment of mental health problems, and new approaches to developing active environments across Europe.

Conor Cunningham is Research fellow in Physical Activity in the School of Medicine, Dentistry, and Biomedical Sciences at Queens University Belfast. Conor completed his PhD studies on children's physical activity and health at Ulster University.

Keith Davids is Professor of Motor Learning at the Centre for Sports Engineering Research, Sheffield Hallam University, UK and holds the position of Finnish Distinguished Professor at the University of Jyvaskyla in Finland. He has extensive experience as a researcher and consultant with high-performance sport organizations in New Zealand (NZ South Island Academy), Australia (Australian Institute of Sport, Cricket Australia, Diving Australia and the Queensland Academy of Sport), and England (English Institute of Sport). His research, in ecological dynamics, examines movement co-ordination and its acquisition with respect to individual and team-sport environments.

Chelsey Dempsey is currently a PhD candidate in the School of Sport, Health, and Exercise Science at Bangor University. She is researching the complex reciprocal relationship between self-efficacy and performance, specifically, the moderators that effect this relationship. Chelsey's other research interests include self-regulation and performance, and psychophysiological measures of effort and anxiety. Chelsey's applied work has been across a variety of sports, including professional basketball, Canadian college ice hockey, Team GB Winter Olympic squads, and elite youth swimming.

Lynne Evans is a Reader in Sport Psychology and Research Excellence Framework (REF) Co-ordinator in the Cardiff School of Sport at Cardiff Metropolitan University. For the last 20 years she has combined her commitment to high-quality research (primarily in the psychology of injuries) with her passion for applied work. She is an Associate Editor for the *Journal of Applied Sport Psychology* and an Editorial Board Member of *The Sport Psychologist*. As a BPS Chartered Sport Psychologist and Registered Sport and Exercise Psychologist (HCPC) she provides sport psychology support to a variety of national sport organizations, NGB's and high-performance athletes.

Ben Lee Fitzpatrick is a Research Associate within the School of Sport at Ulster University and a Registered Nurse specializing in acute medical care. He has worked with people with intellectual disabilities (ID) for over 15 years in various capacities and has applied experience in physical activity, sport and exercise in the community. His current research interests include physical activity levels of vulnerable groups, the relationship between physical activity and psychological wellbeing, and the barriers that prevent vulnerable people leading healthier lives.

Sandy Gordon is a Professor of Sport and Exercise Psychology at the University of Western Australia, Registered Sport Psychologist (WA), Fellow Member of the Australian Psychological Society (APS), and Member of the APS College of Sport and Exercise Psychologists (CoSEP) and Interest Group in Coaching Psychology (IGCP). His current research interests include mental toughness, psychology and sport injury, and applications of positive psychology in both health and sport settings.

Daniel Greenwood is a Senior Skill Acquisition Scientist at the Australian Institute of Sport (AIS). Daniel has worked in applied sport science settings for a decade with roles at the Singapore Sport Council and Queensland Academy of Sport before returning to the AIS in 2014. Daniel has worked at an international level with a variety of team and individual sports, including working with multiple track and field Olympic medalists at the London Olympics in 2012. His current research interests include the combination of coach and scientist knowledge to drive understanding of behaviour in applied contexts, visual regulation of performance, and the representative design of training environments.

Daniel Gucciardi is a Senior Research Fellow in the School of Physiotherapy and Exercise Science, Curtin University, Australia. He has published widely on mental toughness in sport, the most significant of these outputs being lead co-editor for the first research book and author of the mental toughness entry in the first *Encyclopedia of Sport and Exercise Psychology* (Eklund & Tenenbaum, 2014). Daniel was the co-recipient of the Australian Psychological Society Early Career Research Award for 2013.

Bruce Hale is a Professor of Kinesiology at Penn State University. He has been performance-enhancement consulting for 35 years with hundreds of athletes in junior and collegiate sports, several professional teams, and elite national teams such as USA Wrestling, British Biathlon, USA Rowing, TAC, and USA Rugby. He has published two textbooks, a dozen book chapters, and over 35 research articles in sport and exercise psychology. In the area of exercise dependence in bodybuilders, Bruce has published six articles and five chapters.

Richard Hampson is a sport psychologist working with GB Canoeing. He holds an MSc from Loughborough University, and currently works with the GB Canoe Slalom and Paracanoe teams. He has a range of applied experience including work in professional golf, windsurfing and professional football and rowing.

Chris Harwood is a Reader in Applied Sport Psychology at Loughborough University. He is a Registered Sport and Exercise Psychologist (HCPC), Chartered Psychologist, and BASES High Performance Sport Accredited Sport and Exercise Scientist. His research interests focus on the psychological aspects of youth sport with a particular focus on the psychology of parenting and coaching. A former Vice President of FEPSAC, Chris is currently the Chair of the Psychology Division for BASES. As a consultant in sport psychology, he has worked extensively with the Lawn Tennis Association, the Football Association, and several professional football clubs. He holds fellowships of both AASP and BASES for his contributions to applied sport psychology and sport science.

Kate Hefferon is a Senior Lecturer and Chartered Research Psychologist at the University of East London. She has worked on several projects aimed at understanding the links between wellbeing and physical activity within normal and clinical populations. Her research interests lie within the areas of posttraumatic growth, resilience, embodiment, physical activity, and wellbeing.

David Hendry is a doctoral candidate working in the motor skills laboratory at the University of British Columbia in Vancouver, Canada. His main research interests lie in the development of sports expertise, skill acquisition, and sports coaching. He completed his undergraduate degree in Sport Science from Edinburgh Napier University and his MSc in Kinesiology from the University of British Columbia. David has also operated as an elite level soccer coach with Glasgow Rangers FC and the Scottish FA.

Nicola Hodges is a Professor in the School of Kinesiology at the University of British Columbia in Vancouver, Canada. She runs the Motor Skills Lab. which is funded through all three tri-council agencies in Canada (CIHR, NSERC, and SSHRC). She studies processes of motor learning and control and expert performance. Her work looking at practice behaviours involves laboratory experiments and survey work with beginners and elite sports performers. She is in the High Performance Athlete Development Research group of the Canadian Olympic Sport Organization, Own-The-Podium.

Tim Holder is Senior Lecturer in Coaching and Performance at the Institute of Coaching and Performance at the University of Central Lancashire. He is an HCPC Registered Sport and Exercise Psychologist, British Psychological Society Chartered Psychologist, a Chartered Scientist, and a British Association of Sport and Exercise Sciences Accredited Sport and Exercise Scientist. Tim has worked with a number of national governing bodies of sport providing psychological support including table tennis, amateur boxing, swimming, sailing, and synchronized swimming in addition to a range of individual performers across varied individual and team sports. He has worked as a sport psychologist at two Olympic Games and numerous World and European Championships. His research interests include the use of observations in applied practice, coaching, and skill acquisition.

Sophia Jowett is a Reader in Psychology within the School of Sport, Exercise, and Health Sciences at Loughborough University. She is a BPS chartered psychologist with the Division of Sport and Exercise Psychology. Her main research interests revolve around interpersonal relationships in sport with an emphasis on coaching relationships. More recently this work has started to make an impact on other life domains including work (business, organizations) and education (primary and secondary schools). This research is orientated towards 'making a difference' through generating knowledge and understanding the effectiveness of quality relationships.

John Kremer is an Honorary Research Fellow at Queen's University Belfast where he previously lectured in Applied Psychology for over 30 years. He is a Registered Sport and Exercise Psychologist and has either co-authored and/or co-edited a number of texts in sport and exercise psychology. John continues to work with a number of teams and individuals across a wide range of sports.

Keith Lohse is an Assistant Professor in the School of Kinesiology at Auburn University in Auburn, Alabama. He is the principal investigator of the Motor Learning Laboratory and teaches courses on neuromotor control, learning, and biostatistics. His current research focuses on modelling how the dose of physical practice relates to improvements in physical therapy and the use of play/games to facilitate motor learning and rehabilitation.

Elizabeth Loughren is a Research Fellow in the School of Sport and Exercise at the University of Gloucestershire. She has extensive applied experience in health promotion interventions including workplace wellbeing and Arts-on-referral. Her current research interests include the relationship between physical activity and wellbeing, behaviour change, and the use of online technology for physical activity and health promotion.

Ruth Lowry is a Senior Lecturer in Exercise Psychology at the University of Chichester, a Registered Sport and Exercise Psychologist (HCPC), Chartered Psychologist and a Chartered Scientist. She has experience of health promotion intervention evaluation and training of fitness professionals in relation to psychological aspects of physical activity and exercise. Ruth's current research interests include the social influences on health behaviour change, motivation towards physical activity, exercise-related body image issues and the use of drumming for health and wellbeing.

John Mahoney is a doctoral researcher jointly enrolled at the School of Human Movement Studies at the University of Queensland and the School of Sport, Exercise, and Rehabilitation Sciences at the University of Birmingham, as well as a practising psychologist in Australia. He also holds lecturing positions at the Australian Catholic University and the Australian Institute for Applied Counsellors. John's key research interest regards the role of coaches in the development of mental toughness in athletes. He was also the recipient of a Young Investigators Research Grant from the Association for Applied Sport Psychology in 2013.

Andrew Manley is a Senior Lecturer in Sport and Exercise Psychology at Leeds Beckett University. He is also a Registered Sport and Exercise Psychologist with the Health and Care Professions Council, a Chartered Sport and Exercise Psychologist with the British Psychological Society, and a Fellow of the Higher Education Academy. Andrew works with athletes and coaches from a range of backgrounds and sports to enhance psychological aspects of their performance and wellbeing. His primary research examines the impact of specific sources of information (e.g., reputation, clothing) on perception and behaviour within various interpersonal relationships (e.g., coach-athlete, student-teacher, client-practitioner).

Aidan Moran is Professor of Cognitive Psychology and Director of the Psychology Research Laboratory in University College Dublin, Ireland. A Fulbright Scholar, he is the Editor-in-Chief of the

International Review of Sport and Exercise Psychology and co-author (with John Kremer) of *Pure Sport: Practical Sport Psychology* (2nd ed, Kremer & Moran, 2013). He is a former psychologist to the Irish Olympic Squad and has advised many of Ireland's leading professional athletes and teams (e.g., the Irish rugby team). His research investigates mental/motor imagery, attention (eye-tracking) and the cognitive processes underlying expertise in skilled performance.

Robert Morris is a Lecturer in Sport Social Science at Liverpool John Moores University. He is a Registered Sport and Exercise Psychologist (Health and Care Professions Council) and British Psychological Society Chartered Psychologist. Robert has worked with a number of athletes and coaches in the United Kingdom in a range of different sports including golf, football, and rugby. His research interests include athlete career transition, particularly the youth-to-senior and retirement from sport transitions, and organizational psychology and its influence on sport performers.

Colm Murphy is a PhD research student at the Centre for Sports Medicine and Human Performance at Brunel University. He holds BSc in Sport Science and Health from Dublin City University and is a certified performance tennis coach. His current research is exploring the contextual aspect of anticipation in tennis, and the perceptual-cognitive processes underlying expertise in such a skill.

Marie H. Murphy is Professor of Exercise and Health and leads the Centre for Physical Activity and Health Research (CPAHR) at Ulster University. Sheis a Fellow of the American College of Sports Medicine, the British Association of Sport and Exercise Sciences and the Higher Education Academy. Marie's research interests include the role of exercise, in particular walking, on health.

Nikos Ntoumanis is a Research Professor at the School of Psychology and Speech Pathology, Curtin University, Australia. He is a Fellow of the UK's Academy of Social Science and Associate Fellow of the British Psychological Society. He is interested in personal and contextual factors that optimize motivation and promote performance, psychological wellbeing and health-conducive behaviours in various physical activity settings (exercise, sport, physical education). He is the current Editor-in-Chief of *Psychology of Sport and Exercise*.

Susan O'Neill is a Lecturer in the School of Psychology at Queen's University, Belfast, and a Chartered Psychologist with the British Psychological Society and Division of Sport and Exercise Psychology. Susan has applied experience in sport and exercise, with a specific focus on exercise. Her current research interests include understanding the meanings given to the exercise experience and the impact of social-cultural influences on physical activity participation and performance across a range of 'minority' groups.

Chin Wei Ong is currently a PhD candidate in the School of Sport, Health and Exercise Science in Bangor University. Previously, Chin Wei worked with elite youth athletes across various sports as the principal sport psychologist at the Singapore Sports School. His research interests include the dynamic relationship between personality (primarily narcissism) and performance (leadership), psychological aspects of talent development and anti-doping in sport.

Ross Pinder is a Skill Acquisition Specialist with the Australian Paralympic Committee, and has extensive experience across a wide range of sports at national and international level. He completed a PhD in motor learning and skill acquisition before going on to hold research, lecturing, and applied roles, where he has published work in several high-quality international journals and presented at national and international conferences and coaching courses. His research interests include ecological dynamics approaches to perception and action in sport, and he is primarily interested in maximizing skill learning in sport through the use of constraints-led and representative experimental and practice designs.

Ian Renshaw is a Senior Lecturer at Queensland University of Technology. Ian has worked as a skill acquisition specialist with a number of national bodies and sports organizations. Most notable was his work with the Centre of Excellence for Cricket Australia. His current research interests include nonlinear pedagogy, ecological dynamics, decision-making in sports, sports pedagogy, and emotions in learning.

Ross Roberts is a Lecturer in Sport and Exercise Psychology and Co-director of the Institute for the Psychology of Elite Performance (IPEP) at Bangor University. He is an HCPC registered sport and exercise psychologist, an Associate Fellow of the British Psychological Society (BPS), and is accredited by the British Association of Sport and Exercise Sciences. His research interests focus on personality in relation to performance contexts and he has published in a wide range of leading personality, sport psychology, and neuroscience journals. He is also an editorial board member of *The Sport Psychologist*. In his spare time Ross likes to feed his addiction to running in the mountains of Snowdonia.

Christine Selby is an Associate Professor of Psychology at Husson University, United States, and she is a licensed psychologist who maintains a part-time private practice. She is a Certified Eating Disorder Specialist with the International Association of Eating Disorders Professionals and is a Certified Consultant with the Association for Applied Sport Psychology. Christine has published primarily in the area of eating disorders in athletes for largely non-academic audiences. She has also presented locally and nationally on eating disorders and related topics at professional conferences and to allied professionals who work directly with those dealing with eating disorders and related concerns.

Vaithehy Shanmugam is a Lecturer and Programme Director for the BSc in Sport and Exercise Psychology at University of Central Lancashire. She is a BPS chartered psychologist within the Division of Sport and Exercise Psychology and an active researcher and practitioner. Her main research interests revolve around athlete welfare. Specifically, she is interested in understanding the psychological, social, interpersonal, developmental, and environmental etiology and consequences of mental health among athletes. Areas of particular interest include eating disorders, depression, self-harm, and compulsive exercise. She has over eight years of experience working as a practitioner with a diverse range of athletes ranging in both competition level and sport type.

Dave Smith is a Senior Lecturer in Sport Psychology at Manchester Metropolitan University. He is also a British Psychological Society Chartered Psychologist and registered with the Health and Care Professions Council. Dave's research interests include exercise dependence, muscle dysmorphia, drug use, and the psychology of strength sports generally, as well as the use of psychological skills (particularly imagery) and other interventions in sport and health contexts. Dave has also appeared on radio and television all over the world to discuss his work. He has worked with athletes at all levels in various sports, with a particular interest in bodybuilding and strength sports.

Rebecca Symes is Registered Practitioner Sport Psychologist with the Health and Care Professionals Council and a chartered member of the British Psychological Society. She runs her own consultancy,

Sporting Success Ltd, working with a range of elite and professional athletes and teams. Her experience spans across a variety of sports including cricket, archery, mixed martial arts, football, and swimming. Rebecca also does a small amount of work in the corporate sector applying the principles of performance psychology.

Laurence Taggart is a Reader in the Institute of Nursing and Health Research at Ulster University. Laurence's main research interests focus on the physical and mental health of people with learning disabilities, health promotion, the needs of family carers, the training needs of carers, and service developments

Richard Thelwell is Head of the Department for Sport and Exercise Sciences at the University of Portsmouth. He has extensive applied-practitioner experience and is a Registered Practitioner Psychologist with the Health and Care Professions Council, a Chartered Psychologist of the British Psychological Society, and, an Accredited Sport and Exercise Scientist with the British Association of Sport and Exercise Sciences. His current research interests are within the area of coach psychology and in particular the themes of expectation effects, stress, emotion, coping and performance, and psychological skills and behaviour change.

David Tod is a Senior Lecturer in Sport Psychology at Liverpool John Moores University, Liverpool, England. He is a British Psychological Society Chartered Psychologist. David has worked with numerous athletes and coaches across multiple sports in New Zealand, Australia, and the United Kingdom, from weekend warriors to elite and professional performers. His research interests include athlete career transition, expertise in sport psychologists, and the relationship between identity and health behaviour.

Adam Tutton is Head of Education at the Bristol Rovers Community Trust. He leads all classroom and course-work activities for the BTEC Futsal Scholars and Foundation Degree in Community Football Coaching and Development. As a qualified head teacher for 12 years, Adam draws on vast experience to lead various courses and apply to real world settings. In his free time he travels to Cornwall with his family in search of the perfect wave.

Christopher Wagstaff is a Senior Lecturer and Course Director at the University of Portsmouth. His diverse consultancy work spans international, Olympic and Paralympic athletes, coaches and support staff, business executives, senior military officers, and emergency service personnel. He is a Chartered Psychologist and Associate Fellow of the British Psychological Society, a registered Practitioner Psychologist and Partner at the Health and Care Professions Council, and is British Association of Sport and Exercise Sciences accredited. Chris has published widely on organizational psychology in sport and is an Associate Editor of the *Journal of Applied Case Studies in Sport and Exercise Sciences*.

Neil Weston is a Principal Lecturer in Sport Psychology at the University of Portsmouth. He is also a Registered Sport and Exercise Psychologist (Health and Care Professions Council) and British Psychological Society Chartered Psychologist. Neil has worked with a number of athletes and coaches across a range of team and individual sports helping them to optimize their mindset and realize their potential. His research interests include examining the impact of psychological skills interventions upon performance and in particular investigating the psychology of human performance in extreme environments.

Mark Williams is a Professor and Head of Life Sciences at Brunel University. He is a Fellow of the European College of Sport Sciences, the British Association of Sport and Exercise Science, and the British Psychological Society. He is chartered by the British Psychological Society and is accredited by the British Association of Sport and Exercise Sciences to work in high-performance sport. He has published extensively in areas related to anticipation and decision-making, effective practice and instruction, and talent identification and development.

Tim Woodman is a Professor of Sport and Exercise Psychology and an accredited Psychologist with the British Psychological Society (BPS) and the British Association of Sport and Exercise Sciences (BASES). He is the current Director of Bangor University's School of Sport, Health, and Exercise Sciences. He has published over 50 peer-reviewed articles in the flagship journals of personality, social psychology, and sport psychology. He is an Associate Editor for *The Sport Psychologist* and is on the editorial board of *Psychology of Sport and Exercise*. When he is not working, he is often found planning his next adventure in the great outdoors.

Acknowledgements

We would like to take this opportunity to acknowledge the significant contribution made to this text by all of the individual chapter authors. We thank you all for your many hours of hard work throughout the process. We would also like to acknowledge the willingness of the clients who consented to have their experiences told and discussed. Also, thank you to everyone at Wiley for their support and guidance through the process.

Stewart
To my co-editors Neil and Gavin, thank you for all your hard work in making this vision a reality. To the stars that shine brightest in my life, my wife Karen, daughter Isabelle, and son William. I think it is time we spent a summer at the beach!

Neil
I dedicate this book to my parents for their continuous support and encouragement to pursue this highly enjoyable sport psychology career and also to my wife Sarah and three children, Tom, Daisy, and Sophie for the love and fun they bring to my life.

Gavin
I dedicate this book to my parents and six elder brothers for their unending support and encouragement in my career, my wife Emmylou for all her love and guidance, and Aoife and Erin for all the happiness they bring to my life.

About the Companion Website

This book is accompanied by a companion website:

www.wiley.com/college/hewstone.

The website includes:

- All figures/tables
- Talking heads videos
- Sample essay questions
- Links to other/further resources

Part 1 Sport and Performance Psychology

1 Introduction

Stewart Cotterill, Neil Weston, and Gavin Breslin

INTRODUCTION TO THE BOOK

The field of sport and exercise psychology has grown significantly over the last 20 years in line with a notable increase in the number of applied sport and exercise psychology practitioners globally. This growth has, in turn, driven the formalization and enhancement of sport and exercise psychologist training and qualification routes. While there is diversity in the approaches adopted in different countries and across different continents, the ultimate aim is the same, to enhance the quality of the service that we, as sport and exercise psychologists, offer to our clients and organizations.

While these developments are important for the field of sport and exercise psychology, less emphasis has been placed on sharing sport and exercise psychology practitioner experiences. In particular, it is evident that there has been a lack of discussion and dissemination of the different approaches to practice that sport and exercise psychologists have employed to meet the needs of their clients. As a consequence, in our experience trainee sport and exercise psychologists have historically not been exposed enough at a developmental level to the range of possible approaches that might be available to them. This is however changing and a number of education providers are now providing more comprehensive educational programmes for those students/practitioners interested in a career as a sport and/or exercise psychologist.

There has also recently been an encouraging increase in the volume of applied sport and exercise psychology books and peer-reviewed academic journal articles. However the detail as to the interventions employed by the practitioners and the evidence base to justify them, is still insufficient. Hence the present book seeks to overcome these limitations and provide a broad range of sport and exercise case studies covering a range of diverse approaches to practice, and crucially articulating the evidence base underpinning these approaches.

The book is designed to achieve a number of outcomes. First, it provides trainee and qualified practitioners alike with an opportunity to read a wide range of case studies detailing client initial assessment, intervention selection and implementation, as well as the consultant's reflection and evaluation of their experiences. Second, the book seeks to provide readers with an evidence-based approach to the consultancy experience through initial assessment and intervention to evaluation. Third, the book aims to provide a broad range of practitioner approaches to assessing and addressing key performance issues evident in the modern day sport and exercise environments. Finally, authors in each chapter recommend further reading for exploration if the reader is keen to develop a greater understanding of a particular approach or technique.

This book is designed to be a contemporary text, with each chapter integrating both research and applied practice in developing a coherent understanding of current knowledge, future research directions and applied implications within the field. In particular, the text explores issues pertinent to the trainee/applied practitioner/supervisor within the field, and through the use of expert commentary explores potential solutions to many of these key issues.

The specific aims of this book are to:

- Present a range of case studies examining how sport psychology practitioners initially assess the needs of their client(s), in addition to how they approach an intervention to improve the client's situation.
- Provide an evidence-based approach to solving client problems while also allowing practitioners the scope to discuss and reflect upon alternative creative strategies that could have informed their interventions.
- Provide practitioners with a contemporary knowledge base in a range of sport and exercise discipline areas in addition to future research suggestions and applied implications.

- Explore issues pertinent to the applied practitioner/supervisor within the field and through the use of expert commentary explore potential solutions to many of these key issues.

THE NATURE OF APPLIED WORK IN SPORT AND EXERCISE PSYCHOLOGY

Applied practice within the domain of sport and exercise psychology is both diverse and eclectic in its nature. Indeed, the broad range of case studies presented in this book serves to reinforce this view. The domain for the applied practitioner ranges from working with individual athletes, coaches, and patients to teams, clubs, public health organizations, and broader settings. Coupled with this, practitioners can work with current or future Olympic champions, professional athletes, talented young performers, individuals and groups seeking to make healthier life choices, influence public-policy decisions, and to facilitate recovery and adaptation following serious health conditions such as strokes, cancer, and diabetes; and mental health issues such as depression and anxiety disorders. Indeed, the breadth of the field of sport and exercise psychology is truly astounding. Such a range of potential applications of psychology across the sport and exercise field raises questions about whether this can be covered in a single training/development programme. This is though beyond the focus of the current text. This book seeks to explore and highlight the diversity of applied practice facing current sport and exercise psychology practitioners, sharing a range of approaches and crucially their underpinning theoretical and empirical basis.

OVERVIEW OF THE BOOK

The book is comprised of 25 chapters, arranged in four parts: Part I, Sport and Performance Psychology; Part II, Coaching Psychology; Part III, Motor Learning and Control; and Part IV, Psychology of Physical Activity and Exercise. Each chapter is designed to offer the reader an in-depth understanding of the particular case study and approach adopted. Also specific learning outcomes are articulated, and a number of key areas to consider when reading the chapter. Each chapter then presents an overview of the client and the issue before outlining the needs analysis process that guided the decisions regarding the interventions adopted. The framework underpinning the intervention and the associated processes are explained before the authors reflect upon the effectiveness of the approaches adopted. Finally, avenues for further exploration and reading are described to develop a greater understanding of the approaches and interventions presented in the chapter. It is important to state at this point that some of the chapters are real experiences that the clients have given their consent to be published, and some are hypothetical case studies. The chapters are supported by online resources including 'Talking Heads' videos from the authors, sample essays, questions, and further weblinks.

Sport and Performance Psychology

This part of the book explores a range of interventions where the presenting problems are sport and performance focused. In particular, Part I explores psychological factors including managing interpersonal relationships, confidence, concentration and rumination, stress management, personality and group functioning, injury rehabilitation, supporting athletes through career transitions; and the provision of psychological support during major events.

Coaching Psychology

This second part of the book focuses explicitly on the coach, and the potential psychological challenges coaches face. In particular, this part of the book focuses on case studies examining the coach's stress and coping experience, impression management in coach/athlete interactions, creating successful coach/athlete relationships, and nurturing mental toughness through autonomous supportive coaching.

Motor Learning and Control

This part of the book explores motor learning and control and the use of these approaches in applied practice. Specifically, this part of the book explores the cognitive processes involved in the development of motor skills in practice, the development of visual anticipation skills, and the development of perception and action through an ecological-based approach.

Psychology of Physical Activity and Exercise

This final part of the book considers the use of physical activity and exercise as a medium through which a range of health and wellbeing outcomes can be achieved. Specifically, this part of the book explores the challenges of physical activity promotion on a population level, the relationship between exercise and wellbeing, the links between physical activity, self-esteem, and self-concept, intellectual disability and exercise, exercise and body image, exercise dependence, physical activity in children, physical activity and the environment around us, and exercise use in cancer care.

Taking all these chapters collectively, we hope you will enjoy the read and in so doing get a real feeling for the diverse nature of the applied field of sport and exercise psychology. It has been our pleasure working with the authors of each chapter to bring the reader an international, contemporary, informative and diverse textbook.

Stewart, Neil, and Gavin

2 Managing Difficult Interpersonal Relationships: A Basic Psychological Needs Approach

Richard Hampson and Chris Harwood

LEARNING OBJECTIVES

AFTER READING THIS CHAPTER YOU SHOULD BE ABLE TO:

1. Critically understand how a knowledge of Basic Psychological Needs Theory can be used as a motivational tool to help develop professional relationships and performance.
2. Differentiate how psychological need thwarting may present itself in applied situations from challenges associated with low levels of need satisfaction.
3. Critically appreciate the role of the psychologist in mediating conflict when interpersonal challenges arise in elite athlete dyads.
4. Consider the humanistic processes and solution-focused techniques of a consultant involved in an effective dyadic needs analysis and relationship intervention.

AREAS TO CONSIDER WHEN READING THE CHAPTER:

1. The psychological and relational issues that can occur in partnerships at the highest level of elite sport.
2. The benefit of a full-time employed sport psychology practitioner who has the time and availability to offer continued support (as needed) through the athletes' challenging phases.
3. The skill of helping to manage a partnership through facilitation using both athlete-centred and solution-focused principles.
4. The application of consultant support which progresses from proximal to distal (remote) using e-technology.

CLIENT AND BACKGROUND

The two clients involved in this case study are both elite-level canoe slalom athletes. Athlete A (from now on referred to as Joe) was aged 22 at the time of intervention. He had been participating in the sport for over ten years and had represented Great Britain at Under-18, Under-23 and senior level in the team canoe (C2) event. Athlete B (who will be called Robbie from here on) had also been involved in canoeing for over ten years and had represented Great Britain at the same levels in both individual canoe (C1) and C2 Olympic disciplines. As a partnership they had been together for almost four years and had also known each other prior to their formation as a team. At the time of the intervention the pair were preparing to compete for the upcoming summer of international racing that they had recently qualified for by achieving the necessary performance standards at domestic selection trials.

Canoe slalom is a technical, time-based, individual or paired sport. It can be characterized by athletes who compete in either kayak (K) or canoe (C) boats having to make their way down a whitewater course in as quick a time as possible whilst navigating their way through a series of gates which require the paddlers to pass through them either 'downstream' (travelling with the direction of the water) or 'upstream' (having to go past the gate and then coming back up against the river's flow to go through it). Two second penalties are accrued for touching a gate's pole and a 50-second penalty is given if the paddler misses the gate altogether. With regards to the sport's physical components, each 90–120 second performance requires a great level of anaerobic power and endurance. In addition, when one looks towards the mental requirements of athletes in such events, there is a premium placed on good decision-making both (a) in the initial planning of the competitor's strategies to overcome the unique challenges that each course presents and (b) to react to the constantly changing water during the run and then being able to re-focus quickly in such a changeable environment. The competition season runs throughout the course of European summer time and can involve the paddlers travelling to events for weeks and months at a time. As a result of these organizational demands, a great deal of cumulative stress can be placed on any athlete-athlete and/or coach-athlete relationship.

Initially, the work between the athletes and psychologist began when Joe came to the lead author to explain the difficulties that he was currently experiencing within the relationship. The lead author of the current chapter is the psychologist referred to within this case study, and the second author served as the psychologist's supervisor. The psychologist's experience ranged across a number of sports including soccer, golf, windsurfing, and swimming. His work in the organization was undertaken on a full-time basis and, consequently, he came into frequent contact with all of the squad's paddlers. Specifically, at the initial meeting Joe described feeling 'helpless' within the partnership. This was due to a number of reasons which included: (a) not feeling as though he had any input over the team's summer racing and training plans due to Robbie's perceived reluctance to let go of control; (b) his worry that his friendship with Robbie was not as close as it used to be and that Robbie now only saw him as his canoeing partner; and (c) feeling as though he was seen both within the pair and by others outside as the 'second-class citizen' due to the fact that Robbie had qualified to represent the country in both individual and team events this year whereas Joe had only been successful in making the C2 squad. The result of this combination of factors was that Joe was beginning to worry about the future and durability of the partnership. He was also noticing that he was becoming increasingly resentful towards how he felt Robbie was treating him. Furthermore, Joe declared that he felt he had lost a lot of his motivation and drive to train, travel the world, and compete with Robbie over the coming period. Roughly one week later, following an early-season domestic competition, Robbie had also approached the psychologist and identified some worries that he had about the present situation. In particular, he had noticed that Joe's general demeanour had changed both towards him and training. He was worried that the 'lack of effort' which Joe was exerting would lead to the pair underperforming over the summer and that if the relationship carried on in its current manner that he would not enjoy spending time with Joe anymore.

Both initial viewpoints suggested rather fragile states of motivation within the athlete dyad, particularly with respect to the quality and quantity of motivation experienced by Joe. From a theoretical and evidence-based stand-point, a great deal of recent research has highlighted the importance to an individual of satisfying three basic psychological needs (BPNT; Deci & Ryan, 2000). Specifically, this includes the individual's sense of *autonomy* over what is happening in their lives, *competence* within the activities in which they engage, and *relatedness* or sense of belonging and affiliation to those significant others around them. BPNT is a sub-tenet of the long-established Self-Determination Theory (SDT; Deci & Ryan, 1985; Ryan & Deci, 2002). BPNT postulates that the satisfaction of these psychological needs is a central determinant of an individual's cognitive, emotional, and behavioural outcomes and, as Gagné and Blanchard (2007) state, has developed into a popular approach to understanding the antecedents of healthful, effective, and optimal functioning in performance domains. For instance, satisfaction of one's perceptions of autonomy, competence, and relatedness has been shown to predict increased levels of motivation, wellbeing and affect within the sporting context (e.g., Adie, Duda, & Ntoumanis, 2008; Gagné, Ryan, & Bargmann, 2003). Furthermore, a recent investigation by Jackson, Harwood, and Grove (2010) demonstrated how dyadic relationship functioning was impaired when individuals differed in their motivational dispositions and definitions of competence. Specifically, when dyadic partners reported differing achievement goals from one another, lower levels of long-term relationship commitment, and relationship satisfaction emerged in the perceptions of each dyadic member. However, recent research (e.g., Bartholomew, Ntoumanis, Ryan, Thøgersen-Ntoumani & Bosch, 2011) has highlighted an important, further conceptual consideration. Specifically, it has been shown that there is a difference between an individual experiencing a low level of psychological need satisfaction and having one or many of these needs thwarted. Psychological need thwarting (PNT) occurs when a person perceives their levels of autonomy, competence, and/or relatedness as being actively and/or intentionally reduced by someone or something else (e.g., their surrounding environment). Not only is PNT an entirely different experience, but Bartholomew, Ntoumanis, Ryan, and Thøgersen-Ntoumani (2011) have shown it to bring about much more maladaptive personal outcomes. Therefore, once it became clear that Joe might have been experiencing an element of psychological need thwarting within the relationship and his environment, it was deemed important to engage in a more detailed assessment of the dyadic partnership. This would assist in the development of appropriate intervention ideas that would seek to improve individual and interpersonal functioning.

INITIAL NEEDS ASSESSMENT

The core philosophy adopted by the psychologists in their canoe slalom consulting work was reflective of humanistic (or client-centred) psychology. Inspired by Carl Rogers (1961), a humanistic practitioner tends to lead with a focus placed upon fulfilling each individual's potential and emphasizes the importance of and search for self-actualization. It centres around the experiences that a person has had and attempts to guide them to make sense of these and themselves. To achieve this, and in relation to conducting a needs analysis, a humanistic practitioner will typically encourage the individual(s) with whom they are working to examine what they most value and how doing/achieving this allows them to fulfil their potential within life. This is a very different strategy from more cognitive-based approaches (e.g., CBT and REBT) which are based upon deliberately changing faulty/irrational beliefs which may be causing an individual particular distress or discomfort. In such situations the practitioner will begin by identifying the responsible belief(s) and then disturb the foundations of such thoughts with facts, logic, and evidence before replacing them with new, more functional ones.

Within this particular case, elements of a solution-focused model of practice (see de Shazer et al., 1986; Trepper et al., 2012) were also adopted throughout the duration of the intervention and consultations. Solution-focused therapy group treatment is based on over 20 years of theoretical development, clinical practice, and empirical research (e.g., Berg, 1994; De Jong & Berg, 2008; de Shazer et al., 2006). Complimenting a humanistic approach, it differs from traditional treatments that often focus on exploring problematic feelings, cognitions, behaviours, and/or interactions. Instead, the aim of solution-focused work is to guide both individuals to explore what individual and interpersonal outcomes they would like to experience (in this case in order to facilitate a long-term and successful relationship). It was deemed by both authors that in order for *both* athletes to feel a greater sense of need satisfaction (Joe in particular, as will be shown in greater detail later) it was not the case that the psychologist should be dictating what needed to happen. Consistent with solution-focused practice, there was a focus initially on identifying, and then reaching (through the reinforcement of useful behaviours), the desired futures of both individuals (as opposed to spending the majority of the time exploring past problems). With both approaches heavily client-centred, the art of staying true to a humanistic philosophy while applying techniques associated with a solution-focused model of practice will be further illustrated through the intervention.

The initial needs assessment period began with an initial meeting between Athlete A (Joe) and the practitioner. This was followed, shortly after, by a separate discussion between the psychologist and Athlete B (Robbie). These one-to-one meetings were geared towards the psychologist generating a better understanding of how the two individuals (separately) currently saw the situation. These meetings also aimed to illicit what their thoughts and opinions were regarding the partnership, the summer ahead, and how they were currently personally feeling. Following this, a final meeting consisting of both athletes and the practitioner occurred. This allowed the athletes to discuss, in a safe environment, what they wanted to happen or change and then for the partnership (led by the psychologist) to decide how this would be achieved. The following section discusses the process of this case formulation.

The first meeting between Joe and the psychologist followed a request for a conversation by the athlete. It was clearly stated that it would be in relation to an issue that was distinct from the ongoing programme of work that was being carried out between the pair. Once the initial more informal conversations had been engaged in, the formal conversation was prompted by the psychologist asking Joe, 'What do you want from today's session?' This question was asked as it cuts directly to the point and, in the experience of the practitioner, normally prompts the athlete/client to provide two things: (a) what they value that they currently deem to be going 'wrong' or not as expected and (b) what they would like to happen/change. Without gaining both elements of such an answer, a psychologist's job is very difficult to perform optimally. For example, if only part (a) is provided then the professional's choice of intervention may still be inappropriate as two different individuals may want two very different outcomes from the same situation. In contrast, if only part (b) is given then it may be difficult to know where the problem is stemming from and therefore what needs to be addressed first to best/most quickly bring about the desired change(s) and solutions. The canoeist declared that he was 'struggling' with his partner and that he wanted to know what to do to make the situation better and not feel so de-motivated and stressed by current events. Therefore, as planned, Joe had provided me with both his current issue and what he wanted to achieve by working with me. I then asked him to explain exactly what he was currently feeling, how long these symptoms had been present, and what he thought the causes were. He provided the following answers (which were written on the flip chart in the room so that a constant point of reference could be maintained throughout the remainder of the session):

Joe's initial thoughts and feelings:

- Annoyed at Robbie's recent actions towards him.
- That he wasn't looking forward to the summer of competing and training together.
- He was struggling to feel the same motivation and enjoyment for training and the whole process of being an elite-level athlete as he normally did.

His reasons for why the above outcomes were occurring:

- He perceived that Robbie was prioritizing his individual event for the summer rather than the pair's team event. This was due to Robbie's (apparent) greater desire to seek coaching for this event and how any plans with Joe would only be made once he had confirmed things for his individual discipline.
- As a result, he deemed that Robbie was spending much more time training for his C1 event as opposed to the event that they both were competing in. This meant that Joe was not getting as much time practising as he felt necessary and was worrying how this would impact his fitness and ability to perform how he wished.
- That he felt as though he had no say in the pair's plans for the summer due to the fact that everything was being done on the basis that Robbie had two events this summer and those had to take priority over any of his needs and preferences. In turn, this was making him feel as though he wasn't so much part of a team, but was more an 'add-on' or an 'extra'.
- He was concerned that his (usually very close) relationship with Robbie had now been largely reduced to conversations that centred on canoeing. Consequently, he was worried that he might be 'slowly losing a friend'.

Joe later said that he had felt similarly within the relationship at various points in the past but that this was the strongest he had ever experienced the emotional and cognitive consequences that he was currently going through. He declared that this had been the case for around three months. Specifically, he reported experiencing a lower mood than usual, a lack of 'appetite' or motivation to train, and feeling as though he was not being thought about by Robbie which, in turn, led to Joe becoming more irritable with his partner.

Whilst I was listening to Joe and noting these insights for us both to see, the unwanted emotions and thoughts that Joe was experiencing were making more sense (in line with the core concepts of SDT and BPNT) with every new personal insight that was shared. Specifically, it was clear that what he was feeling went further than general low satisfaction of his levels of autonomy (control) in relation to the pair's plans and his lack of participation in key decisions. Instead, he was perceiving his autonomy being deliberately taken away from him in order for Robbie to flourish in all aspects of his competitions. His perceptions of competence and relatedness with his partner were also factors that were becoming progressively more fragile. When I summarized his experiences and clarified my interpretation of what he was going through, he said that he agreed and was glad that he had been understood. At the conclusion of this first meeting, I asked Joe what he would like the next steps to be. Specifically, I recommended that the best chance of the problem reaching (or drawing closer to) a resolution would require both parties first sharing their perspectives on the situation and then working through these issues together, as opposed to dealing with or complaining about them in their separate silos. However, when I then inquired whether he would like to initiate this process or whether he would prefer me to, Joe hinted that he was highly sceptical about the benefits of bringing this topic up with Robbie on his own. This was due to his belief that he had tried to do so already in the past and that his attempts had always fallen on deaf ears. Therefore, it was agreed that during my next regularly scheduled meeting with Robbie I would broach the topic.

To set the scene, Robbie and I were already engaged in regular one-to-one consultations aimed at maximizing his performances in both boats and, in doing so, had developed a relatively strong relationship. As a result of this last fact, I felt confident that he would respond well to any challenging questions that I asked him. I decided that the best place to start would be to make it my aim to gather a representation of how he currently saw the situation and how much this converged with Joe's beliefs. In order for any intervention to meet both partners' needs and produce the best outcomes for the pair as a whole, it was essential that I did not make any assumptions about what was happening based upon only one person's accounts. Therefore, I simply asked Robbie how he felt the relationship and teamwork was at the moment and if he had noticed anything different recently in comparison to normal procedures. This prompted Robbie to explain how he had noticed his partner's behaviour change of late and his frustrations with this. Most notably he described the exact same behavioural outcomes (i.e., a lack of motivation and enjoyment during training sessions) from Joe as had already been explained to me by his partner. He stated that he was concerned about the long-term impact of this 'should Joe not change'. When I asked him if he had any reasons for why this might be occurring he stated 'not really, perhaps he is a bit annoyed that I'm racing in two events this summer and that he isn't my only priority'. That both partners detailed the same behaviours from Joe in addition to Robbie declaring that he had 'no idea' why they were manifesting suggested that helping the pair to understand how their actions influence the other, whilst also encouraging an appreciation of how they can better look after and satisfy each other's needs, would be the most impactful intervention that I could commence at this point in time.

In keeping with the plan outlined above, the final element of the needs assessment was to have a final meeting with both parties together. The efficacy of bringing team members together to openly discuss performance and team functioning has recently been demonstrated to benefit a number of group outcomes including team and social cohesion, mutual trust and confidence by Pain and Harwood (2009). It should be stressed that in this particular case, the individuals involved had worked successfully together in the past and still maintained a desire to do so again. It was their recent actions towards one another (particularly Robbie to Joe) that were causing the current unwanted feelings and behaviours. Therefore, it was noted that trying to identify particular beliefs and then proceed to be relatively direct and dictate what changes needed to occur would not necessarily be the most appropriate method. Rather, it would be more constructive both for the current situation and the pair's long-term relationship to adopt an approach which facilitated them to realize not only what has happened in the past when the relationship has been particularly healthy but also what would need to happen in the future to enable *each* individual to feel happy and secure within the relationship and, therefore, get closer to realizing their full potential both professionally and personally.

This meeting was instigated by asking both parties (Robbie during our meeting and Joe during an informal corridor conversation) to take responsibility for the process moving forwards and arranging a suitable time and place with one another for us all to meet. In line with Beer's (1980) suggestion that team building or development interventions should aim to help groups address the process of evaluating and planning changes to the way that their team members actually work, the two paddlers were encouraged to prepare for the meeting by thinking about what they thought would be most beneficial to the relationship (and to themselves) to disclose to their partner during the meeting at the present moment in time. They were also asked to consider how they would best achieve these benefits and what would be the consequences of not doing so. In line with the guiding approaches of the consultancy, this activity focused on helping Robbie and Joe understand their own values and what they needed to feel happy and fulfilled and then exposing them to situations in which they were encouraged to share this with their partner.

At the subsequent session, I initially attempted to explain that it is difficult to ever fully understand a person's actions until one develops an appreciation for what is happening in their world and how the people and environment around them are having an influence. This concept has been demonstrated recently through the applied research of Holt and Dunn (2006; see also Dunn & Holt, 2004). Their work has provided evidence for the benefit of a personal-disclosure mutual sharing (PDMS) approach initially advocated by Yukelson (1997) and which has been consistently shown to enhance mutual empathy and understanding. Once this had set the scene for the meeting, I then encouraged and facilitated the clients to talk openly and honestly to one another (which hadn't yet happened) about the current situation. I also made a point of referencing back to their individual preparation regarding why this may initially be daunting but what the potential long-term benefits of doing so would be. It was hoped that by this taking place, both would feel as though they had had an opportunity to explain their worries and frustrations (constructively) to the other and, in turn, have a greater empathy for why the recent events had occurred. From there, both could also express what they wanted to change over the coming weeks and months and why they wanted this (both from a professional/athletic and personal/relationship point of view). Finally, once this had happened the pair could input into the plan of how to set about improving the situation, thus allowing both to perceive a greater sense of ownership (autonomy) over the upcoming improvements and feel more motivated to make such changes to their own behaviours.

FRAMEWORK AND INTERVENTION

As noted earlier, before any meeting had taken place as a team, the two individuals were asked to (separately) come up with lists of what they felt needed to occur in order for them to experience a high level of need satisfaction both inside the partnership/canoeing in general and outside this as well. Interestingly, when it came to disclosing their opinions (Holt & Dunn, 2006) over what they would like within the sport, both individuals' lists were very similar. For instance, both identified a desire to be involved in the training and plan-making process, taking responsibility for the organization of other crew matters/tasks and having a mixture of time together as paddlers, but critically as friends as well. However, it was noticeable during the initial follow-up conversations that I conducted with them that the main difference stemmed from the much more rigid and black and white *necessity* that Robbie possessed over these things in comparison to Joe. For instance, both athletes said that being a part of the training-programme planning process was important to them, yet when Robbie discussed this area it became clear that he felt a *need* to be involved in every aspect of it and believed that every session that was put in had a full justification that satisfied his agendas. In contrast, Joe simply wanted to feel as though he understood what was being planned and that he had an opportunity to input into it. In situations when planning took place between the two athletes and their coach, Joe would then describe how Robbie's need to control every element of this time and his determination to fulfil his personal desires would usually lead to Joe backing down and deciding against making any contributions. The long-term consequence of this to Joe was that he would then later regret not 'standing up for himself more' and resent certain sessions when they occurred weeks later as he did not agree with their inclusion in the first instance but never raised these feelings to avoid an argument. This template was used as a reference point throughout the intervention by the practitioner.

Once the pair had each created their list and discussed the rationale behind the various elements within it with myself, the initial meeting was utilized as an opportunity to present it to each other

(Holt & Dunn, 2006; Pain & Harwood, 2009). Whilst doing so, they discussed times that they remembered feeling as though each element was occurring within their relationship in the past, why and how this had a positive influence on them (i.e., its importance), and how the other could facilitate this happening again. More specifically, the pair marked off the factors that they felt their partner had a particularly big influence upon (e.g., Joe deemed that Robbie had a particularly strong influence upon whether or not his need for autonomy and perceiving an element of control over their progress was being satisfied). The other partner was then allowed an opportunity to express how realistic or possible they thought it was for each element to happen. Each subsequently picked three target areas with which they could assist the other partner to help them feel as though their psychological needs were being satisfied to a greater extent (for instance, Robbie chose: Making plans together with Joe, freeing up time to spend together away from canoeing and taking turns to provide feedback during sessions). A weekly 'crew meeting' (myself, Joe, and Robbie together) was then scheduled which would always start off with a 'RAG rating' (red, amber, green) of the effort that each felt they had made to help one another in each of the agreed ways. These specific initiatives drew heavily on the principles and phases of solution-focused group therapy. In this regard, Trepper and colleagues (2012) note the importance of (a) developing a cooperative therapeutic alliance with the client; (b) creating a solution versus problem focus; (c) the setting of measurable changeable goals; (d) focusing on the future through future-oriented questions and discussions; (e) scaling the ongoing attainment of the goals to get the client's evaluation of the progress made; and (f) focusing the conversation on exceptions to the client's problems, especially those exceptions related to what they want different, and encouraging them to do more of what they did to make the exceptions happen.

Having a structure to team meetings has also been reported by athletes as allowing them to feel more able (or 'safe') to express honest thoughts and feelings as in Pain and Harwood's (2009) study. In sum, these sessions were aimed at providing an opportunity to regularly re-align everyone's thinking, discuss and solve any necessary problems and to celebrate the pair's successes. Sessions typically lasted for about 30–45 minutes so that they could be kept lively and interactive whilst also allowing Joe and Robbie the time to discuss any issues or review things that had been done well in sufficient detail. Including this form of process goal monitoring as part of solution-focused work in sessions, made both individuals more accountable for their actions and their influence on the pair's happiness and motivation as opposed to identifying all of the factors and then leaving the desired changes to chance. Indeed, as noted earlier, the existence of dissimilar goals was shown in Jackson and colleagues' (2010) study to provide a potential obstacle to the initial development and then maintenance of dyadic relationships. Equally, research has also indicated that the greater similarity on various constructs including shared attitudes, values, and having a common or united set of goals can have a number of desirable relationship- and team-level outcomes including relationship longevity, satisfaction, and commitment (e.g., Dijkstra & Barelds, 2008; Montoya, Horton, & Kirchner, 2008). The combination of these two factors made the practitioner feel that this part of the intervention to bring together and then track a set of agreed goals and actions would potentially be highly effective in helping to bring about the behavioural and attitudinal changes needed to achieve the pair's relational and performance dreams.

After the first week, the pair had each rated themselves green for the effort that they had made in helping to satisfy the other's basic psychological needs in the three agreed ways. At the same time, both said that they had really enjoyed the past week and had noticed that the atmosphere within the relationship was much more relaxed. Following this initial reinforcement of positive outcomes, each of the partners was given the opportunity to explain (in greater detail) the reasons why the previous actions of their partner had particular effects on them. For instance, Joe explained to Robbie that although he understood the fact that Robbie would be racing in an additional event, he often was left to feel as though he was an unimportant part of Robbie's plans and aims, particularly as Robbie had been so direct about his desire to be successful in his individual competitions. Note during the initial needs analysis there was a clear lack of convergence between the understanding that each other possessed about how their actions affected their partner which, in turn, reinforced a negative cycle. As noted by Yukelson (1997), lack of a mutual understanding and empathy for other members of one's team can lead to a number of maladaptive behavioural and emotional outcomes. In prior discussions, Robbie had openly admitted to the practitioner that he didn't understand why Joe appeared so unhappy during training sessions and that, in his opinion, it was simply the case that Joe 'needed to change'. Whereas, on the other side of the coin, Joe recognized his own behaviours and provided reasons for them (i.e., due to Robbie's actions) but then did not appear to have considered how these had impacted upon Robbie's general demeanour and mentality. As such, a vicious circle had been created which might only be attenuated through enhanced mutual understanding. Therefore, in order for the initial positive changes to continue within the behaviours and overall contentment in the relationship, a real focus on developing a greater empathy and acknowledgement of the other's point of view was deemed essential. Highlighting these points at this time (following a positive week) was deemed important to allow both men to really understand the need for prolonged effort and consideration for each other as opposed to the simple short-term changes that they had experienced.

The second and third weeks of the intervention both resulted in Robbie and Joe rating themselves as green for their effort in satisfying the other's needs more. As expected, their accounts of their enjoyment of paddling together and work ethic served as evidence that they were much higher than pre-intervention levels. Furthermore, in session four the pair also both remarked about times when they had considered how their choice of actions in particular situation(s) may have affected the other. By being able to do this, they had then been able to go against their initial (potentially detrimental) instinct and adopt another way of behaving which would bear a better chance of bringing about a more desired response in their partner. Whilst neither of them was proclaiming himself to be acting desirably in every situation, they acknowledged how the combination of their increased motivation to actively satisfy the other's psychological needs more, in addition to having a better appreciation of how their actions were often the cause of their partner's undesirable responses, was leading to a much more harmonious existence.

Whilst this was happening outside our meetings, the sessions themselves were being used to help the pair better predict how (and why) each other was likely to respond in particular scenarios. This education process involved tasks such as going back over previous instances (from both canoeing and outside life) and reflecting on the triggers and internal interpretations of these triggers that consistently cause both individuals to respond with certain actions and feelings. The principle behind this is that it gave each canoeist a better understanding of not only what scenarios to avoid or create but also how their partner would likely interpret such occurrences and, therefore, why they act in a certain ways. In doing so, both developed a greater appreciation for, and tolerance of the fact that no two people interpret events in exactly the same way.

Following these first four sessions, the hectic period that awaited the pair (which included extensive overseas travel and their first international competition of the season) heavily shaped the structure of the final element of the four-week intervention period and consisted of two parts. First, a summary of the importance of satisfying one's psychological needs (and the consequences of not doing so) was engaged in so that it was fresh in their minds on departure abroad. This was to ensure that the changes in lifestyle did not distract them from the basics which they had recently been doing so well. Second, the pair was also challenged about how they might be able to achieve a greater level of autonomy in satisfying their own needs in addition to their partner making a greater effort to help them as well. The rationale for this was that it was conceivable that at some point during a summer of travelling overseas together one (if not both) of the partners would cease to make such a high effort or be so considerate of the other's plight and could even act in such a way that they could thwart the other's basic needs. Therefore, being better able to look after oneself, particularly for Joe (as opposed to relying on the other's actions) would allow both to understand that they can influence their own cognitive and emotional outcomes. This fact might have been overlooked by the canoeists in light of the recent emphasis that had been placed on adapting actions to help the other person.

Reports from the summer of travelling were very positive. This communication most commonly took the form of a weekly email update with a fortnightly Skype or telephone call with either or (where possible) both individuals. Particularly pleasing was the fact that Joe reported feeling much more confident in his own canoeing ability and his perception of being a stakeholder in the dyad. The best example of this came from one message sent to the practitioner which stated:

> It's been a great week – the whole feel has changed and he's (Robbie) really lightened up to me taking control of things. I even set the training plan – I did check it with him, but only because I thought it right to. We've also adjusted the boat and paddles to the way I've been asking for ages, it feels so much more comfortable now. It's not even been mentioned since!

Joe also noted that he now felt that he had his 'friend back' as well as his racing partner. In addition, Robbie noted Joe's improved overall demeanour and that he no longer had the same doubts over his motivation which had been tangibly lower earlier in the year. Therefore, it was deemed that the initial four-week intervention (following a period of needs analysis) and subsequent follow ups via Skype had been successful. Perhaps most important in this change was that the two young men had become much more self-dependent with regards to their management of each other and the working relationship as a whole than had initially been the case.

REFLECTIONS

The case detailed in this chapter provided many unique challenges (both in terms of the personnel involved and its logistics) and required a range of skills to be utilized by the practitioner. Most importantly, it is the present authors' beliefs that using Basic Needs Theory (BNT; Ryan & Deci, 2000), as the core tenet of the dyadic educational intervention, was effective in aiding the motivational issues faced by the pair. The rationale behind this statement is centred around the benefits that were experienced as a result of initially providing the athletes with the theory's simple framework to aid their understanding of what was happening and how they can better help one another. Once both of the individuals possessed this improved insight into one another, they were then able to start noticing how basic needs were either flourishing in their partner, or not being met or thwarted through the emotional and behavioural consequences that they observed.

Specifically referring back to the basic needs of the two athletes in question, the main two needs which started to be satisfied to a greater extent for Joe as the intervention developed were that of autonomy and relatedness. On reflection as the psychologist involved in this case, it was my sense from our interactions that having his need for relatedness with Robbie – someone who Joe saw as a friend rather than a colleague – being fulfilled to a greater extent was most important to him and which probably had the greatest impact upon his increased happiness and motivation levels. Perhaps both the problem and the solution were, in part, grounded in Joe's overdependence on his relationship with Robbie. As the intervention and individual discussions with Joe (both formal and informal) developed, it became clear that he did not possess an extensive social network to which he could turn. As a result of this, when the personal relationship with his C2 partner was suffering, it brought about an even more significant impact upon his sense of wellbeing than would be likely with other people when in similar situations. Consequently, whilst the current intervention brought about many positive effects in relation to his levels of happiness, future work with Joe may include work which aims to enhance his awareness of the current situation in which he finds himself and its consequences prior to addressing how he could alter this. Should it be the case that there are some unhelpful beliefs existing which are preventing him from opening up to others, then a more CBT-based consultation style might be more appropriate.

Enhancing Joe's perception of his levels of autonomy satisfaction was a more complex operation. This was because facilitating him to feel as though he was able to have a greater input and say with regards to the planning and operating of the team would inevitably involve Robbie having to 'let go' of some of the control which, at the time of initial contact, he was being very protective about. The first step in allowing this to happen was to encourage them to communicate better together and for each partner to explain to the other what they would need in order to feel a sufficient level of control. In doing this, the (often faulty) perceptions of how much 'control' the other would need could be corrected. Further, even if the perceptions were correct, some concessions or minimum standards of 'team work' could then be facilitated to meet one another's needs. This process allowed Joe to immediately feel as though he would be guaranteed more of a say within the relationship and Robbie's fears were soothed in relation to the consequences that he perceived of relinquishing power. In consultation with the psychologist, Robbie frequently mentioned that he simply didn't trust others to always make sensible decisions. In doing so, he never specifically referred to Joe but rather to people in general and could reel off countless memories which reinforced this perception. Turning a critical eye onto this issue, it might have been beneficial to attack this perception and the rationale behind it in more detail on a one-to-one basis (i.e., is this rule applicable to everyone? Or is he taking the actions of a few and generalising them to a larger population?) Positive changes in the current situation for Robbie emerged from developing the communication between the two individuals and helping them to work out ways to maximize their dyadic potential. However, it is debatable how much Robbie would be able to apply his new found trust of Joe to others in similar situations. Neither is it likely that he has altered the very rigid global beliefs that he seemed to possess and, moreover, that he has seen the benefit of ever doing so. However, following the intervention period the pair did both feel as though their basic needs had been sufficiently met and were happier as a unit.

The often unique nature of the intervention sessions required much consideration during the planning stages of this case work. The factors that had to be taken into account were:

- How to appropriately obtain an unbiased/fair representation of the state of the relationship.
- How to create an environment which was perceived as being 'safe' enough for two athletes who had experienced a breakdown in communication to openly share their thoughts and concerns in a non-threatening manner and have them received in the manner intended.
- How to create a forum which is engaging enough to encourage the pair o regularly attend meetings and execute any processes which were put in place for a period of time that was substantial enough to bring about tangible changes.
- How to make the most out of a situation whereby the psychologist would be having to conduct a number of the sessions remotely with the team in a different country.

In answer to the first question, it was deemed best to talk to both parties separately at first following the initial contact from Joe. As the psychologist, this allowed me to see whether the problem was purely one sided or whether both parties detected that something needed to change. This also helped me to be able to facilitate both individuals to make sense of their own thoughts and what points they would want to raise with the other and remove some of the emotion from their thinking before they shared it. This certainly reflected well in the first joint meeting with the pair as they had both clearly planned not only *what* they wanted to say but, critically, *how* they would have to say it in order to have the best chance of experiencing the desired outcome. By doing so, both paddlers: (a) clearly articulated their key points; in (b) a manner that was rarely perceived by the other as a criticism or direct attack. The outcome of this was a very constructive conversation that allowed further positive steps to be made. This individual time allowed both the athletes and the psychologist some crucial planning and thinking time that later resulted in being pivotal in the overall success of the operation. Had the two young men been brought straight together in the first instance without having had the opportunity to discuss and refine their thoughts, it is likely that they would have either barely communicated and shared their feelings with one another or (possibly more catastrophically) exacerbated the situation further via offensive and emotionally impulsive remarks.

With regards to the nature of the subsequent 'crew meetings', the structure – drawn from knowledge of solution-focused principles (Trepper et al., 2012) – that was put in place was highly effective. Having the same outline for each session (which they had contributed to the creation of) meant that the pair knew what to expect, that they would always have an opportunity to offer their perceptions of the week's or fortnight's events and that the meeting, specifically the 'RAG-rating' section of it, would hold them accountable for their actions in the previous week. The format also stood up well to the test of having to be conducted via Skype whilst the team were overseas. This was because most of the session was their platform to review the week and exchange ideas with one another (with me on the other end of the Skype connection). Whilst the nature of having to support from a different country is never as desirable as being with an individual person, the nature of the review meetings provided the two paddlers with a sufficiently supportive and challenging environment to be able to continue their effectiveness as a crew. What was also productive was that while the bulk of the session was about reviewing the previous period, time was also guaranteed to nominate *as a group* the priorities for any actions that needed to be taken in the upcoming seven toe fourteen days (e.g., seeing the physio, preparing the boat, etc.). This ensured that the team were not only becoming more organized and truly performance-focused, but were also provided with a regular opportunity to nurture their perceptions of personal autonomy.

The feedback from the two athletes would also suggest that the 'RAG-rating' system was more enjoyable than the traditional goal-setting interventions that they had experienced in the past. Their feedback indicated that it allowed them to clearly determine the key ways in which they could help one another and, subsequently to see how they had performed in each of these areas during the previous week. The work that had gone into developing the rating system beforehand also meant that there was no room for confusion around what actions were required in order to be classed as performing to a 'red', 'amber', or 'green' level. This allowed both of the partners to feel as though they could more effectively self-regulate as well as critique the other's actions throughout the week by referring back to the scale. They also said that the simplicity of the rating system meant that: (a) it was never considered to be a laborious task to carry out; and (b) it actually generated some intra-group competition in relation to who would get the highest rating each week. In doing so, this made the activities more fun and motivating. This latter point was an unintended sub-effect of the activity but it was pleasing to hear confirmation that seeing how well each other was performing (in relation to team spirit and basic needs management) increased their enjoyment, motivation, and efficacy beliefs towards the project.

A final reflection of both authors to this piece of case work centres around the practitioner style that was adopted. As detailed earlier in the chapter, the humanistic approach to consulting centres around helping the individual(s) to discover what it will take for them to reach their full potential. At times, this was a difficult task to maintain due to the contrasting approaches of the two athletes. Specifically, Robbie tended to demonstrate a very direct and largely outcome-motivated focus for his sport and sport-related interactions. The result of this was that he usually demonstrated a very strong opinion on what he needed to do to be at his best and what he required of others around him. In this regard, using solution-focused principles with goals and scaling that afforded monitoring and measurability to the process appeared to resonate with Robbie's more concrete personality. In comparison, Joe seemed to prioritize the personal journey which he was embarking on and the experiences that came with it as much as the position that the crew finished in any race. A humanistic approach would tend to lend itself very well to the latter mentality by facilitating the client to explore what exactly it is that they value most and how they can take advantage of this enhanced self-awareness to deliver more fulfilling experiences in their day-to-day and sporting lives. As predicted, Joe seemed to especially enjoy the process and working out what was important to him (including the needs that were particularly important and sensitive for his sense of wellbeing). Whilst Robbie seemed to also enjoy this process, it might have been more appropriate to consider a more cognitive approach with him if the sessions had been with Robbie alone. The rationale behind this is that it was often Robbie's more rigid and unhelpful beliefs (along with Joe's sensitivity to Robbie's actions) which were the trigger or cause of many of the misunderstandings and unhappiness. Disturbing these unhelpful beliefs might have been, intervention would have been most effective if i only Robbie had been present. However, cognitive techniques (e.g., CBT) can often be fairly direct and challenging and may have created a perception that the situation between the pair had to be 'managed' rather than enhanced. Furthermore, practising in such a manner could also have been perceived as though Robbie was being singled out as the source of blame for the situation. Given the central focus and importance on the relationship, this type of approach may not have led to the desired outcome. The two varying personalities and needs in this case led to much consideration regarding the methodology employed by the practitioner. Whilst it is acknowledged that other approaches were pertinent to consider, the progression of the pair's happiness, motivation, and co-existence leads the current authors to the conclusion that the right choices were made.

In conclusion, many different factors had to be taken into consideration throughout the course of the intervention and it was only by analysing or assessing the needs of the situation at various stages that allowed the practitioner to make appropriate decisions with conviction. This chapter has attempted to add to the literature by highlighting some of the idiosyncrasies of working closely with small groups (as opposed to one-to-one and large team or squad consulting) both in and out of competition periods. It has also reinforced how a basic needs approach, that considers the premises of need satisfaction and need thwarting, is a useful framework to help generate greater dyadic appreciation and empathy within temporarily strained and fraught relationships.

FURTHER READING

Bartholomew, K. J., Ntoumanis, N., Ryan, R. M., & Thøgersen-Ntoumani, C. (2011). Psychological need thwarting in the sport context: Development and initial validation of a psychometric scale. *Journal of Sport and Exercise Psychology, 33,* 124–145. An interesting paper that introduces the psychological need thwarting scale (PNTS). There is also further articulation regarding how the PNTS can be applied.

Jackson, B., Harwood, C. G., & Grove, J. R. (2010). On the same page in sporting dyads: Does dissimilarity on 2 × 2 achievement goal constructs impair relationship functioning? *Journal of Sport & Exercise Psychology, 32,* 805–827. This study examined the extent to which 2 × 2 achievement goal constructs were associated with key relational perceptions (i.e., relationship commitment, relationship satisfaction) for members of athlete-athlete dyads.

Pain, M., & Harwood, C. (2009). Team building through mutual sharing and open discussion of team functioning. *The Sport Psychologist, 33,* 523–542. This article describes a team-building intervention based on a mutual sharing paradigm with a soccer team during a competitive season.

Rogers, C. R. (1961). *On becoming a person.* Boston: Houghton Mifflin. A very good introduction and overview to client-centred therapy.

REFERENCES

Adie, J., Duda, J. L., & Ntoumanis, N. (2008). Autonomy support, basic need satisfaction and the optimal functioning of adult male and female sport participants: A test of basic needs theory. *Motivation and Emotion, 32*, 189–199.

Bartholomew, K. J., Ntoumanis, N., Ryan, R. M., & Thøgersen-Ntoumani, C. (2011). Psychological need thwarting in the sport context: Development and initial validation of a psychometric scale. *Journal of Sport and Exercise Psychology, 33*, 124–145. Retrieved 8 December 2015 from http://journals.humankinetics.com/jsep

Bartholomew, K. J., Ntoumanis, N., Ryan, R. L., Thøgersen-Ntoumani, C., & Bosch, J. A. (2011). Self-Determination Theory and diminished functioning: The role of interpersonal control and psychological need thwarting. *Personality and Social Psychology Bulletin, 37*, 1459–1473.

Beer, M. (1980). *Organizational change and development: A systems review*. Glenview, IL: Scott, Foresman.

Berg, I. K. (1994). *Family-based services: A solution-focused approach*. New York: Norton.

De Jong, P., & Berg, I. K. (2008). *Interviewing for solutions* (3rd ed.). Belmont, CA: Thomson Brooks/Cole.

de Shazer, S., Berg, I. K., Lipchik, E., Nunnally, E., Molnar, A., Gingerich, W., Weiner-Davis, M. (1986). Brief therapy: Focused solution development. *Family Process, 25* (2), 207–221.

de Shazer, S., Dolan, Y. M., Korman, H., Trepper, T. S., McCollum, E. E., & Berg, I. K. (2006). *More than miracles: The state of the art of solution focused therapy.* New York: Haworth Press.

Deci, E. L., & Ryan, R. M. (1985). *Intrinsic motivation and self-determination in human behaviour*. New York: Plenum.

Deci, E. L., & Ryan, R. M. (2000). The 'what' and 'why' of goal pursuits: Human needs and the self-determination of behavior. *Psychological Inquiry, 11*, 227–268.

Dijkstra, P., & Barelds, D. P. H. (2008). Self and partner personality and responses to relationship threats. *Journal of Research in Personality, 42*, 1500–1511.

Dunn, J. G. H., & Holt, N. L. (2004). A qualitative investigation of a personal-disclosure mutual-sharing team building activity. *The Sport Psychologist, 18*, 363–380.

Gagné, M., & Blanchard, C. (2007). Self-determination theory and well-being in athletes: It's the situation that counts. In M. S. Hagger and L. D. Chatzisarantis (Eds.), Intrinsic motivation and self-determination theory in exercise and sport. Champaign, IL: Human Kinetics.

Gagné, M., Ryan, R. M., & Bargmann, K. (2003). Autonomy support and need satisfaction in the motivation and well-being of gymnasts. *Journal of Applied Sport Psychology, 15*, 372–390.

Holt, N. L., & Dunn, J. G. H. (2006). Guidelines for delivering personal-disclosure mutual sharing team building interventions. *The Sport Psychologist, 20*, 348–367.

Jackson, B., Harwood, C. G., & Grove, J. R. (2010). On the same page in sporting dyads: Does dissimilarity on 2 × 2 achievement goal constructs impair relationship functioning? *Journal of Sport & Exercise Psychology, 32*, 805–827.

Montoya, R. M., Horton, R. S., & Kirchner, J. (2008). Is actual similarity necessary for attraction? A meta-analysis of actual and perceived similarity. *Journal of Social and Personal Relationships, 25*, 889–922.

Pain, M., & Harwood, C. (2009). Team building through mutual sharing and open discussion of team functioning. *The Sport Psychologist, 33*, 523–542.

Rogers, C. R. (1961). *On becoming a person*. Boston: Houghton Mifflin.

Ryan, R. M., & Deci, E. L. (2000). Self-determination theory and the facilitation of intrinsic motivation, social development, and well-being. *American Psychologist, 55*, 68–78.

Ryan, R. M., & Deci, E. L. (2002). Self-determination research: Reflections and future directions. In E. L. Deci & R. M. Ryan (Eds.), *Handbook of self-determination research* (pp. 431–441). Rochester, NY: University of Rochester Press.

Trepper, T. S., McCollum, E. E., De Jong, P., Korman, H, Gingerich, W. J., & Franklin, C. (2012). Solution-focused Brief Therapy treatment manual. In C. Franklin, T. S. Trepper, W. J. Gingerich, & E. E. McCollum (Eds.), *Solution-focused Brief Therapy: A Handbook of Evidence-Based Practice* (pp. 20–38). Oxford: Oxford University Press.

Yukelson, D. (1997). Principles of effective team-building interventions in sport: A direct services approach at Penn State University. *Journal of Applied Sport Psychology, 9*, 73–96. This article is good for reflecting on the development of your own overall framework and delivery.

3 The Use of Team Strengths at a Major Championship

TIM HOLDER

LEARNING OBJECTIVES

AFTER READING THIS CHAPTER YOU SHOULD BE ABLE TO:

1. Appreciate the need to understand the context within which you are working as an applied practitioner.
2. Critically evaluate the sources of information that may assist in the development of contextual intelligence.
3. Critically discuss the range of factors that are important to consider in the delivery of an intervention in a competitive context.
4. Critically discuss the impact of focusing on strengths within a high performance environment.

AREAS TO CONSIDER WHEN READING THE CHAPTER:

1. Consider the amount of contextual information an applied sport psychology practitioner needs to know in order to be effective in the work that they do within that context.
2. In addition to understanding the performer, consider how you might approach understanding the person behind the performer in order to be effective in your role.
3. Consider how you might develop more creativity in your client consultation interactions that are contextually sensitive and scientifically based whilst also suited to the client population needs.

CLIENT AND BACKGROUND

The client group for the case study were the Great Britain synchronized swimming team. Within the Olympic Games competitive programme, synchronized swimming is one of only two sports that involve female only competitors (rhythmic gymnastics being the other). The squad of performers working towards the games were aged between 17 and 24. Many had been training full time since 2007 and had been led by highly experienced and expert coaching staff. This case study charts the use of a strengths-based component of the overall intervention work with the squad in the final period leading up to the 2012 Olympic Games. This specific period was chosen as the work exemplifies what can be achieved in relation to a critical competition (e.g., Gould, & Maynard, 2009; McCann, 2000). Furthermore, the benefits of focusing on strengths at such a critical period in relation to a competitive performance created the fundamental rationale for introducing the intervention. Therefore the case study presents an approach based on recognition of what the group's characteristic strengths were rather than addressing any specific problem or issue.

THE SPORT AND ITS COMPETITIVE STRUCTURE

Synchronized swimming is comprised of movements synchronized to other team members and to accompanying music. The sport requires a range of skills to achieve optimal performance, as evidenced by the judging criteria identified in Table 3.1. There is an aesthetic, performance component, synchronization with the music and other competitors as well as technical precision, physical strength, flexibility, and cardiovascular and muscular endurance.

Performances within the Olympic competition programme are for the duet (two performers) or team (eight performers) (In World and European Championships a solo event (one performer) is also in the competitive schedule). In each competitive event, performances are required in both technical and free routines. In the technical routine a number of components (or elements) of performance are required to be performed. In the free routine there is, as the name suggests, complete freedom to include anything in the performance. The duration of the competitive routines is between 2 minutes 20 seconds (duet technical routine) and 4 minutes (team free routine).

Synchronized swimming is a judged sport and (at the time of the case study) there were five judges each for both technical merit and artistic impression. Judges award scores (out of 10) for the subcomponents of performance (see Table 3.1) based upon internationally recognized criteria.

Table 3.1 *Synchronized swimming judging criteria and weighting (FINA, 2010).*

Technical merit (50%)	*Artistic impression (50%)*
EXECUTION of strokes, figures, and parts thereof, propulsion techniques, precision of patterns	**CHOREOGRAPHY**, variety, creativity, pool coverage, patterns, transition
SYNCHRONIZATION with another and with music	**MUSIC INTERPRETATION**, use of music
DIFFICULTY of strokes, figures and parts thereof, patterns, synchronization	**MANNER OF PRESENTATION**, total command

The high performance centre

The Great Britain synchronized swimming team trained full time and was housed within a lottery funded, World Class Performance Programme (WCPP). The training was undertaken primarily at a high performance centre (based in Aldershot) and comprised of up to 45 hours of training per week. Training was undertaken on five and a half days of the week with one and a half days off. This training and competition schedule resulted in near continual training with approximately 45 weeks of scheduled training per year. The weeks that were designated as not 'formal' training were accompanied with advice and schedules of lighter, or maintenance, training. At the time of the case study, there were 13 performers in the programme.

The high performance centre was staffed by sport specialists employed by British Swimming comprising of a full-time programme manager, national performance director, head coach and assistant coach. In addition to this, specialist consultants would be utilized as and when they could provide additional contributions to programme activities to help achieve the overall programme objectives. These consultants would provide additional coaching expertise such as acrobatics, aesthetic sport experts, or choreographic input to the development of competitive programmes. They would work closely with the full-time staff for short periods of time during the preparation and competition cycles to add to the programme activities within the overall objectives of the programme staff.

Sport science support

In addition, and complementary to the sport specific staff, consultants in sport science and medicine services were supplied through the English Institute of Sport (EIS). The EIS staff contributed to the WCPP in the following areas: physiotherapy (four days a week), strength and conditioning (three days a week), performance lifestyle (two days a week), nutrition (one day a week) and sport psychology (one day a week) as well as access to medical doctors. The author supplied the sport psychology service from January 2011, however prior to this time the squad had been supported by another sport psychologist from the EIS. The psychology work was supported and organized within an internal EIS organizational structure named the 'performance psychology group' which provided services to a number of sports. This group had established meeting points to share current practice and develop expertise. There was also a guiding model of delivery that assisted sports in understanding the types of work that would be delivered within a sport psychology service and some key principles that could be moulded into a bespoke service for the sport. Central to the model was the integration into the performance context and working practices that were coach led. In addition, and important to the case study presented, was the use of a preference indicator profiling system to access personality preferences through the Insights Discovery tool (the Insights Group Ltd).

INITIAL NEEDS ASSESSMENT

Insights Discovery tool

The Insights Discovery preference tool is one of a suite of products produced by the Insights Group Ltd. Their approach is founded in a Jungian philosophy and provides ways in which the principles within such an approach can be used to enhance performance, develop effective relationships, enhance communication, and work effectively with others. The specific discovery tool that is used within the current case study is a personality preference measure. This tool provides a way of understanding the individual

Table 3.2 *Example personality characteristics associated with Insights colour preferences.*

COOL BLUE	FIERY RED
Factual	Action-oriented
Objective	Competitive
Formal	Demanding
Nit-picking	*Aggressive*
Cold	*Controlling*
Reserved	*Intolerant*
EARTH GREEN	SUNSHINE YELLOW
Supportive	Sociable
Caring	Dynamic
Relaxed	Enthusiastic
Bland	*Frantic*
Stubborn	*Hasty*
Reliant	*Flamboyant*

preferences of WCPP athletes for dealing with the world. It can provide sport psychologists with some guidance on the characteristics of those they are working with and help plan for the challenges ahead.

All members of the programme completed the Insights Discovery profile (based on responses to 25 questionnaire items) which resulted in a substantial analysis of how each person prefers to act and react in life situations. This analysis provides a wealth of information about the individual related to their preferences in communication, likely motivation and management approaches, and overall strengths and weaknesses when dealing with others. The profile establishes a colour-coded representation of individual preferences based upon four possible broad types described as cool blue, fiery red, earth green and sunshine yellow. Table 3.2 provides some 'good day' and 'bad day' (in italics) characteristics associated with each of these colour preferences:

The above table indicates that there is a substantial range of preference characteristics possible that influence the way any individual may respond to a situation. In addition there are clearly times when these preferences are associated with responses that may be negative or unhelpful (the 'bad day' characteristics) and others that may be seen as more positive and helpful (the 'good day' characteristics).

The profile helps frame aspects of the intervention in that it identifies the challenges that performers may meet in working with others when their preferences are different. For example, one performer with a strong sunshine yellow profile (where their preference can be sociable and enthusiastic) may find it challenging to deal with another performer who is displaying a strong cool blue profile (where their preference can be more formal and factual). The preferences would lead each of them to approach a particular situation very differently. These preferences may lead to frustrations and an uncoordinated inefficient approach to a performance situation.

The profiles of each individual were shared between performers and staff. The sharing of personality preference profiles enabled a greater understanding of the strengths and challenges within the squad. This enabled a greater self-awareness and understanding as well as understanding of others. Within any group there are clear advantages of having a breadth of preference strengths in appropriately addressing the varied demands and challenges of high performance sport. These advantages were identified and celebrated along with acknowledging the challenges of difference in preference (unfortunately it is beyond the scope of this chapter to provide further details on how this was achieved).

Key to the assessment of the needs within any sporting context is an in-depth understanding of the demands of the sport under consideration. It is only when the sport is understood in addition to the individual performers and support staff, that an effective intervention approach can be truly established (Taylor, 1995). Central to the process of assessment is an objective to gain an understanding of the psychological impacts of the sport demands for those that are performing and working within it. In the present case study a central feature of the WCPP is the centralized training approach that was taken. All the performers were based near to the High Performance Centre (HPC) and trained together on a day-to-day basis. The opportunities provided by such a centralized approach are tempered by the challenges of training within such an environment. The importance in such a situation to have what is known as contextual intelligence (Brown, Gould, & Foster, 2005) cannot be underestimated. The essence of contextual intelligence is contained within the following quote: 'understanding the context in which one operates – knowing what works for which person in which situations. It is more than knowing what to do; it is knowing how to get it done' (Brown et al., 2005, p. 51).

The key challenge for the applied practitioner is not simply understanding the specific demands of the sport, but critically knowing the sport in the situation that you are working in. The key components within the contextual intelligence framework that need to be taken account of are the *language* used within the context, the *structure* of the context in relation to established hierarchies and links between individuals, the *patterns* of information flow between individuals in the context, the *attitudes* and values of key personnel and where the *influence* comes from within the context and how it is demonstrated (Brown et al., 2005).

The contextual intelligence was maximized by the approach taken within the early phases of working with the squad and can be summarized as follows:

1. Search for fundamental knowledge of the sport through various resources from the internet, books and journals to establish some of the competitive performance demands of the sport (although also performed by men, the Olympic event is a women-only event and it is accurate to state that the author's understanding of the sport was not drawing upon personal competitive experiences).
2. Discussions with coaches, performers, and colleagues who had previously (or were currently) working within the sport.
3. Observations of competitive and training environments. During the early weeks of working within the sport the author attended a major competitive event as well as weekly training sessions. Immersion within the sporting context (Bull, 1997) became a key method adopted to develop beyond the basic information, into a more bespoke understanding of the team and their support staff.

The key to establishing a working contextual intelligence is to recognize its dynamic nature. There are a number of significant factors within the context that are pivotal to the understanding of the situation at hand and any one of these factors could change over time. When a pivotal feature shifted it was immensely important for the author to update their understanding of the context. One of the ways in which this was assisted was through the multidisciplinary nature of the sport science and medicine support offered. This approach enabled frequent communication between sport science specialists and also a substantial input from coaches. The multidisciplinary approach to working has significant advantages for the effectiveness of applied practice whilst understanding the potential challenges that emerge from working in this manner (Collins, Moore, Mitchell, & Alpress, 1999; Gustafsson, Holmberg, & Hassmen, 2008; Reid, Stewart, & Thorne, 2004). With this in place, an updating of the current dynamic factors could be established quite readily and responded to accordingly. An exemplar of this would be the communication related to a particular performer's progress within their rehabilitation from injury. Similarly, another example could be something as simple as a coach being away from training for a period of time. There is no doubt that the updating of contextual intelligence was a significant, and ongoing, part of the needs assessment of the WCPP from a sport psychology perspective. It is also worth noting that the work conducted by the author was predominately completed in person for one day a week. Although this was applied flexibly with greater periods of contact possible it is accurate to state that the majority of the work was completed within the contracted day. This part-time, regular contact approach to sport psychology service delivery has advantages over the long term and has been shown to be preferred by athletes and administrators as an effective mode of delivery (Connole, Shannon, Watson, Wrisberg, Etzel, & Schimmel, 2014; Ponnusamy & Grove, 2014). The disadvantage of this could be viewed as the extent to which the author was truly immersed within the sport context. This challenge was somewhat overcome in order to maintain the accuracy and timely updating of contextual intelligence by regular communication and focused observation procedures. The observation intention was to use an informal, contextually led approach. This meant that previous information informed the ongoing observations but the dynamic nature of the situation required an observation strategy that could be open to the reality and complexity of the context rather than reduce the observation focus to a simplified set of behaviours or interactions that could be encompassed within a checklist. This led to an approach demanding the ongoing 'noticing' of a range of factors within the environment (Holder & Winter, under review).

In addition to the immersion, observation, and communication components of the initial assessment, the Insights Discovery tool continued to be used within the context. Philosophical challenges will be reflected upon later but it was clear that, as a tool for establishing self-awareness and understanding of others, the Insights Discovery findings coupled with the language and understanding in relation to the principles of the preference model were well established and part of the culture of the WCPP and those individuals within the HPC. Therefore performers and coaches who had not previously completed the profile were asked to do so and any new members of the WCPP were also requested to complete the profile. This made it possible for a holistic analysis of the preferences of all involved with the HPC to be generated and shared to optimize the understanding of self and others and to establish areas for enhancement and relevant coping strategies.

From the ongoing assessment process the accumulated evidence from observations, interactions with coaches and performers in the form of interviews and other forms of communication, Insights Discovery profiles and shared information (where appropriate) with other support staff culminated in the following key assessment findings:

- The demands of the sport are substantial and are characterized by extensive periods of physical training time within the water where repetition and precision of movements are key.
- The water-based training is supplemented by substantial technical and physical training on land and other support service provision (including sport psychology).
- The absolute duration of training days (approximately 8 or 9 hours per day) led to the requirement for adequate and monitored rest and recovery in order to cope with the demands of a training week, month and year. The need for rest and recovery including optimizing fluid balance and nutritional intake as well as physical and psychological recovery led to significant

impacts on lifestyle as an elite athlete (see Meehan, Bull, Wood, & James, 2004). Opportunities for a lifestyle similar to others of their own age were significantly limited and social lives were almost non-existent for sizeable periods of the competitive cycle.

- Coaches' observation skills were remarkable in their scope and accuracy. These observations invariably were focused on (and intended for) identification of the aspects of performance that needed to be improved. This context of a 'high performance' centre requires the key objective to be focused on high quality of performance and the constant attention to the search for perfection (or at least on the next step towards it). The application of these high standards led to a predominance of corrective feedback as the focus of coach communication with performers.
- Relationships between coaches and performers are critical to the 'feel' and overall effectiveness of the training and competition.
- Relationships between performers clearly have an impact both in and out of the water. The strength and valence of the relationships influence a number of features of the WCPP including open communication, attitudinal shifts influencing effort and persistence and the development of confidence and efficacy at the individual and team level.
- There were a range of individual preferences from the Insights Discovery profiling tool with a large number of members of the HPC with sunshine yellow or earth green as the dominant preference and a small but meaningful group with fiery red as their dominant preference.

Therefore, as a result of the range of evidence collated from the available sources a number of individual, team, and programme-based conclusions could be drawn about the best avenues to influence and enhance the performance of the group. The focus of the work that is being presented here is on the use of a strengths-based approach (Gordon, 2012, Gordon & Gucciardi, 2011) to encourage the maintenance and development of collective efficacy (Myers, Feltz, & Short, 2004; Ronglan, 2007) at a major championship. The links between achieving a collective level of confidence within a team and its performance benefits are clear (Greenlees, Graydon, & Maynard, 1999) as well as understanding that such efficacy needs to be reinforced over time (Ronglan, 2007). The benefits of developing a focus on the strengths of individuals and key processes including training and preparation leading up to this event were clear from the assessment of this high performance context (as identified earlier). In addition the unique dimension of a home Olympic Games for the Great Britain athletes led to the potential for more critical coverage. A renewed focus on the strengths was felt to be an appropriate way to remind performers and staff alike of the significant individual qualities and preparation strategies that had developed within the WCPP in readiness for the London Olympic Games.

Definition box

BOX 3.1

Collective efficacy: 'a group's shared belief in its … capabilities to organise and execute the courses of action required to produce given levels of attainment'.

Source: (Bandura, A. (1997). *Self-efficacy: The exercise of control.* New York: W.H. Freeman and Company 1997, p. 477).

FRAMEWORK AND INTERVENTION

Framework of applied practice

The general approach the author adopts during support work would be termed by many as eclectic. However, the fundamental theoretical framework within which the methods originate is a cognitive behaviourist perspective (Meichenbaum, 1977). It is clear that much of the working practices include a significant influence brought in from humanistic, person-centred approaches (Rogers, 1980). Within this broad philosophical and theoretical framework there were situation-specific features of the case study scenario which further influenced the approaches used with this group. Included in these additional features are two strong themes that emerged more substantially for the author when working within the framework adopted by the Performance Psychology group of the EIS.

First, as mentioned previously, the use of the Insights Discovery tool is well established within the Performance Psychology group and was already in place within the specific sporting context into which the author was engaged. The framework that provided the theoretical grounding for the work of the Insights tools is firmly founded in the psychoanalytic approach taken by Jung. Whilst it is beyond the scope of this chapter to provide details of this approach, there are components within it that deal specifically with the role of the unconscious and the importance of personality on human functioning (Jacobi, 1942). It is certainly not the case that the author considers himself to be a psychoanalytic practitioner and does not possess the training required in order to do so (see Reflections section for further comment). However a period of four days' initial training and two subsequent update training days have been completed by the author in order to be able to use the Insights Discovery preference tool which forms part of the overall Insights portfolio.

Second, the influence of positive psychology approaches (Peterson, 2006; Seligman, 2011) have begun to have noticeable impacts upon the work of the author. In essence the positive psychology approach provides a focus on what the performer can already call their strengths. By doing this, the approach does not only draw upon improvements through developing relative performance weaknesses but significantly highlights the importance of identifying and building on strengths (Gordon, 2012; Gordon & Gucciardi, 2011; Peterson & Park, 2011, 2012). This is most apparent in the current case where the focus is primarily on strengths and the use of those strengths to inform and influence psychological functioning.

It is clear that the fundamental approach to the work the author conducted maintains a driving force and intention for impact (Martindale & Collins, 2005) derived from a cognitive behavioural framework. The additional, context specific elements to the overall approach complement rather than contradict the working practices adopted primarily through the way in which the Insights tool and 'strengths' components are applied through the lens of a cognitive behavioural practitioner.

The intervention

The demands of the sport and the contextual characteristics of the training environment in addition to the uniqueness of the event being a home based Olympic Games (the first since 1948), all had an impact on the specific focus of this competition-based intervention. There were some important principles at the heart of the intended intervention. First, as many of the WCPP team were to be involved in the intervention including team manager, coaches, support staff, and performers themselves. The intention of the intervention was to impact upon the collective efficacy of the broadest group that was possible within the WCPP and who were likely to be influential within the specific competitive context.

Second, the sporting demands previously highlighted, identified a potential gain for the performers, coaches, and support staff in identifying the strengths of each of the individuals and the team as a whole. The author deemed this to be important enough to be a focus of intervention due to the consistent, high performance focus of the programme activities. This led to a regular and meaningful search for performance enhancement by the identification of areas for improvement. This often led to the underplaying of the progress made due to the priority for identification of aspects to improve.

The most common and powerful source of efficacy information is well recognized as performance accomplishments (Bandura, 1986). In many sporting contexts the opportunities for competitive performances are many and often weekly. In synchronized swimming there are extensive periods of time spent training and developing new routines culminating in approximately three or four competitive swims during a season. In a judged sport the importance of performing in front of, and being scored by, judges cannot be underestimated. Needless to say the WCPP provided numerous competitive simulations within the training programme. Due to the relative paucity of competitive performances upon which to base a strong collective efficacy, the intervention attempted to provide reminders of performance-related strengths and tap into other sources of efficacy provided within the activities of the HPC.

The objectives for the intervention were twofold. First, to develop a strength-focused exercise that represented the views of those within the WCPP. These views were focused on the strengths of different individuals in the WCPP and the successful preparation strategies used. These strengths were to be presented in the form of a poster. This poster would be put up in the Olympic village and collated the squad's thoughts about their collective strengths in a visual format and act as a regularly available reminder in the lead up to, and during, the Olympic Games. All members of the squad were also provided with an electronic version of the poster which they could view themselves at any time. Second, the way in which the intervention was delivered was designed to be co-ordinated and facilitated by the author but was implemented and fed back to the author by the group. This was calculated to devolve responsibility for the identification and use of strengths to the performers to enhance their feelings of autonomy and relatedness in addition to the impact on competence (Deci & Ryan, 1985).The culmination of the intervention process was then completed in the form of an A0 (118.9 cm × 84.1 cm) colour poster with the following characteristics instrumental in its design and development:

Overall design – the visual appeal was critical to gaining, and retaining attention to the content of the poster. The visual representation was influenced by the intention to gain access to the creativity within the group (lots of sunshine yellow preference strengths).

Colour – the colour components of the poster were important for two key reasons. The background colour of the poster was altered from the red, white, and blue of a traditional British flag to pink and red. This was important as it tapped into a contextual-specific element of the lead up to the games. For an extended period leading up to the London Olympic Games the last Thursday of the month was designated within the HPC as 'Pink Thursday'. On this day all involved with the programme dressed in pink (purely co-incidentally the author worked mostly on a Friday!). This was not a whimsical idea but was a way of attracting regular local and national press coverage and to enhance the awareness of the sport and its Olympic credentials to those unaware of it in the home nation games year as well as signposting for all within the WCPP the time left before the games (i.e., seven more Pink Thursdays before the games). The second colour aspect of the poster was to represent the dominant Insights colour preference for each individual. This colour formed the background to the information box specific to the individual concerned (e.g., for an athlete who had an earth green dominant preference, the colour green formed the background colour for their individual strengths information; see Figure 3.1).

Size and placement – the size of the poster was A0 (118.9 cm × 84.1 cm) which was designed to dominate within a living space that it was intended to be presented in. In this case the posters were to be placed on the wall in the apartment accommodation in the Olympic village. This also enabled the poster information to be consistently available during the period of preparation and performance at the Olympic Games.

The process of establishing the content of the poster was carried out by the performers, coaches, and support staff at a pre-Olympic training camp in Europe. The author was not present at the time of construction. However, the structure and content were established and communicated by him via email. In two separate sessions, the relevant tasks were led by two performers with the structure and content facilitated by the author through email. The first session was designed to establish the group's input on their perception of the 'edge' and the team strengths at that point in time. This session incorporated the group (including performers, coaches, and support staff) working individually to identify the key strengths they perceived that the team had going into the Olympic Games. In addition individuals identified the elements of their preparation and training that they felt gave them an 'edge' at the home Olympics. These individual viewpoints were then shared and discussed with the rest of the group and sent to the author to collate for presentation in the poster. This aspect of the poster was reflective of an extensive literature that has attested to, and debated the performance advantage gained from performing at home (Neville & Holder, 1999).

The second session was focused on establishing the performers, coaches, and support staff perceptions of other individuals' strengths in terms of characteristics or actions. This session specifically gave the opportunity for the identification of strengths that perhaps were outside the normal thought processes of the individual concerned or which were considered to be 'ordinary' rather than 'extraordinary'. This component was founded on the notions from positive psychology that not all performers will note their own qualities and subsequently will not utilize those strengths to supplement their self-perceptions and therefore limit their flourishing (Fredrickson, 2009).

The content of the poster (see Figure 3.1) was comprised of the following information:

Edge – sources of assistance and preparation that members of the WCPP felt had given the Great Britain team an 'edge' on the opposition. This information was displayed on the poster around the edge of the other content and included: 'Home games', 'Trained in and competed at the Olympic pool', 'Home crowd – experience of it', 'Pink Thursdays', 'Training at home during the games', 'Same time zone', 'Media exposure', 'Volunteers'.

Team strengths – reminders of key preparation outcomes and progressions that the members of the WCPP felt had taken place for the team as a whole. This information was presented as a central column on the poster around which the individual performer strengths could be displayed and included: 'Ranking from 2007–2012, dramatically improved', 'Improved Highlights', 'All the support we have – staff, etc., around the team', 'Improved understanding of every ones personalities', 'Growing in body awareness', 'Physically stronger', 'Family dynamic – close knit team', 'More complicated routines', 'Routine endurance has improved – Can finish strong now', 'Hours of training and years together', 'Winter camps to step forward at the end of the year to keep improving', 'Facilities in Aldershot – pool times, gym access'.

Individual strengths – whereas the team strengths were brought together as a group, the individual strengths were focused on each individual identifying at least two characteristics of each of the other performers, coaches, and support staff that they considered as a personal strength of theirs. Aligned with the individual strengths, was the background colour representing their individual dominant preference as described previously from the Insights Discovery profile along with a headshot photograph of the particular individual to

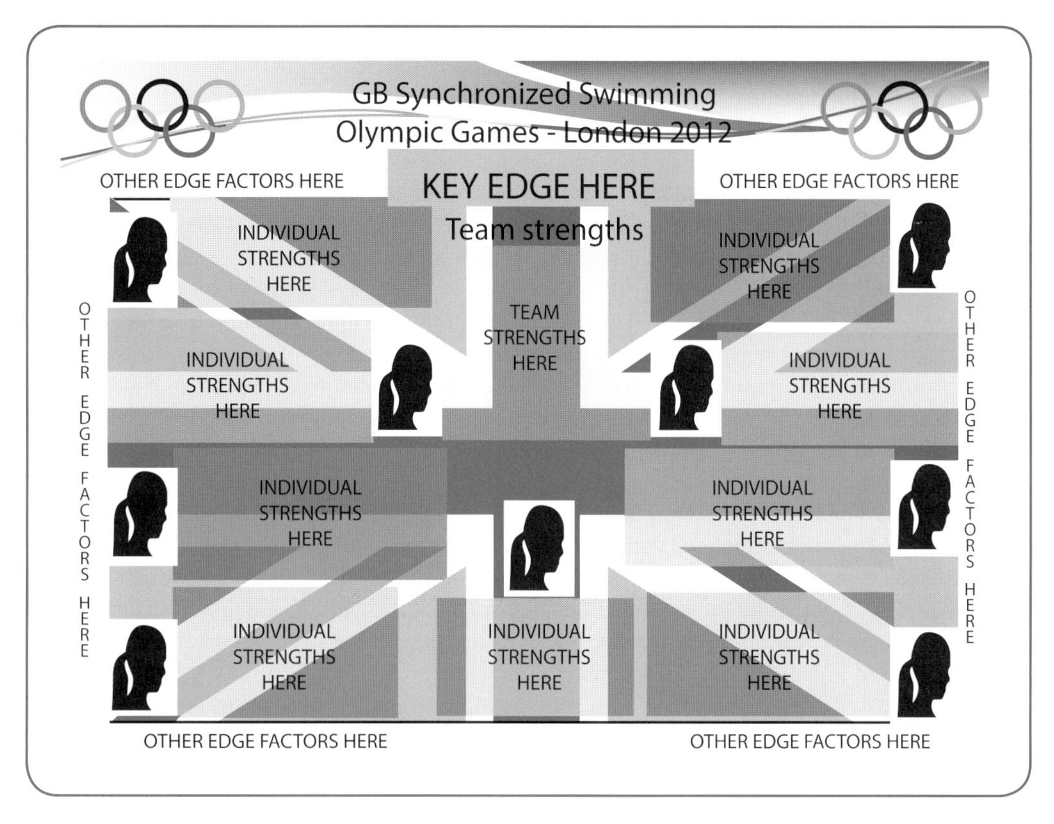

FIGURE 3.1 *Exemplar strengths poster layout*

whom the strengths related. The colour preference background was included as a reminder to all of the preference for each of the performers within the squad. This reminder could feed into how they chose to respond to others within the Olympic environment (for example when under pressure). A sample of the individual strength characteristics of some of the performers was as follows: 'Gratefulness', 'Determined and self-reliant – where there is a will there is a way', 'Dependable, determination/tolerance', 'Precise – you do things properly', 'You have proven great patience and determination', 'I love your witty one liners, I idolize her bravery', 'Great courage', 'Nothing will knock her down', 'Strong', 'Motivated to get what she does right, strong-minded, perseverance'.

Having identified the benefits of working on a strengths-based intervention in the final period leading up to the games, the mode through which this was to be delivered needed to be created. This particular aspect of the intervention could be considered more as the 'art' rather than science of intervention implementation although it is hopefully clear that there was a clear rationale behind the decisions made in relation to the choice of presentation of the collated information. The use of a visual, impactful representation, which could be used as a reminder in the competitive context provided a starting point for the creative component of the intervention. The focus on how the intervention was to be delivered to the specific group receiving it was fundamental to the perceived likely effectiveness.

The importance of performing for Great Britain at an Olympic Games leads to certain pervasive visual images. Primary in this is the use of flags of nations and, for Great Britain, the Union Jack. Butler (1996) had used the flag in an exercise to develop self-belief and this use of the flag as a backdrop to the presentation of strength-based information seemed to be hugely appropriate, visually impactful, and attractive. It is clear that the development and extension of the social identity of the squad was a significant supplementary benefit of the use of the imagery and the content of the strengths-based poster. It is evident that leaders can have an impact on the social identity of a group and practitioners can also influence this through bespoke interventions (Slater, Evans, & Barker, 2013; Pain & Harwood, 2009).

The poster in Figure 3.1 is the one designed for the performers and contains space for content related to the nine performers chosen from the squad of 13 for the Olympic Games. However it is important to note that the same principles (minus the photographs) were applied to smaller scale posters representing the findings for the other two groups engaged with the overall exercise (i.e., the coaching staff and the sport science staff).

Significant components of the poster presentation and content had been supported by team-based sessions delivered by the author throughout the period leading up to the Olympic Games. Although these aspects of the work completed with the WCPP are not the focus of this particular case study, it is important to mention that preparation sessions were conducted based on the individual strengths and weaknesses of particular preferences from the Insights Discovery profiling and enhanced the level of awareness of self and others as well as becoming clear about the opportunities and challenges that would potentially emerge for individuals when under the pressure of a home Olympic environment.

REFLECTIONS

Congruence

An important consideration espoused for applied practitioners is the congruence within applied practice between philosophical frameworks, theoretical foundations, and delivery content and approach (Poczwardowski, Sherman, & Ravizza, 2004; Lindsay, Breckon, Thomas, & Maynard, 2007). Such an approach is consistently presented in the literature as a goal for applied practitioners. The case study presents an example where tension emerged between the philosophical approach of an individual practitioner (the author) and the contextual expectations and common practice of a body of practitioners joined together within a guiding framework (English Institute of Sport). Although the broad foundations of the approach taken by the Performance Psychology group certainly had congruent cognitive behavioural intention and content, the utilization of the Insights Discovery tool with its foundations within a psychoanalytic framework created some initial challenges to the congruence of philosophy and working practice. This philosophical and theoretical incongruence was further exacerbated by the way in which the context within which the author was working had clearly embraced the tool and had influenced the language and interpretation of the discourse around psychology within the HPC. The author was initially unsure of how to move forwards in a situation where such an incongruence was apparent. The decision was taken that to deviate from this accepted approach would be counterintuitive and potentially counterproductive and so the Insights Discovery element of the previous work was incorporated into the author's working practices and delivered within a cognitive behavioural framework. For example, the impacts on thoughts and feelings of differences in preferences were discussed and potential conflicts were identified along with relevant coping strategies.

This issue of congruence highlights a potential limitation of a structured philosophy of approach (Henriksen & Diment, 2011). The notion of a guiding framework within which a variety of practitioners can function with limited incongruence is certainly feasible as long as it is in concert with adaptable practitioners.

Impact of the discovery profiles on the style of service delivery

An interesting by-product of an adaptable approach to the author's delivery of service to incorporate the Insights Discovery profiling was the additional benefits that could be drawn from this profile information. The most striking example was evident in the adaptation of the style of service delivery adopted with individual performers. This was influenced by the recognition, and adaptation to, the preferred communication styles and personality characteristics identified through aspects of the profiling process. For example, those performers with a strong sunshine yellow preference were often provided service on poolside with a more dynamic and staccato delivery style. In contrast, those performers with a strong cool blue preference received service delivery in a more formal setting at appointed times. These examples identify the potential benefits of adapting the style, venue and attitude adopted within service delivery dependent upon performer preferences and characteristics.

Part-time roles

Through working one day a week within the WCPP it became very clear, very quickly that it was hugely important to understand the realistic limitations on effectiveness given the time available. It was important to decide with the coaches, in as planned yet dynamic way possible, what it is that you are going to choose to have an impact on based on your professional judgement and decision making (Martindale & Collins, 2005). Figure 3.2 indicates the reality of the disconnect between the

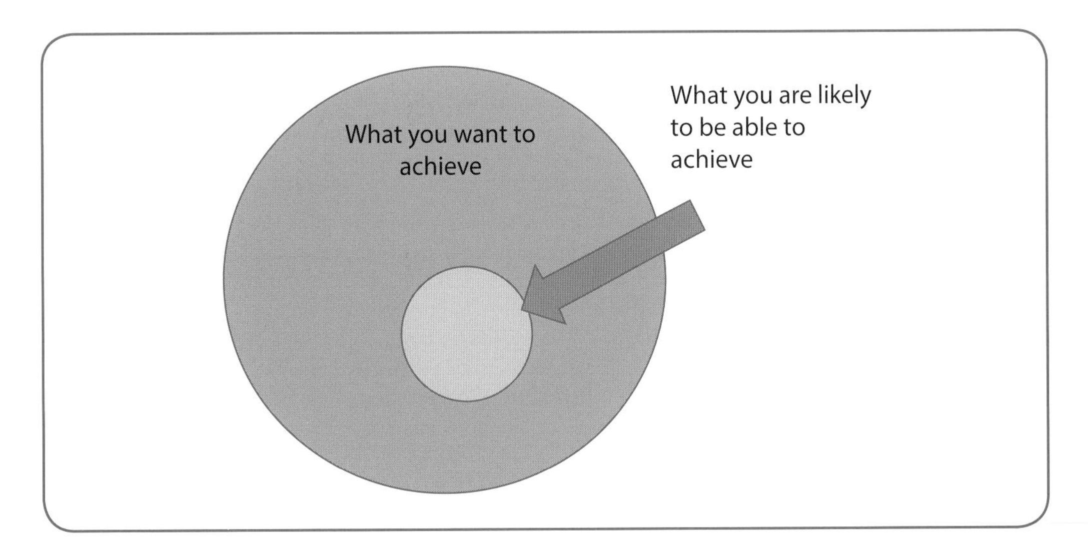

FIGURE 3.2 *'Reality check' of applied practice*

total needs of the working environment that an applied practitioner may desire to impact upon and the proportion of these needs that are able to be serviced. This, of course, is almost always apparent for any practitioner, even those who are employed full time. However the potential frustrations and disappointments that accompany such a disconnect are exacerbated for practitioners in part-time roles. They should be considered in relation to their impact in both the short and long term on both performer and practitioner satisfaction and the potential impacts on client practitioner relationships, rapport and trust (Petitpas, Giges, & Danish, 2009).

Access at competition

Through working with the coaching staff in the WCPP it was decided that the author's work at the games was to be 'available' but not to be present within the village environment. This approach aligned perfectly with the author's philosophy that a key part of the development of performers is to enable them to be more and more independent of the psychological support. The extension of this philosophy was to trust the performers' training and preparation to cope with the demands of the Olympic Games competition. However, the availability of services at the games was made possible as it is evident that in competitive situations it is prudent to plan to offer the opportunity to 'fire fight' as unexpected events may unfold for which the plan does not accommodate.

One of the key reflections based on this experience of 'off site' provision was in getting the balance right. By this I mean establishing a balance between trusting the work that had been done in the years prior to the games whilst maintaining awareness of any emerging issues. The communication between practitioners, coaches, and fellow support service providers was critical in the continual updating of potential need for psychological services and was a key benefit of working in a multidisciplinary team. The personal and professional tension here was in feeling useful by not getting involved – trusting myself to trust the performers. My reflection on this is that it was important for me to 'keep my beak (nose) out and not get put out (offended) by it'. Having the confidence as a practitioner to understand that doing nothing can be exactly what is required.

FURTHER READING

Bond, J. W. (2001). The provision of sport psychology services during competition tours. In G. Tenenbaum (Ed.), *The practice of sport psychology* (pp. 217–230). Morgantown, WV: Fitness Information Technology. This book chapter offers insights into the challenges of working as a sport psychologist whilst a team is competing.

Gordon, S., & Gucciardi, D. F. (2011). A strengths-based approach to coaching mental toughness. *Journal of Sport Psychology in Action, 2*, 143–155. This journal article explores the approaches that applied practitioners could take to the use of strengths-based approaches for a psychological impact related to performance.

Lindsay, P., Breckon, J. D., Thomas, O., & Maynard, I. W. (2007). In pursuit of congruence: A personal reflection on methods and philosophy in applied practice. *The Sport Psychologist, 21*, 335–352. This journal article discusses the importance of considering the philosophy of practice and its role in guiding applied practice in the methods used as well as influencing the style with which applied practice is delivered.

Brown, C. H., Gould, D., & Foster, S. (2005). A framework for developing contextual intelligence (CI). *The Sport Psychologist, 19*, 51–62. This journal article presents an important analysis of the substantial benefits to be gleaned from an understanding of the context within which an applied practitioner works. It establishes key factors to consider about a sporting context that can influence what information an applied practitioner gathers within a performance context and how a practitioner might respond to that information in applied practice.

AUTHOR'S NOTE

This work was completed whilst the author was employed at the University of Chichester and seconded to the English Institute of Sport for one day a week.

REFERENCES

Bandura, A. (1986). *Social foundations of thought and action: A social cognitive theory*. Englewood Cliffs, NJ: Prentice Hall.

Bandura, A. (1997). *Self-efficacy: The exercise of control*. New York: W. H. Freeman and Company.

Brown, C. H., Gould, D., & Foster, S. (2005). A framework for developing contextual intelligence (CI). *The Sport Psychologist*, *19*, 51–62.

Bull, S. J. (1997). The immersion approach. In R. J. Butler (Ed.), *Sports psychology in performance* (pp. 177–202). Oxford: Butterworth Heinemann.

Butler, R. (1996). *Sports psychology in action*. Oxford: Butterworth Heinemann.

Collins, D., Moore, P., Mitchell, D., & Alpress, F. (1999). Role conflict and confidentiality in multidisciplinary athlete support programmes. *British Journal of Sports Medicine*, *33*, 208–211.

Connole, I. J., Shannon, V. R., Watson, J. C., Wrisberg, C., Etzel, E., & Schimmel, C. (2014). NCAA athletic administrators' preferred characteristics for sport psychology positions: A consumer market analysis. *The Sport Psychologist*, *28*, 406–417.

Deci, E. L. & Ryan, R. M. (1985). *Intrinsic motivation and self-determination in human behavior*. New York: Plenum Press.

FINA (2010). *FINA Synchronised swimming manual for judges, coaches and referees*. FINA.org.

Fredrickson, B. (2009). *Positivity*. New York: Three Rivers Press.

Gordon, S. (2012). Strengths-based approaches to developing mental toughness: Team and individual. *International Coaching Psychology Review*, *7*(2), 210–222.

Gordon, S., & Gucciardi, D. F. (2011). A strengths-based approach to coaching mental toughness. *Journal of Sport Psychology in Action*, *2*, 143–155.

Gould, D., & Maynard, I. (2009). Psychological preparation for the Olympic Games. *Journal of Sports Sciences*, *27*(13), 1393–1408.

Greenlees, I. A., Graydon, J. K., & Maynard, I. W. (1999). The impact of collective efficacy beliefs on effort and persistence in a group task. *Journal of Sport Sciences*, *17*, 151–158.

Gustafsson, H., Holmberg, H., & Hassmen, P. (2008). An elite endurance athlete's recovery from underperformance aided by a multidisciplinary sport science support team. *European Journal of Sport Science*, *8*(5), 267–276.

Henriksen, K., & Diment, G. (2011). Professional philosophy: Inside the delivery of sport psychology service at Team Denmark. *Sport Science Review*, *20*, 5–21.

Holder, T., & Winter, S. (under review). The use of observation in applied sport psychology practice: A preliminary investigation.

Jacobi, J. (1942). *The psychology of C. G. Jung*. London: Routledge.

Lindsay, P., Breckon, J. D., Thomas, O., & Maynard, I. W. (2007). In pursuit of congruence: A personal reflection on methods and philosophy in applied practice. *The Sport Psychologist*, *21*, 335–352.

Martindale, A., & Collins, D. (2005). Professional judgement and decision making: The role of intention for impact. *The Sport Psychologist*, *19*(3), 303–318.

McCann, S. C. (2000). Doing sport psychology at the really big show. In M. B. Andersen (Ed.), *Doing sport psychology* (pp. 209–222). Champaign, IL: Human Kinetics.

Meehan, H. L., Bull. S. J., Wood, D. M., & James, D. V. B. (2004). The overtraining syndrome: A multicontextual assessment. *The Sport Psychologist*, *18*(2), 154–171.

Meichenbaum, D. (1977). *Cognitive-behavior modification: An integrative approach*. New York: Plenum Press.

Myers, N. D., Feltz, D. L., & Short, S. E. (2004). Collective efficacy and team performance: A longitudinal study of collegiate football teams. *Group Dynamics: Theory, Research and Practice*, *8*(2), 126–138.

Neville, A. M., & Holder, R. L. (1999). Home advantage in sport: An overview of the studies on the advantage of playing at home. *Sports Medicine*, *28*(4), 221–236.

Pain, M., & Harwood, C. (2009). Team building through mutual sharing and open discussion of team functioning. *The Sport Psychologist*, *23*, 523–542.

Peterson, C. (2006). *Primer in Positive Psychology*. Cambridge: Cambridge University Press.

Peterson, C., & Park, N. (2011). Character strengths and virtues: Their role in well-being. In S. I. Donaldson, M. Csikszentmihalyi, & J. Nakamura (Eds.), *Applied positive psychology: Improving everyday life, health, schools, work, and society* (pp. 49–62). New York: Routledge.

Peterson, C., & Park, N. (2012). Character strengths and the life of meaning. In P. T. P. Wong (Ed.), *The human quest for meaning: Theories, research, and applications* (2nd ed., pp. 277–296). New York: Routledge.

Petitpas, A. J., Giges, B., & Danish, S. J. (1999). The sport psychologist – athlete relationship: Implications for training. *The Sport Psychologist*, *13*, 344–357.

Poczwardowski, A., Sherman, C. P., & Ravizza, K. (2004). Professional philosophy in the sport psychology service delivery: Building on theory and practice. *The Sport Psychologist*, *18*, 445–463.

Ponnusamy, V., & Grove, J. R. (2014). Sport psychology service provision: Preferences for consultant characteristics and mode of delivery among elite Malaysian athletes. *Journal of Sport Science and Medicine*, *13*, 638–644.

Reid, C., Stewart, E., & Thorne, G. (2004). Multidisciplinary sport science teams in elite sport: Comprehensive servicing or conflict and confusion? *The Sport Psychologist*, *18*, 204–217.

Rogers, C. (1980). *A way of being*. New York: Houghton Mifflin.

Ronglan, L. T. (2007). Building and communicating collective efficacy: A season long in depth study of an elite sport team. *The Sport Psychologist*, *21*, 78–93.

Seligman, M. (2011). *Flourish*. New York: Free Press.

Slater, M. J., Evans, A. L., & Barker, J. B. (2013). Using social identities to motivate athletes towards peak performance at the London 2012 Olympic Games: Reflecting for Rio 2016. *Reflective Practice: International and Multidisciplinary Perspectives*, *14*(5), 672–679.

Taylor, J. (1995). A conceptual model for integrating athletes' needs and sport demands in the development of competitive mental preparation strategies. *The Sport Psychologist*, *9*, 339–357.

4 Concentration and Optimal Performance Under Pressure

STEWART COTTERILL AND AIDAN MORAN

LEARNING OUTCOMES

AFTER READING THIS CHAPTER YOU SHOULD BE ABLE TO:

1. Understand the relationship between thinking habits, concentration, and athletic performance.
2. Understand the impact of a lack of quality sleep upon sports performance.
3. Develop a critical understanding of the problem of rumination and its potential impacts upon performance.
4. Understand, describe, and evaluate cognitive therapy-based approaches in sport psychology practice.
5. Critically reflect on the appropriateness of the highlighted cognitive intervention, and to contrast this approach with a mindfulness-based one.

AREAS TO CONSIDER WHEN READING THE CHAPTER:

1. The impact that changes to normal sleeping practices can have upon optimal psychological functioning.
2. What factors influence a consultant's choice of intervention when faced with a client's problems?
3. How do travelling and enforced changes to players' preparation routines affect athletic performance? To what degree do sports teams consider the impacts of travelling and a change to normal routines in their planning and preparation?

CLIENT AND BACKGROUND

The client presented in this case study was, at the time of consultation, a very talented 22-year-old young male cricketer who had been earmarked for future success with his national cricket team. This prediction of future success was in part due to the view that his playing style and technique fitted the 'type' that the national selectors in his sport were seeking for that country's international cricket team at the time of the intervention. Specifically, this player was a fast bowler who, while not having a track record of sustained excellent performances, was deemed to have the necessary basic physical and mental attributes for success. This included the speed at which he could bowl and a technique that could stand up to the pressures of international cricket, a requirement to reach the top in the sport in question.

Although the client (from this point on to be referred to as Chris) in question was seen as being very talented, and as a result earmarked for future success, he was still relatively inexperienced in the world of professional cricket with only one full season playing first-class (professional) cricket in the English County Championship under his belt. At the time of the intervention, he had been playing cricket competitively within the age-group structure of his county for eight years, progressing through the age-group squads and Academy before being offered a professional contract. Chris was viewed by the existing coaching and support staff at his county to be a 'thinker' and while this is often seen as a strength from a strategy perspective, it can also be problematic in other situations. To illustrate the perils of 'over-thinking' more generally in sport, consider the insights of Xavi Hernández, the Spanish soccer player who won both World Cup (2010) and Champions' League (2011) medals; and two-time golf Major winner, Rory McIlroy. When Xavi joined Barcelona football club, he was encouraged to think strategically: 'the first thing they teach is: Think, think, think' (cited in Lowe, 2011, pp. 6–7). In order to prevent himself from thinking too much about the mechanics of his actions, McIlroy distracted himself by speaking to his caddie on his way to victory in the 2011 US Open championship. As he revealed afterwards, 'having a conversation about something completely different is probably the best thing for me as it … stops me getting too involved in what I'm doing' (cited in Irish Times, 2011, p. 20).

Perhaps not surprisingly, Chris was viewed as being 'intelligent' and 'deep' by teammates at his club. Chris's tendency to 'over-think' off the pitch was, at the time, presenting problems for him. For example, he had developed a tendency to ruminate at night, especially before very important matches (such as when he was playing international cricket). This 'over-thinking' was having an impact on the duration and quality of Chris's sleep, which, in turn, was having the 'knock-on' effect of reducing his ability to concentrate as effectively as usual when playing (see Brassington & Goode, 2013, for a good overview of the relationship between sleep and athletic performance). A further outcome of this insufficient sleep was that Chris was showing signs of losing emotional control when playing – an untypical feature of his game. For example, for a player who normally did not display negative emotions, he had developed a tendency to show his frustration by kicking the ground, having verbal outbursts (e.g., swearing), and demonstrating uncharacteristically negative body language (e.g., slumped shoulders and an ungainly posture). As a result of these factors, Chris felt that he was not able to perform to his full ability in big games, which was beginning to erode his confidence ('self-efficacy') in them. This recognition regarding the impact upon performance was the key factor influencing him and his support team to seek a consultation with a sport psychologist for advice on dealing with these problems and performing to his full potential.

INITIAL NEEDS ASSESSMENT

A three-step approach to the initial needs analysis was adopted for this particular case study. The three steps focused specifically on: 1) personality assessment; 2) collecting contextual information from relevant parties; 3) one-to-one discussion with the client. More specifically, the initial needs analysis consisted of Chris completing a Myer-Briggs Type Indicator (MBTi; Myers & Kirby, 1994) personality assessment; discussions with Chris's coaches and support staff; and an initial 2-hour interview session with a sport psychology consultant. This latter session explored a number of different aspects of Chris and his sport including: general background; history in the sport; cricket strengths; general strengths; 'mental game' abilities (e.g., decision-making, concentration, emotional control, motivation, confidence, & resilience); and other mental health and lifestyle issues (e.g., perfectionism, self-efficacy, stress and anxiety, and coping with touring).

The MBTi tool was used as part of the analysis for three specific reasons. First it is very useful in developing a deeper understanding of the client and their preferences for interacting with the world (and the consultant). Second, it formed a core component of the consultant's practice at the time of the case study and third, because it was already extensively used in professional cricket circles in the UK. As a result, this test had popular currency and face validity in cricket (Cotterill, 2012a). The consultant's preference for using the MBTi instrument stemmed from its usefulness in developing a deeper understanding of Chris, his preferences, and the most effective methods to employ when working with him. The MBTi approach was developed by Myers and Briggs (Myers & Kirby, 1994) and is built upon Jung's theory of psychological types (Jung, 1971). The tool categorizes individuals as one of 16 different personality 'types' (see Figure 4.1 for details), which are each composed of

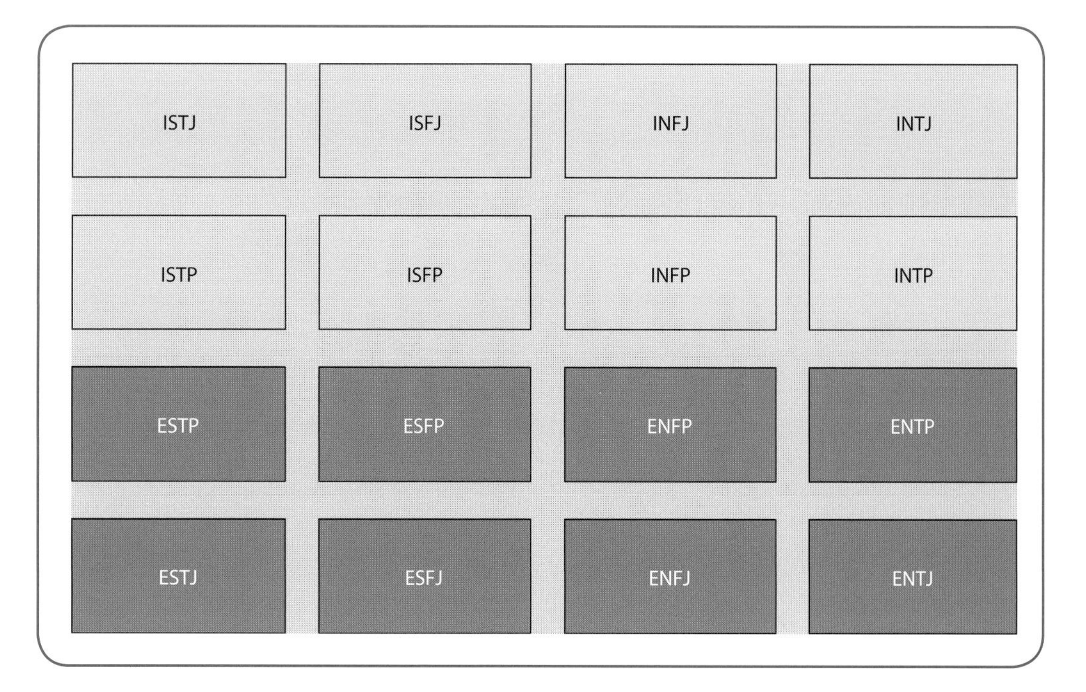

FIGURE 4.1 *MBTi personality types*

four preferences that emerge out of four specific dichotomies (Extraversion-Introversion, Sensing-Intuition, Thinking-Feeling, Judging-Perceiving). See Table 4.1 for further details.

This approach suggests that the personality 'type' that you are determines the way you interact with the world around you. For example, an ISTP likes making decisions on the basis of logic, uses

Table 4.1 *Description of the individual preferences that contribute to the highlighted dichotomies.*

Extraversion (E)	*Introversion (I)*
Tend to act before thinking	Tend to think before acting
Prefer to get into action	Prefer to spend time on reflection
Talk things through	Think things through
More expressive when interacting	More contained when interacting
Gain energy from interactions	Gain energy from concentration
Have a breadth of interests	Have a depth of interests
Sensing (S)	***Intuition (N)***
Want to know the facts	Seek out new ideas
Look at the specifics	Look at the bigger picture
Adopt a realistic approach	Adopt an imaginative approach
Focus on the here and now	Anticipate the future
Ensure things work in practice	Ensure things work in theory
Collect observations	Use conceptual frameworks
Thinking (T)	***Feeling (F)***
Apply logical reasoning	Apply individual values
Use cause-and-effect analysis	Understand others' viewpoints
Seek objective truth	Seek harmony
Decide using impersonal criteria	Decide by personal circumstances
Focus on tasks	Focus on relationship
Provide a critique	Offer praise
Judging (J)	***Perceiving (P)***
Like to come to closure	Keep a range of choices available
Make plans	Remain flexible
Act in a controlled way	Respond to emerging information
Prefer to act within a structure	Prefer to go with the flow
Prefer to schedule activities	Prefer to be spontaneous

objective considerations, is concerned with truth, principles, and justice, is analytical and critical, tends to see the flaws in situations, takes an objective approach. The MBTi tool has been developed and refined since the early 1940s. The current version (M) is composed of 93 items that require responses in a forced choice format. MBTi type has been applied in a wide range of contexts and specifically in developing the individual's understanding of their decision-making, emotional intelligence, communication, conflict resolution, and stress among other areas.

An individual's MBTi type is determined via a three-step process. The first step involves the individual completing a version of the MBTi questionnaire. This provides a score for the individual on each of the eight preferences. As a result, the questionnaire suggests a 'type' for the participant and a 'strength' score (how strong the indication is in each of the four contrasting pairs). The second step in the process involves the individual, working with a qualified MBTi practitioner, to choose which 'type' they think best fits them. This works on the notion that the individual is the expert in themselves, and as such is best placed to decide. The MBTi practitioner's job is to help the individual to reflect and to also present examples to clarify understanding for what the preferences in each dichotomy mean. At the end of this process, once the individual has articulated what they think their preference is, they are presented with the results from the questionnaire. At this point, and the third and final stage, the individual can review both the questionnaire result and their own personal preference, and ultimately make a decision of what they think their overall preference is.

The exploration of the strengths of Chris in the initial needs analysis built upon the work of Linley and colleagues (e.g., Govindji & Linley, 2007; Seligman, Steen, Park, & Peterson, 2005) and Dweck (2006) who each adopted a strengths-based approach to working with clients. This was further informed by the sport-specific strengths work of Gordon (2012) and Gordon and Gucciardi (2011) in cricket. In the current needs analysis this involved asking Chris questions about what his strengths were as a person and as a cricketer.

The discussions about Chris's mental game abilities were underpinned by a pre-existing approach within the performance domain of cricket that focused on the following six key areas of mental game performance: decision-making, concentration, emotional control, motivation, confidence, and resilience (see Table 4.2 for further details).

Chris was provided with a description of each term and was asked to rate his current levels on a scale of 1(very poor) to 10 (excellent) for each of the six areas. This ratings-scale approach to quantifying Chris's perceptions has previously been applied in professional cricket (Cotterill, 2012a). In line with the scenario outlined at the start of the chapter, Chris scored himself low on concentration, emotional control, and confidence. The scores from Chris's self-rating here also formed the core of the subsequent one-to-one discussion between Chris and myself. This approach built upon the performance profiling technique advocated by Butler and Hardy (1992), which was derived originally from Personal Construct psychology (Kelly, 1991). Performance Profiling is a technique that is highlighted as a useful methodology for identifying and understanding the individuals' perceptions of the areas they need to improve or develop (Gucciardi & Gordon, 2009; Kremer & Moran, 2013; Weston, Greenlees, & Thelwell, 2013). Indeed, this specific approach encourages researchers and practitioners alike to regard the client's perception of their own performance and its limitations as an essential source of information for identifying key areas for further improvement/development. A number of benefits of the technique have been highlighted (Gucciardi & Gordon, 2009; Weston, Greenlees, & Thelwell, 2010; Weston et al., 2013) including: raising the individual's self-awareness of their current state, enhancing adherence to programmes of intervention, and increasing the awareness of relevant parties to the players' perceptions of their performance.

Table 4.2 *Mental game assessment descriptors.*

Decision-making	• Will deliver the big performance when it counts • Thinks clearly under pressure • Makes correct decisions and executes relevant plan
Concentration	• Knows both when and how to switch on and off • Also knows what is relevant and important and what's not • Can focus on the right things
Emotional control	• You are able to manage both positive and negative emotions • Can leave emotional events behind them • You are able to achieve good emotional states
Motivation	• You want to be the best and will do everything required to get there • Will always give 100% in training, and will leave no stone unturned in your pursuit of excellence
Confidence	• Are confident in your ability to perform in any situation, and against any opposition • Just know you will succeed
Resilience	• Can take setbacks in their stride, it just makes you more determined • Keeps going whatever is thrown at you

Regarding the mental health and lifestyle components of the initial needs analysis, specific representative questions were asked in order to probe the following areas of Chris's experience: sensation seeking (Do you get bored easily?), perfectionism (How do you feel when you have not done the best that you can?), obsessive-compulsive disorder (Are there things that you do repeatedly/consistently?), self-efficacy (Are you happy in your identity as a cricketer?), stress/anxiety (What aspects of your life do you find most stressful?), and the effect of touring (What do you miss most when you are away from home?). These questions were developed following rigorous consideration of the appropriate mental health literature (Stoeber, 2012) and via sense checking with a clinical psychologist. The rationale for exploring Chris's general mental health was built upon the consultant's belief that a good general level of mental health is crucial for sustained good performance under pressure (Cotterill, 2012b). None of Chris's responses to these questions flagged up any specific mental health concerns.

One core message that emerged from the one-to-one with Chris was a tendency to think and ruminate before trying to sleep. He did acknowledge that this did happen at other times but was more pronounced before sleeping. Rumination is a method of coping with negative mood that involves self-focused attention (Lyubomirsky & Nolen-Hoeksema, 1993). Treynor, Gonzalez, and Nolen-Hoeksema (2003) further suggested that rumination is characterized by self-reflection, as well as a repetitive and passive focus on one's emotions. Based on the initial needs analysis, two specific issues and associated interventions were identified. The first step, in the short term, was to implement strategies for Chris to be able to gain a better quality of sleep. This was designed to reduce the knock-on effects on concentration, confidence, and emotional state. The second step was to resolve the underpinning cause of the sleep issues that related to the rumination or over-thinking. The specific detail that emerged from this discussion, coupled with the information provided by the MBTi assessment and strengths-focus enabled me to gain a better understanding of Chris and his cricket performance. Building upon this information, a specific plan of intervention was formalized.

Understanding 'over-thinking': what is rumination and how can we treat it?

Based on the preceding evidence, we concluded that 'over-thinking' or excessive self-reflection (i.e., focusing too much or too frequently on one's experiences, thoughts and feelings (Nolen-Hoeksma, Wisco, Lyubomirsky, 2008)) played a central role in Chris's performance problems. However, before we outlined a specific intervention plan, additional theoretical knowledge was required. Specifically, we needed to delve deeper into research findings on the nature and treatment of rumination. So, what did we learn from the cognitive and clinical psychological research literature on rumination?

To begin with, we learnt that although the ability to think about ourselves is what makes us distinctive as a species, certain kinds of self-reflection can be counterproductive. In particular, research shows that a type of repetitive thinking known as 'rumination' or 'thinking perseveratively about one's feelings and problems rather than in terms of the specific content of thoughts' (Nolen-Hoeksma et al., 2008, p. 400) is maladaptive in many everyday situations because it encourages brooding rather than action. Interestingly, some researchers (e.g., Treynor et al., 2003) have distinguished between two different types of rumination: An adaptive type called 'reflective pondering' (referring to an attempt to engage in probem-solving to improve one's mood) and a maladaptive type called 'depressive brooding' (or a tendency to focus passively on the symptoms of one's distress). Although both types of rumination involve a focus on one's distress, the brooding type tends to involve more self-critical judgements than the reflective type. Either way, rumination usually involves a tendency to focus on negative thoughts and/or intrusive images arising from real or imagined experiences. Perhaps not surprisingly, rumination is associated with a host of negative psychological and behavioural outcomes. For example, in a recent review of research on this topic, Querstret and Cropley (2013) concluded that rumination was linked to such difficulties as depression and anxiety, increased frequency of intrusive distracting thoughts, increased negative self-evaluation, reduced self-efficacy, and increased feelings of helplessness. Rumination has also been shown to be associated with feelings of self-criticism, hopelessness, dependency, pessimism, neediness, and neuroticism (Nolen-Hoeksma et al., 2008), with impaired problem-solving (Watkins & Moulds, 2005), and, of course, with negative mood (Thomsen et al., 2004).

Next, we explored the mechanisms by which rumination exerts its adverse effects. In this regard, several theories were reviewed. Perhaps the most influential of these accounts is the 'response styles' theory of rumination (RST; Nolen-Hoekesma, 1991). Briefly, this theory suggests that rumination originates in people's misguided assumption that by dwelling on their thoughts, feelings, and behaviours, they will understand themselves better. Unfortunately, the opposite is true. In other words, by ruminating on their distress, people remain fixated on their problems and feelings. Ironically, instead of enhancing self-understanding, rumination actually *exacerbates* and *prolongs* people's distress. These effects of rumination are attributable to several different factors. First, the tendency to ruminate probably amplifies the effects of depressed mood on thinking, thereby increasing the likelihood that people will use prevailing negative thoughts and memories to understand their current circumstances. Second, rumination hampers problem-solving by inducing passivity and fatalistic thinking. Third, rumination interferes with instumental behaviour, thereby leading to increased stress. More recently, an attentional theory of rumination has been postulated – the 'impaired disengagement' hypothesis (Koster, De Lissnyder, Derakhshan, & De Raedt, 2011). Briefly, this theory suggests that attentional mechanisms underlie rumination effects. More precisely, Koster et al. (2011) postulate that 'information-processing impairments make it difficult for ruminators to disengage from negative content' (p. 142). In other words, ruminators tend to have difficulties in paying attention to task-relevant information and in inhibiting task-irrelevant information. Evidence to support this theory comes from various sources. For example, rumination tends to deplete the resources of working memory (the brain's capacity to simultaneously store and process information for short periods of time), making it difficult for people to divide their attention effectively (Joormann & Gotlib, 2008). Also, Davis and Nolen-Hoeksema (2000) found that ruminators committed significantly more perseverative errors and failed to shift mental set significantly more often than did non-ruminators on the Wisconsin Card Sorting Test (WCST; Grant & Berg, 1948), a measure of strategic planning.

If rumination is primarily a cognitive problem, then its treatment is probably best undertaken at the cognitive level also. In this regard, two intervention strategies seem potentially useful: mindfulness training and an application of cognitive therapy through cognitive restructuring. Mindfulness training is an attentional focusing strategy that originated in the Buddhist meditative tradition (Erisman & Roemer, 2010) but which has been applied increasingly to sport psychology (e.g., see Birrer, Röthlin, & Morgan, 2012; Gardner & Moore, 2010). According to Kabat-Zinn (2005), one of the key benefits of mindfulness training is its ability to get an individual to purposefully attend to the present moment, thereby developing 'an openhearted, moment-to-moment, non-judgemental awareness' (p. 24) of oneself and of the world. This type of awareness should be accompanied by an acceptance that one's unpleasant thoughts and feelings are transient phenomena. This emphasis on adopting a non-judgemental orientation to distracting thoughts is important because it distinguishes mindfulness training from other cognitive control techniques such as 'thought suppression' (i.e., the deliberate attempt to remove unwanted thoughts from consciousness). In summary, by urging *acceptance* rather than attempted elimination of intrusive, unwanted thoughts and feelings, mindfulness training purports to help performers to concentrate on the here-and-now.

Mindfulness intervention programmes have been shown to reduce depression (Hofmann, Sawyer, Witt, & Oh, 2010), enhance well-being (Chiesa & Serretti, 2009), and increase calmness (Farb, Segal, & Anderson, 2012). In sport, there has been an upsurge of interest in the evaluation of mindfulness training interventions for athletes (see Birrer et al., 2012; Gardner & Moore, 2012). In a recent experiment, Aherne, Moran, and Lonsdale (2011) investigated the effects of a six-week, compact disc (CD)-based mindfulness training programme on elite athletes' flow experiences in training. Results showed that athletes who underwent this training programme experienced greater flow post intervention than a control group who received no mindfulness instruction. Although this result is interesting, additional research employing larger samples and controlling for the potential effects of increased attention by the experimenter is needed before firm conclusions can be reached regarding the efficacy of mindfulness training in athletes.

The second strategy for counteracting rumination is through 'cognitive restructuring', a technique borrowed from cognitive therapy that helps people to perceive feared situations as controllable challenges (see Moran, 2012, 2014). According to Clark and Beck (2010), cognitive therapy is a problem-oriented form of psychotherapy that helps people (especially those suffering from anxiety and depression) to modify their maladaptive thoughts, attitudes, beliefs, and information-processing biases (e.g., 'if I fail to win an important match, then I'm a failure as a person' or 'we must win this game'). At least three key principles underlie this form of therapy (Dozois & Beck,

2011). First, people's cognition is assumed to affect both their emotions and their behaviour. Second, it is assumed that people can learn to monitor and modify much of their cognitive activity. Third, cognitive therapists assume that by changing one's beliefs, one can achieve desired change in one's behaviour and experience. In summary, the cornerstone of cognitive therapy is the proposition that people can learn to regard their thoughts as *hypotheses* rather than as facts. By testing the validity of these hypotheses empirically, people can 'shift their cognitive appraisals from ones that are unhealthy and maladaptive to ones that are more evidence-based and adaptive' (Dozois & Beck, 2011, p. 30).

Using cognitive restructuring (see Clark & Beck, 2010), athletes can learn to challenge their rumination by looking for evidence that contradicts the 'worst case' scenarios that they brood about. In this way, athletes can learn to evaluate the veracity of their reasoning and to generate alternative conclusions that are more adaptive and plausible than those that first come to mind. For example, Claspell (2010) suggested that athletes could be challenged with questions such as 'What is your evidence to support your catastrophic assumption?' and instructions such as 'Consider alternative explanations for why things in your life are occurring as they are at present.'

FRAMEWORK AND INTERVENTION

Based upon the initial needs analysis an intervention programme was developed that specifically sought to address the performance issues and Chris's tendency to ruminate. This intervention plan was split into two specific parts. The first was a shorter-term 'fix' that focused on developing techniques to help Chris sleep, and as a result diminish the impact that a lack of sleep caused by excessive rumination was having upon performance. The second part of the intervention, which was more long term in its focus, was designed to reduce and ultimately remove Chris's tendency to over-think, particularly before big games.

In the first part of the plan, the focus was on teaching and developing Chris's ability to use and apply a range of practical techniques that are designed to promote sleep. These techniques included controlled (relaxed) deep breathing and developing a simple repetitive mental focus (e.g., focusing on the rhythm of inhaling and exhaling). The notion of counting sheep works on the second principle of a simple and repetitive thought. The rationale for this is that repetitive and rhythmic actions are both physically and mentally relaxing (Page, Berger, & Johnson, 2006).

Also, linked to this first part was an exploration of Chris's behaviours before trying to get to sleep, and seeking to challenge activities that interfere with the ability to descend into a sleep state (Cotterill, 2012c). One of Chris's disclosures during the initial needs analysis had highlighted a tendency for Chris to try to distract himself before trying to sleep (in an effort to not think too much). This 'distraction' took the form of playing on his laptop (watching films, surfing the internet, playing games, etc.). All of which he felt was stimulating his mind and as a result further decreasing the likelihood that he would be able to 'drift off' to sleep easily. This in turn fed his rumination by reinforcing, in his mind that he was not preparing effectively for his upcoming performances.

Sleep has been identified as an important performance factor as it is one of the most important contributors to recovery (Cotterill, 2012c). This 'recovery' can help the player adjust to, and cope with, the physical, neurological, immunological, and emotional stressors that the individual would have experienced during the day (Morin et al., 2006). Griffin and Tyrell (2004) reported that poor sleeping patterns and insufficient rest is associated with individuals who suffer from high levels of anxiety and depression. Griffin and Tyrell further highlighted a link between excessive dreaming, poor sleeping patterns, and depression. Evidence suggests that when players are stressed they spend more time in dream sleep and not enough time in slow-wave sleep where physical regeneration and recovery mainly takes place (Vandekerckhove & Cluydts, 2010). The reason why dreaming can be unhelpful to recovery is that the brain is in a similar state to when it is awake. Essentially, dreaming can be hard work. Dreams are real to your brain, and as such can be hormonally and emotionally draining, resulting in feelings of fatigue in the morning.

Often little consideration is given to achieving optimal sleep in order to facilitate optimal sports performance (Cotterill, 2012c). Humans are generally habitual creatures. As such, individuals have preferred environments and routines that enable them to gain the maximum amount of quality sleep. Changes to these routines can impact on the quality and duration of sleep, and as a result significantly impact upon physical, psychological, and emotional recovery (Samuels, 2008). Teams who travel to away fixtures and stay in hotels need to consider the impacts upon the ability of team members to recover effectively in these changing environments. Changes to the normal sleeping environment can have a negative impact upon the quality and duration of sleep (Savis, 1994). Sleeping on a harder or softer mattress with more or less ambient noise can all impact upon sleep (Bader & Engdal, 2000). This will, in turn, impact upon the amount of stressors the individual can cope with in subsequent days. Travelling to different time zones, which might upset the body clock can be problematic, as can different environmental conditions such as heat and humidity (Okamoto-Mizuno, Tsuzuki, & Mizuno, 2005).

The inability to get to sleep is often classified in the literature as insomnia, which was defined by Roth (2007) as 'the presence of an individual's report of difficulty with sleep' (p.S7). The literature relating to techniques that can be used to treat insomnia and other sleep-related issues suggests six different models of intervention that can be adopted: stimulus control therapy, sleep restriction therapy, relaxation training, cognitive therapy, sleep hygiene education, and cognitive-behaviour therapy (Morin, 2006).

Description box **BOX 4.1**

SLEEP HYGIENE TECHNIQUES

Sleep stimulus control therapy – a set of instructions to re-associate the bed or bedroom with sleep and to re-establish a consistent sleep-wake schedule.

Sleep restriction therapy – a method to cut the time spent in bed to the actual amount of sleep time (if you sleep for 6 hours spend 6 hours in bed).

Relaxation training – aimed at reducing somatic tension (e.g., progressive muscle relaxation, autogenic training) or intrusive thoughts at bedtime (e.g., imagery and meditation) interfering with sleep.

Cognitive therapy – aims at challenging and changing misconceptions about sleep and faulty beliefs about a lack of sleep. Also can seek to reduce excessive monitoring of, and worrying about, insomnia and its consequences.

Sleep hygiene education – linked to health practices (e.g., diet, exercise, substance use) and environmental factors (e.g., light, noise, and temperature) that can promote or interfere with sleep.

Cognitive-behaviour therapy – a combination of any of the above behavioural (e.g., stimulus control, sleep restriction, relaxation) and cognitive procedures.

A combination of some of the approaches outlined was adopted in the current case study, with the interventions specifically focusing on sleep hygiene in the short term and adopting a cognitive-therapy approach in the longer term to challenge the rumination and tendency to over-think and worry. The sleep hygiene part of the intervention built upon the recommendations of Hauri (1991) to successfully impact upon pre-sleep behaviour. Hauri (1991) suggested the following six steps to enhancing sleep hygiene:

1. *Curtail time in bed* – only be in bed for the time you are sleeping.
2. *Never try to sleep* – engage in activities such as reading, watching television, or listening to radio discussions for as long as possible.
3. *Eliminate the bedroom clock* – time pressure is not conducive to sleep.
4. *Exercise in late afternoon/early evening* – linked to producing a core body temperature drop (conducive for sleep) 4–6 hours later.
5. *Avoid caffeine, alcohol, and nicotine prior to bed.*
6. *Regularize bedtime.*

Similar sleep hygiene techniques have been adopted in sport by Hung, Tang, and Shiang (2009) in their work with an Olympic archer in an attempt to reduce the potential impacts of insomnia on performance.

Building upon the existing literature evidence, and mindful of the specific constraints that existed, the following five steps were adopted:

1. To never try to sleep, specifically look to read.
2. To only use the bed for sleep. Owing to the travel required as part of competitive cricket and the significant number of evenings spent in hotels, it was not realistic to only use the bedroom for sleeping. But this could be adapted to only use the bed for sleep and to use the chairs provided for other activities such as watching television.
3. Eliminate the bedroom clock. Set an alarm but not have the time displayed or easily accessible.
4. To remove caffeine and alcohol consumption before going to bed.
5. To engage in some light exercise where possible in late afternoon or early evening.

This plan was developed and implemented before Chris left the United Kingdom on an upcoming overseas training camp. The plan provided an initial three-week implementation period. Chris was provided with a checklist and a diary to record adherence to the plan and to also record the quality of sleep or ease with which sleep was achieved (this was completed the following day). Specific questions (answered as yes or no) included 'Did you feel tired when you went to bed to sleep?', 'Did you use the bed for general lounging?', 'Is the time visible from your sleeping position?', 'Did you consume caffeine between dinner and bed?', and 'Did you engage in light exercise late afternoon or early evening'?

This initial three-week programme was designed to act as a period of embedding and reinforcement to prepare Chris for the subsequent five-week overseas block living in hotel rooms. During the five-week overseas training camp, Chris was also required to continue to keep the sleep hygiene and quality record.

The second, more long-term part of the intervention focused on challenging the beliefs that underpinned Chris's over-thinking and rumination by adopting a cognitive-therapy approach. It was envisaged that while this would potentially take longer to achieve than the 'short-term fix', it would ultimately provide a more lasting solution to the diagnosed issue for Chris. The main focus of this part of the intervention was to understand why the over-thinking and rumination was taking place, what the triggers were, and how to either remove the triggers or to respond to them differently. This part of the intervention was designed to run over a three-month period.

Cognitive therapy has been characterized as 'the fastest growing and most heavily researched orientation on the contemporary scene' (Prochaska & Norcross, 2003: p. 369). Cognitive therapy, in its development around 40 years ago, was influenced by the cognitive revolution in psychology in the 1950s and 1960s. The original approach was based upon the information-processing model (Beck, 2005), and generally stated that processing of external events or internal stimuli is biased and therefore systematically distorts the individual's construction of their own experience. This in turn leads to cognitive errors such as overgeneralization, selective abstraction, and personalization (Beck, 1964). Underlying these distorted interpretations are dysfunctional beliefs incorporated into cognitive structures, or schemas. When these schemas are activated (e.g., by external events) they bias information processes and result in a specific cognitive response (Beck, 2005).

One of the key differences between cognitive therapy and the psychoanalytic approach (Larsen & Buss, 2013) is the focus on present problems as opposed to uncovering hidden traumas from the past (Beck & Ward, 1961). Cognitive behavioural therapy (CBT) and cognitive therapy are often used as synonyms to describe therapies based upon a cognitive model. However, this merging of terms can often be unhelpful as CBT is also used to describe a range of techniques in which cognitive therapy is used in combination with a set of behavioural techniques (Beck, 2005).

First, the individual's cognition is assumed to affect both their emotions and their behaviour. Second, it is assumed that the individual can learn to monitor and modify much of their cognitive activity. Third, cognitive therapists assume that by changing one's beliefs, one can achieve desired change in one's behaviour and experience. In summary, the cornerstone of cognitive therapy is the proposition that people can learn to regard their thoughts as *hypotheses* rather than as facts. By testing the validity of these hypotheses empirically, people can 'shift their cognitive appraisals from ones that are unhealthy and maladaptive to ones that are more evidence-based and adaptive' (Dozois & Beck, 2011, p. 30).

Using cognitive restructuring (see Clark & Beck, 2010), athletes can learn to challenge their rumination by looking for evidence that contradicts the 'worst case' scenarios that they brood about. In this way, athletes can learn to evaluate the veracity of their reasoning and to generate alternative conclusions that are more adaptive and plausible than those that first come to mind. For example, Claspell (2010) suggested that athletes could be challenged with questions such as 'What is your evidence to support your catastrophic assumption?' and instructions such as 'Consider alternative explanations for why things in your life are occurring as they are at present.'

This cognitive therapy approach was applied with Chris in this case study. Specifically, the intervention was applied during the initial five-week training programme. Chris and I engaged in regular meetings (two per week) seeking to challenge Chris's ruminations. Part of this process involved Chris keeping an enhanced personal diary. Alongside the sleep hygiene or quality information, Chris was also required to record the content of his ruminations. This information was then used as the basis for seeking to challenge the content of the thoughts and to see if the evidence supported or contradicted these thoughts. Over the ten sessions that took place there was a shift from a consultant-led challenging of these thoughts to a client-led approach. This was where Chris would record the ruminations then go through the same process in challenging the validity of the statements. The last stage of this process in the final two sessions was for the client to record the ruminations and to challenge them ahead of the sessions. The outcomes and evaluations of this process were then discussed in the timetabled sessions. At the end of this five-week period Chris then continued onto a competitive phase of the NGB development programme that did not include the consultant. Chris though still kept the diary going over the next two months before meeting up again with the sport psychologist on return to the UK to evaluate the progress of the interventions.

REFLECTIONS

As a consultant, this was the first time that I had really sought to explore sleep-related issues in any structured way. After acknowledging that achieving good quality sleep was an issue, I had to do significant searches to acquire the relevant knowledge from which to begin to construct an intervention plan. This was seen as an important 'short-term' approach, as tackling the rumination aspect was going to be more long term. For me there was also an issue in how the work I was doing would be perceived by the coaching staff. The issues highlighted for Chris (emotional control, concentration, and confidence) were very performance related. Getting support and 'buy-in' from the coaches to be focusing on what looked like a sleep issue was important to ensure a consistency of message to Chris regarding the effectiveness of the interventions. This was possible due to the existing relationship I had with the coaches, and the evidence-informed arguments I put forward.

The decision to adopt a cognitive-therapy approach to the underlying psychological factors I think in part reflected my training and development as a sport and exercise psychologist. On reflection, the 'lens' through which my education and professional training as a sport psychologist was presented was fundamentally cognitive. This criticism could be further extended to the sport and exercise psychology literature at the time that advocated cognitive interventions. Indeed, there did not appear to be a gap between cognitive approaches and sport psychology practice. Thankfully this has evolved in recent years with a significant expansion of the debate regarding philosophical approaches in sport and exercise psychology. In my early years of practice, I was a cognitive practitioner by default without knowing that is what I was, or more importantly 'why' that was the case. While I might still adopt the same approach, I have a much clearer appreciation of my professional philosophy as a positive, cognitive, humanist, and the way that this drives the diagnosis I make and the interventions I ultimately choose to adopt.

Feedback from Chris suggested that the interventions had been, at least in part, successful on both counts. First, the sleep hygiene intervention had enhanced the quality of sleep and ease of achieving quality sleep for Chris. He also reported that the effects of the rumination, and indeed the presence of the ruminations had decreased significantly. There were still some isolated episodes, but these were much less frequent and had less of a detrimental effort upon sleep, preparation, and performance. Chris also reported that following the interventions, he was more confident, concentrating better, and not being as emotional as previously was the case. This was also corroborated by the coaches who worked with Chris. In debriefing with the coaches following the overseas competitive element of the programme, the coaches felt there had been an observable decrease in the emotional responses initially reported. There was also a view among the relevant national lead coaches that Chris was also more confident and focused better than had been the case.

Earlier in the chapter, we indicated that mindfulness training could have provided an alternative approach to Chris's problems of over-thinking and rumination. As a result, we will briefly explore how this mindfulness approach could have been adopted with Chris to reduce the episodes of rumination and to improve his quality of sleep. To begin with, we would have given Chris an information sheet which outlined what mindfulness involves (i.e., deliberately paying attention to the present moment in a non-judgemental way; Kabat-Zinn, 2012) and how it could help him to enhance his performance in sport (e.g., by training him to accept distracting events and/or thoughts rather than dwelling on them). We would then have answered any questions that he might have had. After that, we would have introduced him to a six-week programme of guided meditation exercises and somatic (bodily) training based on the work of Kabat-Zinn (2012) and used previously by Aherne et al. (2011). In particular, we would have used such exercises as 'Breath,' 'Breath and Body,' 'Standing Yoga' and 'Body Scan' (see details in Williams, Teasdale, Segal, & Kabat-Zinn, 2007). 'Breath' helps people to become aware of their breathing patterns. Next, 'Breath and Body' teaches a person about the link between breathing patterns and bodily sensations. After that, 'Standing Yoga' elicits awareness of breathing and bodily sensations through a series of stretches. Finally, 'Body Scan' trains participants to become aware of individual bodily parts, one at a time, from lower to upper body. The first three of these exercises typically last about ten minutes each and should be completed once a day. The fourth exercise ('Body Scan') normally takes about 30 minutes and is recommended to be used twice a week on specified days. All four exercises are designed to improve people's awareness of how their bodies feel at any given moment and to improve their ability to focus on their bodily processes as required. To facilitate training exercise compliance, we would have asked Chris to complete a scheduled timetable with a calendar of exercises to tick off when completed. However, to date there are still very few examples of mindfulness techniques being applied in a sports performance setting.

In summary, Chris's case study reinforces that often the 'performance' issues that a performer is experiencing result from fewer performance-focused issues. It is the job of an effective sport psychology consultant to be able to look at the athlete holistically and to correctly diagnose the primary causal factors. Increasingly in sport, elite athletes are being required to travel and stay away from home more and more. As a result, factors such as sleep quality, and general coping abilities are going to become increasingly important to consultants working with these groups. There is still little research exploring the impact of sleep deprivation on sporting performance and crucially strategies that can be utilized to enhance sleep quality, and as a result reduce the potentially detrimental effects upon the individual's performance potential.

FURTHER READING

Beck, A. T. (2005). The current state of cognitive therapy: A 40-year retrospective. *Arch Gen Psychiatry, 62*, 953–959. A good review of the current state of cognitive therapy and its historical development.

Cotterill, S. T., & Barker, J. B. (2013). *The psychology of cricket: Developing mental toughness*. Birmingham: Bennion Kearney. A comprehensive exploration of the psychological factors influencing cricket performance. The book also considers practical techniques and interventions that can be applied to enhance cricketing performance.

Kremer, J., & Moran, A. (2013). *Pure sport: Practical sport psychology* (2nd ed.). Abingdon: Routledge. A good practical guide to applied sport psychology – explaining what works (and what doesn't work) when applying psychological techniques to improve athletic performance.

REFERENCES

Aherne, C., Moran, A. P., & Lonsdale, C. (2011). The effect of mindfulness training on athletes' flow: An initial investigation. *The Sport Psychologist, 25*, 177–189.

Bader, G. G., & Engdal, S. (2000). The influence of bed firmness on sleep quality. *Applied Ergonomics, 31*(5), 487–497.

Beck, A. T. (1964). Thinking and depression: theory and therapy. *Archives of General Psychiatry, 10*, 561–571.

Beck, A. T. (2005). The current state of cognitive therapy: A 40-year retrospective. *Archives of General Psychiatry, 62*, 953–959.

Beck, A. T., & Ward, C. H. (1961). Dreams of depressed patients: Characteristic themes in manifest content. *Archives of General Psychiatry*, *5*, 462–467.

Birrer, D., Röthlin, P., & Morgan, G. (2012). Mindfulness to enhance athletic performance: Theoretical considerations and possible impact mechanisms. *Mindfulness*, *3*(3), 235–246.

Brassington, G. S., & Goode, C. (2013). Sleep. In S. J. Hamrahan & M. B. Andersen (Eds.), *Routledge handbook of applied sport psychology* (pp. 270–281). London: Routledge.

Butler, R. J., & Hardy, L. (1992). The performance profile: Theory and application. *The Sport Psychologist*, *6*(3), 253–264.

Chiesa, A., & Serretti, A. (2009). Mindfulness-based stress reduction for stress management in healthy people: A review and meta-analysis. *Journal of Alternative and Complementary Medicine*, *15*(5), 593–600.

Clark, D. A., & Beck, A. T. (2010). *Cognitive therapy of anxiety disorders: Science and practice*. New York: Guilford Press.

Claspell, E. (2010). Cognitive-behavioral therapies. In S. J. Hanrahan & M. B. Anderson (Eds.), *Routledge handbook of applied sport psychology: A comprehensive guide for students and practitioners*. Abingdon: Routledge.

Cotterill, S. T. (2012a). Experiences of working in an elite sport academy: A case study in professional cricket. *Sport & Exercise Psychology Review*, *8*(1), 45–53.

Cotterill, S. T. (2012b). The challenge of developing cricketers who can play to their strengths. *Sport & Exercise Psychology in Action Conference*, Portsmouth: British Psychological Society Wessex and Wight Branch

Cotterill, S. T. (2012c). *Team psychology in sports: Theory and application*. Abingdon: Routledge.

Davis, R. N., & Nolen-Hoeksema, S. (2000). Cognitive inflexibility among ruminators and nonruminators. *Cognitive Therapy & Research*, *24*, 699–711.

Dozois, D. J. A., & Beck, A. T. (2011). Cognitive therapy. In J. D. Herbert & E. M. Forman (Eds.), *Acceptance and mindfulness in cognitive behavior therapy: Understanding and applying the new therapies* (pp. 26–56). Chichester: Wiley.

Dweck, C. S. (2006). Mindset: *The new psychology of success*. New York: Random House.

Erisman, S. M., & Roemer, L. (2010). A preliminary investigation of the effects of experimentally induced mindfulness on emotional responding to film clips. *Emotion*, *10*(1), 72–82.

Farb, N. A. S., Segal, Z. V., & Anderson, A. K. (2012). The mindful brain and emotion regulation in mood disorders. *Canadian Journal of Psychiatry*, 57(1), 70–77.

Gardner, F. L., & Moore, Z. E. (2010). Acceptance-based behavioural therapies and sport. In S. J. Hanrahan & M. B. Andersen (Eds.), *Routledge handbook of applied sport psychology* (pp. 186–193). London: Routledge.

Gardner, F. L., & Moore, Z. E. (2012). Mindfulness and acceptance models in sport psychology: A decade of basic and applied science advancements. *Canadian Psychology*, *53*(4), 309–318.

Gordon, S. (2012). Strengths-based approaches to developing mental toughness. *Teams and individuals, International Coaching Psychology Review*, *7*(2), 210–222.

Gordon, S., & Gucciardi, D. F. (2011). A strengths-based approach to coaching mental toughness. *Journal of Sport Psychology in Action*, *2*(3), 143–155.

Govindji, R., & Linley, P. A. (2007). Strengths use, self-confidence and well-being: Implications for strengths coaching and coaching psychologists. *International Coaching Psychology Review*, *2*(2), 143–153.

Grant, D. A., & Berg, E. A. (1948). A behavioral analysis of degree of reinforcement and ease of shifting to new responses in a weigl-type card-sorting problem. *Journal of Experimental Psychology*, *38*, 404–411.

Griffin, J., & Tyrell, I. (2004). *Dreaming reality: How dreams keep us sane, or can drive us mad*. Hailsham: HG Publishing.

Gucciardi, D. F., & Gordon, S. (2009). Revisiting the performance profile technique: Theoretical underpinnings and application. *The Sport Psychologist*, *23*(1), 93–117.

Hauri, P. (1991). The sleep disorders. *Current concepts*. Kalamazoo: Scope Publications.

Hofmann, S. G., Sawyer, A. T., Witt, A. A., & Oh, D. (2010). The effect of mindfulness-based therapy on anxiety and depression: A meta-analytic review. *Journal of Consulting and Clinical Psychology*, *78*(2), 169–183.

Hung, T-M., Tang, W-T., & Shiang, T-Y. (2009). A case study of integrated sport sciences for an Olympic archer. *Journal of Medical and Biological Engineering*, *29*(4), 164–171.

Joormann, J., & Gotlib, I. H. (2008). Updating the contents of working memory in depression: Interference from irrelevant negative material. *Journal of Abnormal Psychology*, *117*, 182–192.

Jung, C. G. (1971). *Psychological types*. Princeton, NJ: Princeton University Press. (Original work published 1923).

Kabat-Zinn, J. (2005). *Coming to our senses*. New York: Hyperion.

Kabat-Zinn, J. (2012). *Mindfulenss for beginners*. Boulder, CO: Sounds True.

Kelly, G. A. (1991). *The psychology of personal constructs: A theory of personality (Vol. 1)*. London: Routledge.

Koster, E. H. W., De Lissnyder, E., Derakhshan, N., & De Raedt, R. (2011). Understanding depressive rumination from a cognitive science perspective: The impaired disengagement hypothesis. *Clinical Psychology Review, 31*, 138–145.

Kremer, J., & Moran,. A. (2013). *Pure sport: Practical sport psychology* (2nd ed.). Abingdon: Routledge.

Larsen, R., & Buss, D. (2013). *Personality psychology: Domains of knowledge about human nature*. New York: McGraw-Hill Higher Education.

Lowe, S. (2011). I'm a romantic, says Xavi, heart of the world's best team. *The Guardian* (11 February 11), pp. 6–7 (Sport).

Lyubomirsky, S., & Nolen-Hoeksema, S. (1993). Self-perpetuating properties of dysphoric rumination. *Journal of Personality & Social Psychology, 65*(2), 339–349.

Moran, A. (2012). *Sport and exercise psychology: A critical introduction* (2nd ed.). Abingdon: Routledge.

Moran, A. (2014). Cognitive strategies in sport psychology. In J. L.Van Raalte & B. W. Brewer (Eds.). *Exploring sport and exercise psychology* (3rd ed., (pp. 83–105). Washington, DC: American Psychological Association.

Morin, C. M., Bootzin, R. R., Buysse, D. J., Edinger, J. D., Espie, C. A., & Lichstein, K. L. (2006). Psychological and behavioral treatment of insomnia: Update of the recent evidence (1998–2004). *Sleep, 29*(11), 1398–1414.

Myers, K. D., & Kirby, L. D. (1994). *Introduction to type dynamics and development: Exploring the next level of type*. Mountain View, CA: CPP, Inc.

Nolen-Hoeksema, S. (1991). Responses to depression and their effects on the duration of depressive episodes. *Journal of Abnormal Psychology, 100*, 569–582.

Nolen-Hoeksema, Wisco, B. E., & Lyubomirsky, S. (2008). Rethinking rumination. *Perspectives on Psychological Science, 3*(5), 400–424.

Okamoto-Mizuno, K., Tsuzuki, K., & Mizuno, K. (2005). Effects of humid heat exposure in later sleep segments on sleep stages and body temperature in humans. *International Journal of Biometeorology, 49*, 232–237.

Page, M. S., Berger, A. M., & Johnson, L. B. (2006). Putting evidence into practice: Evidence-based interventions for sleep-wake disturbances. *Clinical Journal of Oncology Nursing, 10*(6), 753–767.

Prochaska, J., & Norcross, J. (2003). *Systems of psychotherapy: A transtheoretical analysis* (5th ed.). Pacific Grove, CA: Brooks Cole.

Querstret, D., & Cropley, M. (2013). Assessing treatments used to reduce rumination and/or worry: A systematic review. *Clinical Psychology Review, 33*(8), 9976–1009.

Roth, T. (2007). Insomnia: Definition, prevalence, etiology, and consequences. *Journal of Clinical Sleep Medicine, 3*(5), S7–S10.

Samuels, C. (2008). Sleep, recovery, and performance: The new frontier in high-performance athletics. *Neurologic Clinics, 26*, 169–180.

Savis, J. C. (1994). Sleep and athletic performance: Overview and implications for sport psychology. *The Sport Psychologist*, 8, 111–125.

Seligman, M. E. P., Steen, T. A., Park, N., & Peterson, C. (2005). Positive psychology progress: Empirical validation of interventions. *American Psychologist, 60*, 410–421.

Stoeber, J. (2012). Perfectionism and performance. In S. M. Murphy (Ed.), *Oxford handbook of sport and performance psychology* (pp. 294–306). New York: Oxford University Press.

Thomsen, D. K., Mehlsen, M. Y., Olesen, F., Hokland, M., Viidik, A., & Avlund, K. et al. (2004). Is there an association between rumination and self-reported physical health? A one-year follow-up in a young and an elderly sample. *Journal of Behavioral Medicine, 27*, 215–231.

Treynor, W., Gonzalez, R., & Nolen-Hoeksema, S. (2003). Rumination reconsidered: A psychometric analysis. *Cognitive Therapy and Research, 27*(3), 247–259.

Vandekerckhove, M., & Cluydts, R. (2010). The emotional brain and sleep: An intimate relationship. *Sleep Medicine Reviews, 14*(4), 219–226.

Watkins, E., & Moulds, M. (2005). Positive beliefs about rumination in depression—A replication and extension. *Personality and Individual Differences*, *39*(1), 73−82.

Weston, N., Greenlees, I., & Thelwell, R. (2010). Applied sport psychology perceptions of the usefulness and impacts of performance profiling. *International Journal of Sport Psychology*, *41*(4), 360–368.

Weston, N., Greenlees, I., & Thelwell, R. (2013). A review of Butler and Hardy's (1992) performance profiing procedure within sport. *International Review of Sport & Exercise Psychology*, *6*(1), 1–21.

Williams, J. M. G., Teasdale, J. D., Segal, Z. V., & Kabat-Zinn, J. (2007). *The mindful way through depression: Freeing yourself from chronic unhappiness*. New York: Guilford.

5 A Search for Meaning: An Integrative Approach to Stress Management Following a Career-ending Injury

CHRISTOPHER R. D. WAGSTAFF

LEARNING OBJECTIVES

AFTER READING THIS CHAPTER YOU SHOULD BE ABLE TO:

1. Define and outline meaning-centred therapy.
2. Outline and use Wong's (2010) ABCDE meaning-centred intervention approach and critically evaluate its utility for sport psychologists.
3. Critically evaluate the potential benefits of narrative approaches to managing traumatic experiences in sport.
4. Discern between a range of possible narrative-based techniques for practice.

AREAS TO CONSIDER WHEN READING THE CHAPTER:

1. What challenges might there be in helping an athlete deal with the stress associated with a career-ending injury?
2. What factors would you need to be mindful of when psychologically supporting an athlete after a career-ending injury?
3. How might you facilitate a narrative approach to help a client deal with an injury trauma, or career transition?

CLIENT AND BACKGROUND

The client, Elliott (pseudonym), at the time of initial consultation was 26 years old and a rugby union player. Prior to our working relationship, Elliott was heavily involved in rugby union. He was a professional player contracted to a club competing in the highest domestic league in England, the Aviva Premiership. Elliott had substantial experience in Europe's elite club competition, the Heineken Cup, and had been selected for England at several representative levels. His professional playing career began shortly after leaving school where he achieved satisfactory A-level grades. His decision to accept a professional contract required him to forgo the opportunity to study for a degree at university in favour of his rugby aspirations. After signing his first professional contract at 18, Elliott spent two years in the club's academy and development sides, before progressing to the first team squad, where he remained for five years before we worked together.

After establishing himself in the starting side of his club during the 2007/8 season, Elliott received glowing performance reviews and a call-up to train with the England squad during 2008/9. His performances were rewarded with an enhanced remunerative contract; however, when a new head coach arrived at the club during the following season his appearances were limited. Halfway through this season, Elliott was told that his contract would not be renewed in May at the end of the domestic season and that he should seek an alternative club. Subsequently, in January of 2010 Elliott instructed his agent that he would be receptive to new offers from premier European clubs. Shortly after, an offer was made by the incoming head coach of a higher placed Premiership club to join them on a much-improved contract for the season 2010/11. In March 2010 preliminary contracts were signed and Elliott was set to join the new club at the end of the 2009/10 season. Specifically, he would be moving house in May and had bought a house in the new city, put his current house up for sale, and his long-term partner had found work in the area of the new club.

In 2010, during a European cup match Elliott was in possession of the ball when an aggressive but legal tackle by an opponent left Elliott with a severe concussion, lacerations of the major neck muscles, and suspected spinal cord damage in the C3/4 region. Numerous tests were carried out to ascertain the extent of the damage to Elliott's spinal cord. Fortunately, no permanent damage had been suffered and Elliott was discharged from hospital after several days. At home Elliott found his day-to-day functioning very limited for several weeks. He suffered frequent headaches, nausea, and blurred vision. Further, these symptoms were exacerbated when Elliott attempted to engage in light physical activity or screen time. For example, climbing the stairs of his house or watching television led to excruciating headaches that commonly resulted in nausea. These symptoms persisted for approximately two months leading the medical team to question their initial diagnosis of the spinal cord and neck injury being the sole cause of Elliott's headaches. Further exploratory brain scans returned equivocal findings.

In October 2010, now out of contract with his old club and unable to fulfil the terms of his new contract, Elliott found himself in limbo and unemployed. The new club gave him three months' unpaid grace and kindly financially supported Elliott to attend specialist private healthcare to optimize his chances of rehabilitation. Sadly, in April 2011 after 12 months' of exploratory tests to identify the source of his ongoing physical symptoms (i.e., headaches) and varied attempts at rehabilitation modes (e.g., neuromuscular consultations, acupuncture, massage, and nutrition), Elliott was advised that he should retire from all forms of rugby on medical grounds.

As a result of his injury and experiences over the 12-month period of attempted rehabilitation, Elliott experienced a range of physical, mental, relational, social, and financial changes. Specifically, the physical symptoms associated with his injury were persistent, debilitating and significantly impacted

Elliott's daily functioning as a human being. As a highly active individual, Elliott was used to physical training at least once per day for several hours; however, following his injury, his symptoms precluded the engagement of even very mild physical activity (e.g., walking his dog). In the short term, this led to rapid muscular atrophy and, in the long term, Elliott's changing body image was instrumental in his experience of reduced self-esteem and fragmented identity. Moreover, due to the uncertainty surrounding the cause of his ongoing symptoms, a reassuring prognosis regarding the cessation of these symptoms or his prospects for returning to competitive rugby were not forthcoming. Elliott perceived his physical symptoms to be imprisoning, reducing his ability and proclivity to mobilize his social support network. He also perceived heightened embarrassment and isolation from his colleagues and fans within the rugby community. This social isolation and reclusive behaviour contributed to Elliott's generally negative affective response to his stress experience. Elliott perceived his interpersonal relationships to have suffered, which culminated in the end of his romantic relationship with his long-term partner four months after his injury. Elliott also stated that he had experienced 'flashbacks' of the injuring incident, which were characterized by unwanted cognitive intrusions with vivid imagery. Finally, without an income beyond a small insurance payout, Elliott was reliant on financial support from his parents and modest income from a property he leased. He was very concerned that changes in his lease agreement, tenancy, or interest rates could force him to forfeit on his mortgage. Elliott contacted me by email, to which I responded via telephone, approximately 13 months after sustaining his injury. At this time he perceived himself to be 'not coping so well with everything', 'feeling completely lost', and having 'some really low points', 'lost sight of who I am and wanted to be' with 'no real structure or meaning left'.

INITIAL NEEDS ASSESSMENT

During initial needs assessment it is imperative to underpin conceptualization and possible intervention content and techniques with empirically-tested research and theory and to align this with one's philosophy of practice. Therefore, I will review relevant literature before giving consideration to the integration of Elliott's needs with my philosophy of practice.

A substantial body of literature exists pertaining to the psychology of sport injury. Several reviews of this literature strongly support the notion that injury is associated with the experience of negative psychological phenomena such as stress, grief, loss, and depression (Brewer, 2007; Evans, Mitchell, & Jones, 2006). Moreover, researchers examining the psychological responses to sport injury have highlighted a range of cognitive, emotional, and behavioural consequences (e.g., Wiese-Bjornstal, Smith, & LaMott, 1995; Wadey & Hanton, 2013), with the difficulties faced by injured sportspeople likely to be exacerbated by the strength of their athletic identity (e.g., Brewer,Van Raalte, & Linder, 1993; Smith & Sparkes, 2004). To this end, and in line with the initial communication between Elliott and myself via email and telephone ahead of our first meeting, I perceived the literatures on injury, stress, and trauma in sport to be pertinent for informing my practice in the present case.

The literature which most strongly informed my conceptualization of Elliott's needs related to research using narrative methods to illuminate the experiences of those encountering serious sport injuries. For example, Smith and Sparkes (e.g., Sparkes & Smith, 2002; Smith & Sparkes, 2004) have conducted a body of research presenting narratives of trauma following spinal cord injuries. Specifically, Smith and Sparkes (2004) highlighted complex positive and negative responses to such events in an exploration of the metaphors used by spinal cord injured (SCI) rugby players in line with Frank's (1995) categories of restitution, chaos, and quest narratives.

The restitution narrative is the most common narrative presented by those who have experienced trauma and might have the tagline 'yesterday I was healthy, today I'm sick, but tomorrow I'll be healthy again' (Frank, 1995, p. 77). The use of restitution narratives might be associated with an affinity for the restored or entrenched self (cf. Charmaz, 1987), that commonly restricts individuals to their past body-self relationships and ways of being in the world in the hope that they will return to this past state. For some, the desire for restitution is compounded by the expectation that other people want to hear restitution stories. In Smith and Sparkes' (2004) study, those using restitution narratives commonly used metaphors that portrayed their injury as a 'war', 'battle', 'struggle', 'fight', and something they had to 'beat'. For Smith and Sparkes, those individuals telling restitution narratives in combination with sport and war metaphors were likely to be inhibited in their attempts to reconstruct their identity by reducing their access to, and flexibility to engage with, others' stories that might assist meaning-making and their own life story. Indeed, Elliott appeared to have found it hard to accept that an alternative body-self narrative might need to be identified and lived, leading him to ignore opportunities to discover an alternative future possible self and grow from his experience. Smith and Sparkes concluded that although restitution narratives can be entwined with hope following injury, a fixation on one kind of body and sense of self is not appropriate when combined with metaphors of sport and war.

Description box **BOX 5.1**

WHAT ARE NARRATIVES?

Narrative approaches are based on the notion that individuals construct experiences and meaning through culturally-mediated social interactions. When lives have been disrupted by trauma or stressors, efforts to create continuity or to 'reorient' oneself, can be viewed as the attempt to reconstruct life story. By uncovering a means of structuring and interpreting our experiences, we become better able to re-establish the relationship between the self, the world and our bodies. This reconstruction is concerned with gaining meaning by placing our experiences within the context of one's own life and reconstructing the narrative of the self (Frank, 1995). Hence, narrative approaches are based on three key assumptions: that people can modify the meaning that they have attached to a given experience, that every narrative has exceptions and alternative stories, and that narratives are cemented by larger power constructs (Brown, Weber, & Ali, 2008).

According to Frank (1995), chaos narratives are the inverse of restitution narratives, since these narratives present a future expectancy and image that one's life will not get better. Such narratives are also characterized by their absence of narrative order and fragmented nature. They are told as the storyteller experiences life; without coherent sequence or discernable causality. Such incoherence is supported by Sparkes and Smith (2002), who highlighted biographical disruption to SCI rugby players who commonly had difficulty in reconstructing or re-storying a self in the face of trauma. Indeed, following injury, those with a chaos narrative might experience what Frankl (1986) labelled an existential vacuum. That is, life is understood as occupying an empty present and future in a fatalistic manner, with little remaining to fill the void left by one's past preferred self. This vacuum also reflects the subjective experience of boredom, anger, and isolation associated with injury (see Evans, Wadey, Hanton, & Mitchell, 2012) and is understandably interwoven with monotony, apathy, emptiness, and meaninglessness. Smith and Sparkes (2004) highlighted a number of vulnerability metaphors associated with chaos narratives including as sense of life being 'choked', experienced in 'solid darkness', and perceptions of being an 'emotionally brittle object'. During my initial communication with Elliott, his narrative lacked coherence, temporal structure, and his reflected vulnerability and confusion. What was apparent was a recent shift from a restitution to a chaos narrative following his medical advice to retire. I was aware that presenting chaos narratives and the vulnerability metaphors may serve to help individuals, acknowledge the need for reconstructing the self and facilitate Elliott's understanding of his loss of physical agency following injury. However, and in line with Smith and Sparkes, chaos narratives might also be constraining for the individual by constricting their field of expression and facilitating the re-enactment of the traumatic events and suffering.

Quest narratives, position trauma as an opportunity to transform the self through a learning (or re-learning) experience or journey toward understanding what is most important in life. The quest narratives told by SCI rugby players in Smith and Sparkes' (2004) study described meeting suffering head on with individuals accepting impairment and disability and seeking to use it in the pursuit of personal growth. Frank (1995) has argued that the actual target of one's quest may never be wholly clear, and that the quest is defined by the person's belief that something is to be gained from the experience. Importantly, the emphasis on a search for meaning or will to growth over a search for happiness is a central component of humanistic-existential psychology (e.g., Frankl, 1986). Within the quest narrative, Smith and Sparkes highlighted metaphors describing participants' injury as being 'reborn', where they were on a 'journey', commonly referring to their 'progress' or 'distance travelled' on this 'rocky road' to an alternative end to that previously expected. As part of this journey, those expressing quest narratives often sought the support of 'guides' for their journey whilst experiencing liberation and empowerment by acting as a social model for others. Although this process of acceptance, transcendence, and reconstruction of the body-self relationship is not easy, quest narratives appear to offer more potential for individuals to engage with the imagination of multiple alternative future stories necessary for developing the self following trauma (cf. Charmaz, 1987). I perceived the re-authoring of Elliott's narrative into a quest one would benefit him.

Despite the possible adaptive benefits associated with quest narratives, positive psychological concepts (e.g., resilience, hardiness, and positive emotional states and self-regulation) have largely been overlooked in the context of sport injury (see Wadey, Evans, Evans, & Mitchell, 2011; Wadey, Evans, Hanton, & Neil, 2012). However, Wadey et al. (2011) recently revealed a number of perceived benefits emanating from sport injury. Specifically, the authors identified several antecedents across three temporal phases at which such perceived benefits might emerge: (a) injury onset (e.g., emotional response), (b) rehabilitation (e.g., free time), and (c) return to competition sport (e.g., reflective practice). Further, Wadey et al.'s findings point to the identification of several mechanisms through which participants derived their perceived benefits including self-disclosure and mobilization of one's social support network. Such findings indicate that although it is common to experience negative psychological responses to sports injury, it is possible for individuals to transform their experience by generating meaning and facilitating psychological growth and development. Moreover, it would appear that self-disclosure and the mobilization of one's support network would assist pursuit.

The notion that individuals might perceive benefits or experience growth following traumatic sport injury had a number of implications for my work with Elliott. First, it would appear that a search for meaning, pursued through the lens of a quest narrative could facilitate the identification of perceived benefits following Elliott's injury. Moreover, as my working relationship with Elliott began sometime after injury onset, efforts to integrate the excellent advice provided by, *inter alia*, Wadey and Evans (2011) for consultation during the injury onset, rehabilitation and return to competition phases proved difficult. Consequently, I supplemented my injury-centric conceptualization of

Elliott's needs analysis with relevant stress management (e.g., Mellalieu, Hanton, Neil, & Wagstaff, 2007; Rumbold, Fletcher & Daniels, 2012) and career transition (e.g., Alfermann, & Stambulova, 2000; Brewer, Van Raalte, & Petitpas, 2000; Wylleman, Alfermann, & Lavallee, 2004) literature that has discussed injury.

In summarizing my initial assessment of Elliott's needs, I centred on a belief that his initial response to his injury was characterized by a restitution narrative (e.g., 'I wanted to return to playing'), which after 12-months of unsuccessful rehabilitation had been re-authored as a chaos narrative (e.g., 'I feel lost, without direction') around the time we began our working alliance. Given this assessment, Elliott's ability to find meaning in his new, chaotic, existence challenged and confused him. Our initial discussions centred on an ambivalence and absence of meaning. Hence, I perceived a need for Elliott to search for meaning through the creation of a life story, aligned with a quest narrative. This transformation of Elliott's fragmented identity into a coherent narrative and gaining of commitment toward a self-regulated will to growth might best align with the humanistic-existential perspective. However, I also believed that Elliott would benefit from a structured process toward meaning-making, more typically associated with positive psychology than humanistic approaches. By identifying strengths and using them in new situations and accepting his traumatic experiences as part of his life story, Elliott could create a new narrative self in order to thrive and flourish. Given the dual meaning-related needs I perceived, the use of a meaning-centred approach offered the most suitable framework for intervention.

In addition to the desire to conceptualize Elliott's needs using extant research and theory, it was important to consider how this aligned with my own philosophy of practice. The potential for Elliott to perceive positive outcomes following his trauma experience aligns with my own perceived value of integrating aspects of humanistic-existential psychology and positive psychology. For example, practitioners aligned with a humanistic-existential perspective have long acknowledged that meaning can emanate from traumatic experiences (e.g., Frankl, 1986). Further, such approaches perceive individuals as autonomous agents, with positive outcomes dependent on one's choice and attendant responsibility to *search for meaning* in one's life. While acknowledging the value of such perspectives, much of my work as a researcher-practitioner (e.g., Wagstaff, Fletcher, & Hanton, 2012a, 2012b, 2012c; Wagstaff, Hanton, & Fletcher, 2013) aligns with a positive psychology perspective, that might argue that Elliott would benefit from identifying and developing character strengths and virtues in order to facilitate the experience of positive emotions. These experiences might serve to broaden Elliott's awareness and encourage novel, varied, and exploratory thoughts and actions. Over time, a broadened behavioural repertoire might build resources such as resilience to deal with stressors and promote a more satisfied life. Hence, it is my belief that positive emotions, strengths, and virtues help buffer against the negative impact of stressors and increase the probability of finding good in one's circumstances. From this perspective, positive outcomes are dependent on a *creation of meaning* in one's life. Therefore, it would appear that a natural confluence was present between Elliott's needs and my practice philosophy regarding the importance of meaning-seeking and meaning-making.

FRAMEWORK AND INTERVENTION

In line with my initial assessment of Elliott's needs and my philosophy of practice, the present case used a meaning-centred framework for intervention. Meaning-centred therapy (MCT) is an integrative, positive, humanistic-existential approach which has its origins in Frankl's (1986) logotherapy. This approach employs personal meaning as its central organizing construct and assimilates various schools of psychology to achieve its therapeutic goal (Wong, 2010). MCT uses the positive psychology lens of promoting factors associated with flourishing whilst accepting that humans experience suffering and trauma. In doing so, it advocates a psycho-educational approach to equip clients with the tools to navigate the inevitable negatives in human existence and create a preferred future (Wong, 2010). Moreover, MCT aims to facilitate clients' hope of finding meaning and purpose, when they encounter overwhelming and undesirable circumstances.

Description box **BOX 5.2**

EXISTENTIALISM

Existential therapeutic interventions operate on the belief that inner conflict within a person is due to predictable tensions associated with confronting the givens of existence (e.g., mortality, freedom, isolation, and meaninglessness). Interventions are aimed at addressing individuals' refusal or inability to deal with the normal existential anxiety that comes from confronting these 'givens' by accepting these feelings rather than trying to change them as if there is something wrong.

MCT offers a conceptual framework with a simplistic focus on internal meaning that is entrenched with the complexities of individual differences to existential givens and belief systems, while seeking and using idiosyncratic strengths toward the facilitation of growth. Wong (2010) proposes that MCT is underpinned by eight core characteristics: integrative, existential, positively oriented, multicultural, narrative, relational and psycho-educational.

MCT is integrative. MCT acknowledges the value in holistic perspectives to psychological intervention for more effective and efficacious practice than when strictly adhering to a single perspective. For example, MCT is primarily based on logotherapy and existential-humanistic psychotherapy, but it also assimilates cognitive-behavioural and narrative approaches (Wong, 2010). Necessarily, the use of an integrated *perspective* or *school* of practice here differs from the salience of a core *philosophy* of practice.

MCT is existential. MCT ascribes to the humanistic-existential traditions of emphasizing the salience of addressing existential anxieties (Yalom, 1980) and the human need for meaning and authenticity (Schneider, Bugental, & Pierson, 2001). The primary existential anxiety is exemplified by an existential vacuum. Such crises are common when people experience a fragmented identity or perceive that their life has no purpose, challenge, obligation, or hope, with no escape from their boredom and pain. Moreover, it is common for individuals to attempt to fill their existential vacuum with material rather than meaningful things including hedonic pursuits, addiction, and unrealistic pursuit of power, wealth, and fame, with such misguided efforts commonly leading to frustration, despair, and depression (Wong, 2010).

MCT is positively oriented. Wong (2010) argued that MCT is inherently positive because of its affirmation of life and the defiant human spirit to survive and flourish in the face of adversity. Moreover, MCT assumes that individuals have unlimited capacity to construct meanings that serve to protect them from inevitable negative life experiences and empower them to make life worth living in the worst of times (Wong, 2010). According to Wong (2010), it is this realistic and dualistic positivity allows individuals to simultaneously embrace the dark side of human existence and the human potential for transformation.

MCT is multicultural. Meaning approaches seek to understand and motivate clients in differing personal circumstances and cultural contexts when faced with universal existential givens (Wong, 2010).

In doing so, MCT aims to help clients define life goals that are consistent with their life experiences, cultural values, and the universal needs for meaning, autonomy, competence, and relationships.

MCT is narrative. Human beings lead storied lives. Therefore, narratives allow rich experiences to emerge from clients. By using story-telling and re-authoring, MCT makes use of such narratives to resonate with clients' values and motivate them to create a preferred future. Thus, MCT aligns with White's (2007) narrative therapy and makes use of the life history interview (McAdams, 1996, 2008) to discover adaptive epithets or formulae that may help restructure the self.

Description box **BOX 5.3**

WHAT IS MEANING-CENTRED THERAPY?

- Meaning-centred therapy or MCT is an integrative, positive, humanistic-existential approach which has its origins in Frankl's (1986) logotherapy.
- This approach employs personal meaning as its central organizing construct and assimilates various schools of psychology to achieve its therapeutic goal.
- MCT advocates a psycho-educational approach to equip clients with the tools to navigate the inevitable negatives in human existence and create a preferred, meaningful future.

MCT is psycho-educational. MCT uses a psycho-educational approach to equip clients with the tools to undertake their change process outside consultancy sessions. Such methods are common to many psychological approaches and empower clients to act in a self-determined manner and embody the change they wish to make. The intended outcome is the emergence of meaning as a result of action.

The strategies incorporated within MCT are guided by two underpinning conceptual frameworks, meaning-management theory and the dual-system model (see Wong, 2012). Meaning-management theory is primarily concerned with meaning-related psychological processes, while the dual-system model is concerned with the self-regulation processes involved in survival and achieving positive life goals.

Meaning-management theory. The meaning-management theory consists of four main components: purpose, understanding, responsible action, and evaluation (PURE). Empirical support for this theory is provided by Wong and Fry (1998) and Wong (2009a). According to Wong (2010) meaning encompasses (a) the human quest for meaning, purpose, and understanding (i.e., meaning-seeking) as well as (b) the human capacity to discover and create meanings out of the perplexing life experiences (i.e., meaning-making). In turn, meaning-management theory hypothesizes that meaning-seeking and meaning-making entail several basic cognitive processes: (a) the automatic adaptive processes of stress appraisal and attribution, (b) the executive decision-making processes of solution-focused problem solving, goal-setting, making commitments, and taking responsible action, and (c) the creative process of symbolization, imagination, and myth making. Such outcomes are possible through the generation of understanding and creation of coherence in the face of uncertainty, chaos, and absurdity. Necessarily, one's world views, values, goals, and morals occupy an important role in how we appraise the circumstances that we encounter and our evaluations of coping resources to manage these.

Importantly for the present case study, meaning-management theory posits that when we cannot make sense or accommodate unexpected, unavoidable, and uncontrollable negative life events, one must accept the negative reality and transcend it through meaning-reconstruction and tragic optimism (Wong, 2009a, 2009b; cf. Frankl, 1986). Importantly, such transcendence also aligns with the expression of a quest narrative.

Dual-system model. The dual-system model is primarily concerned with the 'how to' aspect of adaptation in midst of adversity. The model proposes that the two basic and fundamental psychological processes of approach and avoidance interact with each other to enhance resilience and achieve positive psychosocial outcomes. Specifically, the model emphasizes that employing both approach and avoidance psycho-behavioural processes is the most effective way of buffering against negative responses to adversity whilst broadening one's perspectives in their quest for meaning and fulfilment.

Inherent within this model is the hypothesis that all adverse encounters contain seeds for personal growth and all positive conditions contains hidden dangers. Hence, the dual-system model embraces the paradoxical and contradictory nature of human existence. Indeed, Wong (2010) argues that this dualistic framework integrates psychotherapy with positive psychology in a comprehensive and coherent manner to address clients' predicaments whilst facilitating opportunities to flourish. In order to facilitate the 'how to' of MCT, Wong (2010) proposes the use of a ABCDE intervention process.

The ABCDE meaning-centred strategy. The ABCDE intervention strategy is a tool for coping with protracted negative life experiences and should be distinguished from Ellis's (1987) ABCDE rational-emotive therapy strategy. Indeed, Wong's meaning-centred ABCDE strategy is more similar to acceptance and commitment therapy (Hayes, 2005) and emphasizes action and commitment to values. To elaborate, A stands for *a*ccepting and confronting the reality, B for *b*elieving and affirming that life is worth living, C for *c*ommitting to action and specific goals, D for *d*iscovering new meaning, significance, and understanding, and E for *e*valuating the outcome, enjoying positive results, and self-regulating.

Acceptance. Acceptance of reality and limits is central to MCT. Growth begins by accepting that change is needed. There is a need for practitioners to employ a variety of skills to empower clients to confront reality and awaken their pursuit for positive change. It is important to delineate acceptance from giving up or passivity. Acceptance requires honest recognition and for individuals to confront their limitations in an authentic manner. This important step allowed Elliott to learn how to transcend and transform his future self. In the present case study, tools that were useful for facilitating acceptance included: reviewing the details of the trauma using narrative exposure therapy (NET), Pennebaker's expressive writing paradigm, normalizing adversity, accepting human limitations and weaknesses, practising gratitude, and re-authoring.

Belief and affirmation. According to Wong (2010), acceptance without affirmation exposes individuals to the vulnerability of despair and depression. Hence, if clients are able to affirm that progress is attainable through hope, they are more likely to stick to the regimen of change. A variety of interventions to cultivate hope and affirmation were used with Elliott and included appreciative inquiry, reflective journaling and expressive writing, and imagery.

Commitment. Acceptance and commitment therapy (Hayes, 2005) stresses the importance of action and experience over feeling and thinking. This proposition highlights that change is possible only when one undertakes behavioural steps toward the development of a new self. Here it is salient to foster a commitment to pursuing certain values and taking responsible action for making changes in various areas of one's life. The development of persistence is needed to succeed in making lasting changes and forming new patterns of thinking and behaving. The assignment of further homework was also helpful to assist Elliott to: (a) develop and implement plans of action, (b) set concrete and specific goals, (c) practise small steps towards achieving each goal. In addition to these processes, promotion of the antecedents of self-efficacy (e.g., previous accomplishments, vicarious experience, modelling, and positive reinforcement) benefited the uptake and adherence to planned change.

Discovery. Frankl (1986) emphasized that meaning is discovered as much, if not more than, it is created. Hence, a process of awakening Elliott's will to seek an alternative future self was important. It was also necessary to alert Elliott to the various positive and negative possibilities of such discovery and alternative self. To facilitate such discovery, discussions centred on identifying strengths in narratives, acknowledging the fulfilling aspects of mundane routines, and exploring opportunities for new meaningful experience discovery and creation. Techniques that aided this process included, self-reflection diaries, Socratic questioning, cognitive reframing, meaning construction, and re-storing.

Evaluation. Evaluation represents the affective component of self-regulation. If nothing seems to work and there is no reduction of symptoms and no improvement in the pursuit of positive life goals, then some adjustment is necessary. Wong (2010) proposed that positive emotions such as joy, relief, gratitude, and confidence are inevitable if the previous four strategic steps of ABCDE are successful, and that, in turn, positive feelings and outcomes act as a foil for positive changes.

FRAMEWORK AND INTERVENTION

The intervention outlined here describes the techniques intended to promote meaning-management, the transformation of Elliott's fragmented self into a coherent narrative, and to gain commitment towards a self-regulated will to growth. Specifically, the intervention was characterized by three phases using tools commonly employed to assist individuals experiencing negative responses to life events. First, a life-story interview was conducted to emancipate a realization of pertinent positive and negative life events for later reflection and meaning-making. Second, narrative exposure therapy was used to generate a coherent narrative of these life events and associate factual and affective components of these experiences. Third, expressive writing and positive intervention homework was used to foster long-term reflection and growth in line with the ABCDE model of MCT. It is important to note that these tools can be used interchangeably or in isolation; their combined use here was deemed to be appropriate for supporting Elliott's needs and in light of the central role of narratives in MCT.

Intervention Phase 1: the life-story interview

In my first session with Elliott, I aimed to gain an understanding of his life story through the emancipation of his narrative. The McAdams life-story interview (1996) contains eight steps aimed at encouraging clients to reflect on and communicate their storied life: life chapters, critical events, life challenges, positive and negative influences on life story, stories and the life story, alternative futures for the life story, personal ideology, and life theme. Life stories can contain accounts of highs and lows, as well as key turning points in the formation of one's identity (McAdams, 2008).

In my introductory comments, I asked Elliott to play the role of a storyteller about his life. Understanding that each person's story in a given transaction will be selected, I outlined the structure of the interview and provided assurances regarding the purpose of the session; namely, to understand more about Elliott's unique story and not to analyse, diagnose or answer 'what's wrong with me?' That is, I assured Elliott that the interview was for background research purposes only.

Life chapters. I invited Elliott to begin by thinking about his life as a story with characters, scenes, and plot points or chapters. This included questions such as 'If you were to think of your life as having chapters, what would those chapters be? Could you briefly describe each of these chapters?' Elliott initially found this process unusual and I could sense him questioning the relevance of such tasks. To promote engagement from Elliott, I adopted an open body language, giving frequent verbal (e.g., paraphrasing, seeking clarification) and non-verbal (e.g., gaining eye-contact, nodding, empathetic facial expressions) affirmations associated with active listening. I was particularly interested to observe how Elliott organized and responded to his narrative, therefore I was careful not to influence his organization of this story.

Critical events. The second step in McAdams's life-story interview relates to focusing the narrative lens to focus on significant episodes or memories in the client's life story. I encouraged Elliott to augment these events with details of characters, actions, thoughts, and feelings from these particular standout moments. Specific prompts at this stage included 'for each event, try to describe what happened, where you were, who was involved, what you did, and what you were thinking and feeling. Also try to convey what impact this key event has had in your life and what this event says about who you are or were as a person' (McAdams, 1996, 2008). During this step of the process, questions guided Elliott to focus on experiences according to eight specific events: a peak experience, a nadir experience, a turning point, his earliest memory, an important childhood scene, an important adolescent scene, an important adult scene, and one other important scene.

Life challenge. The third step in the life-story interview is to ask clients to describe the single greatest positive or negative challenge that they have faced. Questions within this step related to short probes such as, 'What were you thinking? What impact has the event had on you? What does it say about who you are? Why is it important?' (McAdams, 1996, 2008).

Positive and negative influences on life story. In the fourth step of McAdams's model, clients are asked to identify the single person, group of persons, or organization/institution that have had the greatest positive influence on their life. This process is repeated for the single negative influence the client perceives. Questions during this step included, 'Can you describe this person, group, or organization and the way he, she, it, or they have had a positive/negative impact on your story?'

Stories and the life story. The fifth step in the interview protocol invites clients to think about stories that have influenced them or that they identify with. Specifically, I encouraged Elliott to consider stories that he had watched (e.g., television, movies, performances), read (e.g., books, magazines, poetry), or heard (e.g., family stories, stories heard). Throughout this step in the process, questions probed Elliott's summary of the story and how he related to it such as, 'Can you tell me why you like or remember that story? What impact has it had on you?' The session ended with a discussion of possible self-directed actions that Elliott might undertake to further facilitate the identification of meaningful stories from his life.

Alternative futures for the life story. The sixth step of the McAdams procedure invites clients to consider two different futures for the story they have outlined, first a realistic, goal-centred positive and then an undesirable or feared negative. In encouraging Elliott to describe a positive future, questions included, 'Can you describe a picture of what you would realistically like to see happen, or even read in the future chapters of your life? In these future scenes, what goals or dreams might you accomplish?' When guiding Elliott to describe a negative future, questions included, 'Could you give me a picture of a future scene or chapter that you fear or one that you want to avoid? This might include a future that could possibly happen, but one that you hope will not occur.' In line with McAdams's guidelines, throughout this step of the interview, I pushed Elliott for as much vivid detail as possible relating to the future scenes and chapters he described. These details were revealed with probes relating to thoughts, feelings, behaviours, characters, situations, places, sounds, smells, images and colours.

Personal ideology. In the penultimate step of the interview, I invited Elliott to give thought to his fundamental beliefs and values relating to religion or spiritual beliefs, political views, and what he perceived to be the most important value in human living to be. Subsequent questions invited Elliott to describe if these beliefs and values had changed over time.

Life theme. The final step in McAdams's interview model is to invite clients to reflect on their past and imagined future life story and to explore common themes. Questions within this step included, 'Reflecting on the story you have spoken about, both past and possible future, do you see any themes, messages, meaning, or ideas that act as a thread piecing the chapters together? What do you see as the major theme of your life story?'

Following our first session, I constructed a written account of the life story Elliott outlined during our interview. At the beginning of our second session I presented this biography to Elliott and invited him to correct or amend it where appropriate. Indeed, from this point, Elliott's story became a live, working document, that was added to, refined and sculpted during future sessions. The main focus of the second session was to return to the biography provided by Elliott and relive his experience using an approach underpinned by narrative exposure therapy (NET).

Intervention Phase 2: narrative exposure therapy

Narrative exposure therapy (NET) is a technique originally developed for trauma-spectrum disorders for survivors of multiple and complex trauma (e.g., refugees, post-traumatic stress disorder sufferers). More recently, it has been successfully used with sub- and non-clinical populations in health-related anxiety such as eating disorders and body dysmorphia (see, for review, Onden-Lim & Grisham, 2013). NET is conceptually underpinned by the theory of dual representation of traumatic memory processing (see, for reviews, Brewin, Gregory, Lipton, & Burgess, 2010; Elbert & Schauer, 2002). Essentially, the dual representation theory proposes that two separate and fragmented mechanisms account for voluntary (e.g., effortful reliving) and involuntary (e.g., intrusive memories and images) memories. In line with dual representation theory, the NET approach seeks to contextualize and transform fragmented sensory, affective, and cognitive elements of clients' experiences into a coherent, chronological narrative. Hence, the use of NET was seen as a complementary extension to the life-story interview initially conducted with Elliott. During NET the client is encouraged to relive emotions experienced when providing the narrative of their storied life whilst retaining an anchor within the 'here and now'. This anchoring is achieved by using frequent reminders by the practitioner that client's responses to the narrative are a result of memories of the experience. The aim of this approach is to link the client's involuntary 'hot' experiences to voluntary 'cold' episodic facts (e.g., time and place), and narrative transformation. Accordingly, the aim is to facilitate meaning-making by revisiting stressful memories, in an attempt to integrate them into a transformed narrative by perceiving the event in the context of their ongoing life, rather than re-experiencing and ruminating over the event in the present.

Activity box **BOX 5.4**

TYPICAL EXPRESSIVE WRITING INSTRUCTIONS

For the next four days, I would like you to write your very deepest thoughts and feelings about the most traumatic experience of your entire life or an extremely important emotional issue that has affected you and your life. In your writing, I'd like you to really let go and explore your deepest emotions and thoughts. You might tie your topic to your relationships with others, including parents, lovers, friends or relatives; to your past, your present or your future; or to who you have been, who you would like to be or who you are now. You may write about the same general issues or experiences on all days of writing or about different topics each day. All of your writing will be completely confidential. Don't worry about spelling, grammar, or sentence structure. The only rule is that once you begin writing, you continue until the time is up.

(Adapted from Pennebaker & Cheung, 2007)

During Elliott's second session, after being presented with the first-person account of his life story, I asked him to continue to narrate his life. This ongoing narration focused both on factual background information and on vividly recorded emotional events surrounding his injury and subsequent behaviours and events. After two sessions of re-authoring his experiences, I noticed that Elliott spoke with more 'cold' episodic and factual acknowledgement about the time of his injury onset and appeared more coherent in his assessment of the role of his subsequent responses to this injury in the context of his subsequent life story.

Intervention Phase 3: meaning-making, homework and growth

During sessions 3 and 4, I was increasingly aware of a more enthused Elliott. He arrived at these sessions with stories and often contacted me in between sessions to describe 'a scene from the new chapter' indicating that meaning-making was occurring. However, I perceived the need for greater focus and structure on setting self-determined goals to facilitate motivation and engage in ongoing meaning-making. Hence, I supplemented discussions in our remaining sessions (5 to 8) with methods from positive psychology such as savouring (cf. Bryant, 2003), identifying, and promoting the development of strengths and gratitude (cf. Seligman, Steen, Park, & Peterson, 2005), and conceiving of a best possible self (cf. King, 2001). In moving forward with these strategies, and in line with the ABCDE model of MCT, I continued to promote the benefits of expressive writing techniques as homework.

I set Elliott homework to complete with differing foci of meaning-searching and meaning-making. Meaning-searching homework related to expressive writing and was heavily-informed by Pennebaker's (1997) expressive writing paradigm. This was used in the present case study by encouraging Elliott to write on one day for consecutive weeks about his deepest thoughts and feelings allied with his injury experience. I encouraged him to associate and integrate this experience with his past, present, and future life story. This included consideration of who Elliott had been, who he currently was, and who he wanted to be. Elliott was informed that the topic of his writing could be the same each day or vary within these guidelines according to his preference (cf. Pennebaker & Cheung, 2007). For example, although Elliott's initial writing focused on his responses to his injury, and subsequent behaviours prior to unsuccessful rehabilitation, the scope of his later writing expanded to include general past and new emotional events.

REFLECTIONS

My approach to evaluating the effectiveness and efficacy of the intervention outlined here was twofold. First, I used informal, qualitative interviews with Elliott and read his narratives to monitor coherence, acceptance, and commitment toward meaning-seeking and making. Second, I quantitatively monitored Elliott's meaning mindset through the use of Wong's (2012) life orientation scale (e.g., 'I can find something meaningful or significant in everyday events'), which indicated a substantial positive trend toward meaning between sessions 3 and 8.

Despite its nascence, MCT provided a valuable framework to integrate the client's needs for meaning-management and my philosophy of practice. While many researchers have called for a dialogue between humanistic-existential and positive psychology (e.g., Robbins & Friedman, 2008; Schneider, 2011), scholars have also suggested that such relationships might be characterized by tension, ambivalence, and philosophical differences (cf. Waterman, 2013). Hence, despite having similar historical lineage, philosophical foundations, and areas of theoretical and applied confluence, caution might be required when developing research agenda or applied practice recommendations that attempt to integrate humanistic-existential and positive psychology perspectives. Despite this caveat, I found MCT to offer a pragmatic and practical guiding framework for applied intervention aimed at managing meaning. I also feel that there are many benefits to the dual-process sub-theory given its integration of techniques from humanistic-existential and positive psychology in view of the narrow-band limitations of using these approaches in isolation (see Waterman, 2013). The pragmatic focus and benefits from the brief use of narrative techniques here allowed me to evade some criticisms levelled at humanistic-existential approaches as lengthy and introspective (see Waterman, 2013). Indeed, the shared goals of understanding and promoting human potential and wellbeing were highly successful in promoting a long-term meaning-management approach and facilitation of growth in the present case.

There are many advantages to using narrative approaches within applied sport psychology practice. The first benefit of using narrative approaches with Elliott was that they allowed him to search the traumatic experience that dominated his life. Experiencing stress or trauma is likely to be challenging for many sportspeople; however, clients might find relief when they are able to rewrite their unfolding life story and take ownership of the authorship of new chapters. Another advantage of using narrative techniques was their flexible use for meaning-management and emphasizing Elliott's strengths and opportunities for growth rather than weaknesses and failures. The narrative techniques used here encouraged Elliott to begin the process of change and re-authoring of a new self and life story. Moreover, such techniques go some way to integrating humanistic-existential phenomena (e.g., the traumatic life) with those aligned with positive psychology (e.g., growth, strengths identification and use) for wellbeing and human flourishing outcomes. While there are various other advantages to this approach, one limitation of this approach relates to the dearth of research examining the efficacy of narrative interventions in sport psychology. Hence, future research on stress management in sport might benefit from empirical examination of the effectiveness of narrative interventions.

Applied implications box **BOX 5.5**

SUGGESTIONS FOR THE USE OF EXPRESSIVE WRITING

- Expressive writing tasks can be set as homework, or can be carried out before, during, or after a session.
- Writing should be carried out in a private, personalised place, free from distractions.
- Encourage clients to write on three or four occasions, usually on consecutive days or weeks.
- Set aside 30 minutes, with 20 minutes for writing and 10 minutes for patients to compose themselves afterwards.
- Let the client select a traumatic/stressful experience. Do not specify a particular topic.
- Allow the client to structure the writing rather than imposing structure.
- If possible, give the client the option to write by hand or on a computer.
- Explain to the clients that their writing is private, for themselves not for you and that confidentiality and anonymity are assured; explain that you will not read their writing unless they want you to.
- Do not give feedback.
- Writing should be kept by the client or separate from the practitioner's file.

(Adapted from Pennebaker & Cheung, 2007)

The narrative techniques employed in the present case equipped Elliott with an understanding and acknowledgement of stress experience. They also equipped him with the skills to motivate and empower himself in his struggle with his transition out of competitive sport and his more holistic pursuit of meaning and happiness. The intervention also allowed me to observe Elliott's capacity for meaning-seeking and meaning-making in order to help him restore purpose, faith and hope in his predicament. Elliott was more educated regarding the likely difficulties and anxieties he might face in the future, but this realization was accompanied by a perception that these anxieties were to be embraced rather than feared due to their reflection of what makes life worth living.

In preparing this chapter, I invited Elliott to provide his own reflections of the consultation process. He now keeps a daily diary to 'map my story with hot and cold distinctions' and to facilitate his 'searching for opportunities for meaning and learning'. A technique he reports regularly using is imagery to stimulate action towards 'a scene from the new chapter' and has passed on the use of this technique to others. Such reflections have reinforced his ongoing adoption of a quest narrative and included statements of intent for learning and growth. This has recently been illustrated by the commencement of a new stage of his journey, with Elliott accepting a place at university to study for a degree in an area he identified as a passion and strength of his during the consultation process. He anticipates that this latest chapter will assist his search for meaning in life through the pursuit of a best possible self and thriving life story.

FURTHER READING

McAdams, D. P. (2001). The psychology of life stories. *Review of General Psychology, 5,* 100–122. An excellent overview of the life history technique and its utility for promoting self-understanding grounded in narrative.

Smith, B., & Sparkes, A. (2004). Men, sport, and spinal cord injury: An analysis of metaphors and narrative types. *Disability & Society*, *19*, 613–626. Essential reading for those with an interest in narrative approaches, meaning and hope in sport. This paper draws on data from a life history study of a small group of men who have suffered spinal cord injury and become disabled through playing sport.

Wadey, R., & Evans, L. (2011). Working with injured athletes: Research and practice. In S. Hanton & S. D. Mellalieu (Eds.), *Professional practice in sport psychology: A review* (pp. 107–132). London: Routledge. An excellent review of extant theory-practice knowledge, with hands-on advice for working with injured athletes in sport.

Wong, P. T. P. (Ed.). (2012). *The human quest for meaning: Theories, research, and applications* (2nd ed.). New York: Routledge. Key reading for meaning-centred therapy and for a basic introduction to applying basic ABCDE intervention strategy to a variety of problems.

REFERENCES

Alfermann, D., & Stambulova, N. (2007). Career transitions and career termination. In G. Tenenbaum and R. C. Eklund (Eds.), *Handbook of sport psychology* (*3rd ed.*, pp. 712–733). New York: John Wiley & Sons, Inc.

Brewer, B. W. (2007). Psychology of sport injury rehabilitation. In G. Tenenbaum and R. C. Eklund (Eds.), *Handbook of sport psychology* (*3rd* ed., pp. 404–424). New York: John Wiley & Sons, Inc.

Brewer, B. W., Van Raalte, J. L., & Linder, D. E. (1993). Athletic identity: Hercules' muscles or Achilles heel? *International Journal of Sport Psychology*, *24*, 237–254.

Brewer, B. W., Van Raalte, J. L., & Petitpas, A. J. (2000). Self-identity issues in sport career transitions. In D. Lavallee and P. Wylleman (Eds.), *Career transitions in sport: International perspectives* (pp. 29–43). Morgantown, WV: Fitness Information Technology.

Brewin, C., Gregory, J. D., Lipton, M., & Burgess, N. (2010). Intrusive images in psychosocial disorders characteristic neural mechanisms and treatment implications. *Psychological Review, 117*, 210–232.

Brown, C. G., Weber, S., & Ali, S. (2008). Women's body talk: A feminist narrative approach. *Journal of Systemic Therapies, 27*, 92–104.

Bryant, F. B. (2003). Savoring Beliefs Inventory (SBI): A scale for measuring beliefs about savouring. *Journal of Mental Health, 12*, 175–196.

Charmaz, K. (1987). Struggling for a self: Identity levels of the chronically ill. In J. Roth & P. Conrad (Eds.), *Research in the sociology of health care: A research manual* (pp. 283–321). Greenwich, CT: JAI.

Elbert, T., & Schauer, M. (2002). Burnt into memory. *Nature, 419*, 883.

Ellis, A. (1987). *The practice of rational-emotive therapy*. New York: Springer.

Evans, L., Mitchell, I., & Jones, S. (2006). Psychological responses to sport injury: A review of current research. In S. Hanton & S. D. Mellalieu (Eds.), *Literature reviews in sport psychology* (pp. 289–319). Hauppage, NY: Nova Science.

Evans, L., Wadey, R. G., Hanton, S., & Mitchell, I. (2012). Stressors experienced by injured athletes, *Journal of Sports Sciences, 30*, 917–927.

Frank, A. (1995). *The wounded storyteller*. Chicago: University of Chicago Press.

Frankl, V. E. (1986). *The doctor and the soul: From psychotherapy to logotherapy (revised and expanded)*. New York: Vintage Books.

Hayes, S. C. (2005). *Get out of your mind and into your life: The new acceptance and commitment therapy*. Oakland, CA: New Harbinger.

King, L. A. (2001). The health benefits of writing about life goals. *Personality and Social Psychology Bulletin, 27*, 798–807.

McAdams, D. P. (1996). Personality, modernity, and the storied self: A contemporary framework for studying persons. *Psychological Inquiry, 7*, 295–321.

McAdams, D. P. (2001). The psychology of life stories. *Review of General Psychology, 5*, 100–122.

McAdams, D. P. (2008). *The life story interview*. Retrieved 8 December 2015 from http://www.sesp.northwestern.edu/foley/instruments/interview/

Mellalieu, S., Hanton, S., Neil, R., & Wagstaff, C. R. D. (2007). Competition and organization stress in sport. *Journal of Sports Sciences, 25*, s33–s34.

Onden-Lim, M., & Grisham, J. R. (2013). Intrusive imagery experiences in a high dysmorphic concern population. *Journal of Psychopathology and Behavioral Assessment, 35*, 99–105.

Pennebaker, J. W. (1997). Writing about emotional experiences as a therapeutic process. *Psychological Science, 8*, 162–166.

Pennebaker, J. W., & Cheung, C. K. (2007). Expressive writing, emotional upheavals, and health. In H. S. Friedman and R. C. Silver (Eds.), *Foundations of health psychology* (pp. 263–284). New York: Oxford University Press.

Robbins, B. D., & Friedman, H. (2008). Introduction to our special issue on positive psychology. *The Humanistic Psychologist, 36*, 93–95.

Rumbold, J. L., Fletcher, D., & Daniels, K. (2012). A systematic review of stress management interventions with sport performers. *Sport, Exercise, and Performance Psychology, 1*, 173.

Schneider, K. (2011). Toward a humanistic positive psychology: Why can't we just get along? *Journal of the Society for Existential Analysis, 22*, 32–38.

Schneider, K. J., Bugental, J. F. T., & Pierson, J. F. (2001). *The handbook of humanistic psychology*. Thousand Oaks, CA: Sage.

Seligman, M. E. P., Steen, T. A., Park, N., & Peterson, C. (2005). Positive psychology progress: Empirical validation of interventions. *American Psychologist, 60*, 410–421.

Smith, B., & Sparkes, A. (2004). Men, sport, and spinal cord injury: An analysis of metaphors and narrative types. *Disability & Society, 19*, 613–626.

Sparkes, A. C., & Smith, B. (2002). Sport, spinal cord injury, embodied masculinities, and the dilemmas of narrative identity. *Men and masculinities, 4*, 258–285.

Wadey, R. G., & Evans, L. (2011). Working with injured athletes: research and practice. In S. Hanton & S. D. Mellalieu (Eds.), *Professional practice in sport psychology: A review* (pp. 107–132). London: Routledge.

Wadey, R. G., Evans, L., Evans, K., & Mitchell, I. (2011). Perceived benefits following sport injury: A qualitative examination of their antecedents and underlying mechanisms. *Journal of Applied Sport Psychology*, *23*, 142–158.

Wadey, R., Evans, L., Hanton, S., & Neil, R. (2012). An examination of hardiness throughout the sport injury process. *British Journal of Health Psychology*, *17*, 103–128.

Wadey, R., & Hanton, S. (2013). Psychology of sport injury: Resilience and thriving. In F. G. O'Conner and R. Wilder (Eds.), *Running medicine* (pp. 921–936). New York: McGraw Hill.

Wagstaff, C. R. D., Fletcher, D., & Hanton, S. (2012a). Positive organizational psychology in sport. *International Review of Sport and Exercise Psychology*, *5*, 87–103.

Wagstaff, C. R. D., Fletcher, D., & Hanton, S. (2012b). Exploring emotion abilities and regulation strategies in sport organizations. *Sport, Exercise and Performance Psychology*, *1*, 262–282.

Wagstaff, C. R. D., Fletcher, D. & Hanton, S. (2012c) Positive organizational psychology in sport: An ethnography of organizational functioning in a national sport organization. *Journal of Applied Sport Psychology*, *24*, 26–47.

Wagstaff, C. R. D., Hanton, S., & Fletcher, D. (2013). Developing emotion abilities and regulation strategies in a sport organization: an action research intervention. *Psychology of Sport & Exercise*, *14*, 476–487.

Waterman, A. S. (2013). The humanistic psychology-positive psychology divide: Contrasts in philosophical foundations. *American Psychologist*, *68*, 124–133.

White, M. (2007). *Maps of narrative practice*. New York: Norton.

Wiese-Bjornstal, D. M., Smith, A. M., & LaMott, E. E. (1995). A model of psychologic response to athletic injury and rehabilitation. *Athletic Training: Sports Health Care Perspectives*, *1*, 17–30.

Wong, P. T .P. (2009a). *The human quest for meaning* (*2nd* ed.). New York: Routledge

Wong, P. T. P. (2009b). Positive existential psychology. In S. Lopez (Ed.), *Encyclopedia of positive psychology* (pp. 148–156). Oxford: Wiley-Blackwell.

Wong, P. T. P. (2010). Meaning therapy: An integrative and positive existential psychotherapy. *Journal of Contemporary Psychotherapy*, *40*, 85–99.

Wong, P. T. P. (2012). Toward a dual-systems model of what makes life worth living. In P. T. P. Wong (Ed.), *The human quest for meaning: Theory, research, and applications* (*2nd* ed., pp. 3–22). New York: Routledge.

Wong, P. T. P., & Fry, P. (1998). *The human quest for meaning: A handbook of psychological research and clinical applications*. Mahwah, NJ: Lawrence Erlbaum Associates.

Wylleman, P., Alfermann, D., & Lavallee, D. (2004). Career transitions in sport: European perspectives. *Psychology of Sport and Exercise*, *5*, 7–20.

Yalom, I. D. (1980). *Existential psychotherapy*. New York: Basic Books.

6 Personality and Group Functioning: Managing a Narcissist's Ego

Chelsey Dempsey, Chin Wei Ong, Ross Roberts, and Tim Woodman

LEARNING OBJECTIVES

AFTER READING THIS CHAPTER YOU SHOULD BE ABLE TO:

1. Evaluate how and why different personalities excel in different roles or environments.
2. Create an unbiased, informed picture of a personality through a triangulation of data (i.e., conducting a needs analysis using several different sources such as teammates, coach, player, observations).
3. Critically discuss narcissism, and the effects of narcissism on group functioning.
4. Construct theoretically driven interventions for a narcissistic athlete.
5. Evaluate different avenues for self-reflection, and understand why a combination of reflective processes may be most beneficial.

AREAS TO CONSIDER WHEN READING THE CHAPTER:

- The sport psychologist's role in helping each personality excel within a team environment.
- How a sport psychologist might determine the effects of personality on performance.
- How a sport psychologist could deal with athletes who have a disruptive personality which negatively impacts the cohesion of the team.

INTRODUCTION

One of the authors of the chapter was invited by a basketball coach to work with the team over the course of a competitive season. Initially, the sport psychology support centred on developing role clarity within the team, although it quickly became apparent that the disruptive influence of the team's captain warranted attention.

The team captain – Ethan – displayed narcissistic[1] characteristics. Narcissism is a personality trait defined as 'a pervasive pattern of grandiosity, need for admiration, and a lack of empathy' (*Diagnostic and Statistical Manual of Mental Disorders*, 5th ed. American Psychiatric Association, 2013, p. 669) and is recognized as a personality disorder should these characteristics become extreme. Morf and Rhodewalt (2001) described narcissists as 'self-aggrandizing and self-absorbing, yet easily threatened and overly sensitive to feedback from others' (p. 117). Thus, although narcissists appear to be confident and self-centred individuals on the outside, there is an insecure and fragile self-image that they wish to protect.

CLIENT AND BACKGROUND

Ethan was 31, originated from Colorado, and had been a professional basketball player for 12 years as a shooting guard (the main objective of a shooting guard is to score points). He was the longest serving player at the club having completed four seasons, three of which as captain. This was considered a long time for an American import player, as the UK league is usually considered a stepping stone toward more competitive leagues across Europe. During his time in the UK, Ethan was often recognized by fans and press alike for his 'flashy' plays and high scores. Two seasons before the consultant's involvement, the team had reached the cup final for two consecutive years, winning one final and losing the other. Ethan was awarded Most Valuable Player (MVP) in both games, which was an impressive achievement since it is especially rare for a player to be recognized as MVP on the losing side.

The case study begins three months into the season, when the team was in eighth position in a league of 12. In the first meeting between the coach and consultant, the coach explained that the league position did not reflect the quality of his team, and wanted some additional guidance to help the players reach their potential. The second meeting was between the team, coach, and the consultant, which gave the opportunity for introductions to take place. The third meeting between the team, coach, and consultant was an observation of a mid-week training session, and was the first time that the consultant witnessed the team in their performance environment. Ethan arrived 15 minutes late to training.

Consultant: Hi Ethan, did you get held up?
Ethan: Nah, I set off late; it's only training.

As the other players were waiting for Ethan to get his trainers on, they began challenging one another to score a basket from the centre circle of the court. One player turned to Ethan and challenged him to take a shot. Ethan began to hurry tying his laces and take his teammate up on the challenge. Everyone watched as he got ready to attempt the notoriously difficult challenge. Ethan

[1]The following chapter will use the term *narcissist* to describe subclinical levels of narcissism, i.e., '"normal" people who simply possess more narcissistic qualities than others' (Wallace, Baumeister, & Vohs, 2005, p. 436).

missed, and attributed his failure to a self-proclaimed lack of preparation, not his lack of skill, 'I haven't warmed up yet! I wasn't ready!'

Ethan's behaviour could suggest a degree of narcissism for several reasons. First, Ethan's attitude toward being late suggests that he is not motivated for training, and even proclaims not to care. The performance of a narcissist is dependent on the level of self-enhancement that is available: opportunities for self-enhancement induce better performance (Wallace & Baumeister, 2002), which is likely caused by an increase in effort (Woodman, Roberts, Hardy, Callow, & Rogers, 2011). An example of a self-enhancement opportunity is performing in front of an audience, or being publicly praised. Typically, training does not present opportunities for self-enhancement (or very few), which may begin to explain Ethan's somewhat blasé attitude.

Second, narcissism has been found to predict overconfidence, whereby narcissists report greater confidence despite performing no better than others (Campbell, Goodie, & Foster, 2004). Furthermore, narcissists base their future performance predictions on their expectations rather than their past performance (Campbell et al., 2004). Thus, although narcissists believe they are exceptional performers, their performance is often no better or worse than their low narcissist counterparts (Gabriel, Critelli, & Ee, 1994).

Although the aforementioned characteristics of a narcissist may appear somewhat negative, there can be advantages to having a narcissist on a team. As mentioned, Wallace and Baumeister (2002) presented evidence that the performance of a narcissist depends on the opportunity for self-enhancement. While depending on an opportunity for self-enhancement may result in limited interest for training, narcissists tend to perform well in competitive situations because the opportunity for self-enhancement is high. Ethan's competitive games are typically in front of 600–700 people, presenting him with an opportunity to demonstrate his (perceived) superiority. The opportunity for self-enhancement could be further increased in high-pressure competition, for instance when competing against the league's best teams. Also, it became clear that his teammates and coach could count on him to perform well in high-pressure situations when others tended to underperform or choke (cf. Roberts, Callow, Hardy, Woodman, & Thomas, 2010; Roberts, Woodman, Hardy, Davis, & Wallace, 2013; Wallace & Baumeister, 2002; Woodman, et al., 2011).

Narcissists also perform well in a team when their individual contribution to the team performance is identifiable. It is important to narcissists that their performance be recognized by others, as narcissists require ongoing attention to reinforce their ego (Morf & Rhodewalt, 2001). Conversely, narcissists are prone to social loafing – a reduction in effort when their individual contribution to the team's performance cannot be identified (Woodman et al., 2011). Woodman et al. demonstrated that narcissists will withhold effort if their individual performance within the team cannot be identified, and will invest effort if their *individual* contribution to group performance is overtly recognized. One would expect social loafing to be scarce in basketball, since it is a sport that is heavily reliant on performance statistics and pre-rehearsed game strategies, and has a small number of players in the team (five).

Since the consultant was not given a specific brief for the season, there was an agreement with the coach to conduct a general team-based needs analysis, before focusing on more specific areas.

INITIAL NEEDS ASSESSMENT

After a discussion with the coach, it was agreed that a team performance profile would be conducted with the squad (Butler & Hardy, 1992; Dale & Wrisberg, 1996). The development of a team performance profile allows the athlete(s) and/or coach to identify and discuss the characteristics needed to execute high performance, and provides a sound basis for any subsequent team-based goal setting or interventions.

Performance profile

The profiling session was conducted largely in line with Butler and Hardy's (1992) three stage recommendations. Below is the final team performance profile (Figure 6.1), which was presented to the team in a follow-up session.

The team agreed that the profile represented its current and ideal levels of performance. The consultant then tried to induce a more in-depth discussion of the results, but the team was reluctant to give any detailed opinions. One difference between the previous session and the current one was anonymity. The individual ratings that each player had previously submitted were anonymous and that same anonymity was not guaranteed in the present environment. Opening up to one another in a team environment to have a discussion about the profile results may have been slightly daunting if sharing their feelings and beliefs about the team was not something that they are used to (Dunn & Holt, 2004; Holt & Dunn, 2006).

The consultant made a recommendation to the coach to follow up the team profile session with one-to-one interviews with each of the players. The interviews were designed to gain more insight into the team ratings, particularly regarding the larger discrepancies in the 'training quality', 'role clarity', 'positive attitude', 'cohesion', and 'game strategy' characteristics. Before conducting the one-to-one interviews, the consultant informed the coach of the interview process and gleaned information from the coach regarding the roles and positions of the players in the squad (e.g., point guard, shooting guard, and centre). Asking for information from the coach in this way proved useful in building rapport between the consultant and coach, and in maintaining the coach's involvement in the intervention. After some time, the conversation turned toward the role of the captain, Ethan.

Coach: Our current captain is Ethan.
Consultant: OK, what is he like as a leader?

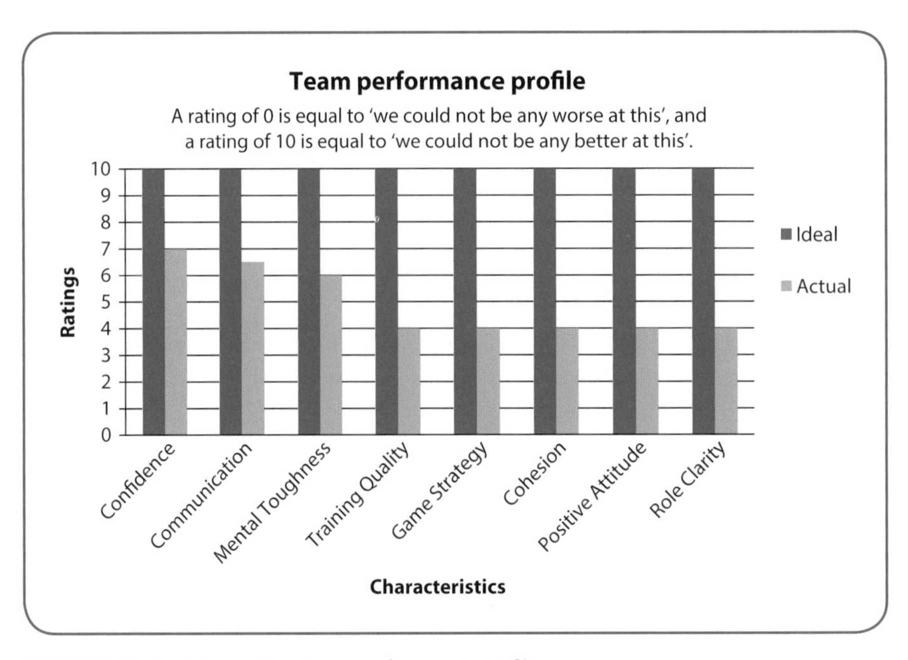

FIGURE 6.1 *Pre-intervention team performance profile.*

Coach: To be honest, he's no captain. I picked him again this year because he's been here the longest. He has been captain since the day I arrived and when I first met him I thought he'd make a great leader, now I'm not sure. I'm hesitant to hand the captaincy to someone else, as he will probably get upset. He's great in the big games, but the rest of the team don't appreciate his attitude in training and how he blames others all the time when things go wrong.

The coach's comments added to the previous evidence regarding Ethan's narcissistic traits. At first, a narcissist is viewed as charismatic (Khoo & Burch, 2008), likeable (Paulhus, 1998), and socially skilled (Oltmanns, Friedman, Fielder, & Turkheimer, 2004). However, as narcissists become more acquainted over time, they score low on observer ratings for the traits of conscientiousness, emotional stability, openness, and adjustment (Paulhus, 1998). Additionally, narcissists' leadership effectiveness dissipates over time (Ong, Roberts, Arthur, Woodman, & Akehurst, in press). These findings were echoed by the coach, who no longer believed that Ethan possessed the suitable leadership qualities necessary for a team captain, now that he had got to know him better. This information was valuable for the consultant before beginning the one-to-one sessions, since there was an opportunity to gain insight into the other players' thoughts regarding Ethan's captaincy.

One-to-one interviews

The interviews were semi-structured (cf. Hutchinson & Skodal-Wilson, 1992), which allowed for an interactive conversation with open-ended questions. This approach facilitates rapport building between the athletes and consultant, and encourages honest exchange regarding the team performance profile (Côté, Salmela, & Russell, 1995; Patton, 1990).

Each player was asked about their role within the team; from which a selection of responses is presented below:

Player 1: I try to be the positive one, picking the guys up when they are down and never give up during a game. To be honest, there is negativity in the team that seems to stem from Ethan.

Player 2: I'm the point guard so I try to keep the guys organized, especially on offence. I pick the plays so I try to identify weaknesses in the opposition. Sometimes I get overruled by Ethan, which is frustrating.

Ethan: I'm the most experienced player here. I have natural leadership qualities, so it's natural for me to lead the others who can learn from me. I have authority over them and they listen to me, most of the time anyway. Sometimes they start moaning when I tell them what to do but if they just did what I say we'd win more often.

Player 3: I just go about trying my best and doing what I can for the team. There tends to be a lot of arguments between Ethan and some of the others players about his big ego. I try to keep out of it.

The comments from the players highlighted a discrepancy in how Ethan viewed himself and how his teammates viewed him. Narcissists are susceptible to deficits in accurate self-perceptions (Campbell et al., 2004), and research has demonstrated that narcissism can account for up to 20% of positive self-perception bias (John & Robins, 1994). Ethan's negative attitude and tendency to take on the roles of other team members could be having a negative effect on the low ratings for positive attitude and role clarity. In addition, his lack of punctuality at training could be negatively influencing the ratings for training quality, since training would often start late because of him. Cohesion might be low because he was not demonstrating social- or task-related commitment toward the team, despite being the captain and claiming to lead by example.

In combining the large discrepancies observed in the team performance profile and the statements in the interviews, the negativity among the squad could be, at least partially, explained by Ethan's displays of narcissism. For this reason, the attention of the intervention was turned towards gathering more evidence relating to Ethan's impact on the squad. This was achieved via systematic observations using evidence-based criteria.

Observations

The consultant performed further observations using one of the most widely used measures for subclinical narcissism, the Narcissistic Personality Inventory (NPI; Raskin & Terry, 1988).[2]

Description box **BOX 6.1**

THE NPI AS AN OBSERVATIONAL TOOL

For each pair of statements, the consultant had to decide which statement corresponds best to the person being rated. For example, the consultant would have to choose between a narcissistic statement ('He/she thinks he/she is an extraordinary person') and a non-narcissistic statement ('He/she thinks he/she is much like everybody else'). One point is scored for each narcissistic statement selected from each pair of statements.

The NPI has 40 items and includes seven sub-scales: authority, exhibitionism, superiority, entitlement, exploitativeness, self-sufficiency, and vanity. The NPI is scored by taking the sum of narcissistic statements selected; the higher the score the more narcissistic the individual. Although the NPI has been used mainly as a self-report measure, it was adapted as an observational tool in the current intervention to identify Ethan's narcissistic behaviours during training and competition. The information obtained from the NPI observational tool was used to triangulate evidence already collected from the team performance profile, coach, and player interviews.

In observing Ethan's responses in the one-to-one interviews, many of the NPI items closely matched Ethan's description of his own leadership characteristics. For example, the narcissistic responses 'I like having authority over people', 'I have a natural talent for influencing people', and 'People always seem to recognize my authority' were displayed by Ethan. In addition, the statements 'I really like to be the centre of attention' and 'I am more capable than other people', might begin to explain why he had overruled the point guard's decisions and wished to be the main player during set plays during competitive games.

The combination of the team profile, one-to-one interviews, and NPI observations provided an accumulation of convincing evidence that an intervention based on narcissism and team functioning was preferable. It was evident that the team dynamic issues were mainly caused by the negative

[2]One may wish to consider using a new measurement for grandiose narcissism, the Grandiose Narcissism Scale (Foster, McCain, Hibberts, Brunell, & Johnson, 2015), when considering which tools to use to aid with observations.

interpersonal relationships within the team, influenced by Ethan's narcissistic personality and behaviour. Thus, an intervention that addressed the aforementioned issues was deemed appropriate.

FRAMEWORK AND INTERVENTION

Service delivery framework

Owing to the complexity and interdependence of issues observed within the team, an intervention that was focused yet flexible in dealing with different relationships within the team was necessary. Additionally, getting the best out of specific individuals through improvements in player relationships was considered a central aim of the intervention. These aims could be achieved by taking a humanistic approach, where each team member was situated at the core of the intervention, and was holistically recognized as a person first and a basketball player second (Poczwardowski, Sherman, & Ravizza, 2004). Being guided by a humanistic framework also helped the consultant to establish a healthy rapport with the team, and emphasize openness to detect potential issues affecting team performances.

The intervention was implemented in two complementary ways. The consultant addressed the issues within the team by working directly with the team members, and also indirectly with the team through the coach. Taking both approaches allowed the consultant to understand and address the intricacies of the player relationships, and also allowed the coach to strengthen his relationships with each player.

Understanding individual differences – a direct approach

One of the most immediate areas to address was the team's understanding of one another's individual differences. There is currently a dearth of literature on the application of personality within group dynamics in sport, which could be attributed to the initial scepticism surrounding the application of personality to explain elite athletic performances (see Beauchamp, Jackson, & Lavallee, 2007) and an overreliance on simple explanations for complex relationships (Roberts & Woodman, in press). Despite the lack of research in the area, theorists have been adamant that an understanding of personality characteristics has an essential role to play in group dynamics in three main ways: 1) Personality is associated with interdependent group outcomes or functioning; 2) the distribution of different personalities within a group might influence group functioning; and 3) having a greater awareness of individual team members' personalities could be used to enhance team functioning (Beauchamp et al., 2007).

The importance of understanding personality characteristics when working with individual athletes is evidenced in research on narcissism in sport. Narcissistic athletes have been found to utilize psychological skills more effectively (Roberts et al., 2010, 2013), respond to leadership characteristics differently from non-narcissistic athletes (Arthur, Woodman, Ong, Hardy, & Ntoumanis, 2011), and perform better when there is an opportunity for personal glory (Wallace & Baumeister, 2002; Woodman et al., 2011). Basketball is an interactive sport where each team member's performance is dependent on other members of the team. A breakdown in this interdependent functioning seemed apparent from the discrepancies in the team performance profile for 'roles', 'positive attitude', 'cohesion' and 'game strategy', which could have contributed to poor team performances. Ethan's narcissistic behaviour has also garnered unfavourable perceptions from individual team members, and could be a destructive force on the interdependent functioning of the team. Therefore, a greater awareness and acceptance of self and others' perceptions of personality could make team members more conscious of their behaviour and its impact on other team members. An intervention was developed to encourage the team to recognize each other's personality and its impact on the team, and a workshop that focused on 'understanding individual differences' was implemented.

Workshop: understanding individual differences. The workshop was designed based on a personal-disclosure mutual-sharing (PDMS) approach (Crace & Hardy, 1997; Holt & Dunn, 2006; Yukelson, 2010), which is a method of team building that encourages individuals to reveal previously unknown stories and information to other members of the team. This technique facilitates mutual communication of personal values, motives, beliefs and attitudes that provide a foundation for the growth of collectively shared constructs and understandings (Ostroff, Kinicki, & Tamkins, 2003; Windsor, Barker, & McCarthy, 2011). PDMS has been linked with improved team functioning, which could result in performance benefits (Evans, Slater, Turner, & Barker, 2013). In order to harness the benefits of PDMS, the workshop was purposefully organized to include opportunities to encourage mutual sharing of experiences.

The workshop consisted of the 'team pictionary' and 'team affirmations exercise' activities. However, due to the lack of engagement in the team profiling earlier, an ice-breaker game preceded the workshop. Ice-breakers can ease individuals into a positive climate for difficult conversations or problem solving and thus were considered appropriate for this workshop (Midura & Glover, 2005). Box 6.2 provides an example of the ice-breaker activity that was designed and used by the consultant.

Description box **BOX 6.2**

ICE-BREAKER GAME: 'YOU AND ME' (30 MINUTES)

Eleven chairs were arranged in a circle and team members were asked to sit on them as quickly as possible. The last team member without a seat had to stand in the centre of the circle. The game then commenced when all the seated team members completed the sentence 'Other than basketball, I love to ...' as honestly and uniquely as possible (e.g., 'Other than basketball, I love to paint.'). Every team member had to pay attention to what everyone else shared, and no identical sentences were allowed. Once the last seated team member in the circle had shared his comment, the consultant asked the player in the centre, 'tell me, who loves to...?' (e.g., 'paint').

If the standing team member answered incorrectly, he would continue standing. If he answered correctly, he could take the seat of a team member of his choice. However, before he was allowed to be seated, the consultant would ask the chosen seated team member, 'tell me, who loves to...', and if he answered correctly, he did not have to give up his seat. The standing team member had to continue choosing other team members until someone who failed to answer correctly had to relinquish his seat. The next round would continue with a new question 'my favourite food is...', 'I dislike...', 'my superhero is...', 'my dream is...', etc.

Learning and discussion points

The purpose of this activity was to promote greater levels of understanding amongst the members of the team. Team members will discover that everyone has something about them, or has experienced something in their lives that makes them either similar to or different from others. This activity also emphasizes the importance of communication in human relationships, particularly active listening.

Activity 1: team pictionary (45 minutes). For this activity, all team members were asked to write down on a piece of paper a word or phrase that best describes their personality and how it positively impacts the team. These phrases were collected and used in an adapted game of pictionary where all the team members had to guess the phrase being drawn on the flipchart by a nominated team member. After guessing each phrase, the team members also had to guess which team member had most likely described himself this way, and explain why they thought so. Afterward, the original team member who submitted the description was revealed and he had to explain why he had described himself in the way he did.

The consultant's aim in this activity was to facilitate frank and open discussion. Before beginning the activity, the consultant informed the team that they could speak honestly and openly, but everything that was said and felt during the activity should remain within the team. However, recognizing that team discussion type activities could potentially lead to heightened emotional intensity within the team (Dunn & Holt, 2004; Holt & Dunn, 2006), the consultant had to ensure that tempers did not fray during the activity. To achieve this, a two-minute time limit was imposed on each team member to speak uninterrupted.

The following outlines Ethan's description as to why he chose the word 'leader' to describe himself:

Ethan: I used the word 'leader' to describe myself, as I am the best player in the team and I always encourage everyone to work to my standards. The team would not stand a chance against the top teams in the league without me.

Player 1: Ethan, you might be the most accomplished player in the team, but that doesn't automatically make you a leader. A true leader is able to command the respect of his team mates. Respect is not earned by displaying immature behaviour like deserting the team when we are down, or playing for personal glory rather than for your team.

Player 2: Yeah I agree, a person who doesn't listen to his team mates and only barks orders all the time is not a good leader.

Player 3: All you do is talk big, but when it comes to the daily grind of training or a game when we aren't at our best, you shirk your responsibilities as captain and blame everyone else.

Ethan: You guys are just jealous that you are not as gifted as me. I'm a natural leader and led this team even before coach arrived. If all of you stuck to your jobs of following my instructions and quit complaining about everything, then maybe we wouldn't be in the position we are.

Consultant: All right gentlemen, thank you, but Ethan your two-minute airtime is up. At this point, I would just like to say that all of you have been great in being frank and open with one another, which is the aim of this activity. A lot of good quality exchanges have emerged so far, and the reason why you have engaged in this activity is because all of you are members of the same team and want your team to do well. We can achieve this together by polishing some of the team processes in our next activity and also with the coach over the course of the season.

Through this activity, it was evident that there was a significant difference between self and peer perceptions of Ethan's leadership. The two-minute rule was particularly useful as it allowed the consultant to take control when the discussion became heated. The exchange between Ethan and other team members was something that stood out from the activity, which not just confirmed earlier reports about Ethan, but also something that required greater attention.

Learning and discussion points. The 'pictionary' activity was aimed at helping team members improve their awareness of one another's personality and how it could be perceived differently by different members of the team. This awareness could act as an antecedent to the recognition of the roles played by the individual team members, which could help to address the large discrepancies for 'roles' and indirectly enhanced 'positive attitudes', 'cohesion' and 'game strategy'. Furthermore, this activity encouraged short dialogues on team members' personal values, motives, beliefs, and attitudes that provided a foundation for the development of shared team values. Therefore, this activity played a significant role in helping team members become more aware of their self and others' perceptions of their personality and contributions to the team.

Activity 2: team affirmations exercise. One of the reasons why Ethan did not get on well with his teammates was because narcissists are generally uncommitted to relationships with others and will engage in relationships primarily for self-enhancement regulation (Morf & Rhodewalt, 2001). For instance, narcissists take credit for success but attribute failure to others (Campbell, Reeder, Sedikides, & Elliot, 2000), only perform when others are noticing (Wallace & Baumeister, 2002), and prefer popular and high-status partners (Campbell, 1999). Although the underlying mechanism for narcissists' lack of commitment to relationships could be attributed to their priority towards self-enhancement, their self-enhancement tendencies are brought about by their need to protect their fragile self-image from potential ego threats (Morf & Rhodewalt, 2001). An example of a narcissist's response to an ego threat was observed in the previous activity when Ethan engaged in a heated argument with other team members after they criticized him. Indeed, ego threats can be derived from criticism (Bushman & Baumeister, 1998), social rejection (e.g., disrespect, Twenge & Campbell, 2003), or a restriction of freedom (Bushman, Bonacci, Van Dijk, & Baumeister, 2003). Therefore, a reduction in ego threat perceptions could possibly attenuate narcissists' chronic self-enhancement, which could in turn promote enhanced team functioning. Reducing ego threats could also inadvertently create an environment that activates communal orientations within the team, which has been shown to be associated with better quality of relationships (Finkel, Campbell, Buffardi, Kumashiro, & Rusbult, 2009).

In order to foster a less ego threatening environment within the team, an activity aimed at providing greater appreciation of each member's value to the team was organized. Using the same phrases/words that were generated in the previous activity, each team member had to provide a positive reason to support why other team members have used certain phrases/words to describe themselves, for example, 'Ethan is a "Leader" because he gives inspirational speeches' (see Table 6.1 for other

Table 6.1 *Team members' self-descriptive words/phrases and the corresponding positive affirmations provided by other team members.*

Self-descriptive words/phrases	*Positive affirmations provided by other team members*
Leader	• Gives inspirational speeches • Gives team confidence and belief in difficult games
Diligent	• Always stays back after training to work on improving skills • Never misses a training session
Team player	• Always happy to play out of position to help the team • Fully committed to team goals and objectives
Mentally tough	• Unfazed by bigger and stronger opposition • Always finds a solution when the going gets tough

examples). These positive statements were then presented to each team member as affirmations of their strengths and how in the eyes of others, they are valuable to the team.

Learning and discussion points. This activity encouraged perspective-taking which has been shown to increase narcissists' empathy (Hepper, Hart, & Sedikides, 2014), and in turn activate communal orientations through better social relations. Additionally, providing positive affirmations have been shown to reduce the impact of ego threats (Thomaes, Bushman, Orobio de Castro, Cohen, & Denissen, 2009), and possibly create a non-ego threatening environment that fosters greater communal orientation. Encouraging narcissists to engage in communal behaviour would result in greater commitment to their relationships (Finkel et al., 2009). Thus, this activity helped the team to recognize one another's strengths, and in doing so, reinforced the development of shared team values initiated in the previous activity by building a more communal culture within the team. Although the outcome of the activity did not instantly resolve the disputes between Ethan and his teammates, it was a step in the right direction for the rest of the season. Any lingering animosity between Ethan and other teammates was diffused through coach-led interventions over the course of the season.

Coach-led interventions – an indirect approach

A major aspect of the coach's role is to manage individual members in the team. The coach-led intervention was a comprehensive programme designed to equip the coach with the knowledge of how one might work with a narcissistic athlete. A similar aim to that of the team workshop was adopted to help the coach realize the significance of understanding personality characteristics in achieving better team performance, with emphasis placed on raising the coach's awareness of narcissism. With an understanding of narcissism, it was possible to identify Ethan's narcissistic traits with the coach, and how they influenced the team. Subsequently, strategies can be employed to harness or downplay these narcissistic traits to improve team functioning. The second aim of the coach-led intervention was to cultivate greater communal orientations within the team. As discussed earlier, this was achieved by reducing the occurrence of ego threats by promoting perspective-taking and other communal behaviour within the team throughout the season.

Central to achieving the aims outlined for the coach-led intervention was the manipulation of self-enhancement. Narcissists engage in agentic self-enhancement to build or maintain their inflated but fragile sense of self, which can be satisfied through both agentic and communal means. Therefore, the intervention included a series of strategies implemented by the coach to create both agentic and communal self-enhancement opportunities, so that Ethan was motivated to engage in tasks that are beneficial to the team.

Description box — BOX 6.3

An individual's agency refers to feelings of competence, extraversion, and uniqueness. Conversely, communal needs refer to one's warmth, agreeableness, and relatedness (Gebauer, Sedikides, Verplanken, & Maio, 2012). One may wish to consider these definitions and how they differ when reading the interventions. Parts of the interventions are tailored to address the team issues via agentic means, whereas other parts of the intervention address the issues via communal means.

(Gibbs, G. (1988). *Learning by doing: A guide to teaching and learning methods.* Oxford: Further Education Unit)

One of Ethan's most important roles was that of team captain. Recent research has shown that narcissists are initially favoured as leaders, but quickly lose this favour over time (Ong et al., in press). That is, narcissists' construal of leadership positions as an opportunity for self-enhancement, coupled with their charisma and social skills among other traits, make them attractive leaders in the first instance and favourable candidates for leader emergence. While narcissists do well to emerge as leaders, their arrogance, insatiable need for superiority and hypersensitivity, could explain why peer perceptions of their leadership effectiveness tend to decline over time (Rosenthal & Pittinsky, 2006). Since Ethan has already been assigned as team captain, the proposed intervention included strategies to arrest the decline of Ethan's leadership effectiveness, which could lead to better team performances.

Player of the month. The first strategy adopted by the coach was to introduce a 'team player of the month' award. This award was voted for by the coaching staff and squad and presented to the team member who has demonstrated the most team contributions over a given month. The award was given out at the last home game of each month. Examples of team contributions were supporting teammates when they are underperforming, helping teammates with extra training, and communicating effectively with teammates and coaching staff. This strategy was aimed at promoting communal orientations within the team. By building a more supportive, less ego threatening environment, Ethan was motivated to satisfy his need to self-enhance by pursuing communal goals.

Team review process. Although encouraging Ethan to fulfil communal goals promoted effective team functioning, the coach recognized that Ethan did sometimes positively contribute to the team when pursuing agentic goals. However, this came at the cost of several of Ethan's relationships with his teammates turning sour. In order to harness the positive aspects of Ethan's agentic self-enhancement, the coach agreed to restructure the team's performance review process by reviewing goals every three weeks as opposed to every three months. Introducing more frequent reviews of goals opened up the opportunity to adjust goals with a view to motivate and challenge Ethan and other team members more optimally. Additionally, more frequent coach reviews enabled more regular assessment of goals, which promoted an increased consciousness of each team member's strengths and weaknesses, and look at ways to improve as a basketball player. For Ethan in particular, conducting frequent reviews with him to constantly assess and readjust goals helped to harness his motivation towards agentic self-enhancement opportunities.

Self-enhancement opportunities in training. The coach also introduced agentic self-enhancement opportunities within aspects of training, where individual performance is less identifiable and opportunities for glory are less abundant. For instance, three new set plays that allowed Ethan to take ownership of the play and make the final shot or key pass were introduced. These plays were rehearsed in training in preparation for Ethan to play a starring role in competitive games. Introducing more opportunities for glory in training did not only increase the commitment of Ethan, but benefited every individual member of the team because when opportunities and rewards were available for team members to aim high in training, the team would be challenged to commit performances to a higher level.

In order to determine if the strategies designed to take advantage of narcissists' motivation toward self-enhancement opportunities were translated into individual contributions towards team performance on the court, the coach agreed to use performance statistics of individual team members more openly and publicly. This was conceptualized and implemented based on the tendency for narcissists to self-handicap when self-enhancement opportunities are not apparent (Wallace & Baumeister, 2002). Williams, Nida, Baca and Latane (1989) found that increasing the identifiability of individual swimmers' performance within a relay race enhanced overall performance. Therefore, making individual performances more openly available could enhance team performance. Adopting such a strategy could potentially backfire if not handled carefully, as narcissists often react negatively to criticism. Kernis and Sun (1994) demonstrated that when a narcissist receives positive feedback they view the evaluation technique as more diagnostic and the evaluator (i.e. the coach) as more competent. Conversely, upon receiving negative feedback, a narcissist would perceive the evaluation technique as less diagnostic and the evaluator as less competent. Thus, it was important for the coach to present any poorer performances not as criticism but as challenges.

REFLECTIONS

In order to reflect on consultant and intervention effectiveness, several methods of self-reflection and feedback from others (peers, athletes, and the coach) were sought. Feedback from the team and coach consisted of a meeting six weeks after the start of the intervention, to discuss its progress and effectiveness. The meeting began with a recap of the intervention aims which was followed by a discussion surrounding the players' thoughts on its effectiveness. Finally, the coach and players (anonymously) provided written feedback using the Sport Psychology Consultant Evaluation Form (Partington & Orlick, 1987). Furthermore, the team re-rated the performance profile constructs (Figure 6.2), so any changes in the team perceptions regarding the core performance constructs could be identified.

Six weeks after the start of the intervention each of the constructs had improved. This feedback was valuable to the consultant, as it indicated whether the intervention was addressing the right issues and impacting the team in the right way.

The main method of self-reflection used was the Gibbs (1988) cycle (Figure 6.3), which was completed within an hour of each workshop or meeting finishing. The cycle allowed the consultant to break an event down into several components before thinking about their own performance.

The first part of the cycle, 'description', may include information such as who was present, where the session was held, what the session or meeting was about, and what was the planned outcome. 'Feelings' allowed me to explore what I was thinking at the time and how it made me feel.

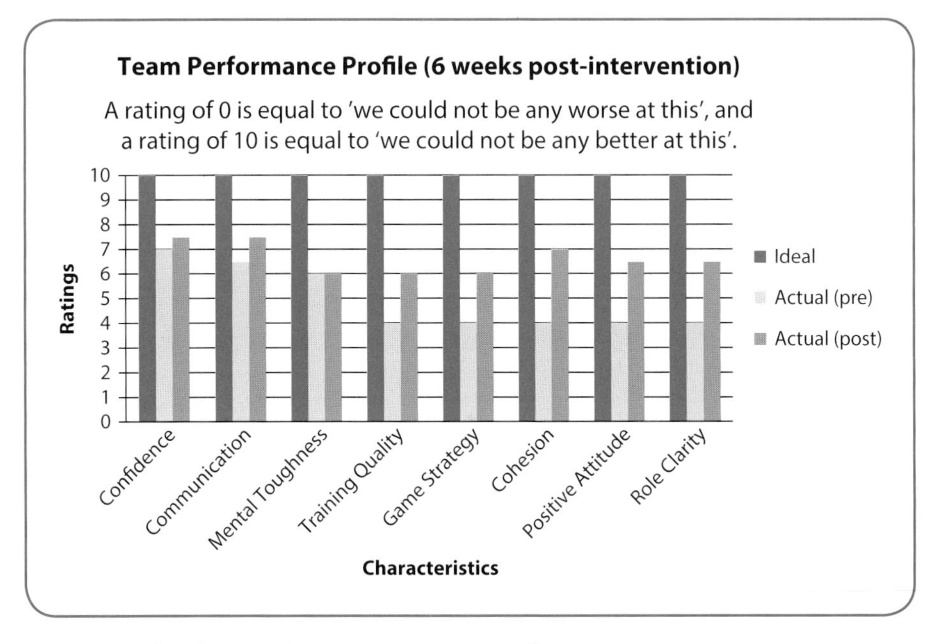

FIGURE 6.2 *Post intervention team performance profile.*

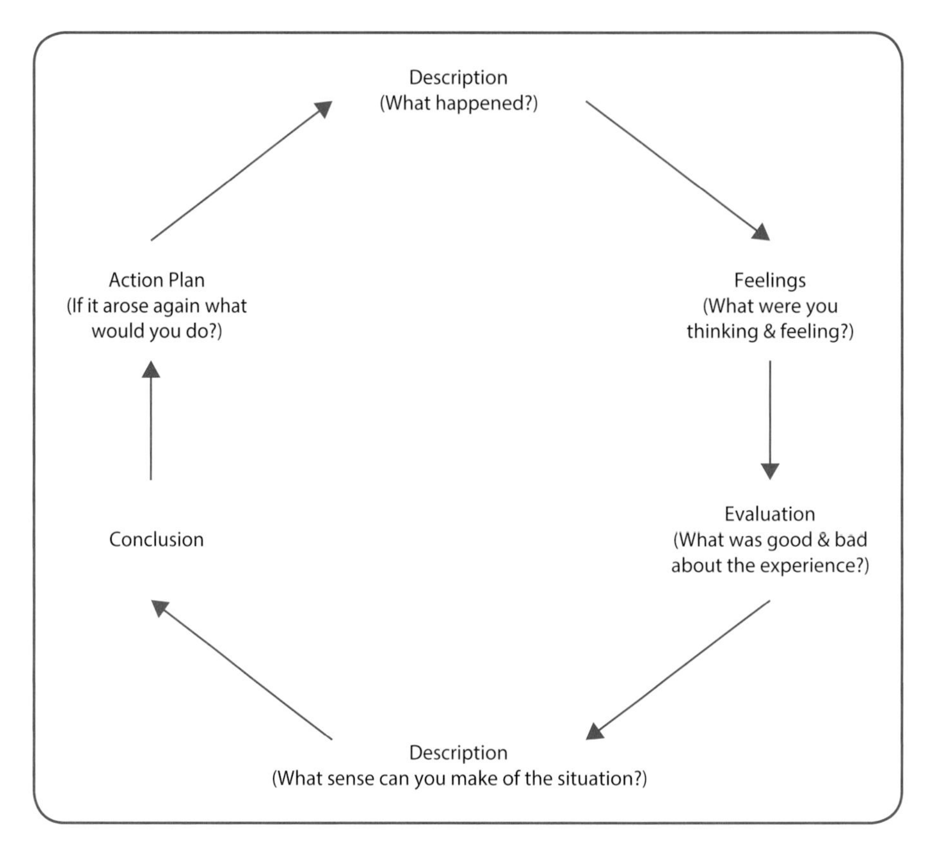

FIGURE 6.3 *Cycle of self-reflection (Gibbs 1988).*

'Evaluation' is a general view of what went well and what could have been done better. The second 'description' then encourages a more in-depth look at the events in the evaluation. If parts of the session went well, what could be replicated elsewhere? Also, if something did not go well, why not? The final two stages, 'conclusion' and 'action plan' allowed me to gather my thoughts about my work and plans for next time. A more accurate conclusion and meaningful action plan can be made when considering feedback from others, since overly positive self-evaluations are common (Taylor & Brown, 1994).

Needs assessment

Description. The needs assessment comprized three sections. The first was a team-based performance profile, the second was the player interviews, and the third was the observation of Ethan.

Feelings. The consultant found it somewhat surprising to be confronted with an issue that was having such a negative impact on the team and performance with no mention of it from the coach. This situation could be a particularly difficult challenge, especially considering the dearth of literature regarding personality and sport. Therefore, the consultant's understanding of the narcissism literature and previous experience as a consultant created the foundation for this intervention. Feelings of apprehension are often normal when one is about to deal with a new situation, but a consultant can take confidence from their ability to problem solve and build rapport with their clients to move toward a common goal.

Evaluation. This situation benefited from the attitude of the coach toward sport psychology. The coach was eager to learn about narcissism and the impact such a personality was having on the team. An understanding coach can make it much easier to express ideas, implement interventions, and get designated time to work with the athletes.

Analysis. With help from the coach, the intervention most likely encountered fewer problems than it could have when dealing with difficult personalities. It was clear that Ethan was the root of the problem, and the issues were dealt with in the best way possible between the consultant and coach. Due to the recent poor performances from the team, the coach was eager to try and change the group dynamic and approach to preparation and reflection of games. Conversely, had the team been performing well and still had these issues, the coach might have been reluctant to make changes to the training and performance environment.

Conclusion. An alternative approach to the issues presented may have been to work directly with Ethan and explain how his behaviour was impacting the rest of the squad. However, upon reading the narcissism literature it was apparent that this would not have been appropriate. Research demonstrates that narcissists are aware that they are not liked and do not particularly mind, as they would rather be admired (Raskin, Novacek, & Hogan, 1991). This suggests that working directly with Ethan might not have attended to the desired outcomes, since it was highly unlikely he would have cared for the opinions of his teammates when challenged about his behaviour. However, by encouraging the team as a whole to understand the different personalities and individual differences within the team, it is possible to adapt the environment to encourage acceptance of one another.

Action plan. Based on previous experience and the current literature, the direct team-based coupled with the indirect coach-based approach was deemed the best way to deal with this particular issue. The evidence at six weeks suggested the intervention was having the desired effects, thus it was deemed appropriate to continue in the same vein as opposed to altering the intervention to confront Ethan about his behaviour directly.

Sport Psychology Consultant Evaluation Form (Partington & Orlick, 1987)

The Sport Psychology Consultant Evaluation Form was completed by the players and coach at the same time the performance profile ratings were re-rated (six weeks after the start of the intervention), in order to gain a triangulation of feedback on the intervention and consultancy work thus far. The form gives the client an opportunity to rate the consultant on a series of statements from 1 (*not at all*) to 10 (*yes, definitely*). Higher ratings indicate that the client felt the intervention was suitable, had a positive impact, and that they have a good working relationship with the consultant. In this instance, all of the ratings were between 7 and 9 (Figure 6.4). A comparison of the ratings across the items enabled me to identify areas that I can further improve upon in future. In addition, the differences in ratings between the players and the coach can give an indication of the areas to improve on when working with either one. For example, I have been rated higher by both players and coach on my ability to relate to the players (item 5) but lower on my ability to provide strategies to improve performance (item 8). This showed that I have established a strong rapport with both players and coach which bodes well for intervention adherence and also future

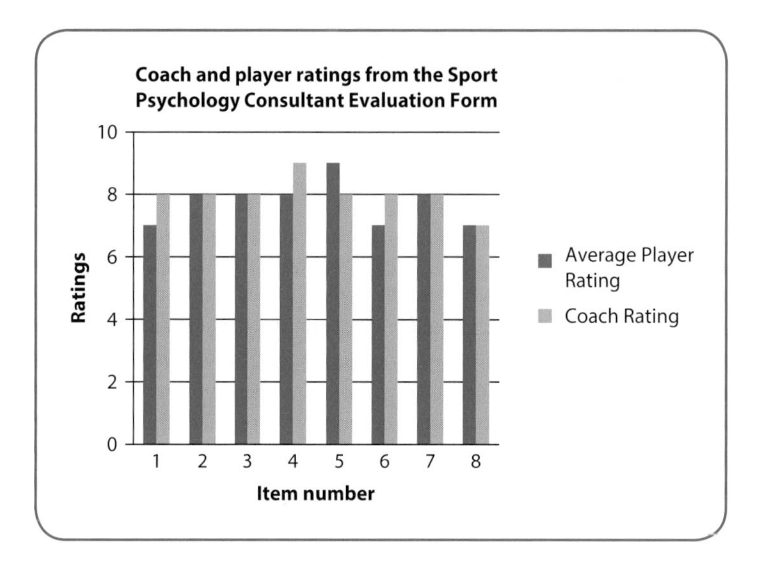

FIGURE 6.4 *Coach and player ratings from the Sport Psychology Consultant Evaluation Form.*

collaborative work. However, the strategies that have been implemented were rated lower and this is also reflected in the post-intervention performance profile (Figure 6.2), where performance ratings although improved, are still some way off the ideal ratings. The coach-led intervention was designed to be a season-long series of practical strategies and I believe both the performance profile ratings and consultant evaluation ratings for item 8 would improve with sustained adherence to the intervention.

Intervention

The interventions were based on the interpretation that Ethan's narcissism characteristics were a significant cause of the large discrepancies identified in the team performance profile. The intervention aimed to address directly the discrepancies observed for 'roles' by generating a greater awareness of personality differences among the team members and coach about narcissism. A greater recognition of team roles in turn resulted in improvements in 'positive attitudes' and 'cohesion' and adherence to 'game strategy'. Greater understanding of Ethan's narcissistic characteristics also allowed the coach to motivate Ethan more effectively in training.

Ice-breaker activity. While the intention of the ice-breaker was to ease the team into the workshop with a greater awareness of individual differences within the team in a light-hearted and non-threatening manner, the team members felt an initial apprehension toward divulging personal information (cf. Dunn & Holt, 2004; Holt & Dunn, 2006). Although the members of the team eventually got more involved in the activity, it would have been better if the ice-breaker was more closely linked to the areas where large discrepancies were presented in the team performance profile. The lack of explanation regarding the personal information sharing during the ice-breaker also resulted in variations in the authenticity of the information shared by some members of the team. This resulted in an observable degree of distrust among certain members when sharing personal information and some members resorted to fabricating information that sounded dubious and ridiculous. However, as the activity was positioned as an ice-breaker to the workshop, the sharing of sometimes dubious information made the session humorous and more light-hearted. It was also a 'test-bed' for the sharing of personal information in the pictionary activity. Therefore, the authenticity of information shared did not negatively impact the aims in this regard.

Team pictionary activity. In the pictionary activity, the team members were more forthcoming with expressing their personality characteristics and their contributions to the team. This led to the smooth running of the activity, which was followed by lively discussion about personality differences and contributions within the team, some of which even broached the topic of roles within the team. However, the open forum that was an unintended outcome of the activity resulted in a concerted attack by a few members of the team on the negative influence of Ethan's behaviour on the team. As expected, Ethan vehemently defended his position as captain and leader of the team and almost turned aggressive. The house rules of amiable discussion and the two-minute time limit for speaking ensured that the discussion remained cordial. If these measures had failed, I could have stepped in as the moderator of this activity. These controls were implemented with the knowledge that PDMS-type interventions could lead to heightened emotional intensity (Dunn & Holt, 2004; Holt & Dunn, 2006). Despite the apparent danger that the discussion might escalate, the activity provided an opportunity for frank and open discussions about how team members felt about one another, and could possibly pave the way for more open communications in the future.

Team affirmations exercise. Although the final team affirmations activity did not resolve the disputes between Ethan and other team members, it helped to calm things down by encouraging the team to engage in perspective-taking. I thought the team affirmations exercise was positively received as many positive behaviours have been picked up by all members of the team (including Ethan). Some have remarked that they did not realize what they were doing was actually having a positive impact on another teammate, which was an indicator that the activity had been a success. This final activity also provided good closure to the workshop and a sound platform for coach-led interventions.

Coach-led intervention. Besides the relationship between Ethan and his teammates, another critical relationship to consider was between Ethan and the coach. The coach-led intervention was administered after the team workshop in order to capitalize on the strengths of Ethan's agentic and communal narcissistic characteristics. Forging a communal environment within the team would minimize ego threats and thus, encourage more communal goal striving by Ethan and also within the team. Additionally, restructuring the team's performance review process by implementing more frequent goal setting and assessments would help the coach to monitor and calibrate goals more effectively. The intervention seemed to have worked, as Ethan has engaged in more communal goals such as organizing extra training sessions, which has seen him being awarded 'team player of the month' twice in the season.

SUMMARY

This case study attempts to demonstrate the importance of understanding how personality can impact team functioning. The interventions focused on enhancing the understanding of the specific personality trait of narcissism, and creating an environment that would manage the personality. It is important to remember that one can only alter an environment, not a personality, and that athletes are people first, athletes second. Therefore, an understanding of personality and performance is paramount in building an effective environment within which all can flourish.

FURTHER READING

Butler, R., & Hardy, L. (1992). The performance profile: Theory and application. *The Sport Psychologist, 6*, 253–264. This paper explains the theory behind the performance profile, before giving several examples of a how a performance profile can be used to aid performance development.

Wallace, H. M., & Baumeister, R. F. (2002). The performance of narcissists rises and falls with perceived opportunity for glory. *Journal of Personality & Social Psychology, 82*, 819–834. This paper demonstrates that narcissists perform better when self-enhancement opportunity is high rather than low. The authors manipulate self-enhancement opportunity in four experiments using different tasks, and find support for their hypotheses in each.

Beauchamp, M., & Eys, M. (2007). *Group dynamics in exercise and sport psychology*. New York: Routledge. This suggested book gives a wide range of topics within group dynamics. Chapters include 'Coach-athlete relationships ignite sense of groupness' and 'Personality processes and intra-group dynamics in sport teams'.

REFERENCES

American Psychiatric Association (2013). *Diagnostic and statistical manual of mental disorders* (5th ed.). Washington, DC: American Psychiatric Association .

Arthur, C. A., Woodman, T., Ong, C. W., Hardy, L., & Ntoumanis, N. (2011). The role of athlete narcissism in moderating the relationship between coaches' transformational leader behaviors and athlete motivation. *Journal of Sport & Exercise Psychology, 33*, 3–19.

Beauchamp, M. R., Jackson, B., & Lavallee, D. (2007). Personality processes and intra-group dynamics in sports teams. In M. A. Eys & M. R. Beauchamp (Eds.), *Group dynamics in exercise and sport psychology: Contemporary themes* (pp. 25–42). New York: Routledge.

Bushman, B., & Baumeister, R. F. (1998). Threatened egotism, narcissism, self-esteem, and direct and displaced aggression: Does self-love or self-hate lead to violence? *Journal of Personality & Social Psychology, 75*, 219–229.

Bushman, B. J., Bonacci, A. M., Van Dijk, M., & Baumeister, R. F. (2003). Narcissism, sexual refusal, and aggression: Testing a narcissistic reactance model of sexual coercion. *Journal of Personality & Social Psychology, 84*, 1027–1040.

Butler, R., & Hardy, L. (1992). The performance profile: Theory and application. *The Sport Psychologist, 6*, 253–264.

Campbell, W. K. (1999). Narcissism and romantic attraction. *Journal of Personality & Social Psychology, 77*, 1254–1270.

Campbell, W. K., Goodie, A. S., & Foster, J. D. (2004). Narcissism, confidence, and risk attitude. *Journal of Behavioral Decision Making, 17*, 297–311.

Campbell, W. K., Reeder, G. D., Sedikides, C., & Elliot, A. J. (2000). Narcissism and comparative self-enhancement strategies. *Journal of Research in Personality, 34*, 329–347.

Côté, J., Salmela, J. H., & Russell, S. (1995). The knowledge of high performance gymnastic coaches: Competition and training considerations. *The Sport Psychologist, 9*, 76–95.

Crace, R. K., & Hardy, C. J. (1997). Individual values and the team building process. *Journal of Applied Sport Psychology, 9*, 41–60.

Dale, G., & Wrisberg, C. (1996). The use of a performance profiling technique in a team setting: Getting the athletes and coach on the 'same page'. *The Sport Psychologist, 10*, 261–277.

Dunn, J. G. H., & Holt, N. L. (2004). A qualitative investigation of a personal-disclosure mutual-sharing team building activity. *The Sport Psychologist, 18*, 363–380.

Evans, A. L., Slater, M. J., Turner, M. J., & Barker, J. B. (2013). Using personal-disclosure mutual-sharing to enhance group functioning in a professional soccer academy. *The Sport Psychologist, 27*, 233–243.

Finkel, E. J., Campbell, W. K., Buffardi, L. E., Kumashiro, M., & Rusbult, C. E. (2009). The metamorphosis of Narcissus: Communal activation promotes relationship commitment among narcissists. *Personality and Social Psychology Bulletin, 35*, 1271–1284.

Foster, J. D., McCain, J. L., Hibberts, M. F., Brunell, A. B., & Johnson, R. B. (2015). The Grandiose Narcissism Scale: A global and facet-level measure of grandiose narcissism. *Personality and Individual Differences, 73,* 12–16.

Gabriel, M. T., Critelli, J. W., & Ee, J. S. (1994). Narcissistic illusions in self-evaluations of intelligence and attractiveness. *Journal of Personality, 62,* 143–155.

Gibbs, G. (1988). *Learning by doing: A guide to teaching and learning methods.* Oxford: Further Education Unit.

Hepper, E. G., Hart, C .M., & Sedikides, C. (2014). Moving narcissus: Can narcissists be empathic? *Personality and Social Psychology Bulletin, 40,* 1–13.

Holt, N. L., & Dunn, J. G. H. (2006). Guidelines for delivering personal-disclosure mutual sharing team building interventions. *The Sport Psychologist, 20,* 348–367.

Hutchinson, S., & Skodal-Wilson, H. (1992). Validity threats in scheduled semistructured research interviews. *Nursing Research, 2,* 117–119.

John, O. P., & Robins, R. W. (1994). Accuracy and bias in self-perception: Individual differences in self-enhancement and the role of narcissism. *Journal of Personality & Social Psychology, 66,* 206–219.

Kernis, M. H., & Sun, C. (1994). Narcissism and reactions to interpersonal feedback. *Journal of Research in Personality, 45,* 430–441.

Khoo, H. S., & Burch, G. S. J. (2008). The 'dark' side of leadership personality and transformational leadership: An exploratory study. *Personality and Individual Differences, 44,* 86–97.

Midura, D. W., & Glover, D. R. (2005). *Essentials of team building: Principles and practices.* Champaign, IL: Human Kinetics,

Morf, C., & Rhodewalt, F. (2001). Unraveling the paradoxes of narcissism: A dynamic self-regulatory processing model. *Psychological Inquiry, 12,* 177–196.

Ong, C. W., Roberts, R., Arthur, C. A., Woodman, T., & Akehurst, S. (in press). The leader ship is sinking: A temporal investigation of narcissistic leadership. *Journal of Personality.*

Ostroff, C., Kinicki, A. J., & Tamkins, M. M. (2003). Organizational culture and climate. In I. B. Weiner, W. C. Borman, D. R., Ilgen, & R. J.Klimoski (Eds.), *Handbook of psychology, Vol. 12: Industrial and organizational psychology* (pp. 565–593). Hoboken, NJ: John Wiley & Sons, Inc.

Partington, J., & Orlick, T. (1987). The sport psychology consultant evaluation form. *The Sport Psychologist, 4,* 309–317.

Patton, M. Q. (1990). *Qualitative evaluation and research methods* (*2nd* ed.). Newbury Park, CA: Sage.

Paulhus, D. L. (1998). Interpersonal and intrapsychic adaptiveness of trait self-enhancement: A mixed blessing? *Journal of Personality & Social Psychology, 74,* 1197–1208.

Poczwardowski, A., Sherman, C. P., & Ravizza, K. (2004). Professional philosophy in the sport psychology service delivery: Building on theory and practice. *The Sport Psychologist, 18,* 445–463.

Raskin, R., Novacek, J., & Hogan, R. (1991). Narcissism, self-esteem, and defensive self-enhancement. *Journal of Personality, 59,* 20–38.

Raskin, R., & Terry, H. (1988). A principle-components analysis of the Narcissistic Personality Inventory and further evidence of its construct validity. *Journal of Personality & Social Psychology, 54,* 890–902.

Roberts, R., Callow, N., Hardy, L., Woodman, T., & Thomas, L. (2010). Interactive effects of different visual imagery perspectives and narcissism on motor performance. *Journal of Sport & Exercise Psychology, 32,* 499–517.

Roberts, R., & Woodman, T. (in press). Contemporary personality perspectives in sport psychology. In S.Hanton & S.Mellalieu (Eds.). *Contemporary advances in sport psychology:* A review. Abingdon: Routledge.

Roberts, R., Woodman, T., Hardy, L., Davis, L., & Wallace, H.M. (2013). Psychological skills do not always help performance: The moderating role of narcissism. *Journal of Applied Sport Psychology, 25,* 316–325.

Rosenthal, S., & Pittinsky, T. (2006). Narcissistic leadership. *The Leadership Quarterly, 17,* 617–633.

Taylor, S., & Brown, J. (1994). Positive illusions and well-being revisited: Separating fact from fiction. *Psychological Bulletin, 116,* 21–27.

Thomaes, S., Bushman, B. J., Orobio de Castro, B., Cohen, G. L., & Denissen, J. J. A. (2009). Reducing narcissistic aggression by buttressing self-esteem: An experimental field study. *Psychological Science, 20,* 1536–1542.

Twenge, J. M., & Campbell, W. K. (2003). 'Isn't it fun to get the respect that we're going to deserve?' Narcissism, social rejection, and aggression. *Personality and Social Psychology Bulletin, 29,* 261–272.

Wallace, H. M., & Baumeister, R. F. (2002). The performance of narcissists rises and falls with perceived opportunity for glory. *Journal of Personality & Social Psychology, 82*, 819–834.

Wallace, H. M., Baumeister, R. F., & Vohs, K.D. (2005). Audience support and choking under pressure: A home disadvantage? *Journal of Sport Sciences, 4*, 429–438.

Williams, K. D., Nida, S. A., Baca, L. D., & Latane, B. (1989). Social loafing and swimming: Effects of identifiability on individual and relay performance of intercollegiate swimmers. *Basic and Applied Social Psychology, 10*, 73–81.

Windsor, P., Barker, J. B., & McCarthy, P. J. (2011). Doing sport psychology: Personal-disclosure mutual-sharing in professional soccer. *The Sport Psychologist, 25*, 94–114.

Woodman, T., Roberts, R., Hardy, L., Callow, N., & Rogers, C.H. (2011). There is an 'I' in TEAM: Narcissism and social loafing. *Research Quarterly for Exercise and Sport, 82*, 285–290.

Yukelson, D. P. (1997). Principles of effective team building interventions in sport: A direct services approach at Penn State University. *Journal of Applied Sport Psychology, 9*, 73–96.

Yukelson, D. P. (2010). Communicating effectively. In J. M.Williams (Ed.), *Applied sport psychology: Personal growth to peak performance* (6th ed., pp. 149–165). New York: McGraw-Hill.

7 Returning to Sport Following Serious Injury: A Case Study of a Professional Rugby Union Player

LYNNE EVANS

LEARNING OBJECTIVES

AFTER READING THIS CHAPTER YOU SHOULD BE ABLE TO:

1. Describe Egan's (2002) Skilled Helper Model.
2. Identify the types of loss associated with injury.
3. Critically discuss ways in which you could alleviate an injured athlete's re-injury anxiety and expedite their successful return to competitive sport.
4. Assess the merits of a uni versus multi-modal intervention approach with an injured athlete.

AREAS TO CONSIDER WHEN READING THE CHAPTER:

1. The factors that give meaning to and influence an injured athlete's injury experience.
2. How the support needs of athletes from other client groups might differ.
3. The role of the sport psychologist in providing support to injured athletes.

CLIENT AND BACKGROUND

This case study provides an insight into some of the most prevalent issues that injured athletes encounter during their return to competitive sport, through the experiences of Alex. Alex is a 25-year-old professional rugby union player who plays for an English premiership club – the top tier of professional rugby in England. He played his age-grade rugby at a rival club, where having progressed through the academy system he secured a senior full-time professional contract at the age of 18. He moved to his present club four years ago, having been attracted by the opportunity to contest his preferred playing position in the starting line-up. Within a short time of being at the club, he established himself as a key player in the team, and prior to his injury, was one of the first names on the team-sheet. Having represented his country at age-grade level, he had aspirations to play senior international rugby.

Alex ruptured his anterior cruciate ligament (ACL) in one of the first few games of the season, and despite his team having had a relatively poor start to the season, Alex had been playing particularly well. Indeed, it was his first run of games for a number of months having lost what he saw as significant game time (six weeks) in the run up to the end of the previous season, a result of some problems with the same knee. Off the back of what he thought had been an exhaustive rehabilitation programme, the current injury was a particularly big blow for him and he had really struggled emotionally to cope with his enforced time out of rugby and the challenge of rehabilitating the knee again – indeed, so much so, that despite no previous experience of sport psychology he had asked the club's physiotherapist if he knew of a sport psychologist that he could speak to.

Alex sustained the injury in the latter stages of a game as the result of an innocuous tackle on him by an opponent. Stretchered off the pitch, he was operated on almost immediately. Although the prognosis for his overall recovery was good, he had never anticipated how arduous the whole experience would be. With his immediate family located some distance away, it rested on his partner to provide much of the support he needed. Initially confined to non-weight bearing activities and constrained by the use of crutches, he was reliant on his partner to help him with even the most mundane of everyday activities. Alex found his initial loss of mobility and independence particularly frustrating and although short-lived it took its toll on him. Unable to drive, he had felt incredibly isolated and in his eyes his teammates and coaches had lost interest in him. During this period he became quite self-absorbed and introspective, with few other interests outside rugby to distract him. With formal rehabilitation came some relief for Alex. Alex invested heavily into his rehabilitation – it gave him a sense of purpose, a means of achieving progress, and some feeling of autonomy and control. With progress came increased motivation to adhere to the programme. However, as rehabilitation progressed Alex became increasingly frustrated with the slowness of his progress, a situation that was exacerbated by a few, albeit minor, but for Alex nonetheless significant setbacks. As a result Alex began to question the effectiveness of the treatment, and lost confidence in the programme and the medical team. He also started to question whether the injury had resulted from a misdiagnosis of his previous knee problems. However, despite these concerns he remained focused on getting back to full fitness for the last few games of the season – a focus that sustained his motivation and engagement with the rehabilitation process.

I met him at his request five weeks before his first scheduled game back. I was greeted by what appeared to be a very considered but focused young man who wanted to do everything he could to ensure that he made an immediate impression on his return from injury over the final few games of the season. In particular, he felt that he needed to allay the doubts that others and he may have harboured about his ability to return to pre-injury levels of performance – to be the same player he was before the injury. During this meeting he explained that his identity was completely wrapped up in him being a rugby player and that he was driven by his ambitions to play senior international rugby, a goal that hitherto he had been confident of achieving. I also learnt of the insecurities he had about his playing contract and what he perceived could be the impact of his recent injury on securing a new one. He was now questioning the diagnosis of his previous knee injury, and the prognosis and rehabilitation of it, which perhaps not surprisingly had had a knock on effect to the current injury and his confidence in the medical support he had received. His overwhelming concerns revolved around his ability to return to pre-injury levels of performance (to achieve his playing aspirations) and the potential for re-injury because of the inability of the knee to stand up to the demands of the game. As a big ball carrier and elusive and pacey runner, his strength in tackle situations had previously been one of his biggest assets as a player – the loss of which could have a significant impact on his playing career. His concerns were further exacerbated by what he saw as a significant loss of overall strength and fitness, the loss of his playing position within the team to a younger talented player (who in his absence has been playing particularly well), the change of head coach at the beginning of the season, and the financial difficulties that the club were experiencing at the time. He admitted that the whole injury experience had drained him emotionally and that he had sought my help because he didn't feel he had anyone he could share his concerns and insecurities with and gain the support from that he needed.

In summary, a number of issues emerged as important to Alex's ability to gain progress and expedite his successful return to playing rugby. Although the most pressing of these appeared to be to help Alex overcome his re-injury anxiety, his loss of confidence in his rehabilitation programme and the medical team, his overall physical fitness and injury status, ability to return to pre-injury levels of performance, contractual concerns and the perception of his status at the club were also salient. The importance of rugby in defining Alex's self-identity and the implications for him with regard to actual and potential loss gave added meaning to the injury, how he had experienced it and responded (cf. Brewer, 1993). By way of contextualizing Alex's case, the issues Alex presented with have been widely acknowledged in the research and professional practice literature to affect injured athletes both during rehabilitation and their return to competitive sport (e.g., Carson & Polman, 2008; Evans, Hardy, & Fleming, 2000; Gould, Udry, Bridges, & Beck, 1997b). For example, slow rehabilitation progress and setbacks, expectations of self and others, playing/performance aspirations, fitness status, and playing contracts have been identified in a number of studies as stressors experienced by injured athletes during their rehabilitation and return to competitive sport (e.g., Bianco, Malo, & Orlick, 1999; Evans et al., 2000; Evans, Wadey, Hanton, & Mitchell, 2012; Hare, Evans, & Callow, 2008; Gould, Udry, Bridges, & Beck, 1997a; Podlog & Eklund, 2006). In addition, feelings of disengagement and isolation (e.g., from coaches and teammates), negative social comparison, lack of confidence in the injured body part and its ability to withstand sporting demands, inadequate levels of informational and esteem support, and re-injury anxiety have been widely acknowledged in a number of bodies of research to detract from athletes' psychological readiness/successful return to competitive sport (e.g., Gould et al., 1997a; Kvist, Ek, Sporrstedt, & Good, 2005; Podlog & Dionigi, 2010; Podlog & Eklund, 2006, 2007; Udry, Gould, Bridges, & Beck, 1997). The present case study, therefore affords an opportunity to consider some of the possible antecedents, mechanisms and effects of some of the most prevalent concerns expressed by injured athletes during their return to competitive sport, as well as ways in which they can be alleviated.

INITIAL NEEDS ASSESSMENT

In essence, any process of assessment involves a decision about what to assess, why, and how. With injured athletes the 'what' is delineated in a way that it may not be with other clients – it involves injury and its effect. So in one sense working with injured athletes may be viewed as potentially less complex than other client groups. However, once you move beyond the 'issue(s)' being injury-related you may find yourself in potentially deeper water. From a personal and professional perspective this water is more easily charted with the right knowledge, understanding, and skills.

So where does the knowledge, understanding and skills come from and how do they impact upon needs assessment? In reality it is difficult and probably not meaningful to separate assessment from the goals of the support or intervention (both in relation to the present case study and injury more generally). Indeed, the helping process from its inception to its conclusion involves interplay between assessment and intervention (Egan, 2002). Context, meaning, and knowledge, both experientially and more formally acquired, shape the basis of the knowledge and understanding that informs both the assessment and intervention or support process. In relation to the current case study, this was predicated on knowledge and understanding of the existing injury-related research literature, my own contribution to this body of knowledge, and my previous experience of working with injured athletes. Having been engaged in research in this area for almost 20 years and worked with injured athletes in a professional support capacity for almost as long, it is difficult to completely delineate between knowledge and understanding derived from scholarship and research as opposed to experiential knowledge through professional practice. Although they are undoubtedly inextricably linked both in terms of the way they inform each other and the process of assessing and supporting athletes, I will, albeit perhaps a little artificially, try to separate out the more formally acquired knowledge into that which has been derived from injury-related concepts, models, and research and that which is more closely aligned to sport psychology service delivery.

In relation to injury-related knowledge, there has been a growing body of research that can guide professional practice, the most influential of which includes models of injury prediction, and response (e.g., Brewer, Anderson, & Van Raalte, 2002; Wiese-Bjornstal, Smith, Shaffer, & Morrey, 1998; Williams & Andersen, 1998) and the concepts of loss and attachment (e.g., Bowlby, 1991; Peretz, 1970). Empirical research (e.g., Carson & Polman, 2008; Evans et al., 2000) and reviews (e.g., Brewer, 2007; Evans, Mitchell, & Jones, 2006), some of which are more easily translatable into professional practice than others, add to this body of knowledge. In terms of guiding assessment (and support), the potential for and actual loss that results from being injured (e.g., self-identity, self-esteem, important ties, relationships, playing status, and performance aspirations) and the influence of a variety of personal and situational factors on a player's appraisal (e.g., personality, injury severity, previous injury history, coping resources, and medical support) provides an important backdrop to understanding how players will respond to and cope with injury (see e.g., Brewer, 2007; Evans & Hardy, 1995; Evans & Hardy, 1999; Wiese-Bjornstal et al., 1998). Although traditionally grounded in psychoanalytic theory, more recent adaptive conceptualizations of loss acknowledge the importance of interactions between social situations and individual perception in determining the significance of loss (Harvey, 1998). Loss, or no longer having 'someone or something that we used to have' (Harvey, 1998, p. 4) can take many forms. In an injury context, actual and symbolic loss can include loss of psychological/mental representations (e.g., loss of self-identity, loss of self-esteem), loss of physical functioning (e.g., strength, fitness, skill execution & performance ability), loss of social interactions and social support (e.g., teammates, coaches), loss of sources of gratification and reinforcement (e.g., performance accomplishment, goal attainment), and more tangible losses (e.g., playing contracts; cf. Brewer, 1993; Evans & Hardy, 1995; Lavallee, Grove, Gordon, & Ford, 1998; Peretz, 1970; Udry, 1997).

The impact of these types of loss for injured athletes, as in the present case, can be considerable and define the actual injury experience. Indeed, to overlook the importance of the threat that injury poses to important attachments and the significance of the potential for and actual loss that it represents, is to neglect the meaning that injury holds, and potentially treat the symptoms not the causes.

Returning to the present case study and the process of needs assessment, I approached the first meeting with Alex in the same way as I would any other client. Specifically, I gleaned as much information in advance of our meeting as I could; and in Alex's case the club physiotherapist who had made the initial contact with me was the primary source of this information. I also conducted a few internet searches to gain some additional insight into the player and his playing history from a developmental perspective. This information served a number of important functions; it provided me with a context to Alex, his injury, and its likely effect in relation to the potential for loss, the personal and situational factors that may be influencing this, and how effectively Alex appeared to have been coping with the injury and the challenges it presented. I also tried to ascertain what support networks Alex had available to him, the extent to which he may have mobilized this support and how effective it was in helping him cope (i.e., how well the support met his needs). Although Alex had asked to see me to help with his return to competitive sport, this background information helped to provide me with a better understanding of what Alex's needs might be and how best to meet those needs, which I find particularly useful in preparing for the initial consultation.

In terms of the initial consultation with Alex, the process of needs analysis was once again informed by my knowledge and understanding of the injury-related literature, but also of the service delivery and counselling literature and the importance of adopting a client-centred philosophy. The need to convey empathy, genuineness, unconditional positive regard, and establish credibility and trust is widely acknowledged in the counselling and service delivery literature and provides a basis for gaining an understanding of the player's perspective about his injury experience (Anderson, Miles, Robinson, & Mahoney, 2004; Egan, 2002; Pocwardowski, Sherman, & Henschen, 1998). This was essential if Alex was to open up and share his thoughts and feelings and where possible the basis of these during our initial consultation. In my experience, it is common for athletes who have sustained severe injuries to feel vulnerable, isolated, and reproach themselves for not being able to cope with their whole injury experience – the result being that they frequently hide their concerns and insecurities 'from the outside world' because they see an inability to cope as a sign of weakness that sets them apart from others. This may be more-so true for sports that have a strong masculine culture (as is the case in rugby football). Such perceptions fuel self-doubts about an ability to cope and to successfully return to sport and pre-injury levels of performance. However, in order to meet Alex's needs not only did I need to understand what his concerns were with regard to returning to sport, but also what the basis of these concerns might be.

The approach to eliciting this information was a simple one. Some may term this an intake interview or clinical interview, but it simply involved engaging Alex in a purposeful non-threatening discussion where he would feel secure in sharing his thoughts and feelngs and their antecedents (ultimately, his injury experience). Indeed, the process was far more organic than the word 'interview' suggests and consistent with the helping approach advocated by Egan (2002). It involved eliciting Alex's injury story through open dialogue. According to Egan's (2002) Skilled Helper Model (Figure 7.1), the first stage of the helping or consulting process involves exploring 'what's going on' or 'what's the present state of affairs' via three steps: Step I-A: help clients tell their stories; Step I-B: help clients break through blind spots that prevent them from seeing themselves, their problem situations, and their unexplored opportunities as they really are; and Step I-C: help clients choose the right problems and/or opportunities to work on. Egan's model provides a flexible framework wherein the use of the various tasks is determined by the client's needs. Box 7.1 contains exemplar questions to facilitate the process of eliciting meaning and gaining progress.

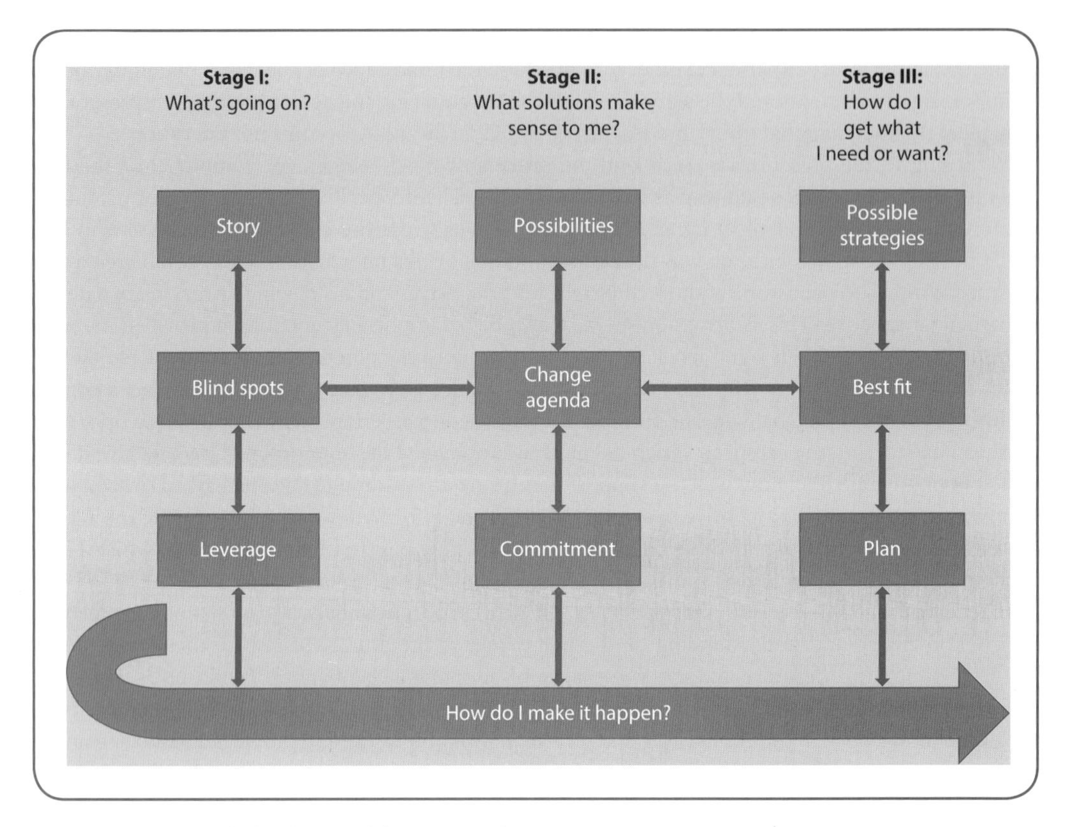

FIGURE 7.1 *The Skilled-Helper Model (Egan, 2002)*

Source: Egan, G. (2002). *The skilled helper: A problem-management and opportunity-development approach to helping*. Pacific Grove, CA: Brooks Cole.

Description box

BOX 7.1

EXAMPLES OF QUESTIONS TO ELICIT MEANING AND GAIN PROGRESS

- Can you tell me about what role 'sport' plays in your life?
- What have you found difficult to deal with since you've been injured?
- The difficulties that you've described are really common among athletes who get injured and many really struggle to cope with them, how well have you coped? Why do you think that is?
- What are your major concerns at the moment?
- What help do you think you'll need for moving forward? How would this help?
- What support do you have available to you?

An important first step in the therapeutic process, and one that is consistent with Egan's framework was to 'normalize' the client's concerns, doubts, and insecurities and to validate these with regard to the extent that injury is a very real stressful and critical life event experience wherein the potential for a heightened sense of self-doubt and inability to cope (because of the potential for loss) is considerable; particularly given that the nature of the demands can be very different from those that they have previously experienced. The added context to this in relation to Alex was that by the time I saw him he had been injured and out of sport for four months. He had found those four months very difficult, constantly reproaching himself for what he saw as a mental fragility and inability to cope. However despite this, and with his projected return fast approaching, he was highly motivated to ensure a successful transition back into competitive sport. As a result, he was very open about how difficult he had found the previous four months, the highs and particularly the lows he had experienced and what had contributed to those. He attributed the lows to what he perceived as a loss of identity and playing status, the slowness and unpredictability of his rehabilitation progress, loss of control, feelings of isolation, and a loss of confidence in his rehabilitation, recovery status, and as a result, his readiness to return to playing competitive rugby (at a level of play that he was happy with). Perhaps not surprisingly, he was very receptive to any suggestions that would give him a sense of control (empower him), help him to make progress, and expedite his successful return to sport.

FRAMEWORK AND INTERVENTION

Cupal (1998) suggested that the fundamental goal of injury interventions (and one with which I align) is:

> To identify the subjective cost of injury to an athlete while concurrently teaching and strengthening coping resources (Heil, 1993; Ross & Berger, 1996). Interventions should consider the personal meaning of injury, as well as empower an individual with appropriate recovery or preventive strategies. (p. 104)

This conceptualization of injury interventions is consistent with a client-centred approach to meeting an injured athlete's needs. It is also in keeping with a humanistic approach (particularly in the initial stages of the consulting process) in that it values and gives primacy to the individual's experience of injury and the personal meaning that it holds for them. To this end, it is important to ensure that the necessary therapeutic conditions are met early on in the consulting process to enable the client (in this case Alex) to feel safe, secure, and free from threat for them to be able to recognize that it is within their control and capacity to move forward and become a 'fully' functioning person (and athlete) again. As the consulting process progresses, a more integrative approach can be and was employed, which drew on a cognitive-behavioural approach – to complement the humanistic one – to help Alex attain specific therapeutic outcomes. In terms of an actual guiding framework, as alluded to earlier, Egan's (2002) Skilled Helper Model provided the overarching framework for the assessment and subsequently the intervention – so in essence the whole support process (see Figure 7.1).

Stage I of the model has already been outlined. Stages II and III together with the action arrow get to the heart of helping and are the most relevant here because they deal with goals, outcomes, and action. To elaborate, Stage I centres on outcomes, goals, and accomplishments. As with the other stages, three steps comprise Stage II; Step II-A focuses on helping clients review possibilities for the future; Step II-B denotes a process for helping clients choose and shape their goals; and Step II-C highlights the importance of goal commitment and what is required for goal achievement. Stage III and the steps that comprise it focus on the activities or work needed to produce the outcomes identified in Stage II. Specifically, Step III-A focuses on helping clients develop the strategies for accomplishing their goals; Step III-B involves choosing the strategies best suited to the client and their needs; and Step III-C helps clients formulate action plans (see Egan, 2002 for a more in-depth discussion of the model). As an aside, it is perhaps surprising that given the utility of Egan's framework for guiding the intervention process, that it hasn't received more widespread support in the sport psychology literature.

Early in the consulting process, helping Alex understand and gain perspective on personal meanings was therefore essential to making progress and the first step to empowering him. It was also fundamental to being able to adopt a model of equal (mutual) expertise to underpin the support process. To this end, as part of the first consultation we discussed the specific challenges that injury presents generally, and for Alex specifically, in a way that would 'normalize' and 'authenticate' his experiences. This process involved facilitating Alex's understanding of his injury experiences in relation to concepts such as loss, attachment, and appraisal, and the effect of factors such as his previous injury, the timing of the injury, his performance status, and his coping skills on the way he derived meaning as well as responded. Reflecting back to Alex what his knowledge and understanding of injury represented in these terms helped him to appreciate why he had struggled to cope and provided him with greater self-awareness of and insight into the basis of his thoughts and feelings and the meanings from which they were derived. Comparisons with other injured athletes provided him with reassurance that he had responded in a way that was completely normal and understandable (normalized things). It also helped him see that there was no reason why these responses would jeopardize his impending progress and/or successful return to sport. As a result, we spent the first part of the initial consultation exploring his injury experience over the preceding months before progressing to what may be perceived as the more pressing issues surrounding his return to competitive sport and five-to-six-week build up to that.

In terms of Alex's immediate concerns, and the ones on which the support was subsequently focused these revolved around re-injury anxiety and the need to attain pre-injury levels of performance; concerns that emanated from a lack of confidence in his knee, his playing/contractual status, loss of fitness (particularly speed and strength), previous injury experience, the unpredictability of his rehabilitation progress, and his perceived loss of autonomy and control. Consistent with previous research and the professional practice literature, a multi-modal approach was adopted to providing support, which comprised social support, goal-setting, imagery and self-talk (e.g., Carson & Polman, 2008; Evans et al., 2000; Johnston & Carroll, 1998). This approach was predicated on Alex's existing knowledge and understanding of the use of mental skills. To elaborate, before I introduced the different strategies, I explored with Alex his knowledge and understanding and previous use of them. Fortunately, for us given the limited time-frame, we had to educate him and safeguard the effectiveness of their use, Alex had a good understanding of the use of mental skills, in particular goals and imagery, which he had used fairly extensively in the past.

A growing body of research has acknowledged the importance of social support in buffering the detrimental effects of injury (e.g., Bianco & Eklund, 2001; Johnston & Carroll, 1998; Mitchell, Evans, Rees, & Hardy, 2014; Rees, Mitchell, Evans, & Hardy, 2010; Udry, 1997). Guided by current multi-dimensional conceptualizations of social support and recent injury-related research, we attempted to increase Alex's perception of available social support, the extent to which he could mobilize this support and the extent to which the perception of available social support as well as received support could best meet his needs (Bianco & Eklund, 2001; Mitchell et al., 2014; Rees et al., 2010). In terms of specific types of support, we focused on informational and esteem support from medical and conditioning personnel, coaches, and players to complement the emotional support that he received from family and friends (e.g., Bianco, 2001; Podlog & Dionigi, 2010; Podlog & Eklund, 2007; Udry, 1997). This support was intended to enhance Alex's knowledge and understanding of how he could optimize his recovery and successful return to competitive rugby, and increase his confidence in his rehabilitation programme, his perception of his recovery status and sense of autonomy and control – ultimately to reduce his re-injury anxiety (e.g., Bianco, 2001; Carson & Polman, 2008; Mitchell et al.,

2014; Podlog & Eklund, 2006, 2007). In order to address Alex's contractual concerns, his expectations with regard to attaining pre-injury standards of performance, and his perceived playing status, we explored the ways in which Alex could improve communication between himself and other players, and the coaching and medical staff (Podlog & Dionigi, 2010; Podlog & Eklund, 2009). The purpose of this approach was to try and ensure that Alex was receptive to and availed of information about his recovery and playing status to avoid returning prematurely, reduce any unrealistic performance expectations and provide him with reassurance about his value and status as a player and team member (e.g., Bianco, 2001; Johnston & Carroll, 1998; Mitchell et al., 2014; Podlog & Eklund, 2006; 2007). It was also anticipated that the information derived from this support would increase his knowledge and understanding of the rehabilitation process, his confidence in his rehabilitation programme and support team, his performance preparation and his sense of autonomy and control. This was considered important, not least because informational and esteem support from medical personnel and coaches can help reduce the risk of re-injury that can result from a premature return, unrealistic performance expectations, and re-injury anxiety (e.g., Bianco, 2001; Carson & Polman, 2008; Podlog & Eklund, 2006; 2007). Having hitherto isolated himself by staying away from the club, this initially meant him spending more time at the club and simply interacting with players, coaches, and other support personal. We also tried to heighten his awareness of the verbal and non-verbal messages that he might be conveying that may discourage the supportive actions of others – with a view to making such messages more positive and encouraging in nature.

Goal-setting complemented the use of, and was underpinned by, informational support. Goals were employed to give structure and focus to Alex's training and build confidence through goal attainment – an approach that was consistent with Alex's previous use of goals and goal-setting (cf. Kingston & Wilson, 2009). In essence, goals provided the stepping stones to expedite recovery and attain performance aspirations by providing increased task focus and enhanced motivation and self-confidence (e.g., Carson & Polman, 2008; Podlog & Eklund, 2006, 2007, 2009). Performance goals provided the basis of performance accomplishment information and process goals helped safeguard a process as opposed to an outcome focus (Evans & Hardy, 2002a, b; Evans et al., 2000). The use of performance and process goals was consistent with evidence that suggests that these types of goals may have particular merit in stressful situations, focusing attention and enhancing self-efficacy through perceptions of autonomy and control (Kingston & Hardy, 1997). Short-term goal attainment provided the motivation to set and achieve subsequent goals. Optimally difficult goals also facilitated increased self-efficacy, and as a result the likelihood of goal attainment – in addition to setting subsequent goals (cf. Kingston & Wilson, 2009). The use of goals also enhanced Alex's treatment and rehabilitation efficacy and perceptions of control and autonomy through his involvement in the goal-setting process (cf. Kingston & Hardy, 1997; Kingston & Wilson, 2009; Evans & Hardy, 2002b). Monitoring goal attainment through completion of a training diary provided Alex with feedback that in-turn enhanced motivation (and confidence). Goal attainment and the associated feedback also formed the basis for verbal persuasion information (i.e., positive/constructive self-talk). The process of goal-setting was co-ordinated by the physiotherapist who ensured that the coaches (including the strength and conditioning coach) had input into it. Examples, of Alex's specific goals are provided in Box 7.2.

Simulation training provided a catalyst for a staged approach to Alex's return to rugby. Simulation training, which involves preparing to meet the demands of specific situations by for example, simulating competition conditions and the associated cognitions and emotions, is an effective way of preparing to meet performance demands (cf. Hardy, Jones, & Gould, 1996). In the current context it was employed to progressively approximate game demands and Alex's ability to successfully meet them. Initially this process focused on general and positional game demands and as the first competitive game approached it shifted to a focus on those aspects of performance particularly associated with Alex's injury occurrence (Evans et al., 2000; Podlog & Eklund, 2007). For example, simulation

Description box

BOX 7.2

EXAMPLES OF GOALS

- Attend squad training sessions twice a week to interact with players and coaches over next two weeks.
- Meet physiotherapist and conditioning personnel to agree goals for build-up to return to rugby.
- Increase focus on technique and form during rehabilitation and training activities.
- Undertake 15 minutes of additional training at the end of a squad training session that simulated full-contact tackle situations with opposing players.
- Incorporate three imagery sessions weekly (15 minutes duration) of game scenarios that involved being tackled in the way that had caused injury, but with a successful outcome (he successfully offloaded the ball and recovered from the tackle to contribute to the next phase of the game).
- Prepare a pre-performance routine that could be used prior to the first few games back to achieve an appropriate activation state through a process focus to offset the potential detrimental effects of re-injury anxiety.

training involved progressing from the use of tackle bags and static tackle situations to situations that more closely mirrored tactical game demands; moving from unopposed non-contact situations to opposed full-contact ones – with the level of the opposition and intensity of the sessions also increasing over time (cf. Podlog & Eklund, 2007). As his first competitive game approached, tackle situations were introduced that directly replicated the situation in which Alex incurred his injury. This approach is consistent with Evans et al. (2000) where physical practice was built up progressively through the use of tackle bags to full-contact situations with opposing players to more closely approximate game demands and situations in which the injury occurred. The use of simulation training served a number of purposes – as a basis for goal-setting it enhanced his motivation and through goal attainment and performance accomplishment information, goal commitment. It also served to increase Alex's confidence in the rehabilitation programme, his physical, technical, and performance status and performance readiness; as well as increased confidence in the rehabilitation support team. However, perhaps most importantly simulation training reduced Alex's re-injury anxiety through increased confidence in the strength and recovery status of the knee and its ability to meet and withstand game demands, particularly those which had the potential to invoke injury and re-injury. In sum it facilitated a state of physical, technical, and psychological preparedness and readiness.

Injured athletes have echoed the benefits of imagery use reported in the sport psychology literature (Evans, Hare, & Mullen, 2006; Hare et al., 2008). Alex reported using imagery quite extensively prior to his injury as part of his preparation for competitive performance to rehearse tactics and set-plays and to achieve what he described as his ideal performance state. He described what appeared to be a very good ability to create and control effective images, an ability he suggested he had developed over years of practice based on trial and error. As a result we decided to use imagery to complement the use of simulation training and goal-setting. Consistent with the research literature and my own professional practice experience we initially decided to use imagery to reinforce the correct technique and successful completion of rehabilitation, training, and performance-related activities, and to foster goal focus and goal attainment (Evans et al., 2000; Evans, 2006; Hare et al., 2008); to increase confidence. As his return to sport approached he also used imagery of the injury withstanding injury-threatening situations, particularly the one in which the injury had originally occurred, and to reinforce a performance process focus (e.g., positioning, defensive alignment and tackling, and his role in set-plays; Evans et al., 2000). Alex's use of imagery served a number of purposes. It reinforced confidence in the injured limb and its ability to withstand potentially injury invoking situations, and increased his confidence in the successful execution of performance-related goals – and as a result his ability to achieve pre-injury levels of performance. In essence, imagery not only reinforced his familiarity with, and overcoming of, anxiety provoking situations associated with the injury occurring, but also his ability to achieve performance-related goals. This use of imagery and its potential effects is consistent with the use and effects of imagery reported in the sport psychology and injury research literature (e.g., Callow, Hardy, & Hall, 2001; Driediger, Hall, & Callow, 2006; Hare et al., 2008; Sordoni, Hall, & Forwell, 2000).

Information derived from a number of sources (e.g., process goals, goal achievement, informational and esteem support from coaches and medical personnel) formed the basis of self-talk. Self-talk served a number of purposes during Alex's return to sport. Specifically, it was used to reinforce a process-oriented attentional focus and the correct execution of skills and techniques; both as part of simulation training and imagery use. However, most importantly it was used to convey positive/constructive self-affirmations while pursuing, and following goal attainment, not least to counteract what had been the debilitating effect of negative self-talk that had reflected his own concerns and self-doubts. The informational support provided by, and feedback received from coaches, players, and medical and conditioning staff was particularly useful as the basis of Alex's self-talk and served to help increase Alex's confidence in his recovery and playing/performance status, which in-turn reduced re-injury anxiety. For example, Alex used the positive feedback from the physiotherapist on rehabilitation progress and players and coaches on his playing progress within his own self-talk to reinforce progress and goal attainment. Despite limited research in this area, the available evidence suggests that self-talk can serve a number of important functions in an injury context akin to those for which it was employed here (e.g., confidence, focus, motivation; Evans et al., 2000; Gould et al., 1997b; Ievleva & Orlick, 1991; Shaffer & Wiese-Bjornstal, 1999).

The above strategies were incorporated over what was a six-week period from the initial consultation to Alex's return to competitive rugby. The approach adopted for the support and intervention process aligned with what may be best viewed as an integrative framework that drew on principles of humanistic and cognitive-behavioural psychology. In terms of the support and intervention process itself, Egan's (2002) Skilled Helper Model helped operationalize the various stages of implementation and the use of the different strategies that comprised the intervention – which was multi-modal in nature. Specifically, a person-centred approach that placed Alex at the centre of the process, ensured goal commitment and subsequently, goal attainment (Egan's model Step II-B and Step II-C). Thereafter, his involvement in the design of the intervention and the skills and strategies that comprised it was reflective of Stage III of Egan's model and the focus on activities/work needed to produce the desired outcomes identified in Stage II (through the use of specific strategies and action plans). Informational and esteem support served an important function in their own right, in addition to providing the basis for positive/constructive self-talk, goal-setting, and goal attainment. The aforementioned were introduced to Alex over the initial consultation at which the physiotherapist was also present. The physiotherapist's involvement at this early stage helped to facilitate the use and effectiveness of informational and esteem support, and fostered a collaborative approach to goal-setting. Liaison between the physiotherapist and coaches helped ensure their involvement in the process and in facilitating Alex's return; specifically through informational and esteem support, which among other things reinforced and provided support for goal attainment.

The two subsequent consultations provided the opportunity to refine the use of these strategies as well as provide Alex with additional support and reassurance about his progress and the use and effectiveness of the different strategies. During the second consultation we also explored the use of imagery to further facilitate his successful return. Once again, informational and esteem support as well as the use of goal-setting helped to empower Alex and increased motivation and confidence to engage in imagery use. Rehabilitation and training activities, and goals and goal attainment provided the initial focus for his imagery, quickly progressing to images of potential injury evoking situations. From the outset I reinforced the importance of psychological readiness in relation to his return to rugby to avoid the potential for injury/re-injury. To this end, I explained the role of psychological factors in predisposing athletes to injury and the mechanisms through which this could occur to increase Alex's knowledge and understanding of the importance of not returning prematurely (Williams & Anderson, 1998). Finally, drawing on the concept of growth following adversity (cf. Wadey, Evans, Evans, & Mitchell, 2011) in order to get buy in from Alex as well as influence his perspective on his injury experience, I introduced and subsequently reinforced the potential to derive benefits from his injury experience. Specifically, I highlighted the potential to improve his repertoire of coping skills as a basis for future enhanced performance (e.g., the use of goal-setting and imagery; Wadey et al., 2011).

To summarize, a number of strategies were employed to help Alex make a successful return to competitive sport, specifically informational and esteem support, goal-setting, simulation training, self-talk and imagery (e.g., Bianco, 2001; Bianco et al., 1999; Evans et al., 2000; Johnston & Carroll, 1998; Podlog & Eklund, 2006; 2007). These strategies were introduced over a six-week period during three separate consultations, with each building on the other(s) and with the focus gradually moving towards preparing for his first competitive game. The involvement of the physiotherapist helped to facilitate the effectiveness of the strategies and served to facilitate an approach that involved fellow players and the medical and coaching staff. Taken together the strategies were intended to engender confidence in Alex's rehabilitation programme and medical and conditioning team, increase confidence in the injured limb to withstand the demands placed on it, increase his overall fitness, and help build belief in his playing potential and value to the club, with the ultimate goal of reducing re-injury anxiety. Put simply the therapeutic approach employed was used to facilitate the necessary conditions that would empower Alex to strive not only to return to his pre-injury levels of performance, but towards becoming a fully functioning person.

REFLECTIONS

This case study provides an overview of the support provided to Alex, a professional rugby player. The support was provided over a six-week period during his return to competitive sport following ACL reconstructive surgery. Alex requested psychological support to help him to deal with his re-injury anxiety, expedite his successful return to playing competitive rugby, and to regain his pre-injury levels of performance. However, it emerged that there were a number of underlying issues that also needed to be addressed. Specifically, Alex had lost confidence in his rehabilitation programme, the medical team, his overall injury, physical fitness, and performance status, and had significant contractual concerns. His re-injury anxiety involved concerns about the ability of the knee to withstand game demands, particularly contact situations in which the original injury occurred. In order to effectively meet Alex's needs, the first part of the support process involved exploring with Alex the meaning that injury held for him; a process that was underpinned by the concepts of loss, attachment, and appraisal. This meaning was considered essential if we were to have a shared understanding of the way Alex had responded to his injury, rehabilitation, and the prospect of his return to competitive sport, along with the underlying causes. Thereafter we adopted a multi-modal approach to the use of informational and esteem support, goal-setting, simulation training, self-talk, and imagery to meet his needs. These strategies were introduced during three face-to-face consultations.

By way of additional background to the case study and support process, I was initially contacted by the physiotherapist on Alex's behalf having previously provided sport psychology support to a few injured and non-injured players at the club over an 18-month period. Largely at the behest of the players involved, this support which had been co-ordinated by the physiotherapist had been carried out very inconspicuously (to other players and coaching personnel). As a result I had already established a working relationship with the physiotherapist who was overseeing Alex's rehabilitation. However, although aware of it in advance of our meeting, I was not involved in the decision for the physiotherapist to be involved in the first consultation with Alex. At this early stage of the process the club coaching staff were not aware that Alex had requested or was receiving sport psychology support. Once the support process was underway the physiotherapist's close contact with Alex during rehabilitation and training sessions at the club enhanced the effectiveness of the support by helping to coordinate and foster a task-oriented process focus, increased adherence, and ongoing feedback, all of which informed progress. Without his involvement, what was in essence a multi-disciplinary (and at times inter-disciplinary) approach to providing support would not have been possible, or as effective. This background information to the case study is important because by providing additional context it enhances meaning – here in relation to reflection.

Feedback on Alex's progress and the effectiveness of the sport psychology support was derived from two primary sources and a number of secondary ones. The primary sources were the physiotherapist and Alex, and the secondary ones the coaches, players, medical staff, and friends and family. In essence, both the physiotherapist and Alex conveyed to me their own feedback and observations, as well as those of others. Alex had provided permission at the start of the consultation process for the physiotherapist and myself to share all information relating to him, which enabled us to have 'no-holds barred' discussions about Alex, the support we were providing, and its effectiveness. Our established professional working relationship (that spanned 18 months) helped to foster openness to our discussions about Alex, the support we were providing, and its effectiveness, which was particularly fruitful. Importantly, these discussions and reflections on the support provided to Alex adopted a 'big picture' perspective that focused on Alex and his needs as a whole, rather than specific component parts and the various types of provision. So in essence, reflection on effectiveness was focused more on the effectiveness of the provision as a whole and how it fitted together in an overall support programme rather than on any specific aspect (e.g., sport psychology). This influenced what I reflected on and how, based on our discussions and my own observations, which contrasts with the approach I might adopt working in other performance settings. In terms of the form and structure of the discussions and communications that informed the reflective process, they took the form of text messages, phone calls, and one face-to-face meeting with the physiotherapist, and face-to-face meetings and text messages with Alex. The content of this feedback subsequently informed the content and provision of the support provided, as well as its timing, but again from a holistic support perspective. It also provided the basis of assessing the effectiveness of the support and the extent to which it met Alex's needs. However, the process of evaluation and reflection, because of the multiple support providers was not and could not be predetermined, developed organically. Nor did it draw on or utilize questionnaires or structured interviews. It occurred somewhat on an ongoing and informal basis as a natural part of the consultative process, shaping the intervention and support as it occurred through enhanced understanding of its meaning, value, and effectiveness.

In terms of the overall effectiveness of the support and how it could have been improved, based on the feedback I received, my own reflections on the process, and in light of my previous professional practice experience (particularly that involving injured athletes) there are a number of features of the process that merit consideration. The goal of the support was to meet the client's needs, in this case Alex, needs that revolved around overcoming re-injury anxiety and attaining pre-injury performance levels. To all intents and purposes the support provided appeared to achieve this goal. In addition, the process by which it was achieved, which was largely dictated by Alex, was from his perspective also effective. For my part, there were a number of factors that influenced the effectiveness of the support that I provided. In any performance environment the role of the coach is paramount and that is no less so when the 'issue' is injury-related. As a result, in both the short and longer term for both Alex's optimal recovery and for the recovery of other injured players in the future, it would have been useful to have the opportunity to increase the coach's knowledge and understanding about his role in the rehabilitation and recovery of injured players. Specifically, it might have been helpful to meet with and discuss the issues with the coach to effect more permanent change at the club in relation to the support provided to injured players and the role of the coaching and medical staff in this process. However, at Alex's request no such discussions occurred and it was left to the physiotherapist to interact with the coaching and conditioning staff as appropriate.

In terms of the support I provided to Alex, and consistent with my previous experience of working with injured athletes I was left with a sense that I could have provided more meaningful support over the period following the player's return to competitive rugby to continue to facilitate his return to pre-injury levels of performance and contribute to optimizing the effectiveness of strategy use for future performance enhancement. However, rightly or wrongly, I have learnt to temper what is in essence a desire to meet my needs (albeit for altruistic reasons) with the reality of the situation, which is about meeting the client's needs, a point that is worth remembering. As a result, my role in providing psychological support ended once Alex had played his first competitive game. By way of a final observation, the present case study is also consistent with my previous experience of providing support to injured athletes in relation to the timing of the request. By this I mean that requests that I have received from injured athletes for sport psychology support have invariably come during athletes' return to competitive sport as opposed to earlier in the rehabilitation process. While I will allow others to draw their own conclusions as to the possible reasons for this, it does remain the case that if support is provided earlier during rehabilitation some of the less than positive effects of the injury experience generally, and rehabilitation specifically, could have been alleviated, both in terms of their impact on the athlete during rehabilitation and their longer-term effect on the athlete's return to competitive sport. To elaborate, if adherence to rehabilitation programmes and treatment efficacy could be enhanced through the use of some of the strategies outlined in this case study earlier in the injury process, then motivation, confidence, and perceptions of autonomy and control (to name but some) could be increased, potentially alleviating re-injury anxiety (see e.g., Brewer et al., 2003; Podlog & Eklund, 2010). This would also increase the perceived benefits that could be derived from what might be otherwise perceived as an adverse and detrimental experience, which may also serve to alleviate some of the challenges that injured athletes face. To conclude, it is worth adding that the experiences discussed here in relation to Alex are extremely common among athletes who have sustained severe injuries. While empirical evidence and professional practice experience supports the efficacy of the strategies described here with an injured athlete during their return to sport, they also have wider application to earlier phases of injury. By way of a final epilogue Alex had a successful return to rugby and went from strength to strength!

FURTHER READING

Egan, G. (2002). *The skilled helper: A problem-management and opportunity-development approach to helping*. Pacific Grove, CA: Brooks Cole. This source provides a fuller understanding of the framework employed for the case study and the role of helping skills in facilitating therapeutic outcomes.

Wadey, R., & Evans, L. (2011). Working with injured athletes: Research and practice. In S. Hanton & S. D. Mellalieu (Eds.), *Professional practice in sport psychology: A review* (pp. 107–132). London: Routledge. This source provides greater insight into some of the challenges injured athletes face during injury onset, rehabilitation and return to sport and some of the strategies that can be employed to address them.

Wiese-Bjornstal, D. M., Smith, A. M., Shaffer, S. M., & Morrey, M. A. (1998). An integrated model of response to sport injury: Psychological and sociological dynamics. *Journal of Applied Sport Psychology, 10*, 46–69. This source provides an overview of a well-established model of response to injury that provides an insight into and overview of factors that might influence athletes' responses to injury and the process by which this is likely to occur.

REFERENCES

Anderson, A., Miles, A., Robinson, P., & Mahoney, C. (2004). Evaluating the athlete's perception of the sport psychologist's effectiveness: What should we be assessing? *Psychology of Sport and Exercise, 5*, 255–277.

Bianco, T. (2001). Social support and recovery from sport injury: Elite skiers share their experiences. *Research Quarterly for Exercise and Sport, 72*, 376–388.

Bianco, T., & Eklund. R. C. (2001). Conceptual consideration for social support research in sport and exercise settings: The case of sport injury. *Journal of Sport and Exercise Psychology, 23*, 85–107.

Bianco, T., Malo, S., & Orlick, T. (1999). Sport injury and illness: Elite skiers describe their experiences. *Research Quarterly for Exercise and Sport, 70*, 157–169.

Bowlby, J. (1991). *Attachment and loss: Vol. 3 Loss, sadness and depression*. London: Penguin.

Brewer, B. W. (1993). Self-identity and specific vulnerability to depressed mood. *Journal of Personality, 61*, 343–364.

Brewer, B. W. (2007). Psychology of sport injury rehabilitation. In G. Tenenbaum & R. C. Eklund (Eds.), *Handbook of sport psychology* (3rd ed., pp. 404–424). Hoboken, NJ: John Wiley & Sons, Inc..

Brewer, B. W., Anderson, M. B., & Van Raalte, J. L. (2002). Psychological aspects of sport injury rehabilitation: Toward a biopsychosocial approach. In D. L. Mostofsky & L. D. Zaichkowsky (Eds.), *Medical and psychological aspects of sport and exercise* (pp. 41–54). Morgantown, WV: Fitness Information Technology.

Brewer, B. W., Cornelius, A. E., Van Raalte, J. L., Petitpas, A. J., Sklar, J. H., Pohlman, M. H., Krushell, R. J., & Ditmar, D. T. (2003). Protection motivation theory and adherence to sport injury rehabilitation revisited. *The Sport Psychologist, 17*, 95–103.

Callow, N., Hardy, L., & Hall, C. (2001). The effects of a motivational general mastery imagery intervention on the sport confidence of high-level badminton players. *Research Quarterly for Exercise and Sport, 72*, 389–400.

Carson, F., & Polman, R. C. J. (2008). ACL injury rehabilitation: A psychological case-study of a professional rugby union player. *Journal of Clinical Sport Psychology, 2*, 71–90.

Cupal, D. D. (1998). Psychological interventions in sport injury: Prevention and rehabilitation. *Journal of Applied Sport Psychology, 10*, 103–123.

Driediger, M., Hall, C., & Callow, N. (2006). Imagery use by injured athletes: A qualitative analysis. *Journal of Sports Sciences, 24*, 261–271.

Egan, G. (2002). *The skilled helper: A problem-management and opportunity-development approach to helping*. Pacific Grove, CA: Brooks Cole.

Evans, L., & Hardy, L. (1995). Sport injury and grief responses: A review. *Journal of Sport and Exercise Psychology, 17*, 227–245.

Evans, L., & Hardy, L. (1999). Psychological and emotional response to athletic injury: Measurement issues. In D. Pargman (Ed.), *Psychological bases of sports injuries* (pp. 49–64). Morgantown, WV: Fitness Information Technology.

Evans, L., & Hardy, L. (2002a). Injury rehabilitation: A goal-setting intervention study.*Research Quarterly for Exercise and Sport, 73*, 310–319.

Evans, L., & Hardy, L. (2002b). Injury rehabilitation: A qualitative follow-up study. *Research Quarterly for Exercise and Sport, 73*, 320–329.

Evans, L., Hardy, L., & Fleming, S. (2000). Intervention strategies with injured athletes: An action research study. *The Sport Psychologist, 14*, 188–206.

Evans, L., Hare, R., & Mullen, R. (2006). Imagery use during rehabilitation from injury. *Journal of Imagery Research in Sport and Physical Activity, 1*, 1–19.

Evans, L., Mitchell, I., & Jones, S. (2006). Psychological responses to sport injury: A review of current research. In S. Hanton & S. D. Mellalieu (Eds.), *Literature reviews in sport psychology* (pp. 289–319). New York: Nova Science.

Evans, L., Wadey, R., Hanton, S., & Mitchell, I. (2012). Stressors experienced by injured athletes. *Journal of Sports Sciences, 30*, 917–927.

Gould, D., Udry, E., Bridges, D., & Beck, L. (1997a). Stress sources encountered when rehabilitating from season-ending ski injuries. *The Sport Psychologist, 11*, 361–378.

Gould, D., Udry, E., Bridges, D., & Beck, L. (1997b). Coping with season ending injuries. *The Sport Psychologist, 11*, 379–399.

Hardy, L., Jones, G., & Gould, D. (1996). *Understanding psychological preparation for sport: Theory and practice of elite performers.* Chichester: John Wiley & Sons, Ltd.

Hare, R., Evans, L., & Callow, N. (2008). Imagery use during rehabilitation from injury. A case study of an elite athlete. *The Sport Psychologist, 22*, 405–422.

Harvey, J. H. (1998). *Perspectives on loss: A sourcebook.* New York: Routledge.

Heil, J. (1993). A framework for psychological assessment. In J. Heil (Ed.), *Psychology of sport injury* (pp. 73–88). Champaign, IL: Human Kinetics.

Ievleva, L., & Orlick, T. (1991). Mental links to enhanced healing: An exploratory study. *The Sport Psychologist, 5*, 25–40.

Johnston, L. H., & Carroll, D. (1998). The provision of social support to injured athletes: A qualitative analysis. *Journal of Sport Rehabilitation, 7*, 267–284.

Kingston, K., & Hardy, L. (1997). Effects of different types of goals on processes that support performance. *The Sport Psychologist, 11*, 277–293.

Kingston, K., & Wilson, K. (2009). The application of goal setting in sport. In S. D. Mellalieu & S. Hanton (Eds.), *Advances in applied sport psychology* (pp. 75–123). New York: Routledge.

Kvist, J., Ek, A., Sporrstedt, K., & Good, L. (2005). Fear of re-injury: A hindrance for returning to sports after anterior cruciate ligament reconstruction. *Knee Surgery, Sports Traumatology, Arthroscopy, 14*, 393–397.

Lavallee, D., Grove, J. R., Gordon, S., & Ford, I. W. (1998). The experience of loss in sport. In J. H. Harvey (Ed.), *Perspectives on loss: A sourcebook* (pp. 241–252). New York: Routledge.

Mitchell, I., Evans, L., Rees, T., & Hardy, L. (2014). Stressors, social support and the buffering hypothesis: Effects on psychological responses of injured athletes. *British Journal of Health Psychology, 19*, 486–508.

Peretz, D. (1970). Development, object-relationships, and loss. In B. Schoenberg, A. C. Carr, D. Peretz, & A. H. Kutscher (Eds.), *Loss and grief: Psychological practice in medical practice* (pp. 3–19). New York: Columbia University Press.

Pocwardowski, A., Sherman, C. P., & Henschen, K. (1998). A sport psychology service delivery heuristic: Building on theory and practice. *The Sport Psychologist, 12*, 191–207.

Podlog, L., & Dionigi, R. (2010). Coach strategies for addressing psychosocial challenges during the return to sport from injury. *Journal of Sports Sciences, 28*, 1197–1208.

Podlog, L., & Eklund, R. C. (2006). A longitudinal investigation of competitive athletes' return to sport following serious injury. *Journal of Applied Sport Psychology, 18*, 48–68.

Podlog, L., & Eklund, R. C. (2007). Professional coaches' perspectives on the return to sport following serious injury. *Journal of Applied Sport Psychology, 19*, 207–225.

Podlog, L., & Eklund, R. C. (2009). High-level athletes' perceptions of success in returning to sport following injury. *Psychology of Sport and Exercise*, *10*, 535–544.

Podlog, L., & Eklund, R. C. (2010). Returning to competition after a serious injury: The role of self-determination. *Journal of Sports Sciences*, *28*, 819–831.

Rees, T., Mitchell, I., Evans, L., & Hardy, L. (2010). Stressors, social support psychological response to sports injury in high and low-performance standard participants. *Psychology of Sport and Exercise*, *11*, 505–512.

Ross, M. J., & Berger, R. S. (1996). Effects of stress inoculation on athletes' post-surgical pain and rehabilitation after orthopedic injury. *Journal of Consulting and Clinical Psychology*, *64*, 406–410.

Shaffer, S. M., & Wiese-Bjornstal, D. M. (1999). Psychosocial interventions strategies in sports medicine. In R. Ray & D. M. Wiese-Bjornstal (Eds.), *Counseling in sports medicine* (pp. 41–54). Champaign, IL: Human Kinetics.

Sordoni, C., Hall, C., & Forwell, L. (2000). The use of imagery by athletes during rehabilitation. *Journal of Applied Sport Psychology*, *3*, 329–338.

Udry, E. (1997). Coping and social support among injured athletes following surgery. *Journal of Sport and Exercise Psychology*, *19*, 71–90.

Udry, E., Gould, D., Bridges, D., & Beck, L. (1997). Down but not out: Athlete responses to season-ending injuries. *Journal of Sport and Exercise Psychology*, *19*, 229–248.

Wadey, R., Evans, L., Evans, K., & Mitchell, I. (2011). Perceived benefits following sport injury: A qualitative examination of their antecedents and underlying mechanisms. *Journal of Applied Sport Psychology*, *23*, 142–158.

Wiese-Bjornstal, D. M., Smith, A. M., Shaffer, S. M., & Morrey, M. A. (1998). An integrated model of response to sport injury: Psychological and sociological dynamics. *Journal of Applied Sport Psychology*, *10*, 46–69.

Williams, J. M. & Anderson, M. B. (1998). Psychosocial antecedents of sport injury: Review and critique of the stress and injury model. *Journal of Applied Sport Psychology*, *10*, 5–25.

8 Transition Indecision: A Case Study of an Athlete's Move from Playing to Coaching

ROBERT MORRIS AND DAVID TOD

LEARNING OBJECTIVES

AFTER READING THIS CHAPTER YOU SHOULD BE ABLE TO:

1. Identify and understand factors that influence the quality of athletes' retirement from sport.
2. Interpret signs athletes are experiencing a negative transition.
3. Evaluate the use of an eclectic framework to support athletes in transition.
4. Discuss ways that practitioners influence service delivery.
5. Discuss ways that practitioners change as they gain client experience.

AREAS TO CONSIDER WHEN READING THE CHAPTER:

1. Factors that might influence athletes' retirement from sport.
2. Advantages and disadvantages of working from an eclectic framework.
3. Ways that sport psychology practitioners (e.g., their histories, needs, desires, perceptions) influence service-delivery processes and outcomes.

CLIENT AND BACKGROUND

James was coming towards the end of his career in professional football when he first contacted me (Robert) to ask for sport psychology services. I was in the early stages of my career as an applied practitioner, and like many early career practitioners had anxieties about my own skills and knowledge (Tod, Anderson, & Marchant, 2011). James was in his mid-thirties and had competed at the highest level of his sport; he had played in the English Premier League and for his country numerous times. He had decided to retire from sport, but had no idea what he wanted to, or could, do next. In the first part of the chapter, we present the case, including the context, assessment, and interventions, along with the reasons for my decisions and actions at the time. In the reflection section we discuss (a) how I evaluated my effectiveness as a consultant, (b) challenges I experienced working with James, (c) why I selected the intervention model and associated issues, and (d) how I might work with James differently today.

James had approached me because he felt his playing career was over due to his age, and he had no idea what he was going to do next in his life. He was anxious and worried, and despite being financially independent, recognized that boredom would likely lead to issues that he wanted to avoid. Specifically, in his words, he wanted to be a 'good person', and not 'get involved in all the bad stuff that goes on when people retire from sport', such as drugs and alcohol abuse (Stambulova, 2000). As we talked about his thoughts of retirement and what he perceived was available to him, it was apparent that James might experience a 'negative transition' (Stambulova, 2003) if he did not get the support he needed. Researchers (e.g., Alfermann, 1995; Grove, Lavallee, & Gordon, 1997) have highlighted that retirement from sport is often rocky with approximately 15% of athletes experiencing serious psychological maladjustment (e.g., depression, anxiety, Wippert & Wippert, 2008; Wylleman, 1995).

Definition box **BOX 8.1**

Schlossberg (1981, p. 5) suggested transition is 'an event or non-event [which] results in a change in assumptions about oneself and the world, and thus requires a corresponding change in one's behaviour and relationships'.

Park, Lavallee, and Tod (2013) identified characteristics associated with career termination, including: (a) pre-retirement planning, (b) sport-career achievement, and (c) availability of psychosocial support. We use these characteristics as a way to structure James' case. Pre-retirement planning positively influences transitions from sport if it provides athletes with clear goals on their life after sport and feelings of comfort. James had not identified post-retirement goals before he approached me, six months before the season and his career ended. He had started to panic about the situation indicating he was experiencing worry and was continuously feeling run down from thinking about what he was going to do next. Having left school at the age of 16, James believed he had no academic qualifications that could help him to get a 'normal' job after retirement. He considered normal jobs to be those such as teaching and nursing. James also felt that he did not have good personal contacts within the business world, and that this might hinder him when he retired.

James mentioned that he felt his performances on the pitch were suffering, and that he wanted to 'get things sorted' so that he could focus on performing well in the final few months of his career. Despite being a successful athlete throughout most of his career, and having achieved the majority of the goals he had set when he turned professional, James thought he was a failure because he had not achieved many goals he had set over the past three seasons, including winning specific (high-end) competitions and scoring a specified number of goals. Park et al. (2013) suggested that athletes who achieve their career goals would experience a better quality of transition from their sport than those who perceive they had not. Reflecting on his failure to attain his recent goals had lowered James' self-esteem and increased his competitive anxiety. James continually kept asking, 'What had I done for the team' and 'What can I do for the team?'

Additionally, similar to many elite athletes (Park et al., 2013), James had developed a strong identity as a footballer, one that others, such as his coach, parents, and schoolteachers, had reinforced over the years. In his mind, James had linked his worth as a person to his ability to play football. He feared that if he did not achieve his goals, his parents, and others important to him (e.g., his coach), would think he was a failure, and he would risk losing their approval.

Psychosocial support was another factor apparent in James' case. James came from a sporting background and a strong family unit. Most of his friends also came from football. Although he hoped otherwise, he thought it inevitable he would lose these friends when he was no longer part of the sport. In addition, James said his employer would not provide support to help him with his retirement. For these reasons, James felt worried about his future. He constantly referred to worrying about 'feeling lonely' and 'being on my own' when he retired.

INITIAL NEEDS ASSESSMENT

Prior to conducting an intake interview, I spoke to James on the phone after he had made initial contact with me. This first conversation was brief, because James was insistent that we meet to talk about his issues, rather than discussing them on the phone. During our first face-to-face meeting, I used Taylor and Schneider's (1992) sport-clinical intake protocol to assess James and his presenting issues. The protocol contains interview prompts in seven areas including: (a) cursory description of the presenting problem, (b) description of athletic history, (c) family and social support, (d) health status, (e) important life events, (f) changes prior to the onset of presenting problem, and (g) details of the presenting problem. I thought the protocol was useful with James, because it allowed me to explore his background and sport career in detail, and helped me to collect relevant information in a semi-structured interview fashion. The protocol also provided a balance between making the interview structured (and overly clinical) and allowing James to discuss topics he believed were important. I was also able to structure my case notes efficiently around the schedule. The protocol also reassured me, because it acted like a checklist and gave me confidence that I was not missing relevant details. Following Taylor and Scheider's (1992) protocol meant that I was able to manage my doubts associated with collecting relevant information in sufficient detail, a commonly reported view among early career practitioners (Tod et al., 2011).

I also had to decide where the interview would occur. When deciding, I remembered from my training that interviews should happen in environments where clients felt comfortable, so that they feel more able to open up to probing questions (Steptoe, Barker, & Harwood, 2014). Interviewing James in a busy 'public' environment (e.g., café) seemed inadvisable: he may not open up to me sufficiently. He was a well-known public figure and there were potential negative ramifications if the information he disclosed was overheard or got into the wrong hands (e.g., the media). I asked James if he could identify somewhere to meet. James recommended a golf club near to his home, where we subsequently met and played a round of golf while discussing his issues. The golf course was a place where James felt comfortable and able to talk freely, because it was away from prying eyes and ears. We often met at the golf course for subsequent meetings. Although this environment was the one where James felt comfortable, it also presented difficulties for me as an applied consultant. For example, how was I going to remember all the areas of Taylor and Schneider's (1992) sport-clinical intake protocol and everything James said in response? To ensure that I remembered to ask questions in all areas of the protocol, I used the 'notes' function on my mobile phone, with the note including the protocol areas needing to be covered. To remember information James was telling me, I resorted to trying to ensure that I remembered the most important points, paying particular attention to factors that could potentially influence his retirement from sport. After the round, I placed more notes in my phone, indicating what I felt were the key points of my meeting with James that I would use for subsequent conversations. Additionally I am a competitive person and I realized that I had to control my desire to win so that I stayed focused on helping James. At this time, I was starting to appreciate in greater depth that as the instrument of service delivery, I had to be aware of how my needs, desires, and history influence client interactions. To help James effectively, I needed to be aware of, and manage, my tendency to approach golfing situations competitively.

Another strategy I used in the initial stages (and throughout my time) working with James was observation of his training and competitive performances. I was (and still am!) aware of the necessity of building rapport with athletes (e.g., Sharp & Hodge, 2011; Tod & Andersen, 2012). With James, I believed one way to build rapport was to observe him during training and competitive matches. There was no structure to my observations and no literature informed my approach at that time. I had obtained the idea from my master's degree lecturers at Liverpool John Moores University. Since then I have read literature to help inform my observations (e.g., Watson & Shannon, 2010). In addition, several clients had previously communicated that they believed I cared about them, and had a genuine interest in their development, because I had been prepared to attend their events, especially when I had done so during the weekend or I had paid to see the competition. Further, I interpreted attending events as indicating that I was dedicated to my job and acting in a professional manner. I quickly also realized that observing clients helped me understand the demands of their sports, along with their behaviours, interactions with others, and coping strategies, and allowed me to identify areas of conversation that I could raise with athletes during formal one-to-one sessions. With James, the observations revealed that he was a hardworking and sociable person, who interacted and supported younger players in their development whenever possible. By observing his performances, I was able to generate discussion in our subsequent conversations, asking James questions such as, 'Do you enjoy supporting the younger players?' and 'What do you feel you are offering when giving advice to the younger players?'

FRAMEWORK AND INTERVENTION

In supporting James, I used an eclectic model (see Kerr, 2010, for a description) to sport psychology consultation, underpinned mainly by my understanding of the humanistic person-centred approach (Buhler, 1971) and other frameworks as needed (e.g., mental skills training underpinned by the cognitive-behavioural approach; Dobson, 2009). An eclectic approach resonated with my views regarding how to help people and it had been a main feature of my academic training. For example, I believed the underpinning feature of humanistic psychology that people are innately good and we should help them achieve self-actualization (Rogers, 1959). I also believed, however, that there are occasions where skills and techniques from other frameworks (e.g., goal setting, mental imagery, etc.) could, and should be, used if they have a solid evidence base and will benefit the client. In James' case, as discussed earlier, he wanted me to help him be a 'good person' (which echoed to me a parallel with humanistic psychology). Equally, however, there was the immediate issue of his impending retirement from sport, and a cognitive-behavioural approach often lends itself to dealing with time-limited issues (i.e., there were only a few months before James retired; Beck, 1995).

I employed Stambulova's (2010) five-stage career planning strategy with James. Stambulova's counselling-based framework draws on the humanistic and cognitive-behavioural approaches to help athletes in transition. A mapping exercise focusing on athletes' past, current, and perceived future takes place during the first four stages. The fifth stage involves bridging the athlete's past, present, and perceived future and generating a goal-setting programme that can guide their future actions. Researchers believe such career planning helps athletes to self-explore, become self-aware, and make informed decisions (Petitpas, Brewer, & Van Raalte, 2009; Stambulova, 2010).

Definition box

BOX 8.2

Stambulova's five-stage career planning strategy is a counselling framework for helping athletes with career transitions. The first four stages involve mapping out the client's past experiences, current situation, and perceived future. The fifth stage involves integrating their past, present, and projected future into a career and life strategy that includes goals the athlete aims to achieve.

In the first stage (create a framework) consultants ask athletes to draw a timeline of their lives. Stambulova (2010) suggested placing on this timeline athletes' birth date and present age, dividing the timeline into the past, present, and future.

Stambulova (2010) proposed asking athletes in the second stage (structure your past) to describe the most important events of their lives and note them on their timelines. The events do not have to be sport-related, but can include any experiences that athletes believe have been important in their lives and development. Stambulova (2010) suggested that this stage of the model allows consultants to gain a comprehensive outline of the client's background, and can be useful for informing later decisions (e.g., exploration of future job opportunities). In James' situation, the majority of the events were from his sporting career. Making his professional first team debut, winning the English League Cup, and playing in European football were the first three events James added to his timeline. I asked James if there were other events. He then added experiences such as meeting and marrying his wife, and having children.

The third stage of the model (structure your present) involves athletes rating the most important domains of their current life on three different scales: subjective importance, time spent, and stress level. The domains that James ranked were his sport, family, peers, and future job prospects. Subjective importance (athletes rank the domains in order of importance) outlines how athletes view each domain in relation to others (Stambulova, 2010). In exploring these domains, James believed that his family and family life were of utmost importance to him, followed by his sport, peers, and his future job prospects (in that order).

Regarding the time-spent category, athletes rank the domains starting with the area in which they spend the most time (Stambulova, 2010). In contrast to the subjective importance dimension outlined above, James indicated that he spent little time with his family, and he spent most of his time playing football or training to improve his fitness and performance levels. He also spent a lot of his free time with his peers playing golf and snooker, which he had classed as team bonding and 'part of the job'. James had also spent no time exploring job prospects despite worrying about his future, and instead he preferred to 'live in the moment'. After we discussed these factors, James concluded that he needed to spend more time with his family after he retired and more time now considering future job opportunities. He believed that he had put too much responsibility on his wife to bring up their children. Now he was retiring he wanted to spend time watching his children grow up, but at the same time, he believed he had to stay employed to prevent himself becoming bored, isolated, and a 'bad person'.

Finally, 'stress level' reflects the anxiety athletes experience in relation to the domains they consider important in their lives. James felt most stressed about not having a job post-retirement. Equally, he believed that he did not feel any real stress in relation to his sport career, because this was something he had done for a number of years and he was used to success and setbacks in equal measure. Stress levels associated with spending time with peers and family were reasonably low, according to James.

Description box

BOX 8.3

Presented here are the five stages of Stambulova's (2010) framework used to support James in transition. Using this framework may help to support others in similar situations with their retirement from sport.

Step 1: Make a Framework
- Athletes draw a life/timeline and mark their birth (e.g., the year) as an initial point on the left and their current age (or year) as the second point on the line.

↓

Step 2: Structure Your Past
- Athletes think about and discuss with practitioners the most significant points in their life and mark these time points on the lifeline.

↓

Step 3: Structure Your Present
- Assessment of the most meaningful domains of athletes current lives.
- Ranking of life domains on three different scales:
  (a) personal importance
  (b) time spent
  (c) stress level
- Analysis of ranking: Do athletes devote enough time to their priorities?

↓

Step 4: Structure Your Future
- Assessment of the most significant events athletes desire/expect in the future, which are then marked on the lifeline. Athletes think about events across their lives, and the next 10, 5, 3, and 1 years.

↓

Step 5: Bridge Your Past, Present, and Future
- Split into three sub-steps, the first sub-step involves athletes going "from the present to the past and back to the present," focusing on their key experiences, the lessons learned, and the coping resources developed.
- The second sub-step involves clients setting goals, analysing resources and barriers that may influence goal achievement, and developing an action plan.
- The third sub-step is aimed at helping athletes balance their current priorities with their future goals. To reach this balance, sport psychologists encourage athletes to reconsider their plans for the next three to five years and answer two questions: "can you do anything today to prepare for the forthcoming events?" and "do you still think that you have the right priorities today?"

Source: Stambulova, N. B. (2010). Counseling athletes in career transitions: The five-step career planning strategy. *Journal of Sport Psychology in Action*, *1*(2), 95–105.

In stage four (structure your future), athletes outline the important events they expect to happen in the future. Athletes predict events across their remaining lifespans, in ten, five, three, and one-year periods. This stage allows athletes and sport psychologists to plan and arrange forthcoming priorities (Stambulova, 2010). James found this stage difficult, because he had not thought about such things before. Although I had developed an understanding of James, I realized that I was not capable of making predictions regarding what may happen in his life. Instead, I encouraged him to consider important areas, by asking: 'what events do you think will happen in ten years' time?' I probed him to think further about his 'family, work, and personal life'. Still nothing, this stage was going to be a challenge!

I encouraged James to go away from this session and consult with important others (e.g., his wife, friends, and teammates) to see if they might be able to highlight important events that may occur.

Two weeks later we met to review the events James had identified. James had developed a new timeline with a number of additional events, including starting a new job in less than six months' time, moving home in a year's time, and retirement (from his new job) in approximately 25 years' time. Additionally, James had realized that there were going to be a number of changes that would occur in his children's lives. They would go to secondary school, start new jobs, maybe enter higher education, and leave home. When I asked James about the significance of these events, he got emotional and said: 'doing this task and talking to you previously has made me realize that my kids are everything ... I have missed a number of years of their lives playing football and now I want to be there all the time for them.' I asked him to explain further and he said that because he spends much time away from home travelling to and from matches, home and abroad, he was often absent from his children. He also said he had never done the 'school run' (took his children to school), and this was something that he wanted to do more often moving forward.

The fifth stage (bridge your past, present, and future) includes three sub-steps. The first sub-step involves the client going 'from the present to the past and back to the present,' focusing on their key experiences, the lessons learnt, and the coping resources developed. The main aim of this sub-step is to get athletes to identify and review the coping resources they have developed (Stambulova, 2010).

I encouraged James to think about the most difficult times in his life, such as when he was unsuccessful in sport (e.g., during periods of continual poor performances), or successful (e.g., when winning trophies, being selected for the team, and signing contracts), and what he had learnt from these experiences. James talked about developing his ability to block out negative thoughts when he was unsuccessful or in difficult situations. He had also learnt this strategy was sometimes not effective if it did not help him deal with the underlying issues affecting his performance. He soon realized that he needed to talk to his peers about the anger and disappointment he felt when they lost a game, if only to understand that everyone was feeling anger and disappointment at their performances. Equally, he realized that his success was due, in part, to working as part of a productive team. Reflecting back upon these experiences, James realized that the main coping resources he had developed and relied on were his family and peers, people with whom he could discuss difficult times and celebrate success. Thinking forward, James said he wanted to keep these resources available, because he believed this support had helped him achieve his goals.

Stambulova's (2010) second sub-step of the fifth stage involves the client setting goals, analysing resources and barriers that may influence goal achievement, and developing an action plan. This sub-step was useful for helping James clarify his immediate plans post-retirement. He had already discussed retiring from sport, but he had few ideas about what he was going to do for a career after he retired. During our conversations, James continually talked about how his experiences and knowledge all related to football. I tried to help James understand that what he had learnt from football could apply to other life domains. I asked questions such as 'How do you think these experiences, and the knowledge you have gained, may transfer to other areas of your life?' Through such questioning and additional probing (e.g., 'tell me more about that situation'), James talked about how he had learnt to communicate with fellow players, discuss ways peers could perhaps enhance their performances, and offer suggestions about what could be improved by the team in future performances. James recalled one time when he had identified a weakness in a new teammate (a defensive player who positioned himself too square when attempting to stop an attacker, making it easy for the opponent to get past him). James suggested one way he could improve (practice opening up his body to give him the freedom to twist and turn whatever way the attacker went). James believed he was required to support teammates, but he also enjoyed doing so. I wondered aloud if coaching could be something James might consider doing in the future. James was unsure about his ability to coach to a high level because he believed that he did not have the capabilities or knowledge to be successful, but acknowledged that he enjoyed coaching. Indicative of his enjoyment was his working towards Union of European Football Associations (UEFA) coaching qualifications; he had completed his A Licence, and had started his Professional Licence. I reminded James about what he had said regarding his communication skills and the way he had identified how other players could improve, and how much he had enjoyed doing so, aspects central to coaching. After discussing these factors, James started to highlight where his experiences could help others. He said he wanted to discuss the possibility of coaching with his colleagues, friends, and family before meeting with me next time.

During our next session, James said, 'Do you know what? ...I've found a career I want to do.' Over the next hour, James discussed how our last conversation had stimulated his thoughts, and he had considered in more detail a coaching career. He wanted to find out if coaching was a career he would enjoy. I sought clarification from him that I had not 'forced' him down this career path; he responded by saying no, it was what he personally had decided to do and he felt that our conversation had helped him realize how he could use the skill set he had developed as a player to his advantage after retirement. James also mentioned that he was also prepared to step away from coaching if he felt he was not being successful in the role. Although he had made a decision about his short-term plans, he appreciated that he still had to do a lot of work before he knew if coaching was what he was going to do for the rest of his working life. James had discussed his decision with his wife, and she could not think of him having anything other than a job in football. She also suggested that by being a coach he would be able to spend more time with his children, because he may not need to attend as many 'social' events as he used to, or do extra training. James had also approached his manager and asked for recommendations about coaching. James' manager had immediately said the club would be more than happy to take him on in a coaching role. His manager had reiterated the skills, knowledge, and qualifications James had, and how beneficial these assets would be for the club, which James had acknowledged made him feel more confident about the role. The coach said he had always wanted to keep James, despite James not having shown great interest in coaching previously. James mentioned the conversations with his wife and manager had inspired him to consider a career in coaching, because now he thought he would see his children more often than currently, he could still see his friends, he had the qualifications, and he had the skills and knowledge.

The conversations that James held away from our one-on-one sessions reinforced to me that he was an engaged client; regularly completing tasks that we (he) had considered useful to him. In this situation, he had spoken to relevant people who could help him make decisions about his future. This level of engagement helped with the overall therapeutic process and completion of the intervention, because it meant we could discuss and expand on any exercises he had completed or conversations he had had between sessions (Tod & Andersen, 2012).

We were now able to help James set goals. James set three main objectives for the forthcoming months, which included short-, medium-, and long-term goals. His short-term goal (within two weeks) was to meet the head coach to agree his specific role in the club and sign his contract (i.e., whether he would be working with the youth team or the senior players or working with players in specific playing positions or the whole team). James believed that having some certainty about his role, and having a contract in place, would be a relief for him, and he wanted this to happen quickly to give himself clarity on his future. His medium-term goal (within four months) was to establish himself in the coaching role. When I asked what he meant by establishing himself, and how he would know that he had, he responded that he knew many of the players as teammates, whereas now he needed to gain their respect as their coach. James believed he could evaluate his success through gaining the players' and his manager's opinions. His long-term goal (within two years) was to complete his UEFA Professional Licence. The Professional Licence involves a number of regular residential gatherings, and overseas travel, and can take two years to complete. James had only started his licence in the past five months and wanted to complete it in as short a period as possible, but he also wanted to make sure he gained as much knowledge and applied experience from completing it.

The third sub-step of the fifth stage of Stambulova's (2010) intervention framework brings athletes back from the future to the present and the aim is to help them balance their current priorities with their future goals. To reach this balance, sport psychologists encourage athletes to reconsider their plans for the next three to five years and answer two questions: 'Can you do anything today to prepare for the forthcoming events?' and 'Do you still think that you have the right priorities today?' When athletes answer 'no' to the latter question, Stambulova (2010) suggests sport psychologists help clients to identify ways to start working towards their goals. Athletes and sport psychologists also decide whether to set a future date to review the client's progress.

James already believed that he had started preparing effectively for forthcoming events, because he had established what he wanted to do with his future career. He had started to develop his skills in this area, and he had chosen a career that would allow him to spend more time with his family. When I asked the second question about his priorities, James replied that he had got his priorities right; from now on spending time with his family would be his main priority.

REFLECTIONS

In the following paragraphs we discuss (a) how I evaluated my effectiveness as a consultant, (b) challenges I experienced working with James, (c) why I selected Stambulova's (2010) model and associated issues, and (d) how I might work with James differently today.

I evaluated the intervention and my time with James primarily from his verbal feedback, the observation that he kept coming back for more sessions, his willingness to undertake homework exercises, and his payment for my services. Although not directly targeted by the intervention, during the final months of the season prior to his retirement, James indicated that he felt more relaxed and had performed much better than in previous seasons. He believed that he was 'valuable' to the team again, and it did not matter whether this value was in a playing or support role. I knew, however, improved performance was not strong evidence that I had been helpful, because there were other uncontrolled factors that may have had a greater influence. For example, James also realized he had more psychosocial support available to him than he had previously believed (the level of psychosocial support had not changed; however James' awareness of his access to it had increased). To illustrate, he gave the example of speaking to his coach about what he was going to do post-retirement (using his coach for support was something he had never previously considered doing). Additionally, James believed his engagement in the consultancy process meant that he felt much more prepared for his transition from playing elite sport because he felt more in control of his decisions and committed to his goals.

Over the forthcoming months as he moved from his playing to coaching roles within the club, we met at least once a month to discuss potential and actual difficulties. James, however, kept reiterating that he felt comfortable in his new role, and that he believed his engagement in the process outlined above had allowed him to manage challenges that arose. For example, James was unsure of how he would cope operating in an authoritative role, and perhaps having to discipline players with whom he used to play. In such situations, James reminded himself of our previous conversations, during which he had identified personal strengths, such as his communication skills, he could use to explain why he was annoyed, rather than responding with rage. On reflection, I could have helped James with such situations through role-plays and discussing ways he has previously handled conflict.

I experienced several challenges in working with James. At the outset of our relationship, I knew I had to develop a collaborative rapport with James to facilitate any assessment I undertook or intervention we tried. It took some time, regularly interacting with James and observing his performances, before he felt comfortable to open up to me. Reflecting back, I often wonder if I tried to get James to do and say too much too soon. As an elite footballer in the UK, James may have had interactions with others who wanted to use him for their own agendas. I appreciate now that even though he approached me, he was probably evaluating the degree to which I focused on serving his interests rather than my own. The Health and Care Professions Council, who regulate the sport and exercise psychology profession in the United Kingdom, outline in their *Standards of Conduct, Performance, and Ethics* (2012) that psychologists must act in the best interests of their clients, rather than acting in a way which helped them achieve their own interests. When working with James I did harbour thoughts that he may be wondering if I was a clingy fan or someone who might use him for personal gain, and that this may be hindering the development of rapport. The fact James kept coming back to our sessions, and started to reveal more and more information about himself each time we met indicated, however, that this was not the case. As we developed a stronger relationship we were able to explore in more depth aspects around James' retirement, and reflecting back I now realize rapport and consultancy go hand in hand – as rapport is developed, more can be done with clients, and the more that is done the better the rapport becomes (Bordin, 1994; Horvath & Bedi, 2002; Tod & Andersen, 2012). There is also a need to progress at the client's pace. Effective sport psychology consultation occurs when the consultant builds a connection with the athlete to create positive change, and the relationship meets the athlete's needs (Sharp & Hodge, 2011; Tod & Andersen, 2012). In James case, a good relationship allowed me to offer my interpretations and suggestions (e.g., coaching) without James thinking I was trying to force a solution, and he knew I was comfortable with him leaving the session and seeking assistance from other people (e.g., when he talked to his family about important events in his life). Looking back, I am now sure that James did not think I was a clingy fan. Rather, because I was a new person in his life, there was no requirement for him to open up to me about things that were personal to him, prior to him establishing for himself that I was a suitable person with whom to talk!

I found this period of the consultancy challenging because we were just months away from James' retirement and I was impatient (a major error on my part), thinking that he was going to retire without a back-up plan in place. When I now consider the situation James was in (he was financially stable and appeared to have a settled family life) and his disposition, perhaps he could have coped being without a job for a short period of time. I learnt valuable lessons from this experience: consider each person based on their own situation, and interventions can take a while to bear fruit, but that does not mean they will not be effective.

Another challenge for me was working and dealing with a well-known and highly successful athlete. This was my first 'big' job as a sport psychology practitioner and I felt responsible for ensuring James achieved his goals. My grappling with responsibility reflects a common theme among neophyte practitioners. Trainees typically take too much responsibility for service-delivery outcomes (Tod et al., 2011). In addition, he was telling me information that could potentially ruin his public reputation, relationships with his family members, and his links with his teammates if it got into the wrong hands (e.g., the press, opposition players, and even teammates). This insight had an effect on my service delivery; I was excited to know all I could about this person on a personal level (something many others could only dream about) which could have distracted me from the real reason I was dealing with him in the first place. Learning to deal with the 'glamour' of working with elite and well-known athletes is another lesson trainee practitioners learn (Tod et al., 2011). I also realized that if I did a good job with James, I could generate more work for myself. A recommendation from James would carry a lot of weight. This realization meant that, on occasions, I might have been less likely to take risks with the interventions, because I did not want to upset and alienate my client. Starting with James, and with subsequent elite athletes, I remind myself that I am employed to serve their interests and I implement interventions that (we) believe will help them, and I am more comfortable suggesting interventions or offering alternative interpretations of their situations as long as I believe there is a good relationships between us. As discussed earlier, the Health and Care Professions Council's *Standards of Conduct, Performance, and Ethics* (2012) outline the importance of psychologists ensuring they are serving the best interests of the client. The British Psychological Society, which is also a leading organization within psychological practice in the United Kingdom, also highlight in their *Code of Ethics and Conduct* (2009) the need forpsychologists to work in the best interests of the client. With James, I soon realized how valuable serving the needs of my client was and would be within my future work as a sport psychology practitioner because I could support the client to achieve their personal goals, and get a sense of self-fulfilment that I had helped him do just that.

Reflecting on the start of our relationship, it would have been easy for me as a sport psychology practitioner to try to work through each individual problem that James was experiencing and try to change (perhaps via the use of a life skill development intervention, and/or education sessions) the way he was thinking or approaching those situations (i.e., adopt a problem-solver persona). Equally, it would also have been easy to use exclusively mental skill techniques, such as progressive muscular relaxation, imagery, and self-talk, to manage anxieties around his retirement, because I was familiar with these interventions and anxiety management. By taking a person-centred approach with James, however, the sessions were client- rather than practitioner-led (Andersen, 2000), and we were able to discuss and manage aspects he believed were most meaningful to him and his life. For example, we were able to focus on how important James's family was to him and what he could do to spend more time with them, something which would not have been raised if I had taught him a series of progressive muscular relaxation techniques (or similar).

Although I used Stambulova's (2010) intervention with James, I could have used other approaches (or a combination of more than one framework) derived from alternative transition models (e.g., Schlossberg, 1981; Taylor & Ogilvie, 1994). I selected Stambulova's (2010) intervention because: (a) there was flexibility in the way it could be administered; (b) it provided a holistic perspective on the possible transitions athletes face; (c) it was structured in a way that I could follow; and (d) it suited James' needs and provided a framework that allowed us to address his issues in a collaborative manner. Additionally, by following Stambulova's (2010) framework, which had structure, was based on research, and resonated with my approach to sport psychology, I had confidence that I was able to help James and act as a professional. Similar to many trainee practitioners, I had doubts about my competence, because I had not yet fully demonstrated to myself, through client experience, that I had the wherewithal to help James (and others). With my earliest clients, I was rigid in my approach. For example, with James I would have a copy of Stambulova's (2010) framework in front of me to ensure I was implementing strategies correctly and asking the right questions. Part of the reason why it was necessary to justify interventions theoretically was to demonstrate I was a *bona fide* helper who offered a professional service. If I helped James today, I would be more relaxed about drawing upon other ways I could help him, even if that meant there had been sessions where I did not offer any advice or help, but had just been a sounding board. If I believed there were no ethical violations, and from theory it made sense that a strategy would likely be helpful, then I would be happy to use such methods. In addition, I have more client experience now than I did when working with James, and I would be more capable than I was of adapting strategies in my repertoire to fit James' needs. Murphy (2000) wrote that reflecting on reading *Doing Sport Psychology* (Andersen, 2000) had caused him to 'observe how infrequently I ever do straightforward interventions such as those we see studied so often in our journals' (p. 276). I take comfort from those words because I now realized that for interventions to be helpful, they needed to be adapted to fit clients and their situations.

There are, however, some issues associated with Stambulova's (2010) model that I needed to consider to ensure its effectiveness. It is not a quick fix, and there needs to be a good practitioner-client relationship due to the personal information the client is asked to provide in the early stages. With James, although there was an effective outcome from the consultancy, we covered a number of personal topics in a short time period, during which we were developing trust in each other. I needed to demonstrate clearly that I was a likeable and trustworthy person. Stambulova (2010) also suggested the athlete's age, maturity level, and mental health status influence her model's effectiveness. James' potential negative mental health status (e.g., his anxieties about what to do after retiring) could have influenced his thoughts and clarity when working through his issues with me. I needed to monitor his anxiety levels in case they caused functional or social impairment and specific interventions were required.

In summary, if working with James now, I would be more: (a) patient with him; (b) client, rather than intervention, led; (c) flexible, perhaps integrating ideas from other frameworks (e.g., Taylor & Ogilvie, 1994) and using a wider range of interventions; and (d) aware of how my own needs, tendencies, and history may influence the service-delivery process, relationship, and client outcomes. These changes reflect the individuation process (Rønnestad & Skovholt, 2013; Tod, 2014), whereby practitioners develop methods of working congruent with their world views. When working with James I was an inexperienced practitioner and anxious to operate as a competent professional as defined by my teachers, mentors, the literature, and professional bodies' codes of conduct. Today, I would be less anxious to ensure that I was a competent professional, because I have a greater understanding of what that involves, and I have more confidence that I can be effective. Greater confidence means that if I consulted with James today, my internal voices would distract me less as I focused on being present with him, listening to his story, and helping him resolve his issues and work towards his goals, perhaps using a greater range of techniques and interventions than I did.

Activity box

BOX 8.4

Read Tod (2007) in the Further Reading list at the end of the chapter in which he identifies the typical changes practitioners experience in their service delivery practices and perceptions as they gain client experience. Discuss with a peer which of those changes are present in the current case study.

SUMMARY

Like many clients, James has stayed in my memory because working with him exposed me to issues, and necessitated that I consider service-delivery processes I had not yet experienced at that stage in my professional life. It has been enjoyable and worthwhile revisiting and reflecting on his case to compare how my thinking has changed. I have a broader set of skills and a better appreciation of service delivery today than when working with James. Despite my inexperience and anxieties at the time, however, I helped James achieve his goals and address his issues. For us, that is a great message for the trainees and inexperienced practitioners who will carry the field forward in the future. Old dogs with new tricks are not necessarily more effective than young dogs with old tricks, as long as those old tricks are the fundamental skills and processes that allow practitioners to help clients gain happiness, find meaning, and live more adaptive lives.

FURTHER READING

Park, S., Lavallee, D., & Tod, D. (2013). Athletes' career transition out of sport: A systematic review. *International Review of Sport and Exercise Psychology, 6*, 22–53. This article presents a systematic review of the factors associated with the quality of athletes' sport-career termination.

Stambulova, N. B. (2010). Counseling athletes in career transitions: The five-step career planning strategy. *Journal of Sport Psychology in Action, 1*(2), 95–105. This article outlines the intervention of transition used in the current case study.

Stambulova, N. B., & Ryba, T. V. (2013). *Athletes' careers across cultures.* Abingdon: Routledge. This book outlines and discusses a number of aspects of careers in sport in relation to different cultures across the world, including retirement from sport transition.

Tod, D. (2007). The long and winding road: Professional development in sport psychology. *The Sport Psychologist, 21*, 94–108. This article details the major ways that sport psychologists' service delivery perceptions and style evolve as they gain client experience.

Wylleman, P., Alfermann, D., & Lavallee, D. (2004). Career transitions in sport: European perspectives. *Psychology of Sport and Exercise, 5*, 7–20. This article provides a summary of some of the main career transitions in sport literature.

REFERENCES

Andersen, M. B. (2000). Beginnings: Intakes and the initiation of relationships. In M. B. Andersen (Ed.), *Doing sport psychology* (pp. 3–16). Champaign, IL: Human Kinetics. Alfermann, D. (1995, July). *Career transitions of elite athletes: Drop-out and retirement. Paper presented at the 9th European* Congress of Sport Psychology, Brussels.

Beck, J. S. (1995). *Cognitive therapy: Basics and beyond.* New York: Guilford. Bordin, E. S. (1994). Theory and research on the therapeutic working alliance: New directions. In A. O. Horvath & L. S. Greenberg (Eds.), *The working alliance: Theory, research, and practice* (pp. 13–37). Chichester: John Wiley & Sons, Ltd.

British Psychological Society. (2009). *Code of ethics and conduct.* Leicester: BPS.

Buhler, C. (1971). Basic theoretical concepts of humanistic psychology. *American Psychologist, 26*, 378–386.

Dobson, K. S. (2009). *Handbook of cognitive-behavioral therapies.* New York: The Guilford Press.

Grove, J. R., Lavallee, D., & Gordon, S. (1997). Coping with retirement from sport: The influence of athletic identity. *Journal of Applied Sport Psychology, 9*, 191–203.

Health and Care Professions Council (2012). *Standards of conduct, performance, and ethics.* London: HCPC.

Horvath, A. O., & Bedi, R. P. (2002). The alliance. In J. C.Norcross (Ed.), *Psychotherapy relationships that work: Therapist contributions and responsiveness to patients* (pp. 37–69). New York: Oxford University Press.

Kerr, J. H. (2010). An eclectic approach to psychological interventions in sport: Reversal theory. *The Sport Psychologist, 7*, 400–418.

Murphy, S. M. (2000). Afterword. In M. B.Andersen (Ed.), *Doing sport psychology* (pp. 275–279). Champaign, IL: Human Kinetics.

Park, S., Lavallee, D., & Tod, D. (2013). Athletes' career transition out of sport: A systematic review. *International Review of Sport and Exercise Psychology, 6*, 22–53.

Petitpas, A., Brewer, B., & Van Raalte, J. (2009). Transitions of the student-athlete: Theoretical, empirical, and practical perspectives. In E. F.Etzel (Ed.), *Counseling and psychological services for college student-athletes* (pp. 283–302). Morgantown, WV: Fitness Information Technology.

Rogers, C. R. (1959). A theory of therapy, personality, and interpersonal relationships, as developed in the client-centered framework. In S.Koch (Ed.), *Psychology, a study of a science. Vol. III: Formulations of the person and the social context.* New York: McGraw-Hill.

Rønnestad, M. H., & Skovholt, T. H. (2013). *The developing practitioner: Growth and stagnation of therapists and counsellors.* New York: Routledge.

Schlossberg, N. (1981). A model for analyzing human adaptation to transition. *The Counseling Psychologist, 9*, 2–18.

Sharp, L. A., & Hodge, K. (2011). Sport psychology consulting effectiveness: The sport psychology consultant's perspective. *Journal of Applied Sport Psychology, 3*, 360–376.

Stambulova, N. B. (2000). Athlete's crises: A developmental perspective. *International Journal of Sport Psychology, 31*, 584–601.

Stambulova, N. B. (2003). Symptoms of a crisis-transition: A grounded theory study. In N. Hassmen (Ed.), *Svensk idrottspykologisk förening* (pp. 97–109). Örebro, Sweden: Örebro University Press.

Stambulova, N. B. (2010). Counseling athletes in career transitions: The five-step career planning strategy. *Journal of Sport Psychology in Action, 1*(2), 95–105.

Steptoe, K., Barker, J., & Harwood, C. (2014). Enhancing the performance of individual athletes and teams: Considerations and challenges for the delivery of sport psychology services. In J. Gualberto Cremades & L. S. Tashman (Eds.), *Becoming a sport, exercise, and performance psychology professional: A global perspective* (pp. 77–84). Abingdon: Routledge.

Taylor, J. & Ogilvie, B. (1994). A conceptual model of adaptation to retirement among athletes. *Journal of Applied Sport Psychology, 6*, 1–20.

Taylor, J., & Schneider, B. A. (1992). The sport-clinical intake protocol: A comprehensive interviewing instrument for applied sport psychology. *Professional Psychology: Research and Practice, 23*, 318–325.

Tod, D. (2007). The long and winding road: Professional development in sport psychology. *The Sport Psychologist, 21*, 94–108.

Tod, D. (2014). Daddy and the meaning of service delivery. In P. McCarthy & M. Jones (Eds.), *Becoming a sport psychologist* (pp. 38–45). Abingdon: Routledge.

Tod, D., & Andersen, M. B. (2012). Practitioner-athlete relationships in applied sport psychology. In S. D. Mellalieu & S. Hanton (Eds.), *Advances in applied sport psychology professional practice: A review* (pp. 273–306). Abingdon: Routledge.

Tod, D., Andersen, M. B., & Marchant, D. B. (2011). Six years up: Applied sport psychologists surviving (and thriving) after graduation. *Journal of Applied Sport Psychology, 23*, 93–109.

Watson, J. C., II., & Shannon, V. (2010). Individual and group observations: Purposes and processes. In S. J. Hanrahan & M. B. Andersen (Eds.), *Routledge handbook of applied sport psychology* (pp. 90–100). Abingdon: Routledge.

Wippert, P., & Wippert, J. (2008). Perceived stress and prevalence of traumatic stress symptoms following athletic career termination. *Journal of Clinical Sport Psychology, 2*, 1–16.

Wylleman, P. (1995, July). *Career transition of athletes*. Symposium presented at the IXth European Congress of Sport Psychology, Brussels, Belgium.

9 Ahead of the Competition: Anxiety Control in Archery

JOANNE BATEY AND REBECCA SYMES

LEARNING OBJECTIVES

AFTER READING THIS CHAPTER YOU SHOULD BE ABLE TO:

1. Critically appreciate the challenges associated with developing high-functioning performance routines.
2. Identify and evaluate how professional philosophy impacts upon all aspects of practice (i.e., initial needs analysis, assessment, intervention, etc.).
3. Critically consider the benefits and drawbacks of adopting a humanistic philosophy with the athlete.
4. Recognize how relaxation interventions might be introduced and developed for use in elite level competition.
5. Have confidence to employ a series of relaxation strategies with athletes.

AREAS TO CONSIDER WHEN READING THE CHAPTER:

1. Consider the challenges of working in elite sport with limited time available.
2. Consider how encouraging athletes to work away from sessions can enhance effectiveness.
3. Be aware of viewing the athlete as an individual and not just an athlete and therefore exploring beyond their sporting identity.

CLIENT AND BACKGROUND

The first author began working with Freddie (a pseudonym) during the spring of 2010. At that time and aged 16, Freddie had been on the Great Britain archery development squad for two-and-a-half years. He had already travelled to several Junior European competitions and was a well-seasoned competitor domestically. His ambition was to qualify for a World Junior competition in the next two years. He had been shooting since he was ten and his love and enthusiasm for the sport was apparent in our initial meeting. Upon asking him what he got out of archery his response was to ask, 'What don't I get out of it?' He then listed a number of positive benefits such as enjoyment, motivation, and a love for the technical aspects of the sport.

Freddie's experience of sport psychology had been limited since there had not been a psychologist attached to the development squad previously. However, he was excited to begin work on this aspect of his performance. He also informed me that he had a pre-shot routine (PSR) in place. Upon further examination, this PSR consisted solely of focusing attention on the key technical aspects of each shot and was outcome focused (i.e., engage scapula and shoot 10s). It also became clear that the routine was extremely lengthy and made Freddie susceptible to becoming over analytical about each component of the shot resulting in a loss of fluidity in competitive situations.

I had been working with Freddie for over a year before the intervention outlined in this chapter was introduced. During that time we reduced the length of his PSR and had worked closely together in the performance environment (in both training and competition) to establish what thoughts and feelings were occurring during his shooting. We subsequently recognized Singer's (1988) five-step approach to develop a new routine which integrated a number of psychological skills techniques (i.e., thought stopping, imagery, and a version of Stratton, Cusimano, Hartman, & DeBoom's (2005) 3Rs). We also developed within performance routines for between ends (in a ranking round after each archer has shot six arrows they walk to the target to score and collect their arrows), between distances (for Freddie this was 36 at each distance of 90m, 70m, 50m, 30m), and for breaks in competition.

However, after travelling with the team to a number of domestic and international competitions, it became clear that a pattern was emerging. Freddie would shoot well in the qualifying rounds of the competition where there was no elimination and little pressure, and would report running his performance routines successfully and without too much thought, just like in training. However, in the elimination rounds he often shot below par and appeared to lose his ability to complete his shots with such fluidity. In archery, elimination rounds are termed 'head-to-heads' and consist of two archers lining up against each other. They shoot up to five ends of three arrows scoring two points for each end won and 1 point for a drawn end. The first up to six points progresses to the next stage with the loser exiting the competition. In the case of a tied score after five ends, there is a one arrow shoot-off where the highest arrow closest to the middle wins.

Freddie had never won a head-to-head at an international competition. He spoke of feeling increased tension when shooting in these situations and reported perceptions of increased heart rate and a more powerful heartbeat. The resulting pounding sensation in his chest subsequently impacted on both his emotional and cognitive control. Specifically, he was worried about being able to maintain a sufficiently steady posture to execute the shot smoothly and struggled to concentrate on executing his performance routines. This led him to doubt his ability to execute a good shot, resulting in him trying to overly control his shot. It was therefore clear that Freddie was experiencing many of the symptoms of both cognitive (e.g., worry and apprehension) and somatic (e.g., increased heart rate, muscular tension) anxiety (Weinberg, 2010). Freddie's decreased performance during these situations seems to fit with Fazey and Hardy's (1988) Catastrophe Theory which contends that when physiological arousal is high, increased cognitive anxiety will impair performance. Hillman,

Apparies, Janelle, and Hatfield (2000) reported in their research with skilled marksmen, that it is not unusual for athletes in these types of sports to be susceptible to over arousal.

Definition box

BOX 9.1

Cognitive anxiety: mental component of anxiety involving negative concerns about performance

Somatic anxiety: physiological components of anxiety involving perceptions of autonomic arousal

Master's (1992) theory of conscious processing seeks to explain why this performance impairment is to be expected. During the skill acquisition process, learning has been considered to take place in three stages (Fitts & Posner, 1967). During the initial cognitive stage learners are said to place emphasis on rules and instructions thus ensuring a slow and effortful performance. As the individual builds up experience of the skill they move to an associative stage whereby practice is needed to ensure the skill is refined and movement patterns begin to flow. Finally, the learner reaches the autonomous stage, where the skill becomes controlled by an unconscious process resulting in a smooth and effortless performance (Masters, 1992). Thus in the early stage, knowledge may be said to be explicit whereas by the final stage implicit knowledge dominates. Given that Freddie was part of a Junior National squad he would have been operating within the autonomous stage of learning.

Master's (1992) theory posits that during the autonomous stage, performance may become impaired if performers revert to focusing on the rules originally used to develop the skill (i.e. reverting to an earlier stage of learning in an attempt to gain control over their actions). Master's termed this 'reinvestment' and this process is most likely to occur in pressurized situations. The theory also suggests that some individuals are more likely to reinvest than others due to certain personality factors such as cognitive failure, emotional rehearsal, and self-awareness. Much research into sports performance supports the assertions of Master's (1992) theory including Lam, Maxwell, & Masters (2009), Gucciardi & Dimmock (2008) and Chell, Graydon, Crowley, and Child (2003).

Cognitive failure addresses individuals' proneness to have 'slips of action' (i.e. likelihood of actions not occurring in the planned manner); emotional rehearsal suggests that individuals who rehearse emotional events are more likely to experience anxiety in a stressful situation (Roger & Jamieson, 1988) and self-awareness theory (Wicklund, 1975; Duval & Silvia, 2001) stipulates that (a) specific situations force people to become inwardly self-focused and, (b) that certain individuals are predisposed to be more self-focused than others (Brehm, Kassin, & Fein, 2002). Thus, individuals scoring highly on measures of these personality factors are most likely to reinvest under pressure. Whilst the Reinvestment Scale (Masters, Polman, & Hammond, 1993) was not used with Freddie, my existing knowledge about him suggested that he was prone to reinvestment which was likely to occur in times of high physical arousal and high cognitive anxiety (i.e. international head-to-heads).

Whilst it was useful to know how this increased tension manifested itself and what might be happening from a theoretical standpoint, I was also interested in exploring its genesis. Further discussion in one-to-one conversations revealed that Freddie felt under pressure due to being the last remaining member of the more established athletes on the development squad not to win an international head-to-head. He explained that sometimes wearing a GB shirt could feel 'heavy' if you did not feel you deserved to wear it. Further examination of this issue revealed that meeting other people's expectations was very important to Freddie and that failure to do so was alien to him. He was also an individual who admitted to a history of being too proud to ask for help. He was a high achiever both in archery and in the academic domain having never received lower than an A* grade across 14 GCSEs and 3 A-levels. Additionally he was seen as a role model within the archery squad and was given the role of a leader within the programme (cf. Cope et al., 2011). Cope, Eys, Beauchamp, Schinke, and Bosselut (2011) claim that such informal roles are common within sports teams. In their research identifying types of informal roles that athletes occupy, Freddie seemed to fulfil the role of 'mentor'. Specifically this describes, 'an athlete who acts as a trusted counsellor or teacher ... This athlete has usually been in the team for a few years and has experience and wisdom to teach the less experienced athlete(s)' (Cope et al. 2011, p. 24). Outside the archery domain, Freddie was very close to his single mother and wanted to make her proud of him. Therefore whilst it was apparent that Freddie's future was permeated with high expectations, his past indicated that he was able to achieve and meet those expectations. Consequently he had little experience of failure in which to build up the skills of resilience. Collins and MacNamara (2012) assert that an element of failure, challenge, and trauma along the way can help athletes to succeed as these experiences enable athletes to build up the necessary coping skills. However when Freddie encountered these unfamiliar feelings of anxiety, pressure, and failure, he was not able to cope and thus his performances were not matching his obvious potential.

Discussion points box **BOX 9.2**

- Why is it important to get to the root cause of a problem and not just provide a short-term solution that will help current performance?
- What implications might there be for needing/wanting to do more exploratory work with an athlete?
- When might it be appropriate to just provide an initial solution?

INITIAL NEEDS ASSESSMENT

Assessment in sport psychology comes in many guises, partly as a result of the varied training backgrounds of applied practitioners and partly because operating within real-world settings creates specific challenges for assessment (Vealey & Garner-Holman, 1998; McCann, Jowdy, & Van Raalte, 2003). Most practitioners now advocate the use of several assessment methods in order to develop a comprehensive understanding of athletes, although assessment choices undoubtedly remain influenced by the professional philosophy of the sport psychology consultant (see Poczwardowski, Sherman, & Ravizza, 2004; Poczwardowski, Sherman, & Henschen, 1998). Frameworks and guidelines designed to help practitioners assess athletes effectively have also been well documented in the literature (see Davies & West, 1991; McCann et al., 2003; Murphy, 1995; Vealey & Garner-Holman, 1998) and underline the importance of appropriate assessment for subsequent intervention and evaluation.

The assessment approach I adopted with Freddie was multifaceted and evolved over time. I believe working with athletes over a number of years necessitates such a flexible and organic approach. To illustrate this, it is worthy of note that each of the four areas which Vealey and Garner-Holman (1998) outlined in their multi-domain assessment framework (i.e., athlete characteristics, contextual characteristics, organizational culture of the sport, and consultant characteristics) changed throughout our time working together, and cognizant of that, so too did my methods of assessment. Nonetheless, the most frequent forms of assessment I used were interviews and observations, a pattern which reflects the most well-used types of assessment in the literature on this area (Vealey & Garner-Holman, 1998; Fifer, Henschen, Gould, & Ravizza, 2008). Whilst some practitioners might view using interviews as time-consuming, I believe them to be a fundamental tool in developing rapport, gaining a holistic understanding of athletes, and laying the foundations for a trusting relationship, a position endorsed by many well-known practitioners in the field (e.g., Andersen, 2000; Ravizza, 2002; Fifer et al., 2008). Furthermore, I believe that multiple interviews can help consultants to conceptualize the issue, a process that Poczwardowski (1998) identified as occurring between the assessment and implementation of an intervention programme. Martingdale and Collins (2010) have called for a greater examination of the metacognition which underpins an intervention in order to make visible the judgements, decisions, and problem-solving strategies employed by sport psychology consultants throughout the conceptualization process. Certainly a greater examination of this area is warranted, and would be especially useful to novice practitioners since often the root causes of athletes' issues are not easily identified during the early stages of assessment and therefore taking time to conceptualize a client's issues can increase intervention efficiency.

Freddie and I had several meetings during which I explored a number of key areas with him and began to understand him as both an archer and a person. Exploring the multiple contexts operating in an athlete's life has been advocated by Whelan, Meyers, and Donovan (1995), whilst others have devised useful assessment approaches and frameworks to help guide practitioners to do just that (e.g., Hellstedt, 1995; Lazarus, 1976). Philosophical discussions have also highlighted that consultants who recognize the importance of exploring multiple selves are most likely to convey to their athletes that they care about them as a person and not just an athlete (Friesen & Orlick, 2010). This has been claimed to have positive implications for athletes' commitment and adherence to future intervention work and adds credence to Ravizza's contention that athletes have to 'know you care before they care what you know' (2002, p. 7).

I also spent many hours observing Freddie during practice and competition simulation. Investing in such 'face time' has been viewed as essential in developing rapport and trust between athlete and practitioner (Watson & Shannon, 2010) and is considered a useful strategy to use alongside more traditional forms of assessment (Gardner & Moore, 2005). Furthermore, such observational analysis demonstrates awareness on the part of the practitioner that sport does not operate in a vacuum and that social influences not present in a more formal type of assessment may be noted in the training environment (Watson & Shannon, 2010). Whilst I did not utilize a formal observational checklist, there may be merit in using such a tool in order to ensure consistency across observations (see Watson & Shannon (2010) for an example). Nonetheless, I was interested in seeing how Freddie responded to pressure and stress, what his work ethic was like, how he operated around competitors and team mates, how receptive he was to coaching generally and to specific members of the coaching team, and how easily distracted he was. I was also alert to noticing discrepancies between what he reported to me in our more formal meetings and his behaviours in the training and competition environment. It was during these observations that I also began to look for evidence of the PSR which Freddie had told me he was using. I noticed that he often shot more slowly than the other archers and that his timing between shots varied considerably. Furthermore, his behaviour and attention between shots was far from uniform. After gaining (with appropriate consent) some footage of him shooting in training, I raised this issue with Freddie and shared both my observations and the footage. Whilst it had taken us some time to get to this point (a luxury that sport psychology consultants do not always have), I was aware of the cautionary words from Partington and Orlick (1991) which advised against imposing a standard intervention package too soon. Such sentiments are echoed by Danish, Petitpas, and Hale (1993, p. 407) who contended that 'When a problem-solving approach is initiated prematurely, the development of rapport is impeded, self-exploration is curtailed, and the therapeutic relationship is jeopardized.'

In parallel with conducting my own independent assessment of Freddie, I also worked with a small team of consultants who had been tasked with providing an assessment strategy that could be implemented across all Great Britain archery squads (Olympic, Paralympic, and development). Developing this strategy was twofold. First, it entailed an examination of the literature on peak performance including the development of psychological characteristics generally (see Orlick & Partington, 1998; Gould, Diffenbach, & Moffett, 2002; Durand-Bush & Salmela, 2002; MacNamara, Button, & Collins, 2010; Williams & Krane, 2010) and in archery and related disciplines more specifically (Robazza & Bortoli, 1998; Hung, Lin, Lee, & Chen, 2008). Second, we utilized the access we had to Olympic and Paralympic competitors and medalists and spoke to them in focus-group settings to ascertain their beliefs regarding the characteristics and qualities necessary to train and compete at the highest level. The culmination of this research was the creation of a psychological profile consisting of five key themes that were then broken down into a number of qualities and skills required to be an elite archer and presented to the athletes in the form of a table. Some of these qualities and skills were as follows: determination, drive, and commitment to achieve; self-awareness of ideal shooting state; embracing challenge and discomfort; taking responsibility, retaining perspective and life balance; preparing thoroughly for competition; and excellent emotional control and composure in competition. Athletes rated their level of proficiency in each domain on a scale of 1–10 for each skill/process and then detailed what they thought they needed to do to improve this area in a parallel column labelled 'action plan'. Such self-reflection and self-monitoring techniques are commonly used in applied sport psychology and are considered to be central to enhancing athlete motivation and achievement behaviour (Bandura, 1986). Research has also indicated that the development of sport-specific measures by consultants remains popular and that their use is increasing (O'Connor, 2004).

Each athlete was informed why they were being assessed, how the process would help them, and how the assessment information would be used and disseminated. Athletes were subsequently encouraged to discuss each aspect of their action plans with the relevant people and were aided in setting goals around self-improvement. The process was to be monitored by both the sport psychologist for each squad and the athlete's personal coach. The psychological profile was also to be repeated every three months in order to provide feedback to athletes regarding their progress (something that is highlighted as important by Beckmann and Kellmann (2003)) and was to be submitted to the performance director to inform discussions related to athlete progression. In some ways the process undertaken was reminiscent of the performance profile (Butler, 1989) although it clearly lacked the element of self-determination inherent in the original tool since the archers played a passive role in the creation of the psychological profile against which their progress would be judged.

As a result of completing the psychological profile it was apparent that Freddie scored lowest on the qualities contained within the competition toughness section. Specifically, this section was made up of (a) excellent emotional control and composure in competition; (b) retaining a task focus; and (c) performing under pressure. These findings echoed discussions that Freddie and I had been having during training camps about his ability to perform well when it mattered most and demonstrated a clear overlap between the individual-level assessment being conducted with Freddie, and the multi-squad assessment tool designed by the applied sport psychology team. It therefore underlined that the work we were doing together was underpinned by appropriate assessment and conceptualization and thus the efficiency of any subsequent interventions was enhanced.

By this stage Freddie and I had been working for a number of months during the off-season on developing his PSR. This had culminated in him reporting a more process-based task focus and more control over unhelpful thoughts and images. Performance data recorded during training sessions and simulated competition also showed that he was recovering more quickly from bad shots (one bad shot tended not to follow another as frequently) and he demonstrated more consistent timing between shots. As a result, Freddie's training scores had been much more consistent. Executing a shot with consistent timing has been viewed as a critical aspect of archery performance. In their work with the Taiwanese Olympic archery team Hung, Lin, Lee, and Chen (2008) demonstrated how consistent routines, including shot timing improved performance and that inconsistent aiming time was linked to poor performance. Nonetheless, as we moved into the competitive season, Freddie reported the issue outlined previously (i.e., that he was able to maintain his PSR in the qualifying rounds but once it came to head-to-heads he felt increased tension in his upper body and a simultaneous pounding in his chest).

FRAMEWORK AND INTERVENTION

The overarching framework used when working with Freddie was humanistic and was underpinned by both my core beliefs and values (see Poczwardowski et al., 2004) and my aim to create an environment that nurtured performance enhancement and self-growth. Such holistic development of an individual's potential is the primary concern of humanistic practitioners (Hill, 2001) and is reflected in aspects of the assessment approach outlined earlier. Throughout our time working together, I felt as though we developed the supportive, non-judgemental environment that Bruno (1977) advocated as necessary to allow clients to reach their full potential. Evidence of this was reflected in Freddie's openness in sessions and his engagement in following and determining his programme outside our contact time.

Many of the discussions surrounding Freddie's sporting performance centred on him aspiring to live in the present when he competed. Additionally, they involved his commitment to a process of change that would allow him to reach his future potential as an Olympian. Such aspirations reflect the beliefs of some of the most influential figures in humanistic psychology (e.g., Rogers, 1961; Maslow, 1954; Seligman, 1998) and interestingly also suited Freddie's personality. Freddie was one of very few athletes I have worked with who, right from the outset, did not view sport psychology intervention as a 'quick fix'. Whilst he was clearly ambitious and motivated, he recognized that he was engaging in a process of development, and was interested in evolving both within and outside his athletic self. We had many conversations about how he might use the attitude developed in sessions to approach situations differently in his academic and family life. I also encouraged Freddie to begin to take ownership of his sessions with me. Facilitating such autonomy on the part of the client is characteristic of humanistic theory that focuses on the client as the agent for change and espouses a self-determining philosophy (Walker, 2010). Therefore Freddie increasingly played a role in determining how he wanted our sessions to be structured and to progress. He often set the agenda (emailing me details beforehand) and would arrive having read something he would like to discuss or implement into his training. One example of this was Freddie coming to me having completed and scored the Test of Performance Strategies (TOPS; Thomas, Murphy, & Hardy, 1999) which he had found online.

Working in this way demonstrated congruence between my underpinning philosophy, the framework I adopted, and my subsequent methods of assessment and intervention. This congruence is something that Lindsay, Breckon, Thomas, and Maynard (2007) highlight as of great importance. However I believe that for this approach to be most effective the consultant needs to be working with a client who is also comfortable and committed to working in this way. I was fortunate that

Freddie was engaged in a process of change that necessitated a mindset of continual evolution and development.

Nonetheless, as will become apparent, some of the intervention work outlined in this chapter is based on the acquisition and development of psychological skills training strategies pertaining to relaxation. Whilst this type of intervention might seem incongruent with the humanistic framework detailed above, such a composite approach is not unusual. Indeed, whilst it has been acknowledged that such an integrative approach is difficult to develop, it has also been identified as being entirely appropriate for use in the applied sport psychology domain (Poczwardowski et al., 1998). Different types of eclecticism have even been identified by Young (1992) which include synthetic eclecticism (using a fusion of theoretical frameworks), technical eclecticism (using one overarching theory but multiple techniques from a variety of frameworks), and atheoretical eclecticism (drawing from manifold theoretical frameworks).

Following the synthetic eclectic approach, another framework that guided aspects of the intervention with Freddie was the cognitive-behavioural framework. This emphasizes how thought patterns and mental habits (cognitive) as well as the social environment (behavioural) influence actions and feelings (Hill, 2001). Or to put it another way, it addresses the relationship between thoughts, feelings, and behaviours. In contrast to a client-centred approach like humanism, cognitive-behavioural approaches take a more prescriptive avenue with a client, often through giving them specific education, skills, and strategies (Martindale & Collins, 2005). One of the advantages of this approach is that it more readily lends itself to use in time-bound conditions, therefore whilst an overall framework might be of a humanistic nature, at points in the consulting process, specific interventions may be required to fit within a timescale. A second advantage to this approach is that it is appropriate with younger athletes who might have little experience in the mental side of performance and therefore need some guidance. Third, a cognitive-behavioural approach, through its emphasis on goal setting and measurable outcomes might be appropriate for clients who yearn to see more tangible progress and results. As mentioned, whilst Freddie understood that this was not a 'quick fix' process, he was driven by meticulous planning, setting goals, and measuring his progression. Therefore when it became apparent that he needed to manage his anxiety in competition, an intervention specifically for this purpose fitted well. In essence, whilst I was determined to understand and address the root cause of his anxiety, Freddie needed a process he could learn to use in competition as necessary and he was keen to be able to work on his mental performance at home. This fits with the idea of cognitive-behavioural therapy giving clients 'homework'. Thus I decided upon the use of progressive muscular relaxation (PMR) (Jacobson, 1938), which originates from a cognitive-behavioural background, as one aspect of our work.

The aim of PMR is to train an athlete to elicit a relaxed state by developing sensitivity to muscular tension. In short, this involves isolating different muscle groups, contracting and relaxing those muscles and then learning to become aware of the differences (for a detailed PMR script see Williams, 2010). The majority of research into PMR has centred on its function to help athletes cope with the debilitative effects of competition-related anxiety, with most research supporting its effectiveness in doing so (e.g., Lanning & Hisanaga, 1983; Greenspan & Feltz, 1989; Pawlow & Jones, 2005). However, there is some evidence that PMR might have other psychological functions and benefits. Johnson (2000) found that when the technique was implemented in sport rehabilitation settings injured athletes reported both enhanced mood states and perceptions of readiness. Furthermore, in research with women with breast cancer, Tacón, Caldera, and Ronaghan (2004) reported increased perceptions of an internal locus of control. Such enhanced mood state and perceptions of readiness and control are also likely to be of benefit to athletes in competition environments, and therefore extending the range of research on the functionality of PMR in competitive settings beyond that associated with anxiety would seem to be warranted.

Whilst it is important to have an understanding of your overarching framework, there are a number of other things that are central to a sport psychologist's effectiveness, the biggest of which is often said to be the relationship between the sport psychologist and athlete. This is influenced by the psychologist's needs, personality, how they relate to athletes, how athletes relate to them, their fears, their responses to athletes' success and failure and their strengths and weaknesses (Andersen, 2000). Additionally, knowing and trusting your judgement and intuition is important for effectiveness (Fifer et al., 2008). These areas are intertwined since the framework(s) you are using can guide your judgement whilst your intuition is likely to be influenced by your level of experience and your relationship with the client.

Activity box **BOX 9.3**

How important is it to know the philosophical framework you are working from as an applied practitioner? And why?

Can you provide a brief outline of the main types of frameworks sport psychologists might work from?

INTERVENTION

Prior to detailing the intervention undertaken with Freddie, there are two points of note. First, the strategies and techniques outlined here were part of a wider stress management training (SMT) programme designed to help Freddie cope better with competition demands in head-to-head situations. Many of the SMT intervention strategies (e.g., cognitive restructuring, imagery) formed part of his performance routines (between arrows, between ends, and between distances). Second, there were some uncontrollable contextual factors present which impacted on the delivery of the intervention and determined what could be done and when. Specifically these were the time in the season (new psychological skills and strategies were only to be introduced in the off-season) and the time allocated for sport psychology input. Thus a flexible, multi-pronged approach was necessary.

Discussion box **BOX 9.4**

Why might the governing body have suggested the off-season is the time to implement new skills and strategies?

What are the advantages and disadvantages of this approach?

Given that Freddie first reported his anxiety in head-to-head situations two-thirds of the way through a competitive season, the first strategy was to attempt to replicate a competition environment at a number of training camps and thus recreate the stress response. This entailed using environmental stimuli such as PA announcements, music, flags, and scoreboards. The setting was structured so that head-to-heads were practised continually and willing members of the current Olympic squad were also recruited to shoot against Freddie in these situations. Finally, self-imposed consequences for poor performance were introduced or privileges were removed (e.g., not going to the cinema with the rest of the squad). Whilst it was challenging to simulate a competition environment in what was a familiar training venue, providing opportunities for young athletes to develop resilience in talent developments pathways has been advocated by Collins and MacNamara (2012) as critical for their development. Furthermore, Deinstbier (1989) claims that intermittent exposure to challenging situations (with subsequent periods of adjustment) develops skills, attitudes, and hormonal responses to stress that result in a more solution-focused perception.

Freddie wore a heart rate monitor during training camps to see if the perceived elevation in heart rate was borne out during head-to-head scenarios and to ascertain whether heart rate had a real or imagined impact on Freddie's performance scores. Whilst heart rate was slightly elevated in head-to-head situations, Freddie reflected that it was generally insufficient in magnitude and consistency to mimic the feelings he experienced in competition. However, he did claim that shooting against Olympic archers and knowing there were consequences attached to poor performance went some way to replicating the muscular tension he had felt. He also reported being more focused than usual and feeling more prepared for upcoming competitions as a result of this type of practice.

At the end of the competitive season I began working with Freddie on a modified version of PMR identified in Williams (2010). This time in the season had been identified by Archery GB as the prime time to introduce changes to technical, strategic, and psychological aspects of performance. Given that the relaxation response can take many weeks to master and to mould into a competition-friendly skill, it was also considered that introducing it at this juncture would enable Freddie to commit fully to the process and not feel under any significant time pressure to master it. Described as the 'gold standard' of relaxation techniques (Weinberg, 2010), PMR seems best suited to self-paced sports such as archery where there are natural breaks between both each shot and shooting generally. Consideration of Davidson and Schwartz's (1976) matching hypothesis also underlined the appropriateness of such a technique to address the muscular tension and increased heart rate Freddie reported. More contemporary research has also highlighted that PMR can decrease pulse rate more effectively than other types of relaxation intervention (Khanna, Paul, & Sandhu, 2007). However, it was recognized that disentangling the somatic and cognitive aspects of anxiety would be both difficult and naïve. It was true that Freddie's awareness of muscular tension triggered his worry and apprehension and therefore addressing the somatic component first was warranted, but later work with this client also addressed the cognitive element.

Definition box — BOX 9.5

Progressive muscular relaxation (PMR) is designed to train an athlete to elicit a relaxed state by developing sensitivity to muscular tension. In the end a PMR routine can be as little as a few seconds.

Historically criticisms of PMR have predominantly centred on its lack of utility in a performance environment (Morris & Thomas, 1995; Balague, 2005). However this criticism is perhaps a little myopic given that once well learnt, those athletes who are competent in PMR should be able to scan their bodies for feelings of tension and subsequently relax specific muscles. It perhaps also dismisses the additional benefits that learning PMR might have for athletes. These include a heightened awareness about the difference between feelings of tension and of relaxation (Williams, 2010), the therapeutic effects of using PMR (such as using it the night before an important competition to facilitate sleep) (Burton & Raedeke, 2008; Williams, 2010), the 'domino effect' learning PMR might have for athletes to more expediently learn shorter techniques oriented for use in competition environments (Burton & Raedeke, 2008; Williams, 2010), and the promotion of enhanced recovery times from training and injuries (Burton & Raedeke, 2008; Williams, 2010) One of the primary functions of relaxation as reported by athletes in Kudlackova, Eccles, and Dieffenbach's (2013) research, was in its ability to help them cope with everyday anxieties. Given that Freddie had very high expectations of himself both inside and outside archery, this research may be especially pertinent to consider. Pawlow and Jones (2005) have also found that PMR enhances the immune system by stimulating immunoglobulin levels, something which is also worth consideration for athletes, particularly during the competitive season.

In the first instance Freddie and I ran through the PMR process in a quiet room familiar to him whilst at a training camp. I provided Freddie with an audio of the exercise for his smartphone which used my voice. I did this because several athletes have relayed that they struggle to relax to the sound of their own voice on audio file. Freddie was encouraged to practise the 25–30 minute PMR each day for two to three weeks. The enhanced body awareness reportedly felt by athletes has meant some literature has suggested a two-to-three-week time frame for learning PMR is suitable with this population (Burton & Raedeke, 2008). However, studies detailing the time spent teaching participants PMR have varied between ten days to a number of weeks (Jones, 1993; Khanna et al., 2007; Hanafi, Hashim, & Ghosh, 2011) with some applied research failing to report on this at all (e.g., Blakeslee & Goff, 2007; Hashim, 2011). After three weeks Freddie reported that he was often asleep prior to the end of the exercise. Given that he seemed able to achieve a deep state of relaxation at this point we next implemented Ost's (1988) shorter version of PMR. Over the next four weeks we moved from a 15-minute version, to a five-minute version (which included saying 'relax' to himself on each exhalation), to a two-minute version. This reduction in time spent relaxing as the skill is mastered has been advocated by Bernstein, Borkovec, and Hazlett-Stevens (2000) as appropriate and were supplemented with continuing to use the full-length version twice a week (Jones, 1993). Freddie then began using the two-minute version whilst at training camps and when training at home. Generally this involved him using it before training began, after breaks and between distances. He reported feeling extremely competent with the shortened technique and also reported increased perceptions of confidence and control.

The next stage was to further reduce the time required to achieve this relaxed, confident and controlled state so that Freddie could recognize a relaxation strategy in competitive situations when time is at a premium. As Ravizza has noted, 'basic relaxation skills are important but eventually they must be applied in the act of performance' (Fifer et al., 2008, p. 362). Consequently Freddie was introduced to the technique of centring which has been defined as 'a breathing technique designed to promote physical balance and mental focus' (Nideffer, 1994, p. 127). Considered to be one of the easiest ways to reduce arousal, breath control techniques have also been reported to have interactive effects across both cognitive and somatic symptoms of anxiety (Weinberg, 2010). Despite the technique itself being predominantly somatically-based, Weinberg (2010) contends that using it can also facilitate a reduction in negative thoughts simply because it provides the athlete with something else to focus their attention on. Whilst research on centring remains scant, the technique has generally been found to have a positive effect (Huang & Lynch, 1994; Nideffer, 1994; Patrick & Hrycaiko, 1998, Rogerson & Hrycaiko, 2002; Haddad & Tremayne, 2009) and its brevity has resulted in athletes reporting using this type of relaxation more in competition environments (Wadey & Hanton, 2008; Kudlackova et al., 2013).

Freddie worked on his diaphragmatic breathing by being focused on both the inhalation and exhalation phases. Specifically, this involved inhaling through the nose (expanding the abdomen first and then gradually filling the lungs until the chest and shoulders are raised), then exhaling through the mouth slowly and with strength whilst imagining any tension leaving the body. The exhalation was also recommended to be about double the length of the inhalation with Freddie saying 'relax' to himself as he exhaled. There are many guidelines for centred breathing (e.g., Kremer & Moran, 2008; Weinberg & Gould, 2011), but I have found many of them confusing to use with athletes. Some seem overly focused on pushing the abdomen out on the inhalation whilst simultaneously keeping the chest and shoulders still (e.g., Kremer & Moran, 2008). I have found this unhelpful in promoting a relaxation response with athletes since they tend to hold the chest and shoulders rigid and not fully inhale. Thus the guidelines outlined above are a combination of different instructions that I have found to work best in my experience.

Freddie and I worked closely together throughout a training camp to help him implement centred breathing at every opportunity. We also recreated the competition environment once more and got him to practice his centring under head-to-head conditions. His recorded heart rate was lower and he reported greater perceptions of control. This strategy then became integrated into part of a larger performance routine which provided Freddie with structured, systematic ways of thinking and behaving throughout competition and enabled him to maintain a task-relevant focus and a sense of control. He also maintained the use of the longer versions of relaxation (usually the two-minute version) between breaks in competition and between distances. The PMR was not to be used on competition days, but he often continued to use this the night before competitions in order to facilitate sleep. In total it took us three months to reach a stage where Freddie could attain a relaxed state within a few seconds in the performance environment.

Whilst Freddie had learnt a variety of relaxation techniques which he reported were helping him to manage his physical, emotional, and cognitive control, I was also cognizant that his performance decrement in high-pressure situations was likely to be symptomatic of a more complex, ingrained issue. I therefore asked him to explore his present situation with regard to his fear of falling short of other people's expectations in more detail. For Freddie 'other people' constituted the other archers in the squad and his mother. Fear of failing to meet the expectations of his peers is unsurprising given that support and social networks are said to generally become more peer-focused between the ages of 15 to 20 (Voorhees et al., 2005). Nevertheless, it is also likely that Freddie's mother continued to play an important role in his perception of self since Lowry and Bond (2010) demonstrated that British junior archers' social networks tended to remain characterized by relationships with adults, specifically parents and national coaches. Freddie was highly motivated to understand more about this and identified that he wanted to speak to his mother which he subsequently did.

Freddie's self-determination to pursue this route, combined with his confidence to act on what instinctively felt right, demonstrated to me that he was engaged in a process of change. His motivation to do so seemed governed by a desire to be closer to what Rogers (1961) would term his 'ideal self'. The conversation with his mother led both of them to recognize that he had adopted the role of the 'sensible son' who never let her down. In the absence of a father in the house, and with an elder brother who was a little wayward, Freddie realized that his desire not to cause his mother any stress had manifested itself in him working hard in every aspect of his behaviour to make her proud of him. This had culminated in him being a high achiever both academically and in his sport and consequently being a stranger to failure. Freddie told me that having this conversation with his mother allowed him to feel a sense of freedom. Whilst he was aware that his mother just wanted him to enjoy his archery, this enjoyment was threatened by a manifestation of achievement related beliefs about not letting her down. Subsequently, it seemed as though the conversation had led to them having a new understanding of each other. Freddie said he felt as though a weight that he did not even know existed had been taken from his shoulders. In humanistic terms it seemed as though this critical self-reflection had allowed him to become more congruent as he moved closer towards the self he wanted to be.

REFLECTIONS

Reflective practice received scant attention in applied sport psychology until the late 1990s. The surge of interest that emerged at the turn of the century (e.g., Lindsay, Breckon, Thomas, & Maynard, 2007; Cropley, Miles, Hanton, & Niven, 2007; Tod, 2007; Woodcock, Richards, & Mugford, 2008) coincided with a growing awareness of the importance of the processes which influence sport psychology service delivery (Simons & Andersen, 1995) alongside the general adoption of a more athlete-centred approach to consultancy (Holt & Strean, 2001). Generally the focus on reflective practice has been well received within sport psychology although Martingdale and Collins (2005, 2007) have vociferously argued for clearer criteria to be developed against which practitioners should reflect, alongside a greater focus on the content of reflection as opposed to the process.

According to Andersen, Knowles and Gilbourne (2004) engaging in self-reflection is an attitude as opposed to a collection of techniques and requires practitioners to be open and questioning, examine their practice, and lay themselves open to feeling uncomfortable and vulnerable. Nonetheless, reflection can occur through written reflections, journal writing, and conversations and is often strengthened by aligning itself to some criteria. Novice practitioners might consider using Ghaye's (2001) reflective questions as a starting point to examine their practice, with more experienced practitioners directed towards Johns' (1994) more detailed model.

The effectiveness of the intervention was predominantly assessed by continually monitoring that Freddie perceived it to be doing what he needed it to do. This information was gained in a number of ways. First, Freddie and I would sit down at a training camp each month and one of the things we would discuss was his progress with the intervention. Each time we met I would complete a write-up of our session detailing the focus of discussion and actions to address (see appendix II). The content of this was subsequently emailed to Freddie and some of the information was also shared with Freddie's coach (with his consent). Second, Freddie maximized the remote support offered to him and therefore email and Skype contact was frequent between training camps. In this way I was able to monitor Freddie's progress with the PMR and subsequent relaxation interventions and gauge when the time was right to move things forward. I also continued to observe Freddie in training, competition simulation, and competition environments, travelling with the squad to both domestic and international competitions. I was therefore able to see when Freddie was implementing his relaxation interventions and speak to him regularly about their effectiveness. I always shared detailed observations and feedback with Freddie as soon as possible so it maintained maximum relevance in both our minds and was easier to recollect. I was also keen to avoid the warning from McCann et al. (2003, p. 302) that 'failure to provide comprehensive feedback can leave athletes and coaches unwilling to work with sport psychologists because they took a lot of our time, collected a bunch of data, and we never got to see any results'.

At an organizational level each athlete in the Great Britain archery development squad also had to submit various pieces of paperwork designed to monitor their progress. These consisted of extensive self-report logs which included a weekly periodization planner, quarterly updates about each aspect of their training (e.g., strength and conditioning, psychology), and post-competition reports. This information was shared with the performance director and this might of course have generated some response bias in the form of social desirability. However, I saw no disconnect between what Freddie was reporting at an organizational level and what I was recording through various types of assessment. I simply used this information for evaluation and monitoring purposes, to establish intervention plans, or simply to confirm my observations. In addition to this, Freddie completed ongoing goal-setting logs (see appendix III) with me. He set medium-term goals (three months) and short-term goals (weekly) and then assessed his progress towards these. Freddie was meticulous at completing these and this information was very useful to me since it provided an overview of how he was progressing in all aspects of the psychological work we were undertaking and not just the relaxation intervention outlined in this chapter. He also reported that he found the goal-setting logs motivational and had used them to reflect on his progression at times when he would otherwise have thought he was plateauing. In my experience however these goal-setting logs have not been universally popular with athletes since they require a substantial and continual time commitment. However, fortunately Freddie went against the maxim stated in Beckmann and Kellmann's work that 'athlete's hate paperwork' (2003, p. 338).

Whilst it might seem unusual that so much athlete monitoring, evaluation, and reflection was conducted through self-report and proformas as opposed to more psychometric measures of psychological change it is actually quite common. Many examples of bespoke survey questionnaires exist which are generally designed to facilitate athlete self-awareness and feedback and allow sport psychology consultants to evaluate the effectiveness of their interventions. For example, Ravizza (2010) has used a performance feedback sheet, and Orlick's (1986) competition reflections questionnaire has been widely adopted by applied sport psychology consultants (see Vealey & Garner-Holman, 1998). Additionally, research that has used more empirical methods (e.g., CSAI-2; Martens, Vealey, Burton, Bump, & Smith, 1990) to measure changes in psychological processes as a result of psychological intervention has produced equivocal results. Many have not found significant changes even when athletes have relayed that they perceived the intervention to be helpful (Vealey & Garner-Holman, 1998). One explanation for this has been that the psychobehavioural changes emanating from interventions might not easily be detected by measuring instruments designed for research purposes (Vealey & Garner-Holman, 1998).

My self-reflection was further enhanced through taking part in regular peer reflection sessions with two other applied sport psychologists who also worked within the sport of archery. These sessions allowed me to consider my practice through reflecting on my methods and philosophy in a non-judgemental environment. Poczwardowski et al. (1998) suggests that addressing such issues has been advocated to maximize the professional growth and development of practitioners whilst Simons and Andersen (1995) advocated that sport psychology consultants should follow the advice of Socrates and 'know thyself' through engagement in such processes. Specifically this process allowed me to reflect on the intervention I was conducting with Freddie and my role within this as a facilitator for change and growth.

Self-reflection can generate possible alternatives to the ways in which consultations are approached. Starting therefore at the beginning of the process, one of the assessment methods used was to get Freddie to complete a profile, rating himself on five pre-determined themes. Having pre-determined themes goes against concepts of both cognitive-evaluation theory (Deci & Ryan, 1985) and self-determination theory (Deci & Ryan, 1985,) which posit that having a sense of perceived control or autonomy will enhance intrinsic motivation. Since Freddie was given no choice to determine the areas he deemed to be important to his performance it raises questions around his intrinsic motivation towards improving those areas. Second, there might have been some merit in additionally gaining coach ratings for Freddie as this has been shown to enable athletes and coaches to have more open discussions and establish aligned starting points for progression (Dale & Wrisberg, 1996).

Moving on to the intervention itself, an area to consider is whether the interaction between psychological stress and physiological arousal could have been exploited further. Whilst basic heart-rate measures were taken, it would be interesting to see how the theory of challenge and threat states in athletes (TCTSA; Jones, Meijen, McCarthy, & Sheffield, 2009) would have applied. The TCTSA stipulates that in competitive situations, athletes will make evaluations about the demands of the situation based on the extent to which it promotes perceptions of danger (physical or esteem), uncertainty and effort (physical and psychological). Consequently, an evaluation of the resources available to cope with the demands will then be made, based upon self-efficacy, perceptions of control and achievement goals. In short, the greater the levels of self-efficacy, the higher the perception of control and the greater the focus on approach goals, the more likely it is a challenge (adaptive responses to stress) state will be evident. Conversely, lower levels of self-efficacy, lower perceptions of control, and a focus on avoidance goals will point towards a threat (maladaptive responses to stress) state (Turner et al., 2013). Both these challenge and threat states have different patterns of cardiovascular activity, which can be measured through the use of biofeedback equipment, and differing implications for performance. For example, challenge states are associated with improved decision-making, effective cognitive function, reduced likelihood of reinvestment, and efficient self-regulation with threat states resulting in the opposite (e.g., reduced decision-making capabilities, increased cognitive function, increased likelihood of reinvestment, and inefficient self-regulation; Jones et al., 2009).

Whilst it could be assumed from Freddie's own description of what he was experiencing during international head-to-head matches that he was in a threat state, being able to provide some psycho-physiological markers of this would have provided additional insight into what was happening for him during this time. In turn this would also provide some baseline data that could then be used to establish if interventions such as PMR were being effective at helping transition from a threat state to a challenge state, which in theory should lead to a better performance. Based on the work of Turner et al. (2013), a protocol for this could be to set up a simulation competition (e.g., Freddie to shoot a series of head-to-heads against Olympic archers) and prior to this record cardiovascular measures that differentiate challenge and threat including heart rate, total peripheral resistance, and cardiac output. Included within this would be a baseline measure, and then a measure after inducing the stressor (e.g., an audio recording outlining the series of head-to-heads Freddie was subsequently due to participate in). Freddie would then take part in the head-to-heads with performance being recorded and correlated with the biofeedback data. This same process could then be re-employed at a later date after an intervention so that progress could be monitored more scientifically. With Freddie's personality whereby he likes data and information and his desire to improve his approach he would likely be fully engaged in this way of working and benefit from the evidence based methodology.

Adopting this approach would of course require some financial investment since one would need to engage the service of research consultants with the appropriate equipment and expertise to interpret the findings. Additionally, as previously mentioned in this chapter, attempts to create a competition scenario in a familiar environment and with competitors that are known to Freddie can be difficult. Time would need to be put into considering the most effective and realistic way of doing this since the only way the biofeedback approach could be effective is if heart rate is elevated as otherwise challenge and threat cannot be determined. This could be done at a live competition such as an international hosted in the UK but this would need to be considered carefully to ensure the testing didn't interfere with key performance preparations.

Another way the current intervention could have been enhanced is to have matched best performance with arousal levels more solidly which Weinberg (2010) suggests gives a fuller picture of the arousal-performance relationship. It is recognized that individual athletes have different levels of optimal arousal for best performance (see Hanin, 1997) and whilst the PMR intervention was aimed at helping to evoke the appropriate arousal levels for Freddie, at no point was this explicitly linked to his performance nor were any measures used to establish what his individual zone of optimal functioning was. Measures such as the Positive and Negative Affect Scale (Watson, Clark, & Tellegan, 1988) could have been used to measure emotional states and then performance measures could have been taken via an agreed rating system either by Freddie and/or his coach. As Weinberg (2010) suggests, this rating system could have looked at how Freddie performed compared to how he usually performed (e.g.,

1 = much worse than usual; 10 = much better than usual) or through breaking down his performance into individual components such as pre-shot focus, hand position, timing, release, and so on,. and rating his execution of these areas, or even more objectively through his competition scores. The emotional states and performance measures could then be jointly assessed to see what states are associated with Freddie's best performance. This would then have given a clear picture of Freddie's individualized zones of optimal functioning, which would be a humanistically orientated perspective of arousal since focus is on individual uniqueness, self-actualization, and the unity of the person (Hill, 2001).

The intervention with Freddie initially focused on the somatic component of his anxiety; however it was recognized that there was a cognitive element triggered by the awareness of muscular tension.

Where currently the approach was to work first with the somatic component, it was recognized that the awareness of muscular tension triggered the anxiety. Initially it was not appropriate to start PMR due to it being two-thirds of the way through the season so in this intervening time, it would have been interesting to begin to address the cognitive elements first to see what impact that had. It would also be worth considering Rational Emotive Behaviour Therapy (REBT; Ellis, 1995) with Freddie since this aims to reduce irrational beliefs and cognitive anxiety. Whilst there is little research behind REBT in sport, there is some supporting evidence for its efficacy with youth athletes (Turner & Barker, 2013). This particular research employed a three-week brief REBT intervention with elite youth cricketers that consisted of one 20-minute counselling session a week for three consecutive weeks and two homework assignments. Results showed players experienced a reduction in irrational beliefs and cognitive anxiety. With greater sport psychologist resource, this could have fitted neatly into the timeframe, particularly given that brief REBT can be as effective as long-term REBT (Palmer, 1995).

It is also worthy of note that the majority of Freddie's training was undertaken at home or at his local archery club and not at the main Archery GB training facility. Consequently it would be worth considering interventions that could have been used when Freddie was training on his own at these venues. For example, basic ways to increase his heart rate and perceptions of stress in these environments such as through aerobic exercise, listening to high-tempo music, using energizing imagery, throwing die to replicate an opponent's score, and recording different scenarios which could be sent to his smartphone prior to training sessions (and which he didn't access until he was shooting) could all be considered. Such arousal-inducing techniques have been advocated by Weinberg (2010) to be of value.

Activity box — BOX 9.6

What other ways can you think of that could have helped Freddie when he was training at home or his club to simulate pressure training?

Be aware, that you're not trying to recreate the environment but the response (i.e. increased heart rate, sweating, etc.).

Whilst so far the focus of this discussion has been on relatively cognitive-behavioural approaches to the intervention, with more time, it would have been appropriate to extend the humanistic and counselling approach, especially in relation to Freddie's views around expectations, pressure, and his relationship with his mother and how these influence his current view of the world. This would start to establish a greater understanding of the underlying reasons behind Freddie's performance lapses. Whilst this area was explored (e.g., Freddie began to speak to his mother more openly), this was limited by time constraints and therefore never reached the level that could potentially have had the biggest impact. In my experience, this can often be the case in sport when time and financial aspects get in the way and therefore many interventions are designed around maximum impact with the least amount of time and also focus on short-term solutions more so than longer-term ones.

A final point of reflection relates to the fact that peer supervision took place with other psychologists working within archery. I would raise the question as to whether in addition to this, engaging in peer supervision with psychologists working in other sports and potentially other sports of a similar nature (e.g., shooting or golf) would have expanded the richness of the discussions and helped to generate new ideas and viewpoints. Sometimes one can get stuck in a particular way of thinking about how to approach a situation or be reluctant to deviate from tried and tested methods, so the influence of outside voices should not be underestimated. After all, 'it's good to talk'.

FURTHER READING

Hanrahan, S. J., & Andersen, M. B. (Eds.) (2010). *Routledge handbook of applied sport psychology: A comprehensive guide for students and practitioners.* New York: Routledge. This text provides an excellent contemporary resource overviewing a number of key issues for psychologists working in the applied domain.

Hill, K. L. (2000). *Frameworks for sports psychologists: Enhancing sport performance.* Champaign, IL. Human Kinetics. This text provides a good insight into the different frameworks available to applied sports psychologists.

Collins, D., & MacNamara, A. (2012). The rocky road to the top. Why talent needs trauma. *Sports Medicine, 42*(11), 1–8. This article is useful for people working on talent development programmes or pathways.

Poczwardowski, A., Sherman, C. P., & Henschen, K. P. (1998). A sport psychology service delivery heuristic: Building on theory and practice. *The Sport Psychologist, 12*, 191–207. This article is good for reflecting on the development of your own overall framework and delivery.

Poczwardowski, A., Sherman, C. P., & Ravizza, K. (2004). Professional philosophy in the sport psychology service delivery: Building on theory and practice. *The Sport Psychologist, 18*, 445–463. This article is good for reflecting on the development of your own overall framework and delivery.

REFERENCES

Andersen, A. G., Knowles, Z., & Gilbourne, D. (2004). Reflective practice for sport psychologists: concepts, models, practical implications and thoughts on dissemination. *The Sport Psychologist, 18*, 188–203.

Andersen, M. (2000). Beginnings: Intake and the initiation of relationships. In M. Andersen (Ed.), *Doing sport psychology* (pp. 3–16). Champaign, IL: Human Kinetics.

Balague, G. (2005) Anxiety: From pumped to panicked. In S. Murphy (Ed.), *The sport psych handbook: A complete guide to today's best mental training techniques* (pp. 73–92). Champaign, IL: Human Kinetics.

Bandura, A. (1986). *Social foundations of thought and action: A social cognitive theory.* Englewood Cliffs, NJ: Prentice-Hall.

Beckmann, J., & Kellmann, M. (2003). Procedures and principles of sport psychological assessment. *The Sport Psychologist, 17*, 338–250.

Bernstein, D. A., Borkovec, T. D., & Hazlett-Stevens, H. (2000). *New directions in progressive relaxation training: A guidebook for helping professionals.* New York: Praeger.

Blakeslee, M. L., & Goff, D. M. (2007). The effects of a mental skills training package on equestrians. *The Sport Psychologist, 21*, 288–301.

Brehm, S. S., Kassin, S. M., & Fein, S. (2002). *Social psychology.* Boston: Houghton Mifflin.

Bruno, F. J. (1977). *Human adjustment and personal growth: Seven pathways.* New York: John Wiley & Sons, Inc.

Burton, D., & Raedeke, T. D. (2008). *Sport psychology for coaches.* Champaign, IL: Human Kinetics.

Butler, R. J. (1989). Psychological preparation of Olympic boxers. In J. Kremer and W. Crawford (Eds.), *The psychology of sport: Theory and practice* (pp. 74–84). Leicester: British Psychological Society.

Chell, B. J., Graydon, J. K., Crowley, P. L., & Child, M. (2003). Manipulated stress and dispositional reinvestment in a wall-volley task: An investigation into controlled processing. *Perceptual and Motor Skills, 97*, 435–448.

Collins, D., & MacNamara, A. (2012). The rocky road to the top. Why talent needs trauma. *Sports Medicine, 42*(11), 1–8.

Cope, C. J., Eys, M. A., Beauchamp, M. R., Schinke, R. J., & Bosselut, G. (2011). Informal roles on sport teams. *International Journal of Sport and Exercise Psychology, 9*(1), 19–30.

Cropley, B., Miles, A., Hanton, S., & Niven, A. (2007). Improving the delivery of applied sport psychology through reflective practice. *The Sport Psychologist, 21*, 475–494.

Dale, G., & Wrisberg, G. (1996). The use of a performance profiling technique in a team setting: Getting the athletes and coach on the 'same page'. *The Sport Psychologist, 10*(3), 261–277.

Danish, S. J., Petitpas, A. J., & Hale, B. D. (1993). Life development intervention for athletes' life skills through sports. *The Counseling Psychologist, 21*, 352–385.

Davidson, R. J., & Schwartz, G. E. (1976). The psychobiology of relaxation and related states: A multi-process theory. In D.Mostofsky (Ed.), *Behavioral control and modification of physiological activity* (pp. 399–442). Englewood Cliffs, NJ: Prentice-Hall.

Davies, S., & West, J. D. (1991). A theoretical paradigm for performance enhancement: The multimodal approach. *The Sport Psychologist, 5*, 167–174.

Deci, E. L., & Ryan, R. M. (1985). *Intrinsic motivation and self-determination in human behavior.* New York: Plenum.

Deinstbier, R. A. (1989). Arousal and physiological toughness: Implications for mental and physical health. *Psychology Review, 96*, 84–100.

Durand-Bush, N., & Salmela, J. H. (2002). The development and maintenance of expert athletic performance: Perceptions of world and Olympic champions. *Journal of Applied Sport Psychology, 14*, 154–171.

Duval, T. S., & Silvia, P. J. (2001). *Self-awareness and causal attribution: A dual-systems theory.* Boston: Kluwer Academic.

Ellis, A. (1995). Changing Rational-Emotive Therapy (RET) to Rational Emotive Behavior Therapy (REBT). *Journal of Rational-Emotive and Cognitive-Behavior Therapy, 13*, 85–89.

Fazey, J. A., & Hardy, L. (1988). *The inverted-U hypothesis: A catastrophe for sport psychology.* British Association of Sports Sciences Monograph, No. 1. Leeds: The National Coaching Foundation.

Fifer, A., Henschen, K., Gould, D., & Ravizza, K. (2008). What works when working with athletes. *The Sport Psychologist, 22*, 356–377.

Fitts, P. M., & Posner, M. I. (1967). *Human performance.* Oxford: Brooks and Cole.

Friesen, A., & Orlick, T. (2010). A qualitative analysis of holistic sport psychology consultants' professional philosophies. *The Sport Psychologist, 24*, 227–244.

Gardner, F., & Moore, Z. (2005). *Clinical sport psychology.* Champaign, IL: Human Kinetics.

Ghaye, T. (2001). Reflective practice: *Faster, Higher, Stronger, 10*, 9–12.

Gould, D., Diffenbach, K., & Moffett, A. (2002). Psychological characteristics and their development in Olympic champions. *Journal of Applied Sport Psychology, 14*, 172–204.

Greenspan, M. J., & Feltz, D. L. (1989). Psychological interventions with athletes in competitive situations: A review. *The Sport Psychologist, 3*, 219–236.

Gucciardi, D. F., & Dimmock, J. A. (2008). Choking under pressure in sensorimotor skills: Conscious processes or depleted attentional resources? *Psychology of Sport and Exercise, 9*, 45–59

Haddad, K., & Tremayne, P. (2009). The effects of centering on the free-throw shooting performance of young athletes. *The Sport Psychologist, 23*, 118–136.

Hanafi, H., Hashim, H., & Ghosh, A. (2011). Comparison of long-term effects of two types of relaxation techniques on choice reaction time and selected psychophysiological variables following repeated sub-maximal intensity exercises in school level athletes. *International Journal of Applied Sports Sciences, 23*, 183–197.

Hanin, Y. L.(1997). Emotions and athletic performance: Individual zone of optimal functioning. *European Yearbook of Sport Psychology, 1*, 29–72.

Hashim, H. (2011). The effects of progressive muscle relaxation and autogenic relaxation on young soccer players' mood states. *Asian Journal of Sports Medicine, 2*, 99–105.

Hellstedt, J. C. (1995). Invisible players: A family systems model. In S. M. Murphy (Ed.), *Sport psychology interventions* (pp. 117–146). Champaign, IL: Human Kinetics.

Hill, K. L. (2001). *Frameworks for sports psychologists: Enhancing sport performance.* Champaign, IL: Human Kinetics.

Hillman, C. H., Apparies, R. J., Janelle, C. M., & Hatfield, B. D. (2000). An electrocortical comparison of executed and rejected shots in skilled marksmen. *Biological Psychology, 52*, 71–83.

Holt, N. L., & Strean, W. B. (2001). Reflecting on initiating sport psychology consultation: A self-narrative of neophyte practice. *The Sport Psychologist, 15*, 188–204.

Huang, C. A., & Lynch, J. (1994). *Thinking body, dancing mind.* New York: Bantam Books.

Hung, T, M., Lin, T. C., Lee, C. L., & Chen, L. C. (2008). Provision of sport psychology services to the Taiwan archery team for the 2004 Athens Olympic Games. *International Journal of Sport and Exercise Psychology, 6*, 308–318.

Jacobson, E. (1938). *Progressive relaxation.* Chicago, IL: University of Chicago Press.

Johns, C. (1994). Guided reflection: In A. Palmer, S. Burns, & C. Bulman (Eds.), *Reflective practice in nursing* (pp. 110–130). Oxford: Blackwell Science.

Johnson, U. (2000) Short-term psychological intervention: A study of long term injured competitive athletes. *Journal of Sport Rehabilitation, 9*, 207–218.

Jones, G. (1993). The role of performance profiling in cognitive behavioural interventions in sport. *The Sport Psychologist, 7*, 160–172.

Jones, M., Meijen, C., McCarthy, P. J., & Sheffield, D. (2009). A theory of challenge and threat states in athletes. *International Review of Sport and Exercise Psychology, 2*, 161–180.

Khanna, A., Paul, M., & Sandhu, J. S. (2007). Efficacy of two relaxation techniques in reducing pulse rate among highly stressed females. *Calicut Medical Journal, 5*(2), 2.

Kremer, J., & Moran, A. P. (2008). *Pure sport: Practical sport psychology.* London: Routledge.

Kudlackova, K., Eccles, D. W., & Dieffenbach, K. (2013). Use of relaxation skills in differentially skilled athletes. *Psychology of Sport and Exercise, 14*, 468–475.

Lam, W. K., Maxwell, J. P., & Masters, R. S. W. (2009). Analogy learning and the performance of motor skills under pressure. *Journal of Sport and Exercise Psychology, 31*, 337–357.

Lanning, W., & Hisanaga, B. (1983). A study of the relation between the reduction of competition anxiety and an increase in athletic performance. *International Journal of Sport Psychology, 14*, 219–227.

Lazarus, A. A. (1976). *Multimodal behavior therapy.* New York: Springer.

Lindsay, P., Breckon, J. D., Thomas, O., & Maynard, I. W. (2007). In pursuit of congruence: A personal reflection on methods and philosophy in applied practice. *The Sport Psychologist, 21*, 335–352.

Lowry, R., & Bond, K. (2010) Mapping the social world of high performing youth athletes: Ego network analysis of junior British archers. *Association for Applied Sport Psychology*, 27–30 October, Providence, RI.

MacNamara, A., Button, A., & Collins, D. (2010). The role of psychological characteristics in facilitating the pathway to elite performance. Part 1: Identifying mental skills and behaviors. *The Sport Psychologist, 24*, 52–73.

Martens, B., Vealey, R. S., Burton, D., Bump, L. A., & Smith, D. E. (1990). Development and validation of the Competitive State Anxiety Inventory-2 (CSAI-2). In R. Martens, R. S. Vealey, & D. Burton (Eds.), *Competitive anxiety in sport* (pp. 117–190). Champaign, IL: Human Kinetics.

Martindale, A., & Collins, D. (2005). Professional judgement and decision making: The role of intention for impact. *The Sport Psychologist, 19*, 303–317.

Martindale, A., & Collins, D. (2007). Enhancing the evaluation of effectiveness with professional judgment and decision making. *The Sport Psychologist, 21*, 458–474.

Martindale, A., & Collins, D. (2010). But why does what works work? A response to Fifer, Henschen, Gould, and Ravizza 2008. *The Sport Psychologist, 24*, 113–116.

Maslow, A. (1954). *Motivation and personality.* New York: Harper & Row.

Masters, R. S. W. (1992). Knowledge, nerves and know-how: The role of explicit versus implicit knowledge in the breakdown of a complex motor skill under pressure. *British Journal of Psychology, 83*, 343–358.

Masters, R. S. W., Polman, R. C. J. & Hammond, N. V. (1993). 'Reinvestment': A dimension of personality in skill breakdown under pressure. *Journal of Personality and Individual Differences, 14*, 655–666.

McCann, S. C., Jowdy, D. P., & Van Raalte, J. L. (2003). Assessment in sport and exercise psychology. In J. L.Van Raalte., & B. W. Brewer. (Eds.), *Exploring sport and exercise psychology* (2nd ed., pp. 291–305). Washington, DC: American Psychological Association.

Morris, T., & Thomas, P. (1995) Approaches to applied sport psychology. In T. Morris. & J. Summers (Eds.), *Sport psychology: Theory, applications and issues* (pp. 215–258). Chichester: John Wiley & Sons, Inc.

Murphy, S. M. (1995). (Ed.). *Sport psychology interventions*. Champaign, IL: Human Kinetics.

Nideffer, R. M. (1994). *Psyched to win*. Champaign, IL: Leisure Press.

O'Connor, E. A. Jr. (2004). Which questionnaire? Assessment practices of sport psychology consultants. *The Sport Psychologist, 18*, 464–468.

Orlick, T. (1986). *Psyching for sport: Mental training for athletes*. Champaign, IL: Human Kinetics.

Orlick, T., & Partington, J. (1998). Mental links to excellence. *The Sport Psychologist, 2*, 105–130.

Ost, L. (1988). Applied relaxation: Description of an effective coping technique. *Scandinavian Journal of Behavior Therapy, 17*, 83–96.

Palmer, S. (1995) Brief therapy: A rational-emotive behavior approach. Dr Stephen Palmer interviews Dr Albert Ellis. *The Rational-Emotive Behavior Therapist, 3*, 68–71.

Partington, J., & Orlick, T. (1991). An analysis of Olympic sport psychology consultants' best-ever consulting experiences. *The Sport Psychologist, 5*, 183–193.

Patrick, T., & Hrycaiko, D. (1998). Effects of a mental training package on an endurance performance. *The Sport Psychologist, 12*, 283–299.

Pawlow, L. A., & Jones, G. E. (2005). The impact of abbreviated progressive muscle relaxation on salivary cortisol and salivary immunoglobulin a (sigA). *Applied Psychophysiology and Biofeedback, 30*, 375–387.

Poczwardowski, A., Sherman, C. P., & Henschen, K. P. (1998). A sport psychology service delivery heuristic: Building on theory and practice. *The Sport Psychologist, 12*, 191–207.

Poczwardowski, A., Sherman, C. P., & Ravizza, K. (2004). Professional philosophy in the sport psychology service delivery: Building on theory and practice. *The Sport Psychologist, 18*, 445–463.

Ravizza, K. (2002). A philosophical construct: A framework for performance enhancement. *International Journal of Sport Psychology, 33*, 4–18.

Ravizza, K. (2010). Increasing awareness for sports performance. In J. M. Williams (Ed.), *Applied sport psychology: Personal growth to peak performance* (6th ed., pp. 189–200). New York: McGraw-Hill.

Robazza, C., & Bortoli, L. (1998). Mental preparation strategies of Olympic archers during competition: An exploratory investigation. *High Ability Studies, 9*, 219–235.

Roger, D., & Jamieson, J. (1988). Individual differences in delayed heart-rate recovery following stress: The role of extraversion, neuroticism and emotional control. *Journal of Personality and Individual Differences, 9*, 721–726.

Rogers, C. (1961). *On becoming a person: A therapist's view of psychotherapy*. London: Constable.

Rogerson, L. J., & Hrycaiko, D. W. (2002) Enhancing competitive performance of ice hockey goaltenders using centering and self-talk. *Journal of Applied Sport Psychology, 14*, 14–26.

Seligman, M. (1998). The gifted and the extraordinary. *APA monitor, 29*(2).

Simons, J. P., & Andersen, B. M. (1995). The development of consulting practice in applied sport psychology: Some personal perspectives. *The Sport Psychologist, 9*, 449–468.

Singer, R. N. (1988). Strategies and meta-strategies in learning and performing self-paced athletic skills. *The Sport Psychologist, 2*, 49–68.

Stratton, R. K., Cusimano, K., Hartman, C., & N. DeBoom, (2005). In J. Taylor & G. Wilson (Eds.), *Applying sport psychology: Four perspectives* (pp. 51–63). Champaign, IL: Human Kinetics.

Tacón, A. M., Caldera, Y. M., & Ronaghan, C. (2004). Mindfulness-based stress reduction in women with breast cancer. *Families, Systems & Health, 22*(2), 193–203.

Thomas, P. R., Murphy, S. M., & Hardy, L. (1999). Test of performance strategies: Development and preliminary validation of a comprehensive measure of athletes' psychological skills. *Journal of Sports Sciences, 17*, 697–711.

Tod, D. (2007). The long and winding road: Professional development in sport psychology. *The Sport Psychologist, 21*, 94–108.

Turner, M., & Barker, J. J. (2013). Examining the efficacy of Rational Emotive Behavior Therapy (REBT) on irrational beliefs and anxiety in elite youth cricketers. *Journal of Applied Sport Psychology, 25*, 131–147.

Turner, M. J., Jones, M. V., Sheffield, D., Slater, M. J., Barker, J. B., & Bell, J. J. (2013). Who thrives under pressure? Predicting the performance of elite academy cricketers using the cardiovascular indicators and challenge and threat states. *Journal of Sport and Exercise Psychology, 35*, 387–397.

Vealey, R. S., & Garner-Holman, M. (1998). Applied sport psychology: Measurement issues. In J. L.Duda (Ed.), *Advances in sport and exercise psychology measurement* (pp. 433–446). Morgantown, WV: Fitness Information Technology.

Voorhees, C. C., Murray, D., Welk, G., Birnbaum, A., Ribier, K. M., & Johnson, C. C., et al. (2005). The role of peer social network. Factors and physical activity in adolescent girls. *American Journal of Health Behavior, 29*, 183–190.

Wadey, R., & Hanton, S. (2008). Basic psychological skills usage and competitive anxiety responses: Perceived underlying mechanisms. *Research Quarterly for Exercise and Sport, 79*, 363–373.

Walker, B. (2010). The humanistic/person-centered theoretical model. In S. J. Hanrahan & M. B. Andersen (Eds.), *Routledge handbook of applied sport psychology: A comprehensive guide for students and practitioners* (pp. 123–130). New York: Routledge.

Watson II J. C., & Shannon, V. (2010). Individual and group observations: Purposes and processes. In S. J.Hanrahan, & M. B.Andersen (Eds.), *Routledge handbook of applied sport psychology: A comprehensive guide for students and practitioners* (pp.90 100). New York: Routledge.

Watson, D., Clark, L. A., & Tellegan, A. (1988). Development and validation of brief measures of positive and negative affect: The PANAS scales. *Journal of Personality and Social Psychology, 54*, 1063–1070.

Weinberg, R. S. (2010). Activation/arousal control. In S. J. Hanrahan, & M. B. Andersen (Eds.). *Routledge handbook of applied sport psychology: A comprehensive guide for students and practitioners* (pp. 471–480). New York: Routledge.

Weinberg, R. S., & Gould, D. (2011). *Foundations of sport and exercise psychology* (5th ed.). Champaign, IL: Human Kinetics.

Whelan, J. P., Meyers, A. W., & Donovan, C. (1995). Competitive recreational athletes: A multisystematic model. In S. M.Murphy (Ed.), *Sport psychology interventions* (pp. 71–116). Champaign, IL: Human Kinetics.

Wicklund, R. A. (1975). Objective self-awareness. In L.Berkowitz (Ed.), *Advances in experimental social psychology* (pp. 233–275). New York: Academic Press.

Williams, J. M. (2010). Relaxation and energizing techniques for regulation of arousal. In J. M.Williams (Ed.), *Applied sport psychology: Personal growth to peak performance* (6th ed., pp. 247–266). New York: McGraw-Hill.

Williams, J. M., & Krane, V. (2010). Psychological characteristics of peak performance. In J. M. Williams (Ed.), *Applied sport psychology: Personal growth to peak performance* (6th ed., pp. 169–188). New York: McGraw-Hill.

Woodcock, C., Richards, H., & Mugford, A. (2008). Quality counts: Critical features for neophyte professional development. *The Sport Psychologist, 22*, 491–506.

Young, M. E. (1992). *Counseling methods and techniques: An eclectic approach*. New York: Macmillan.

Part 2 Coaching Psychology

10 Impression Management in Professional Football: A Case Study from the Coach's Perspective

ANDREW MANLEY AND RICHARD THELWELL

LEARNING OBJECTIVES

AFTER READING THIS CHAPTER, YOU WILL BE ABLE TO:

1. Critically evaluate relevant theories and frameworks that attempt to explain how athletes form initial expectancies and impressions of coaches.
2. Summarize and critique existing, up-to-date evidence regarding the potential consequences of expectancies within the context of coach-athlete interactions.
3. Appreciate and justify why coaches should be mindful of the ways in which athletes create and update their impressions and expectancies.
4. Critically evaluate interventions designed to help coaches manage interactions with athletes and teams in order to optimize the interpersonal impressions and expectancies created.

AREAS TO CONSIDER WHEN READING THE CHAPTER:

1. What key sources of information can a sports coach harness for the purposes of creating favourable impressions and expectancies with members of his or her team?
2. In addition to initial interactions with athletes and teams, when else might sports coaches need to facilitate the creation of optimal expectancies?
3. Beyond coaches of athletes and teams, who else might benefit from the information provided within this chapter?

CLIENT AND BACKGROUND

The client is a 36-year-old male football coach who has recently been appointed as first-team coach for a professional team in the second tier of the English Football League. The client has completed all relevant coaching qualifications endorsed by professional organizations (e.g., the Football Association), and has over ten years' experience of working with high-performing Academy teams. He also has experience as a professional footballer, having represented three different clubs across the second and third tiers of the English Football League during his seven-year playing career as a central midfielder. The client's new appointment represents his first opportunity to fulfil the role of first-team coach with a high-performing senior squad. Having obtained the relevant contact details from a former colleague, the client approached the sport psychologist via email to enquire about the kind of support that could be offered to help him prepare for his new role. Following initial email correspondence, the client and practitioner met in person to discuss the client's psychological support needs and the ways in which they may be able to satisfy these needs within their work together. This initial meeting took place one month prior to the commencement of the client's new role as first-team coach.

During the first meeting (often referred to as an intake interview), the client mentioned that he felt '*very uncertain*' about how to approach his new role as first-team coach, which prompted him to independently seek out the services of a sport psychologist. Whilst the client expressed that he felt confident in his ability to fulfil the duties and roles of his new position to an excellent standard, he remained concerned about his ability to create the appropriate first impressions with his new players. This thought appeared to be particularly salient to the client, who stated that the previous first-team coach had a reportedly very good rapport with the players and support staff, many of whom have recently signed new contracts and will, therefore, remain with the club. The client was clearly aware of the importance of first impressions and expectancies to his own performance as well as that of his players, but he seemed unsure as to how he could manage the initial interactions with his squad for optimal and mutual benefit. Poignant questions which the client asked during the first meeting (e.g., 'How can I quickly get the trust and respect of the players?', 'How can I get the players and support staff to 'buy-in' to my coaching methods from the word 'go'?') reflected this primary concern. Furthermore, the client's appointment as new first-team coach for the professional club in question had attracted a significant degree of media attention, which had been perceived as an exciting yet novel and potentially threatening experience for the client. This was apparent in the first meeting by the client's apparently jovial yet repeated references to the prospect of losing his job and establishing a largely negative reputation should the team not perform well (e.g., 'I reckon the knives'll be out for me within the first few weeks if we don't get a couple of wins under our belt').

In digesting the key issues presented above, we can glean initial encouragement from the fact that the client decided to seek the services of a sport psychologist independently as opposed to being referred by a third party. For one reason or another, a client who is encouraged to speak with a sport psychologist by someone else may experience and display emotions which make the client appear indifferent, reluctant, or even hostile towards the practitioner. This can make it very difficult and time-consuming for the practitioner to forge an effective working relationship with the client (Speed, Andersen, & Simons, 2005). In contrast, the above information gave the practitioner confidence from the outset that the client was at best fully aware of the specific role a sport psychologist would be able to fulfil, and at worst was eager to obtain a more detailed understanding of the potential support the practitioner may be able to provide. With the client appearing relatively acknowledging, open, and curious about apparent links between psychology and his own coaching practice, an effective and trusting relationship between client and practitioner was relatively easy to establish and maintain. This was further facilitated by the formulation and agreement of appropriate expectations (e.g., frequency of contact, specific aims of the support programme) within this intake interview and the wider initial needs assessment (Wrisberg, Loberg, Simpson, Withycombe, & Reed, 2010).

The key issues highlighted above did much to indicate that the client saw himself as a performer in his own right, an idea that is becoming more prevalent within the coaching science literature (e.g., Cassidy, Jones, & Potrac, 2009; Giges, Petitpas, & Vernacchia, 2004; Potrac, Jones, & Armour, 2002; Thelwell, Weston, Greenlees, & Hutchings, 2008a; 2008b). Like elite athletes, high-performance coaches are expected to perform in highly pressurized environments, often whilst under extensive scrutiny from various stakeholders including colleagues, employers, and the media. Furthermore, a coach's performance is likely to be evaluated based on (and, in part, determine) the degree to which his/her athletes realize their own performance goals. By looking more closely at the key issues, we know that the client was fully aware of his need to manage the beliefs and expectancies of his players and staff (as well as the media) by 'creating the appropriate first impression'. Given that this seemed to be the primary concern for the client, it was this performance role that was agreed to be the principal focus for the support work and subsequent intervention. In professional environments, making a good first impression can be important for developing effective working relationships with players and staff, and even maintaining employment! Thus, it made sense to try and manage these impressions and expectancies as well as possible from the outset. The ideas and evidence presented in the remainder of this chapter will describe a holistic framework broadly relating to the management and exhibition of verbal and non-verbal cues during initial interpersonal interactions between particular stakeholders within a professional football club. This information will be complemented by an overview of some example processes and practical resources that a practitioner could apply in supporting clients similar to the coach described within this case study.

INITIAL NEEDS ASSESSMENT

As with any initial needs assessment, the practitioner considered carefully the specific context within which he was required to work with his client. One of the first contextual issues or constraints identified within this case study was the available timeframe for the completion of the initial needs assessment and intervention development/delivery. An approach similar to a 'crisis intervention' model of consultancy seemed appropriate. This was not because of the severity of the circumstances associated with the case, as crisis intervention models are typically employed to help individuals deal with the immediate effects of a major trauma such as the death of a teammate (e.g., Buchko, 2005). Rather, the 'crisis' here was a reference to the timeframe within which the practitioner was requested to intervene, as the client was due to commence his role as first-team coach within one month of the intake interview. Moreover, first impressions and initial expectancies, no matter how fleeting the interactions on which they are based, can have important immediate and long-lasting impacts on interpersonal relations (Jussim & Harber, 2005). As a result, the initial needs assessment and intervention development had to be completed in time for the client's first official day in his new role. Another key contextual issue worthy of consideration was the client's own expectations of consultancy. A short-term, intensive approach such as that reflected in 'crisis intervention' models seemed appealing given that sports coaches have been reported to be 'more willing to seek ... services if they had more frequent contact with the SPC [sport psychology consultant]' (Wrisberg et al., 2010, p. 489). The practitioner concluded that by aligning (where appropriate) his practical approach with the client's own preconceptions and preferences, the working relationship between client and practitioner would be optimized, which would have beneficial implications for any interventions employed.

The initial needs assessment phase (see summary in Table 10.1) consisted of three main objectives:

1. Educating the client about the frameworks, processes, and potential consequences inherent in impression management and expectancy formation;
2. Identifying aspects of the client's self-concept and the self-concepts of his players/staff that are likely to influence and direct impression management motives and behaviours;
3. Developing a series of cognitive-behavioural strategies and resources tailored to help the client facilitate the creation of favourable impressions and expectancies by players and staff.

One of the immediate aims of the intervention was to help the client develop an appreciation of the ways in which he could actively manage the first impression he creates in the presence of others. This concept is defined by Leary and Kowalski (1990) as 'Impression Management', but is also often referred to in the literature as 'Self Presentation' (Leary, 1992). Leary and Kowalski's two-component model of impression management provided a useful framework for the present case study. According to this model, the client's ability and willingness to manage the impression he creates is determined by the balance between two components: *impression motivation and impression construction*. Impression motivation represents the extent to which the client is motivated to control how others perceive him. Impression construction, on the other hand, refers to the kind of impression that the client is trying to convey to a particular audience. Within their model, Leary and Kowalski list five factors that are suggested to influence impression construction:

1. *Self-concept* (i.e., an individual's sense of the kind of person they are or aspire to be);
2. *Desired and undesired identity images* (i.e., qualities and behaviours that are either congruent or incongruent with the self-concept a person holds or wishes to exhibit);
3. *Role constraints* (i.e., an individual's efforts to display characteristics and attributes they believe to be associated with their particular role);
4. *Values and expectancies of the target audience* (i.e., a person's attempts to tailor publicly exhibited images to the values and preferences of significant others within their social or professional network);
5. *Current or potential social image* (i.e., how a person believes they are or will be perceived by others).

With this in mind, the practitioner reasoned that if the client:

i) Can develop a strong, positive sense of his own *self-concept* where he is clear about the kind of coach he is/wants to be;

ii) Can develop the ability to recognize and effectively exhibit ways of *promoting desired identity images whilst avoiding undesired identity images* associated with his *role as first-team coach* and;

iiii) Can feel confident in his ability to reflect the *values and expectancies of his players and staff*...

...then he will be well placed to create a favourable first impression and prompt the formation of positive expectancies by players and staff.

The activity outlined in Box 10.1 was used as a simple and accessible means of introducing the above concepts and processes of impression management to the client. By working through the various scenarios and orienting questions over the course of two one-hour sessions, the practitioner helped the client to identify and explain the thoughts, emotions, behaviours, and outcomes of positive (and negative) past experiences. In addition, the activity likely helped the client adopt a more empathic perspective, allowing him to obtain a greater awareness and understanding of behaviours which may

Table 10.1 *Schedule of activities completed by client and practitioner during the initial needs assessment phase.*

Session No.	Activity (i.e., "What")	Methods (i.e., "How")
1	Intake interview, contracting, and initial rapport building	Informal discussion with client to obtain background information and understand client's motives for seeking support. Client provided with information regarding the role of the practitioner and professional codes of ethics and conduct/standards of proficiency (e.g., BPS, HCPC) to which the practitioner is required to adhere. Mutually agreed terms of consultancy developed, which formed the basis of a formal contract (sent via email immediately following conclusion of first session). Duration: 90 minutes.
2 3	Signing of contract; initial needs assessment of client's impression motivation and understanding of related concepts	2 × 1-hour sessions, the first of which began with Q & A around the content of the formal contract before it was signed by the client and practitioner. The remainder of these sessions were devoted to assessing (and enhancing where necessary) the client's understanding of key concepts related to impression management (see activity outlined in Box 10.1).
4	Identification of client self-concept as a coach	The session began with verbal feedback/discussion based on issues/outcomes covered in Sessions 2 and 3. Remainder of the session consisted of the client completing the 'strengths categorization' activity. The practitioner provided the client with a photo and diagram of his resulting strengths profile (e.g., Figure 10.1) to prompt further consideration or reflection prior to the next session.
5	Identification of priority strengths, qualities and attributes for development	The client was asked to nominate 'green', 'amber', and 'red' strengths/qualities/attributes. The client was also asked to provide explanations/justifications for each nomination.
6 7	Planning a good first impression	2 × 1-hour sessions, which involved completion of the activities outlined in Box 10.2. Following the second of these sessions, the practitioner compiled an initial report based on the needs analysis activities conducted, and shared this with the client via email ahead of the next session.
8	Dissemination of initial needs assessment report	The practitioner outlined and explained the content of the initial needs assessment report, providing further clarification where necessary as to how it would be used to inform the development/delivery of the intervention.

(Sessions 1–8 span: 2 weeks)

Note: Unless stated, all sessions lasted for one hour and took place in a private environment where client comfort and confidentiality was assured.

be exhibited by both players and staff during his initial interactions with them (Lorimer & Jowett, 2009). After all, the client is unlikely to be the only person motivated to manage his initial impressions.

In conjunction with the activity outlined in Box 10.1, the practitioner decided to provide the client with an opportunity to clearly define the kind of coach they saw themselves to be, as adherence to a clear coaching philosophy has been reported as vital to effective coaching performance (Burton & Raedeke, 2008). Such an activity allowed the client and practitioner to obtain a detailed understanding

Activity box

BOX 10.1

IMPRESSION MANAGEMENT SCENARIOS

Starting at the top and working your way to the bottom, imagine that you are keen to create a favourable impression to others in each of the situations listed below (you can reflect on actual past experiences if that helps):

- i) Entering a room full of strangers
- ii) Going on a first date
- iii) Delivering a presentation or completing an oral exam
- iv) Performing in a sport where a crowd was watching
- v) Attending a job interview
- vi) Working with a colleague whom you have worked with for a long time
- vii) Being introduced to a new colleague for the first time
- viii) Coaching a player or team whom you have worked with for a long time
- ix) Coaching a player or team for the first time

For each situation, write down some brief notes in relation to the following questions, explaining the reasons behind your answers wherever possible:

- a) What would you be *thinking* in this situation? (For example, what sort of impression would you like to create? What kind of characteristics and qualities would you be keen to exhibit?)
- b) What would you be *feeling* in this situation? (For example, what kind of emotions would you be likely to experience? How confident would you be in your ability to create the desired impression?)

How would you *behave* in this situation? (For example, what kind of actions would you be likely to display or exhibit, either intentionally or unintentionally?

of the strength of the client's own self-concept, a factor likely to influence the client's capacity to create the appropriate first impression (Leary & Kowalski, 1990). There are myriad ways of describing and defining strengths and attributes in relation to the self-concept of great coaches, but despite the work of numerous researchers (e.g., Abraham, Collins, & Martindale, 2006; Becker, 2009), obtaining an exhaustive and universal definition has proved problematic. Given that the client appeared confident in his ability to fulfil the duties and roles of his new position to an excellent standard, the practitioner deemed it prudent to ask him to list and define all the positive qualities and attributes he believed he either possessed or would ideally like to develop over the course of his coaching career. The attributes generated were transferred to individual 'key strengths' cards and used as part of a 'strengths categorization' exercise. Through this activity, the client and practitioner worked collaboratively within a one-hour consultancy session to clearly identify the strengths, qualities, and attributes which:

1. Most closely aligned with the client's self-concept;
2. The client felt confident in exhibiting during initial interactions with players and staff;
3. The client was motivated to exhibit to players and staff, provided he could develop the ability to do so consistently.

Figure 10.1 depicts how the practitioner conducted the 'strengths categorization' exercise with the client. The circumplex grid displays four main quadrants within which the client was asked to

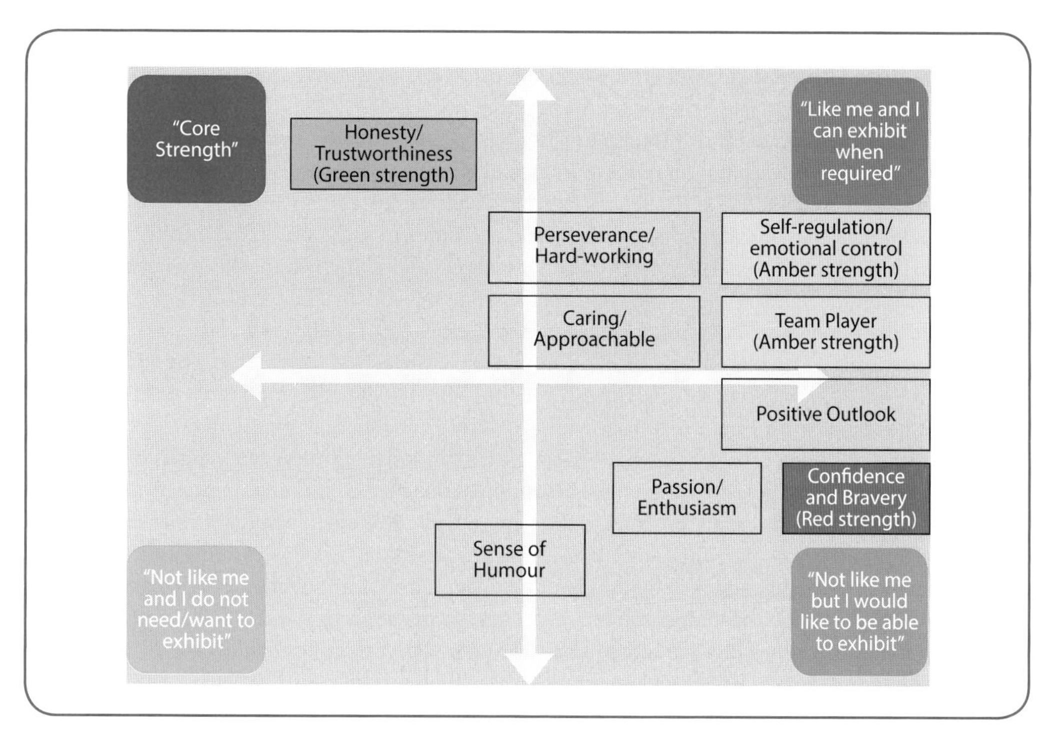

FIGURE 10.1 *Strengths, qualities, and attributes identified by client during 'strengths categorization' activity.*

place his previously-generated 'key strengths' cards depending on how he thought they should be categorized (notice that some cards overlap more than one quadrant, which reflects the client's indecisiveness during the task). Once all the cards had been categorized by the client, the practitioner asked him to identify a total of four strengths according to the extent to which he would be able to exhibit them confidently and consistently. These are colour-coded as follows:

'Green strength': Represents the one 'strength' the client felt most closely represented his 'core strength' (or self-concept) and should be easy to identify / exhibit during initial interpersonal interactions.
'Amber strengths': Represents the two 'strengths' which the client believed he would be able to display / exhibit often, but could do more to develop / enhance them further.
'Red strength': Represents a single strength which the client deemed important to display / exhibit during initial interactions, but at the time did not feel confident in his ability to do so clearly or consistently.

This task was developed based on principles adhered to within Positive Psychology (i.e., the study of human flourishing). In direct contrast to models of practice that emphasize pathology, disease, and the treatment of symptoms, Positive Psychology adopts a focus on health and growth through the pursuit of positive affect (e.g., Aspinwall & Tedeschi, 2010; Peterson & Seligman, 2004; Seligman, 2002). Instructing the client to choose a total of four qualities on which to focus on is not an arbitrary decision, but one that is informed by the Broaden-and-build Theory of Positive Emotions (Fredrickson, 2001). Recent studies have tested this theory with a range of participants including work-based teams (e.g., Losada & Heaphy, 2004), married couples, and individuals (e.g., Fredrickson & Losada, 2005). The findings of these studies provide empirical support for a positivity ratio of 3:1 (i.e., three positive emotions are sufficient to combat the deleterious effects of a single negative emotion). In the context of the present case study, the green and amber strengths listed above represent the three positive emotions identified (i.e., qualities which the client felt confident he could exhibit), while the red strength has the potential to be associated with more negative emotions (e.g., doubt, lack of confidence in the client's perceived ability to display this quality). This combination of positive thought and emotion in conjunction with a necessary experience of stress or adversity is believed to be central to the development of psychological resilience (Fletcher & Sarkar, 2013).

Having identified the key strengths, qualities, and attributes that the client was motivated and/or confident to exhibit during initial interactions with his players and staff, the initial needs assessment was almost complete. The final step was to raise the client's awareness of what he could do to not only create a favourable first impression, but also manage the expectancies that his players and staff might form as a consequence. This was achieved through the completion of the activity outlined in Box 10.2. Over the course of two one-hour sessions, this activity assisted the client in identifying influential sources of information that he could control and use to his advantage during initial interactions with players and staff.

The activity depicted in Box 10.2 was inspired by the contention that people (e.g., sports coaches) can use verbal and non-verbal cues to enhance the first impressions they create, and thus exert control over the expectancies which others (e.g., players, staff) generate about them. The practitioner deemed this to be a fundamental aspect that should be addressed within the initial needs assessment, since the initial impressions and expectancies created by the client could have important consequences regarding players' attention to the clients' coaching instruction, players' acquisition of specific skills, and the nature of the working relationships that are subsequently developed between the client, his staff and his athletes (e.g., Higgins & Bargh, 1987; McPherson, 1994; Manley, Greenlees, Smith, Batten, & Birch, 2014).

Activity box **BOX 10.2**

PLANNING A GOOD FIRST IMPRESSION

As well as identifying your own thoughts, feelings and behaviours that are likely to have an impact on the initial impressions you create, when planning a good first impression, it is useful to spend a little time considering what the expectancies of others (i.e., players, staff) are likely to be. To help with this, please take a moment to consider the following questions, making brief notes if deemed useful:

i) What do you think your *players* will look for when forming initial impressions and expectancies of you as the new first-team coach?
   - What attributes and qualities do you think players will expect or want you to display?
   - What sources of information (i.e., verbal and non-verbal) might players use to judge whether or not you possess certain attributes/ qualities?*
   - Which of these sources of information can be controlled and adapted by you?

ii) What do you think your *staff* will look for when forming initial impressions and expectancies of you as the new first-team coach?
   - What attributes and qualities do you think that staff will expect or want you to display?
   - What sources of information (i.e., verbal and non-verbal) might staff use to judge whether or not you possess certain attributes/ qualities?*
   - Which of these sources of information can be controlled and adapted by you?

*Manley et al.'s (2008) Information Sources Scale could be used to facilitate the identification of influential verbal and non-verbal cues.

FRAMEWORK AND INTERVENTION

A primarily cognitive-behavioural approach to consultancy was adopted within this case study. In other words, the strategies employed were intended to facilitate beneficial change through the identification and modification of the client's context-specific thought processes (i.e., cognition), emotional responses, and behaviours (Hemmings & Holder, 2009; Hill, 2001). The cognitive-behavioural approach was particularly apparent in the initial needs assessment activities outlined in Boxes 10.1 and 10.2. Within these activities, the client was asked to describe, challenge, and evaluate his thoughts, beliefs (i.e., cognitions), and emotions (i.e., affective responses) regarding his own self-concept as a coach and the coaching environment within which he was required to perform.

Following this phase of consultancy, the practitioner's work with the client focused on the development and delivery of intervention strategies designed to help the client modify his thoughts (e.g., understanding of the impression management process), feelings (e.g., confidence in managing impressions and expectancies), and behaviours (e.g., context-specific performance behaviours) to maximize the chances of him creating a favourable first impression within his new coaching role. Although the practitioner predominantly adhered to cognitive-behavioural principles and methods, complementary perspectives and approaches to consultancy (e.g., Positive

Description box **BOX 10.3**

WHAT ARE 'EXPECTANCIES', AND HOW DO ATHLETES FORM INITIAL IMPRESSIONS AND EXPECTANCIES OF COACHES?

Expectancies are defined as 'beliefs about a future state of affairs' (Olson, Roese, & Zanna, 1996, p. 211) that allow individuals to develop rules and make predictions about the world around them. Olson et al. (1996) proposed a model of expectancy processes stipulating that expectancies, or predictions about the outcome of a given event, are developed as a result of the perceiver's attention to, and encoding of, the stimuli available in the surrounding environment. The subsequent expectancies that are formed are proposed to have the potential to influence the cognitive, affective, and behavioural responses of the perceiver. In an effort to build on previous attempts to classify the sources of information utilized in person perception (e.g., Becker & Solomon, 2005; Cook, 1971; Olson et al., 1996), Manley et al. (2008) identified three main categories of informational cues that are used by athletes when creating first impressions and expectancies of a new coach:

a) *Dynamic behavioural cues* (i.e., episodic and controllable behaviours that are amenable to change over the course of short-term interactions – these include eye contact, tone of voice, facial expressions, and body language/posture).
b) *Static cues* (i.e., stable sources of information which are generally uncontrollable – examples include gender, race, ethnicity, and age).
c) *Third-party reports* (i.e., written or verbal information ordinarily conveyed to the athlete by a third party rather than directly by the coach – examples include information regarding a coach's qualifications, reputation, previous experience, or success).

Psychology; see 'strengths categorization' exercise outlined above) were drawn upon where appropriate, thus reflecting a somewhat integrative and pragmatic approach to consultancy.

The findings of this and subsequent experimental studies (e.g., Manley, Greenlees, Smith, & Thelwell, 2010; Manley et al., 2014; Thelwell, Weston, Greenlees, Page, & Manley, 2010) have indicated that, as broad categories, dynamic behavioural cues and third-party reports appear to have the greatest impact on athletes' first impressions and expectancies of coaches, with static cues having least influence.

The three activities outlined in the previous section represent a kind of profiling tool by which the needs of the client and the demands of the situational context were identified and assessed. From the data obtained during the initial needs assessment phase, a three-pronged intervention (see summary in Table 10.2) was implemented, which consisted of the following:

1. Selection of controllable sources of information which allowed for the demonstration of key strengths, qualities, and attributes aligned to the client's self-concept;
2. Enhancement and monitoring of the client's ability to confidently and consistently exhibit controllable cues in the presence of players and staff;
3. Evaluation of players' and coaching staffs' responses to the behaviours exhibited by the client during meetings and coaching sessions.

Table 10.2 *Schedule of activities covered by client and practitioner during the delivery, monitoring, and evaluation of the intervention.*

	Session No.	Activity (i.e., "What")	Methods (i.e., "How")
2 weeks	1	Selection of behaviours for impression management training programme	For the sake of clarity and to manage client expectations, intervention objectives were summarized at the start of this session. Practitioner worked with client to complete the PBeST (see Table 10.3) within the session. The PBeST was completed twice: once in relation to interactions with players, and again from the perspective of creating favourable impressions with coaching staff. The client was encouraged to canvass opinion from other coaching colleagues where possible to inform the selection of appropriate performance behaviours. Duration: 90 minutes.
2 weeks	2 3	Develop performance behaviour training and assessment protocols	2 × 1-hour sessions. Based on the outcomes and data obtained in the previous session, the PBeAT was finalized. In confirming the content of the PBeAT, the client and practitioner not only identified key performance behaviours which would be the focus of the impression management training programme, but also developed an appropriate tool for the monitoring and evaluation of the client's performance behaviour. The client and practitioner also discussed likely scenarios which formed the basis of authentic role-play training and assessment activities.
	4 5 6 7	Role-play scenarios for the training and assessment of key performance behaviours	4 × 1-hour sessions. Within each session, the client attempted to exhibit specific performance behaviours within a series of authentic role-play scenarios identified in the previous sessions. The client, practitioner, and coaching colleagues (where available) assessed the behaviour of the client using the PBeAT (see Table 10.4). Sessions were video recorded to assist the client's self-reflection outside the sessions. In addition, the client was encouraged to practise the execution of key performance behaviours (i.e., physical and mental rehearsal) on a daily basis (minimum 10 minutes), and directed to complete the PBeAT on each occasion. Completed PBeATs were reviewed at the start of each session with the practitioner.

Session No.	Activity (i.e., "What")	Methods (i.e., "How")
8	Preparation for initial meeting with new coaching team	Planning for initial consultation with client's new coaching team; discussion of SDT as the underpinning framework for conducting this meeting.
9	Initial consultation with client's new coaching team	Rationale for collaborative work between client and practitioner (i.e., manage initial impressions, expectancies, and working relationships with new players) explained to the coaching team. This also provided an ideal opportunity for exhibition or evaluation of the client's key performance behaviours in managing initial impressions of new colleagues. Location: club meeting room
10	First day in new post; initial training session with new players	Initial introductions; first opportunity for client to exhibit target performance behaviours in presence of entire team of players and staff. Evaluation by client and practitioner using PBeAT following this session. Duration: 2 hours. Location: club meeting room/training ground.
11 12 13 14 15	Video recording of training sessions and analysis of performance behaviours	5 × 2–3 hour training sessions. All sessions video recorded for purposes of observation and analysis of client's performance behaviour during interactions with players and staff. State space grids (see Figures 10.2 and 10.3) used in conjunction with PBeAT to monitor and evaluate performance behaviour. Between training sessions, client and practitioner met in person or engaged in discussion of data remotely (e.g., phone, email, Skype). Location: club meeting room/training ground.
16	Formal evaluation of intervention	Evaluation against key objectives (i.e., review of PBeAT/SSG data, repeat of strengths categorization task). Final report compiled and support formally concluded. Duration: 2 hours.

4 weeks (sessions 10–16)

Despite appearing highly motivated to develop his impression management skills, the client clearly indicated a lack of confidence in his ability to create appropriate first impressions with new players and coaching staff. This lack of confidence had implications for the design and implementation of the intervention, as high motivation coupled with low confidence can often result in increased levels of stress and anxiety (e.g., Bray, Martin, & Widmeyer, 2000; James & Collins, 1997), and in turn, reduced performance (in this case, the facilitation of undesired impressions and expectancies formed by players and staff). Consequently, it was crucial that any potential strategies considered ways in which the client's confidence in managing initial impressions could be enhanced.

Activities such as those conducted within the initial needs assessment (see Boxes 10.1 and 10.2) had been designed to lay the foundations for the development of client-tailored, context-specific strategies that could be used to enhance the client's impression management confidence and 'performance' during the initial meetings and interactions with his players and staff.

Given the needs of the client (i.e., confidence in coaching ability but a lack of confidence in creating favourable initial impressions) in conjunction with the limited time available to address these needs, a sole focus on developing, implementing, and evaluating strategies designed to support the creation of appropriate impressions and expectancies was warranted. In other words, the practitioner's role here was not to adapt or advise on the coaching methods and style deemed to be appropriate in the eyes of the client (that was the expertise of the client himself). Rather, the practitioner's role was to help identify and develop skills related to the control of verbal and non-verbal cues to optimize players' and staff members' initial impressions and expectancies of the client. Both the client and practitioner believed that the effective management of these impressions and expectancies would have a range of beneficial implications for the client (e.g., reduce the time required to forge effective intra-team relationships).

To achieve the first of the intervention objectives (i.e., selection of controllable sources of information for the demonstration of key strengths, qualities, and attributes aligned to the client's self-concept), the activity outlined in Box 10.2 was briefly revisited. With reference to the data initially provided by the client on completion of this activity, the client and practitioner worked together within a single 90-minute session to complete the Performance Behaviour Selection Tool; PBeST – see Table 10.3).

By assisting the client to complete the PBeST, the practitioner was able to facilitate the selection of (a) dynamic behaviours, (b) verbal cues, (c) aspects of physical appearance, and (d) positive reputation information that were not only under the direct control of the client, but also offered a suitable way of making previously identified strengths, qualities and attributes observable to the client's players and coaching staff during initial interactions with them. The left-hand column of the PBeST displays the potential sources of information that were identified by the client during this first session within the intervention programme. The PBeST enabled the client to systematically assess each of these sources of information in terms of the extent to which it was perceived to be under his control (middle column), and the degree to which he believed it would allow him to display each of the four strengths identified as integral to his coaching self-concept (right-hand column). This simple method of helping the client to rank each of these informational cues in terms of controllability and relevance to his self-concept as a coach was vital to building his confidence regarding his ability to create the desired first impression with his new colleagues. In addition, it helped both the practitioner and the client to identify the specific behaviours that the intervention should prioritize for development, implementation, and evaluation over the course of the weeks leading up to and following the official start of the client's new role.

As well as building the client's confidence in demonstrating specific strengths and attributes through the performance behaviours identified, another primary aim of the intervention was to maximize consistency/minimize variability in the client's exhibition of these behaviours. Researchers and educators of sport coaching (e.g., Becker, 2009; Potrac et al., 2002) have referred to the importance of consistent coaching behaviours when interacting with players in particular, arguing that if coaches are perceived to be (inappropriately) unpredictable in the behaviours they exhibit, players may deem the coach's words and actions to be both surprising and out of place. Such an interpretation can present a potent barrier to the coach acquiring the players' trust and respect. Of course, the coaching process is a complex one, as highlighted by recent qualitative and theoretical studies (e.g., Bowes & Jones, 2006; Jones, 2004), which point to the degree of flexibility necessary for successful coaches to respond effectively to highly dynamic situations and environments. However, evidence from observations of coach-athlete interactions within elite and youth sport contexts (e.g., D'Arripe-Longueville, Saury, Fournier, & Durand, 2001; Erickson, Côté, Hollenstein, & Deakin, 2011; Saury & Durand, 1998) suggests that part of a coach's success and effectiveness may be due to his or her ability to respond consistently to a wide variety of circumstances. When considering this evidence in conjunction with findings advocating that a perceiver's acceptance of information is more robust when it is perceived to

Table 10.3 *Performance Behaviour Selection Tool (PBeST) showing client's ratings.*

Performance behaviours identified as potentially influential (players and staff)	***Controllability rating*** *Use the scale below to indicate how controllable you perceive each of the performance behaviours to be:* *Not at all controllable 1 2 Somewhat controllable 3 4 Completely controllable 5*	***Strength exhibition rating*** *Use the scale below to indicate the extent to which you feel the performance behaviour reflects each of the four strengths:* *Strength not at all reflected 1 2 Strength somewhat reflected 3 4 Strength completely reflected 5*			
		Honesty/ trustworthiness	**Self-regulation/ emotional control**	**Team player**	**Confidence and bravery**
Direct eye contact when speaking	5	5	4	4	5
Direct eye contact when listening	5	5	4	5	4
Confident speech (no 'ums' and 'ahs'; well-projected)	5	4	5	4	5
Clear speech/instructions (language that is to the point and jargon-free; no ambiguity)	5	4	4	5	4
Controlled speech (not rushed)	5	5	5	4	5
Controlled/even breathing	4	3	5	3	4
Professional appearance – grooming (e.g., clean-shaven, brushed hair)	5	5	5	4	5
Professional appearance – clothing (e.g., clean, appropriate to context)	5	4	2	4	3
Lean, athletic physique	4	2	4	4	2
Reputation as a talented former player	3	2	4	5	4
Positive/confident/open body language (upright posture/not leaning, head up, hands by side/out of pockets/arms not folded)	5	5	5	5	5
Warm facial expressions (smiling when greeting others; no 'hard' frowning)	5	5	5	5	5
Firm handshake when greeting others	5	5	4	4	5
Acknowledging effort (e.g., thank you/applause at end of session; praise where appropriate)	5	4	4	5	3
Acknowledging conflict/lack of effort (e.g., instructional feedback; addressed privately)	5	5	4	5	5

be familiar (e.g., Park & Reder, 2003) or congruent with initial impressions and expectancies held by the perceiver (e.g., Harrison, 2001), the decision to focus on the development of consistent patterns of verbal and non-verbal behaviour was justified within the context of the present case study.

Once the PBeST had been completed, the client and practitioner used the responses and ratings as the basis for the development and implementation of an impression management training protocol. The final training protocol, which was developed over the course of two one-hour sessions, consisted of five sessions which were conducted over a ten-day period. By this stage of the intervention, the client's first official day in his new role was about two weeks away, meaning that the protocol needed to be short and concise (in keeping with the 'crisis intervention' approach). Although the protocol was context-specific and, therefore, unique in its design, some of the methods employed (e.g., use of role-play scenarios; video analysis of behaviours) were inspired by those described by Hackfort and Schlattmann (2005) for the purposes of training athletes in the self-presentation of emotions.

The impression management training protocol focused on developing the client's ability to demonstrate the performance behaviours which he deemed to be both highly controllable and highly reflective of his key strengths, qualities, and attributes (i.e., characteristics which the client saw as central to his self-concept as a coach, and thus important for him to exhibit clearly and consistently in his initial interactions with members of his new team). Table 10.4 displays the Performance Behaviour Assessment Tool (PBeAT), which was used to help the client practice and evaluate his demonstration of these performance behaviours. The left-hand column of the PBeAT includes the ten performance behaviours which, based on the ratings from the PBeST, were deemed to be most under the client's control and most reflective of the four key strengths he was motivated to exhibit in his observable behaviour within the coaching context. The middle and right-hand columns provide the client with the opportunity to rate his performance in demonstrating these behaviours according to consistency and confidence, respectively. Initially, the PBeAT was used by the practitioner and client to evaluate the extent to which the client was able to consistently and confidently execute the desired behaviours as part of a rehearsal or role-play activity (as indicated by the 'situation / context' provided in Table 10.4). For example, during certain sessions within the training protocol, the practitioner assumed the role of a player or member of coaching staff, and actively assessed the client's performance behaviours using the PBeAT. In conjunction with the practitioner's assessment, the client also used the PBeAT to self-assess his performance following such role-play activities, thus allowing for comparison and discussion between client and practitioner. In addition, rather than relying on the practitioner to assume the hypothetical role of player or staff member within every simulation / role-play scenario, the client was encouraged to draw on his existing coach networks and ask for the support of fellow professionals with whom he has built up a trusted relationship. Support and input of this nature from like-minded peers seemed to be invaluable in helping the client to obtain in-depth and authentic feedback during this preparatory phase of the intervention, and also appeared to be crucial in building the client's confidence in the lead-up to the first meeting with his new team of players and coaching staff.

Ultimately, the client was prompted to view this initial stage of the intervention in the same way as he would the planning phase for any coaching session – by planning and preparing himself as much as possible ahead of the first meeting, the more confident he was likely to be in his ability to perform as required.

Even when the first day of the client's new job finally arrived, he was encouraged to continue using the PBeAT on a regular basis as a means of monitoring his ability to consistently and confidently execute the desired performance behaviours. For example, several copies of the PBeAT were formatted as a booklet and given to the client for use as a kind of reflective diary, with one PBeAT being recommended for completion within 24 hours of each meeting or coaching session as a structured and formalized part of the intervention process (Cropley, Hanton, Miles, & Niven, 2010). In the initial days of his new role, these written self-reflections (in conjunction with discussions with the practitioner)

Table 10.4 *Performance Behaviour Assessment Tool (PBeAT) showing client's (and practitioner's) ratings of client performance*

Performance behaviours deemed controllable and reflective of key strengths, qualities and attributes (i.e., Honesty/trustworthiness; Self-regulation/emotional control; Team player; confidence and bravery)	***Consistency rating*** *Use the scale below to indicate how consistent you think you were in exhibiting each of the performance behaviours: Not at all consistent 1 2 Somewhat consistent 3 4 Completely consistent 5*	***Confidence rating*** *Use the scale below to indicate how confident you felt in exhibiting each of the performance behaviours: Not at all confident 1 2 Somewhat confident 3 4 Completely confident 5*
Direct eye contact when speaking	3 (3)	4 (4)
Direct eye contact when listening	4 (3)	4 (4)
Confident speech (i.e., no 'ums' and 'ahs'; well-projected)	3 (3)	5 (4)
Clear speech/instructions (i.e., language that is to the point and jargon-free; no ambiguity)	5 (4)	5 (5)
Controlled speech (i.e., not rushed)	4 (5)	5 (5)
Positive/confident/open body language (i.e., upright posture/not leaning, head up, hands by side/out of pockets/arms not folded)	4 (4)	4 (5)
Warm facial expressions (i.e., smiling when greeting others; no 'hard' frowning)	3 (3)	4 (3)
Firm handshake when greeting others	5 (5)	5 (5)
Acknowledging effort (e.g., thank you/applause at end of session; praise where appropriate)	4 (3)	5 (4)
Acknowledging conflict/lack of effort (e.g., instructional feedback; addressed privately)	3 (4)	3 (4)

Situation/Context: Role play of first meeting with players and staff in meeting room at Club Training Ground.

Note: ratings outside parentheses are self-report assessments of the client's performance; ratings in parentheses were provided by the practitioner based on client observation represented the main source of evidence of the client's performance. However, to adequately monitor and assess the client's performance behaviours and interactions with players and staff in a meaningful and reliable way, the practitioner requested the opportunity to attend and record video footage during specific coaching sessions so that interactive behaviours between the client and his players/staff could be subsequently observed and analysed. In facilitating these observation opportunities, it was imperative that the practitioner and client worked collaboratively in planning how the practitioner would be introduced to the client's new team to avoid the potential for confusion and/or conflict being expressed by players or coaching staff. Self-determination Theory (SDT) represents a specific theoretical framework that proved useful within this context. According to SDT (Deci & Ryan, 2000), we as humans are motivated to fulfil three fundamental needs:

Autonomy (i.e., the need to feel in control of one's decisions);

Relatedness (i.e., the need to feel related to others and the tasks in which they engage);

Competence (i.e., the need to feel competent and display the ability to learn and/or perform relevant tasks).

By fully briefing the coaching staff in the first instance of the limited and non-invasive nature of the practitioner's proposed involvement during specific coaching sessions, whilst also affording coaching staff the opportunity to consent/agree to the suggested action, the client was able to demonstrate that he:

1. Had a clear willingness to listen to any ideas or objections his fellow coaches may have had (i.e., reinforced staff's sense of *autonomy*);
2. Valued what was important to both the players and his coaching staff (i.e., reinforced staff's sense of *relatedness*), and;
3. Recognized the skills and qualities that his fellow coaches were in a position to offer (i.e., reinforced staff's sense of *competence*).

In addition, this initial consultation with the new coaching staff gave the client a perfect opportunity to clearly demonstrate all four key strengths (i.e., honesty/trustworthiness, self-regulation/emotional control, team player, confidence, and bravery) to some extent, and he reported it gave him a greater sense of control over proceedings within the initial meeting with his players and staff. A similar briefing with the players was also planned to take place soon after the client had begun his new role as head coach, but this did not materialize for logistical reasons. However, by briefing his coaching staff in the first instance, the client was able to ensure that players observed consistency and agreement in the verbal and non-verbal behaviours exhibited by both him and his support staff.

As outlined in Table 10.2, the client's interactions with players and staff were observed and assessed by recording video footage of five separate coaching sessions over a period of four weeks. In conjunction with self-report measures (i.e., regular completion of the PBeAT), direct observation of *in vivo* behaviour was intended to give both the client and practitioner more robust and objective information regarding the degree to which the client was improving his ability to display appropriate performance behaviours confidently and consistently. This was deemed to be particularly important in light of previous reports (e.g., Curtis, Smith, & Smoll, 1979) of large discrepancies between coaches' self-reported behaviour and that which was observed directly. Furthermore, when implementing strategies for the direct observation of client behaviour in the field, the practitioner needed to carefully account for the extent to which demand characteristics such as self-presentational bias (Nicols & Maner, 2008) might influence the thoughts, feelings, and behaviours of both the client and the people with whom the client was expected to interact. Thus, in line with the recommendations of Smith, Smoll, and Hunt (1977), the first coaching session that was filmed served as an opportunity for coaches and athletes to acclimatize to the presence of the practitioner and the video recording equipment in an effort to minimize reactivity. Footage from the remaining four coaching sessions was observed and evaluated using the State Space Grid (SSG) methodology (Hollenstein, 2007; Lewis, Lamey, & Douglas, 1999).

Rather than relying on unidirectional observations of coach-athlete interactions (e.g., coach behaviours towards the athlete only), SSGs offer a method for examining dynamic and interactive systems such as that represented by the reciprocal and interdependent relationship which exists between athletes and coaches (e.g., Poczwardowski, Barott, & Jowett, 2006). Until recently, SSGs had been used primarily in laboratory-based settings to examine developmental interactions such as those which occur between parents and their children (for a useful review, see Hollenstein, 2007). However, researchers have started to successfully apply the SSG methodology in order to reveal specific patterns of behaviour reflective of productive coach-athlete (Erickson et al., 2011) and peer interactions (Murphy-Mills, Bruner, Erickson, & Côté, 2011) within youth sport settings. Employed in accordance with the methods outlined by Erickson et al. (2011), the SSGs created within this case study allowed for the identification and interpretation of behaviours exhibited by the client, his players, and his fellow coaches during dyadic and small-group interactions. More specifically, the SSGs enabled the practitioner and client to assess these observable behaviours in terms of:

1. *Consistency* (i.e., were the behaviours exhibited consistently in all interactions, or did they vary across interactions?);
2. *Recurring patterns and transitions* (i.e., which behaviours were frequently observed in a specific and predictable sequence?).

The main drawback to using SSGs for the purposes of direct observation is the time required by the practitioner in familiarizing him/herself with the method and coding the data. For example, in the context of this case study, the practitioner needed to devote a significant amount of time to develop the relevant SSGs and learn how to record observations from video footage. In addition, despite the existence of freely available software which can be used for the purposes of analysing and displaying the coded data (e.g., GridWare is available from www.statespacegrids.org), the actual process of coding video footage and recording it within the SSG is often highly time-intensive, particularly for those who are relatively unfamiliar with the methodology (Erickson et al., 2011). Therefore, in order to make the time demands of this technique more manageable and practical within the context of this particular case study, 'pockets' or 'snap-shots' of footage (e.g., 20 × 1 minute clips of interpersonal interaction) were selected at regular intervals across each of the filmed coaching sessions. Ultimately, even though used sparingly, the SSG methodology was deemed to be a useful adjunct to the self-report data obtained from the client's own evaluations and reflections (i.e., completed PBeAT forms).

In order to implement the SSG methodology, the practitioner was first required to develop an appropriate 'grid' within which the 'state space' could be recorded. For example, in the case of dyadic interactions between the client and one of his players, the SSG consisted of the client's performance behaviours which had been previously agreed as the focus of the intervention (displayed on the x-axis in Figure 10.2), and relevant player behaviours which might be observed at any one time during the coach-player interactions (displayed on the y-axis in Figure 10.2). Note that because the behaviours included in the SSG need to be mutually exclusive, performance behaviours were combined to form more holistic categories of observable non-verbal behaviour (i.e., *congruent* or *incongruent* with target performance behaviours). The two axes combine to form co-ordinates for the behaviours displayed by both client and player during a specific interaction, with additional grids developed for examination of coach-staff interactions and coach-team interactions.

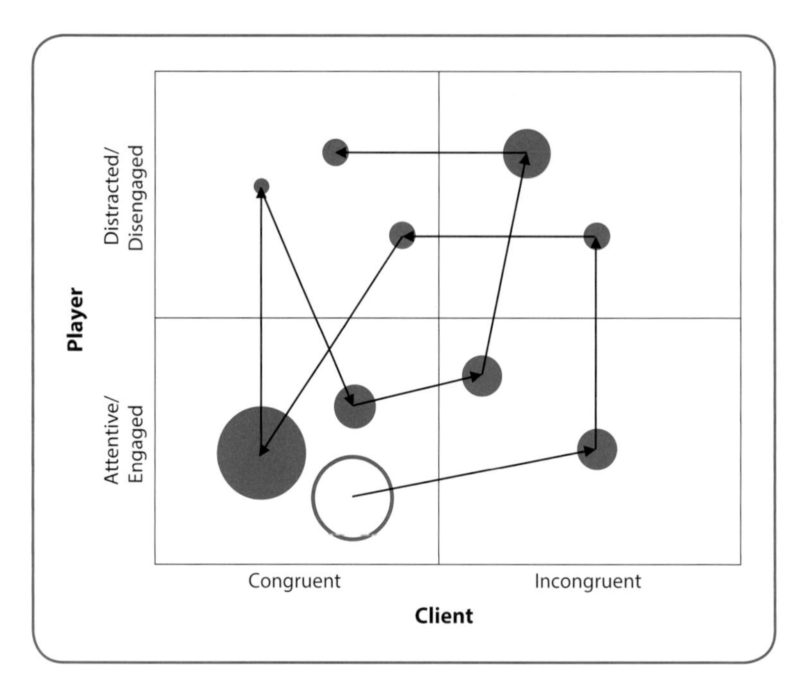

FIGURE 10.2 *State space grid depicting behaviours exhibited by the client and one of his players during the course of a 1-minute dyadic interaction within the second observed coaching session.*

Note: observed behaviour is in the 'congruent-attentive/engaged' quadrant 61% of the time, and in the 'incongruent-distracted/disengaged' quadrant 17% of the time.

Figure 10.2 provides an example of how an SSG was used to depict the behaviours and responses displayed within a short interaction (around 1 minute) between the client and one of his players during the second coaching session. Not only does the SSG outline the trajectory of the interaction over time (starting at the hollow circle), it also displays the length of time each dyadic interaction was observed (represented by the size of the circle in each cell). For example, the data displayed in Figure 10.2 shows that the coach displayed non-verbal behaviour which was highly congruent with target performance behaviours (e.g., direct eye contact, upright stance, warm facial expressions) for the majority of the interaction with the player's response to this fluctuating between highly attentive/engaged (e.g., direct eye contact, nodding) and distracted/disengaged (e.g., looking away from the coach, fidgeting).

The SSG method of observation allowed for the visual and statistical analysis of interactive patterns of behaviour displayed between the client and members of his team within real time (e.g., identifying the impact of the consistent execution of positive performance behaviours on behaviours exhibited by players and/or coaches). Just like data obtained through the use of the PBeAT, the practitioner used data generated by the SSGs to challenge the client's self-reported behaviour, to monitor progress, and adapt the focus of the intervention where deemed necessary. The data provided by the SSGs also allowed the practitioner to identify aspects of the client's behaviour which appeared to have been exhibited consistently during specific interactions, which in turn, was intended to help enhance the client's confidence in his ability to perform these target behaviours. Furthermore, by acknowledging the response of players and staff to these performance behaviours, the data appeared to facilitate the identification of specific patterns of behaviour which were most conducive to effective interaction with certain team members at particular times. For

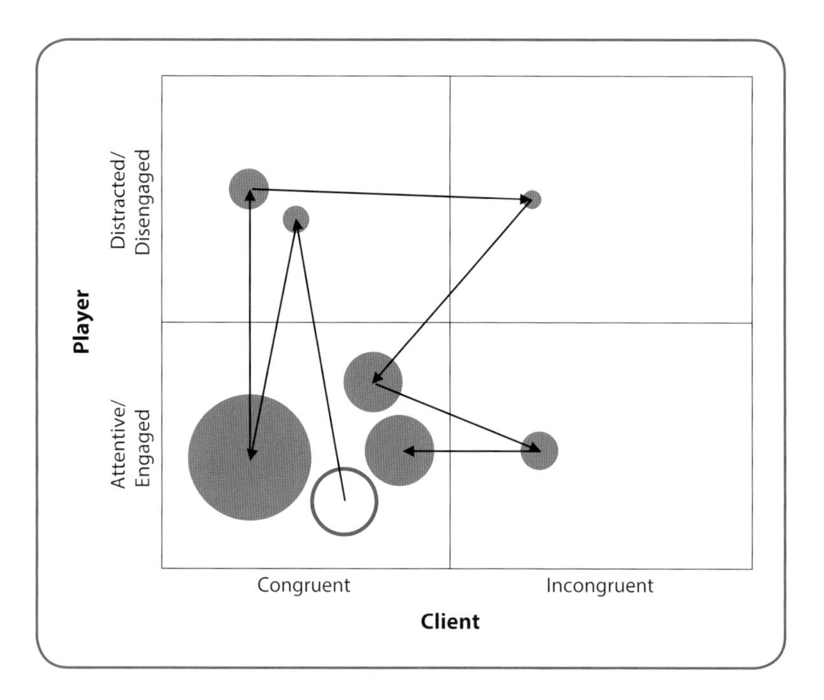

FIGURE 10.3 *State space grid depicting behaviours exhibited by the client and one of his players during the course of a 1-minute dyadic interaction within the fifth observed coaching session.*

Note: observed behaviour is in the 'congruent-attentive/engaged' quadrant 72% of the time, and in the 'incongruent-distracted/disengaged' quadrant just 4% of the time.

example, following discussion of the SSG data presented in Figure 10.2, the client made a concerted and conscious effort to display congruent performance behaviours more consistently towards his players in subsequent coaching sessions. The SSG displayed in Figure 10.3 indicates that by the fifth coaching session, the client's efforts had paid dividend. Increased levels of congruent performance behaviours were not only exhibited by the client, but they were accompanied by higher levels of attentive / engaged player behaviour than had been witnessed in the second coaching session (i.e., Figure 10.2).

In addition to data obtained from completed PBeATs and SSGs, the final evaluation session (see Table 10.2) incorporated a repeat of the 'strengths categorization' activity as a means of assessing the extent to which the client's self-concept may have been influenced during the course of the intervention. Although drastic shifts in the client's reported strengths were not observed (unlikely within such a short timeframe), the activity provided a basis for open discussion between the client and practitioner regarding the extent to which the intervention had helped to reinforce or increase the client's confidence in his ability to showcase some of the key strengths, qualities, and attributes identified as important to his identity as a coach. Following the final evaluation session, a report was compiled for and sent to the client consisting of an overview of the agreed aims of the intervention, and a summary of the progression observed during the course of the intervention in relation to each of these aims. Data from the measurement tools employed (e.g., 'strengths categorization' activity; PBeAT; SSGs) were used to evidence progression in terms of the client's confidence and consistency in exhibiting appropriate coaching behaviours. The final session with the client allowed for a discussion of the anticipated conclusions of the report and the formulation of an action plan based on these conclusions. Although not taken up by the client, suggested actions included the potential to extend the practitioner's involvement to some degree (e.g., fortnightly or monthly observation and/or review). The practitioner had made the client aware of the anticipated timeframe for the intervention at key stages of the consultancy process (e.g., during the intake interview, at the end of the initial needs assessment phase), However, from an ethical standpoint, it was important that the practitioner made arrangements for the fulfilment of any additional needs that client may have had before formally concluding the consultancy relationship (Moore, 2003).

REFLECTIONS

This chapter has provided an overview of an intervention that the authors believe was effective in addressing the specific needs of the client described at the outset. However, the intervention and approach described does not represent the only way in which a practitioner could have supported the client successfully. The authors acknowledge that there are a range of other avenues which would have been worthy of exploration in attempts to support and optimize the performance of the client (see Box 10.4 for an alternative approach which could have been employed).

Description box **BOX 10.4**

MANAGING EXPECTATIONS BY DEVELOPING OF A CODE OF CONDUCT

Research from teaching (e.g., Fink & Siedentop, 1989) has shown that during the first weeks with a new cohort of students, expert teachers focus on developing the boundaries of acceptable behaviour. During this time, teachers actively reward students for working effectively within these boundaries, while punishing actions that go beyond the realms of agreed and acceptable behaviour. Taking such an approach has been shown to be effective for creating a clear and shared set of expectations, such that punishment for exhibiting behaviour which veers outside these accepted norms is seen as not only fair, but also predictable. Furthermore, developing such an environment has been shown to have a positive impact on learning. Interestingly, there are examples where similar approaches to expectation management have been adopted in professional sport. We need look no further than Sky ProCycling Team's 'Rider's Rules' (http://roadcyclinguk.com/tech/tech-features/interview-life-on-the-road-with-team-sky-bus-driver-chris-slark.html), a list of 17 core principles, generated primarily by the riders themselves, which emphasize the importance of characteristics such as 'honesty', 'respect', and 'communication'. Sir Clive Woodward also employed a similar method while he was coach of the World Cup-winning England Rugby Union team. In his autobiography (Woodward, 2004), Sir Clive talks of allowing his players to develop a 'players' handbook' that included expectations of what it meant to be an England player. In fact, Woodward identifies how the players actually began to police themselves, a strategy that would fit well with Deci and Ryan's (2000) Self-determination Theory.

Activity box

BOX 10.5

CODES OF CONDUCT

Some orienting questions to consider:

1. What other professionally-recognized 'codes of conduct' or 'standards of proficiency' exist which are applied within the context of sport?
2. How might existing 'codes/standards' be of use to coaches as a guiding framework for their own practice and performance?
3. Is it possible/necessary to develop a generic 'code of conduct' to which all coaches should adhere, or would 'codes/standards' need to be specific to the sport, person and/or environment?

Other feasible and appropriate interventions might have consisted of supporting the client to acquire and implement a range of emotion-regulation strategies in conjunction with their new role as first-team coach. For example, recent studies (e.g., Chan & Mallett, 2011; Tamminen & Crocker, 2013) have outlined the need for coaches to possess high levels of emotional intelligence (i.e., 'the ability to monitor one's own and others' feelings and emotions, to discriminate among them and use this information to guide one's thinking and actions' (Salovey & Mayer, 1990, p. 189) in order to successfully manage interpersonal relationships within high-performance environments. Therefore, the label of the football coach or manager has a much broader meaning if we think about 'management' in terms of the awareness and regulation of emotions in relation to the self and others. This view of coaching performance may have had a number of important implications for the client described in the present case study, especially in relation to his cognitive, behavioural, and emotional regulation prior to, during, and following initial coaching sessions with players and staff. Therefore, an intervention designed to focus more heavily on these aspects of performance as opposed to the creation of desired impressions and expectancies could quite easily have been justified. Additionally, although media attention was alluded to within the key issues section at the start of the chapter, the intervention described within this case study did not focus directly on the types of impressions and expectancies that the client might have created via the exhibition of specific behaviours in his interactions with the media. However, an intervention similar to that outlined in this chapter but with a focus on media-friendly performance behaviours could be useful, especially as a means of helping the client deal with this particular source of organizational stress (Fletcher & Wagstaff, 2009).The practitioner employed a variety of methods for obtaining and evaluating client-related data over the course of the support programme, from intake interview through to final report. However, a range of other tools and resources, some of which were considered for use during the course of the intervention, may have been appropriate for inclusion and implementation. For instance, in the context of the current case study, it seemed that the client had a high level of *impression motivation* (Leary & Kowalski, 1990), which from an intervention adherence perspective was considered to be good news by the practitioner. However, as a means of triangulating some of the self-report data provided by the client during the intake interview, a validated psychometric measure such as the Impression Motivation in Sport Questionnaire-Team (IMSQ-T; Payne, Hudson, Akehurst, & Ntoumanis, 2013) could have been employed.

The IMSQ-T is a 15-item questionnaire that assesses impression motivation across four main dimensions or objectives:

1. *Self-development* (i.e., awareness that the reactions of others to self-presentations may impact on a person's self-concept or view of themselves);
2. *Social identity development* (i.e., establishment of a positive impression);
3. *Avoidance of negative outcomes* (i.e., motivation to avoid creating an undesirable impressions that may lead to adverse consequences);
4. *Avoidance of damaging impressions* (i.e., self-presentational efforts to avoid harmful evaluative reactions from significant others).

Although developed specifically for athletes competing in team sports, parallels with Leary and Kowalski's (1990) model mean that the IMSQ-T could have been adapted and used to more accurately quantify the strength of the client's impression motivation. The data obtained may have allowed the practitioner to feel more confident in the subsequent content of the intervention. There are other validated questionnaires which could have been utilized for similar triangulation purposes. For example, the Self-Presentation in Sport Questionnaire (SPSQ; Wilson & Eklund, 1998), which was developed specifically for use with athletes in competitive sporting contexts, could have been slightly revised and applied as a way of assessing the client's self-presentational concerns more objectively. It could be argued that the incorporation of such quantitative measures alongside some of the interview techniques would have offered an efficient balance to the initial needs assessment phase.

To complement the use of SSGs as a means of evaluating players' responses to the client during coaching sessions, the practitioner considered asking the coaching team to collect quantitative data regarding players' perceptions of the client's coaching competence. A validated measure such as the Coaching Competence Questionnaire (Myers, Feltz, Maier, Wolfe, & Reckase, 2006; Myers, Wolfe, Maier, Feltz, & Reckase, 2006) could have been used for this purpose, and would have given the practitioner access to potentially useful insights regarding players' evaluations of the coach across four main competency areas:

1. *Character-building competence* (i.e., the client's ability to promote virtues such as fair-play);
2. *Game strategy competence* (i.e., the client's ability to make effective decisions regarding tactics and strategy during matches);
3. *Motivation competence* (i.e., the client's ability to motivate his players);
4. *Technique competence* (i.e., the client's ability to teach his players technical skills).

However, the practitioner decided against the use of such a measure, deeming it unlikely that 'paperwork' of this nature would have been perceived by the players as familiar, appealing, or worthwhile within the context of coaching sessions (e.g., Beckmann & Kellmann, 2003).

The previous chapter has outlined some of the methods by which the client's progression and thus the success of the intervention were monitored and evaluated. For example, a combination of client self-report (i.e., completed PBeAT worksheets in the form of a reflective diary) and objective observation of client behaviour (i.e., SSGs) was monitored throughout the course of the first few weeks of the intervention (i.e., immediately before and after the client started in his new role as head coach). Given the needs of this particular client and the decision to implement a 'crisis intervention' approach, the practitioner, on reflection, deemed it wise to try and provide feedback or data to demonstrate at the earliest opportunity that progression was being made. A process-driven manner of monitoring and evaluation was adopted, and seemed to be useful in the initial sessions of the intervention. This involved the setting of process goals for the client to complete each day (e.g., rehearsing performance behaviours as part of role-play exercises to evaluate performance using the PBeAT). Such goals were highly controllable to the client and were used as a means of building the client's confidence in the intervention, even in the very early education and acquisition stages (Burton & Raedeke, 2008). In addition, by providing some tangible and immediate feedback on progress made by the client in completing his initial goals, the practitioner optimized the client's adherence to the proposed intervention. However, the practitioner was always mindful of the potential for some of the monitoring tasks, especially the self-reflective PBeAT diary, to be perceived as fairly monotonous and repetitive after just a few completions. With this in mind, the practitioner ensured that the client's perceptions and experiences of both the intervention strategies and the interpersonal support provided by the practitioner were assessed at key intervals (i.e., a frequency of every two weeks seemed appropriate given the short-term nature of the proposed intervention). Moreover, the practitioner ensured that for every task or activity given to the client, there was always a related action point for the practitioner to complete themselves. On reflection, the practitioner believes that this approach impacted positively on the client's adherence to the intervention, as he quickly realized that he was never being asked to do something that the practitioner was not willing to do himself.

A specific tool that was not used but could have been beneficial on a number of levels is Partington and Orlick's (1987) Consultant Evaluation Form (CEF). Since its development, the CEF has been used by a large number of sport psychology consultants to obtain evaluative feedback with regard to the client's satisfaction and perceived effectiveness of the support they have received (Hemmings & Holder, 2009). In respect of the present case study, the CEF would have not only allowed the practitioner to obtain feedback necessary for the successful and appropriate adaptation of service delivery, but it would also have provided an opportunity to reinforce the importance of self-evaluation and reflection, something which the practitioner had asked the client to engage in as a key aspect of the intervention. Thus, within the context of this particular case study, the CEF could have been used as an effective means of not only monitoring and evaluating the practitioner's performance, but also building rapport with the client by actively demonstrating similarities between them.

ACKNOWLEDGEMENTS

The authors would like to thank Andy Abraham, Gareth Morgan, and Julian North for their thoughts and contributions that informed certain aspects of this case study.

FURTHER READING

Gladwell, M. (2005). *Blink: The power of thinking without thinking.* London: Penguin. This stimulating and accessible book considers the positive and negative consequences of initial impressions, particularly those that are formed either, subconsciously, under time pressure, or with very little information available. The relevance of this text to the current case study is probably best summed up in the words of the author, Malcolm Gladwell, himself: 'Our first impressions are generated by our experiences and our environment, which means that we can change our first impressions by changing the experiences that comprise those impressions ...Taking rapid cognition seriously – acknowledging the incredible power, for good and ill, that first impressions play in our lives – requires that we take active steps to manage and control those impressions' (p. 97).

Horn, T. S. (2008). *Advances in sport psychology* (3rd ed.). Champaign, IL; Human Kinetics. This edited text covers a range of contemporary issues in sport psychology, many of which have some relevance to the case study presented within this chapter. However, the chapter entitled 'Coaching effectiveness in the sports domain' (cited in the main reference list) will probably resonate most with those who found the above case study particularly interesting.

Horn, T. S., Lox, C., & Labrador, F. (2010). The self-fulfilling prophecy theory: When coaches' expectations become reality. In J. M. Williams (Ed.), *Applied sport psychology: Personal growth to peak performance* (6th ed.), 81–105. Boston: McGraw-Hill. Another contribution from Thelma Horn that is well worth a read. This chapter explores the phenomenon known commonly as the 'self-fulfilling prophecy', sometimes referred to as the 'Pygmalion Effect'. This particular brand of expectancy effect is considered within the context of sports coaching. The research evidence and recommendations provided are likely to be of use to coaches who are motivated to avoid making errors in judgement that may have important consequences for the development of their athletes.

Knapp, M. L., & Hall, J. A. (2002). *Nonverbal communication in human interaction* (5th ed.). New York: Wadsworth/ Thomson Learning. An excellent text for anyone interested in understanding more about the ways in which non-verbal behaviour can be exhibited and harnessed during interpersonal interactions within a wide range of contexts.

Jowett, S., & Lavallee, D. (2007). *Social psychology in sport*. Champaign, IL: Human Kinetics. Another edited text that provides a useful overview of how elements commonly referred to within the study of social psychology manifest themselves within sport settings. Specifically, Iain Greenlees' chapter on 'Impression formation in sport' is of particular relevance to many of the issues and concepts presented within the present case study.

REFERENCES

Abraham, A., Collins, D., & Martindale, R. (2006). The coaching schematic: Validation through expert coach consensus. *Journal of Sports Sciences*, *24*(6), 549–564.

Aspinwall, L. G., & Tedeschi, R. G. (2010). The value of positive psychology for health psychology: Progress and pitfalls in examining the relation of positive phenomena to health. *Annals of Behavioral Medicine*, *39*(1), 4–15.

Becker, A. J. (2009). It's not what they do, it's how they do it: Athlete experiences of great coaching. *International Journal of Sports Science and Coaching*, *4*, 93–119.

Becker, A. J., & Solomon, G. B. (2005). Expectancy information and coach effectiveness in intercollegiate basketball. The Sport Psychologist, *19*, 251–266.

Beckmann, J., & Kellmann, M. (2003). Procedures and principles of sport psychological assessment. *The Sport Psychologist*, *17*, 338–350.

Bowes, I., & Jones, R. L. (2006). Working at the edge of chaos: Understanding coaching as a complex, interpersonal system. *The Sport Psychologist*, *20*, 235–245.

Bray, S. R., Martin, K. A., & Widmeyer, W. N. (2000). The relationship between evaluative concerns and sport competition state anxiety among youth skiers. *Journal of Sports Sciences*, *18*, 353–361.

Buchko, K. J. (2005). Team consultation following an athlete's suicide: A crisis intervention model. *The Sport Psychologist*, *19*, 288–302.

Burton, D., & Raedeke, T. D. (2008). *Sport psychology for coaches*. Champaign, IL: Human Kinetics.

Cassidy, T., Jones, R., & Potrac, P. (2009). *Understanding sports coaching: Social, cultural, and pedagogical foundations of coaching practice* (2nd ed.). Abingdon: Routledge.

Chan, J. T., & Mallett, C. J. (2011). The value of emotional intelligence for high performance coaching. *International Journal of Sports Science & Coaching*, *6*(3), 315–328.

Cook, M. (1971). *Interpersonal perception*. Harmondsworth: Penguin Education.

Cropley, B., Hanton, S., Miles, A., & Niven, A. (2010). Exploring the relationship between effective and reflective practice in applied sport psychology. *The Sport Psychologist*, *24*(4), 521–541.

Curtis, B., Smith, R. E., & Smoll, F. L. (1979). Scrutinizing the skipper: A study of leadership behaviors in the dugout. *Journal of Applied Psychology, 64*, 391–400.
D'Arripe-Longueville, F., Saury, J., Fournier, J. F., & Durand, M. (2001). Coach-athlete interaction during elite archery competitions: An application of methodological frameworks used in ergonomics research to sport psychology. *Journal of Applied Sport Psychology, 13*, 275–299.
Deci, E. L., & Ryan, R. M. (2000). The 'what' and 'why' of goal pursuits: Human needs and the self determination of behaviour. *Psychological Inquiry, 11*(4), 227–268.
Erickson, K., Côté, J., Hollenstein, T., & Deakin, J. (2011) Examining coach-athlete interactions using state space grids: An observational analysis in competitive youth sport. *Psychology of Sport and Exercise, 12*, 645–654.
Fink, J., & Siedentop, D. (1989). The development of routines, rules, and expectations at the start of the school year. *Journal of Teaching in Physical Education, 8*(3), 198–212.
Fletcher, D., & Sarkar, M. (2013). Psychological resilience: A review and critique of definitions, concepts, and theory. *European Psychologist, 18*(1), 12–23.
Fletcher, D., & Wagstaff, C. R. D. (2009). Organizational psychology in elite sport: Its emergence, application and future. *Psychology of Sport and Exercise, 10*, 427–434.
Fredrickson, B. L. (2001). The role of positive emotions in positive psychology: The broaden-and-build theory of positive emotions. *The American Psychologist, 56*(3), 218–225.
Fredrickson, B. L., & Losada, M. F. (2005). Positive affect and the complex dynamics of human flourishing. *The American Psychologist, 60*(7), 678–686.
Giges, B., Petitpas, A. J., & Vernacchia, R. A. (2004). Helping coaches meet their own needs: Challenges for the sport psychology consultant. *The Sport Psychologist, 18*, 430–444.
Hackfort, D., & Schlattmann, A. (2005). Self-presentation with a special emphasis on emotion-presentation: Concept, methods, and intervention strategies. In D. Hackfort, J. L. Duda, & R. Lidor (Eds.), *Handbook of research in applied sport and exercise psychology: International perspectives*. Morgantown, WV: Fitness Information Technology.
Harrison, L. (2001). Understanding the influence of stereotypes: Implications for the African American in sport and physical activity. *Quest, 53*, 97–114.
Hemmings, B., & Holder, T. (2009). *Applied sport psychology: A case-based approach*. Oxford: Wiley-Blackwell.
Higgins, E. T., & Bargh, J. A. (1987). Social cognition and social perception. *Annual Review of Psychology, 38*, 369–425.
Hill, K. L. (2001). *Frameworks for sport psychologists: Enhancing sport performance.* Champaign, IL: Human Kinetics.
Hollenstein, T. (2007). State space grids: Analyzing dynamics across development. *International Journal of Behavioural Development, 31*, 384–396.
James, B., & Collins, D. (1997). Self presentational sources of competitive stress during performance. *Journal of Sport & Exercise Psychology, 19*, 17–35.
Jones, R. L. (2004). Coaches' interactions. In R. Jones, K. Armour, & P. Potrac (Eds.), *Sports coaching cultures: From practice to theory* (pp. 135–149). London: Routledge.
Jussim, L., & Harber, K. D. (2005). Teacher expectations and self-fulfilling prophecies: Knowns and unknowns, resolved and unresolved controversies. *Personality and Social Psychology Review, 9*, 131–155.
Leary, M. R. (1992). Self-presentational processes in exercise and sport. *Journal of Sport & Exercise Psychology, 14*, 339–351.
Leary, M. R., & Kowalski, R. M. (1990). Impression management: A literature review and two-component model. *Psychological Bulletin, 107*(1), 34–47.
Lewis, M. D., Lamey, A. V., & Douglas, L. (1999). A new dynamic systems method for the analysis of early socioemotional development. *Developmental Science, 2*, 457–475.
Lorimer, R., & Jowett, S. (2009). Empathic accuracy, meta-perspective, and satisfaction in the coach-athlete relationship. *Journal of Applied Sport Psychology, 21*(2), 201–212.
Losada, M., & Heaphy, E. (2004). The role of positivity and connectivity in the performance of business teams. *American Behavioral Scientist, 47*(6), 740–765.
Manley, A. J., Greenlees, I., Graydon, J., Thelwell, R., Filby, W. C. D., & Smith, M. J. (2008). Athletes' perceived use of information sources when forming initial impressions and expectancies of a coach: An explorative study. *The Sport Psychologist, 22*(1), 73–89.

Manley, A. J., Greenlees, I. A., Smith, M. J., Batten, J., & Birch, P. D. J. (2014). The influence of coach reputation on the behavioral responses of male soccer players. *Scandinavian Journal of Medicine and Science in Sports, 24,* e111–e120.

Manley, A. J., Greenlees, I. A.,Thelwell, R. C., & Smith, M. J. (2010). Athletes' use of reputation and gender information when forming initial expectancies of coaches. *International Journal of Sport Science & Coaching, 5,* 517–532.

McPherson, S. L. (1994). The development of sports expertise: Mapping the tactical domain. *Quest, 46,* 223–240.

Moore, Z. E. (2003). Ethical dilemmas in sport psychology: Discussion and recommendations for practice. *Professional Psychology: Research and Practice, 34*(6), 601–610.

Murphy-Mills, J., Bruner, M. W., Erickson, K., & Côté, J. (2011). The utility of the state space grid method for studying peer interactions in youth sport. *Journal of Applied Sport Psychology, 23*(2), 159–174.

Myers, N. D., Feltz, D. L., Maier, K. S., Wolfe, E. W., & Reckase, M. D. (2006). Athletes' evaluations of their head coach's coaching competency. Research Quarterly for Exercise and Sport, *77,* 111–121.

Myers, N. D., Wolfe, E. W., Maier, K. S., Feltz, D. L., & Reckase, M. D. (2006). Extending validity evidence for multidimensional measures of coaching competency. *Research Quarterly for Exercise and Sport, 77,* 451–463.

Nicols, A. L., & Maner, J. K. (2008). The good–subject effect: Investigating participant demand characteristics. *The Journal of General Psychology, 135*(2), 151–166.

Olson, J. M., Roese, N. J., & Zanna, M. P. (1996). Expectancies. In E. T. Higgins & A. W. Kruglanski (Eds.), *Social psychology: Handbook of basic principles* (pp. 211–238). New York: The Guildford Press.

Park, H., & Reder, L. M. (2003). Moses illusion. In R. F. Pohl (Ed.), *Cognitive illusions* (pp. 275–292). New York: Psychology Press.

Partington, J., & Orlick, T. (1987). The sport psychology consultant evaluation form. *TheSport Psychologist, 1,* 309–317.

Payne, S. M., Hudson, J., Akehurst, S., & Ntoumanis, N. (2013). Development and initial validation of the Impression Motivation in Sport Questionnaire-Team. *Journal of Sport & Exercise Psychology, 35,* 281–298.

Peterson, C., & Seligman, M. E. P. (2004). *Character strengths and virtues: A handbook and classification.* New York: Oxford University Press.

Poczwardowski, A., Barott, J. E., & Jowett, S. (2006). Diversifying approaches to research on athlete-coach relationships. *Psychology of Sport and Exercise, 7,* 125–142.

Potrac, P., Jones, R., & Armour, K. (2002). It's all about getting respect: The coachingbehaviors of an expert English soccer coach. *Sport Education and Society, 7*(2), 183–202.

Salovey, P., & Mayer, J. D. (1990). Emotional intelligence. *Imagination, Cognition and Personality, 9,* 185–211.

Saury, J., & Durand, M. (1998). Practical knowledge in expert coaches: On-site study of coaching in sailing. *Research Quarterly for Exercise and Sport, 69,* 254–266.

Seligman, M. (2002). *Authentic happiness.* New York: Free Press.

Smith, R. E., Smoll, F. L., & Hunt, E. B. (1977). A system for the behavioural assessment of athletic coaches. *Research Quarterly, 48,* 401–407.

Speed, H. D., Anderson, M. B., & Simons, J. (2005). The selling or telling of sport psychology: Presenting services to coaches. In M. B. Anderson (Ed.), *Sport psychology in practice* (pp. 1–16). Champaign, IL: Human Kinetics.

Tamminen, K. A., & Crocker, P. R. E. (2013). 'I control my own emotions for the sake of the team': Emotional self-regulation and interpersonal emotion regulation among female high-performance curlers. *Psychology of Sport and Exercise, 14,* 737–747.

Thelwell, R. C., Weston, N. J. V., Greenlees, I. A., & Hutchings, N. V. (2008a). A qualitative exploration of psychological-skills use in coaches. *The Sport Psychologist, 22,* 38–53.

Thelwell, R. C., Weston, N. J. V., Greenlees, I. A., & Hutchings, N. V. (2008b). Stressors in elite sport: A coach perspective. *Journal of Sports Sciences, 26*(9), 905–918.

Thelwell, R. C., Weston, N. J. V., Greenlees, I. A., Page, J. L., & Manley, A. J. (2010). Examining the impact of physical appearance on impressions of coaching competence. *International Journal of Sport Psychology, 41,* 277–292.

Wilson, P., & Eklund, R. C. (1998). The relationship between competitive anxiety and self-presentational concerns. *Journal of Sport & Exercise Psychology, 20,* 81–97.

Woodward, C. (2004). *Winning.* London: Hodder and Stoughton.

Wrisberg, C. A., Loberg, L. A., Simpson, D., Withycombe, J. L., & Reed, A. (2010). An exploratory investigation of NCAA Division-I coaches' support of Sport Psychology Consultants and willingness to seek mental training services. *The Sport Psychologist, 24,* 489–503.

11 Managing Coach Stress in Teams Through Enhanced Role Clarity and Communication

NEIL WESTON

LEARNING OBJECTIVES

AFTER READING THIS CHAPTER YOU SHOULD BE ABLE TO:

1. Identify the variety of factors that can contribute to coach stress.
2. Critically evaluate the literature examining coach stress and coping.
3. Critically consider the theoretical underpinning of role clarity, acceptance, and performance.
4. Understand the characteristics and impact of a cancerous player in addition to how coaches might deal with such players.

AREAS TO CONSIDER WHEN READING THE CHAPTER:

1. What factors do you think influence the strain professional coaches experience?
2. How might you help a coach who is suffering from strain?
3. How might you improve the clarity and performance of roles within a sport team?
4. How might you deal with a negative, disruptive player within a sport team?

CLIENT AND BACKGROUND

The hypothetical client, Steve (40 years old) is a professional head coach with a Championship rugby union club in the second tier of English rugby. Prior to coaching, Steve had a very successful playing career spanning 15 years which resulted in 34 caps for his country, three English Premiership titles, and one European Cup victory. He played scrum half with his home club for the entirety of his career. For the final five years of Steve's professional playing career, he fulfilled the role of captain for his team and very much enjoyed the responsibility of leading the team both on and off the field of play. Steve retired from playing the sport five years ago and moved directly into a coaching role as academy director at the same club, a role that he relished. The club gave him a significant amount of autonomy in terms of structuring the development of the young talented players at the club. This autonomy extended to player and coach recruitment to the academy team in addition to implementing a player development programme that incorporated physical, technical, tactical, and psychological aspects of performance. Having successfully completed the Rugby Football Union (RFU) Level 3 coaching qualification towards the latter part of his playing career, Steve enrolled on and successfully completed the RFU Level 4 qualification alongside his academy job. Steve acknowledged the very useful knowledge and skills he learnt as part of the course, in addition to the opportunity to discuss elite coaching practices with leading coaches in his field.

Steve coached the academy team for three years achieving a good deal of success (one semi-final and two runner ups in the U18 Academy league) and he helped to develop several players that progressed into the senior team. This success resulted in Steve being promoted to assistant coach with the senior team but unfortunately the team was relegated in his first season in the role resulting in the head coach being dismissed. Steve was offered, and accepted, the head coach position with the goal to gain promotion back to the Premiership competition in his first season.

In his role as academy director, Steve had employed a sport psychologist to work with his players in order to address their mental frailties and to strengthen their mental toughness. It was through this association that Steve contacted the same sport psychologist mid-way through his first season as head coach to work with him to facilitate a more productive state of mind. In particular, Steve was concerned with the building pressure associated with the head coach position and the strong desire from his Board of Directors, the fans and local media to achieve promotion. This pressure was creating a great deal of strain which he acknowledged manifested itself in the form of some negative behaviour and communication which he felt helpless to resolve. In appreciating there were problems that he did not have the necessary skills to address, Steve contacted the sport psychologist in the hope that they could help 'sort his mind out' and modify his behaviour to help cope with the strain he was experiencing.

At the time of initial contact with the sport psychologist, the team was placed fifth in the league and nine points adrift of the team in first position, and two points behind the team placed fourth with ten games remaining. In the English Championship competition, teams are allocated four points for a win with a bonus point awarded to either team that scored four tries or more. The losing team would also receive a bonus point should they be within seven points of their opponent at the end of the match.

Only one team was eligible for promotion to the Premiership and this would be determined by the four top-placed teams at the end of the season competing in play-off matches (semi-final and then final), the winner of which would be promoted. While it was essential for his team to be in the top four places at the end of the season and thus enter the play-offs, being in either the first or second position would result in being able to choose whether they played home or away in the first leg of the play-off tie. Steve indicated that it would be advantageous to have such a choice and indeed research in soccer has revealed teams playing at home second in a tie had a higher probability to win the tie overall (Page & Page, 2007). Hence the opportunity to choose the order of the location of the play-off matches would be likely to increase the team's chances of winning the play-off matches. In appreciating the benefit of being placed first or second at the end of the season, Steve had thus set this goal as a precursor to the overall goal of achieving promotion to the Premiership.

A review of the team's performance up to this point revealed the team had won seven of their 12 matches with a draw and four losses. However closer inspection revealed the team's frailty at home having lost three matches and drawn one out of the six played. This form is contrary to the substantial body of literature which suggests there is a home advantage in sport generally (Carron, Loughhead, & Bray, 2005; Pollard & Pollard, 2005) and in rugby (Luis, Carreras, & Wilbur, 2012; Morton, 2006; Thomas, Reeves, & Bell, 2008). Allied to this form, Steve revealed that he felt under greater pressure to win home matches, yet the performances were just not happening for the team. This desire and drive to be more assertive and offensive at home aligns with research findings with ice-hockey coaches where the coaches adopted significantly more assertive tactics at home rather than away (Dennis & Carron, 1999). Steve remarked that the pressure he was experiencing was manifesting itself in him displaying maladaptive communication and behaviour that was compromising his ability to motivate, instil confidence, and generally facilitate the team's performance. The experience of stress is not an unusual occurrence in professional sports coaches (Frey, 2007; Olusoga, Butt, Maynard, & Hays, 2010; Thelwell, Weston, Greenlees, & Hutchings, 2008) and indeed has been shown to result in a number of negative cognitive, emotional, and behavioural outcomes (Fletcher & Scott, 2010; Hudson, Davison, & Robinson, 2013). The next section will describe the initial assessment conducted by the sport psychologist in addition to presenting the key findings to emerge from that analysis.

Definition box

BOX 11.1

The *stress experience* is a dynamic, complex, and multidimensional psychological process (Fletcher & Scott, 2010) which at times has led to contradictory definitions of key terms. Recent literature in this area has tended to align with the definitions provided by Fletcher, Hanton, and Mellalieu (2006, p. 329) which are provided below:

Stressors: 'Environmental demands encountered by an individual'.

Stress: 'An ongoing process that involves individuals transacting with their environments, making appraisals of the situations they find themselves in, and endeavouring to cope with any issues that may arise'.

Strain: 'An individual's negative psychological, physical and behavioural responses to stressors'.

INITIAL NEEDS ASSESSMENT

Beckmann and Kellmann (2003) assert that a systematic rigorous psychological assessment is an essential starting point in the development of a client-centred intervention. Through such assessments psychologists can increase their understanding of their client in terms of their personality, preferences, ambitions, perceived weaknesses, and strengths. The process can also be enlightening for the client as they clarify their current situation and become more self-aware of themselves and their sport. Overall the aim of an initial assessment is to resolve any difficulties and improve the client's ability to function effectively and thus better enjoy what they are doing. With this in mind, a multimodal initial assessment approach was adopted with Steve to delve more deeply into the underlying reasons for his stress experience.

In initiating such consultations, it is important to be mindful of the need to develop a good working alliance with the client (Andersen, 2000) which Sharp and Hodge (2011) define as a 'collaborative relationship between the therapist and his or her client, where both individuals are working together to address whatever concerns are impeding the growth and functioning of the client' (p. 362). In order to facilitate such relationships, it is incumbent on the sport psychologist to demonstrate a number of key characteristics and qualities. These include being honest, personable, trustworthy, approachable, perceptive, positive, a good communicator and knowledgeable of the sport and sport psychology (Anderson, Miles, Robinson, & Mahoney, 2004; Cropley, Miles, Hanton, & Niven, 2007). Furthermore, it is important that practitioners adhere to appropriate professional body codes of ethical and professional conduct (in this case the British Psychological Society (2009); Code of Ethics and Conduct and the Health and Care Professions Council (HCPC; 2012a) Standards for Conduct, Performance and Ethics).

More specifically, with coach client populations it is important to understand the breadth of roles that coaches typically have to fulfil including being 'performers, educators, administrators, leaders, planners, motivators, negotiators, managers, and listeners' (Giges, Petitpas, & Vernacchia, 2004, p. 431). Giges et al. further highlight that in their experience, coaches need to feel a sense of meaning, purpose, security, autonomy, competence, relatedness, and general worthiness and thus practitioners must be aware of such needs. Sharp and Hodge (2013) add that for a successful coach-psychologist working relationship to flourish, the psychologist must possess good knowledge of the sport, sport psychology, and of their client in addition to being trustworthy, flexible, and willing to understand and embed themselves within the team's culture. Fortunately in this situation the working alliance and associated understanding of the client had had time to develop as the psychologist had worked with Steve in his previous time as academy director. That being said, a specific assessment of Steve's current position as head coach was needed to ascertain the key issues being experienced from which a targeted intervention could be developed to improve the situation.

Hence following an initial telephone conversation where Steve outlined his general concerns and need for help, I asked him to complete a modified version of the Coaching Issues Survey (CIS; Kelley & Baghurst, 2009) and return it to me in advance of our first face-to-face meeting five days later. The CIS provides a measure for identifying sport coaching issues that might lead to strain. Coaches are asked to complete 30 items on a five-point Likert scale (ranging from 1 = no stress to 5 = extreme stress) as to the degree to which each issue (item) causes them, or produces, stress in their coaching situation. For the purposes of the present consultation, and being mindful of the current definitions of stress and strain, the Likert scale was amended to replace the term 'stress' with 'strain' and provide Steve with the definition of strain (see Box 11.1) so that he was clear as to the criteria he was rating the various items against. Furthermore, an additional five-point Likert frequency scale was employed (1 = never to 5 = always) where the coach was asked to rate how often they had experienced each issue in the competitive match environment (Fletcher & Scott, 2010). Three items were removed from the questionnaire (other sports or campus events conflicting with my team's use of facilities, not successfully fulfilling my responsibilities outside my coaching duties (teaching), and inadequate travel budget for contests with highly competitive teams) as they were deemed inappropriate to the coach's current situation. A summary of the coach's responses is available in Table 11.1.

Table 11.1 *Summary of the coach's modified CIS responses in order of those that contribute to the highest to lowest strain.*

Item	*Intensity*	*Frequency*
Not reaching my coaching goals.	5	4
Players' inconsistency in executing the fundamental skills or game plan.	5	3
Not having enough time to devote to my coaching responsibilities.	4	4
Placing pressure on myself to win.	4	4
Handling defeat.	4	3
Negative media coverage.	4	3
Making decisions which are not popular with my players.	4	3
The expectation to win a contest in which my team is predicted to win by a close score.	4	2
Personality conflicts with my players.	4	2
Injury to one of my starters or top players.	4	2
Inconsistent judgement calls during a contest.	4	2
Momentum turning against my team in a contest.	4	2
Budget limitations hampering recruiting.	4	2
Being unable to recruit the key personnel that my team needs to be successful.	4	2
Substantial number of hours spent working in a day.	3	4
The expectation to win a contest in which my team is predicted to win by a large margin.	3	3
My career as a coach interfering with family and/or social life.	3	3
The expectation to win a contest in which my team and the opposing team are evenly matched.	3	3
The expectation to win a contest in which my team is predicted to lose by a close score.	3	2
Not having enough time for recruiting.	3	2
Not successfully fulfilling my responsibilities outside my coaching duties (e.g., speaking engagements, committee assignments, etc.).	3	2
Being concerned that my players might not return to the club for the next season.	3	2
Not having time for myself.	2	4
Understanding my athletes' emotional responses and motivations.	2	2
Not knowing the criteria by which I will be judged.	1	1
Not being able to hire adequate assistant coaches and support staff.	1	1
Being a source of help to my athletes.	1	1

As can be seen by the data in Table 11.1, a number of issues were causing Steve concern and leading to strain including the worry about not reaching his goals, an inconsistency in the players' ability to execute the fundamental skills or game plan, not having sufficient time to devote to his coaching responsibilities, placing pressure on himself to win, struggling to handle defeat and the worry associated with negative media coverage and making decisions that were not popular with his players.

In advance of our face-to-face meeting, I asked Steve if I could observe him at the next competitive home league match which was due to be held in three days' time to help inform our subsequent discussion. His team was playing the third-placed team and lost by a narrow margin. Similar to many professional coaches, Steve wore a microphone and headset to communicate with coaching staff during matches and so I requested, and was granted, access to those communications in real time so that I could hear how he communicated with his staff and players during the match. In order to maintain anonymity in my role at this stage in the consultation and to not unduly influence anyone's behaviour, I observed from a distance in the main stand.

Tkachuk, Leslie-Toogood, and Martin (2003) state that behavioural assessment 'involves the collection and analysis of information and data in order to identify and describe target behaviours, identify possible causes of the behaviours, select appropriate treatment strategies to modify the behaviours, and evaluate treatment outcomes' (p. 104). Behavioural observation can provide practitioners with valuable real-time information on what, when, and how a performer acts but importantly does not allow them to infer an individual's reasons for, or cognitive reaction to, a lived experience. In the present case, my approach to observation was informed by elements of Bloom, Crumpton, and Anderson's (1999) Revised Coaching Behaviour Recording Form. Particular categories used to record my observations included: technical instruction (encompassing technical instruction and correction), tactical instruction (information communicated to inform tactical decision-making), hustles (communication to activate or energize athletes), praise (positive, supportive comments towards athletes), verbal scolds (negative critical communications), non-verbal behaviours (gestures that either were supportive or critical e.g., pat on the back, smile, scowls, gesticulations etc.), humour (verbal content designed to relax and lighten the mood), and others (any other behaviours not included in the other categories). These categories were constructed into an observation checklist where a quantitative tally could be recorded for each area, in addition to any relevant qualitative comments.

The findings from the competitive observation and responses to the modified CIS were further explored during a face-to-face meeting with Steve held five days after the telephone conversation and two days following the observed match at a location convenient to him and away from the club environment. The initial focus of this first meeting followed the guidelines of Giges et al. (2004) to assist Steve in becoming more aware as to how his mind influenced his coaching. A sample of the typical questions asked can be found in the Giges et al. paper. However the items included areas such as his reasons and ambitions for coaching, sources of enjoyment in coaching, coaching priorities, what facilitated and hindered his coach effectiveness, what upsets him as a coach and the subsequent impact this had on his emotions and behaviour, and what he'd like to change to improve his situation. This line of questioning initially allowed me to re-calibrate my understanding of Steve's ambitions and goals following a period of not seeing him since his academy director role. Latterly in consultation with Steve's modified CIS findings and my observations during the competitive match, we started to tease out some of the issues he was experiencing and how they were impacting upon his mind and behaviour. In particular, we focused on the stressors he was experiencing and their impact in addition to examining the coping strategies that he had attempted to employ to help deal with stressful situations.

In summary, the findings of these discussions revealed a coach under significant pressure at certain times in his work and that his experience of strain was triggered by identifiable stimuli. Discussions with Steve uncovered a broad range of stressors impacting upon his stress experience which aligns with the findings of other professional sport coach research (Olusoga, Butt, Hays, & Maynard, 2009; Thelwell, et al., 2008). These stressors varied in their intensity and frequency but all contributed to him feeling significantly under pressure to deliver on the team's goals. Recurrent but maybe less significant stressors included managing board expectations and issues, administrative responsibilities, the coaching and medical staff, and player injuries, as well as the significant time required to fulfil daily tasks and the associated guilt of not spending more time with family and friends. Whilst these stressors were less influential in their ongoing intensity, the volume of stressors experienced by Steve led him to feel under constant pressure to the meet the multiple demands of his role.

More prominent factors contributing to Steve's stress experience, and the area in which our immediate focus would be directed, related to player and coach-specific performance stressors. Player related-stressors were highlighted by Steve as probably the most significant and consistent issue that led him to feel frustrated, disappointed, and generally anxious. More specifically, Steve indicated that certain players' inability to consistently execute the core skills was compromising the team's performances and win/loss ratio. My observations of Steve during the competitive match reinforced his frustration in this area with some clear verbal (e.g., a focus on errors during the match and at half time, swearing) and non-verbal communications (e.g., various negative gestures from the touchline). Furthermore, his perceived inability to get the most out of those players and facilitate more consistent performances was weighing on his mind. Our conversation led us to ascertain what positive strategies could be implemented to try to improve this area of performance. In doing so we focused on controllable strategies that would enable the players to feel a greater clarity of what was expected of them and a greater ownership to fulfil those expectations. This led me to conclude that a focus on developing role clarity, acceptance, and performance in addition to Steve's competence at communicating player roles could help the team to function more effectively and thus alleviate some of the strain being experienced by Steve.

A significant secondary issue that had been festering for some time in the performance environment was the disruptive influence of one of the older more experienced players who, in Steve's opinion, had been slowly manipulating player opinions against him. This player had been at the club for a couple of years and was an experienced international player (albeit now retired from international rugby) who as a consequence of their status in the game garnered the attention of the younger players in the squad. Having initially been brought in as an important player to help lead and develop the relatively inexperienced player group, this player had not been delivering the necessary performances to warrant a starting place and as such had taken offence to 'warming the bench'. This player's dissatisfaction at their current substitute role had been voiced directly to Steve and whilst feeling that he had explained his decisions to the player, Steve indicated that the player was not in agreement with his assessment of the situation and thus was creating problems in training and off the field of play. This manipulative and disruptive behaviour was having a negative impact on team unity and needed to be resolved in order to ensure a more cohesive and productive training and competitive environment. Hence the secondary intervention for the team would focus on managing the disruptive influence of this player.

In summary, Steve was experiencing an all-encompassing broad range of stressors, from multiple sources which whilst fluctuating in their intensity, maintained a constant pressure on his time and energy which was mentally taxing. His frustration at not being able to facilitate consistent high level performances from his team resulted in performance outcomes which were contrary to those expected by the media, supporters, and club's board. Thus a multimodal intervention targeting controllable actions focused on developing clear roles and responsibilities in his playing staff in addition to clearer lines of communication from himself was initiated. Aligned to this approach was a specific intervention focused on dealing with the disruptive influence of the senior player.

FRAMEWORK AND INTERVENTION

Smoll and Smith (2010) and Luiselli (2012) emphasize the importance of evidence-based practice approaches to intervention delivery which provide clear, concise, jargon-free instructions in a language that the intended recipients are able to comprehend. This philosophy aligns closely with my own, in that I believe a practitioner's work should, wherever possible, be informed by appropriate literature whilst also allowing the flexibility to develop creative solutions to resolve client problems. Indeed this approach is central to the recommendations provided by the governing body for practice in the UK (HCPCb, 2009). The framework for which my delivery style is more closely aligned to is that of a cognitive behavioural approach (Scott & Drydon, 2003). Principally I'm interested in examining the interplay between a client's cognitions, emotions, and behaviours and how they impact upon client functioning. This relates not only to situations when these areas are having a disruptive influence on a client's wellbeing, but also importantly celebrating and emphasizing situations when they are having a powerful positive impact upon a client's performance. I would also say that the humanistic framework (Hill, 2001) which places an importance on the holistic development of a human being through self-awareness, actualization, and fulfilment, is one that influences my practice too.

With the above delivery philosophies in mind, the present two-pronged intervention approach sought to help Steve cope with the strain he was experiencing by enacting controllable intervention strategies to improve the productivity of his playing staff both individually and collectively. First, we sought to introduce an intervention to improve Steve's communication of the roles he wished his players to fulfil, in addition to helping to clarify player roles and improve their acceptance and performance of those roles. A second intervention focused on dealing with the negative disruptive influence of a senior player and creating a more cohesive and player involved performance development environment.

Role performance and communication intervention

Steve admitted that he was struggling to manage the strain he was experiencing which principally manifested itself in maladaptive communications with his players during and after matches. This was confirmed in my observations of Steve where he demonstrated quite a few instances of negativity in both his verbal and non-verbal communications. Steve wasn't happy with such behaviours and to a certain extent felt a little out of control of the situation and wanted to regain control and display greater composure, authority, and positive direction for his team. It was important at this stage to emphasize to Steve that his responses to stressful experiences were no different to those experienced by professional coaches in other sports (see Olusoga et al., 2010). However we acknowledged the importance of reducing the frequency and intensity of these reactions to maintain greater order and control of leadership interactions with his players.

Communication is recognized as an essential part of sport team functioning (LeCouteur & Feo, 2011; Sullivan & Feltz, 2003; Yukelson, 2010) and has been defined as 'a process that involves sending, receiving, and interpreting messages through a variety of sensory modalities' (Crocker, 1990; Harris & Harris, 1984, cited in Yukelson, 2010, p. 150). These messages can be sent via verbal or non-verbal means (e.g., behaviours, gestures, body positions, or language) and will be influenced by the context in which they are delivered in addition to the receiver's capacity to listen and interpret the message being sent. Yukelson (2010) asserts that in order for coach-athlete communication to flourish, the coach must be approachable and engage in clear, open, honest, and fair communication that is tailored to suit the individual and is mindful that the athlete is an equal partner in a two-way reciprocal relationship. In doing so, coaches increase their chances of being trustworthy and credible in the eyes of their players.

With this knowledge in mind, we began this first part of the intervention by discussing how approachable and useful Steve's players might view his communication style. By asking Steve to put himself in the shoes of some of his players, we talked through his recent interactions with these players (in training and competition situations) and reflected upon the impact his communication may have had in helping the athlete understand what was expected of them in addition to how such communication may have impacted upon the athlete's motivation, confidence, and general emotional wellbeing. In a rather honest exchange, it was clear that Steve appreciated that he needed to be more mindful of individualizing his communication to suit the personality and preferences of each athlete. Furthermore, he acknowledged he could improve communications with players to more clearly articulate what he expected of them in their positional roles in order for those players to perform those roles more effectively. We devised a general player communication plan whereby Steve identified a set of controllable principles that he would seek to adhere to when communicating with his players and indeed staff (see Box 11.2). It was agreed that we would meet to discuss his progress towards achieving these objectives every other week and modify and add to the principles following time for reflection.

Description box **BOX 11.2**

STEVE'S PRINCIPLES OF COMMUNICATION

1. Tailor my communication style to suit the individual.
2. Look at, and actively engage with, what the other person is saying.
3. Be attentive, non-judgemental, and supportive.
4. Acknowledge what they have said.
5. Behave in a positive and engaging manner.
6. Deal in facts and when needed substantiate the facts with evidence (e.g., performance statistics, etc.).
7. Where problems emerge identify solutions or strategies that the player can use.
8. Be positive and encouraging in my communications.
9. Seek opportunities to motivate and build my athletes' confidence.

An additional element to this intervention was initiated to supplement the above approach and enable Steve to develop a greater sense of control over his understanding of player roles and responsibilities. It was hoped that clarifying, communicating, and then monitoring role performance within the team would provide Steve with a sense of control and ownership over his management of player development. This approach mirrors the suggested strategies employed by world-class coaches when attempting to cope with stressful situations (Olusoga et al., 2010).

Roles are defined as the pattern of behaviour expected of an individual within a social setting (McGrath, 1984). Early differentiations as to these roles aligned to task (e.g., captain) and social (e.g., comedian) categorizations (Bales & Slater, 1955), however the more recent and accepted conceptualization relates to those roles that are formal or informal (Mabry & Barnes, 1980; Cope, Eys, Beauchamp, Schinke, & Bosselut, 2011). Cope et al. (2011) define formal roles as a set of behaviours or actions expected of an individual that are directly established by the group/organization and are typically linked to its instrumental objectives (e.g., goal kicker, penalty taker, etc.). Whereas informal roles result from interactions within the group that are not formally prescribed or expected by the organization (Cope et al., 2011). These range from positive informal roles such as social co-ordinator, comedian, mentor and spark plug to negative roles such as malingerer (i.e., prolongs injury or problem to garner sympathy or attention), distractor (i.e., disrupts team-mates, focus), and cancer (i.e., expresses negative emotions that spread destructively throughout the team) (Cope et al., 2011).

The clearer an athlete understands their role responsibilities (i.e. role clarity) and accepts the role (i.e. role acceptance), the more likely they are to perform the role effectively (Beauchamp, Bray, Eys, & Carron, 2002), have stronger task cohesion, and self-efficacy (Eys & Carron, 2001) and be satisfied in the role (Eys, Carron, Bray, & Beauchamp, 2003b). Indeed, research by Høigaard et al. (2010) found the more athletes experienced role ambiguity, the less satisfied they were and thus the more social loafing they reported.

Kahn, Wolfe, Quinn, Snoek, and Rosenthal (1964) proposed their Role Episode Model which was adapted to a sport environment by Eys, Carron, Beauchamp, and Bray (2005) to explain the communication of role responsibilities. The model proposes that the transfer of role information begins with the role sender (typically the coach) spending time determining the expectations for the role and who might fulfil it. This is then followed by the role sender communicating the role to the focal person (in this case the athlete) to then review and hopefully accept and comply with the role expectations. The final element of the model involves the role sender interpreting and feeding back on the focal person's responses in the role. Critical to the effectiveness of this process is the coach's ability to engage in clear and effective role communication with the athlete (Eys, Schinke, & Jeffery, 2008). Furthermore, Deci and Ryan's (1985) Cognitive Evaluation Theory would suggest that developing the athlete's sense of autonomy and ownership of the role responsibilities should help in enhancing their intrinsic motivation to fulfil the role and thus perform it.

Hence, if Steve is able to clearly define the roles he expects of his players on the field of play, identify suitable athletes to fulfil these roles, communicate the role requirements in a clear, coherent, and supportive manner, and encourage athlete involvement in the determination of the role responsibilities, then the research would suggest that a more task cohesive, satisfied, and better performing group of athletes would result.

Mindful of this knowledge, the next stage of the intervention focused on me carrying out a briefing session with Steve whereby the above information was discussed with a view to educating him as to the importance and potential impact of role clarity, communication, and performance. Steve was then asked to reflect upon the roles necessary for each positional aspect of the team and to define what he wanted from those positions given the different aspects of performance (e.g., attack and defence, set pieces, etc.). This role analysis was expanded to encompass formal roles in the team (e.g., goal kicker, captain, vice-captain, etc.).

Eys, Carron, Beauchamp, and Bray (2003a) assert that such an activity is most effective towards the start of a group forming (in this case the start of the season). However whilst not an ideal timing, Steve indicated that the activity would provide a useful mid-season point of evaluation and reflection in order to initiate some positive change and impetus for the second half of their season. We both agreed that this activity would require some time to complete on his own and that consultation with his coaching staff would help in spreading the workload as well as engaging and motivating his coaches in the process. We devised a short briefing paper for the coaching staff to outline the basis of the activity, what each coach needed to do and by when. Each coach (including Steve), depending upon their specialism, was allocated a defined number of positions and formal roles and asked to review the role requirements and come prepared to discuss their thoughts at a coach staff meeting. I then facilitated this meeting with the goal of developing a clear list of role responsibilities from which Steve and his coaches could then disseminate to the players. An important aspect of this discussion was how the role responsibilities would be communicated with the players, how player acceptance and satisfaction of their roles would be ascertained and also how role performance would be monitored and discussed with players between now and the end of the season. Furthermore, it was important to re-consider and clearly communicate the team's goals for the remainder of the season to act as a key structure within which the player roles would sit. My role in this process also involved taking notes of the various discussions and summarizing the role requirements, goals, and methods of dissemination and monitoring.

The next phase in the intervention involved Steve presenting the information derived in the coach meeting to the playing staff (with coaches present). Steve emphasized to me the importance of him assuming more control over how he presented himself to his players and coaches in this session and to ensure that the key messages were delivered in a clear, confident and considered manner so as to form the right impression to his players (see Box 11.3). Furthermore, he felt that he needed to make sure that the players were made fully aware as to what he and his coaching staff had been doing, why they had been doing it, and what he hoped would result from these activities.

Activity box

BOX 11.3

In the present scenario we have considered how Steve could communicate more effectively with his playing and coaching staff in order to facilitate a more effective and productive performance environment. Aligned to this, and discussed in more detail in Chapter 10 of this book, is the growing body of literature examining coach impression formation and management. Some informative research by Manley and colleagues (2008) examining the information sources that athletes use to inform their initial impressions and expectancies of their coaches could also provide a valuable focus for a supplementary intervention with Steve. Whilst wishing not to cover similar ground in the present intervention to that in Chapter 10, it would be useful to consider how such research might inform how Steve could approach the current situation.

Steve began by reaffirming the team's goals and general values that had been set at the beginning of the season asking the team to re-assess the standards they expected of one and other (see the second intervention below for more details). This led nicely into a mid-season evaluation of the team's performance to date and the underlying reasons for the current situation. An essential element of this part of the presentation was to develop a plan for the second half of the season and a clear articulation of the way forward (i.e., role clarification exercise). Despite some apprehension on the part of Steve prior to leading the team meeting, the meeting was generally well received by the playing staff. In line with our discussion about the importance of player input to such activities, Steve encouraged players to comment on the team's progress and of the roles that had been developed by the coaching staff. Following the conclusion of the team meeting, Steve and his coaching staff had identified a schedule to meet with the players individually to discuss and agree upon their role responsibilities and develop a training plan to support players in fulfilling their roles.

Cancerous player intervention

The second intervention aligns closely to that of the first and indeed was delivered along similar timelines in order to feed into the above team meeting. The focus here was in trying to help Steve deal with the negative disruptive influence of a senior experienced team player. Steve acknowledged that this player had significant playing experience up to and including international rugby and as such garnered the respect and attention of many of the players particularly when he first joined the club a couple of years previously. While his performances in the early stages of his contract had been to a high and consistent standard, these had declined in the last six months. A possible contributing factor to this performance decline was the breakup of the player's marriage which had clearly distracted him from his playing responsibilities. As a consequence, this player had been a substitute this season more than a starter and thus his resultant lack of playing time had corresponded with a more negative disruptive influence in training and on match day. Whilst they had a few honest and frank discussions with one and other, Steve was aware that the player was beginning to undermine his leadership authority within the playing group resulting in some younger more impressionable players being led down a path that was contrary to the key club values determined in pre-season. Steve, with the support of his coaching staff, was of the clear view that the situation needed to be resolved in order to improve team cohesion and performance.

Research by Cope and colleagues (2010, 2011) provides a useful basis from which to understand the characteristics of the player's behaviour and to help formulate a solution to the problem. In 2011 the authors examined the type of informal roles that were evident within sport teams identifying 12 informal roles including nine categorized as beneficial and three deemed detrimental. Of these negative informal roles, two correspond closely to the behaviour of the current player that being 'the distractor' defined as 'an athlete who draws away or diverts the attention of other team-mates decreasing their focus', and 'cancer': 'an athlete who expresses negative emotions that spread destructively throughout a team' (p. 24).

Cope et al. (2010) provides a useful reference point from which to explore this cancer role in more detail and thus help to inform an intervention with the present troublesome player. The authors interviewed ten intercollegiate male coaches to ascertain their thoughts on the characteristics, emergence, consequences, and management of a cancer player. The findings of these interviews (i.e., categories and sub-categories) were then further scrutinized by another ten coaches. The characteristics identified of cancer players included being manipulative, negative, narcissistic, blame shifting, and distracting. The findings also revealed that the cancer role is likely to emerge in individuals who lack confidence in their ability, are emotionally immature, have narcissistic personalities, initially find it difficult to fit into the group (and thus respond in such a way to try to fit in), have coaches that are lenient in enforcing team rules, or have significant external pressures from friends, family, or coaches that force them to act in this way. Interestingly, Benson, Eys, Surya, Dawson, and Schneider (2013) in their research examining athlete perceptions of role acceptance, suggest that players that do not accept their role are likely to engage in behaviours indicative of the 'cancer' role.

The possible consequences of the cancer role include the development of cliques, a reduction in cohesion and performance, general distractions away from the core team tasks, attrition from the group, and detrimental impressions of the coaches' competence should the cancerous influence not be resolved. Importantly and essential in informing my work with Steve, were the findings relating to how the coaches believed a cancer player needed to be managed for the good of the team. Key strategies included using direct communication with the player to highlight the negative influence of their behaviour and try to work with them to resolve the situation; using indirect communication in developing team expectations and rules for behaviour which can then provide the basis from which to discipline those players not adhering to the agreed behaviours, utilizing the wider coaching group to manage cancerous players, using disciplinary consequences for disruptive behaviour, and using the team to 'neutralize' the negative influence.

With this knowledge in mind, I discussed with Steve how we might attempt to approach this situation from team and individual perspectives. We began by agreeing that it would be useful to reaffirm with the playing squad the key values and behaviours expected of the team both on and off the field of play. Shoenfelt (2010) asserts that team values are underlying, guiding principles that assist teams in meeting their objectives and provide a foundation for building trust, rapport, and cohesion within teams. Hence a team-based approach reiterating team values would have clear benefits for the team whilst also not singling out and embarrassing the player in question in front of his peers. It would also allow the players to agree and then monitor and deal with any individuals stepping out of the agreed team values and behaviours. Whilst this activity had been enacted in pre-season, the monitoring of these values had recently been ignored leading to some player behaviour contrary to those initially agreed. By getting the players to reaffirm these core values and re-establish the punishments for not adhering to them, we would empower the team to set the standards and police player behaviour thus hopefully resulting in more consistent and productive on and off-field performances. This approach aligns to the philosophy evident in the highly successful New Zealand All Blacks rugby union team where player empowerment, responsibility, and accountability were central elements in creating the necessary environment for consistent high-level performances (Hodge, Henry, & Smith, 2014).

Alongside this team-based approach, Steve acknowledged that he would need to meet with the player and try to resolve their issues in order to more closely understand why he was behaving in the way that he was. This direct communication approach aligns to the advice provided by coaches in the Cope et al. (2010) research. Furthermore, the work of Benson et al. (2013) suggests that cancerous player behaviour may be a response to an athlete not accepting the role provided to them.

Steve admitted that he had been unable to invest as much time as he would have liked to talk to his players on a one-to-one basis due to the volume of roles and tasks he needed to fulfil as head coach. Thus he felt that if he invested more time speaking to the player, empathizing with their current situation and understanding their dissatisfaction with their role within the club, then he might be able to improve the player's behaviour and influence on the team. Indeed, Steve recognized that the player, given his experience and knowledge of the game, could be a real asset in helping to develop the younger players and thus a realignment of his role towards a more player development leadership/mentor role may help to modify his behaviour.

It was important that Steve did his homework on the player to ensure that he was informed as to his background and current off-field situation in addition to being mindful of the player's strengths. In the course of this information gathering, it was evident that the player had being talking with others about moving into a coaching capacity when his playing career ended. This information could prove to be invaluable in helping to realign the player's role within the club towards more of a mentorship/leadership role in developing the younger players. Indeed, Steve's experience of transitioning from player to coach would help him to empathize with the present player's situation in addition to providing the opportunity to develop the player's coaching experience and competence. Hence Steve would approach his interaction with the player with a view to moving them from assuming a 'distractor' or 'cancer' informal role to more of a positive 'mentor' role (Cope et al., 2011) whereby they could assume responsibility for providing advice, support, and guidance for the less experienced members of the squad.

Therefore, a meeting was arranged with the player with the aim of discussing the player's current situation. Rather than directly confronting the negative, disruptive influence that Steve perceived the player was having on the team, he focused more on empathizing with the player's recent off-field problems, understanding his aspirations for the remainder of his playing career as well as his future career plans (for a more detailed discussion on transitions from athlete to coach see Chapter 8). Similar to the intervention with the team, an important objective of these discussions was to establish what roles the player could fulfil to benefit the team and themselves moving forward, in addition to ensuring the player had the necessary available support to embrace and perform the new responsibilities. Broaching this difficult conversation with the player required a great deal of tact on the part of Steve's communication style in addition to requiring the player himself to open up and reflect on where he currently was in his career and where he wanted to go. This was achieved over the course of three one-to-one sessions with the player where it was agreed that he would take on an influential mentor role for a set number of younger players (in line with the work of Cope et al., 2011). As part of that discussion, Steve and I worked with the player to establish the key characteristics that a mentor should demonstrate in order to have a useful impact upon their mentees. In determining the list of characteristics, I then typed them up and provided them to the player in a small laminated reminder card to act a useful cue when he sought to interact with his mentees. We also all agreed that he would benefit from getting involved in coaching the Academy squad as well as enrolling on a relevant RFU coaching course. Finally, Steve agreed to mentor the player to provide advice and support as and when it was required.

REFLECTIONS

Given the hypothetical nature of this case study, I have chosen to focus upon detailing the interventions in terms of their rationale and make up without necessarily going into the outcomes that might materialize. It is hoped that coaches and practitioners alike can appreciate the characteristics of the situations presented and thus be better prepared should they have to deal with them in the future. This section of the chapter will briefly reflect upon and evaluate the interventions chosen and in particular discuss how the approaches adopted could be monitored to evaluate their effectiveness.

Luiselli (2012) highlights the importance of intervention integrity which relates to how accurately a client implements the intervention that they have been taught. There are several ways in which this integrity can be monitored such as asking the client to record and evaluate their activities in the form of a diary or observing the client in training or practice whilst they enact the intervention strategies and recording the adherence to the planned activity (see Luiselli for his 'Intervention Integrity Recording Form'). In the context of the present consultation with Steve, several monitoring procedures could have been implemented to evaluate the intervention integrity and obtain feedback as to whether the intended progress and outcomes were being realized.

First, in the context of the Communication Principles intervention (see Box 11.2), I would provide the coach with a short checklist evaluation form which would ask him to record on a ten-point Likert scale (ranging from 1 = very poor to 10 = excellent) how effective he felt he was in adhering to, and enacting, the various principles. This form would allow for a short qualitative section whereby he could record his thoughts on the interaction with the player and any areas he felt required improvement in any future interactions.

Through the initial assessment it was clear that Steve's general communications pre, during and post game could be more effective in order to maximize his impact upon the team. Whilst not the direct focus of the present intervention approach, a similar evaluation of his match-day communications could be enacted whereby Steve and myself could rate his ability to provide clear, informative, positive, and helpful communication to his players. This could align to the above format or the recommendations of Luiselli (2012) and Smoll and Smith (2010).

In line with the team-based intervention to clarify team values and adherence to those values, a small player leadership group could be established with the remit to monitor the team's adherence to the agreed values and report back in a weekly team meeting those players clearly demonstrating the values as well as disciplining those who do not. This monitoring approach would reinforce the player -centred philosophy to being more accountable and involved in the team's development and thus instil a more intrinsically motivated player environment.

With respect to the role-performance intervention approach, it would be essential to monitor each player's perception regarding the clarity, acceptance, satisfaction, and efficacy of the role(s) they were seeking to fulfil, in addition to tracking the player's performance of that role. Performance analysts at the club could be utilized to provide objective performance statistics for the coaches and players to help monitor player role performance. Furthermore, player perceptions of role clarity, acceptance, satisfaction, and efficacy could be monitored on a periodic basis via the use of a short simple questionnaire measuring the key variables.

An important individual (e.g., psychologist or assistant coach) could be assigned the responsibility for handing out, collating, analysing, and feeding back the questionnaire findings to Steve in tandem with a summary of the performance data derived from the performance analysts. Steve would then be adequately informed to prioritize his communications with key players who needed to improve their role acceptance, performance, satisfaction, and/or efficacy. Drawing upon the work of Benson et al. (2013), it is essential for Steve to use these role communication opportunities to reinforce to each player the importance of their role in helping the team to realize their social and task goals. Aligned to this, is the need for Steve to acknowledge within team meetings the contribution of different roles (and in particular the less recognizable or glamorous roles) in helping the team achieve their objectives (Benson et al.).

In summary, it is clear from the literature that professional sport coaches experience a variety of stressors (Frey, 2007; Olusoga et al., 2010; Thelwell et al., 2008) which if not dealt with appropriately can lead to negative cognitive, emotional, and behavioural outcomes (Fletcher & Scott, 2010; Hudson et al., 2013). Given this knowledge, it is essential that coaches develop a pre-emptive plan to deal with the range of stressors they are likely to encounter. Whilst a significant proportion of the stress and coping sport literature has focused on helping athletes, Thelwell et al. (2008) argue that coaches should be viewed as performers in their own right. As such, organizations employing professional coaches should seek to invest in expertise to assist coaches in becoming more knowledgeable of, and competent in, dealing with the stressful nature of professional sport coaching. Furthermore, it is incumbent in coaches themselves to acknowledge, and not ignore, the strain associated with their job and ensure that they have the necessary support around them, and skills within them, to adequately cope with the stressors. Support can come in the form of family, friends, and coaching mentors, as well utilizing the support of their coaching staff. Clearly sport psychologists, with their expertise in understanding the stress and coping process, can provide coaches with valuable knowledge and skills to assist them in proactively coping with, and responding to, stressful sport situations. Hence the development of a coach-psychologist working alliance could be a valuable asset to any sport organization in order to help the coach and thus the club to realize their potential.

ACKNOWLEDGEMENT

The author would like to thank Ian Davies for his feedback on earlier chapter drafts.

FURTHER READING

Luiselli, J. K. (2012). Behavioral sport psychology consulting: A review of some practice concerns and recommendations. *Journal of Sport Psychology in Action, 3*, 41–51. Simple and effective summary of how evidence-informed, clear, and concise approaches to behavioural assessment can help consultants evaluate intervention effectiveness, including some useful example checklists and forms.

Smoll, F. L., & Smith, R. E. (2010). Conducting psychologically orientated coach-training programs: A social-cognitive approach. In J. M. Williams (Ed.) *Applied sport psychology: Personal growth to peak performance* (pp. 392–416). New York: McGraw-Hill. This book chapter provides useful guidance on how to facilitate and optimize coaching behaviours and effectiveness.

Olusoga, P., Butt, J., Maynard, I., & Hays, K. (2010). Stress and coping: A study of world class coaches. *Journal of Applied Sport Psychology, 22*, 274–293. This paper provides a useful overview of how coaches respond to stressful situations in addition to providing a summary of the range of coping strategies employed to deal with such situations.

REFERENCES

Andersen, M. B. (2000). Beginnings: Intakes and the initiation of relationships. In M. B. Andersen (Ed.), *Doing sport psychology* (pp. 3–16). Champaign, IL: Human Kinetics.

Anderson, A., Miles, A., Robinson, P., & Mahoney, C. (2004). Evaluating the athlete's perception of the sport psychologist's effectiveness: What should we be assessing? *Psychology of Sport and Exercise, 5*, 255–277.

Bales, R. F., & Slater, P. E. (1955). Role differentiation in small decision-making groups. In T. Parsons and R. F. Bales (Eds), *Family socialization and interaction process* (pp. 259–306). Glencoe, IL: The Free Press.

Beauchamp, M. R., Bray, S. R., Eys, M. A., & Carron, A. V. (2002). Role ambiguity, role efficacy, and role performance: Multidimensional and mediational relationships within interdependent sport teams. *Group Dynamics: Theory, Research, and Practice, 6*, 229–242.

Beckmann, J., & Kellmann, M. (2003). Procedures and principles of sport psychological assessment. *The Sport Psychologist, 17*, 338–350.

Benson, A. J., Eye, M., Surya, M., Dawson, K., & Schneider, M. (2013). Athletes' perceptions of role acceptance in interdependent sport teams. *The Sport Psychologist, 27*, 269–281.

Bloom, G. A., Crumpton, R., & Anderson, J. E. (1999). A systematic observation study of the teaching behaviors of an expert basketball coach. *The Sport Psychologist, 13*, 157–170.

British Psychological Society (2009). *Code of ethics and conduct*. Leicester: BPS.

Carron, A. V., Loughhead, T. M., & Bray, S. B. (2005). The home advantage in sport competitions: Courneya and Carron's (1992) conceptual framework a decade later. *Journal of Sports Sciences, 23*, 395–407.

Cope, C. J., Eys, M. A., Beauchamp, M. R., Schinke, R. J., & Bosselut, G. (2011). Informal roles on sport teams. *International Journal of Sport and Exercise Psychology, 9*, 19–30.

Cope, C. J., Eys, M. A., Schinke, R. J., & Bosselut, G. (2010). Coaches' perspectives of a negative informal role: The 'Cancer' within sport teams. *Journal of Applied Sport Psychology, 22*, 420–436.

Crocker, P. (1990). Facial and verbal congruency: Effects on perceived verbal and emotional feedback. *Canadian Journal of Sport Science, 15*, 17–22.

Cropley, B., Miles, A., Hanton, S., & Niven, A. (2007). Improving the delivery of applied sport psychology support through reflective practice. *The Sport Psychologist, 21*, 475–494.

Deci, E. L., & Ryan, R. M. (1985). *Intrinsic motivation and self-determination in human behavior*. New York: Plenum Press.

Dennis, P. W., & Carron, A. V. (1999). Strategic decisions of ice hockey coaches as a function of game location. *Journal of Sports Sciences, 17*, 263–268.

Eys, M. A., & Carron, A. V. (2001). Role ambiguity, task cohesion, and task self-efficacy. *Small Group Research, 32*, 356–373.

Eys, M. A., Carron, A. V., Beauchamp, M. R. & Bray, S. R. (2005). Athletes' perceptions of the sources of role ambiguity. *Small Group Research*, *36*, 383–403.

Eys, M. A., Carron, A. V., Beauchamp, M. R. & Bray, S. R. (2003a). Role ambiguity in sport teams. *Journal of Sport and Exercise Psychology*, *25*, 534–550.

Eys, M. A., Carron, A. V., Bray, S. R., & Beauchamp, M. R. (2003b). Role ambiguity and athlete satisfaction. *Journal of Sports Sciences*, *21*, 391–401.

Eys, M. A., Schinke, R. J., & Jeffery, S. M. (2008). Role perceptions in sport groups.In M. R. Beauchamp & M. A. Eys (Eds.), *Group dynamics in exercise and sport psychology* (pp. 99–115). New York: Routledge.

Fletcher, D., Hanton, S., & Mellalieu, S. D. (2006). An organizational stress review: Conceptual and theoretical issues in competitive sport. In S.Hanton & S. D.Mellalieu (Eds.), *Literature reviews in sport psychology* (pp. 321–373). Hauppauge, NY: Nova Science.

Fletcher, D., & Scott, M. (2010). Psychological stress in sports coaches: A review of concepts, research and practice. *Journal of Sports Sciences*, *28*, 127–137.

Frey, M. (2007). College coaches' experiences with stress – 'problem solvers' have problems, too. *The Sport Psychologist*, *21*, 38–59.

Giges, B., Petitpas, A. J., & Vernacchia, R. A. (2004). Helping coaches meet their own needs: Challenges for the sport psychology consultant. *The Sport Psychologist*, *18*, 430–444.

Harris, D. V., & Harris, B. L. (1984). *Sports psychology: Mental skills for physical people*. Champaign, IL: Leisure Press.

Health and Care Professions Council (2012a). *Standards of conduct, performance, and ethics*. London: HCPC.

Health and Care Professions Council (2012b). *Standards of proficiency*. London: HCPC.

Hill, K. L. (2001). *Frameworks for sport psychologists: Enhancing sport performance*. Champaign, IL: Human Kinetics.

Hodge, K., Henry, G., & Smith, W. (2014). A case study of excellence in elite sport: Motivational climate in a world champion team. *The Sport Psychologist*, *28*, 60–74.

Høigaard, R., Fuglestad, S., Peters, D. M., Cuyper, B., De Backer, M., & Boen, F. (2010). Role satisfaction mediates the relation between role ambiguity and social loafing among elite women handball players. *Journal of Applied Sport Psychology*, *22*, 408–419.

Hudson, J., Davison, G., & Robinson, P. (2013). Psychophysiological and stress responses to competition in team sport coaches: An exploratory study. *Scandinavian Journal of Medicine & Science in Sports*, *23*, 279–285.

Kahn, R. L., Wolfe, D. M., Quinn, R. P., Snoek, J. D., & Rosenthal, R. A. (1964). *Organizational stress: Studies in role conflict and organizational psychology*. Chicago: Rand McNally.

Kelley, B. C., & Baghurst, T. (2009). Development of the Coaching Issues Survey (CIS). *The Sport Psychologist*, *23*, 367–387.

LeCouteur, A., & Feo, R. (2011). Real-time communication during play: Analysis of team-mates' talk and interaction. *Psychology of Sport & Exercise*, *12*, 124–134.

Luis, V., Carreras, D. & Wilbur, K. (2012). Analysis of the effect of alternating home and away field advantage during the Six Nations Rugby Championship. *International Journal of Performance Analysis in Sport*, *12*, 593–607.

Luiselli, J. K. (2012). Behavioral sport psychology consulting: A review of some practice concerns and recommendations. *Journal of Sport Psychology in Action*, *3*, 41–51.

Mabry, E. A., & Barnes, R. E. (1980). *The dynamics of small group communication*. Englewood Cliffs, NJ: Prentice Hall.

McGrath, J. E. (1984). *Groups: Interaction and performance*. Englewood Cliffs, NJ: Prentice Hall.

Morton, H. R. (2006). Home advantage in southern hemisphere rugby union: National and International. *Journal of Sports Sciences*, *24*, 495–499.

Olusoga, P., Butt, J., Hays, K., & Maynard, I. W. (2009). Stress in elite sports coaching: Identifying stressors. *Journal of Applied Sport Psychology*, *21*, 442–459.

Olusoga, P., Butt, J., Maynard, I., & Hays, K. (2010). Stress and coping: A study of world class coaches. *Journal of Applied Sport Psychology*, *22*, 274–293.

Page, L., & Page, K. (2007). The second leg home advantage: Evidence from European football cup competitions. *Journal of Sports Sciences*, *25*, 1547–1556.

Pollard, R., & Pollard, G. (2005). Long-term trends in home advantage in professional team sports in North America and England (1876–2003). *Journal of Sports Sciences*, *23*, 337–350.

Scott, M. J., & Drydon, W. (2003). The cognitive-behavioural paradigm. In R. Woolfe, W. Dryden, & S. Strawbridge (Eds.), *Handbook of counselling psychology* (pp. 161–179). London: Sage.

Sharp, L., & Hodge, K. (2011). Sport psychology consulting effectiveness: The sport psychology consultant's perspective. *Journal of Applied Sport Psychology, 23*, 360–376.

Sharp, L., & Hodge, K. (2013). Effective sport psychology consulting relationships: Two coach case studies. *The Sport Psychologist, 27*, 313–324.

Shoenfelt, E. L. (2010). 'Values added' teambuilding: A process to ensure understanding, acceptance, and commitment to team values. *Journal of Sport Psychology in Action, 1*, 150–160.

Smoll, F. L., & Smith, R. E. (2010). Conducting psychologically orientated coach-training programs: A social-cognitive approach. In J. M. Williams (Ed.), *Applied sport psychology: Personal growth to peak performance* (pp. 392–416). New York: McGraw-Hill.

Sullivan, P., & Feltz, D. L. (2003). The preliminary development of the scale for effective communication in team sports (SECTS). *Journal of Applied Social Psychology, 33*, 1693–1715.

Thelwell, R. C., Weston, N. J. V., Greenlees, I. A., & Hutchings, N. V. (2008). Stressors in elite sport: A coach perspective. *Journal of Sports Sciences, 26*, 905–918.

Thomas, S., Reeves, C., & Bell, A. (2008). Home advantage in the Six Nations rugby union tournament. *Perceptual and Motor Skills, 106*, 113–116.

Tkachuk, G., Leslie-Toogood, A., Martin, G. L. (2003). Behavioral assessment in sport psychology. *The Sport Psychologist, 17*, 104–117.

Yukelson, D. P. (2010). Communicating effectively. In J. M. Williams (Ed.), *Applied sport psychology: Personal growth to peak performance* (pp. 149–165). New York: McGraw-Hill.

12 Training a Coach to be Autonomy-Supportive: An Avenue for Nurturing Mental Toughness

John W. Mahoney, Daniel F. Gucciardi, Sandy Gordon, and Nikos Ntoumanis

LEARNING OBJECTIVES

AFTER READING THIS CHAPTER YOU SHOULD BE ABLE TO HAVE:

1. An understanding of mental toughness and factors that lead to its development.
2. An understanding of self-determination theory.
3. The ability to recognize coaching behaviours that support or thwart psychological needs.
4. Awareness about how to implement coaching behaviours that support individuals' psychological needs with the intention of enhancing mental toughness.

AREAS TO CONSIDER WHEN READING THE CHAPTER:

1. What is mental toughness?
2. How would you assess an athlete's mental toughness?
3. You've been asked by a sport organization to create an intervention or programme aimed at developing mental toughness in athletes. How would you approach this request for developing mental toughness (e.g., content, structure)?
4. What role do coaches play in the development of mental toughness?
5. Which coaching behaviours foster or forestall mental toughness development?

INTRODUCTION

Attaining and sustaining high performance is a defining characteristic of athletic pursuits. Although the formula for reaching such standards is open to considerable debate, most athletes and coaches would agree that physical, technical, tactical, and psychological skills are key ingredients to the recipe. Recently, researchers have sought to conceptualize key psychological characteristics under a single banner, namely *mental toughness*. For over a decade, researchers (e.g., Jones, Hanton, & Connaughton, 2002) have invested considerable effort towards defining and conceptualizing mental toughness and, even more recently (e.g., Connaughton, Wadey, Hanton, & Jones, 2008), determining the factors that contribute to its development. Despite this growing knowledge base, little effort has been made to translate this research into practice. Indeed, to our knowledge, there are only two published experimental trials (Bell, Hardy, & Beattie, 2013; Gucciardi, Gordon, & Dimmock, 2009) in which scholars have evaluated interventions aimed at developing mental toughness. These two studies are noteworthy examples of athlete-centred programmes delivered by a practitioner directly to athletes (Gucciardi et al., 2009) or indirectly by altering the training environment by a multidisciplinary team including coaches, ex-players, psychologists, medical staff and administrators (Bell et al., 2013). Aligned with these recent efforts, we contest that mental toughness can also be developed through the provision of particular coach-mediated learning environments. These claims are founded on previous research which has supported the important role of coaches in mental toughness development (Connaughton et al., 2008; Gucciardi, Gordon, Dimmock, & Mallett, 2009), as well as theory and research from broader fields of psychological enquiry that are consistent with this point of view (e.g., Mageau & Vallerand, 2003; Mahoney, Gucciardi, Ntoumanis, & Mallett, 2014). Thus, the purpose of this chapter is to introduce readers to a coach-centred intervention for enhancing mental toughness and to highlight the theoretical underpinnings and implementation of our proposed intervention through a case study example.

CLIENT AND BACKGROUND

Roger (pseudonym), the 51-year-old head coach of a women's crew at an English-based rowing club, approached the lead author with regard to sport psychology support. Roger coached ten female rowers of varying ages (M = 23.90 years, range = 17–38 years) and experiences (M = 4 years' rowing experience, range = 2–9 years); several of whom had achieved representative honours during their career. Specifically, four rowers had competed at a regional level and two had competed at a national level. However, except for one national representative, the rowers were competing solely at a club level when Roger sought psychological support.

Roger had sought psychological support for the crew for two main reasons. The first of these reasons related to recent changes within the crew. A number of rowers had been recruited to the squad after graduating from the club's junior programme and, as such, Roger perceived this occasion as an opportunity to introduce new training initiatives. The second reason Roger sought support stemmed from his desire to involve expert practitioners and leverage off their expertise to enhance the crew's performances. Roger had already employed a sport nutritionist and exercise physiologist, and believed a psychologist was also central to his objectives. Although interested in employing a psychologist, Roger had not contemplated a specific topic for intervention. As such, Roger and the psychologist (henceforth, the practitioner) discussed and explored possible avenues for intervention.

Roger identified that the crew had under-achieved at a number of recent regattas and, based on their track-record as individuals (e.g., regional and national representation), they were capable of better performances. He explained that occasionally the crew would perform to their abilities, but that they were often unable to repeat such performances; thus, performance consistency was a key consideration. Roger illustrated this point by recounting the crew's previous eight competition times and placings. The crew had achieved two second-place finishes in their previous eight races, but had also finished second last on three occasions (all races were against the same group of six opposition crews). Their race times were equally inconsistent; however, variances in course and weather conditions mean that race times are often poor indicators of performance in rowing, so Roger preferred to compare placings because crews typically competed against the same opposition. Based on this discussion and the evidence provided by Roger, the concept of mental toughness was introduced and suggested as a possible intervention topic.

A BRIEF DEFINITION AND CONCEPTUALIZATION OF MENTAL TOUGHNESS

Mental toughness has been defined as a personal capacity to produce consistently high levels of subjective (e.g., personal goal achievement) or objective (e.g., race times) performance despite everyday challenges and stressors as well as significant adversities (Gucciardi, Hanton, Gordon, Mallett, & Temby, 2015). A recent synthesis of the literature identified that researchers commonly conceptualize mental toughness as comprising eight personal characteristics: optimistic thinking, resilience, self-belief, handle challenge, winning mentality, context intelligence, attentional control, and emotional awareness, and regulation (Gucciardi, Mallett, Hanrahan, & Gordon, 2011). This definition resonated with Roger's description of the crew's experiences and the conceptualization served as a means to operationalize and measure the rowers' levels of mental toughness. Indeed, performance (in)consistency was central to Roger's overall assessment of his squad. Roger expressed great interest in mental toughness as a focus for intervention following the presentation of this definition and conceptualization.

Researchers have suggested that a number of factors contribute to mental toughness development. For example, in a study by Connaughton et al. (2008), mental toughness development was suggested to be contingent on factors such as competitive experiences, mental preparation, physical preparation, social support, vicarious experiences, mastery experiences, enjoyment, critical incidents (e.g., overcoming adversities), psychological skills (e.g., imagery), pre-performance routines, simulation training, and parental focus. Other researchers (Thelwell, Such, Weston, Such, & Greenlees, 2010; Weinberg, Butt, & Culp, 2011) have recorded similar lists, however, with such a diverse and exhaustive range of factors, it is difficult to conceive a parsimonious intervention for the development of mental toughness. A possible alternative to an intervention that encompasses all or many of these factors is one that focuses on a unifying concept that is prevalent in the literature, but also encapsulates a number of other factors. We believe one such factor is the coach-mediated learning environment.

Coach-mediated learning environments have been discussed in all previous studies that have identified the factors that contribute to mental toughness development. Further, coach-mediated learning environments can also encompass and/or influence a number of other factors identified in mental toughness research including the provision of competitive, vicarious, mastery, critical, and simulated experiences, as well as athlete enjoyment, pre-performance preparation, and social support. With this knowledge in mind, the practitioner suggested that Roger undertake a coach-centred intervention that sought to enhance his knowledge of, and abilities to, implement the learning environments that promoted mental toughness.

INITIAL NEEDS ASSESSMENT

To form a clear understanding of the coaching environment and to identify the appropriateness of a coach-centred intervention for mental toughness development, Roger and the rowers were first asked to complete a battery of questionnaires (see Table 12.1). The primary goal with this initial assessment was to gather an understanding of the different types of pressures that may influence Roger's coaching practice. Broadly speaking, these pressures can occur from above (i.e., culture of the rowing context), within (i.e., Roger's own personal attributes or dispositions), and below (i.e., perceptions of the rowers, such as their attitudes, beliefs and motivations; Reeve, 2009). As the practitioner could have little influence over organizational issues that may be created from pressure from above (e.g., expectations of club administrators), the initial needs assessment process targeted pressures from within and below.

In order to determine the appropriateness of a coach-centred intervention, as well as help evaluate the effectiveness of such an intervention, Roger was asked to complete a series of questions pertaining to his typical motivational orientations. The General Causality Orientations Scale captures the relatively enduring features of people's understanding of what causes the initiation and sustainment of behaviour, and reflect three categories of individual differences in the degree to which the sources of behaviour are interpreted as self-determined or not (Deci & Ryan, 1985a). Controlled orientations refers to the tendency to experience behaviour as originating from internal or external pressures (e.g., threats, rewards, expectations), and is therefore a low degree of internalization. The propensity towards a high degree of internalization is referred to as autonomy orientations, whereby behaviour is driven by a sense of volition and choice, and an awareness of personal values or interests. Impersonal orientations refers to the tendency to interpret the causes of behaviour as largely unknown to the individual or being beyond one's intentional control. Controlled (rather than autonomous) orientations may create pressure from within, and therefore lead to the adoption of controlling coaching behaviours (Reeve, 1998) such as intimidation, negative conditional regard, and excessive personal control (Bartholomew, Ntoumanis, & Thøgersen-Ntoumani, 2009).

Roger's responses suggested that he was predominately oriented towards intrinsically motivating environments (60 out of 84, where higher scores reflect stronger autonomy orientations), indicating that he preferred to engage in novel and personally interesting activities. In comparison, Roger scored low on controlling orientations (40 out of 84, where higher scores reflect stronger orientations towards controlling motivational environments) and lowest on impersonal orientations (24 out of 84, where higher scores reflect stronger orientations towards impersonal motivational environments), suggesting that he was generally less inclined to place importance on extrinsic factors (e.g., winning, fame) or believe that his and others' actions were ineffectual. These self-perceptions were promising findings with regards to implementing a coach-centred intervention as they suggested that Roger would willingly engage in a programme directed at his personal development. The rowers also completed a battery of questionnaires to provide an insight into possible pressures from below. Broadly speaking, this aspect of the needs assessment focused on the perceived quality of Roger's interpersonal style on a continuum ranging from supportive to controlling, as well as a personal quality of the

Table 12.1 *Descriptions, examples, and results of the coach and athlete questionnaires.*

Measure	*Aim*	*# of items*	*Example item*	*Scale*	*M (SD)*
General Causality Orientation Scale (Deci & Ryan, 1985a)	Measure of three motivational orientations (autonomous, controlling, impersonal) in coaches	36	*You are embarking on a new career. The most important consideration is likely to be: how interested you are in that kind of work.*	1 (*Very unlikely*) – 7 (*Very likely*)	N/A
Sport Climate Questionnaire – Short Form (adapted from Williams & Deci, 1996)	Measure of perceptions of autonomy support in sport environments	6	*I feel understood by my coach*	1 (*Strongly disagree*) – 7 (*Strongly agree*)	4.51 (1.31)
Controlling Coach Behaviour Scale (Bartholomew et al., 2010)	Measure of athletes' perceptions of sport coaches' controlling interpersonal styles	15	*My coach only rewards/praises me to make me train harder*	1 (*Strongly disagree*) – 7 (*Strongly agree*)	2.82 (0.70)
Basic Needs Satisfaction in Sport Scale (Ng, Lonsdale, & Hodge, 2011)	Measure of athletes' perceptions of autonomy, competence, and relatedness in sport	14	*I am skilled at my sport*	1 (*Not at all true*) – 7 (*Very true*)	5.00 (0.90)
Psychological Needs Thwarting Scale (Bartholomew, Ntoumanis, Ryan, & Thøgersen-Ntoumani, 2011)	Measure of athletes' perceptions of needs thwarting	12	*I feel pushed to behave in certain ways*	1 (*Strongly disagree*) – 7 (*Strongly agree*)	3.01 (1.42)
Mental Toughness Index (Gucciardi et al., 2015)	Measure of the eight personal characteristics of mental toughness proposed by Gucciardi et al. (2011)	8	*I bounce back from adversity*	1 (*False 100% of the time*) – 7 (*True 100% of the time*)	4.66 (1.09)

rowers that may potentially influence Roger's coaching behaviours. To achieve this aim, rowers completed questionnaires that pertained to their perceptions of Roger's coaching behaviours, satisfaction of their psychological needs (this notion is discussed in greater detail later, Deci & Ryan, 1985b; Deci & Ryan, 2000), and perceived levels of their mental toughness. When social contexts undermine or thwart peoples' psychological needs to feel autonomous, competent, and related to others, such conditions can result in feelings of alienation, burnout, and disengagement (Deci & Ryan, 2000), which in turn can create pressure for leaders to adopt a controlling style to manage these individuals (Sarrazin, Tessier, Pelletier, Trouilloud, & Chanal, 2006). Aside from the being the primary outcome variable for this intervention, it was also considered important to gauge the rowers' mental toughness as some coaches believe a controlling style (e.g., yelling, criticism) is required to develop this personal quality in their athletes (Kerr & Stirling, 2012).

The results of this initial assessment identified that Roger was perceived as demonstrating a mixture of coaching behaviours that supported or thwarted individuals' psychological needs. Further, rowers' results suggested that their psychological needs were moderately satisfied, as well as thwarted, and that they perceived themselves as possessing moderate levels of mental toughness (for a summary of results, see Table 12.1). Collectively, the rowers' perceptions of their coach, the satisfaction of their psychological needs, and their mental toughness levels appeared worthy of attention.

FRAMEWORK AND INTERVENTION

To the best of our knowledge only two studies to date have evaluated mental toughness programmes. Gucciardi, Gordon, and Dimmock (2009) developed an athlete-centred mental toughness programme and evaluated its effectiveness against a traditional psychological skills training programme. These researchers' found that both the mental toughness and the traditional psychological skills programme were equally effective in enhancing athletes' perceptions of mental toughness. Although their work represented a useful starting point for intervention-based research, the content of both programmes overlapped considerably, meaning that it is difficult to identify the benefits of the mental toughness programme over other approaches or narrow in on the effectual components of the intervention. Bell et al. (2013) also evaluated a mental toughness programme and unlike Gucciardi and colleagues. They designed a programme informed by personality theory and stress inoculation research. Athletes were exposed to pressurized performance environments with the intention of enhancing their abilities to overcome obstacles and re-engage with performance-related tasks. This performance environment was moulded by a multidisciplinary team of coaches, ex-players, psychologists, medical staff, and administrators. Compared to a control group, athletes in the mental toughness programme demonstrated a significant improvement in performance. Although a novel approach, Bell et al.'s mental toughness programme was largely founded on the use of extrinsic punishments and controlling sanctions. Environments that are extrinsically regulated and undermine individuals' perceptions of internal control have been associated with a number of negative outcomes such as burnout, dropout, disengagement, and resignation of effortful action (for a review, see Bartholomew, Ntoumanis, & Thøgersen-Ntoumani, 2009). As such, Bell et al.'s proposed programme might produce positive performance-related results in the short-term, but have far-reaching negative emotional, behavioural, and performance consequences in the long-term.

In light of Bell et al.'s (2013) findings, there is impetus to investigate whether or not an intervention designed to develop mental toughness can improve performance and performance consistency, whilst also preserving (or enhancing) individuals' psychological functioning (e.g., psychological wellbeing, vitality). We believe that, contrary to Bell et al.'s intervention, training environments can be designed as supportive and nurturing contexts for the development of mental toughness. In support of this contention, researchers (Gucciardi, Gordon, Dimmock et al., 2009) have shown that coaches believe that they are likely to facilitate mental toughness through supportive and nurturing training environments. In particular, coaches believe that establishing trusting and respectful relationships with athletes, constructing challenging and novel training environments, subscribing to athlete-centred philosophies, and encouraging athletes to be involved in learning and development contribute to mental toughness development. Contrary to Bell et al.'s protocols, Gucciardi and colleagues also found that coaches believed they could inhibit mental toughness development by prioritizing success over athlete development, setting low or unrealistically high expectations, and prescribing to a weakness-focused, as opposed to strengths-focused approach (i.e., conditions that externally regulate behaviour). Interestingly, coaches' perceptions of mental toughness development appear to resonate closely with theory and research from other areas of established psychological enquiry. In particular, the coaching behaviours, process, and strategies identified by Gucciardi and colleagues complement self-determination theory (Deci & Ryan, 1985b, 2000) literature. Below we detail self-determination theory and highlight how we employed knowledge from this field to inform our coach-centred mental toughness intervention.

Self-determination theory in a nutshell

According to self-determination theory (SDT), human functioning and psychological health is predicated by the satisfaction of individuals' psychological needs for *autonomy* (i.e., the perception that one's actions and decisions are volitional), *competence* (i.e., the perception that one's actions are efficacious), and *relatedness* (i.e., the perception that ones' actions and roles are valued by wider social networks). When individuals' *psychological needs* are satisfied, they are more likely to perceive an internal locus of control. That is, they believe that they are able to personally influence the events in their lives. When individuals hold such perceptions they engage in behaviours that are energizing, interesting, engaging, and reaffirming (Deci & Ryan, 2000). In support of these contentions, researchers have reported that psychological needs satisfaction is associated with greater levels of task engagement, more effortful actions, task persistence, deeper levels of cognitive processing, and greater levels of concentration (Amoit, Gaudreau, & Blanchard, 2004; Boggiano, Flink, Shields, Seelbach, & Barrett, 1993; Boiché, Sarrazin, Grouzet, Pelletier, & Chanal, 2008; Ryan & Deci, 2000). In comparison, when individuals' psychological needs are thwarted they are more likely to perceive that others or circumstances out of their control influence the events in their lives. A lack of perceived personal control commonly results in feelings of disinterest, anxiety, and hopelessness (Bartholomew et al., 2009). In addition, researchers have reported that psychological needs thwarting is associated with burnout, dropout, emotional upheaval, and, in extreme cases, psychopathology (Adie, Duda, & Ntoumanis, 2012; Deci & Ryan, 2000; Quested & Duda, 2011). Importantly, the conditions that support or thwart psychological needs are consistent with Gucciardi, Gordon, and Dimmock's (2009) interviews with coaches and, as such, form the foundations of the programme employed with Roger.

The conditions that enhance and inhibit psychological needs satisfaction are outlined within a micro-theory of SDT, namely, *basic psychological needs theory* (BPNT, Deci & Ryan, 2002). According to BPNT, psychological needs satisfaction is determined by the provision of environments that support perceptions of autonomy, competence, and relatedness. In a meta-analysis by Su and Reeve (2011), five conditions were found to enhance individuals' perceptions of psychological needs satisfaction: offering choices, providing meaningful rationales, acknowledging negative feelings, using non-controlling language, and nurturing inner motivational resources. These five behaviours are consistent with previous research (Gucciardi, Gordon, Dimmock, et al., 2009) on coaching behaviours that promote mental toughness and, as such, provide a conceptual bridge that helps inform our coach-centred intervention.

Further, Bartholomew and colleagues (Bartholomew, Ntoumanis, Ryan, & Thøgersen-Ntoumani, 2011; Bartholomew, Ntoumanis, & Thøgersen-Ntoumani, 2010) have explored the conditions that result in psychological needs thwarting. They reported that controlling use of rewards (e.g., promising and awarding prizes for desired actions), negative conditional regard (e.g., withholding of attention when athletes do not display desired behaviours), intimidation (e.g., threatening athletes with physical punishment if they do not meet expectations), and excessive personal control (e.g., interfering with athletes' lives outside sport) were likely to undermine individuals' psychological needs. These behaviours are also consistent with Gucciardi, Gordon, Dimmock et al.'s (2009) findings regarding coaching behaviours that undermine mental toughness development. Comparable findings in SDT and mental toughness research informed the design of the present intervention and the objective of enhancing Roger's awareness of environment conditions that facilitate both psychological needs satisfaction and mental toughness development.

A coach-centred intervention for developing mental toughness

Roger and the practitioner met on four occasions over a two-month period (approximately one-hour meetings). During these meetings, Roger and the practitioner discussed theory and research from SDT, the conditions that satisfy and thwart psychological needs satisfaction, and the application of autonomy-supportive coaching behaviours to Roger's coaching. The practitioner's consultations with Roger were underpinned by principles consistent with a humanistic model. Consistent with a humanistic approach, the practitioner was guided by the belief that individuals (in this instance, both Roger and the athlete group) continue to develop across all stages of life, and that personal worth and dignity are central to this development (for detail about humanistic philosophies see, Jacobsen, 2007). Below is a detailed description of each session.

Session 1. Following the initial needs assessment, this session commenced by feeding back the findings of the coach and athlete questionnaires to Roger including a description of each variable. Roger agreed with the results (i.e., highest on autonomous, low on controlling, and lowest on impersonal motivational orientations) and expressed his contentment with what they likely meant for the intervention. Roger was then presented with the findings of the athlete questionnaires. In summarizing the athletes' responses, Roger was informed that he exhibited facilitative coaching behaviours, but that there were areas where he could improve his coaching to promote the development of mental toughness in the rowers.

At this stage, the practitioner presented Roger with a lay introduction to SDT and how the provision of particular coaching behaviours could promote athletes' perceptions of psychological needs satisfaction. In an attempt to introduce these topics, Roger was asked to consider two athletes – one 'mentally tough' and one 'mentally weak' – and to contemplate how a coach might have contributed to each athletes' development. The intention of this activity was to encourage thoughts about coaching behaviours – particularly those consistent with self-determination theory research – that either promote or inhibit mental toughness development. To reinforce these ideas, a list of the behaviours identified by researchers (Bartholomew et al., 2009; Gucciardi, Gordon, Dimmock et al., 2009; Su & Reeve, 2011) were presented and discussed (see Table 12.2). These behaviours formed the basis of discussions for the current and subsequent sessions.

Table 12.2 *Types, descriptions, and examples of coaching behaviours/philosophies that support athletes' psychological needs.*

Behaviour/Philosophy	*Description*	*Example*
Providing meaningful rationales [A]	Explaining the purpose for a task in a way that connects with individuals' personal values/goals	'We're going to work on this skill today because it is related to your performance goals.'
Acknowledging negative feelings [R]	Expressions that demonstrate an understanding of, and legitimize, individuals' perspectives	'I understand what you're saying. You don't want to do this drill because it's difficult. I agree, it is difficult.'
Use of non-controlling language [A,C]	Avoiding language that induces pressure (e.g., should, must, have to) and using language that conveys choice and flexibility.	'What have you learnt that you could use in this situation?'
Offering choice [A]	Providing options and encouraging choice-making	'Which of the following tasks would you like to complete today?'
Nurture inner motivation resources [A,C,R]	Attending to individuals' psychological needs during task engagement	Creating choice-filled, challenging, and purposeful activities
Weekly challenging tasks [C]	Set challenging, performance-related tasks for athletes to complete over a short period of time (i.e., 1 week). Tasks should target the upper limit of athletes' abilities and not over or under challenge them	A team or squad could be challenged to complete a set amount of time or distance completing a difficult task (e.g., fitness, advanced skills)
Simulated performance experiences [C]	Create training environments that simulate pressure-filled performance experiences and clearly identify performance-related goals	One group of athletes, outnumbered by another group of athletes, has to maintain a lead whilst their opposition has to come from behind to win
Relate positively with athletes [R]	Establish and maintain positive relationships by opening lines of communication and offering both informational and emotional support	Approach athletes individually to gauge their perceptions about their sport participation. Ask about their enjoyment and pleasure in sport, but also the obstacles and challenges they are facing
Prioritize athlete development over coaching success [A,R]	Construct holistic athlete development plans that attend to athletes' sporting and personal goals, while avoiding placing too strong an emphasis on performance outcomes	Demonstrate an interest in athletes' lives outside sport and make concessions where necessary to allow athletes to pursue goals across a number of contexts

Note. A = behaviour/philosophy addressing autonomy; C = behaviour/philosophy addressing competence; R = behaviour/philosophy addressing relatedness.

In the interest of time and to simplify content, only coaching behaviours that have been shown to support perceptions of autonomy were presented during this first session. Coaching behaviours that support perceptions of competence, relatedness, and need thwarting behaviours, formed the topics of discussion during the subsequent three sessions respectively. Roger was first presented with a description and examples of autonomy. Autonomy was described as the view that one is self-directing, makes his/her own decisions, and chooses his/her own actions (Deci & Ryan, 2000). Two examples of autonomy presented to Roger included a rower who plans her race tactics (e.g., when she will increase her stroke rating) and a rower who chooses her warm-up routine. Following this introduction, Roger was asked to consider why being autonomous would promote mentally tough actions such as effort and persistence. The objective of this discussion was to help Roger understand how self-direction increases individuals' perceptions of internal control, which, in turn, promotes engagement in energizing, interesting, engaging, and reaffirming actions and tasks (Mahoney et al., 2014). It is this explanation that forms the fundamental link between SDT and mental toughness. With this knowledge, Roger was then asked to design a training programme to be completed before the next session that integrated notions of autonomy. To facilitate this training programme, Roger was asked to illustrate how he would introduce, coach, and debrief the training session using the training course layout (see Figure 12.1). Finally, Roger was asked to offer a summary of the session to demonstrate his learning, as well as highlight his intentions to implement his knowledge.

Session 2. The second session began by debriefing the training programme Roger had planned and administered following Session 1. He had intended to allow the crew to select between three skill-based options at the start and mid-point of training. In discussing this strategy, Roger noted that some rowers disagreed with the training choices of their peers. He further noted his concern that the strategy he used might undermine some rowers' perceptions of autonomy. In response, Roger was encouraged to allow different rowers or groups of rowers to select training programmes on different occasions. For example, if future disagreements arise among the rowers, Roger could allow one group to decide on one training activity and then allow another group to decide the subsequent activity. In addition, Roger was encouraged to communicate the value of tasks to individuals who disagreed with the selected training programme and to encourage rowers who chose training tasks to provide rationales for their selections over other options. For example, when rowers were not able to decide on the training task, Roger could have stressed, 'the drill is important to helping you balance the boat, which helps with momentum and increases your speed. If you can improve balance, you're more likely to reach your goal of moving the boat faster'. If the provision of choices is unachievable, coaches can still encourage athletes to engage with effort on tasks by providing a rationale for their involvement that is consistent with their personal values (Hagger & Chatzisarantis, 2007).

Following this introduction, the practitioner directed the discussion to the primary topic of the session, namely, coaching behaviours that enhance perceptions of competence. As an introduction to this topic, Roger was presented with the following description of competence: the view that one can bring about desired outcomes with his/her actions (Deci & Ryan, 2000). Examples of competence were also presented including a rower who achieved a self-set performance goal (e.g., reducing her 2 km ergometer time by 3 seconds over a 10-week period) and a rower who mastered a new skill or process goal (e.g., learning to engage her legs before her arms through the *drive* phase of the stroke). As with discussions from the first session, Roger was asked to contemplate why perceiving oneself as competent would promote mental toughness. The intention of this discussion was for Roger to acknowledge that competence, like autonomy, fosters perceptions of internal control, which, in turn, promotes effortful action, as well as task engagement and persistence (Mahoney et al., 2014). Gucciardi, Gordon, Dimmock et al.'s (2009) strategies for creating challenging training environments were presented in order to illustrate how Roger might enhance perceptions of competence among the crew. Specifically, the practitioner presented ideas about challenging athletes' limits (e.g.,

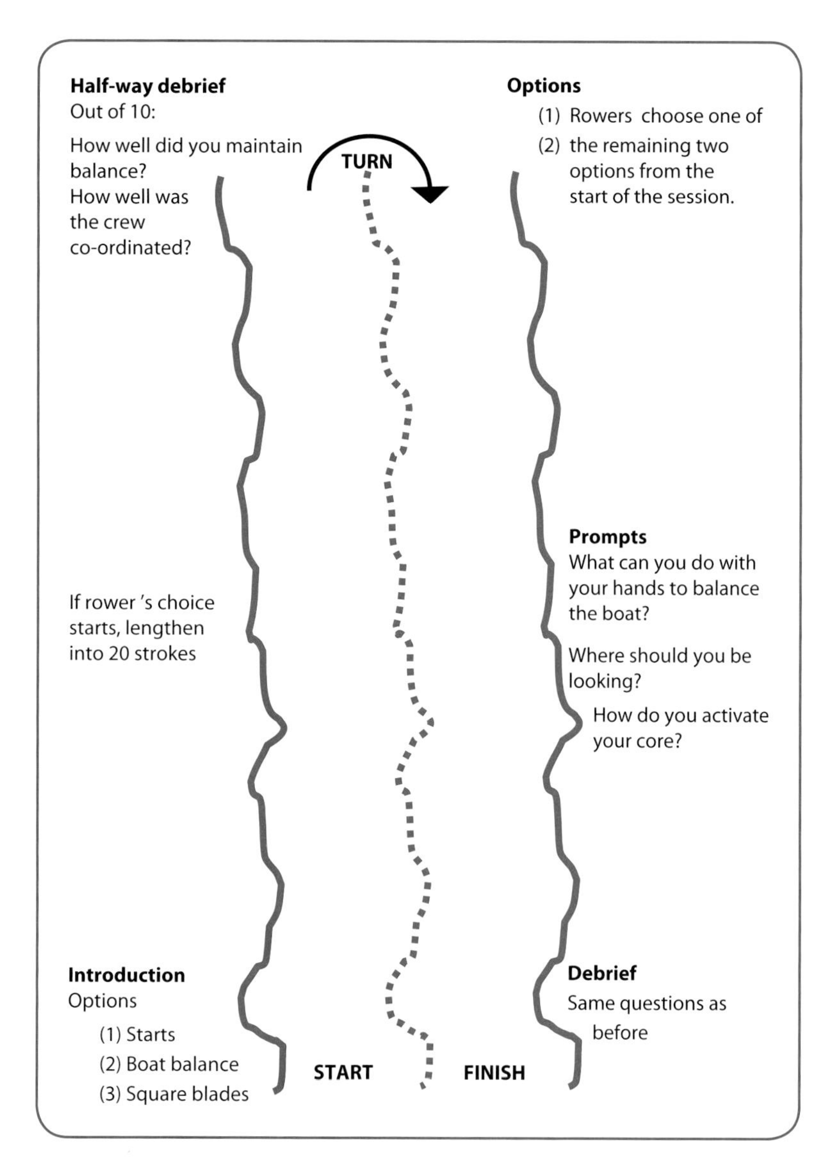

FIGURE 12.1 *Roger's proposed plan for implementing coaching behaviours that support athletes' need for autonomy.*

encouraging them to row a moment longer than initially planned when exhausted), setting weekly tasks and challenges (e.g., completing a set time or distance in training), and architecting pressure-filled training environments (see Table 12.2). The latter was discussed in light of Bell et al.'s (2013) intervention and Roger was encouraged to minimize pressure-filled tasks that undermined athletes' psychological needs. Roger was again encouraged to incorporate these strategies (along with those learnt in Session 1) into a training plan to be conducted before the subsequent session. An illustration of Roger's proposed training programme is presented in Figure 12.2. To end the discussion, Roger was again asked to provide a summary of the session and detail his intentions to implement his knowledge.

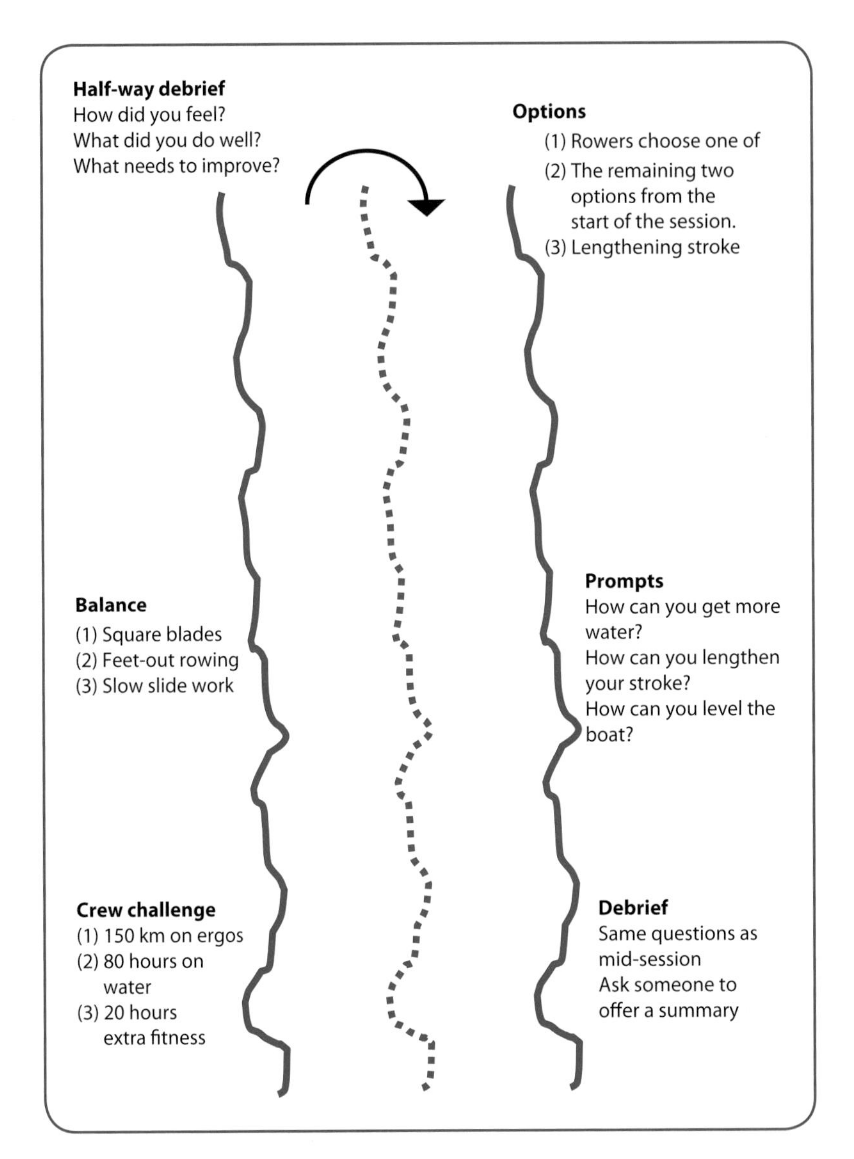

FIGURE 12.2 *Roger's proposed plan for implementing coaching behaviours that support athletes' need for autonomy and competence*

Session 3. The third session began with a discussion about the implementation of Roger's proposed training programme. Compared to the previous training programme, Roger perceived a relative amount of ease implementing his intended strategies. He expressed that the rowers appeared more engaged with the decision-making opportunities afforded to them and more willing to discuss their perceptions of their performances following training tasks. Roger also identified that he allowed different individuals and groups from the previous week to make decisions, as well as provided rationales for training drills, especially for athletes who disagreed with the drill selected.

Following this introduction, the practitioner directed discussions to coaching behaviours that enhance perceptions of relatedness. Relatedness was described as the view that one is connected to a wider social network and holds personally valued roles within such groups (Deci & Ryan, 2000).

A cohesive crew that demonstrates camaraderie towards each other (e.g., encouraging each other after mistakes, congratulating each other after successes) and a crew captain who fulfils her leadership responsibilities (e.g., empathizes with others during times of uncertainty) were provided as examples consistent with notions of relatedness. Roger was asked to contemplate why enhanced perceptions of relatedness would promote higher levels of mental toughness. The intention of this discussion was to help Roger identify two points: first, that a sense of belonging fosters individuals' perceptions that they are needed, and are responsible and accountable for their actions; and second, that role identification promotes beliefs that individuals contribute meaningfully to the pursuits and achievements of groups to which they belong (Mahoney et al., 2014).

Subsequent to these discussions, Roger was presented with ideas about how to enhance perceptions of relatedness among the rowers (see Table 12.2). Drawing again from Gucciardi, Gordon, Dimmock, et al. (2009), creating an open line of communication with and between rowers (e.g., asking athletes if they have any questions or comments, approaching athletes individually to discuss obstacles to performance), as well as offering and providing informational (e.g., advice about technique) and emotional (e.g., acknowledge negative emotional states and that the coach is there to help) support were proposed as possible ideas for enhancing rowers' perceptions of relatedness. In addition to these recommendations, and consistent with SDT, role identification was detailed as an approach that formally and explicitly singles out meaningful contributions individuals make within a group. This approach involves sport-specific role identification such as the specific contributions different sporting positions make to performance (e.g., the *stroke* seat in rowing) and sport-general role identification such as the delegation of leadership responsibilities (e.g., coxswains in rowing).

The practitioner suggested that Roger might incorporate these ideas by concluding training sessions with a brief team meeting. Team meetings were suggested because they are useful platforms for enhancing perceptions of relatedness as they offer an open forum within which individuals are afforded opportunities to build strong collegiate bonds and identify the meaningful contributions they make to the wider group. Based on the practitioner's suggestions, Roger decided to reserve the final 15 minutes of each training session for crew discussions.

Session 4. The final session began by inviting Roger to discuss his experiences of implementing coaching behaviours intended to enhance athletes' perceptions of relatedness. Prior to this session, Roger had implemented his team meeting strategy on two occasions. On reflection, Roger believed that the discussions had been successful in enhancing the rowers' perceptions of belonging. He noted that the time spent formally acknowledging the insights of the rowers, and explicitly detailing his beliefs about the roles of particular athletes helped to clarify the responsibilities of individuals and the shared direction of the crew.

To conclude the coach-centred intervention, the practitioner presented a number of coaching behaviours that were associated with psychological needs thwarting. Consistent with the literature (Bartholomew, Ntoumanis, Ryan, Bosch, & Thøgersen-Ntoumani, 2011), these behaviours are typically referred to as controlling coach behaviours. This topic was presented last so that Roger had time to develop a number of new, more effective coaching behaviours to replace these other behaviours. Consistent with Bartholomew and colleagues (Bartholomew, Ntoumanis, Ryan, & Thøgersen-Ntoumani, 2011; Bartholomew et al., 2009), Roger was informed that coaches can thwart athletes' psychological needs by using rewards to control behaviours (e.g., promising rewards for correct stoke technique), communicating negative conditional regard (e.g., ignoring rowers until they execute correct stroke technique), using intimidation (e.g., yelling at rowers who fail to execute correct stroke technique), and excessively controlling individuals' personal lives (e.g., demanding that rowers practise their stroke technique during their discretionary time). When presented with these ideas, Roger identified that it was common practice for rowing coaches to threaten athletes with physically demanding training sessions if they lacked effort or did not perform to expectations, and dictate what athletes should eat and drink, as well as how much they should sleep for recovery. Indeed, Roger confessed employing several of these controlling coach behaviours previously in his practices.

Roger's confessions prompted a discussion about why coaches might employ controlling coach behaviours. The practitioner acknowledged that there are a number of personal and contextual factors that led to the use of coaching behaviours that thwart psychological needs (see, Mageau & Vallerand, 2003). Considering Roger scored low on controlling and lowest on impersonal motivational orientations, it is more likely that contextual factors such as expectations of athletes and management, constraints on training times, Roger's own experiences as an athlete, and delinquent athlete behaviour might better explain his use of such behaviour. These topics formed the basis of the discussions between Roger and the practitioner.

Discussions around reasons why coaches typically engage in behaviours that thwart individuals' psychological needs provided Roger with the opportunity to reflect on his coaching practices and the reasons why he engaged in certain behaviours. The practitioner made a point of emphasizing that coaches who engage in controlling coach behaviours are likely to undermine mental toughness development because individuals' perceptions of control and meaning are forestalled. As a result, athletes are less likely to be effortful and persistent in their goal pursuits, and may withdraw their participations with time (Mahoney et al., 2014). These discussions offered an appropriate summary to the coach-centred intervention and afforded Roger an opportunity to contemplate how he could continue to pursue coaching behaviours that support others' psychological needs, whilst avoiding those behaviours that thwart them. As this session ended the intervention programme, the practitioner encouraged Roger to summarize his knowledge and competencies across the entire coach-centred intervention.

REFLECTIONS

The coach-centred intervention described above is a novel approach to developing mental toughness in athletes and the selection of a coach-centred intervention extends previous research in this area, which has identified the key role of coaches in mental toughness development (Connaughton et al., 2008; Gucciardi, Gordon, Dimmock et al., 2009). More importantly, the intervention complemented the needs of the client and married well with Roger's personal orientations. Nevertheless, although the selection of a coach-centred intervention appeared appropriate, it is necessary to reflect on the sessions, the dialogue with Roger, and the practitioner's perceptions of the therapeutic process in order to inform future practice and refine coach-centred interventions for the development of mental toughness. Largely, the reflections below are based on the practitioner's self-reflections, as well as some discussions with an informed colleague (the last author). The process of self-reflection involves observing and interpreting one's own actions. As such, self-reflections are useful for uncovering knowledge and critically contemplating one's motives and thoughts (Von Wright, 1992). In this instance, we took a phenomenographic approach to self-reflection, meaning we attempted to characterize different events according to theoretically similar conceptions (Storey, 2007). To facilitate this phenomenographic approach, we decided to follow a *good, better, how* structure, where *good* refers to the notable positive experiences from the intervention, *better* to the areas that could be addressed in future interventions, and *how* to our recommendations about how practitioners and coaches could improve on our approaches (Nilsson & Marriott, 2005).

Good

On reflection, the primary strength of the intervention was Roger's engagement both during each session and with the take-home activities. There appeared to be two primary reasons why Roger engaged so willingly with the intervention. First, are Roger's motivational orientations. Across all areas of psychological practice, it is necessary to match the selected intervention with the values, personal principles, and general orientations of the client (Beutler & Consoli, 1993). Incongruence between the intervention and the client can jeopardize the likelihood that intended positive outcomes will follow. Roger's responses to the General Causality Orientation Scale were a useful indication that an intervention of the nature detailed above would be warmly received. Indeed it was. Roger engaged in discussions, prepared materials voluntarily, completed take-home tasks, and integrated information competently. We acknowledge that not all coaches will approach interventions as Roger did; it is more likely that Roger is an exception to the rule. If Roger had been less likely to respond to a autonomy-supportive coach-centred intervention, it is more likely that we may have pursued an athlete-centred intervention.

We believe that the simplicity of the guiding theoretical framework (i.e., SDT) and its practicality supported Roger's learning and engagement. Roger quickly formed a clear understanding of the three basic psychological needs. For example, he was able to quickly determine how to integrate coaching behaviours that supported both autonomy and competence following Session 2. He also recognized the central outcomes associated with needs satisfaction (i.e., effort, persistence, psychological functioning). The simplicity of the SDT framework allowed for clear coaching behaviours to be identified, defined, and implemented. Further, the link to SDT principles meant that the majority of time in the sessions was spent discussing how Roger could implement specific coaching strategies as opposed to detailing theoretical concepts. The simplicity and direct link of SDT principles to practice is an improvement on other mental toughness programmes (e.g., Gucciardi, Gordon, & Dimmock, 2009) that have included a variety of concepts and behaviours that, arguably, are likely to overwhelm some individuals and only scratch at the surface rather than provide a detailed insight in the concepts and applications.

Finally, there was evidence to suggest that the coach-centred intervention successfully enhanced rowers' perceptions of psychological needs satisfaction and facilitated mental toughness development. Although not a complete representation of the crew, four rowers completed the athlete battery of questionnaires four weeks following the completion of the intervention and again eight weeks later (the remaining six rowers were not present during all three data collection points). Their results, including their original questionnaire scores, are illustrated in Figures 12.3 to 12.7. All four rowers reported initial increases in perceptions of autonomy-supportive coaching environments, psychological needs satisfaction, and mental toughness. Three of the rowers also reported initial decreases in perceptions of controlling coaching environments and psychological needs thwarting. Additionally, these four rowers' responses indicated the successes of the programme were, to some extent, maintained across time. In particular, there was evidence to suggest that autonomy-supportive environments and mental toughness levels were maintained 12-weeks after the completion of the coach-centred intervention. Although appearing to support the implementation of a coach-centred intervention, several other findings call into question the success of the programme and prompt recommendations for future practice.

Better and how

We have collapsed the *better* and *how* sections of our reflection in order to simultaneously identify aspects of the intervention that could be improved and suggest recommendations for practitioners to

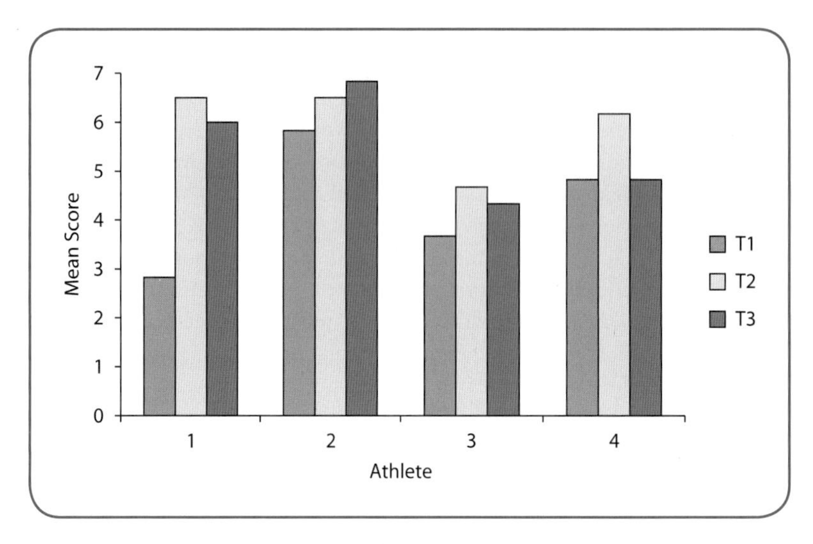

FIGURE 12.3 *Athletes' perceptions of needs-supportive coaching environments over time.*

heed in the future. A primary limitation of our intervention was the lack of in situ training undertaken with Roger. On reflection, we believe that greater learning might have occurred if the practitioner had consulted Roger during training. For example, the practitioner could have provided feedback, insight, and suggestions to Roger following interactions with the crew over the course of each training session. In attending to this suggestion, practitioners could use a number of practices that support reflection during action, such as revising coaching behaviours after audio- and/or video-recording training sessions. Approaches such as reflective practice (Cropley, Miles, & Nichols, 2015) could have augmented Roger's learning, as well as assisted him overcome barriers to implementing particular coaching behaviours. For example, during Roger's debrief of his take-home task following Session 1,

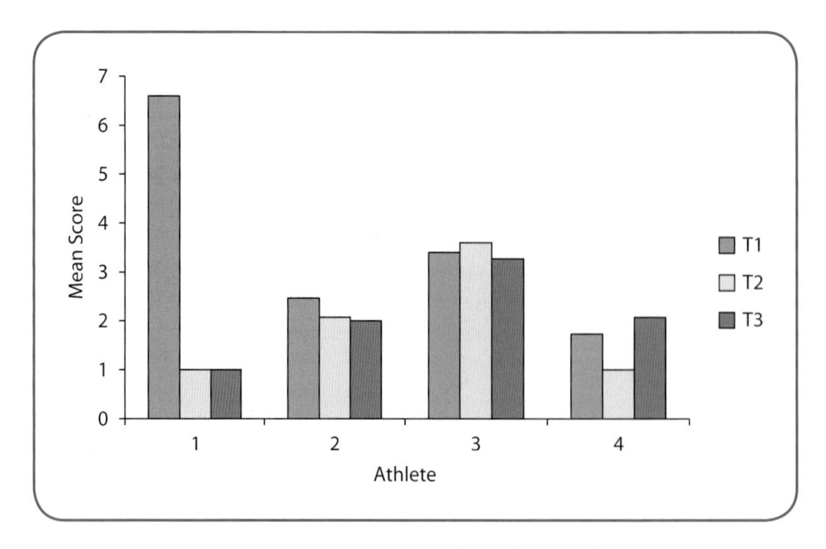

FIGURE 12.4 *Athletes' perceptions of needs-thwarting coaching environments over time.*

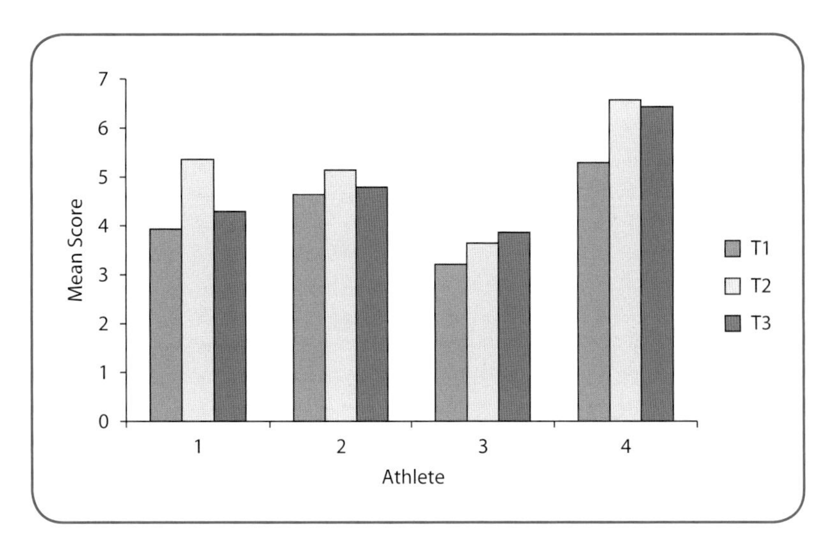

FIGURE 12.5 *Athletes' perceptions of psychological needs satisfaction over time*

he identified that he resorted to his previous coaching behaviours when he was unable to garner athletes' responses to his questions. Without being in the situation, it was difficult for the practitioner to determine what contributed to Roger's difficulties (e.g., poor questioning, distracted athletes, Roger's impatience). In the future, practitioners could follow-up information sessions and individual consultations with coaches by attending training sessions and acting as an advisor, as well as using innovative reflective techniques (e.g., audio- or video-recording training sessions).Interested readers are referred elsewhere for an introduction to the principles of reflective practice (Cropley et al., 2015).

A second issue that arose from the intervention concerns the sustainability of some of the changes observed following the intervention. As illustrated in Figures 12.3 to 12.7, some rowers'

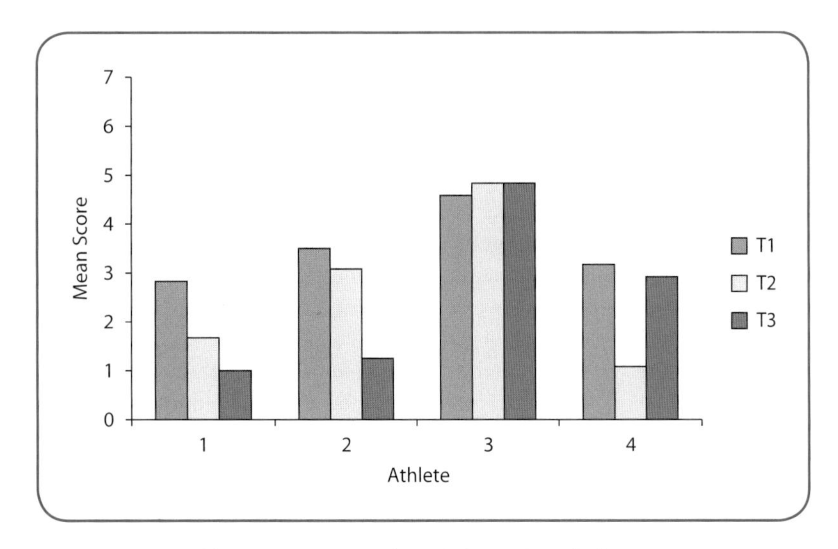

FIGURE 12.6 *Athletes' perceptions of psychological needs thwarting over time.*

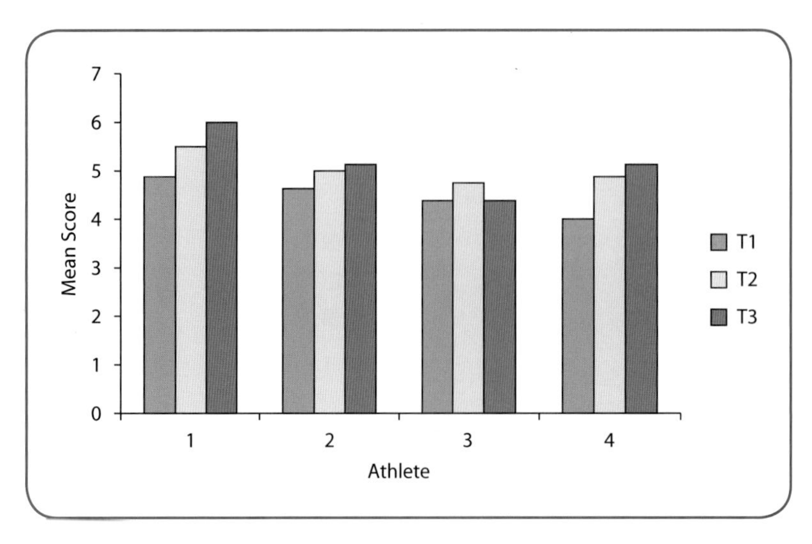

FIGURE 12.7 *Athletes' self-reported levels of mental toughness over time.*

perceptions of the coaching environments that thwart psychological needs, as well as the degree to which their psychological needs were being satisfied or thwarted, were not sustained over time. This discontinuity in the athletes' perceptions might be explained by changes in training content. Specifically, due to winter weather around the final data time point, the crew were predominately participating in indoor ergometer training sessions (compared to on-water training), which can be tedious, exhausting, and not enjoyable. Subsequently, the temporary changes in athletes' perceptions might be a reflection of the training content and context rather than the processes evident in the coaching environment alone. Face-to-face interviews could have been employed to investigate these assumptions. Nevertheless, coaches need to be aware of how certain training protocols might thwart athletes' psychological needs and how to implement strategies to overcome such issues. It would have been useful to have continued to consult with Roger during this transition in training content and to have advised him about how to create autonomy-supportive environments when faced with intuitively tedious, exhausting, and unenjoyable tasks. For example, Roger could have been encouraged to clearly detail the value of ergometer training to rowing performances (e.g., 'successes in ergometer training directly translate to improvements in on-water rowing performance bad help fulfil your performance goals'), set meaningful, enjoyable, and challenging weekly tasks for the crew (e.g., 'your challenge as a crew this week is to complete between 60–80 hours on the ergometers'), and build a cohesive social culture (e.g., the rowers had previously stated that they enjoy having social gatherings following training; Roger could have coordinated a social event following a testing ergometer training session). In the future, practitioners should be more vigilant in addressing the implementation of autonomy-supportive environments across a number of training and competitive contexts.

A final point is the potential for programmes such as the one detailed in this chapter to undermine the psychological needs of coaches. Essentially, the programme can be manipulated into a form of behaviour control. That is, practitioners can impose the knowledge detailed above in a way that is threatening, coercive, and intimidating. That is, practitioners can make coaches feel pressured into employing autonomy-supportive behaviours if they are manipulative in the manner in which they communicate the importance of these strategies. Practitioners, themselves, have to support the psychological needs of coaches when communicating SDT principles. Specifically, as was attended to when working with Roger, practitioners need to provide choices about how coaches can engage in particular coaching behaviours (i.e., support autonomy), reinforce when coaches have demonstrated learning and effort (i.e., support competence), and form strong therapeutic relationships (i.e., support relatedness). By adhering to SDT principles in their own practices, it is more likely that practitioners will nurture coaches' psychological needs and promote their willingness and commitment to implementing worthy strategies.

SUMMARY

Our intentions in this chapter were to introduce the reader to a contemporary definition and conceptualization of mental toughness, and to illustrate how practitioners might develop mental toughness through a coach-centred intervention. The coach-centred intervention we detailed was founded on SDT principles and aimed to increase the use of behaviours that supported athletes' psychological needs for autonomy, competence, and relatedness, as well as decreased the use of behaviours that thwart these needs. In light of the points raised in the self-reflection above, as well as evidence from four rowers, the intervention appears an attractive means for developing aspects of mental toughness. Additionally, practitioners need to be aware of the shortcomings of our intervention, as identified in the *better and how* section, and to improve upon these in the future to better support the needs of coaches and athletes. By doing so, practitioners are more likely to effectively promote mental toughness development and, consequently, facilitate the consistent achievement of high performance standards in athletes.

FURTHER READING

Mahoney, J., Ntoumanis, N., Mallett, C., & Gucciardi, D. (2014). The motivational antecedents of the development of mental toughness: A self-determination theory perspective. *International Review of Sport & Exercise Psychology, 7,* 184–197. This conceptual paper ties together the principles that underscore self-determination theory and previous research on mental toughness. In particular, the authors argue that mental toughness can be conceptualized by notions of *striving, surviving,* and *thriving*, and that literature regarding self-determination theory is generative in understanding both the antecedents and consequences of these three notions.

Mahoney, J. W., Ntoumanis, N., Mallett, C. J., & Gucciardi, D. F. (2014). Mental toughness in sport: Motivational antecedents and associations with performance and psychological health. *Journal of Sport & Exercise Psychology, 36,* 281–292. This empirical study explored that associations between autonomy-supportive environments, psychological needs satisfaction, mental toughness, and related outcome variables (i.e., positive and negative affect; performance). The authors identified that psychological needs satisfaction (through the provision of autonomy-supportive environments) indirectly relates to adaptive outcomes through mental toughness.

Ntoumanis, N., & Mallet, C. (2014). Motivation in sport: A self-determination theory perspective. In A. Papaioannou & D. Hackfort (Eds.). Routledge companion to sport and exercise psychology: Global perspectives and fundamental concepts (pp. 67–82). Abingdon: Taylor & Francis. This chapter is a useful resource for individuals interested in further readings and information about how to change motivational environments from a SDT perspectives.

REFERENCES

Adie, J. W., Duda, J. L., & Ntoumanis, N. (2012). Perceived coach-autonomy support, basic need satisfaction and the well- and ill-being of elite youth soccer players: A longitudinal investigation. *Psychology of Sport and Exercise, 13*, 51–59.

Amoit, C. E., Gaudreau, P., & Blanchard, C. M. (2004). Self-determination, coping, and goal attainment in sport. *Journal of Sport & Exercise Psychology, 26*, 396–411.

Bartholomew, K. J., Ntoumanis, N., Ryan, R. M., Bosch, J. A., & Thøgersen-Ntoumani, C. (2011). Self-determination theory and diminished functioning: The role of interpersonal control and psychological need thwarting. *Personality and Social Psychology Bulletin, 37*, 1449–1473.

Bartholomew, K. J., Ntoumanis, N., Ryan, R. M., & Thøgersen-Ntoumani, C. (2011). Psychological need thwarting in the sport context: Assessing the dark side of athletic experience. *Journal of Sport & Exercise Psychology, 33*, 75–102.

Bartholomew, K. J., Ntoumanis, N., & Thøgersen-Ntoumani, C. (2009). A review of controlling motivational strategies from a self-determination theory perspective: Implications for sports coaches. *International Review of Sport and Exercise Psychology, 2*, 215–233.

Bartholomew, K. J., Ntoumanis, N., & Thøgersen-Ntoumani, C. (2010). The controlling interpersonal style in a coaching context: Development and initial validation of a psychometric scale. *Journal of Sport & Exercise Psychology, 32*, 193–216.

Bell, J. J., Hardy, L., & Beattie, S. (2013). Enhancing mental toughness and performance under pressure in elite young cricketers: A 2-year longitudinal intervention. *Sport, Exercise, and Performance Psychology, 2*, 281–297.

Beutler, L. E., & Consoli, A. J. (1993). Matching the therapist's interpersonal stance to clients' characteristics: Contributions from systematic eclectic psychotherapy. *Psychotherapy: Theory, Research, Practice, Training, 30*, 417–422.

Boggiano, A. K., Flink, C., Shields, A., Seelbach, A., & Barrett, M. (1993). Use of techniques promoting students' self-determination: Effects on students' analytic problem-solving skills. *Motivation and Emotion, 17*, 319–336.

Boiché, J. C. S., Sarrazin, P. G., Grouzet, F. M. E., Pelletier, L., & Chanal, J. P. (2008). Students' motivational profiles and achievement outcomes in physical education: A self-determination perspective. *Journal of Educational Psychology, 100*, 688–701.

Connaughton, D., Wadey, R., Hanton, S., & Jones, G. (2008). The development and maintenance of mental toughness: Perceptions of elite performers. *Journal of Sport Sciences, 26*, 83–95.

Cropley, B., Miles, A., & Nichols, N. (in press, 2015). Learning to learn: The coach as a reflective practitioner. In J.Wallace & J.Lambert (Eds.), *Becoming a sports coach*. London: Routledge.

Deci, E. L., & Ryan, R. M. (1985a). The general causality orientations scale: Self-determination in personality. *Journal of Research in Personality, 19*, 109–134.

Deci, E. L., & Ryan, R. M. (1985b). *Intrinsic motivation and self-determination in human behavior.* New York: Plenum.

Deci, E. L., & Ryan, R. M. (2000). The 'what' and 'why' of goal pursuits: Human needs and the self-determination of behavior. *Psychological Inquiry, 11*, 227–268.

Deci, E. L., & Ryan, R. M. (2002). Self-determination research: Reflections and future directions. In E. L.Deci & R. M.Ryan (Eds.), *Handbook of self-determination research* (pp. 431–441). Rochester, NY: University of Rochester Press.

Gucciardi, D. F., Gordon, S., & Dimmock, J. (2009). Evaluation of a mental toughness training program for youth-aged Australian footballers: I. a quantitative analysis. *Journal of Applied Sport Psychology, 21*, 307–323.

Gucciardi, D. F., Gordon, S., Dimmock, J., & Mallett, C. J. (2009). Understanding the coach's role in the development of mental toughness: Perspectives of elite Australian football coaches. *Journal of Sport Sciences, 27*, 1483–1496.

Gucciardi, D. F., Hanton, S., Gordon, S., Mallett, C. J., & Temby, P. (2015). The concept and measurement of mental toughness: Test of dimensionality, nomological network and traitness. *Journal of Personality, 83*(1), 26-44.

Gucciardi, D. F., Mallett, C. J., Hanrahan, S. J., & Gordon, S. (2011). Measuring mental toughness in sport: Current status and future directions. In D. F. Gucciardi & S. Gordon (Eds.), *Mental toughness in sport: Developments in theory and research* (pp. 108–132). Abingdon: Routledge.

Hagger, M. S., & Chatzisarantis, N. (2007). *Intrinsic motivation and self-determination in exercise and sport*. Champaign, IL: Human Kinetics.

Jacobsen, F. J. (2007). *Invitation to existential psychology*. Chichester: John Wiley & Sons, Ltd.

Jones, G., Hanton, S., & Connaughton, D. (2002). What is this thing called mental toughness? An investigation of elite sport performers. *Journal of Applied Sport Psychology*, *14*, 205–218.

Kerr, G. A., & Stirling, A. E. (2012). Parents' reflections on their child's experiences of emotionally abusive coaching practices. *Journal of Applied Sport Psychology*, *24*(2), 191–206

Mageau, G. A., & Vallerand, R. J. (2003). The coach-athlete relationship: A motivational model. *Journal of Sports Sciences*, *21*, 883–904.

Mahoney, J. W., Gucciardi, D. F., Ntoumanis, N., & Mallett, C. J. (2014). Antecedence and consequences of mental toughness: A self-determination theory approach. *International Review of Sport & Exercise Psychology*, *7*(1), 184–197.

Ng, J. Y. Y., Lonsdale, C., & Hodge, K. (2011). The Basic Needs Satisfaction in Sport Scale (BNSSS): Instrument development and initial validity evidence. *Psychology of Sport and Exercise*, *12*, 257–264.

Nilsson, P., & Marriott, L. (2005). *Every shot must have a purpose*. New York: Penguin.

Quested, E., & Duda, J. L. (2011). Antecedents of burnout among elite dancers: A longitudinal test of basic needs theory. *Psychology of Sport and Exercise*, *12*, 159–167.

Reeve, J. (2009). *Understanding motivation and emotion (5th edn)*. Chichester: John Wiley & Sons.

Ryan, R. M., & Deci, E. L. (2000). Self-determination theory and the facilitation of intrinsic motivation, social development, and well-being. *American Psychologist*, *55*, 68–78.

Sarrazin, P., Tessier, D., Pelletier, L., Trouilloud, D. & Chanal, C. (2006). The effects of teachers' expectations about students' motivation on teacher's autonomy-supportive and controlling behavior. *International Journal of Sport and Exercise Psychology*, *4*, 283–301.

Storey, L. (2007). Doing interpretative phenomenological analysis. In E. Lyons & A. Coyle (Eds.), *Analysing qualitative data in psychology* (pp. 51–64). London: Sage.

Su, Y. L., & Reeve, J. (2011). A meta-analysis of the effectiveness of intervention programs designed to support autonomy. *Educational Psychology Review*, *23*, 159–188.

Thelwell, R. C., Such, B. A., Weston, N. J. V., Such, J. D., & Greenlees, I. A. (2010). Developing mental toughness: Perceptions of elite female gymnasts. *International Journal of Sport and Exercise Psychology*, *8*, 170–188.

Von Wright, J. (1992). Reflections on reflection. *Learning and Instruction*, *2*, 59–68.

Weinberg, R., Butt, J., & Culp, B. (2011). Coaches' views of mental toughness and how it is built. *International Journal of Sport and Exercise Psychology*, *9*, 156–172.

13 Creating a Successful and Effective Coaching Environment through Interpersonal Sports Coaching

VAITHEHY SHANMUGAM AND SOPHIA JOWETT

LEARNING OBJECTIVES

AFTER READING THIS CHAPTER YOU SHOULD BE ABLE TO:

1. Demonstrate an understanding of the context of interpersonal sports coaching within a university context.
2. Appreciate the importance of providing psychological support to professional coaching staff operating in competitive sport.
3. Outline and evaluate theories underpinning the coach-athlete relationship.
4. Outline and appraise a range of relationship management techniques that can be utilized by coaching staff to create a positive interpersonal coaching environment.

AREAS TO CONSIDER WHEN READING THE CHAPTER:

1. The complex and multidimensional factors that contribute to successful and effective interpersonal relationships with significant others within your sporting environment (coaches, managers, directors, sport science support personnel, athletes, teammates).
2. The strengths and weaknesses of your communication skills, and how they affect and are affected by your relationship with significant others.
3. How you communicate, relate, interact with others, as well as how you respond to, manage with, and prevent interpersonal conflict with significant others.

CLIENT AND BACKGROUND

Jim is a 30-year-old Caucasian Rugby coach. He recently joined a university to coach the women's team. The university has a fine record of performances in this sport (e.g., a string of success in British Universities and Colleges Sports (BUCS), a number of players in the team represent their nations at U18, U21 and Senior. This is his first full-time professional coaching job at this performance level and within the university context, having previously coached as a part-time university assistant coach and prior to that, at a grass-roots level. Jim, himself, was a competitive rugby player, representing the first team of his university for four years. After completing university, he represented the local county club while in full-time employment. He currently doesn't play. Jim is also married with a young daughter. In the first meeting, Jim expressed his concerns about settling into the coaching position. In particular, he was thoroughly enjoying his time and was pleased to be part of the university's sport, though he was somewhat concerned about replacing a coach whose reputation and coaching has led the team to winning various titles and accolades. He was aware that he had to get to know each one of his athletes both personally and professionally sooner than later, as well as getting them to function and operate as a team. His main concern was that developing good working relationships with his athletes takes time, time that he did not feel he had. He was concerned about developing and fostering good effective relationships with his team and between members of the team, especially given that the members of squad changed every year. In particular, he was aware that some of the best athletes had left the team (due to completing their studies), disrupting the dynamics and connections formed within the team. With that in mind, Jim posed to us with a number of questions, 'How can I as a coach nurture and rebuild relationships with each player in the team effectively and efficiently?', 'How can I instil trust and respect?', 'How can I make the team committed to a performance vision?', How can I create an environment in which everyone works hard to achieve their individual and team's goals?'. Jim was clearly keen to maximize his coaching effectiveness and we were enthusiastic to support him by utilizing our knowledge and understanding of the research conducted in the area of coach-athlete relationships. Thus the following sections of this chapter will outline the work that we implemented with Jim over the course of a season.

Definition box **BOX 13.1**

THE RELEVANCE OF THE COACH-ATHLETE RELATIONSHIP IN SPORT:

Coach-athlete relationship
A situation in which coaches' and athletes' feelings, thoughts, and behaviours are mutually and causally inter-connected. (Jowett, 2007)

> He's the sole reason why I was successful at Manchester United and successful in my career ... You see so many young players fall by the wayside but under the boss that was never going to happen. He looked after us all and gave us everything we needed to become the players and the men that we are today.
>
> (David Beckham on Alex Ferguson)

Over the course of their sporting career, athletes form many significant and interdependent relationships, but it is the relationship that they form with their coach that is perceived to be central in determining their skill development, physical performance, and psychosocial growth and development (see Jowett, 2007). In recent years, the coach-athlete relationship has been perceived as a social situation in which coaches' and athletes' interpersonal feelings of closeness, thoughts of commitment, and behaviours of complementarity or cooperation are mutually and causally inter-connected (Jowett & Felton, 2014). This conceptualization and operationalization of the coach-athlete relationship is known as the 3+1Cs (Jowett & Felton, 2014). The 3+1C model proposed that the quality of the relationship between a coach and an athlete is developed through four key relational components of closeness, commitment, complementarity, and co-orientation (see Jowett, 2005; 2007; Jowett & Felton, 2014). Closeness reflects the strength of the affective bond within the dyadic relationship. Specifically, it is the interpersonal feelings that the coach and athlete attach to their relationship (i.e., the extent to which they like, respect, appreciate, and trust each other). Commitment relates to the members' motivation to maintain their close relationship in both the short and long term. Committed coach-athlete relationships are likely to be determined to continue their working partnership, while a lack of commitment in the relationship is evident when neither member wishes to continue their working partnership. Complementarity refers to the relationship members' cooperative and corresponding behaviours of affiliation (e.g., being responsive and friendly). High level of complementarity is evident in the relationship when both members engage in corresponding and reciprocal behaviours (Yang & Jowett, 2013). Finally, co-orientation reflects the degree to which an athlete and coach have developed a common ground reflected in their perceptual similarity and understanding for the relationship they have formed. Accordingly, scientific evidence has demonstrated that the manner in which the coach interacts, relates, and communicates with their athlete defines the quality and the nature of the athlete's and coach's sporting experiences, be it interpersonal, intrapersonal, or environmental (see Jowett, 2007; Jowett & Felton, 2014).

Coaches and athletes need to maintain a long-term relationship, one that is stable and satisfying for both members (Rhind & Jowett, 2012). Interdependent relationships that last over time should be satisfying and fulfilling (Jowett, 2007; Jowett & Nezlek, 2012). Relationship maintenance is defined as the strategies that coaches and athletes use to keep their relationship in a desired state (i.e., fulfilled and satisfied; Rhind & Jowett, 2010). Accordingly, the maintenance of the relationship in the specified/desired state is considered to be complex, involving the conscious effort of both the coach and the athlete. Specifically, in their COMPASS model, Rhind and Jowett (2010) proposed that coaches and athletes utilize seven key communication strategies to maintain their relationship in their desired state. These include strategies related to conflict management (e.g., identifying, discussing, resolving, and monitoring of potential areas of conflict and disagreement), openness (e.g., promotion of open lines of communication), motivation (providing reasons for the other partner to stay in the relationship), preventative (discussion of expectations and what to do if these are not met), assurance (e.g., demonstrating commitment to the relationship), support (e.g., helping each other through difficult times) and social networks (e.g., socializing together to maintain a common social network).

The use of such strategies is considered to help maintain a close, committed, complementary and co-orientated coach-athlete relationship, while the absence of these strategies are associated with relationships that may be underlined by emotional distance, lack of commitment, cooperation, and common ground. For example, Rhind and Jowett (2011) found that high levels of closeness in the coach-athlete relationship was related to the use of strategies which promoted openness and social network, such as socializing with each other and having open channels of communication. Commitment was related to the use of motivational, assurance, and support strategies such as providing support to each other during times of need, demonstrating that the other relationship member can count on them and providing reasons to stay in the current partnership. Finally, the relationship construct of complementarity was maintained through preventative and conflict management strategies, such as coaches and athletes discussing their expectations and resolving and managing any areas of conflict and disagreement.

It is very common for sport psychology consultants to work with athletes and coaches in an attempt to psychologically empower (e.g., mental skills training) athletes with the aim of performance enhancement (e.g., Post & Muncie, 2012). However, there is limited evidence on psychologically empowering coaches (e.g., interpersonal skills, improved communication) with the aim of performance enhancement and increased wellbeing for themselves and their athletes (e.g., Holder, 2009; Kleinert et al., 2012; Langan, Blake, & Lonsdale, 2013). The available evidence-based interventions that target coaches include the Coaching Effectiveness Training (CET; Smith, Smoll, & Curtis, 1979), Mastery Approach to Coaching (MAC; Smith, Smoll, & Cumming, 2007) and more recently, the Promoting Adolescent Physical Activity (PAPA; see Duda, 2013). All of these schemes aim to improve the sporting experiences of young athletes, by targeting coaches and their coaching practices. Whilst these interventions are delivered to coaches in order to foster positive experiences in athletes (e.g., enhanced enjoyment of sport, self-esteem, skill development) the effects of such programmes on coaches' wellbeing and sporting experiences remain uncertain. Moreover, these interventions have been developed and implemented predominately with young athletes in mind – thus they are rarely applied within senior sport settings. Considering the lack of professional interventions for coaches operating in adult sport or competitive sport context (regardless of the age group of athletes) and the high demand for delivering services to coaches that aim to enhance their performance and their wellbeing (which we ourselves have experienced when working with coaches or their athletes), the case study and intervention presented aims to bridge that gap.

Although the scope of our service was to provide Jim with the appropriate training and knowledge about fostering harmonious and effective relationships with his athletes, it was crucial to consider and take into account the context in which Jim operates as well as the associated demands that he faced. Only when these were better understood, could the development and implementation of an appropriate and tailored programme which aimed to target the central issues raised by Jim be probed. If the demands faced by Jim were not appropriately recognized and understood, the outcome of the programme or service supplied would have been doubtful. The assessment of contextual demands has been thought to be critical when delivering psychological support to any client (e.g., athletes, coaches, or sport organizations) across any sport (see Holder, 2009).

The demands of a university coach

Coaches who work within a university setting are presented with a number of demands that are unique to this setting. Common requirements of university coaches and coaches operating within different contexts (e.g., club, national) are to recruit, train, and coach the athletic members of the squad whilst also provide pastoral care. University coaches are also expected to coach a forever changing squad where each squad year on year is different. This may be viewed as a unique phenomenon for university competitive sport whereby a number of athletes, usually the most experienced (and possibly the most talented), leave at the end of every academic year having spent around two to three years with the squad. Last but not least, one primary concern of university coaches is to ensure that their athletes for the short length of time they work together (usually maximum of three years) are achieving and improving not just athletically, but also academically. Considered together, university coaches are presented with substantive challenges that are determined by the unique setting within which they operate.

INITIAL NEEDS ASSESSMENT

Assessment of the coaching environment: profiling interpersonal relationships

Following the guidelines of Kleinert et al. (2012), the following assessment took place. The focus of the needs assessment was primarily on the interpersonal relationship between Jim and his athletes. Appraisal of Jim's current coaching behaviours, relationships, interaction, and communication styles (e.g., strengths and weaknesses), and readiness to change was achieved through two in-depth intake interviews. This allowed for an insight into how Jim perceived his current coaching behaviours, as well as his intentions to engage without reservation in the current programme, which has been found to be critical in ensuring the effectiveness of interventions (e.g., Weinberg & Williams, 2006). Open questions aimed at gathering, probing, and clarifying responses and information were asked during these intake interviews. Examples of questions included 'What is your overarching coaching philosophy, vision, values, focus ...?', 'How would you describe your current coaching styles, behaviours, leadership, relationship?', 'How would you describe your current connection with your team?', and 'In the past how have you resolved any incompatibility, disagreement, misunderstanding, conflict or other negative interpersonal issues in the team?'

Next, the Direct and Meta versions of the Coach-Athlete RelaTionship Questionnaire (CART-Q; Jowett, 2009; Jowett & Ntoumanis, 2004) and the Coach-Athlete Relationship Maintenance Questionnaire (CARM-Q; Rhind & Jowett, 2011) were administered to both Jim and his athletes. The CART-Q assessed the quality of the coach-athlete relationship in terms of closeness, commitment, complementarity, and co-orientation. Scores were calculated by deriving the sum of scores for each component, with high scores reflecting high-quality relationships, while low scores reflected a poor-quality coach-athlete relationship. Specifically, scores ranging from 1 to 2 represented low or poor levels of emotional closeness, commitment, and complementarity, while scores of 3 to 5 represented moderate levels, and scores of 6 and 7 represented high or excellent levels. The CARM-Q on the other hand assessed the communication strategies used by coaches and athletes to maintain relationship quality (Rhind & Jowett, 2012). Scores were derived from averaging the sum of scores for each communication strategy, which high scores (6 to 7) reflecting engagement in communication strategies, while low scores (1 to 2) reflected low engagement in such strategies, and moderate scores (3 to 5) reflected neither high nor low engagement in communication. Administering both these questionnaires served multiple purposes (i.e., diagnostic-current state, prognostic-future potential, state and educational-interventional purposes). First, they allowed an insight into how Jim perceives his relationship with his athletes, but also how athletes perceive their relationship with Jim (see Figure 13.1). But more importantly, it allowed for an insight into any discrepancies in how both athletes and Jim perceived their relationship (see Figures 13.2 to 13.6). Given, that coaches and athletes often find it difficult to communicate when they are dissatisfied with each other (Collins & Durand-Bush, 2010), by generating these dyadic maps, it visually (and objectively) highlighted the degree to which the relationships appear to function effectively (Jowett, 2005; Rhind & Jowett, 2012). In particular, the comparison of the results gained from the Direct and Meta perspective versions of the CART-Q highlighted the degree to which Jim and each one of his athletes have common ground or shared knowledge, and understanding about the relationship developed thus far (see Jowett, 2009).

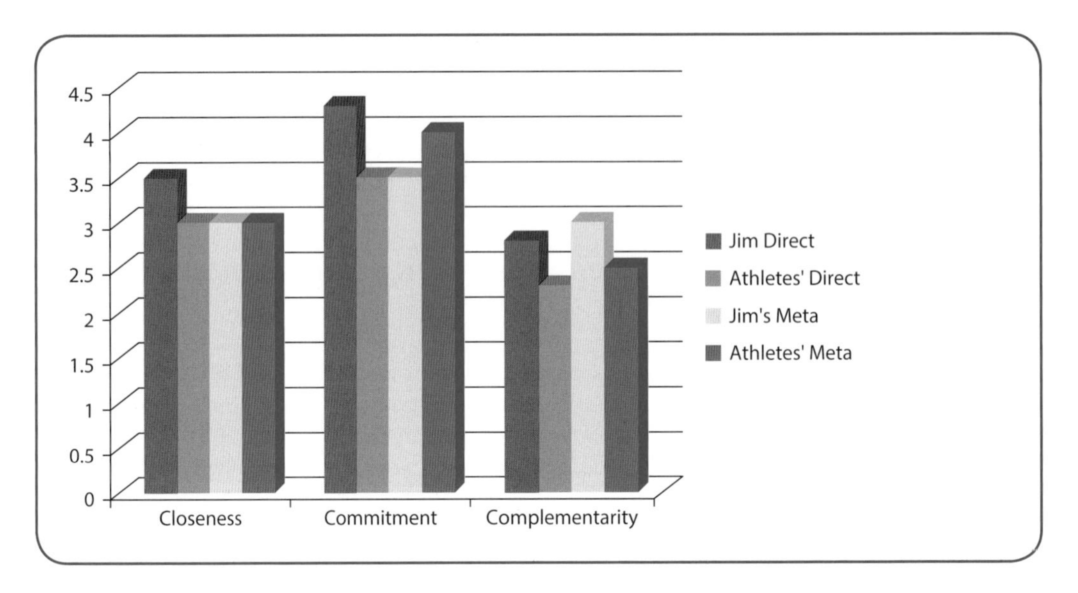

FIGURE 13.1 *Representation of Jim's and his athletes' scores on the direct and meta CART-Q.*

As shown in Figure 13.1, it was clear from Jim's scores on the direct CART-Q, that he perceived his relationship with athletes with moderate levels on the component of commitment, but low levels of emotional closeness and complementarity. These findings indicated that while Jim felt committed to his athletes, he did not feel emotionally attached to his athletes or felt that his athletes were being responsive to his coaching behaviours. However, these low scores could be a reflection of Jim's recent employment, as he had only been working with this group of athletes for a short period of time. Similarly, from looking at the average direct scores of Jim's athletes, they also reported somewhat similar perceptions of their relationship with Jim, with low levels across all three relationship dimensions: emotional closeness, thoughts of commitment, and complementary behaviours. In terms of Jim's and his athletes' meta perspective, results indicated low levels of emotional closeness, commitment, and complementarity in the coach-athlete relationship. This suggested that both Jim and his athletes perceived the other member to view their coach-athlete relationship as lacking in these relationship functions. While there were no discrepancies of significance (i.e., discrepancies of 2 points and higher), it should be noted that the scores reported by Jim and his athletes were below 5, which indicated that there is room for improvement via a relationship-focused intervention.

The comparison between Jim and his athletes' direct perspective of the 3Cs as demonstrated in Figure 13.2, indicated the degree to which both parties felt close, thought to be committed and behaved in a complementary way (i.e., how actually similar their perceptions were). The comparison of athletes' Direct and Meta perspective (Figure 13.3) indicated how similar the athletes assumed their perceptions to be with Jim's (athletes' assumed similarity). Similarly, the comparison between Jim's Direct and Meta perspective (Figure 13.4) indicated how similar he perceived his perceptions to be his athletes (coach's assumed similarity).

The comparison of the athletes' direct perspective data with the meta perspective data derived from Jim indicated (Figure 13.5) the (lack of) correspondence between the two relationship members (coach's empathic understanding of athletes' perceptions about relationship quality). Correspondingly, the comparison of the coach's direct perspective data with the meta perspective data derived

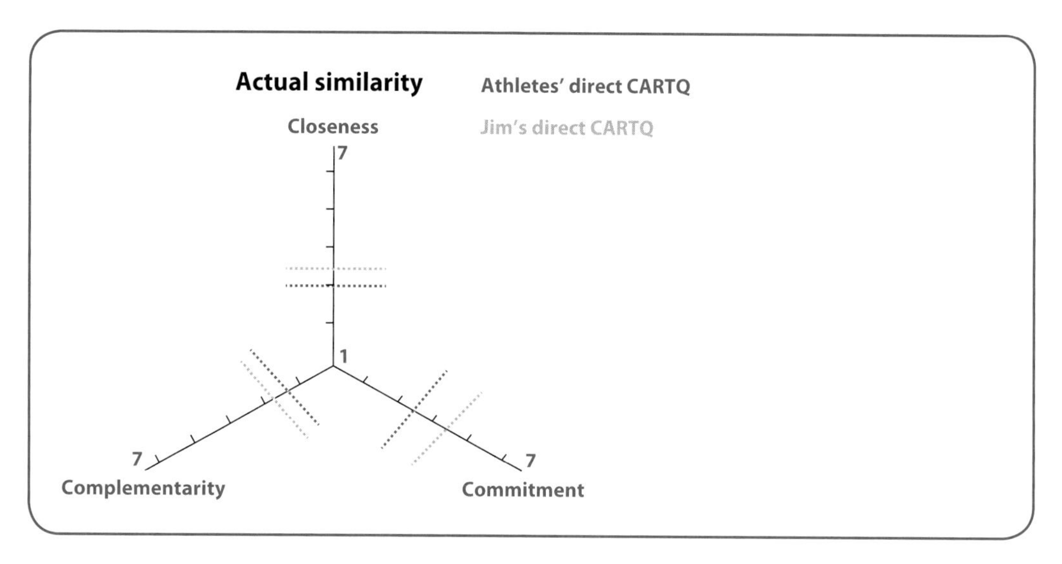

FIGURE 13.2 *Actual similarity in the coach-athlete relationship between Jim and his athletes.*

from athletes' indicated (Figure 13.6) the (lack of) correspondence between the two relationship members (athletes' empathic understanding of coach's perceptions about relationship quality).

Results generated from the CARM-Q indicated that both Jim and his athletes engaged in some key communication strategies such as conflict management and motivational more frequently than others such as openness, assurance, preventative, support and social networks, which were either poorly or moderately employed (see Figure 13.7).

Using the results generated from the completion of the CART-Q and CARM-Q measures to identify/diagnose areas of interpersonal strengths and weaknesses, interviews were subsequently

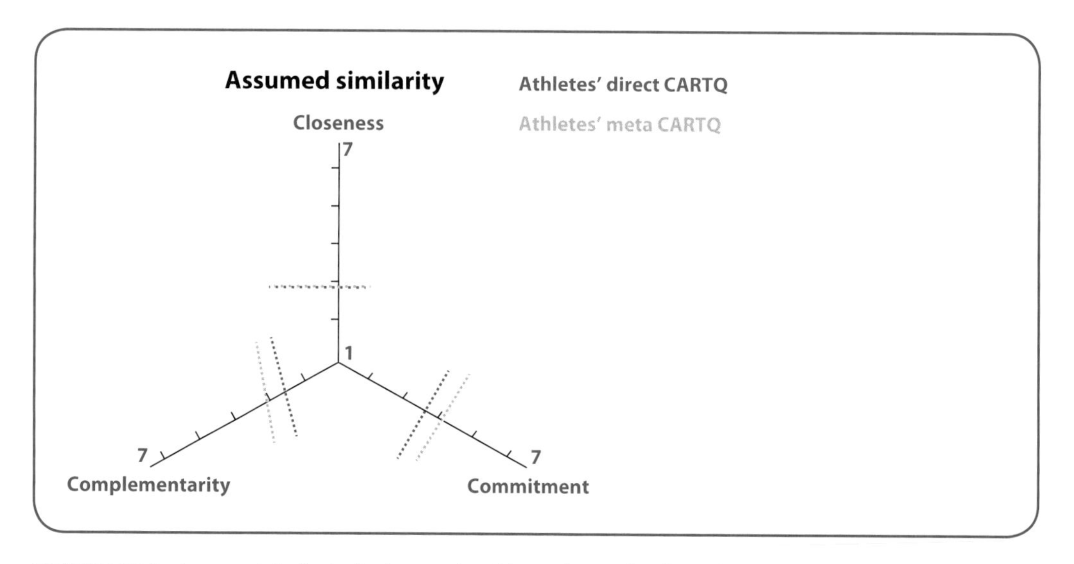

FIGURE 13.3 *Assumed similarity in the coach-athlete relationship from the perspective of his athletes.*

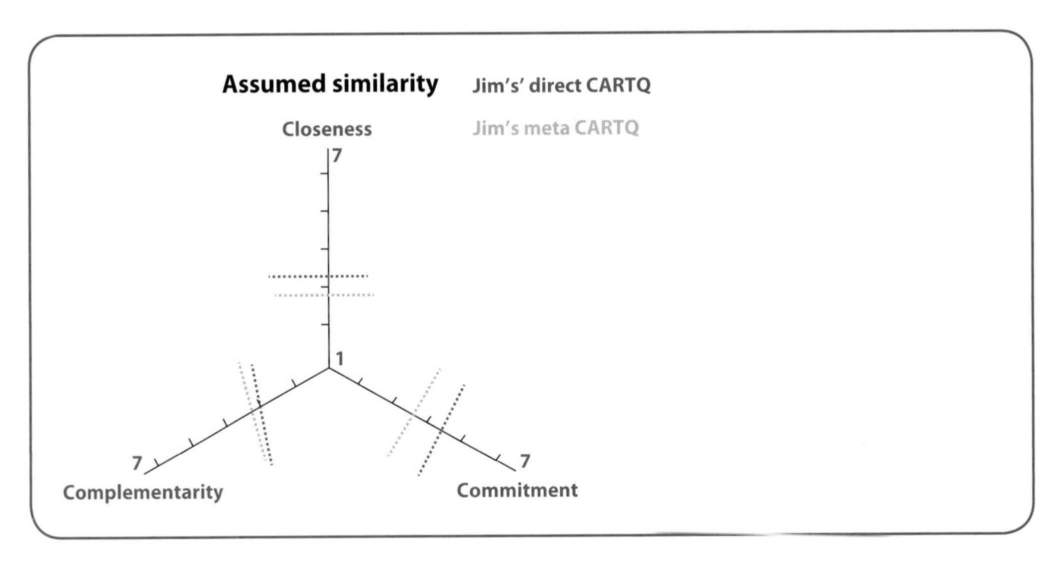

FIGURE 13.4 *Assumed similarity in the coach-athlete relationship from Jim's perspective.*

conducted with athletes and other support staff about Jim's coaching behaviours, relationships, interactions and communication style as well as about their preferences for interpersonal qualities in their coach (e.g., what they are looking for in a performance coach). This allowed us to gain an understanding about how athletes and relevant others within the coaching environment perceived Jim including his interpersonal qualities, competences, and effectiveness as a coach. Such interviews were deemed critical as it has been found that athletes' perceptions and appraisal of the coach shape athletes' sporting experiences such as their satisfaction with the coach, sport enjoyment, and the effort invested into the sport (e.g., Davis & Jowett, 2010; Smith 2007). Examples of questions asked to athletes and

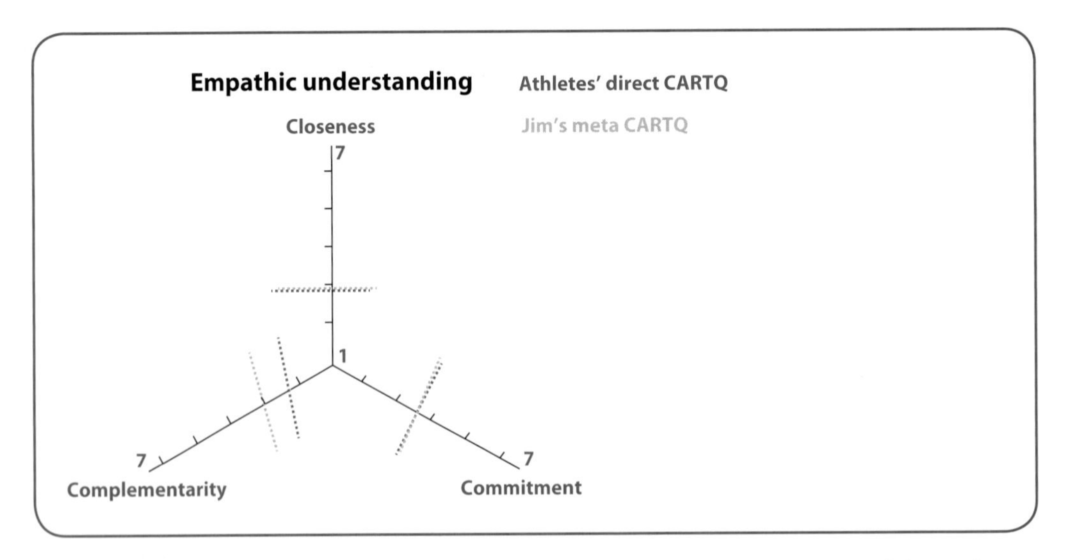

FIGURE 13.5 *The degree to which Jim understands his athletes' perceptions of the quality of the coach-athlete relationship.*

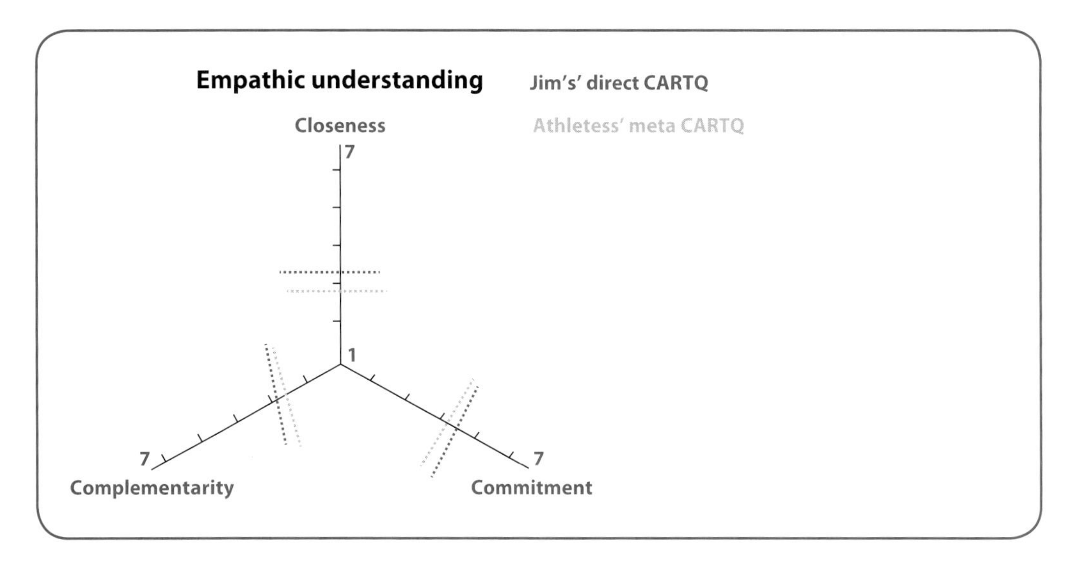

FIGURE 13.6 *The degree to which athletes understands Jim's perceptions of the quality of the coach-athlete relationship.*

other support staff included 'How would you describe Jim as a coach?', 'In your daily interactions, what type of behaviours would you like to see more and/or less of?', 'How have you experienced his instructions, direction, and leadership', 'How do you feel the team is likely to perform in the short and long future given his current coaching approach'.

Observations of Jim interacting with his athletes during training and competition (including before, after and timeouts) as well as outside sport (e.g., social events, team meetings) were also conducted. This provided communicative/conversational and behavioural data on his coaching practices. This added to perceptual data collected via the questionnaires and interviews. Together these data

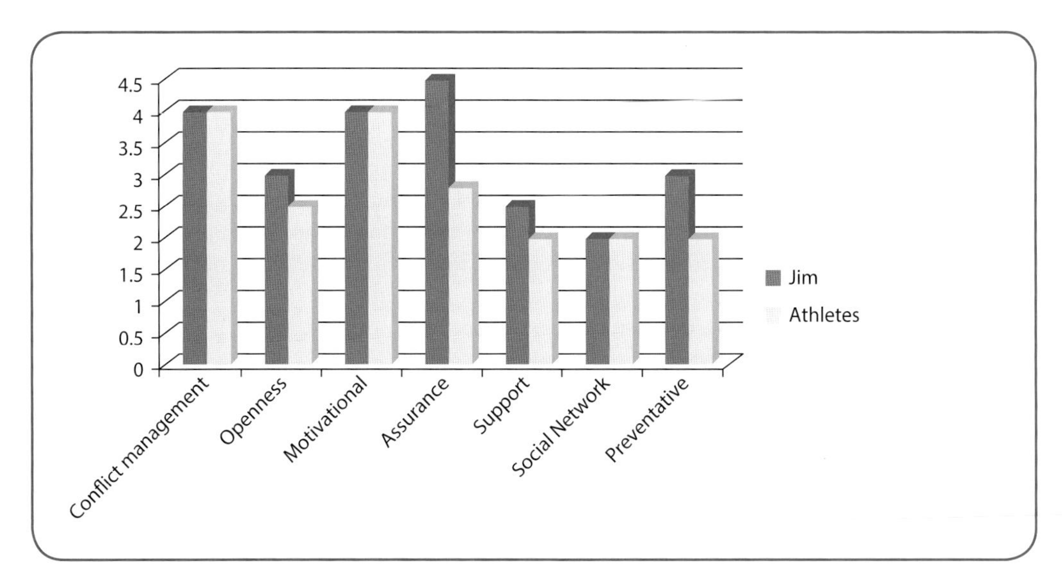

FIGURE 13.7 *Communication strategies employed by Jim and his athletes.*

substantiated and in some cases explained how and why Jim coached the way he did and how and why he was perceived by his athletes in a certain way. Direct observation of such interactions was deemed important as there is evidence to suggest that there is little congruence between coaches' observed behaviours and their athletes' self-reported behaviours (see Smith, 2007). Both informal and formal systematic observation methods were used. Specifically, to understand and attain behavioural data on his coaching practices, the Coaching Behavioural Assessment System (CBAS; Smith et al., 1979) was used during training and competitions. The CBAS allows the direct observation and coding of coaches' actions and behaviours (see definition, Box 13.2). Using a frequency recording sheet, during competitions and training, the number of times that Jim engaged in these behaviours were recorded to highlight the behaviours he frequently engaged in and those that he rarely engaged in. From the feedback generated from the CBAS, on average, it was evident that Jim frequently engaged in reactive behaviours such as providing positive reinforcement in response to desirable performance, as well as mistake-contingent encouragement and mistake-contingent technical instruction in response to errors, or following mistakes on the field. However, he scored low on keeping control of his team in response to misconduct, providing and assigning roles and duties to athletes and general communication about issues unrelated to the game, training, and competition. Informal observations were conducted by the authors especially focusing on conflictual situations. Specifically, the authors noted down verbal (i.e., tone of communication, content of communication) and non-verbal (i.e., body language) cues related to Jim's communication style. It was evident at times that Jim responded abruptly, loudly, unpleasantly, unfriendly, antagonistically, and aggressively. At times it was uncertain whether he was trying to correct athletes' behaviour, gain their attention, show annoyance, and demonstrate a level of control. Subsequent discussions with Jim made us realize that there was an element of lacking emotional control in most cases and lack of knowing how to assert in a positive manner without altering the positive tone of the coaching environment unintentionally.

In summary, the findings from the needs analysis indicated that as a whole, Jim had a less than desirable quality working relationship with his athletes (see Table 13.1 for a breakdown). It was clear from the data generated from the psychometric measures that while Jim was committed to his athletes and furthering his athletes' sporting career and partnership, he was not emotionally attached to them nor was he responsive to their behaviours and needs. This was corroborated by the results generated from his athletes. Furthermore, while he engaged in some communication strategies to enhance the quality of his relationships such as conflict management and prevention, the use of other strategies such as providing openness, support, and assurance on and off the sporting field were lacking. Such psychometric data were further reinforced and strengthened by the findings of the observations, whereby Jim was noted to provide technical support and encouragement, but rarely enquired about the academic or personal lives of his athletes (e.g., general communication). Thus on this premise, it was thought best to devise an intervention that focused on improving the areas that Jim was lacking in, but also providing advice on areas that he was doing well, to optimize the effectiveness of these strategies and qualities even further. The focus of our intervention aimed at improving the quality of coach-athlete relationships through the delivery of an evidence-based coach training psycho-educational programme.

Definition box

BOX 13.2

COACHING BEHAVIOURAL ASSESSMENT SYSTEM (CBAS; SMITH ET AL., 1979) (ADAPTED FROM SMITH, 2007)

Smith, R. E., Smoll, F. L. & Curtis, B. (1979). Coach effectiveness training: A cognitive behavioural approach to enhancing relationship skills in youth sport coaches. *Journal of Sport Psychology*, *1*(1), 59–75.

Source: Smith, A. L. (2007). Youth peer relationships in sport. In S. J. Jowett & D. Lavallee (Eds.), *Social psychology in sport* (pp. 41–54). Champaign, IL: Human Kinetics.

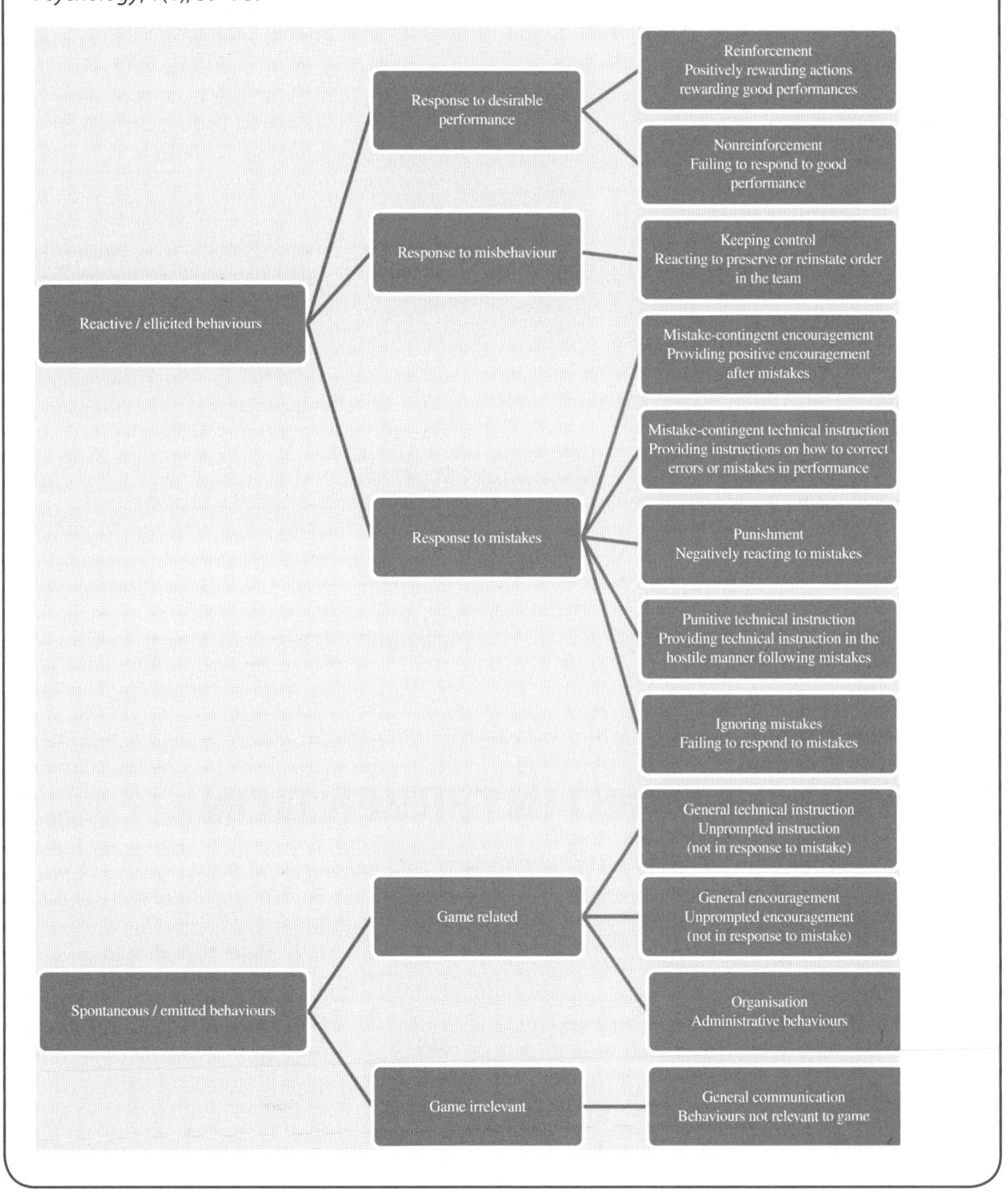

Table 13.1 *A summary of the key findings from needs analysis.*

Needs analysis	*Strengths*	*Weaknesses*
CARTQ	Jim showed moderate levels of commitment to his athletes.	Both Jim and his players perceived low levels of emotional closeness and complementarity in their relationship.
CARMQ	Jim and his players engaged in a moderate level in conflict management, preventative, and motivational communicational strategies.	Engagement in communication strategies such as open channels of communication, assurance, and support was low. Jim and his athletes did not engage in social activities or interact with each other away from the training environment or engage in interactions that promote openness in the relationship.
Observations	Jim frequently engaged in reactive behaviours such as providing positive reinforcement, mistake-contingent encouragement and mistake contingent technical instruction.	Low levels of spontaneous behaviours were noted. Jim found it difficult to control his team in response to misconduct, providing and assigning roles and duties to athletes and general communication about issues unrelated to the game, training, and competition.
	The content of Jim's communication was clear to understand, and usually displayed positive body language.	Jim's tone and nature of communication was sometimes strained, especially during times of conflict or misconduct. Jim was noted at times to ignore conflict between teammates.
Interviews with support staff	Jim was noted as technically sound, with good ideas for improving the ability of the athletes.	Jim was noted as inexperienced in managing conflict with this athletes and didn't get to know his players on a personal level.
Interviews with athletes	Jim was perceived as a good coach and committed to helping athletes improve technically. He was committed to them and their athletic partnership.	Jim was perceived as unapproachable, especially if they wanted to discuss issues related to school or personal issues. Jim did not engage in any team socials. Athletes weren't comfortable to be open with him and this was perceived to be a possible area of conflict in the future.

FRAMEWORK AND INTERVENTION

The cognitive-behavioural and humanistic approaches guided the current intervention. Cognitive-behavioural approaches (Beck, 1993, 2008) postulate that our cognitions are central to our feelings and behaviours. Specifically, these approaches propose that our automatic thought processes are subject to cognitive distortions such as negative, dichotomized, personalized, and overgeneralized thinking (see Henriksen, Diment, & Hansen, 2011). The cognitive-behavioural approach further suggests that the events of our life do not directly disturb us, rather our perceptions and interpretations of these events. Thus a central role of the sport psychologist is to empower athletes and coaches to be in control of their thought processes, raise their awareness, and help them understand how their interpretations impact their effort, performance, and wellbeing. Therefore, through the identification and modification of these distorted thought patterns, and the formulation of rational and functional thoughts, individuals can enhance their personal and athletic development (Henriksen et al., 2011). More recently, the cognitive-behavioural approach has embraced more humanistic features, with an emphasis on 'personal choice and the value of collaboration [between therapist and client]' (Ivey, Ivey, & Simek-Morgan, 1993, p. 217). Specifically, the driving force of the humanistic approach is that it is non-directive, whereby the practitioner follows the direction of the client. Furthermore, the humanistic approach focuses on the current experiences of the individual, specifically their current interpersonal relationships, and the 'here and now' experiences of individual. An underlying tenet of the humanistic approach is that every individual is unique and perceives and construes the world and their encounters in a way that is meaningful to them. Thus by examining individuals' distinctive perceptions, they can be equipped with resources which promote responsibility, personal growth, and self-actualization (Poczwardowski et al., 2004). The aim of the humanistic approach is not to treat the issues, but rather raise awareness and allocate new meanings to these issues. Thus we consider this dualistic framework to complement the current issues raised by Jim.

Based on the findings of the initial needs analysis, and guided by relevant the research, it was evident that creating an interpersonal, positive, purposeful, safe and caring coaching environment was fundamental. As a result, an 'interpersonal sport coaching' (ISC) educational programme was developed to help Jim facilitate and maintain effective and harmonious relationships with his athletes. This programme was delivered to Jim initially, through two interactive educational workshops, both lasting three hours each. The first workshop focused on understanding the role, significance, functions, quality, and content of coach-athlete relationships. The second workshop focused on utilizing communication strategies aimed at maintaining harmonious and effective relationships with his athletes. The first workshop was delivered at the start of the second month in the season in order to help Jim appreciate the power and purposefulness of relationships for successful coaching. The second workshop was implemented shortly after the first session in order to facilitate the development and maintenance of good-quality relationships with each one of his athletes in the squad.

The ISC educational programme was derived from recent theoretical and empirical evidence, which has highlighted the role and significance of quality coach-athlete relationships and the potential usage of communication strategies to maximize their effectiveness (e.g., Jowett, 2009; Rhind & Jowett, 2012). Specifically, the basis of this educational intervention was grounded in the psychosocial-cognitive-affective-behavioural principles of the 3+1 Cs and COMPASS model (Jowett, 2007; Rhind & Jowett, 2012).

Given that recent literature has highlighted that the use of a 'one-off' coaching educational workshop is only beneficial for 'short term retention knowledge' (Langan et al., 2013, p. 48), and advocated the use of situated learning formats within workshops to promote learning, the current intervention targeted the above mentioned properties of relationship quality and communication strategies through a variety of methods including role plays, modelling, observations of own short interactions in video form, discussions of favourable and unfavourable coach-athlete interactions, and problem solving. In particular, guidelines that promote desirable relational behaviours formed the foundation of the ISC workshop. Moreover, to further reinforce the implementation of such techniques within his coaching environment, Jim was asked to identify and incorporate up to three of these relational strategies, relevant to his team, in his future interactions. Accordingly, the following remaining segment of this section will provide an overview of the content embedded within both these interactive workshops.

Content of Workshop 1: facilitating and developing effective coach-athlete relationships

The first interactive workshop aimed to articulate and convey the theoretical and research evidence to Jim, while emphasizing the significance of fostering and developing effective relationships with his athletes, as well as guidelines on how to develop high-functioning relationships, so that he is better resourced to develop conducive relationships. First, there was an introduction into the role and significance including the content and functions of coach-athlete relationships for enhancing professional and personal development of Jim and his athletes. This focused, among others (evidence from anecdotal examples and empirical research), on distinguishing between effective and ineffective coach-athlete relationships. Second, an introduction was provided on the key relational components of closeness, commitment, complementarity, co-orientation, and communication, which have been highlighted to be conducive for professional and personal development. This also enabled an exploration of Jim's current perception of his relationships with his athletes (derived from the needs analysis) and his athletes' perception of their relationship with Jim. Third, a discussion into the strategies that Jim had employed to develop relationships with his athletes (currently or in the past) was also explored. With the guidance of the consultants, Jim was encouraged to actively engage in developing potential strategies or ways to enhance the quality of his relationships with his athletes, in particular, with those that he has less than desirable relationships with. Examples of such strategies are provided below. Finally, a discussion was conducted into understanding the feasibility of employing such strategies with his current athletes along with facilitating a contingency plan on how such strategies could be implemented with current squad.

Developing effective closeness with athletes

- Provide constructive feedback, praise, encouragement, and support to athletes in training, competition, and non-sport related contexts.
- Show recognition and investment (e.g., remembering birthdays and the academic course that athletes are doing).
- Promote open channels of communication (e.g., make small talk, short generic exchanges) and disclosure of personal feelings and thoughts to enhance closeness within the dyadic relationship but also among the team members.
- Engage in team-building and social activities to spend with one another, and with mutual friends (other coaches, athletes), to create opportunities for interaction and disclosure of information (un)related to sport.
- Show athletes that you care about them as an individual (not just as an athlete). Displaying commitment to the athletes
- Demonstrate commitment, confidence, and certainty to the team and individual players (mainly these players than needing these more) by attending both training and competitions.
- Be on time for training (e.g., being the first to arrive and last to leave).
- Deliver organized and prepared training sessions.
- Be prepared to sacrifice and give up time for the sake of the team (and individual players) and improving performance such as staying longer on the sport field to practise, receive and give instruction or feedback, and scheduling or attending extra sessions.

- Ensure that training sessions are focused, engaging, challenging, but enjoyable.
- Set specific individual goals and team targets.

Facilitating complementarity between the coach and athletes

- Create a coaching environment that is characterized by mutual responsibility, collaboration and accountability.
- Establish clear team rules and expectations (e.g., code of conduct that all members, both coaches and athletes have to adhere to as well as the consequences if these are not followed).
- Allow athletes to provide input and actively participate in the training sessions.
- Achieve a balance between order and freedom.
- Ensure that you and your athletes' role and responsibilities are well understood (e.g., athletes will need to understand that they need to be actively involved in the process of their development, and that they need to actively engage in the various tasks, self-responsibility and ownership).

Promoting co-orientation and effective communication

- Set clear and achievable personal and team goals for all members to strive towards. Ensure whatever goals are set (individual and team) are agreed by each individual player in the team and are entirely in line with everyone's capabilties, expectations, hopes, aspirations.
- Engage in verbal interchange about sport and non-sport related issues. Try to find out as much as you possibly can for each one player that may be relevant for coaching the indvidual athlete, team. Identify likes, dislikes, fears, preferences, weaknesses...
- Ask questions and actively listen to athletes' response.
- Encourage athletes to discuss concerns with you at an appropriate venue.
- Encourage freedom to express struggles and engage in problem resolution.
- Be sensitive, empathic to athletes' needs; try to understand your athletes from their viewpoint. Though don't hesitate to express your viewpoints and engage in a dialogue that allows reaching a common ground especially when viewpints are discrepant.

Content of Workshop 2: communication strategies to maintain effective coach-athlete relationships

The second interactive workshop aimed to articulate and convey the significance of the key communication maintenance strategies to Jim, so that he was better resourced to maintain the relationships that he has established with his athletes in the desired state. In particular, the content of the second workshop targeted several communication strategies that could be utilized by Jim. We considered the proposed communication strategies as independent tools in the coach's toolbox which could be used as and when an appropriate situation arose.

In this workshop, the significance of relationship maintenance to enhance personal and professional development for both Jim and his athletes was introduced. It also focused on the key communication strategies that have been found to be utilized by coaches and athletes to maintain their relationship in their desired state. First, the key relational strategies that have been found to be utilized by coaches and athletes to maintain their relationship in their desired state was discussed. This also enabled an exploration of the relational strategies that Jim currently uses to maintain his relationship with athletes. Second, guidelines were provided to Jim as to how to employ these key communication strategies to help maintain a quality relationship, examples of which are provided below. Finally, there was a discussion was into the current relational issues that Jim felt he needed to direct his attention to, in addition to understanding the feasibility of employing such strategies with his current athletes. Here he was also asked to develop a contingency plan to determine how such strategies could be implemented with the current squad.

Management and resolution of relational conflict. Jim knew that an effective and harmonious relationship is not characterized by the absence of conflict and disagreement, but rather the deployment of effective processes to manage and resolve conflict and disagreement (Rhind & Jowett, 2010). Various areas within his sport and organization that have the potential to result in conflict or disagreement with his athletes (e.g., training expectations, tactics, feedback, role clarity, player selection and deselection, etc.) were highlighted and discussed. Jim was trained to explore and identify the underlying issues that were manifesting as interpersonal conflict in the relationship through the use of case studies, which he was asked to work through. Rather than treating the symptoms, he was encouraged to identify the source of the problems using problem-solving techniques. Once the source was identified, he was encouraged to find appropriate solutions with the input of the athlete.

Keeping the lines of communication open. Extending from the information from Workshop 1, promoting the disclosure of personal feelings and thoughts to enhance openness within the dyadic relationship was reinforced further. Jim was encouraged that such disclosure processes are not a one-off event, but should occur regularly throughout the season (e.g., weekly one-to-one meetings or in an open forum).

Providing assurance and support to athletes. Jim was encouraged to create a coaching environment that is supportive, nurturing, and encouraging. Specifically the principles of achievement theory (Ames, 1992; Nicholls, 1984) and Basic psychological needs (Ryan & Deci, 2001) was reinforced. Areas of focus included providing task-involving motivational climate, ensuring that athletes' basic psychological needs of competency, relatedness, and autonomy were being met. Here Jim also explored and reflected upon how he currently provides support and feedback to his athletes when they come to see him with concerns.

Encourage athletes' motivation to commit to the coach-athlete partnership for the long term. Jim was trained the possible strategies that he could employ with athletes whom they feel are less committed to their working partnership. This includes enhancing athletes' level of enjoyment when training and the setting and adjusting of goals to aid achievement.

Use of preventative strategies to manage athletes' expectations. Jim was encouraged to focus on setting clear and manageable expectations with his athletes as well as communicating the consequences if they were not met. He was encouraged to create an expectations contract in consultation with his athletes, which would be signed by both parties (see Box 13.3).

Description box

BOX 13.3

GUIDELINES FOR DEVELOPING AN EXPECTATIONS CONTRACT WITH ATHLETES (SEE AMERICAN SPORT EDUCATION PROGRAM, 2007)

- **Create an inclusive team environment.**
  Invite and include all members of team to discuss and consult in the development of the expectation contract. This includes any assistant coaches, reserve players, and other professionals involved with the running of the team. This is essential to ensure all members of the team feel involved and contribute to the formulation of the expectation contract.
- **Consider the purpose, function, and content of the contract.**
  It is critical that all members involved are aware that this contract serves to outline how athletes and staff are expected to behave and conduct themselves as well as the consequences when such expectations are not met. The contract can cover behaviours and conduct during training ground and competitions. Deliberate the areas that need to be covered (i.e., roles and responsibilities, sportspersonship behaviours, conflict resolutions) and the areas that do not need to be covered (i.e., athletes' behaviours and relationships outside sport, personal beliefs and attitudes).
- **Consider the importance of the expectations set.**
  It is unlikely that all aspects of staff and athletes' behaviours can be covered nor should the expectation contract seek to legislate every aspect of coaches' and athletes' conduct. Therefore when contemplating and choosing the expectations, take into account the importance of these expectations. Only include expectations that comprise of pertinent issues which impact how the team operates.
- **Reflect on the appropriateness of the consequences for unmet expectations.**
  When selecting the consequences for failing to meet expectations, reflect on the appropriateness of the consequence. They should be in line with the severity and the frequency of the misconduct (i.e., turning up to training late for the first time could equate to extra laps around the track, repeatedly turning up late could resultsin a financial penalty). In addition, have procedure/process in place if staff and athletes want to contend the consequence, especially if they do not think they have violated an expectation. Such process should allow them to voice and treat their concerns in a fair and objective manner.
- **Ensure that all expectations within the contract are clearly explained.**
  Clearly explained expectations will reduce the likelihood of potential misunderstanding, conflict between staff and athletes as well as any breaking of expectations.
- **Review expectations contract at the end of the season:**
  At the end of the season, it is advisable to review the contract set for staff and athletes and reflect how well they were adhered to. This is a forum to discuss whether changes need to be put in place for the forthcoming season (i.e., making aspects of the contract clearer or adding/removing issues of contention).

Source: American Sport Education Program. (2007). Coaches' guide to team policies: Code of conduct for creating a positive environment. Champaign, IL: Human Kinetics.

Strengthening the coach-athlete network. Jim was encouraged to engage in team-building and social activities to promote and further develop his interactions with athletes in line with the recommendations of Paradis and Martin (2009).

REFLECTIONS

As frequently suggested in applied sport psychology literature, it is critical to monitor, evaluate, and reflect on the effectiveness of the psychological support provided to clients (e.g., Thelwell, 2009). Accordingly, the following section will outline the experiences and challenges faced by the consultants, the strategies employed to evaluate the effectiveness of the ISC coaching workshop, and the consultants, before concluding with reflections on alternative interventions that could have been potentially employed with the current client.

Experiences and challenges faced by the consultants

Working with Jim to help raise his awareness and knowledge about forming and maintaining harmonious relationships with his athletes for enhanced performance and wellbeing has been enriching (for all involved). First, it was a valuable experience for us as consultants, because it gave us a direct platform to use theory and research. Second, it was refreshing to work with a very receptive coach and a team (who wanted to learn, wanted to succeed), which allowed us to work closely with them in a non-hindered or controlled way, in particular, noticing and receiving feedback from Jim and his team about how he has re-evaluated his coaching practices and interactions. Specifically, an improvement in his relationship, leadership, management, and coaching and communication skills were noted by players and the coaching staff. Players commented on the fact that Jim was more approachable after the intervention and took time to talk to them about issues unrelated to sport. All parties involved in the team reported that Jim was also more effective and efficient in managing interpersonal conflict within the team. Specifically, Jim commented that he had set up rules about conflict resolution with the team as part of their contract. He had set up a 48-hour rule for all conflict resolution (i.e., athletes and coaches (if involved) had 48 hours to resolve any conflict within the team, before he would get involved). It was quite reassuring and encouraging for us to see Jim actively engage and incorporate our strategies into his coaching behaviours and attitudes.

Although the intervention appeared to be effective, there were a number of challenges and issues that we experienced during this process. First, given the dearth of interventions about interpersonal coaching environments, there was lack of relevant literature to guide and shape our efforts/intervention. However, this challenge gave us the opportunity to be creative and unrestricted in the ways we approached the 'issues'. Another challenge was getting all athletes to engage fully in the intervention. Some athletes were aware of what we were doing and participated in the study by taking part in the interviews and offering us some real insight into the coaching environment. However, others were reluctant and found that engagement in such intervention, infringed on their training time (i.e., completing psychometric questionnaires before or after training). Upon reflection, we considered that the main reason for the disengagement for these athletes, could be due the fact that they didn't benefit much from the workshop, because it was aimed more at Jim. This highlighted to us that we need to continue our effort with the team and implement the intervention with the athletes and other coaching staff. As even one bad relationship can cause a major drift or ripple effect on the entire team and thus attending to this small number of partnerships is exceptionally important for a high-performing team.

Evaluation of the effectiveness of the ISC programme

In order to establish the effects of the ISC education programme, the following assessments was conducted pre, during (e.g., four months post intervention) and post season (end of academic year).

First, questionnaires reflecting of the quality of the coach-athlete relationship and sporting experiences were completed by the athletes and coach. Specifically, the measures assessed the quality of the coach-athlete relationship (e.g., CART-Qs; Jowett, 2009; Jowett & Ntoumanis, 2004; Leadership in Sport Scale; LSS; Chelladurai & Saleh, 1980), satisfaction/enjoyment, motivation, and engagement in sport and coaching (i.e., Athlete Satisfaction Questionnaire: ASQ; Riemer & Chelladurai, 1998), self-esteem (i.e., Rosenberg's Self-esteem Scale; RSES: Rosenberg, 1962), physical self-concept (i.e., Marsh, Hey, Roche, & Perry, 1997) group cohesion (i.e., Group Environment questionnaire; GEQ; Carron, Widmeyer, & Brawley, 1985) and intention to remain training and coaching with the team (i.e., single item enquiring about athletes' and Jim's intention to return the following season). The aim of this profiling and re-profiling technique was to capture any notable improvements in functioning of the coach-athlete relationships, but also in the athletes' and Jim's sporting experiences.

Second, interviews were employed with Jim, other coaching staff, and athletes post season and compared to the initial findings of the need analysis. Similar to the needs analysis, the post-season interviews addressed Jim's post-educational programme coaching behaviours, the quality of their coach-athlete relationship, and communication, as well as their evaluation of their sporting experiences. In the post-season athlete interviews, following the guidelines of Smith and colleagues (1979) athletes were asked to reflect and recall the number of times that Jim interacted in a way that was highlighted in the coaching education educational programme. Generating the behavioural feedback from the other coaches and athletes illustrated changes in Jim's interactions with his team. Finally, during the post-season interviews, Jim was interviewed in relation to his current coaching behaviours, his perception of his relationships with his athletes, as well as whether there have been any behavioural changes in their relationship.

Evaluation of the effectiveness of the sport psychology consultants

As practitioners, not only do we have a responsibility to be aware of the effectiveness of the support that we provide to clients but also recognize and be aware of the effectiveness of the mechanisms and processes involved in our service delivery (Lindsay, Breckon, Thomas, & Maynard, 2007). Accordingly, a team approach was utilized to monitor our effectiveness as practitioners to further aid our development. Specifically, we involved Jim, his athletes, supporting coaches, each other, as well as other sport psychologists in the evaluation process. For example, we had discussions with Jim about our conduct, behaviours, and interactions at the end of each workshop as well as at the end of the season. In addition to this, Jim was asked to complete an informal self-developed feedback sheet, on which he was asked to rate the content of the workshops (i.e., was it applied, was it relevant), our mode of delivery (i.e., presentation style, communication skills), and areas that we could improve upon. Finally, he completed a Consultant Evaluation Form (CEF: see Partington & Orlick, 1987) at the end of the season and rated the amount and type of contact we formed, as well as our knowledge, our ability to provide an individualized programme, our personal qualities such as being open, flexible, empathetic, and approachable. To further complement this, we also conducted informal discussions with the athletes and members of Jim's team about our conduct and our ability to integrate and connect with the team.

One of the advantages of providing psychological support to Jim as part of a team of sport psychology consultants was that it offered the opportunity for peer supervision and generated immediate feedback for each other, from each other. This is a tool which is routinely employed within counselling settings (Cross, 2011). Peer supervision is considered to increase skill development, self-monitoring, personal growth, and instructive feedback (Borders, 1991). Although there appears to be a literature stressing the importance and usefulness of peer supervision within the sport psychology literature (e.g., Andersen & Williams-Rice, 1996; Walker & Waumsley, 2012), there is a lack of clear guidelines on how to implement peer supervision with sport psychology. Thus, we adopted the dyadic peer supervision implemented by Cross (2011). The dyadic peer supervision consisted of five phases; (1) the presentation of the case or issue and request for assistance statement, (2) the questioning period and identification of focus, (3) the feedback statement, (4) the supervisee response, and (5) optional discussion period. Each session took around 40 minutes and was employed routinely over the course of the consultation period. Embedded within the peer supervision, we also used peer observations. Specifically, this involved both consultants jointly deciding on the areas that each other would observe and focus on a backdrop of agreed criteria, followed by constructive feedback, and discussion. The themes from the discussion were then used to formulate future strategies and developments.

Reflections on providing an alternative mode of delivery

Coaches and athletes develop a two-way relationship whereby their feelings, thoughts, and behaviours are reciprocally related (Jowett, 2005; Rhind & Jowett, 2012). Bearing this in mind, it is clear that we only offered psychological support to one member of the relationship, namely the coach. While we aimed to empower and equip Jim with the resources to relate with his athletes more effectively and efficiently, we neglected the responsibility and contribution of the athletes in the development and maintenance of this powerful relationship. Moreover, this relationship does not exist in isolation. Rather there are a number of other social influences (e.g., coaching staff, parents, athletic directors). Accordingly, these social agents have the capacity to influence the coach-athlete relationship. Thus, it might have been beneficial to deliver the proposed workshops to Jim, his athletes, coaching team, parents, and athletic directors, so that they are aware of their role in the development of meaningful coach-athlete relationship. Moreover, given that interventions are considered to be more effective if the client has social support and encouragement from their social network (e.g., Côté, 1999), it is possible that by incorporating significant others and raising their awareness of the principles, that they can work together to maximize the development of an effective coach-athlete relationship.

Reflections on providing an alternative intervention

There are number of different avenues that we could have taken with Jim in terms of intervention. Rather than focusing on improving the quality of the coach-athlete relationship dyad, we could have taken an approach to change the environment in which the coach and the athletes are embedded. Specifically, we could have focused on improving the team dynamics (with Jim included) and changing the climate of sporting environment in which they operate, rather than dyadic relationships that make up the team. Drawing from the group cohesion literature it has been suggested that the ability of a team to foster unity, emotional closeness, commitment to each other and promote togetherness and teamwork is the most salient variable in enhancing performance in sport teams and favourable athletic, personal, and group outcomes (e.g., Carron, Eys, & Burke, 2007). Thus it may have been beneficial for Jim, his athletes and those that work closely with the team to work together to promote the development of a cohesive team. The common and effective method of enhancing cohesion is through team-building exercises such as setting team goals, enhancing interpersonal relationships, engaging in adventure experiences, and activities that encompassed the development of team roles, environment, and processes (Martin et al., 2009). Thus we could have employed team-building exercises with Jim and his entire team to improve the environment in which they operate.

SUMMARY

The significance of coach-athlete interactions has been highlighted to be critical in determining the athletic and psychosocial development of athletes and coaches. While it is common for sport psychology consultants to work with athletes, coaches, support staff, and sport organizations to help improve athletes' performance, providing sport psychology support to empower coaches is an area that has received minimal attention. Thus the chapter outlined the role of sport psychology consultants in providing psychological support to a coach operating within a university setting. Drawing upon the current evidence-based theoretical frameworks of 3+1C and COMPASS model, we described the delivery of an informal two-part interactive Interpersonal Sport Coaching workshop aimed at helping the coach in developing and maintaining effective and harmonious relationship with his athletes. The focus on developing quality relationships was thought important as it would help accelerate the development of a positive purposeful environment early in the season which would ultimately serve as a sound foundation to achieve specific goals including skill development, performance success, and personal growth of both relationship members.

Discussion box

BOX 13.4

1) Discuss the contribution of the 3+1c and COMPASS model in enhancing our understanding of the significance of the coach-athlete relationship for personal and professional development.
2) What factors might influence the effectiveness of sport psychologists in terms of working with a university coach?
3) What are the practical difficulties associated with delivering psycho-educational workshops?
4) Consider the limitations of using retrospective recall as a method to evaluate the effectiveness of the intervention. What can be done to minimize the effects of such recall?
5) Consider how this intervention can be applied with other coaches or athletes across different sports, contexts, performance levels.

Key future research box

BOX 13.5

Understand the content of conflict, its nature and processes, including antecedents and consequences of coach-athlete interpersonal conflict.

How specific events such as success/failure, the incidence of eating disorders, injury and burnout can influence the quality of the coach-athlete relationship.

How individual difference characteristics (e.g., gender) especially personality play a role in the quality and functions of the coach-athlete relationship as well as communication patterns.

FURTHER READING

Jowett, S. (2007). Interdependence analysis and the 3 + 1Cs model in the coach-athlete relationship. In S. Jowett & D. Lavallee (Eds.), *Social psychology in sport* (pp. 15–27). Champaign, IL: Human Kinetics. This chapter provides a comprehensive overview of the theoretical framework underpinning the coach-athlete relationship as well as the supporting empirical evidence. It guides the reader through from the conceptualization of the coach-athlete relationship, the development of instruments to assess the presence of the key relational components as well as the factors that affect and are affected by coach-athlete relations.

Langan, E., Blake, C., & Lonsdale, C. (2013). Systematic review of the effectiveness of interpersonal coach education interventions on athlete outcomes. *Psychology of Sport and Exercise 14*, 37–49. This article provides a comprehensive review of all the informal psycho-educational coaching interventions conducted within the sporting context. It examines the underlying theories that which have guided such as interventions as well as a look into effectiveness of these outcomes on athletes' physical and psychosocial development.

Jowett, S., & Felton, L. (2014). Relationships and attachments in teams. In M. Beauchamp & M. Eys, *Group dynamics advances in sport and exercise psychology* (2nd ed., pp. 73–92). New York: Routledge. This chapter provides a comprehensive review of the 3+1Cs model as well as the conceptualization of the coach-athlete relationship from an attachment theory perspective. It further provides an overview of the research underpinning both these theoretical models.

Sullivan, P., Jowett, S., Rhind, D. (2014). Communication in sport teams. In A. Papaioannou & D. Hackfort (Eds), *Routledge companion to sport and exercise psychology: Global perspectives and fundamental concepts* (pp. 559–570) . London: Routledge. In this chapter, the emphasis is placed on understanding communication in team sports. It includes theoretical and empirical information on the COMPASS model and CARM-Q.

REFERENCES

Ames, C. (1992). Achievement goals, motivational climate, and motivational processes. In G. C. Roberts (Ed.), *Motivation in sport and exercise* (pp. 161–176). Champaign, IL: Human Kinetics.

Andersen, M. B., & Williams-Rice, B. T. (1996). Supervision in the education and training of sport psychology service providers. *The Sport Psychologist, 10*, 278–290.

Beck, A. T. (1993). Cognitive therapy – past, present, and future. *Journal of Consulting and Clinical Psychology, 61*, 194–198.

Beck, A. T. (2008). The evolution of the cognitive model of depression and its neurobiological correlates. *American Journal of Psychiatry, 165*, 969–977.

Borders, D. L. (1991). A systematic approach to peer group supervision. *Journal of Counseling and Development*, 69(3), 248–252.

Carron, A. V., Eys, M. A., & Burke, S. M. (2007). Team cohesion: Nature, correlates and development. In S. Jowett and D. Lavellee (Eds.), *Social Psychology in Sport* (pp. 91–101). Champaign, IL: Human Kinetics.

Chelladurai, P., & Saleh, S. D. (1980). Dimensions of leader behavior in sports: development of a leadership scale. *Journal of Sport Psychology, 2*, 34–45.

Collins, J., & Durand-Bush, N. (2010). Enhancing the cohesion and performance of an elite curling team through a self-regulation intervention. *International Journal of Sports Science and Coaching, 5*, 343–362.

Côté, J. (1999). The influence of the family in the development of talent in sport. *The Sport Psychologist, 13*(4), 395–417.

Cross, A. (2011). Self- and peer-assessment: The case of peer supervision in counselling psychology. *Investigations in University Teaching and Learning, 7*, 1740–5106.

Davis, L., & Jowett, S. (2010). Investigating the interpersonal dynamics between coaches and athletes based on fundamental principles of attachment. *Journal of Clinical Sport Psychology*, 4(2), 112–132.

Duda, J. (2013). The conceptual and empirical foundations of empowering coaching: Setting the stage for the PAPA project. *International Journal of Sport and Exercise Psychology, 11*, 311–318.

Henriksen, K., Diment, G., & Hansen, J. (2011). Professional philosophy: Inside the delivery of sport psychology service at team Denmark. *Sport Science Review. Volume XX*, 5–21.

Holder, T. (2009). Developing coach education materials in table tennis – applying a cyclical model of performance. In B.Hemmings & T.Holder (Eds.), *Applied sport psychology: A case-based approach* (pp. 162–166). Chichester: John Wiley and Sons, Ltd.

Ivey, A. E., Ivey, M. B., & Simek-Morgan, L. (1993). *Counseling and psychotherapy. A multicultural perspective* (3rd ed.). Boston: Allyn and Bacon.

Jowett, S. (2005). Partners on the sport field: The coach-athlete relationship, *The Psychologist, 18*, 412–415.

Jowett, S. (2007). Interdependence analysis and the 3 + 1Cs model in the coach-athlete relationship. In S. Jowett & D. Lavallee (Eds.), *Social Psychology in Sport* (pp. 15–27). Champaign, IL: Human Kinetics.

Jowett, S. (2009). Validating the coach athlete relationship measures with the nomological network. *Measurement in Physical Education and Exercise Science, 13*, 34–51.

Jowett, S., & Felton, L. (2014). Relationships and attachments in teams. In M. Beauchamp & M. Eys (Eds.), *Group dynamics advances in sport and exercise psychology* (*2nd* ed., pp. 73–92). New York: Routledge.

Jowett, S., & Nezlek, J. (2012). Relationship interdependence and satisfaction with important outcomes in coach – athlete dyads, *Journal of Social and Personal Relationships, 29*, 287–301.

Jowett, S., & Ntoumanis, N. (2004). The Coach-athlete Relationship Questionnaire (CART – Q): Development and initial validation. *Scandinavian Journal of Medicine and Science in Sports, 14*, 245–257.

Kleinert, J., Ohlert, J., Carron, B., Eys, M., Feltz, D., & Harwood, C., et al. (2012). Group dynamics in sports: An overview and recommendations on diagnostic and intervention. *The Sport Psychologist, 26*(3), 412–434.

Langan, E., Blake, C., & Lonsdale, C. (2013). A systematic review of the effectiveness of interpersonal coach education programmes on athlete outcomes. *Psychology of Sport and Exercise, 14*, 37–49.

Lindsay, P., Breckon, J., Thomas, O., and Maynard, I. (2007). In pursuit of congruence: A personal reflection upon methods and philosophy in applied practice. *The Sport Psychologist, 21*(3), 273–289.

Martin, L. J., Carron, A. V., & Burke, S. M. (2009). Team building interventions in sport: A meta-analysis. *Sport and Exercise Psychology Review, 5*(2), 3–18.

Nicholls, J. (1984). Conceptions of ability and achievement motivation. In R. Ames & C. Ames (Eds.), *Research on motivation in education: Student motivation* (Vol. *1*, pp. 39–73). New York: Academic Press.

Partington, J., & Orlick ,T. (1987). The sport psychology consultant: Analysis of critical components as viewed by Canadian Olympic athletes. *The Sport Psychologist, 1*(1), 4–17.

Poczwardowski, A., Sherman, C. P., & Ravizza, K. (2004). Professional philosophy in the sport psychology service delivery: Building on theory and practice.*The Sport Psychologist, 18*(2), 445–463.

Post, P., & Muncie, S. (2012). The effects of imagery training on swimming performance: An applied investigation'.*Journal of Applied Sport Psychology, 24*, 323–337.

Riemer, H. A., & Chelladurai, P. (1998). Development of the athlete satisfaction questionnaire. *Journal of Sport and Exercise Psychology, 20*(2), 127–156.

Rhind, D. J. A., & Jowett, S. (2010). Relationship maintenance strategies in the coach–athlete relationship: The development of the COMPASS model. *Journal of Applied Sport Psychology, 22*, 106–121.

Rhind, D. J. A., & Jowett, S. (2011). Linking maintenance strategies to the quality of coach-athlete relationships, *International Journal of Sport Psychology, 42*(1), 55–68.

Rhind, D., & Jowett, S. (2012). Development of the Coach-Athlete Relationship Maintenance Questionnaire (CARM-Q), *International Journal of Sports Science and Coaching,7* (1), 121–137.

Ryan, R. M., & Deci, E. L. (2001). On happiness and human potentials: A review of research on hedonic and eudaimonic well-being. In S.Fiske (Ed.), *Annual review of psychology* (pp. 141–166). Palo Alto, CA: Annual Reviews, Inc.

Smith, A. L. (2007). Youth peer relationships in sport. In S. J. Jowett & D. Lavallee (Eds.), *Social Psychology in Sport* (pp. 41–54). Champaign, IL: Human Kinetics.

Smith, R. E., Smoll, F. L., & Cumming, S. P. (2007). Effects of a motivational climate intervention for coaches on young athletes' sport performance anxiety. *Journal of Sport and Exercise Psychology, 29*(1), 39–59.

Smith, R. E., Smoll, F. L., & Curtis, B. (1979). Coach effectiveness training: A cognitive behavioural approach to enhancing relationship skills in youth sport coaches. *Journal of Sport Psychology*, *1*(1), 59–75.

Thelwell, R. (2009). Team goal setting in professional football. In B. Hemmings & T. Holder T. (Eds.), *Applied sport psychology: A case-based approach* (pp. 161–180). Chichester: John Wiley & Sons, Ltd.

Walker, N., & Waumsley, J. (2012). Peer supervision beyond training in sport psychology consulting – lessons from counselling psychology. In BPS DSEP Conference, London, 18–20 April 2012, London.

Weinberg, R. S., & Williams, J. M. (2006). Integrating and implementing a psychological skills training training program. In J. M. Williams, (Ed.), *Applied sport psychology: Personal growth to peak performance* (pp. 425–457). Palo Alto, CA: Mayfield.

Yang, S. X., & Jowett, S. (2013). Conceptual and measurement issues of the complementarity dimension of the coach-athlete relationship across cultures, *Psychology of Sport and Exercise*, *14*, 830–841.

Part 3 Motor Learning and Control

14 The Role of Psychology in Enhancing Skill Acquisition and Expertise in High Performance Programmes

Keith Davids, Ian Renshaw, Ross Pinder, Dan Greenwood, and Sian Barris

LEARNING OBJECTIVES

AFTER READING THIS CHAPTER YOU SHOULD BE ABLE TO:

1. Critically evaluate weaknesses of traditional models of skill acquisition that over-emphasize the role of repetitive practice of a common optimal movement template.
2. Develop understanding of key concepts in ecological dynamics, a theoretical framework for conceptualizing athletes as complex, adaptive systems.
3. Understand why an ecological dynamics conceptualization of practice in sport involves the search for functional movement solutions, under changing performance conditions.
4. Reflect on how practice task constraints can be designed to be *representative* of performance task constraints, so that faithful simulations of competitive contexts can be created.

AREAS TO CONSIDER WHEN READING THE CHAPTER:

1. What is your model of the learner?
2. What is your model of the learning process?
3. How can practice task constraints be made more faithful as simulations of competitive performance environments?
4. How can psychologists encourage athletes to be more adaptive and innovative in performance?

CLIENTS AND BACKGROUND

Case Study 1: maximizing representativeness in practice to learn to face fast bowling

Problem: Preparing batters to face fast bowling
Setting: Senior representative cricket team
Constraints: Access to fast bowlers

The coach of the County U-19 yrs cricket team, Scotty Turner, had a problem. As county U-19 champions from the previous season, his team were invited to represent the country in an off-season international competition in South Africa with the opposition consisting of state and regional representative teams from all around the world. While excited and honoured to be coaching a team representing his country, Scotty is also worried that his team won't be able to compete at this new level of performance. Through his contacts across the world, Scotty has found out that at least three of the teams have fast bowlers who can bowl 150 km·h-1. While Scotty's team had some good medium-pace bowlers, none of them could bowl at that sort of pace. He wondered how he could prepare the young batters in the team for this baptism of fire.

Scotty's first thought was to 'borrow' the fast bowlers from the club's senior men's teams, one of whom had previously played for England while another was pushing international selection. He asked the coaches about their availability, but, frustratingly one had a long-term back injury and was rehabilitating while the other one was spending the winter in Australia.

His next idea was to replicate the demands of facing the fast bowler by using the available bowling machine. He did not particularly like using the machine as his instincts told him that using the machine led to changes in the co-ordination of batters as they often moved early into position, predicting the release of the ball, and were 'lying in wait for the ball' (Renshaw et al., 2007). He could not see much of an alternative.

Scotty realized that he needed to gain a better understanding of psychological research on processes of skill acquisition to enable him to design faithful practice tasks for his cricketers. He mulled over a couple of ideas he had gained from reading around the psychology literature on designing practice tasks for enhancing skill acquisition in sport. One source that proved to be particularly useful was a new blog site on constraints-led cricket coaching (ianrensh.wordpress.com). Interestingly, the first psychological study he read discussed the use of bowling machines, which intrigued him. Much as his instincts had told him, it provided empirical evidence that removing the information available in a bowler's actions led to detrimental performance changes in batter's timing and co-ordination (see Pinder et al., 2009). Two further psychological studies he read piqued his interest, discussing an integration of video images and ball projection technology to develop perception-action couplings (Pinder et al., 2011a; Stone et al., 2014). These articles seemed perfect for Scotty's needs. They made him realize that he needed a strong theoretical rationale and research evidence from psychology to develop his understanding of how to systematically prepare batters to face fast bowling. The final article considered a concept called *The BattleZone*, which was a small-sided, constraints-led games approach that takes place inside a modified net placed on the 30 m one-day circle in cricket (Renshaw & Chappell, 2010). Scotty decided to use a combination of the three approaches to prepare the batters for the competition in South Africa. He needed to balance the needs of the batters to face real bowlers with the workload demands of the team's medium-pace bowlers.

Before training commenced in preparation for the tournament, Scotty decided to measure the speeds of the faster bowlers using a speed gun he had borrowed from a friend in the local university sport science department. A sport psychologist there had been experimenting with the use of a small camera (MiSite® technology: www.eyeman.com.au). He lent the equipment to Scotty who placed it on the first and second XI batters' helmets, revealing footage of their fast bowlers.

With the bowling speed data he had collected, Scotty used the speed conversion table he had found on the blog (see Table 14.1) to work out the distance the bowlers would need to bowl from in order to replicate the temporal demands of facing the 150 kmh1 bowlers in the tournament. He measured out distances and drew lines on the pitch indicating where the batters should stand for each bowler. He then designed constraints-based practice tasks using the BattleZone concept which he set up in the large indoor school with all the nets pulled back. He gave the bowlers a script that replicated the typical strategies of fast bowlers (e.g., a series of short balls into the ribs of the batters to try and get catches for fielders positioned close in on the legside, before following up with a well-pitched up delivery to try and catch the batter on the crease). These practice task constraints provide a faithful simulation of the competitive performance environment in cricket, by enabling batters to experience the feelings of facing very fast bowlers and helping them to develop strategies to find the best way for them to deal with fast bowling.

In line with the psychology research on video-based training, Scotty initially had to hire a large screen and projector to help demonstrate his training design. Using simple maths he was able to provide a realistic image of the bowlers on the screen based on the height of the bowler and distance of the batsmen from the screen (see Pinder et al., 2011b). When the club noted how successful the video-based training was, the high-performance department released funds to buy the large screen and projector, and Scotty used the video screen extensively throughout the programme. Through careful editing Scotty created training sets designed to simulate the same game scenarios he had set up in the BattleZone games. Importantly, for each set, he knew the landing points of each delivery and was able to assess whether the batters were organizing movements accordingly. In one psychology article, Scotty had read about *representative design* of practice tasks and, to further increase the *representativeness* of his practice tasks, Scotty asked the players to bat in pairs, just like they would in a game. The non-batting partner stood behind the batter and between them they adjudged the success of their responses. He observed from the video-based training that the batters were able to 'face' the really quick first and second XI bowlers on screen by attuning to the bowler's actions and the release point of the delivery. For example, Will Springer was a promising batter, but the previous summer he'd had a lot of trouble against quicker bowlers. Scotty had read in some media articles that the national team tended to practise extensively against a ball projection machine whenever they experienced technical problems. He encouraged Will to do the same, but he didn't seem to be getting any better. After reading the psychological research on perception-action coupling, Scotty understood why Will had looked tentative when facing the fast bowlers, and didn't appear to have time to organize his responses particularly when trying to play forward. Scotty knew that to progress past this stage would take a considerable amount of time facing the bowlers so that he could judge the length of the ball quickly by attuning to information from the ball release points of the bowlers. He saw this as an ideal opportunity to make use of the video-based projection technology and test its usefulness. Will trained regularly to couple his batting actions with images of the first and second XI fast bowlers on the video screen and was soon able to move either forward or back quickly and not get 'stuck on the crease'. Having built up his confidence from repeatedly judging the length and line of deliveries, Scotty helped Will to use this knowledge to face the 'real' fast bowlers in the shape of his team mates bowling from the reduced delivery distances. He quickly adapted to the greater temporal demands and moved back behind short balls or well forward into deliveries to hit the ball straight back passed the bowler.

Table 14.1 *Bowling distances-speed conversion chart: for example, if a coach wants a batter to learn to face 140 km h^{-1} bowlers but only has a 125 km h^{-1} available then you look up the full distance (1) time to contact for the 140 km h^{-1} bowler (0.45 s) and then look up the temporal equivalent for the 125 km h^{-1} bowler (2). The distance the bowler should deliver the ball from is therefore 15.68 m.*

		full		25cm		50cm		75cm		1m		1.25m		1.50m		1.75m		2m	
km h	msec	distance	time	distance	time	distance	time	distance	time	distance	time	distance	time	distance	time	distance	time	distance	time
50000	13.89	17.68	1.27	17.43	1.25	17.18	1.24	16.93	1.22	16.68	1.20	16.43	1.18	16.18	1.16	15.93	1.15	15.68	1.13
55000	15.28	17.68	1.16	17.43	1.14	17.18	1.12	16.93	1.11	16.68	1.09	16.43	1.08	16.18	1.06	15.93	1.04	15.68	1.03
60000	16.67	17.68	1.06	17.43	1.05	17.18	1.03	16.93	1.02	16.68	1.00	16.43	0.99	16.18	0.97	15.93	0.96	15.68	0.94
65000	18.06	17.68	0.98	17.43	0.97	17.18	0.95	16.93	0.94	16.68	0.92	16.43	0.91	16.18	0.90	15.93	0.88	15.68	0.87
70000	19.44	17.68	0.91	17.43	0.90	17.18	0.88	16.93	0.87	16.68	0.86	16.43	0.84	16.18	0.83	15.93	0.82	15.68	0.81
75000	20.83	17.68	0.85	17.43	0.84	17.18	0.82	16.93	0.81	16.68	0.80	16.43	0.79	16.18	0.78	15.93	0.76	15.68	0.75
80000	22.22	17.68	0.80	17.43	0.78	17.18	0.77	16.93	0.76	16.68	0.75	16.43	0.74	16.18	0.73	15.93	0.72	15.68	0.71
85000	23.61	17.68	0.75	17.43	0.74	17.18	0.73	16.93	0.72	16.68	0.71	16.43	0.70	16.18	0.69	15.93	0.67	15.68	0.66
90000	25.00	17.68	0.71	17.43	0.70	17.18	0.69	16.93	0.68	16.68	0.67	16.43	0.66	16.18	0.65	15.93	0.64	15.68	0.63
95000	26.39	17.68	0.67	17.43	0.66	17.18	0.65	16.93	0.64	16.68	0.63	16.43	0.62	16.18	0.61	15.93	0.60	15.68	0.59
100000	27.78	17.68	0.64	17.43	0.63	17.18	0.62	16.93	0.61	16.68	0.60	16.43	0.59	16.18	0.58	15.93	0.57	15.68	0.56
105000	29.17	17.68	0.61	17.43	0.60	17.18	0.59	16.93	0.58	16.68	0.57	16.43	0.56	16.18	0.55	15.93	0.55	15.68	0.54
110000	30.56	17.68	0.58	17.43	0.57	17.18	0.56	16.93	0.55	16.68	0.55	16.43	0.54	16.18	0.53	15.93	0.52	15.68	0.51
115000	31.94	17.68	0.55	17.43	0.55	17.18	0.54	16.93	0.53	16.68	0.52	16.43	0.51	16.18	0.51	15.93	0.50	15.68	0.49
120000	33.33	17.68	0.53	17.43	0.52	17.18	0.52	16.93	0.51	16.68	0.50	16.43	0.49	16.18	0.49	15.93	0.48	15.68	0.47
125000	34.72	17.68	0.51	17.43	0.50	17.18	0.49	16.93	0.49	16.68	0.48	16.43	0.47	16.18	0.47	15.93	0.46	15.68	0.45
130000	36.11	17.68	0.49	17.43	0.48	17.18	0.48	16.93	0.47	16.68	0.46	16.43	0.45	16.18	0.45	15.93	0.44	15.68	0.43
135000	37.50	17.68	0.47	17.43	0.46	17.18	0.46	16.93	0.45	16.68	0.44	16.43	0.44	16.18	0.43	15.93	0.42	15.68	0.42
140000	38.89	17.68	0.45	17.43	0.45	17.18	0.44	16.93	0.44	16.68	0.43	16.43	0.42	16.18	0.42	15.93	0.41	15.68	0.40
145000	40.28	17.68	0.44	17.43	0.43	17.18	0.43	16.93	0.42	16.68	0.41	16.43	0.41	16.18	0.40	15.93	0.40	15.68	0.39
150000	41.67	17.68	0.42	17.43	0.42	17.18	0.41	16.93	0.41	16.68	0.40	16.43	0.39	16.18	0.39	15.93	0.38	15.68	0.38
155000	43.06	17.68	0.41	17.43	0.40	17.18	0.40	16.93	0.39	16.68	0.39	16.43	0.38	16.18	0.38	15.93	0.37	15.68	0.36
160000	44.44	17.68	0.40	17.43	0.39	17.18	0.39	16.93	0.38	16.68	0.38	16.43	0.37	16.18	0.36	15.93	0.36	15.68	0.35

FIGURE 14.1 *Integration of video images with ball projection technology to help a cricketer learn how to use anticipation processes from pre-ball flight information from a bowler in co-ordinating their actions.*

The video-based training was always linked to regular BattleZone practice where batters were required to link in these judgements (e.g., attempting to change the pace on the ball, or working the ball into specific gaps or avoiding close catchers placed on the legside) and practise running between the wickets (see Renshaw & Holder, 2010). A range of practice designs helped to counter the constraints Scotty faced. Using a combination of innovative and imaginative representative practice tasks, the county U19s were well prepared for the challenges of the international tournament and Scotty and his batters were confident they could handle anything that the opposition fast bowlers threw at them. Having developed a theoretical model of how each learner acquires movement skill as a result of experience and practice, Scotty now felt that he had a principled-base programme to help him solve performance problems like this in the future.

Case Study 2: harnessing adaptive movement variability in sports training

Problem: Encouraging elite athletes to change practice styles
Setting: A national high-performance training programme in springboard diving
Constraints: Designing practice task constraints that simulate competitive performance conditions in springboard diving

A training intervention was designed in an elite springboard diving training programme to encourage divers to explore the variability of the dive take-off and continue with dives where they would normally baulk (for details of the full intervention, see Barris et al., 2014). Divers were asked to continue with normal prescribed practice, aiming for good-quality dive entries on each dive, but to continue with the dive approach and take-off regardless of their perceived quality. We sought to observe whether the athletes would acquire the ability to adapt to their environmental conditions and complete a consistent entry of the water regardless of the quality of the hurdle take-off. This strategy gave the divers the opportunity to explore a larger range of movement solutions to successfully complete a dive. The performance of each elite athlete was monitored throughout all training sessions (ten per week) for one week, to record any baulks that occurred in both aquatic and dry-land environments (springboards set up over foam pits and crash pads in a gymnasium). To minimize any influence on performance, the athletes were initially unaware that the frequency of baulks was being recorded. These observations were used as a reference for the intervention. Experiential knowledge offered by the elite athletes (n = 4) during training sessions prior to the training programme, provided some insights into their attitude towards baulking:

> I baulked four times in training, then in comp ('competition') I was too far forward, but I had to go ... I would have baulked again if it was training. (Personal communication, Participant 1 Augus 2011)

Additionally, Participant 4 shared her feelings about baulking in training:

> I know it's wrong but it seems like a waste to go on a bad hurdle, I have to get out and dry myself; it takes longer, so it's easier to baulk while you are on the board and start again ... It makes sense to me that I should only go off good hurdles, I only want to practise the good ones. (Personal communication, Participant 4, September 2011)

At the end of the observation week, a meeting was held with the divers to explain the details of the intervention and why it was important for them to change their training behaviours. The athletes were told to follow their normal coach prescribed training programme, and received feedback from the coach about their performance as normal. Specifically the athletes were given the following instructions.

- Avoid baulking except in situations where you feel unsafe.
- Instead of baulking, use poor hurdles and get off the springboard by completing any dive, for example these completion strategies might include: a double bounce on the board, performing a dive with a lower degree of difficulty instead, implementing dives from a different dive group. On every entry (whether it was the intended dive or not), they were encouraged to work hard for the best possible entry into the water. The purpose of this re-emphasis on learning design was to shift the focus of the athletes away from seeking a consistent take-off, to seeking a consistent entry into the water.

The progressiveness of daily diving practice (increasing the complexity of the skills from simple to most complex) allowed the divers to safely prepare for this movement adaptation approach by starting with more simple dives first:

- As the intervention progressed, the athletes were encouraged to complete an intended dive regardless of take-off (except in unsafe situations).
- On every entry (whether it was the intended dive or not), they were encouraged to work hard for the best possible entry.

Use of ball projection machines in practice?

May 23, 2008

Hockey machine helps England to catch on

"A machine constructed to hone the skills of hockey goalkeepers is being used by England to improve catching and Richard Halsall, the new fielding coach who presented it to the squad during the build-up to the npower Test series, is planning to "pinch" from more sports before the season is out."

From *The Times*

http:/www.smh.com.au/sport/cricket/ponting-risking-his-legacy-by-inviting-tap-on-shoulder-benaud-20111114-1nflo.html

Ponting risking his legacy by inviting tap on shoulder: Benaud

Sydney Morning Herald, November 15, 2011

'Ricky just looks all at sea, that might be a bit harsh but he's not the player he was, as you would expect. I just think he runs the risk of it all ending in tears if he's not careful.'

Ponting, however, has left no stone unturned in his bid to rediscover his form, spending at least an hour-and-a-half batting in front of a bowling machine under the watch of coaches Dene Hills and Justin Langer.

Arthur directs his blundering Test batsmen to training camp

Chris Barrett

Excerpts from the *Sydney Morning Herald* 15 December 2011

'We're going to practise against the swinging ball'... Mickey Arthur.

Batting camps are generally reserved for schoolboy and junior cricketers not the likes of Ricky Ponting, Australia's greatest swinger of the blade since Bradman. Yet that is exactly what is in store for Australia's batsmen after the calling of a three-day camp in Melbourne in the lead-up to the Boxing Day Tests against India. Ponting will be joined by Test captain Michael Clarke, Michael Hussey, Brad Haddin, as well as Dan Christian, Shane Watson, and possibly Shaun Marsh in the MCG nets from next Tuesday.
Clarke and Warner aside, Australia's batsmen have not been in the finest of touch of late, capitulating infamously for 47 in Cape Town last month and playing a central part in an embarrassing seven-run defeat to New Zealand in Hobart on Monday.

The Melbourne batting summit, coach Mickey Arthur said, is simply being arranged to sharpen the focus on the headline act of the summer. "What we're going to do at the batting camp is we're going to talk about the Indian bowlers, we're going to set up bowling machines a la Ishant Sharma, guys like that," he said.

"We're going to practise against the swinging ball and get our basics right before Boxing Day. There's no major reconstruction of anyone's technique - it's literally getting our guys thinking about the Test match, thinking as a group and honing our four-day skills to get the guys best prepared to play on Boxing Day. We're not reshaping anybody's technique or anything."

http://www.smh.com.au/sport/cricket/arthur-directs-his-blundering-test-batsmen-to-training-camp-20111214-1ouze.html#ixzz1gjuYU6bW

FIGURE 14.2 *Media documentation of assumptions of sport practitioners and common misconceptions of the role of ball projection machines. Note that in the first example, it is clear that the ball projection machine is being used to practise a variety of interceptive actions (fielding practice as well as batting). Regardless, the same problem arises in that affordances for a* batting action *are not provided for fielders to learn to anticipate characteristics of a stroke (e.g., anticipating impending ball trajectory from speed and angle of bat orientation). In the third example the notion that ball projection technology can be used to practise against specific opponents is a misconception. Without pre-flight information,* the actions of a specific bowler *cannot be factored into this practice aim. We have limited our analysis to exemplar sources in England and Australia in the past six years.*

Table 14.2 *Self-reporting of athletes' dive completions during a training intervention.*

Name	*Completed*	*Uncomfortable*	*Baulk*
SB	*1, 2*	*4, 5*	*3*

During each training session, participants were asked to record their perceptions of each dive in chronological order in one of three columns (completed, uncomfortable, baulk) on a whiteboard positioned at the base of the springboard. Dives where the athlete felt comfortable and completed the intended action were recorded in the completed column. Dives perceived as uncomfortable were classified as those where the athlete would previously have baulked, but instead in the new training programme attempted a dive (regardless of whether it was an intended dive or not). Finally, baulked dives were those where the athlete aborted the take-off. For example, if a diver completed five dives and the first two were completed successfully, the third one was a baulk and the fourth and fifth were uncomfortable (i.e., the athlete would complete the board as shown in Table 14.2).

Over the period of the intervention we hoped to see a progressive decrease in baulks and an increase in uncomfortable dives, followed by a decrease in dives rated uncomfortable and an increase in completed dives. The athlete's scores were recorded to track progress, and feedback was provided to them at regular intervals. Individual athlete performances throughout the training programme were considered as line graphs in the post-intervention period of reflection (see Figure 14.3).

As part of this process, each diver also took part in 16 simulated competitions where one attempt at each dive was filmed from the judges' seating location for retrospective analysis. The average score for each participant's reverse and back dives are presented in Figure 14.4.

The average back dive score is reported as a control, because it was practised as much as the other dives (front and reverse). But it was not part of the training intervention as it did not require a forward (hurdle) approach.

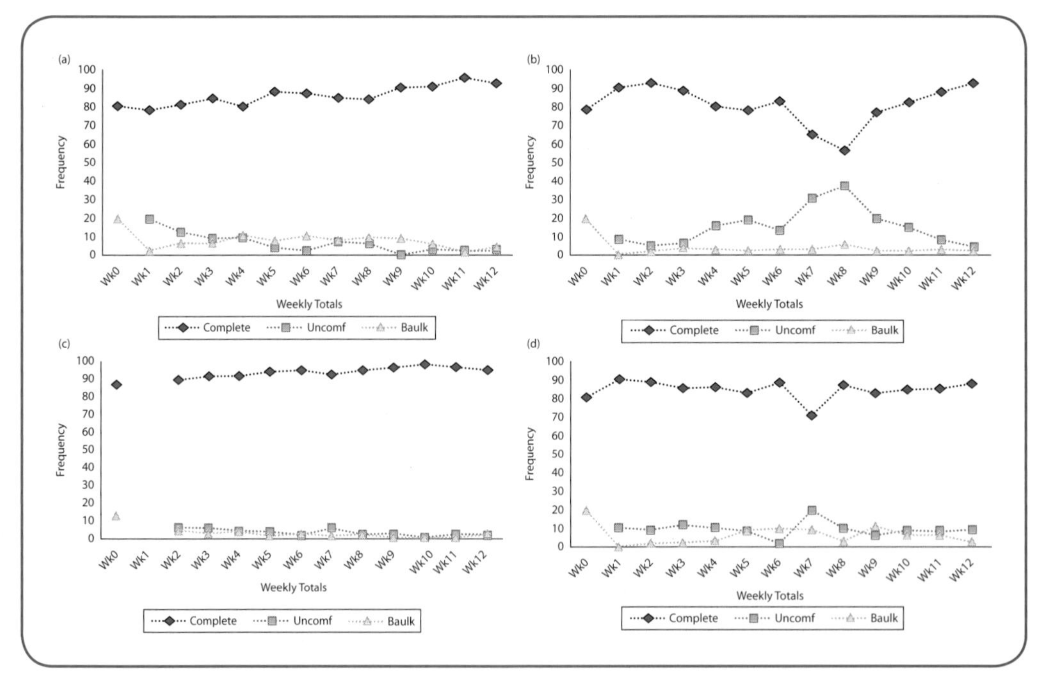

FIGURE 14.3 *Frequency of completed, uncomfortable, and baulked dives by four elite springboard divers over a 12-week training intervention.*

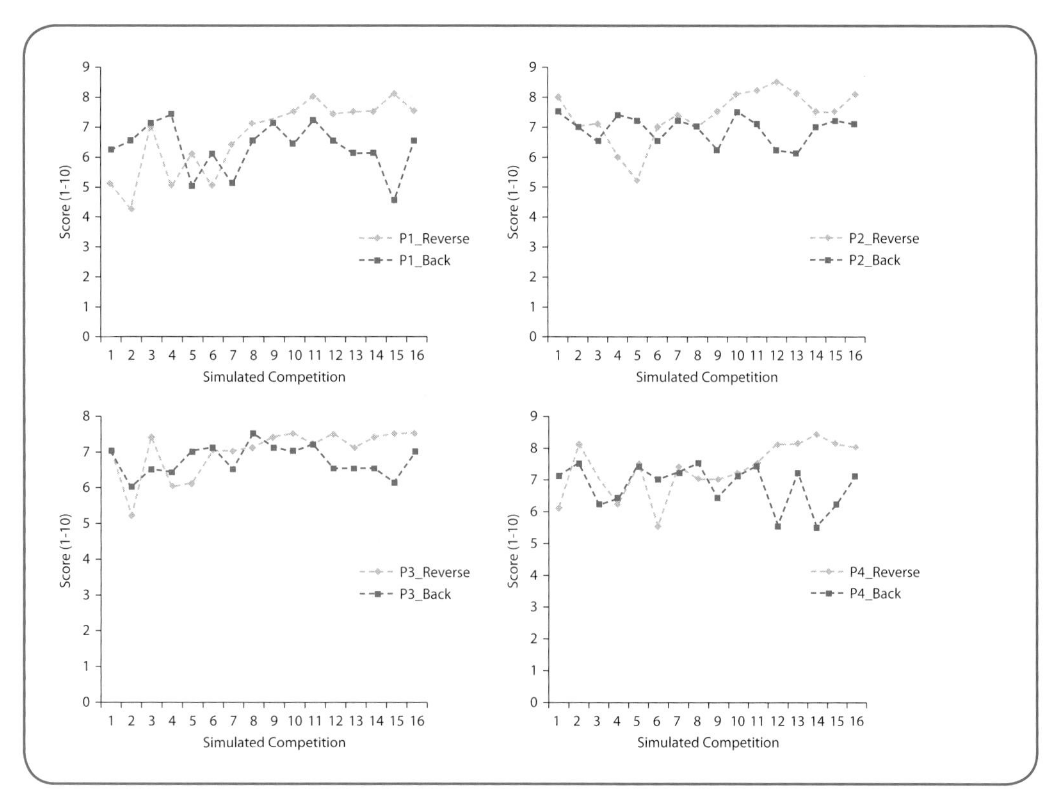

FIGURE 14.4 *Performance scores of intervention (reverse) and control (back) dives of four elite springboard divers over a 12-week training intervention.*

FRAMEWORK AND INTERVENTIONS

Our interventions with elite athletes have investigated and implemented learning design from an *ecological dynamics* perspective, examining its effects on movement co-ordination and control and the acquisition of expertise. Ecological dynamics is a systems-oriented theoretical rationale for understanding the emergent relations in a complex system formed by each performer and a performance environment. This approach has identified the individual-environment relationship as the relevant scale of analysis for modelling how processes of perception, cognition, and action underpin expert performance in sport (Davids et al., 2013; Zelaznik, 2014). In this chapter we elucidate key concepts from ecological dynamics and exemplify how they have informed our understanding of relevant psychological processes including: movement co-ordination and its acquisition, learning and transfer, impacting on practice task design in high-performance programmes.

The challenge for psychologists

How do athletes become expert in their discipline? How do they acquire such exquisite timing and gain efficiency, fluidity, and elegance in their movements? To effectively answer these questions psychologists need a model of movement co-ordination and control during performance, and their acquisition. Such a model should provide theoretical insights on how actions are co-ordinated and controlled with respect to important events, objects, features, and significant others in specific performance environments (Davids et al., 2012). Further, the model should yield principles for informing the design of skill acquisition programmes at sub-elite and elite levels of performance, with significant implications for the conduct of performance evaluation tests in talent development programmes (Pinder et al., 2013; Vilar et al., 2013).

Many theories of skill performance and acquisition currently exist, providing psychologists with a challenge in deciding which to use in their evidence-based practice. Recently, questions have been raised over traditional approaches to motor behaviour, which have emphasized the role of internal representations in information processing and cognitive neuroscientific accounts (e.g., Davids & Araújo, 2010; Zelaznik, 2014). For example, one of the most influential traditional models, from cognitive psychology, has proposed that expertise can only emerge after athletes have accumulated 10,000 hours of deliberate practice (Ericsson et al., 1993), an idea that has begun to be widely rejected (for pertinent criticisms see Davids, 2000; Tucker and Collins, 2012; Hambrick et al., 2014). In a study of chess masters, an astonishing range of 3,016–23,608 hours has been reported for the achievement of expertise (e.g., Grandmaster level). Rather, our work in ecological dynamics conceptualizes practice as a process of 'repetition without repetition' (Bernstein, 1967). It emphasizes each learner's search for functional co-ordination solutions, rather than the repetition of a single ideal movement pattern during practice (Davids et al., 2012). This is an important challenge in designing practice tasks in high-performance programmes, since too much repetitive practice of multi-articular actions could lead to increased risk of over-use injuries, especially in developing athletes undergoing rapid growth and maturation (Davids et al., 2013).

Similar criticisms can be directed towards some biomechanical models of skill performance and learning which have advocated the development of 'standard models of motion' as *templates* for performance of specific actions (e.g., Yada et al., 2011). The main issue with such traditional approaches is that they tend to promote a rather mechanistic view of human behaviour, failing to consider the array of constraints that impinge on an individual's learning and performance including psychological and neurobiological factors (Davids & Araújo, 2010; Seifert et al., 2013). These criticisms of traditional theories have particularly relevant implications for understanding the design of those practice and training programmes in sport which emphasize the invariant repetition of an 'optimal movement pattern' or an 'idealised technique' to which all individuals should aspire (Brisson & Alain, 1996; Schöllhorn et al., 2012).

A challenge for collaborating teams of psychologists, biomechanists, coaches and teachers, sport scientists, and performance analysts, is to understand how to design practice tasks that simulate key features of competitive sport performance (Seifert et al., 2013). In our work with coaches and athletes, a significant challenge for us concerned how we could identify the key perceptual variables that athletes in different competitive performance contexts use to regulate their actions. We resolved this issue by adopting a two-pronged approach in which distinct, yet complementary, sources of knowledge have been harnessed to provide evidence-based learning designs. First, we have attempted to verify the key perceptual variables used by athletes to regulate actions by developing *experimental knowledge* in a classic psychological approach (e.g., Pinder, Davids, Renshaw, & Araújo, 2011a). In this empirical research programme we developed theoretical models of performance and tested them in investigations (for reviews see Davids et al., 2012, 2013). Second, because of the limitations of using an experimental approach in some sport performance environments, we also sought to interrogate the *experiential knowledge* of highly-skilled coaches to determine which perceptual variables they perceived as significant in athletic performance (e.g., Greenwood et al., 2013). Elite coaches are in an influential position to contribute to knowledge on learning design, given their extensive training and daily experience in high-performance and talent development programmes. In the following sections, we discuss how *an integration* of experiential and empirical knowledge has helped us to resolve practical problems of learning design in high-performance programmes in simulating competitive environments. The integration of these knowledge sources to influence planning and organization of practice task constraints is the most important point to emerge in our research programme. As exemplified in this chapter, our work has identified how experiential knowledge of high-performance coaches can sometimes lack an evidence-based foundation. When complemented with empirical data, we show how experiential knowledge can provide an enormously valuable foundation for practical applications in learning design (Greenwood et al., 2014). The examples we have selected from our studies highlight the value of an ecological dynamics rationale in underpinning manipulation of practice task constraints to provide faithful simulations of competitive performance environments in cricket batting, springboard diving, and controlling the run-up in the long jump.

Examples of learning design issues

How should ball projection machines be used in cricket batting practice? When a cricketer encounters problems of form in batting, how should practitioners intervene to re-instate previous performance levels? Analysis of media documentation reveals that, traditionally in cricket, *practice volume* (reminiscent of deliberate practice) has been emphasized through use of ball projection technology (see Figure 14.1, for some examples).

What model of the learner and the learning process underpins these important performance-related decisions? An empirically supported advantage of practising against ball projection machines is that they alleviate workload required of bowlers during batting practice, with over-use injuries being a major concern[1] (Dennis, Finch, & Farhart, 2005). Projection machines can also provide relatively consistent conditions for practising batters, which a developing bowler may not be able to provide. However, the over-reliance on ball projection technology in practice has been questioned in recent times. Concerns have been raised whether projection machines provide faithful simulations of competitive performance constraints in cricket batting (Pinder et al., 2011b). This is because batting against a ball projection machine actually removes critical information sources (i.e. affordances) present when facing a bowler during competitive performance (e.g., removal of information from a bowler's prior movements such as body orientation and angle of arm at ball release). Due to high ball velocities generated by fast bowlers during performance, batters often need to attune to information from bowlers' actions *prior to ball release* which is available in competitive performance environment. These critical information sources are obviously not available under practice task constraints involving ball projection machines. Psychological research has investigated whether, in cricket, batting against a bowling machine is representative of batting against a bowler in a performance environment (Pinder et al., 2009; 2011a). Clear distinctions have been observed in emergent movement patterns under the two distinct task constraints, predicated on a batter's capacity to use information from a bowler's actions. Against a ball projection machine, cricket batters could only rely on ball-flight information. These findings also suggested that prolonged exposure to ball projection machines during practice may lead cricket batters to attune to informational variables which are difficult to access in performance environments (Renshaw, et al., 2007; Pinder et al., 2011a). The implication from these data is that the tendency to design simplistic and highly controlled practice drills, emphasizing practice volume, may not accomplish the requisite level of *representative design* to enhance learning in cricket batting (Pinder et al., 2011a).

---

[1]These concerns are real in high performance development programmes. For example, Cricket Australia's Centre of Excellence in Brisbane limits the workload of young fast bowlers to only 36 deliveries per practice session to avoid over-use injury risk.

Description box

BOX 14.1

WHAT IS REPRESENTATIVE DESIGN AND WHY IS IT IMPORTANT?

Representative design was originally proposed by Ego Brunswik (e.g., 1956) to refer to the design of experimental task constraints so that they *represent* a behavioural setting to which empirical results are intended to be generalized (Araújo, Davids, & Passos 2007; Davids, 2015). *Representative learning design* (Pinder et al., 2011) is a term which captures how psychologists and performance specialists might use Brunswik's (1956) insights to advise coaches how to design practice and training-task constraints that are representative of competitive environments in individual or team sports (Pinder et al., 2011). A key principle of ecological dynamics for the design of representative practice tasks in individual and team sports is that practice-task simulations should be based on a detailed sampling of the information variables available in specific performance environments for athletes to use in regulating their behaviours. A most important point is that representative practice tasks need to ensure that each athlete's processes of cognition, perception, and action are functionally integrated during performance (Pinder et al., 2011).

REFLECTIONS

The ability to adapt movements as circumstances in performance environments change is important in learning sports skills, regardless of whether they are more dynamic or stable. Research has shown that practising skills with high levels of variability can result in an increased ability to perform in competition as well as the ability to adapt to unique situations which may emerge during competition. By only practising a dive in perfect conditions, athletes can only expect to perform the dive to a high standard in *identical perfect* conditions. These conditions may appear quite rarely during competitive performance.

Analysis of methods of approach in both presented case studies shows how a model of the learner and the learning process from an ecological dynamics perspective can help to resolve the performance issues discussed. This theoretical framework emphasizes the importance of simulating, in practice task constraints, the information that athletes use to regulate performance in competitive environments. This is a non-trivial issue that can impact on effective and efficient use of time and effort expended in practice, perhaps explaining why some athletes may not need 10,000 hours of practice time to become expert. The coupling of *information and action* underpins performance in sport and can be acquired under practice task constraints which provide a positive transfer between training simulations and specific performance environments (Davids et al., 2013; Seifert et al., 2013). The implication of these ideas for psychologists is that skill acquisition interventions need to be based on empirical verification of information sources used by athletes to support their actions. An important task is to ascertain how these sources need to be *represented* in simulated practice environments. In particular, there are two important theoretical concepts from ecological dynamics that can help psychologists gain a better understanding of skill acquisition processes in sport: *attunement to affordances and adaptive variability* (Davids, Button, & Bennett, 2008).

Affordances and expertise acquisition in sport

The concept of affordances provides a powerful way of coupling perception and action in human behaviour, since 'within the theory of affordances, perception is an invitation to act, and action is an essential component of perception' (Gibson, 1979, p. 46). In order to establish functional perception-action couplings which successfully regulate behaviours, performers need to be able to become perceptually attuned to informational constraints of the performance environment, as well as acquire the ability to scale information to their own action capabilities (i.e., calibration) (Fajen et al., 2009). Affordances are perceived in relation to the relevant properties of each individual including the scale of key body dimensions (e.g., limb sizes), or action capabilities (e.g., speed, strength) (Fajen et al., 2009). These ideas have important implications for psychologists working with developing or ageing athletes whose body dimensions and action capabilities change as they undergo growth spurts, for example during adolescence, or through the natural ageing process. As expertise in sport is enhanced, informational constraints designed into practice tasks should progressively lead an individual to *specifying* information sources that invite the organization of *specific actions* and enhance their capacity to adapt to changes in a competitive performance environment. We have examined this idea in our work on the sport of ice climbing (Seifert et al., 2013), with climbers of varying expertise who differed in the movements they used with ice picks and crampons to climb the surface of an ice fall. We observed that expert ice climbers displayed a greater *dependence* on specifying properties of frozen water falls when climbing, compared to less skilled climbers. Movement patterns were subtly adapted as the experts perceived variations in key environmental properties due to differences in ice fall shape and steepness, and temperature, thickness, and density of ice. The perception of different affordances by the expert climbers allowed them to explore greater levels of variability in their upper- and lower-limb co-ordination tendencies. Their movement patterns varied as the climbers explored horizontal, oblique, vertical, and crossed-limb angular locations, which allowed them to swing their ice tools to create different anchorages and to hook existing holes in the ice fall structure. In contrast, less skilled climbers tended to display higher levels of movement pattern stability and fewer exploratory activities. They only relied on horizontal and oblique angles of the upper and lower limbs. Their ascent patterns resembled the rather rigid action of 'climbing a ladder'. Their main intention was to maintain stability on the ice fall and they could not detect the affordances for climbing offered by ice fall properties.

The role of movement pattern variability in practice

The findings of our work with ice climbers illustrated for us that expert performance is characterized by stable and reproducible movement *performance outcomes* which are consistently achieved over time under different task and environmental constraints. In contrast, *movement patterns* that achieve performance consistency are not stereotyped and rigid, but flexible and adaptive. This capacity in complex neurobiological systems benefits from an inherent property known as system *degeneracy*, a technical definition for 'the ability of elements that are structurally different to perform the same function or yield the same output' (Edelman & Gally, 2001, p. 13763). An important aspect of degeneracy is that two or more independent information-regulated co-ordination structures can be used to achieve the same function, if needed, providing athletes with wonderful performance flexibility.

However, traditionally in psychology (and other disciplines such as biomechanics), variability has been viewed as a 'noise' component of performance and learning (Davids & Seifert, 2014). This conception has led to the design of repetitive, structured practice tasks in the quest for repeatable movements (and hence consistent performances). For example, in springboard diving, many elite coaches have stressed the need for athletes to develop stable, invariant movement patterns during the approach phase on the board during practice (Barris et al., 2013). In the face of performance challenges like these (e.g., see also run-ups in cricket bowling and the athletic jumps, Greenwood et al., 2013), there is always some variability in initial conditions of body position and postural orientation of an athlete. To resolve these issues, traditional practice strategies tend to seek athletes to develop a 'repeatable action', with most coaching books providing detailed examples of putative 'ideal' performance models or movement templates (e.g., Woolmer et al., 2008).

These ideas are also highly relevant for understanding how to perform hitting or catching actions in ball games, where psychologists have been interested in performance of dynamic interceptive actions (Savelsbergh & Bootsma, 1994). In order to successfully co-ordinate and organize interceptive actions with respect to the environment, performers need to: a) ensure that they contact an object at the appropriate moment in time, b) contact with optimum velocity and force, and c), ensure that they contact the object with the required spatial orientation (Savelsbergh & Bootsma, 1994). To accomplish this task, performers need to be able to pick up and use precise and accurate information to support their resulting actions. For example, elite cricket batters, who can face bowling speeds of up to 160 $km \cdot h^{-1}$, need to differentiate trajectories in depth of ball to a 0.5° precision. Additionally, Regan (1997) demonstrated that response timing precision have margins of failure at these extremes of ± 2.5 ms at movement execution. Severe time constraints on action provide an opportunity to analyse the mechanisms involved in the regulation of movement responses to successfully satisfy specific task constraints (Davids et al., 2005; Renshaw & Davids, 2006). Temporal demands of fast-ball sports go beyond intrinsic neurobiological limitations in visuo-motor delays and movement times (van der Kamp et al., 2008). Researchers have, therefore, concluded that information available *before* the onset of ball flight is essential to success in fast-ball sports. Consequently over the past few decades there has been a significant increase in research focusing on visual anticipation, defined as the accurate prediction of future events based on partial or incomplete sources of visual information (Poulton, 1957). The idea of information-movement coupling can be generalized across many different sports. Our research has helped us to reflect on how practice tasks could be designed to provide affordances for elite athletes to explore adaptive movement behaviours to resolve performance challenges. We have achieved this understanding by working on the design of representative task constraints in training environments which contain information sources as affordances to be perceived and used to support adaptive behaviours. The data from our case studies of training practices in cricket batting and elite springboard diving programme were presented to illustrate how psychologists might provide advice on how emergent movement pattern variability could be harnessed during training to enhance athlete performance. These case studies highlighted how teams of psychologists, coaches, and sport scientists could work together to reconsider the traditional focus in practice on repetitive reproduction of invariant movement patterns during training. Rather the aim should be to help coaches and athletes understand how to search for, discover, and exploit functional movement solutions, which might involve performance of adapted movement patterns from trial to trial. Previous work on the role of ball projection machines illustrated the complexity of using this technology to develop batting skill in learners. Reflecting on research in ecological dynamics, it is apparent that ball projection technology provides only one type of general transfer between practice and performance: lateral transfer emphasizing general processes (Issurin, 2013). Lateral transfer refers to the transfer of a broad range of general skills, processes and knowledge to a range of tasks, all with similar levels of complexity and challenge. This process could be emphasized in the design of practice tasks such as static drills or generic tasks such as practising to intercept a moving ball. Through exposure to lateral transfer an athlete can gain experience of the *generic process* of coupling information and action which are challenging when batting in the nets against a projection machine and against bowlers in the cricket square. Although movement organization processes differ, there is some value in performers learning to couple their actions to information sources such as ball flight. Another example of lateral transfer processes involves the use of a climbing wall to train for climbing on outdoor rock surfaces. Vertical transfer is altogether more powerful for learning and refers to applying what we have already learnt to a more complex task (Issurin, 2013). Vertical transfer could occur when one trains on a slight inclined ice slope as practice for climbing a steep-ice water fall or when a cricketer faces a bowler out on the middle wicket (*Battlezone*), rather than a projection machine.

These ideas suggest that psychologists need to understand when and how to use lateral and vertical transfer processes during skill acquisition. An important question to reflect on is what transfers? An ecological dynamics perspective proposes that it is the *information-action relationship* that is transferred between training and performance environments. This is a key idea in practice design from an ecological dynamics viewpoint. It implies that psychologists need to study the information present in the performance environment and to ascertain how it needs to be represented in a practice environment. We also noted that Issurin (2013) proposes that low- to medium-skilled individuals can gain a lot from training with general (non-specific) information sources (i.e., being exposed to lateral transfer processes), whereas highly-skilled individuals need exposure to very specific information sources during practice (i.e., vertical transfer).

Psychological interventions have also revealed how functional variability can provide the adaptability in movement performance that can underpin successful performance outcomes in sport. Movement pattern variability can enhance sports performance by facilitating the emergence of adaptive and creative performance behaviours, without detriment to performance consistency. Reflecting on ideas discussed in this chapter, it seems apparent that high-performance athletes need to be continually exposed to task constraints that allow them to practise adapting their movement patterns. Training, from this perspective, should be viewed as an opportunity to engage in exploratory movement behaviours.. The implications from the case study on springboard diving are not limited to that sport alone. These finding may be applied to the practice of many different types of sports skills. For example, volleyball servers need to learn to adapt to small variations in the ball toss phase, long jumpers need to visually regulate gait as they prepare for the take-off, and cricket bowlers need to adapt the bound phase to their run-up variations. It is important for a coach to appreciate the role of movement variability and relay the expected performance and movement responses to athletes during interventions.

The springboard diving training intervention facilitated elite athletes in learning how to adapt their movement patterns during preparation to perform a complex task (the approach and hurdle phases of a multi-somersault springboard dive take-off). The effect was to provide a strategy that helped the divers to stabilize the key performance outcome (entry into the water), rather than them having to remove the effects of variability in performance by baulking. In the early stages of the training intervention, athletes attempted to change their previous training behaviours and use their poor hurdles to complete any dive. This approach was observed in all participants during the first four weeks, where the number of uncomfortable dives recorded was greater than the number of baulked dives (see Figure 14.4). The divers' reflections were obtained on implementation of the new training strategy to attempt to harness adaptive movement variability in allowing a dive to emerge from the preparation phase, regardless of whether it was perceived as ideal or not. During this time the athletes reported feelings of nervousness and discomfort but also greater concentration and awareness. 'It makes me feel more cautious, like I am in competition' (Personal communication, Participant 3, October 2011). This feeling was echoed in comments by Participant 2, who added: 'I feel so tired after training ... I think it's because I have to think so much, I'm concentrating so much harder now' (Personal communication, Participant 2, October 2011).

Although each participant responded differently during the training programme (varying the time taken to adapt to the new training regime), the data suggested that these high-performance athletes were all able to adapt their movements to the emergent variability in the preparatory phase. They displayed the flexibility required to complete good-quality dives under more varied take-off conditions. By practising without baulking, the divers were able to develop the capacity to adapt their performances, exploring different strategies and exploiting the most functional performance behaviours (Barris et al., 2014).

These adaptations were exemplified by changes in the number of reported uncomfortable dives (increase in uncomfortable dives as they attempt to stop baulking, followed by an increase in completed dives, as the uncomfortable take-offs become easier). The few baulks that did still occur were largely due to perceptions of the need for safety by athletes. In the final week of the training programme, we asked athletes to reflect on how they felt about the training programme they had been participating in. They typically responded in a positive way. 'It works; sometimes I forget and then I baulk, and then I remember after that I'm supposed to not baulk; and I don't know why I did it, but I know I should try harder; because it does work' (Personal communication, Participant 4, December 2011). Additionally, Participant 2 reported greater feelings of confidence because 'Good or bad, I know I can go on any hurdle now' (Personal communication, Participant 2, December 2011). Finally, Participant One described her feelings in an actual competition: 'It was such a bad hurdle, I was hanging ten (toes over the edge of the board) and in the corner, but I knew what to do, it had happened in practice before, so I didn't panic, I just waited for the board and squeezed (into a really tight pike)' (Personal communication, Participant 1, December 2011).

Of interest, was a temporary regression in feelings of comfort (observed as a decrease in completed dives and increase in reported uncomfortable dives) by Participants 2 and 4 during weeks 7 and 8. This regression coincided with the final week of preparation before the National Championships (a National Team selection event), suggesting that although elite athletes were able to modify their behaviour during the training programme, perturbations, such as additional stress or anxiety can cause them to revert back to their original perception of what constitutes an uncomfortable dive.

Importantly, the introduction of functional variability in diving performance during practice appears to have had little impact on the emergent movement pattern and the experts' scoring (see Figure 14.5). Although no improvements were made in the quality of movement pattern execution (e.g., magnitude of scores did not improve), this was not our expectation. After all, the athletes were practising the same diving movement patterns during training. However, towards the end of the training programme, as the athletes became more confident diving from uncomfortable hurdle steps, all athletes became more *consistent* in their reverse dive execution, which was reflected in the consistent scoring by the experts (even though they did not view the diving events sequentially). Consequently, it seems that the benefit of achieving performance outcome consistency during competition (avoiding any minor point deductions that may be associated with deviation from the movement criteria guidelines) outweighed the severe penalties imposed for either baulking or executing a poor dive from an uncomfortable, unpractised take-off. Conversely, the judged scores for the four participants' back two and half somersault dives were inconsistent and fluctuated greatly from test to test throughout the training programme. The ability of the athletes to execute both dives well, may be attributed to the large training volume, high repetition of skills and expert coaching. However, it is possible that the consistency in execution of the reverse dive may have been the result of the training programme, where the divers, like skilled athletes in other studies, were able to demonstrate stability in performance outcomes by compensating for variability detected in the take-off.

In addition, there have been some significant practical implications for these participants in training and competition. This study was initially designed as a five-week training programme, however, the duration was extended by the head coach as the athletes showed improvements in their ability to adapt to poor-quality take-offs. Consequently, at the Australian Olympic Team Trial, two participants successfully performed dives from uncomfortable preparatory phases, which resulted in both of them qualifying for the 3 m Springboard events at the London 2012 Olympics.

To summarize, the clear implication of theoretical ideas in ecological dynamics is that high-performance practice programmes need to be carefully designed to allow athletes to exploit inherent co-ordination tendencies. The ideas pose major questions for traditional ideas of practising to stabilize a movement template, common optimal movement pattern, or standard motion model. Instead an ecological dynamics rationale emphasizes the significance of the specific relationship created between an individual athlete and a performance environment.

FURTHER READING

Davids, K. (2015). Athletes and sports teams as complex adaptive systems: A review of implications for learning design. *RICYDE. Revista internacional de ciencias del deporte, 39*(11), 48–62. These are two highly readable articles from a special issue on motor behaviour which both examine how ecological dynamics provides a model of the learner and learning process to help psychologists understand the processes of affordance perception and adaptive movement variability in individual and team sports settings, as players continuously interact with each objects, surfaces and critical others during performance.

Davids, K., Hristovski, R., Araújo, D., Balague-Serre, N., Button, C. & Passos, P. (Eds.) (2014). *Complex systems in sport.* Abingdon: Routledge. This is a useful textbook which can help students to develop and generalize the ideas gained from reading the current chapter and the interventions discussed (cricket batting and springboard diving) to other sports and activities. Key concepts in ecological dynamics are developed in depth by world class experts in the field.

Passos, P., & Davids, K. (2015). Learning design to facilitate interactive behaviours in Team Sports. *RICYDE. Revista Internacional de ciencias del deporte, 39*(11),18–32.

REFERENCES

Barris, S., Farrow, D. & Davids, K. (2013). Do the kinematics of a baulked take-off in springboard diving differ from a completed dive? *Journal of Sports Science 31*, 305–313.

Barris, S., Farrow, D. & Davids, K. (2014). Increasing functional variability in the preparatory phase of the takeoff improves elite springboard diving performance. *Research Quarterly for Exercise and Sport, 85*, 97–106.

Bernstein, N. A. (1967). *The control and regulation of movements.* London: Pergamon Press.

Brisson, T., & Alain, C. (1996). Should common optimal movement patterns be identified as the criterion to be achieved? *Journal of Motor Behavior, 28*(3), 211–224.

Davids, K. (2000). Skill acquisition and the theory of deliberate practice: It ain't what you do it's the way that you do it! Commentary on Starkes, J. 'The road to expertise: Is practice the only determinant?'. *International Journal of Sport Psychology, 31*, 461–465.

Davids, K., & Araújo, D. (2010). The concept of 'Organismic Asymmetry' in sport science. *Journal of Science and Medicine in Sport, 13*(6), 633–640.

Davids, K., Araújo D., Hristovski, R., Passos, P. & Chow, J.-Y. (2012). Ecological dynamics and motor learning design in sport. In A. M. Williams & N. Hodges (Eds.), *Skill acquisition in sport: Research, theory and practice* (2nd ed., pp. 112–130). London: Routledge.

Davids, K., Araújo, D., Vilar, L., Pinder, R. & Renshaw, I. (2013). An Ecological Dynamics approach to skill acquisition: Implications for development of talent in sport. *Talent Development and Excellence, 5*, 21–34.

Davids, K., Button, C., & Bennett, S. (2008). *Dynamics of skill acquisition: A constraints-led approach*. Champaign, IL: Human Kinetics.

Davids, K., Renshaw, I., & Glazier, P. (2005). Movement models from sports reveal fundamental insights into coordination processes. *Exercise and Sport Science Reviews, 33*(1), 36–42.

Davids, K., & Seifert, L. (2014). Functional variability. In R.Eklund & G.Tenenbaum *Encyclopedia of Sport and Exercise Psychology* (Vol. *1*, pp. 301–303). Thousand Oaks, California: Sage.

Dennis, R. J., Finch, C. F., & Farhart, P. J. (2005). Is bowling workload a risk factor for injury to Australian junior cricket fast bowlers? *British Journal of Sports Medicine, 39*(11), 843–846.

Edelman, G. M., & Gally, J. A. (2001). Degeneracy and complexity in biological systems. *Proceedings of the National Academy of Sciences of the United States of America, 98*(24): 13763–13768.

Ericsson, K. A., Krampe, R. T., & Tesch-Romer, C. (1993). The role of deliberate practice in the acquistion of expert performance. *Psychological Review, 100*(3), 363–406.

Fajen, B. R., Riley, M. A., & Turvey, M. T. (2009). Information, affordances, and the control of action in sport. *International Journal of Sport Psychology, 40*(1), 79–107.

Gibson, J. J. (1979). *The ecological approach to visual perception*. Boston: Houghton Mifflin.

Greenwood, D., Davids, K., & Renshaw, I. (2013). Experiential knowledge of expert coaches can identify informational constraints on performance of dynamic interceptive actions. *Journal of Sports Sciences*.

Greenwood, D., Davids, K., & Renshaw, I. (2014). Experiential knowledge of expert coaches can help identify informational constraints on performance of dynamic interceptive actions. *Journal of Sports Sciences, 32*(4), 328–335.

Hambrick, D. Z., Oswald, F. L., Altmann, E. M., Meinz, E. J., Gobet, F., & Campitelli, G. (2014). Deliberate practice: Is that all it takes to become an expert? *Intellligence, 45*, 34–45.

Issurin, V. (2013). Training transfer: Scientific insights and insights for practical application. Sports Medicine, 43(8), 675–694.

Pinder, R. A., Davids, K., Renshaw, I., & Araújo, D. (2011a). Manipulating informational constraints shapes movement reorganization in interceptive actions. *Attention, Perception & Psychophysics, 73*(4), 1242–1254.

Pinder, R. A., Davids, K., Renshaw, I., & Araújo, D. (2011b). Representative learning design and functionality of research and practice in sport. *Journal of Sport & Exercise Psychology, 33*(1), 146–155.

Pinder, R. A., Renshaw, I., & Davids, K. (2009). Information-movement coupling in developing cricketers under changing ecological practice constraints. *Human Movement Science, 28*(4), 468–479.

Pinder, R., Renshaw, I., & Davids, K., (2013). The role of representative design in talent development: A comment on 'Talent identification and promotion programmes of Olympic athletes'. *Journal of Sports Sciences, 31*(8), 803–806.

Poulton, E. C. (1957). On prediction in skilled movements. *Psychological Bulletin, 54*, 467–478.

Regan, D. (1997). Visual factors in hitting and catching. *Journal of Sports Sciences, 15*(6), 533–558.

Renshaw, I., & Chappell, G. S. (2010). A constraints-led approach to talent development in cricket. In L. Kidman & B. Lombardo (Eds.), *Athlete-centred coaching* (2nd ed., pp. 151–172). Christchurch, NZ: Innovative.

Renshaw, I., & Davids, K. (2006). A comparison of locomotor pointing strategies in cricket bowling and long jumping. *International Journal of Sport Psychology, 37*(1), 1–20.

Renshaw, I., & Holder, D. (2010). The Nurdle to leg and other ways of winning cricket matches. In I.Renshaw, K.Davids & G.Savelsbergh (Eds.), *Motor Learning in Practice: A constraints- led approach*. London: Routledge.

Renshaw, I., Oldham, A. R. H., Davids, K., & Golds, T. (2007). Changing ecological constraints of practice alters coordination of dynamic interceptive actions. *European Journal of Sport Science, 7*(3), 157–167.

Savelsbergh, G. J. P., & Bootsma, R. J. (1994). Perception-action coupling in hitting and catching. *International Journal of Sport Psychology, 25*, 331–343.

Seifert, L., Button, C. & Davids, K. (2013). Key properties of expert movement systems in sport: An ecological dynamics approach. *Sports Medicine, 43*, 167–172.

Schöllhorn, W. I., Hegen, P., & Davids, K. (2012). The nonlinear nature of learning – a differential learning approach. *The Open Sports Sciences Journal, 5*, 100–112.

Stone. J. A., Panchuk, D., Davids, K., North, J. S., Fairweather, I., & Maynard I. W. (2014). An integrated ball projection technology for the study of dynamic interceptive actions. *Behavior Research Methods, 46*, 984–991.

Tucker R., & Collins, M. (2012).What makes champions? A review of the relative contribution of genes and training to sporting success. *British Journal of Sports Medicine*, *46*(8),555–561.
van der Kamp, J., Rivas, F., van Doorn, H., & Savelsbergh, G. (2008). Ventral and dorsal contributions in visual anticipation in fast ball sports. *International Journal of Sport Psychology*, *39*(2), 100–130.
Vilar, L., Araújo, D., Davids, K., & Renshaw, I. (2013). The need for 'representative task designs' in evaluating efficacy of skills tests in sport: A comment on Russell, Benton and Kingsley (2010). *Journal of Sports Sciences*, *1–4*. 1731–1733.
Woolmer, B., Noakes, T. D., & Moffett, H. (2008). *Bob Woolmer's art and science of cricket*. London: New Holland.
Yada, K., Ae, M., Tanigawa, S., Ito, A., Fukuda, K. & Kijima, K. (2011). Standard motion of sprint running for male elite and student sprinters. *Portuguese Journal of Sport Science*, *11*(2), 583–585.
Zelaznik, H. (2014). The past and future of motor learning and control: What is the proper level of description and analysis? *Kinesiological Reviews*, *3*, 38–43.

15 Developing Motor Skill in Practice: A Case of Mastering 'Heelflips'

KEITH LOHSE AND NICOLA J. HODGES

LEARNING OBJECTIVES

AFTER READING THIS CHAPTER YOU SHOULD BE ABLE TO:

1. Have a more mechanistic understanding of the perceptual, cognitive, and motor demands that are required in learning a complex skill.
2. Be able to explain how different practice and instructional methods can facilitate learning for people of varying skills, who are practising skills of varying difficulty.
3. To develop an awareness of motor learning principles that guide best practice with respect to challenge and constraints.

AREAS TO CONSIDER WHEN READING THE CHAPTER:

1. Motor skill learning is a complex proposition, with constraints from the learner, the task, and the environment. How can we modify these constraints to optimize learning?
2. Our best models of learning (e.g., computational, psychological, physiological) come from reductive, controlled experiments. In contrast, most learning occurs in more complex skills in more complex environments. We argue that the generalization from the laboratory to 'the street' is good, but what do you think?
3. Faced with performers of different abilities, where one person wants to refine an existing skill (i.e., perform it more accurately and consistently) and one wants to acquire the skill (i.e., learn how to do it), how might your recommendations about how to practise differ across the two individuals?

CLIENT AND BACKGROUND

We present the case of an amateur skateboarder, JB, who wanted to significantly improve his skateboarding skills and was prepared to invest a considerable amount of time practising to achieve this aim. This case was appealing to us in the Motor Skills Laboratory at the University of British Columbia, because the acquisition of novel, complex, and potentially risky skills defines many sporting situations (e.g., skating, diving, snowboarding, gymnastics). Despite its applicability, the initial acquisition stage, when a performer is learning to successfully and repeatedly perform a new, complex skill, has received relatively little empirical attention in the motor learning literature. As should become increasingly apparent in reading this chapter, this process was a dynamic and dyadic process that involved learning on both our parts. Whilst there are certain known principles that appear to guide motor skill acquisition, rarely are these principles studied interactively in laboratory work (where the goal is mostly one of isolating specific variables and effects to make conclusions about causes). Moving from the laboratory to the field presents unique challenges, and as became clear to us as we embarked on this challenge, our role was mostly one of offering JB new ways to approach thinking about problems and solutions and help in framing the understanding of why current methods appear (or not) to work.

JB was a 29-year-old amateur skateboarder, living in Washington DC when this consultation began, but who is now living the skateboarding dream in Venice, California. A decade ago, he skated regularly, spending an estimated 3–5 hours per day, five days per week, over the span of four years. While his time investment in practice was considerable, JB attested that his practice was not what is now defined as 'deliberate practice' (Ericsson, Krampe, & Tesch-Romer, 1993) that is, effortful practice, designed specifically to improve performance. Thus, ten years later, JB was interested in returning to/surpassing his former level of skill by focusing on deliberate practice using motor learning principles. Taking a remarkably proactive and scientific approach to his training, JB contacted several motor learning researchers via email to solicit their feedback in designing his practice (prior to contacting our research group).

JB begun this new practice regime with a few ideas of how to interleave the order of the tricks he was practising and began collecting some of his own data (the number of practice attempts, the number of successes) to track his progress. His first goal was to relearn basic flip tricks that form the basis for other, progressively more complex tricks in skateboarding. Re-acquiring older skills was proceeding smoothly, but a major hurdle for JB occurred in trying to learn heelflips, shown in Box 15.1. Heelflips are a type of flip trick in which force from the fore-foot or side of the foot rotates the board around its long axis in mid-air before landing. Although JB felt successful in relearning other flip tricks, such as kickflips, JB found heelflips especially difficult; performing approximately 100 attempts in a session, but only successfully landing 1–4 attempts. JB filmed himself, engaged in explicit error-analysis between attempts, and used visualization as a strategy to overcome these failed attempts. Unfortunately, over the next few months, JB continued to struggle with heelflips, failing to land the trick despite his increase in deliberate practice.

JB subsequently contacted the Motor Skills Laboratory for our input on his practice regimen and advice that we might have on how he could better structure his practice sessions (in April, 2013). JB's practice on heelflips provided an interesting and unique case study for motor learning research. In experimental studies of learning, researchers often ask participants to learn a skill by scaling or refining an existing action in a novel context (e.g., the simple action of a button press must be strung together in a novel pattern for sequence learning tasks; the simple action of a reach must be adapted to visual or dynamic distortions in adaptation learning). Although a number of authors have studied how practice variables affect the acquisition of more complex skills, such as balancing on a stabiliometer

Description box

BOX 15.1

AN ILLUSTRATION OF SELECT STAGES OF A HEELFLIP

(1) In the approach, the feet are near the back of the board. (2) As the board is propelled off the ground, the forefoot is slid toward the nose of the board. (3) Force is applied to the edge of the board with the foot from a 'kick', which starts the board to rotate around its long axis. (4–5) Momentum carries the board forward as it continues to rotate. (6) As the board completes a 360° rotation, the rider lands on the board.

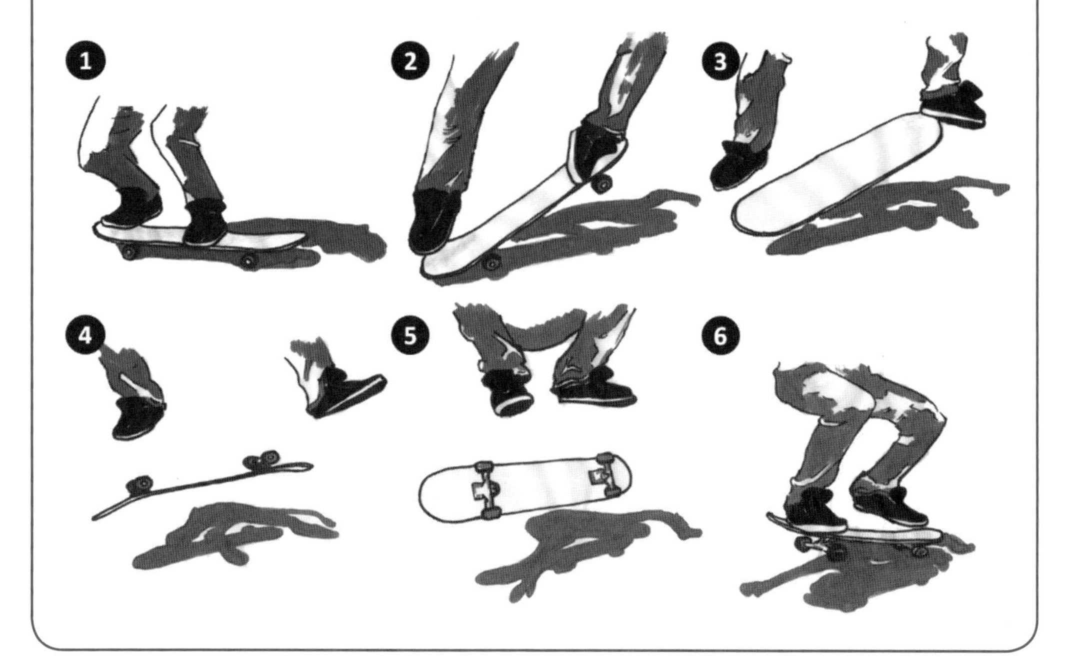

(e.g., McNevin, Shea, & Wulf, 2003), learning to juggle (e.g., Anshel & Singer, 1980), or co-ordinate both arms under difficult timing constraints (e.g., Hodges & Franks, 2002), this initial stage of going from failure to success of an action, at least within the laboratory setting, has received relatively little attention. In JB's case, he certainly had familiarity with other skateboarding tricks, but not heelflips specifically. Thus, although some knowledge from previous skills might positively transfer, learning heelflips was largely learning 'from scratch'.

Learning a truly novel skill poses a lot of interesting theoretical questions. Certainly it is difficult to fathom how the motor system can correct errors in truly novel movements when there is no reference (even an approximate reference) for what the correct movement should be. Furthermore, although the amount of practice is one of the best predictors of success/competence in a skill, there is tremendous variability in the amount of practice needed to attain a certain skill level and a myriad of variables that can enhance or hinder learning on any given attempt (Schmidt & Lee, 2011). Initial acquisition of a skill is not defined by a monotonic, linear relationship between practice and performance (e.g., Newell et al., 2001; Dickinson et al., 2004), such that practice is only beneficial once an individual gets close to the target skill. In JB's case, considerations about learning must also be balanced against considerations for safety and injury prevention. Although the risk of injury is not a common theme in motor learning research, safety is an important consideration when learning many complex and dynamic skills in both sport (e.g., for gymnasts, free-runners, or snowboarders) and occupational settings (e.g., for firefighters, military personnel, or police).

Our aim in this chapter is to present evidence-based practice pertaining to motor skill learning and principles of practice based on how to structure practice, how to instruct, and what and when to watch and receive feedback. Skill acquisition specialists need to be familiar with aspects of practice that pertain to a variety of skills, a variety of skill levels and that have generality across a range of sports. We try to address key motor learning concepts in this chapter, but more comprehensive reviews can be found in the suggested readings at the end of the chapter.

INITIAL NEEDS ASSESSMENT

Despite investing considerable time in researching how to structure his practice, JB was struggling to learn how to heelflip. JB's errors varied from attempt to attempt and day to day, but ultimately he was not consistent (and often not even successful) in landing the heelflip. He reported that often he could fix a problem on one day to have a new problem arise the next. We discussed his current practice schedule to see if we could offer advice on motor learning principles that he could incorporate into his practice sessions. In a series of email exchanges, we identified a few key areas of discussion that could be informed by empirical research on motor learning:

- Deliberate practice and amount of practice (e.g., the number of tricks to practice in a session).
- Practice scheduling: the order in which tricks were being practised (e.g., practising complex tricks at the beginning of a session to avoid fatigue).
- Part-whole practice and natural skill progressions (i.e., how best to break skills down into simpler components).
- Demonstrations and feedback (i.e., how and when to supplement physical practice with observational practice).
- Attentional focus (i.e., where best to direct attention during performance attempts).
- Pressure/anxiety and safety (i.e., potential ways of decreasing fear and anxiety during performance/practice).

After JB told us about his current practices over email and some relatively broad comments were made in response, members of the Motor Skills Laboratory met to discuss this problem as a group and suggest evidence-based interventions that could help JB learn heelflips (and potentially other tricks). Before our intervention, JB had roughly designed his practice session to complete approximately 100 heelflip attempts in each session. Beyond simply making these attempts, having read about the value of deliberate practice, JB would attempt three, reflect on any mistakes, visualize a solution to that mistake and then attempt to implement the solution on the next three attempts. He even reported filming himself and then looking at the footage frame-by-frame to identify errors in his movement. JB reported that this strategy was mildly successful as it would help him fix a particular mistake in subsequent attempts. However, if he managed to fix one mistake another problem would emerge.

JB also reported that he was attempting to break the skill down into component parts (e.g., squatting over the board to make sure his weight distribution was correct, jumping without a board flip) and practising those skills in isolation. JB reported practice for several days with this method. Over the course of six practice days, JB landed zero of an estimated 500 full heelflip attempts using these methods.

Following several more weeks of practice (and about 700 attempts), JB was still struggling to land heelflips (approximately ten successful landings in 700 attempts). In correspondence, he suggested that, 'maybe it's just an irrational fear of falling' that was specific to that trick. The anxiety appeared to be specific to heelflips as JB was able to land other similar tricks (e.g., a kickflip) and performed other tricks that had a high risk of injury (e.g., jumping stairs, grinding hand rails, dropping in on steep ramps).

FRAMEWORK AND INTERVENTION

We created a list of motor learning principles that we thought would be relevant for JB. These principles were related to the topics outlined in the previous section but more specifically concerned three major themes: (a) effective feedback and providing relevant and useable demonstrations, (b) scheduling practice to best promote learning (and avoiding fatigue/boredom), and (c) creating optimal task difficulty. These three themes seemed to capture the essence of the topics detailed above as well as being themes that have received considerable attention in motor learning research. Our theoretical framework was primarily one based on information-processing theory and cognitive-behavioural interventions, although we also considered how a constraints-based framework of practice would complement these potential interventions. We then wrote to JB with recommendations and ideas based on these practice principles and maintained a dialogue (over email) for how these practice principles might best be implemented. Each principle and JB's experience trying to employ it are discussed below.

EFFECTIVE FEEDBACK

Bringing in a coach. There was general agreement in the laboratory that JB would benefit from having a knowledgeable skateboarder with him who could watch and evaluate his heelflip from different angles. Intuitively, the idea of having an expert partner/coach to facilitate learning is appealing, but this practice is also grounded in motor learning research. Motor learning, after all, is a highly complex process in which a redundant system with many degrees of freedom (joints, limbs, and muscles) must be controlled in order to generate very precise movements in the environment (Guigon, Baraduc, & Desmurget, 2007). Furthermore, feedback from the environment seldom makes it clear what corrections need to be implemented in the motor system. This disconnect between errors (detected through sensory feedback) and which aspect/s of motor control need to be changed is referred to as the 'credit assignment' problem (Wolpert, Diedrichsen, & Flanagan, 2011). Accurate credit assignment is probably the greatest help that a coach can provide. An expert who has an understanding of the mechanics of the action, experience performing and watching successful and unsuccessful attempts, and (critically) experience in successful interventions, can help an athlete identify what is going wrong in a movement that is ultimately affecting the outcome. Error-detection, credit assignment, and error-correction can happen endogenously (i.e., internally generated processes, outside conscious control) as illustrated by the white boxes in Box 15.2. However, externalizing some of these processes, by bringing in an expert partner or coach can expedite the learning process (we illustrate in Box 15.3 at what stages of execution certain coaching methods might best enhance these more endogenous processes, but we provide more detail pertaining to these two figures in subsequent sections).

Description box **BOX 15.2**

A SCHEMATIC OF A SIMPLIFIED MOTOR SYSTEM

A schematic of a simplified motor system, showing approximate stages (in dark blue boxes) and underlying representations of endogenous processes (in white boxes) involved in motor control. Lines represent abstract transformations that occur between stages. Comparisons (indicated by Xs) between the desired state, predicted state, and the actual state of the motor system (estimated through afferent feedback) generate error signals that can be used to tune perceptual-motor transformations (black arrows between stages). Accurately tuning these transformations so that the actual state reliably resembles the desired state is part of the motor learning process.

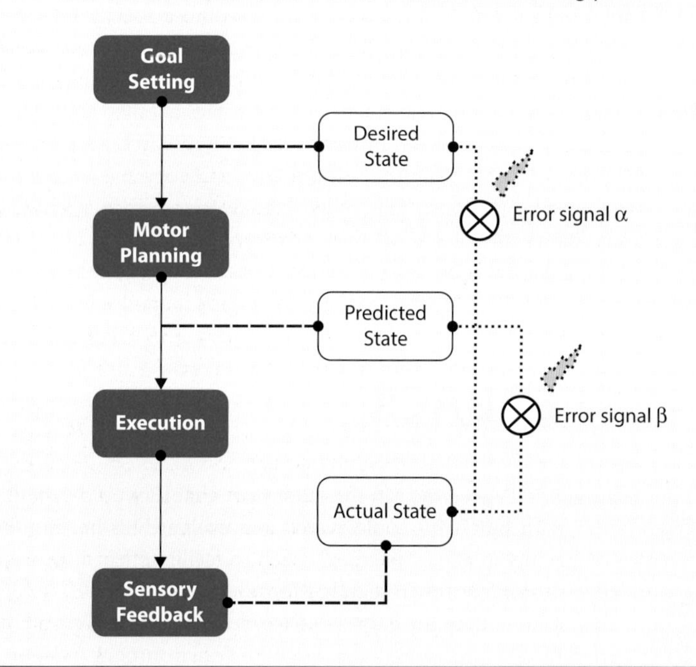

The suggestion to bring in a coach might seem too self-evident to be useful, but JB's response surprised us. Although he agreed that effective feedback was a critical element of deliberate practice, JB said that skateboarding, in general, resisted the idea of coaches. In skateboarding, the culture appears to prefer autonomous skill development and discovery learning (consistent with a larger rejection of organization and authority in the sport, Beal & Weidman, (2003), although there is evidence that this might be changing with certain cities publicly offering coaching clinics for adults). While codified skill progressions and drills might not be part of skater culture, observation and feedback do often come from peers when skaters skate together. In JB's case, however, he was skating after work on his own (the only skater in his current peer group), making it difficult to find a partner to train with. However, JB did have access to numerous online videos that showed successful and

Description box

BOX 15.3

Building on the 'endogenous' motor system schematic shown in Box 15.2, this figure shows how endogenous error signals might be augmented or supplemented by changes to the practice environment. Based on the examples in the chapter we detail how external feedback, video demonstrations, assistive devices, and manipulations to the practice schedule can impact various processes of control. Appropriate application of motor learning principles can improve the quality of error signals and/or how those error signals are used, resulting in accelerated learning. Although the complexity of the motor system is tremendously scaled-down in the figure, we hope to illustrate the applied value of integrating basic science in motor learning and control with the practical tools available to coaches and athletes

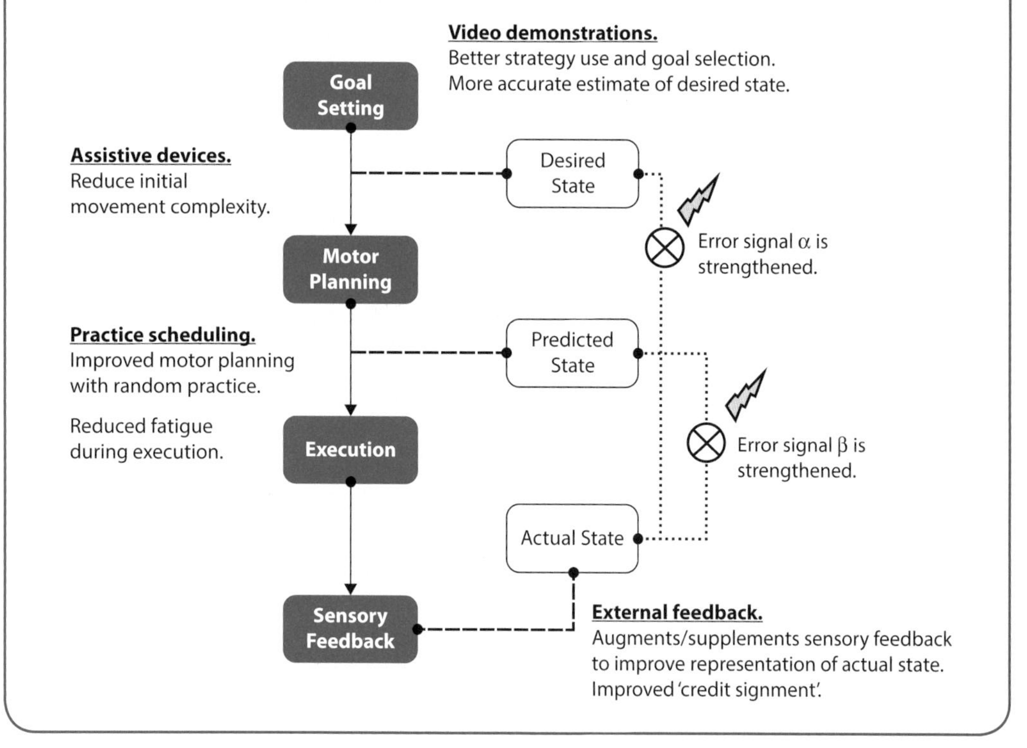

unsuccessful heelflips performed by both expert and novice skateboarders. JB also had the capability to record his own attempts. Thus, we tried to provide JB with principles for the effective use of video feedback (when watching his own attempts) and video demonstrations (when watching the attempts of others).

Video feedback and demonstrations. One of the difficulties in early skill learning is how to form a good approximation of what action is required (what some people have referred to as a 'reference of correctness' or 'perceptual blueprint'), then in translating this reference into motor commands and hence successful execution (Adams, 1986; Sheffield, 1961; Schmidt, 1975; Willingham, 1999; Wolpert et al., 2011). We know that in early learning much of the information that is extracted from a demonstration is strategic in nature, mainly reflective of the positioning and timing of limbs (e.g., keep the knees bent; don't rotate the head) and that feedback which helps to alert the learner to these strategic features is generally a good tool for learning (see Magill & Anderson, 2012; Hodges & Franks, 2008). JB mentioned that he was interested in watching YouTube videos of others and filming himself for reflection and to get augmented feedback about things he might not be seeing (see website reference list below for some examples). There is evidence that coupling demonstrations with self-referenced video feedback aids the potential of both these instructional methods (e.g., Hodges, Chua, & Franks, 2003).

Beyond a strategic role, the function of demonstrations in aiding learning has recently been debated. Although one might have a vague understanding of what is being done when watching someone perform a novel and relatively complex skill (such as heelflips, or an ice-skating or gymnastic stunt), arguably this level of understanding is quite vague. This is of course one of the major problems facing new learners, how to understand what is being done such that the demonstration can be transformed to the appropriate movements. We now know that a person's motor capabilities inform their understanding (and arguably this transformation); such that when you cannot perform an action, then in some ways, you cannot perceive it appropriately either (e.g., Calvo-Merino et al., 2005, 2006). In this regard, the informative nature of demonstrations should be viewed as dynamic, changing as the skills of the learner change, but also limited prescriptively with respect to early skill learning. In a recent two-ball juggling study, although observers thought they were learning from repeated demonstrations, these capability judgements were overly optimistic compared to actual success after watching (Hodges & Coppola, 2014).

Somewhat contrary to the statement above regarding overly optimistic perceptions of competence following successful demonstrations, when performers are allowed to physically practise, there is evidence that they are quite good judges of when feedback or a demonstration is needed. In research on self-scheduling of feedback and demonstrations, people have tended to request feedback and demonstrations on a relatively small percentage of trials (approximately 10%, e.g., Wulf, Raupach, & Pfeiffer, 2005, although this increases to about 20% for more skilled individuals; Hodges, Edwards, Luttin, & Bowcock, 2011). This relatively low frequency of presentation is often shown, however, to be as effective as giving feedback or demonstrations more frequently (but as prescribed by the 'teacher'). Interspersing physical practice attempts with observation of others (or of oneself) also seems to be a good practice technique (see Ong & Hodges, 2012 and Hodges & Ste-Marie, 2013 for reviews). Watching demonstrations early in practice, rather than later, seems to be best, at least for acquisition of relatively simple skills (Weeks & Anderson, 2000). Of course, some idea of what the goal of the action is needed for learning to occur, yet how demonstration might work to best convey this goal is rather murky. Combining different types of models, particularly learning or novice models with more skilled models has been shown to be a good method (e.g., Rohbanfard & Proteau, 2011). In this way, the learner gets to see what is 'correct' or a potential solution, as well as engage in the problem-solving process of other learners and potentially learning what is not working. Seeing errors in others' performance might help make errors in one's own performance more salient.

To best optimize long-term learning, it appears that showing a demonstration after a performance attempt might be better than prescribing what to do before each attempt (e.g., Richardson & Lee, 1999). That is, try achieving the desired performance goal (e.g., flipping the skateboard in the air using the foot and landing), before seeing how it should (or could) be done. Although this may be a more effortful way of learning (i.e., thinking about what to do and trying one's own solution before being told what to do), there is considerable evidence in the learning research that this type of practice is good for memory retention of the skill. In some ways, the demonstration then acts as feedback, rather than merely something to passively copy.

Scheduling of practice: integrating old and new techniques

Reflecting on JB's practice schedule, we presented some advice on how to organize practice more effectively. Specifically, we recommended integrating more repetitions of successful tricks and, when practising heelflips or other new tricks, breaking attempts into *practice* trials and *test* trials. The intention in practice trials would be to de-emphasize success as a goal, instead focusing on exploration and experimentation with the technique. Conversely, on test trials, success would be the goal and we encouraged JB to adopt an external focus of attention on the movement of the board (see Wulf, 2007). That is, in these test trials, we encouraged JB to focus more attention on successfully landing the flip and what the board had to do, rather than his technique and his body movements (with the latter being defined as an internal focus). JB took these recommendations, developed a practice schedule roughly like the one below, and recorded observations about the effectiveness of this method:

1. Warm-up
2. Learning or acquisition phase (practising new tricks).
   a. Five practice trials for new Trick A.
   b. One test trial for new Trick A.
   c. Five practice trials for new Trick B.
   d. One test trial for new Trick B.
   e. Repeat as desired ...
3. Refining or diagnostic phase (practising 'successful' tricks, that is tricks with a relatively high success rate).
   a. Approximately ten attempts at each known trick, randomly interleaved practice of different tricks.
   b. Occasionally increasing trick difficulty (e.g., clearing obstacles, etc.).

During the learning phase, new tricks were repeated in combinations of blocked (i.e., repetitive) practice trials followed by test trials, until JB was gaining success in landing that trick. Once some success was obtained (e.g., landing a trick more consistently), then we recommended that a new trick (e.g., Trick C) could be added to the rotation. In practice trials, the emphasis was on attempting the trick, or parts of the trick, with less focus on the success of the trick and more focus on exploring the movement. Test trials, conversely, put the emphasis on successfully landing the trick, allowing JB some feedback as to how close he was getting to correctly performing the trick. In the test trials, JB was encouraged to focus externally on the skateboard and/or on the desired landing spot (see Wulf, 2007). There is a significant body of research showing that attending to the effects of the action on the environment (rather than the movement and its mechanics), allows for a smoother and more automatic mode of control, better performance, and potentially better skill retention (e.g., Lohse, Wulf, & Lewthwaite, 2012). During the refining phase, old tricks would be practised in a more random or interleaved fashion with added difficulty (as scheduled by JB on that day).

Practice was structured in this way for a number of reasons. First, we felt that the volume of practice for JB's previous sessions was quite high. JB also practised heelflips (his most challenging skill) later in the practice session, when fatigue (either physical or mental) would potentially hinder success. Thus, we suggested that JB move the acquisition of new skills to earlier in practice following his warm-up (advice that JB found really useful). Although previous research in simple laboratory tasks

Description box **BOX 15.4**

WHAT IS THE CONTEXTUAL INTERFERENCE EFFECT?

The contextual interference or CI' effect is a practice organization effect that matters when people need to schedule their practice of multiple, related skills. Essentially, it is a comparison of high-interference practice, characterized by frequent switching across skills or tasks, or what has been termed random practice, and low-interference practice, characterized by repetitive, blocked practice of different skills within or across practice sessions. The easier (low CI) blocked practice, typically results in more obvious performance gains during practice in comparison to the essentially more challenging (high CI) random practice. Importantly, however, these results are reversed when retention is looked at a day or so later. In retention, a more random type of practice results in better long term learning than the easier, low interference schedule.

Example of 2 different types of practice schedules for 3 skills (A,B,C):

Random practice: skill A, skill B, skill A, skill C, skill A, skill C, skill B, skill B, ...

Blocked practice: skill A, skill A, skill A.... skill B, skill B, skill B.... skill C, skill C ...

The CI effect was first defined (and illustrated) by Battig (1966) in the verbal learning domain. It has since been replicated numerous times with motor tasks, although the effects do seem to be somewhat dependent on the skills of the learner and the demands of the tasks (for a more recent review see Lee, 2012 as well as Guadagnoli & Lee, 2004).

References

Battig, W. F. (1966). Facilitation and interference. In E. A. Bilodeau (Ed.), *Acquisition of skill* (pp. 215–244). New York: Academic Press.

Guadagnoli, M. A., & Lee, T. D. (2004). Challenge point: A framework for conceptualizing the effects of various practice conditions in motor learning. *Journal of Motor Behavior, 36*, 212–224.

Lee, T. D. (2012). Contextual interference: Generalizability and limitations. In N. J. Hodges & A. M. Williams (Eds.), *Skill acquisition in sport: Research, theory, and practice*. London and New York: Routledge.

suggests that fatigue negatively affects performance more than it affects learning (Alderman, 1965; Carron, 1969; Schmidt, 1969), we reasoned that the intensity and complexity of the trick might make it a skill more constrained by fatigue.[1]

Second, in view of research on contextual interference (see Box 15.4 for a description of this effect and references) and its dependence on the demands of the skill for the performer (e.g., Guadagnoli, Holcomb, & Weber, 1999; Porter & Magill, 2010), we thought that JB's previous practice schedule had too much interleaving of heelflips with other skills. In general, schedules of practice that are high

[1]The tasks used in previous laboratory experiments on fatigue and motor learning were continuous tasks in which participants were still, arguably, successful but more errorful under fatigue. That is, in a pursuit rotor task, participants showed larger errors post-fatigue, but were still able to track the target. In the heel-flip, however, JB was not simply showing movement errors in an otherwise successful attempt; JBs attempts were failing. Thus, we thought that if we could improve JB's performance by reducing fatigue, increasing the likelihood of a successful trial, this might be beneficial to learning as well. The difference between errors and failures as well as the influence of fatigue on learning skills that require powerful movements are, to our knowledge, not well studied.

in CI (i.e., random or interleaved practice of different skills), lead to better long-term retention than schedules of practice that are low in CI (i.e., repetitive, blocked practice of one skill before moving onto practice of the next). This is despite the fact that performance improvements seem to be more pronounced, at least within practice, with the low CI, blocked schedule. Although there is considerable evidence that long-term learning is aided by bringing interference into practice, this type of practice is most beneficial when the learner has some experience successfully performing these skills. With less experience, or higher complexity of skill, progressing from a more blocked to random type of practice within or across practice schedules is arguably a better technique (see Guadagnoli & Lee, 2004 for rationale).

Thus, even though JB might attempt 100 heelflips within a session, these attempts occurred in the larger context of practice, such that they were interleaved in a relatively random fashion throughout the practice session. Thus, to reduce the contextual interference between trials, we suggested the balance of five practice trials and one test trial for each skill, with no more than two new skills practised within a session. This makes the practice more blocked in nature, decreasing the challenge associated with moving between numerous skills from trial to trial, and allowing JB time to cognitively process errors and make changes to the same skill across practice attempts.

Third, in addition to moving the older skills to the end of the practice session, JB was encouraged to occasionally add challenges to these successful tricks in order to keep their functional difficulty high. The goal of encouraging JB to add degrees of difficulty (or interference) to these already successful tricks was to allow learning or refining of these skills to continue (see Guadagnoli & Lee, 2004). Progressive increases in task-relevant difficulty (or challenge) have been shown to be beneficial for experimental studies of learning in the laboratory and in applied physical therapy sessions (e.g., Pollock, Boyd, Hunt, & Garland, 2014). JB commented that practising skills in an environment that required the clearing of obstacles, or following lines, although adding difficulty, positively aided his attentional focus. Focusing on clearing a beverage bottle (what he referred to as 'open' conditions, and what is referred to in the literature as an external focus) appeared to help the fluidity of his movements, whereby 'my eyes have to shift away from the board and onto the obstacle, such that the throw is more or less running on instinct'. JB also noted that the type of practice schedule we had devised resembled similar recommendations by the skateboarder (and cartoonist) Christopher Chann (see website references). We reasoned that it was encouraging that someone from 'inside' the skateboarding community (an expert skateboarder, yet a novice motor learning theorist) had made similar recommendations to us (non-skateboarders, yet motor learning experts)!

Optimal difficulty: simplifying a complex skill

JB had questions about reducing the difficulty of the skill by decomposing the heelflip into constituent elements. We cautioned against this, however, as part-skill practice is often less effective than whole-skill practice when the stages of the skill depend on each other (for a review see Lee, Chamberlin, & Hodges, 2001). With independent stages, it can be appropriate to break a skill down into constituent elements and practise these stages individually. In the heelflip, however, timing and balance at each stage are dependent on the step before. Thus, we advised JB not to simplify the skill by removing critical elements of the trick, but to use assistive devices or environmental constraints to help simplify the skill, yet at the same time, keeping the skill (and balance constraints) relatively intact (such as practising on a softer surface or without wheels; see Davids et al., 2010). In this case, JB started holding onto a handrail while attempting the trick.

Using the handrail to give JB additional control in the air (and alleviate fears associated with landing 'primo' – when the board lands on its side causing pain to the arch of the foot) helped considerably. He reported that he was able to land about 20% of his attempts while holding onto the handrail (although he was cognizant of the fact that he would use the rail to aid his jump height, such that forcing himself to only put one hand on the rail would prevent this temptation). He also noted that interleaving assisted trials with unassisted trials improved the unassisted trials. Although he was still not landing heelflips in the unassisted trials, JB reported that his form and the motion of the board were improved (i.e., more elevation of the board and the board spinning closer to his feet).

Increased success while using an assistive device (e.g., the hand rail) is promising, but research on assistive technologies in motor learning has shown that transfer from assisted to unassisted situations is not always substantial (for a recent review of the physical guidance literature see Hodges & Campagnaro, 2012). Furthermore, continued training with an assistive device may lead to dependence on the device, because a learner fails to develop internal error-detection and correction mechanisms when training with physical guidance (Winstein, Pohl, & Lewthwaite, 1994). Thus, major concerns when incorporating assistive devices into training are the amount of physical guidance that the device provides and the regularity with which the device is used. Experimental data suggest that progressively fading out the use of an assistive technology is beneficial because early use of the device facilitates learners' performance early, but reducing the use of the device over time allows learners' to develop their own error-detection and correction mechanisms that they can rely on when the device is no longer being used. In JB's case, he limited himself to only using one hand on the rail, rather than both, to prevent this dependence and extra height boost that both hands on the rail gave him. Sports with a high risk of physical injury, such as gymnastics, have taken advantage of this principle for many years, using manual guidance early in practice to reduce the risk of harm while giving learners physical guidance through the movement (Arkaev & Suchilin, 2004). The principles underlying constraints-based methods of instructions are also based on the premise that physical constraints can help bring about desirable movements. For example, using a soft bar to jump over might help the performer concentrate on height and the lift of the board, rather than the mechanics of the flip. Defining a narrow space for landing the board might also help to bring about a more effective (tight) technique, merely through a focus on landing within a boundary. This also has the advantage of keeping attention focused on an external outcome effect, rather than on the mechanics of the movement.

In a skill with a high risk of injury like skateboarding, the learner's level of arousal is understandably high. Heightened arousal from somatic threat can greatly reduce the efficacy and efficiency of motor behaviours, generally making movements slower (Pijpers, Oudejans, & Bakker, 2005), and can also change gaze behaviour (Nieuwenhuys, Pijpers, Oudejans, & Bakker, 2008), altering the availability and quality of perceptual information to the motor system. These changes to both action execution and perception clearly have the potential to interfere with learning. As such, dangerous skills might be a particular case where assistive devices not only improve the learner's safety during training, but also facilitate learning specifically because they ameliorate some of the negative effects of arousal on the perceptual-motor system (see also Heinen, Pizzera, & Cottyn, 2009 who showed that assistive guidance led to a reduced fear of injury for certain gymnastic skills). That is, assistive devices need to allow a learner to perform an approximate movement for learning to occur, but beyond repetition of the appropriate movement, the reduced anxiety experienced during training can also positively impact learning.

REFLECTIONS

Working with the revised schedule of practice, where we recommended practising difficult skills at the beginning of practice, a mix of practice trials and test trials for heelflips, progressively fading out the use of assistive devices (in this case, a hand rail), and the use of video demonstrations and feedback to aid in detection and correction of errors, JB started landing heelflips in approximately four weeks of continued practice. By JB's count, he was landing heelflips 40–60% of the time following the intervention (compared to about 1–2% before the intervention). As this was a case study, it is not possible to establish if the evidence-based prescriptions in our intervention caused JB to improve, but it is reassuring that he did!

As research continues in motor control, motor learning, neurophysiology, and experimental psychology, we are also seeing a growing role for skill acquisition specialists in applied settings (see Button & Farrow, 2012; Williams, Ford, Causer, Logan, & Murray, 2012). Connecting laboratory and field-based research can be challenging, as in the laboratory, reductionist approaches are used to mechanistically study the relationships between a limited number of variables, whereas in applied settings, complex interactions between personal, environmental, and task constraints make it difficult to tell what part/s of an intervention are having an effect and why. This knowledge translation is not insurmountable, however, and in Boxes 15.2 and 15.3 we present schematics that connect the motor learning principles applied in this intervention to computational models of motor control and learning (see Wolpert et al., 2011).

As articulated by Willingham (1999) and Hollerbach (1982), the problem of motor control can be thought of as the transformations that occur between the formulation of a movement goal and the muscle activations that result in movement. Motor learning can then be framed as the problem of tuning these transformations to create relatively permanent changes in the capability for behaviour. As shown in Box 15.2, high-level 'goals' (e.g., 'ollie', meaning get the board off the ground with the feet still planted) are transformed into 'motor plans' (e.g., the sequence of sub-movements required to ollie) which are transformed into 'execution' of the movement (e.g., activation of particular muscles involved in the ollie) resulting in physical movement of the body and the skateboard which are perceived through sensory receptors. What is important from a learning and instructional standpoint is how the error signals that are generated during movement can be refined and decreased with practice. Shown in Box 15.2 (white boxes), these error signals can occur endogenously, outside awareness. These error signals have been described in detail elsewhere, but here we list them as signal α and signal β. Signal α is a result of the comparison between the desired end-state of a movement to the actual end-state of the movement. This signal will have a magnitude (e.g., very wrong, less wrong, mostly correct, correct) but it can also have a direction (e.g., moved too far or close, joint angle was too obtuse or acute, etc.). Signal β is due to a comparison of the predicted state (formulated after the motor plan has been sent) to the actual state. This signal will similarly have a magnitude and a direction, but it represents whether a movement did what the motor system 'thought' it would do based on the plan that was sent and executed.

As an explanatory example, if I am borrowing my friend's skateboard it is going to be different from my own and, as such, slightly different motor commands will be required to accurately control it. If my friend's skateboard is heavier than mine, more force will be required to ollie. On my first attempt, I apply my typical motor commands for an ollie and the board barely leaves the ground. Signals α and β are generated. Signal α generally suggests that something wrong happened during execution. Signal β clarifies what went wrong by suggesting that our predicted outcome (the usual large jump we get when we ollie) did not match the actual outcome (the shallow ollie we just did). This information can be used to modulate the appropriate level of force on the next attempt. This is just one example of how α and β error signals can be used to refine motor control processes during learning. In Table 15.1 we have illustrated how various degrees of error in either of these processes will implicate performance and ultimately learning. The key thing to consider is that error signals exist on a continuum from large to small. By combining error signals, we can reduce some uncertainty in what aspects of motor control need to be corrected, but even then, the appropriate correction is often far from clear based on this endogenous information alone.

Table 15.1 *Different types of error signals and how they combine to influence learning.*

Movement	*Error signal α*	*Error signal β*	*Interpretation*
#1	Larger	Larger	The predicted outcome did not occur, neither did the desired outcome. From this error it is not clear if prediction or control processes need to be updated.
#2	Smaller	Larger	The movement produced the desired outcome, but not what was predicted. Prediction processes need to be updated.
#3	Larger	Smaller	The movement resulted in the predicted outcome, but not the desired outcome. Goal selection and/or control processes need to be updated.
#4	Smaller	Smaller	This is a well-calibrated movement.

We have shown how changes in the practice environment might augment or supplement endogenous information, leading to more reliable or more informative error signals. For instance, external feedback provided by a coach or via video feedback, might provide a better estimation of the actual state of the motor system (e.g., 'your foot is not far enough forward on the board'). External feedback and instructions might make this error signal more interpretable and also improve how this error signal is used through better credit assignment. That is, a coach can help you detect that your balance is shifted too far backward, but also can help you pinpoint when and where this error starts to occur in the movement.

Similarly, video demonstrations by experts or even by novices, provide a 'reference of correctness' for how the movement (or stages of the movement) should or should not look. This can be conceptualized in the model as a more accurate estimate for the desired state of the system and a clearer 'goal' focus. A more accurate representation of the desired state could alter motor planning and execution transformations in the 'down-stream' efferent pathway. A more accurate representation could also lead to a more informative error signal because a more valid desired state is being compared to the actual state of the system.

Assistive devices can provide safety during the execution of dangerous skills but can also help to reduce the complexity of the movement, reducing the number of transformations required during motor planning and making the next state of the system easier to predict. Gradually fading out the use of assistive devices allows the learner to improve the accuracy of some transformations, bringing the desired state closer to the actual state, before all of the relevant motor transformations need to be handled at once (when the assistive device is completely removed).

Finally, moving more complex skills to early in the practice session means that there is less neuromuscular fatigue during movement execution. Reduced fatigue could help ensure that the actual movement is more commensurate with the intended movement, bringing the actual state closer to the predicted state. Changing the number and order of skills being practised affects these processes as well. By bringing in more interference between the practice of various skills as the skills become more successful, will ensure that the planning processes are improved from trial to trial, keeping cognitive effort between trials high, aiding long-term retention.

Thus, in many ways, we felt that the intervention was successful, but there are number of things we would prefer to do differently, if we had full control of the situation. Although we were generally satisfied with being able to bring motor learning theory to the table to answer JB's questions and design an effective practice schedule in concert with him, it would have been far preferable to work with JB personally, rather than over email, and track his performance data with greater rigour. It might have also been helpful to get some feedback from other skateboarders about their experience learning these tricks, or indeed, from athletes in similar extreme or high-risk sports (such as snowboarding or diving). We asked JB to give us some reflection on our motor learning feedback and his experiences with acquiring the heelflip and motor learning in general. We close with JB's response.

> I think switching the sessions around so that the task to be acquired was early in the session was probably the most useful advice. This focus on a more difficult trick earlier in practice, particularly in a long session, did however come at the expense of accurate reflection in the diagnostic section, in that fatigue, carrying over from the previous sections, reduced performance. So, for example, I'd miss lots of backside 180s and record these as misses, even though the faults were more related to fatigue rather than about me not knowing how to do the trick. For feedback, I agree that coaching is probably the best route for improvement, since it's immediate and less time consuming than waiting until I get home, looking through videos, and getting feedback far removed from the actual practice session.
>
> As far as external focus, I think I more or less focus on how tricks ought to 'intuitively feel' rather than a strictly external focus (i.e. I want to flip this board in such a way) though I do use this external approach when initially 'forming' a new trick. This 'intuitive feel' is also what I tend to visualize when watching how to execute a new trick (i.e., I imagine how the side of the board feels against the base of my pinky toe). When freely skating, my eyes are usually looking ahead and I 'recreate' the sensation of a trick, for example a 'pop shove it' (i.e., when you stay in relatively the same spot and the board does a 180° flip so you land on the other end of the board). Oddly enough, I was just reading research on language learning (http://time.com/3013439/language-trying-hurts-learning/) and I think this is also applicable here, though I probably differentiate between sensing how things ought to feel, and say a procedural 'internal focus' (i.e., I need to move my foot to such a spot) which probably isn't as productive. I'm reminded of when I was learning how to drive a stick-shift manual car and kept stalling. Someone took my hands and applied pressure on my left to mirror the clutch, and my right as the accelerator. I took those signals in that example and successfully applied that in the car I was driving.
>
> What would be great is a machine that would apply the 'sensation' of a heelflip to a beginner's feet to provide a model. Perhaps a robotic device that could apply touch and pressure at the appropriate times. I have a feeling this would seriously reduce the time it takes to learn complex motor skills. I know for heelflips, I think what really might have helped is knowledge of the 'sensation' needed for this weird back lean or front foot snap, as this wasn't originally in my mental model of the sensation of a heelflip. I also find logging my practice hours and tricks time consuming and I think an activity monitor device, such as the one now manufactured by Kickstarter © called 'Trace' would be useful in freeing my mental resources to just focus on the task at hand rather than data collection: https://www.kickstarter.com/projects/activereplay/trace-the-most-advanced-activity-monitor-for-action.

ACKNOWLEDGEMENTS

Special thanks to JB for his outreach, his insightful and difficult questions, his continued willingness to provide feedback and contribute to this project, despite all the demands on his time. We sincerely hope you fulfil your dreams!

We would also like to acknowledge the initial thoughts and considerations of people in the Motor Skills Laboratory in 2012, that provided the groundwork for this chapter.

Acknowledgement also goes to the three tri-council funding agencies in Canada (NSERC, SSHRC and CIHR) which have provided the last author, NH, money and time to conduct research and write articles such as these that contribute to our understanding of motor learning.

FURTHER READING

Davids, K., Savelsbergh, G., & Renshaw, I. (2010). *Motor learning in practice: A constraints-led approach*. Abingdon: Routledge. A series of chapters on different sports where a constraints-based or ecological framework has been adopted to explain or guide the research.

Farrow, D., Baker, J. & MacMahon, C. (2013). *Developing sports expertise: Researchers and coaches put theory into practice* (2nd ex.). Abingdon: Routledge. These authors have edited a couple of books on the development of sport skill, which have an applied focus and contain a coach's perspective on empirical research.

Hodges, N., & Williams, M. (2012). *Skill acquisition in sport: Research, theory, and practice.* Abingdon: Routledge. An edited volume with chapters written by experts in various fields related to motor learning and expert performance (see also 2004).

Klawans, H. L. (1996). *Why Michael couldn't hit and other tales from the neurology of sports.* London: W. H. Freeman & Company. A series of case studies, in accessible, non-academic descriptions, to explore the neurophysiology of sport.

Schmidt, R. A., & Lee, T. (2011). *Motor control and learning: A behavioral emphasis* (5th ed.). Champaign, IL: Human Kinetics. A comprehensive academic textbook on the topic of motor learning and control.

REFERENCES

Adams, J. A. (1986). Use of the model's knowledge of results to increase the observer's performance. *Journal of Human Movement Studies, 12*, 89–98.

Alderman, R. B. (1965). Influence of local fatigue on speed and accuracy in motor learning. *Research Quarterly for Exercise and Sport, 36*, 131–140.

Anshel, M. H., & Singer, R. N. (1980). Effect of learner strategies with modular versus traditional instruction on motor skill learning and retention. *Research Quarterly for Exercise & Sport, 51*, 451–462.

Arkaev, L., & Suchilin, N. (2004). *Gymnastics: How to create champions*. Indianapolis, IN: Cardinal Publishers Groups.

Beal, B., & Weidman, L. (2003). Authenticity in the skateboarding world. In R. E. Rinehart & S. Syndor (Eds.), *To the Extreme: Alternative Sports Inside and Out* (pp. 337–352). Albany, NY: State University of New York Press.

Button, C., & Farrow, D. (2012). Working in the field (Southern Hemisphere). In N. J. Hodges and A. M. Williams (Eds.), *Skill acquisition in sport: Research, theory, and practice*. Abingdon: Routledge.

Calvo-Merino, B., Glaser, D. E., Grèzes, J., Passingham, R. E., & Haggard, P. (2005). Action observation and acquired motor skills: An fMRI study with expert dancers. *Cerebral Cortex, 15*, 1243–1249.

Calvo-Merino, B., Grèzes, J., Glaser, D. E., Passingham, R. E., & Haggard, P. (2006). Seeing or doing? Influence of visual and motor familiarity in action observation. *Current Biology, 16*, 1905–1910.

Carron, A. V. (1969). Physical fatigue and motor learning. *Research Quarterly for Exercise and Sport, 40*, 682–686.

Dickinson, J., Weeks, D., Randall, B., & Goodman, D. (2004). One-trial motor learning. In A. M.Williams & N. J.Hodges (Eds), *Skill acquisition in sport: Research, theory and practice* (pp. 63–83). Abingdon: Routledge.

Ericsson, K., Krampe, R., & Tesch-Romer, C. (1993). The role of deliberate practice in the acquisition of expert performance. *Psychological Review, 100*, 363–406.

Guadagnoli, M. A., W. R. Holcomb, & T. J. Weber. (1999). The relationship between contextual interference effects and performer expertise on the learning of a putting task. *Journal of Human Movement Studies, 37*, 19–36.

Guadagnoli, M., & Lee, T. (2004). Challenge point: A framework for conceptualizing the effects of various practice conditions in motor learning. *Journal of Motor Behavior, 36*, 212–224.

Guigon, E., Baraduc, P., & Desmurget, M. (2007). Computational motor control: Redundancy and invariance. *Journal of Neurophysiology, 97*, 331–347.

Heinen, T., Pizzera, A., & Cottyn, J. (2009). When is manual guidance effective for the acquisition of complex skills in gymnastics? *International Journal of Sport Psychology, 40*, 1–22.

Hodges, N. J., & Campagnaro, P. (2012). Physical guidance research: Assisting principles and supporting evidence. In N. J.Hodges and A. M.Williams (Eds.), *Skill acquisition in sport: Research, theory, and practice*. Abingdon: Routledge.

Hodges, N. J., Chua, R., & Franks, I. M. (2003). The role of video in facilitating perception and action of a novel coordination movement. *Journal of Motor Behavior, 35*, 247–260.

Hodges, N. J., & Coppola, T. (2014). Probing how we learn and what we think we learn from observational practice of a novel action. *Psychological Research*. DOI: 10.1007/s00426-014-0588-y.

Hodges, N. J., Edwards, C., Luttin, S., & Bowcock, A. (2011). Learning from the experts: Gaining insights into best practice during the acquisition of three novel motor skills. *Research Quarterly for Exercise and Sport, 82*, 178–188.

Hodges, N. J., & Franks, I. M. (2002). Learning as a function of coordination bias: Building upon pre-practice behaviours. *Human Movement Science, 21*, 231–258.

Hodges, N. J., & Franks, I. M. (2008). The provision of information. Essentials of performance analysis (pp. 21–9). Abingdon: Routledge.

Hodges, N. J., & Ste-Marie, D. (2013). Observation as an instructional method. *Developing sport expertise: Researchers and coaches put theory into practice* (2nd ed., pp. 115–128). Abingdon: Routledge.

Hollerbach, J. (1982). Computers, brains and the control of movement. *Trends in Neurosciences, 5*, 189–192.

Lee, T. D., Chamberlin, C. J., & Hodges, N. J. (2001). Arranging practice conditions and designing instruction. In R. N. Singer, H. A. Hausenblas, & C. Janelle (Eds.), *Handbook of research on sport psychology* (2nd ed.). New York: John Wiley & Sons, Inc.

Lohse, K. R., Wulf, G., & Lewthwaite, R. (2012). Attentional focus affects movement efficiency. In N. J. Hodges and A. M. Williams (Eds.), *Skill acquisition in sport: Research, theory, and practice*. Abingdon: Routledge.

Magill, R. A., & Anderson, D. I. (2012). The roles and uses of augmented feedback in motor skill acquisition. In N. J. Hodges & M. A.Williams (Eds.). *Skill acquisition in sport: research, theory and practice* (pp. 3–18). Abingdon: Routledge.

McNevin, N. H., Shea, C. H., & Wulf, G. (2003). Increasing the distance of an external focus of attention enhances learning. *Psychological Research, 67*, 22–29.

Newell, K. M., Liu, Y-T., & Mayer-Kress, G. (2001). Differential time scales of change to learning frequency structures of isometric force tracking. *Psychological Review, 108*, 57–82.

Nieuwenhuys, A. Pijpers, J. R., Oudejans, R. R. D., & Bakker, F. C. (2008). The influence of anxiety on visual attention in climbing. *Journal of Sport & Exercise Psychology, 30*, 171–185.

Ong, N. T., & Hodges, N. J. (2012). Mixing it up a little. How to schedule observational practice. *Skill acquisition in sport: Research, theory and practice* (2nd ed., pp. 22–39). Abingdon: Routledge.

Pijpers, J. R., Oudejans, R. R. D., & Bakker, F. C. (2005). Anxiety-induced changes in movement behaviour during the execution of a complex whole-body task. *Quarterly Journal of Experimental Psychology Section A: Human Experimental Psychology, 58*, 421–445.

Pollock, C. L., Boyd, L. A., Hunt, M. A., & Garland, S. J. (2014). Use of the challenge point framework to guide motor learning of stepping reaction for improved balance control in people with stroke: A case series. *Physical Therapy, 94*, 562–570.

Porter, J. M., & Magill, R. A. (2010). Systematically increasing contextual interference is beneficial for learning sport skills. *Journal of Sports Sciences, 28*, 1277–1285.

Richardson, J. R., & Lee, T. D. (1999). The effects of proactive and retroactive demonstrations on learning signed letters. *Acta Psychologica, 101*, 79–90.

Rohbanfard, H., & Proteau, L. (2011). Learning through observation: A combination of expert and novice models favors learning. *Experimental Brain Research, 215*, 183–197.

Schmidt, R. A. (1969). Performance and learning a gross motor skill under conditions of artificially-induced fatigue. *Research Quarterly for Exercise and Sport, 40*, 185–190.

Schmidt, R. A. (1975). A schema theory of discrete motor skill learning. *Psychological Review, 82*, 225–260.

Schmidt, R. A., & Lee, T. (2011). *Motor control and learning: A behavioral emphasis* (5th ed.). Champaign, IL: Human Kinetics.

Sheffield, F. D. (1961). Theoretical consideration in the learning of complex sequential task from demonstration and practice. In A. A.Lumsdaine (Ed.), *Student response in programmed instruction* (pp. 13–32). Washington, DC: National Academy of Sciences.

Weeks, D., & Anderson, P. (2000). The interaction of observational learning with overt practice: effects on motor skill learning. *Acta Psychologica, 104*, 259–271.

Williams, A. M., Ford, P., Causer, J., Logan, O., & Murray, S. (2012). Translating theory into practice: Working at the 'coal face' in the UK! In N. J. Hodges and A. M. Williams (Eds.), *Skill acquisition in sport: Research, theory, and practice*. New York: Routledge.

Willingham, D. (1999). Neural basis of motor-skill learning. *Psychological Science, 8*, 178–182.

Winstein, C., Pohl, P., & Lewthwaite, R. (1994). Effects of physical guidance and knowledge of results on motor learning: Support for the guidance hypothesis. *Research Quarterly for Exercise & Sport, 65*, 316–323.

Wolpert, D. M., Diedrichsen, J., & Flanagan, J. R. (2011). Principles of sensorimotor learning. *Nature Reviews Neuroscience, 12*, 739–751.

Wulf, G. (2007). *Attention and motor skill learning*. Champaign, IL: Human Kinetics Press.

Wulf, G., Raupach, M., & Pfeiffer F. (2005). Self-controlled observational practice enhances learning. *Research Quarterly for Exercise & Sport, 76*, 107–111.

16 Improving Anticipation in Racket Sports: An Evidence-based Intervention

DAVID T. HENDRY, COLM MURPHY, NICOLA J. HODGES, AND A. MARK WILLIAMS

LEARNING OBJECTIVES

AFTER READING THIS CHAPTER YOU SHOULD BE ABLE TO:

1. Provide a brief overview of the importance of advanced cue utilization in dynamic interceptive sports such as tennis.
2. Describe the primary methods used to assess anticipatory performance in racket sports.
3. Detail evidence-based skill-acquisition principles that can be used to improve anticipation in the laboratory and field.
4. Explain how methods of instruction and practice structure can help to make anticipatory skills more resistant to psychological stress.

AREAS TO CONSIDER WHEN READING THE CHAPTER:

1. The temporal demands of tennis dictate that anticipatory decisions must be made in advance of ball-racket contact.
2. Methods used to improve advance-cue utilization help to ensure a fast and effective response in the performer, as long as the cognitive demands are minimized.
3. While advanced cue usage is important, other perceptual-cognitive and motor skills will impact on anticipatory processes.

CLIENT AND BACKGROUND

In tennis, the time taken for the ball to travel from one opponent to the other is commonly faster than the combined sum of the player's reaction and movement times. Consequently, in order to make an effective return, players must be able to initiate a response in advance of the opponent actually striking the ball (Williams, Davids, & Williams, 1999). The ability to effectively anticipate upcoming events and adapt accordingly is commonly acknowledged as being a strong contributing factor to expert performance (for a review see, Abernethy, Farrow, Gorman, & Mann, 2012). The expert advantage in anticipation tasks has been regularly demonstrated in a variety of domains including sport (Roca, Ford, McRobert, & Williams 2013; Williams, Huys, Cañal-Bruland, & Hagemann, 2009). Training programmes that attempt to improve anticipation by highlighting associations between key postural cues, such as trunk and shoulder position, and shot outcomes, have resulted in significant improvements in response accuracy, response time, or both in racket-sports players (Smeeton, Williams, Hodges, & Ward, 2005; Hagemann, Strauss, & Cañal-Bruland, 2006). The effectiveness of such training methods have been evaluated with particular emphasis on the instructional approach taken (Smeeton et al., 2005; Abernethy, Schorer, Jackson, & Hagemann, 2012).

The following case study presents a hypothetical example of a professional tennis player named 'Andrew', who is having problems anticipating shots at the net. He started playing tennis at the age of five, resulting in approximately 20 years 'playing experience. He has been competing internationally for Great Britain since the age of 12 and has been playing professional tennis for seven years. At the time of the intervention, Andrew was ranked by the Association of Tennis Professionals (ATP) within the top 250 players in the world, a ranking which he had quite steadily maintained over the previous two years. However, he was finding it difficult to break into the top 200 in the world. This barrier is a milestone which his coach believes he can reach and which carries great importance in relation to the grade of tournaments the player can enter. He and his coach described his game-style as 'aggressive baseline'. During his professional career he has risen through the ranks due to his ability to control points, forcing mistakes from his opponents and finishing points from the mid-court.

Initial contact came through a passing conversation with Andrew's coach. This conversation took place during the player's hard court competition season. Andrew was due to return from competition to his training centre in two weeks for a four-week training block. The coach mentioned how Andrew was performing well in competition but was missing out on some crucial wins which would improve his ranking. He suggested that for him to reach the next level he needed to be able to 'finish more important points at the net'. He identified poor anticipation as the reason for this weakness. With the ball having to travel a much shorter distance between players in net-point situations, than in baseline exchanges, the ability to anticipate effectively is of the utmost importance. Upon further questioning, the coach suggested that the player makes the correct judgement about the direction of the shot, but, that he is too slow in arriving at this decision and executing the return. As a result, the coach reported that the player had become increasingly anxious about his performance at the net.

Performance profiling of Andrew was conducted on a regular basis. Physical testing is carried out twice a year to monitor the player's physical condition and susceptibility to injury. Technical analysis was carried out by the coach using video and mental evaluations were carried out by a sports psychologist. The tactical element of Andrew's game was largely based on statistical information from performance analysis of matches. It was through these analyses that Andrew's poor win: loss ratio from plays at the net (from net points) in comparison to norms was identified. The coach was adamant that Andrew's technique was not influencing this win:loss ratio. This belief was verified in part by Andrew's unforced errors percentage at the net, which was no higher than the norms in that situation. Andrew was arriving at the ball too late, which too often resulted in him being passed or lobbed due to a lack of conviction on the original volley.

INITIAL NEEDS ASSESSMENT

Expert athletes across a variety of sports, including tennis, appear to have superior ability to make faster and more accurate anticipatory responses compared with novices or less-expert athletes (see, Abernethy, Farrow, Gorman, & Mann, 2012). This advantage does not stem from experts' visual 'hardware', such as visual acuity, depth perception, and peripheral visual field (for a review, see Williams, Davids, & Williams, 1999; Ward, Williams, & Bennett, 2002). The discriminating factor between skill classes is more likely related to superior 'software', leading to enhanced anticipation and decision-making (for a review, see Williams, Ford, Eccles, & Ward, 2011). These software characteristics have been defined as superior: (a) *postural cue usage*, which is the ability to pick up early visual information from an opponent or teammate's body movements prior to a key event (Müller, Abernethy, & Farrow, 2006; Williams & Davids, 1998); (b) *pattern recognition*, which is the capacity to recognize an evolving pattern of play early in its development (e.g., Williams & Davids, 1995; Williams, Hodges, North, & Barton, 2006); and (c) *knowledge of situational probabilities*, which is the ability to make or form 'a priori' expectations or decisions about the potential options that may occur in any given situation (e.g., Crognier & Féry, 2005; Ward & Williams, 2003).

The nature of anticipation in tennis is complex and multifaceted, with each perceptual-cognitive skill interacting with the other in a dynamic nature (e.g. Williams, et al., 1999). It is beyond the scope of this chapter to adequately outline all potential testing procedures and intervention strategies for all perceptual-cognitive skills. Consequently, in this chapter we will focus on methods used to measure and improve anticipation by enhancing the player's ability to use advanced visual cues.

The first step in analysing Andrew's anticipatory performance was to conduct orientation meetings between the skill-acquisition specialist, Andrew and his coach. Four important factors were highlighted that are relevant to Andrew's training: a) to break into the top 200 in the world Andrew must improve upon his ability to win points at the net; b) Andrew is technically and physically capable of making effective plays; c) at the net, Andrew is often able to make contact with the ball but appears to be a split second away from making an effective play; and d) Andrew has become increasingly anxious due to his inability to finish important points at the net.

Performance analysis techniques have helped to highlight the importance of various shots and strategies used in professional tennis to win points or matches (e.g., O'Donoghue & Brown, 2008; O'Donoghue & Ingram 2001; Gillet, Leroy, Thouvarecq, & Stein, 2009). Six of Andrew's recent competitive hard court matches were analysed (three wins and three losses) using frame-by-frame analysis on Dartfish ©. All situations in which Andrew had approached the net in these matches were 'tagged' for further analysis. The statistics included net points won or lost, volley success rate, successful passing shots from the opponent, and frequency of observable anticipation behaviour. Observable anticipation behaviours were measured as any lateral movement which occurred 160 milliseconds or earlier, following the opponent's racket-ball contact (considering a visuo-motor delay of approximately 200 milliseconds, Le Runigo, Benguigui, & Bardy, 2010). Movements made thereafter were considered reactive (Triolet et al., 2013). Performance statistics were then compared with norms from professional tennis players (with an ATP ranking within the top 200) for net points won and volley success rate (see Table 16.1).

Table 16.1 *Anticipation performance assessment.*

Anticipation performance assessment	Pre-intervention	Post-intervention	Normative data
No. of matches analysed	6	6	n/a
Matches won (%)	50	50	n/a
No. of net points analysed	48	48	n/a
Net points won (%)	45	64	64
No. of volleys analysed	60	60	n/a
Unforced errors (%)	15	15	15
Opponent successful passes (%)	40	21	21
No of observable anticipation behaviour occurrences	3	12	12
Correct anticipation responses (%)	97	97	97

Temporal occlusion

We used a temporal occlusion paradigm (e.g., Abernethy, Wood, & Parks, 1999) to assess how early in the action sequence Andrew was able to make correct anticipatory judgements. This technique involved filming an action sequence from the position normally occupied by the performer (i.e., what the player is able to see). Filming was recorded from the perspective of a player situated at the net viewing an ability-matched opponent making a passing shot from the baseline. This 'first-person' viewing perspective ensured ecological validity (i.e., a good match between the training session and competition where similar visual scenes are encountered). First-person perspective training has also been shown to lead to faster and more accurate decision-making in comparison to an external viewpoint (i.e., third-person perspective, Petit & Ripoll, 2008). A series of clips were then selectively edited to present varying degrees of information about the unfolding shot using a repeated measures design, whereby the same action sequence was shown occluded at different points. In previous studies with racket sports, temporal occlusion points have been presented approximately every 80 milliseconds, from about a quarter of a second before racket-ball contact up until and following racket-ball contact (Abernethy, Gill, Parks, & Packer, 2001; Cañal-Bruland, et al., 2011). Anticipatory behaviours occurring before 240 milliseconds are considered to be related to tactical judgements as opposed to advanced cue utilization. Film clips were projected onto a large screen to further simulate competitive situations at a viewing angle similar to that normally encountered at the net. Andrew was then required to respond verbally, while additionally making a movement response in the anticipated direction. An illustration of edited video frames similar to those used in the temporal occlusion paradigm are presented in Figure 16.1.

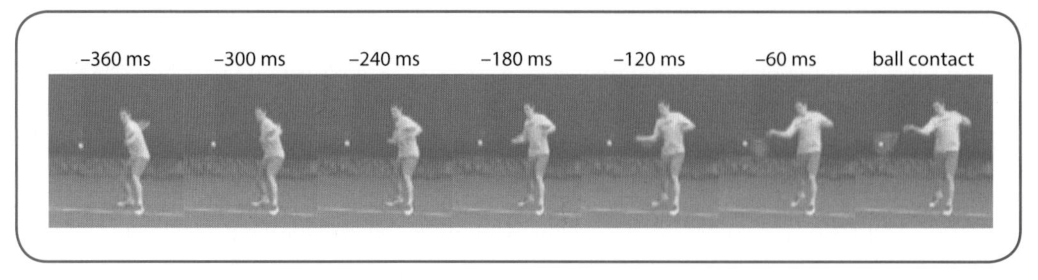

FIGURE 16.1 *Static frames as examples of various temporal occlusion points that may be employed in a forehand passing shot simulation.*

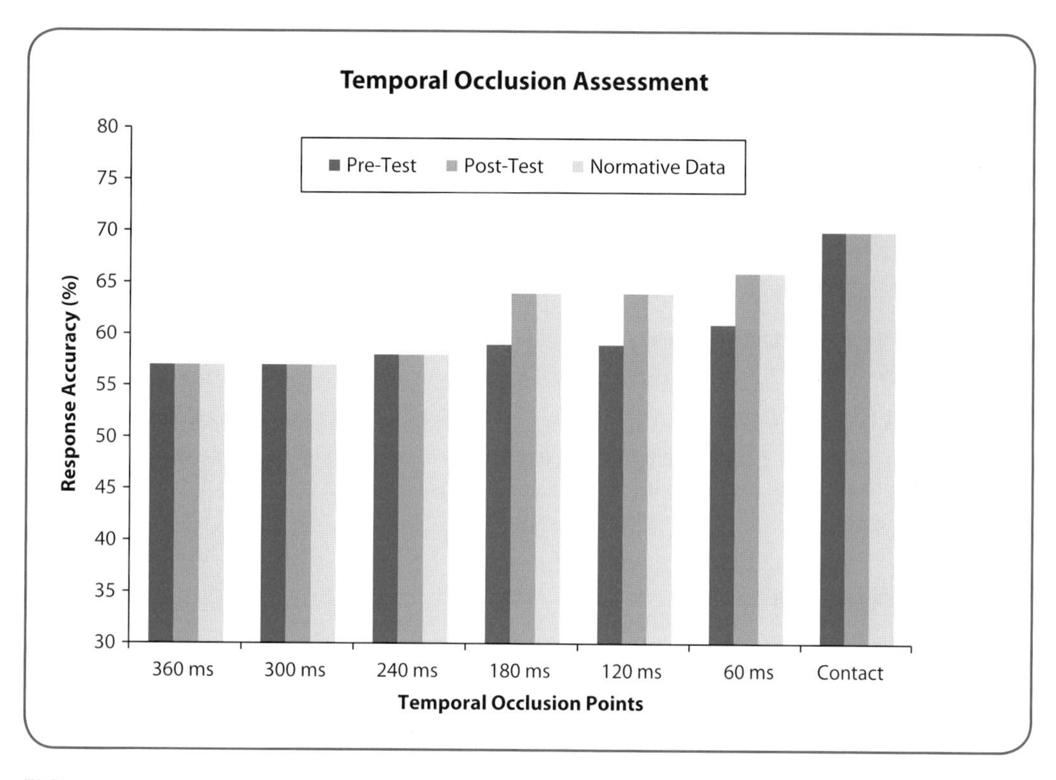

FIGURE 16.2 *Temporal occlusion assessment results (response accuracy) for time points before and at racket-ball contact.*

Researchers using this temporal occlusion paradigm have shown that expert tennis players are better able than novices to predict shot outcomes at an earlier point in the action sequence (i.e., before ball-racket contact, Farrow, Abernethy, & Jackson, 2005). This advantage dissipates as a function of extended viewing (i.e., ball-racket contact and post-contact). The superior ability of experts to predict shot outcomes of an action with relatively little information present (i.e., at an early occlusion point) suggests that they are better able to use advanced cues to prepare and execute appropriate responses.

Andrew's anticipatory judgements at the net were less accurate, 180 milliseconds to 60 milliseconds before racket-ball-contact, in comparison to normative data derived from similarly ranked players (see Figure 16.2).

Definition box

BOX 16.1

Temporal occlusion involves selectively editing film clips at approximately 180 milliseconds and 60 milliseconds intervals to provide varying degrees of information from an action sequence. Expert performers are generally able to make correct anticipatory decisions earlier than novices, typically based on postural information rather than positional information related to the racket or ball.

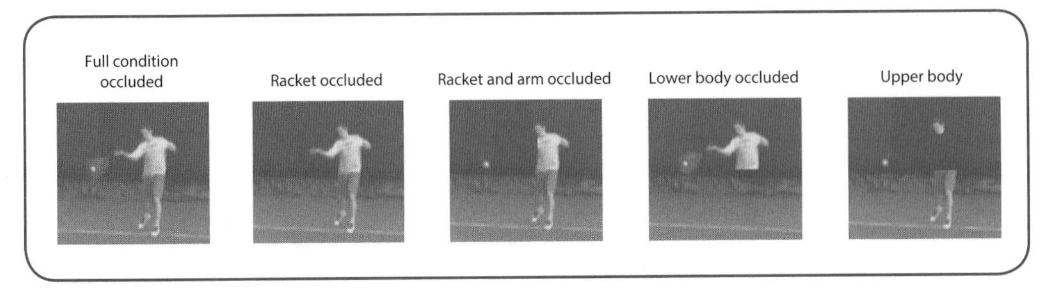

FIGURE 16.3 *Examples of spatial occlusion conditions that may be employed in a tennis player hitting a forehand passing shot.*

However, he was not different from similarly ranked players before 240 milliseconds, which effectively ruled out a deficiency in his ability to use tactical information to facilitate anticipatory response (Triolet et al., 2013). These results confirmed the coach's suspicion that Andrew was not anticipating efficiently at the net.

Spatial occlusion

Since we were able to show deficiencies in Andrew's ability to make correct anticipatory judgements at relatively early stages in the action sequence, we then needed to diagnose the antecedents of his weakness. We therefore used the spatial occlusion technique (e.g., Williams & Davids, 1998) to identify the specific information cues Andrew based his anticipatory judgements on during net plays. In this paradigm, video footage of the action remained constant (e.g., ball-racket contact). However different areas of the display were occluded throughout the duration of the presented action sequence (e.g., the opponent's arm or racket during a tennis serve, see Figure 16.3).

Decrements in Andrew's performance that were related to the occlusion of a particular area of the display (e.g., head, arm, racket) relative to a control condition (i.e., full vision), provided insight into the relative importance that this particular body segment had as a source of information (e.g., Williams & Davids, 1998; Müller et al., 2006).

A repeated measures design was employed where Andrew was shown the same filmed action sequence under different occlusion conditions. Spatial occlusion studies in tennis have typically shown that experts are better able to extract information from more proximal parts of the body (e.g., shoulders and trunk) providing earlier information about movement outcomes, thus facilitating experts' superior ability over novices to pick up relevant information earlier in the movement sequence (Huys, et al., 2009; Cañal-Bruland & Williams, 2010). Andrew performed poorly relative to norms when more distal sources of information were occluded (e.g., racket, racket arm) compared to more proximal sources of information (i.e., trunk and shoulder) but the racket and racket arm remained visible (see Figure 16.4).

These findings suggest that Andrew was making anticipatory judgements based upon more distal cues, which may contribute to his problems returning shots at the net.

Definition box — BOX 16.2

Spatial occlusion film clips are edited to occlude different body segments (e.g., trunk and hips) from the display. This allows practitioners to assess which postural cues players are basing their anticipatory judgements upon.

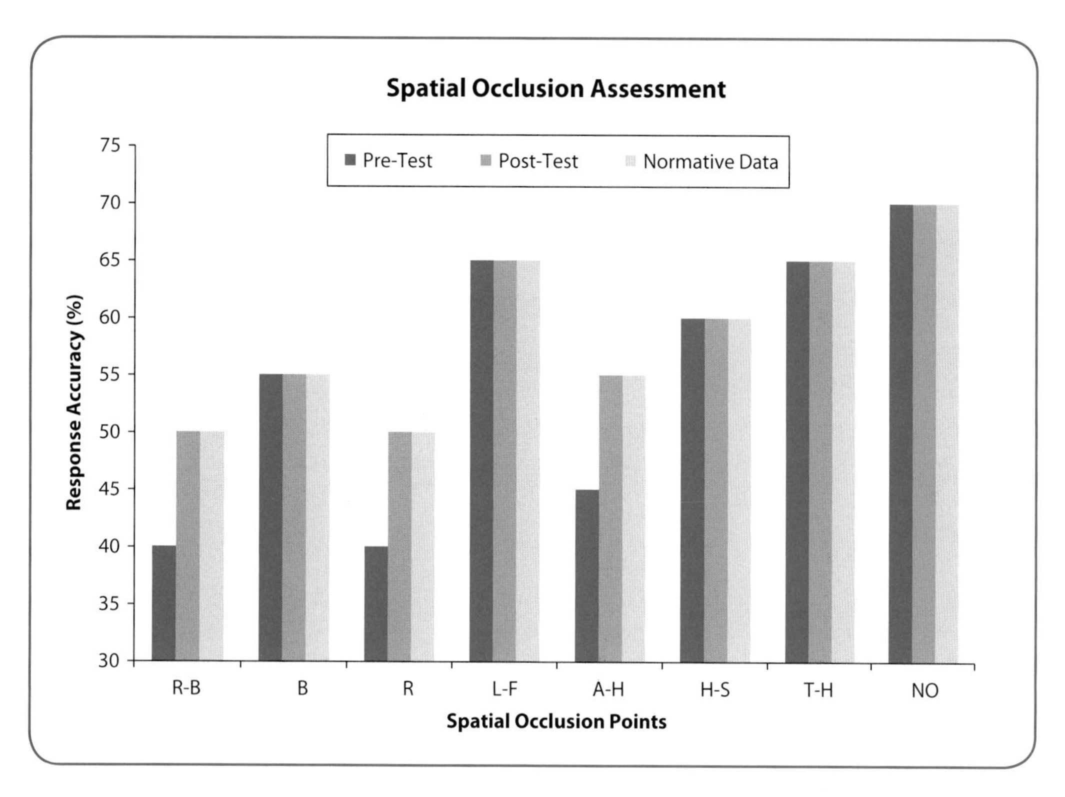

FIGURE 16.4 *Spatial occlusion assessment results (response accuracy) when various body parts, racket, and ball are occluded from the display.*

Visual search behaviour

In order to glean more information about what informational cues Andrew was attending to at the net, we used a mobile, head-mounted eye movement registration system to study his visual search behaviour (for a review, see Causer, Janelle, Vickers, & Williams, 2012). According to Williams (2012), skill-acquisition specialists are able to make inferences as to the degree of processing engaged in by athletes from the duration of eye fixations, with longer fixations suggestive of increased cognitive demands, while an athlete's point-of-gaze provides an index of key spatial information. Although the eye movement registration system can be used on court (Singer et al., 1998), we collected data in the laboratory whilst Andrew watched edited videos of opponents attempting passing shots. In tennis, skilled players tend to focus gaze on the shoulder rather than the racket of an opponent (Goulet, Bard, & Fleury, 1989; Williams, et al., 2002). This tendency for experts to focus on more proximal information sources as opposed to distal is thought to facilitate anticipatory response time (Abernethy et al., 2012). Analysis of Andrew's visual search behaviours highlighted an inefficient strategy in that his gaze tended to shift from more proximal sources of information (e.g., trunk and hips) to more distal sources (e.g., arm and racket) earlier in the action sequence compared to his peers (see Figure 16.5).

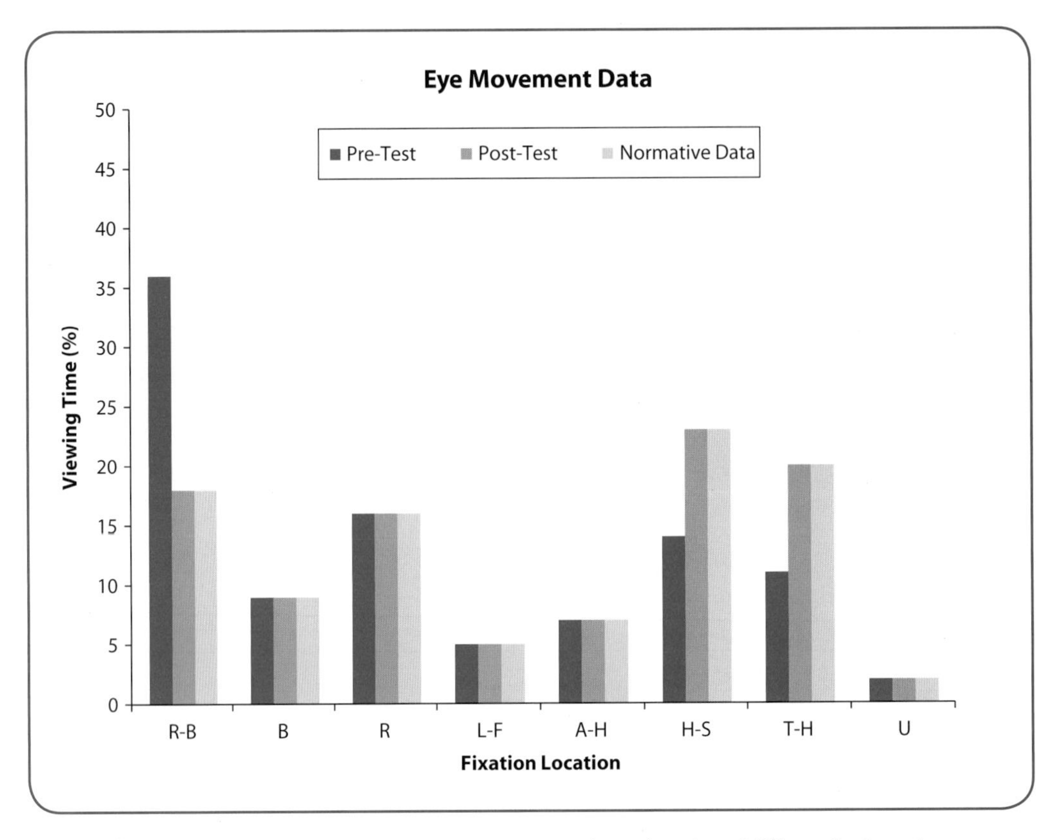

FIGURE 16.5 *Eye-movement data (percentage viewing time) as a function of different body-racket locations.*

This finding corroborated the spatial occlusion results, showing that Andrew may not be focusing on the most relevant postural cues of his opponent.

While expert sport performers are more efficient with their visual search strategies, changes in search behaviours are noted when athletes are placed under conditions involving emotional or physiological stress (e.g. Causer, Holmes, Smith, & Williams, 2011). Specifically, players have been shown to increase their rate of search (e.g., Williams, Vickers, & Rodríguez, 2002) and reduce the duration of their final fixation point before ball contact (known as the Quiet eye period, e.g., Vickers, 1996). Andrew recorded a greater number of fixations of shorter duration than his peers, which may be indicative of heightened anxiety or a less efficient scan pattern (e.g., Williams, Vickers, & Rodríguez, 2002).

One potential limitation of analysing visual search behaviours is that it is difficult to differentiate between what the player is 'looking at' and what they are 'seeing' (Williams & Ericsson, 2005). Moreover, evidence exists pertaining to expert performers' ability to extract relevant information using a more 'global' rather than a 'local' perceptual strategy (for a review, see Williams & Ward, 2007). Rather than focusing on specific, isolated areas, skilled athletes seem better able to pick up relevant information from several areas simultaneously (e.g., Huys et al., 2009). For example, experts are more likely to fixate centrally and use this strategy to gather information about an unfolding action, such as picking up an opponent's overall body kinematics based on peripheral vision.

FRAMEWORK AND INTERVENTION

Rationale for intervention

The general pattern of results outlined above provided a rationale for our intervention. This intervention was designed to redirect attention towards more proximal postural cues. We expected that such an intervention would result in faster anticipatory response times, leading to improved performance at the net. Since the coach has noticed signs of heightened anxiety in Andrew, and competition demands an ability to perform under pressure, intervention strategies more resistant to psychological stress were employed.

Framework overview

To measure improvement in Andrew's anticipatory performance, we used a typical experimental design consisting of a pre-test, training phase, post-test, and transfer test (i.e., performance analysis of net shots won during competitive play). The training phase combined both on and off-court practice. A number of skill-acquisition principles relating specifically to instructions, feedback, and practice organization were applied.

The time period of previous intervention studies have varied from a single 60-minute session (e.g., Williams et al., 2003) to 20 sessions conducted over a four-week period (Abernethy, Woods, & Parks, 1999). In accordance with the typical tournament schedule of our elite tennis player, the intervention took place over four weeks and involved two 45–60-minute sessions, consisting of one *on-court*, and one *off-court* practice session per week. The on and off-court training methods are detailed below along with a brief explanation of the underlying skill-acquisition principles applied to ensure optimal retention and transfer to the dynamic demands of competitive tennis.

Off-court practice intervention

In previous off-court (laboratory-based) interventions, improvements in anticipation have been evidenced by methods that highlight relationships between key postural cues and shot outcomes (e.g., Christina, Barresi, & Shaffner, 1990: Singer, et al., 1994; Williams & Burwitz, 1993; Williams et al., 2003, Smeeton et al., 2005). This latter method has shown practical utility in its transfer to field settings (e.g., Williams & Ward, 2003; Williams, Ward, & Chapman, 2003). The method of instruction used to highlight these associations can impact learning. An overview of the off-court intervention is presented in Table 16.2.

Method of instruction

An important question underpinning each of the off-court (and on-court) training intervention(s) was how the information should be conveyed. Traditional approaches rely on explicit instruction delivered by the coach to the learner (e.g., Williams & Hodges, 2005). However, 'explicit' (e.g., conscious, rule-based, verbalizable) instructional techniques are less resistant to psychological stress than more 'implicit' (i.e., no or low conscious awareness, non-verbalizable) instructions (for a recent review, see Masters & Poolton, 2012). When placed under stressful or cognitively demanding conditions, players taught using explicit instructions are prone to 'reinvest' attention away from automatic processes, towards previously learnt, technical aspects of the action (analogous to an earlier stage of learning).

Table 16.2 *Overview of off-court methods employed to highlight relationships between advanced visual cues and shot outcomes.*

Method	*Week 1*	*Week 2*	*Week 3*	*Week 4*
Temporal and spatial occlusion Verbal and physical response	Temporal occlusion only Range 180–60 ms before ball-racket contact	Temporal occlusion only Range 200–60 ms before ball-racket contact	Temporal and spatial occlusion Range 180–60 ms before ball-racket contact Racket and racket arm occluded	Temporal and spatial occlusion Range 200–60 ms before ball-racket contact Racket and racket arm occluded
Instructional technique	Guided-discovery			
Feedback	Positive social comparative Average over 10 trials	Summative and bandwidth	Bandwidth	Bandwidth and self-regulated
Shot presentation	**Medium variability** Single player Variety of passing shots **Low-medium CI** Blocked-serial order	**Medium variability** Single player Variety of passing shots **Medium CI** Serial order	**High variability** Multiple players Variety of passing shots **High CI** Random order	**High variability** Multiple players Variety of passing shots **High CI** Random order

CI = Contextual interference

Acquiring a greater number of explicit rules during practice results in a greater inclination to reinvest, resulting in performance decrements during pressure situations (e.g., Liao & Masters, 2002; Masters, 2000; Maxwell, Masters, & Poolton, 2006).

A guided-discovery approach to instructing has been compared to one based on explicit instruction among groups of skilled tennis players (Williams, et al., 2002). In the explicit instruction condition, key postural cues were highlighted during training, such that explicit links were made between particular postural positions and outcomes (e.g., open hip leads to a forehand shot directed down the line). In the guided-discovery condition, players were only directed towards potentially informative areas of the display, such as the trunk or hips, but they were not told specific outcomes associated with these areas and were instead encouraged to discover meaningful relationships between postural cues and shot outcomes. Both instructional-method groups improved their anticipatory performance in comparison to control groups, both in off-court (film-based) and on-court (physical response to a live feed) tests, but there were no differences between the groups. In a follow-up study, intermediate junior tennis players were studied over a longer period of time and under anxiety-provoking conditions (Smeeton et al., 2005). Players in the explicit instruction and guided-discovery groups improved at a faster rate during practice than a discovery-learning group (no instructions). During the anxiety-provoking transfer test, the explicit instruction group exhibited a significant increase in decision times compared to the guided-discovery and discovery groups. Based upon these findings we employed a guided-discovery instructional technique throughout each component of the on and off-court intervention detailed below.

Spatial and temporal occlusion training. To improve Andrew's ability to recognize advanced postural cues at an earlier point in the action sequence, a mixture of different presentation techniques including progressive spatial occlusion and temporal occlusion were used. First, a series of tennis action sequences were filmed from a first-person perspective using a head-mounted camera. Each action sequence consisted of a ball being played to either an opponent's deuce or advantage side, followed by an approach to the net or approach shot, before an opponent performed either a forehand or backhand passing shot. Each filmed action sequence was selectively edited in accordance with the temporal and spatial occlusion paradigms. The player was required to respond by stepping off force-sensitive pads placed underfoot to others placed either side of him in the direction of the anticipated shot and swinging his racket as though he was hitting a volley, whilst also providing a verbal response. This method of physically responding to a stimulus is thought to keep the coupling between perception and action relatively congruent to real-world responses (e.g., Savelsbergh, Haans, Kooijman, & van Kampen, 2010).

Presentation of clips

During the first off-court intervention session, the temporal occlusion paradigm was used with action sequences edited to occlude at time points between 180 milliseconds and 60 milliseconds before racket-ball contact. A series of six blocks of 16 action sequences was presented to the player over a 1-hour period. Initially, each block consisted of a single player, performing an equal number of forehand and backhand shots directed cross-court or down the line. The presentation order (e.g., forehand cross-court, backhand line, backhand cross) and occlusion period of clips (200–60 milliseconds) was provided in a serial order before being gradually more random (for an example, see Table 16.3). Presenting clips in this manner is supported by the contextual interference (CI) effect, a learning phenomenon associated with how a person best learns when practising multiple skills (Lee, 2012). Although presenting action sequences in a mixed or random order (or high CI) has been shown to lead to a slower acquisition rate (compared to blocked or low CI), it generally leads to better retention. The benefits of the CI effect are thought to be due to the strengthening of retrieval processes whereby 'forgetting' and 'recalling' skills across practice attempts aid the later retrieval of the different skills. In this case, learning the relationships between different postural cues and their outcomes are strengthened from practising them in a mixed order.

To progressively challenge the player, a combination of temporal and spatial occlusion techniques was employed during subsequent off-court sessions. Filmed action sequences were occluded at a series of points between 200–60 milliseconds prior to ball-racket contact over the intervention period. However, these clips were edited to delete the opponent's racket arm and racket. The intention of occluding this information was to guide Andrew's visual search towards more proximal spatial locations, thus speeding up his anticipatory response time. This process of behaviour change was not

Table 16.3 *Clip presentation order for a typical block during the* off-court *intervention.*

Week	*Clip presentation order*
1	AAAA, BBBB, CCCC, DDDD.*
2	ACBD, ACBD, ACBD, ACBD.
3	ACBC, DDAB, ABDA, ABCB.
4	DBBC, DACB, CDAC.

*A = Forehand, down the line, B = Forehand, cross-court, C = Backhand, down the line, D = Backhand, cross-court.

explicitly directed, but occurred as a function of the information (or lack thereof). While potentially more time consuming it was thought to ultimately be more resistant to psychological stress (Masters & Poolton, 2012).

Film clips from a number of different opponents were progressively added to the off-court intervention. Although most elite tennis players have similar strokes, each player's individual movement pattern has its own nuances that may have interfered with Andrew's ability to pick up advanced postural cue information. Presenting clips of various players invoked more variable practice conditions (i.e., performing a singular skill with multiple variations in conditions) which have learning advantages over constant or low variation practice (e.g., Salmoni, Schmidt, & Walter, 1984). Presenting clips of numerous opponents facilitated Andrew's ability to filter out extraneous contextual information (such as opponents' uniform and racket colour) and develop an adaptable anticipation response, able to account for changes in opponent characteristics (e.g., handedness, physical size, parameter adjustments in form or swing kinematics).

Feedback

The delivery of augmented feedback can significantly influence learning. In our intervention, the primary source of feedback was response times (i.e., Andrew's ability to read, interpret, and physically respond to the action stimulus). Andrew's elite status required that feedback be provided sparingly, so as to maintain and enhance his ability to detect and correct errors (for a review, see Magill & Anderson, 2012). To keep feedback to a minimum, we initially only provided delayed feedback after each block of trials (see Anderson, Magill, & Sekiya, 1994), which was expressed as an average score (e.g., Young & Schmidt, 1992). To further fade out feedback provision during weeks 3 and 4, feedback from the coach was only provided when it fell below 'acceptable' parameters (Sherwood, 1988) or when the player chose to ask for feedback (for a review of self-directed practice benefits and mechanisms, see Sanli, Patterson, Bray, & Lee, 2013).

To help reduce anxiety at the net, we actively worked on Andrew's perception of competence in these circumstances. Positive normative feedback, indicating better than average performance, has resulted in better retention than situations where this type of positive feedback is not provided, or feedback indicating below average performance is given (Ávila, Chiviacowsky, Wulf, & Lewthwaite, 2012; Lewthwaite & Wulf, 2010; Wulf, Chiviacowsky, & Lewthwaite, 2010). We speculated that this method would, to an extent, ameliorate anxiety related to competence at the net. This feedback method was systematically delivered, but faded out over subsequent sessions.

On-court practice intervention

On-court training sessions provided opportunity for Andrew to apply principles from the off-court sessions in an ecologically valid environment. To ensure that anticipatory improvements were relatively resistant to psychological pressure, we employed a guided-discovery approach to instruction and practice. Practice sessions were primarily based upon the constraints-led approach to learning (e.g., Newell, 1986; Davids, Button, & Bennett, 2008) during which key practice parameters were selectively manipulated to guide the player towards faster anticipatory responses. These practice parameters or constraints were suitably organized to ensure that the player's perceptual-cognitive and perceptual-motor skills were optimally challenged (Guadagnoli & Lee, 2004).

The need to engage in relevant forms of practice is fundamental to skill acquisition and transfer to the competitive environment. In our on-court intervention, 'relevant' referred to games-based practice activities that closely mimic match play and include perceptual (e.g., visual search), cognitive (e.g., decision-making) and motor (e.g., technique) elements of the sport (for a review, see Williams, Ford, Eccles, & Ward, 2011). Practice methods currently employed in a number of sports predominantly fail to incorporate perceptual-cognitive skills into training sessions and instead focus primarily on perceptual-motor skills (Ford et al., 2010; Low et al., 2013). We used modified games, matches, and the competition format of the sport (referred to as 'playing form' activities, Ford et al., 2010), in order to continuously place the player into situations with similar underlying structures to that of competition (for a review, see Williams et al., 2011).

The use of adapted games is grounded in the constraints-led approach to skill teaching (e.g., Davids et al., 2008). In this approach, learning is thought to occur as a consequence of the interactive relationship between the performer and the environment. We systematically manipulated the environmental (e.g., lighting), individual (via visual occlusion goggles) and task (e.g., rules or court dimensions) constraints to effect this relationship. This approach to learning is again low on explicit guidance, instead promoting a more discovery or guided-discovery approach to learning.

A number of task constraints were employed to maintain the structural integrity of the game whilst increasing the frequency of net plays (e.g., Ford & Williams, 2013). Practice sessions began with a modified game during which an opponent was instructed to play a moderately short ball at any point during a baseline rally. Andrew then played an approach shot before attempting to finish the play at the net. Since much of the perceptual training occurred in the off-court sessions, Andrew's opponent was permitted to use any variety of passing-shot techniques. Other task constraint manipulations were used including double points for winning shots at the net and conditioned points to mimic important points in matches, (e.g., match point or break point). By awarding double points at the net, we increased the frequency and incentive of net shots. Match or break points further acclimatized Andrew towards making more effective anticipatory responses during pressure situations.

Visual occlusion goggles were used to constrain Andrew's ability to focus on more proximal advanced cues (see Farrow & Abernethy, 2003). These glasses work in a similar manner to the temporally occluded video clips, in that the glasses can be triggered to occlude at various time points in the action sequence. We attempted to occlude information at time points similar to those used in the off-field intervention (e.g., 180 milliseconds–60 milliseconds before racket-ball contact). For safety reasons, a familiarization period was required before the glasses were gradually introduced to the on-court intervention. Similarly, dark coloured glasses that matched the surroundings of the indoor training facility, ball colour, and the opponent's racket and sleeves (all dark blue), but not the opponent's kit (white shorts and t-shirt) were used to help guide Andrew towards advanced visual cues (see Button & Farrow, 2012). This method, whilst not empirically tested, was thought to constrain Andrew's ability to pick up information from the racket arm and racket and focus attention towards the shoulders and trunk.

Activity box — BOX 16.3

Considering both a games-based approach to learning and the challenge point framework, explain how you might adapt constraints to improve anticipation for novice and intermediate tennis players?

A games-based approach to learning also encouraged variable and random practice conditions. Not only did this type of practice structure lead to greater retention and transfer to the competitive arena, but it provided an appropriate level of challenge relative to Andrew's tennis skill (Guadagnoli & Lee,

2004). According to the challenge point framework, there exists a theoretical 'optimal challenge point' in which the constant amount of task difficulty, regardless of the participant or condition (nominal task difficulty), and the degree of task difficulty in relation to the performer's skill level (functional task difficulty) interact to produce peak learning and performance benefits. For accomplished players such as Andrew, it is hypothesized that adding variability and randomness to practice can increase the challenge in the task and lead to superior learning benefits. Based upon this framework, we systematically tailored challenge over the intervention to ensure optimal benefits. For example, Andrew was progressively matched against more skilled opponents throughout the intervention, with opponents given increasing incentive to go for 'winners'.

REFLECTIONS

Performance analysis of match play during weekly practice was the primary strategy used to monitor the player's progress throughout the intervention. Analysis was concentrated on the player's win: loss ratio on net points, number of times passed at the net, as well as the total number of observable anticipation behaviours (e.g., Triolet et al., 2013) compared to before the intervention. We analysed these parameters during six games immediately after the four-week intervention period, comparing the results with those recorded pre-intervention. Additionally, longitudinal tracking of the total number of games won and ATP world ranking provided useful information as to the efficacy of the programme (see Table 16.1).

A modified version of Cox and colleagues' (2003) Revised Competitive Anxiety Inventory-2 (CSAI2-R) was used to measure changes in this construct. Feelings of competence should be enhanced through the training and the use of positive social comparative feedback (e.g., Chiviacowsky, Wulf, & Lewthwaite, 2012) aiding perceived self-efficacy and potentially ameliorate anxiety (e.g., Bandura, 1997). We also used an adapted version of the Basic Needs Satisfaction in Sport (Ng, Lonsdale, & Hodge, 2011) questionnaire to directly assess changes in perceived competence. Questionnaires were administered at a) the beginning of the intervention to establish a baseline level, b) after completion of the last session to assess the efficacy of the intervention and c) immediately before Andrew's first competitive game to assess transfer to competition.

An evaluation of each individual session took place between the skill-acquisition specialist, the coach and the player to assess the relative strengths and weaknesses of the intervention. In addition, a separate weekly meeting between the skill-acquisition specialist and the coach took place to outline the week's objectives and the underlying principles pertaining to feedback, instruction, and practice methods.

Limitations

We endeavoured to provide evidence-based rationale for the assessment and intervention of anticipation skill in tennis. However, there are a number of potential limitations in this hypothetical case study. Primarily these limitations are related to the complex nature of anticipation and the limited amount of applied research studies conducted with expert sport players.

There is a dearth of scientific literature as to how experts re-learn or modify existing techniques or how elite athletes learn (for exceptions, see Coughlin, Williams, McRobert, & Ford, 2013; Hodges, Edwards, Luttin, & Bowcock, 2011). Arguably this stems from the law of diminishing returns in which improvements in experts are likely to be fractional, (i.e., not statistically significant and therefore unlikely to be published), or improvements take place over prolonged periods (i.e., well beyond the time span of normal learning studies). Consequently, our review of the skill-acquisition literature relies primarily upon learning studies conducted with novice or intermediate skill level athletes.

Much of the rationale for the proposed perceptual-cognitive skills interventions has its roots firmly planted in motor learning. Although much of this literature is based on rather reductionist simple motor tasks (e.g., key pressing or tracking tasks), there is little reason to think that the general mechanisms uncovered from these tasks will not up-scale to more complex tasks or transfer to other perceptual-cognitive tasks (for a discussion of this point in reference to the contextual interference effect, see Lee, 2012).

Translatory research, focusing on the applicability of learning principles to performance settings, has taken place over the last decade (e.g.,; Smeeton et al., 2005; Williams & Ford, 2009). However, skill-acquisition specialists are still required to make significant leaps with respect to the applicability of some of the research findings into real-world settings. The challenge for practitioners working in the field is to take the general learning principles and apply them to the unique context of their sport. In this regard, there is a requirement for a more interactive exchange between researchers in the laboratory and field practitioners (e.g., Ericsson & Williams, 2007). Bridging the gap between the laboratory and the performance environment requires more bidirectional consultation between parties. As outlined above, the perceptual-cognitive processes involved in anticipation in tennis are multifaceted, complex, and interrelated. Consequently, a holistic approach to the study of anticipation, integrating pattern recognition, situational probabilities, and shot sequencing, may help to identify interrelated weaknesses. For example, deficiencies in a player's knowledge that a drop shot is about to be hit, relative to their position on the court (i.e., situational probability) is likely related to their visual search strategy and the pick-up of relevant perceptual cues, indicating that a drop shot is about to be played

Attempting to improve the anticipatory response time of a professional tennis player over a four-week period was a challenging task. In deciding the duration of the intervention we made reference to previous intervention studies and the player's competitive schedule. The four-week period accommodated both aspects. While we achieved anticipatory improvements after the intervention, it must be acknowledged that a longer intervention period may be required (Abernethy et al., 2012). In this respect, coach education of the underlying skill-acquisition principles applied is crucial in bringing about long-term behaviour change. Analysis of practice activities across the developmental continuum by a skill-acquisition specialist could in theory help prevent perceptual-cognitive skill deficiencies by systematically integrating them into regular practice.

Future directions

Considerable scope exists for scientists and practitioners to develop novel training methods and measures of anticipation. Although in the current case study we focused on advanced cue utilization, situational and contextual information should be considered when designing testing and training interventions in dynamic, interactive sports such as tennis (e.g., Abernethy et al., 2001; Crognier & Féry, 2005). It is now becoming more widely appreciated that motor experience (as well as perceptual experience) plays a direct role in predicting action outcomes in sports (e.g., Aglioti, Cesari, Romani, & Urgesi, 2008, Mulligan & Hodges, 2014; Urgesi, Savonitto, Fabbro, & Aglioti, 2012). When experts are anticipating the effects of an observed action it is thought that their motor system activates as though they were performing the action themselves. In this way, anticipatory predictions are made based on a low-level simulation of the observed action in the observer (e.g., Jeannerod, 2001; Knoblich & Flach, 2001). The closer the match between the observer's motor capabilities and the observed action, the better they will be at understanding and predicting the outcome of actions.

In a bid to create more ecologically valid testing and training environments for the player which simulate in-game performance, virtual reality techniques have been used to create sport environments in the laboratory (for a review, see Miles, Popa, Watt, Lawrence, & John, 2012). Immersive, interactive, virtual reality could allow for a more realistic viewing perspective as well as the creation of optic flow and depth perception, which is generally missing from current testing and training procedures (Craig & Watson, 2011). Similarly, advances in technology such as global position systems (GPS) allow for player movements to be recorded in real-time. These data can be used to target contextual or situational information such as court positioning, shot sequencing, and patterns of play (e.g., Loffing & Hagemann, 2014). At the non-behavioural level, neuroscience methods are being increasingly employed to further the understanding of the perceptual-cognitive processes underlying anticipatory decisions of expert athletes (e.g. Wright, Bishop, Jackson, & Abernethy, 2010; Yarrow, Brown, & Krakauer, 2009).

Performance analysis techniques are also becoming more accessible and less arduous to use. Advances in social media and portable devices are constantly making these methods more accessible. Multi-media software applications 'apps' such as 'coaches eye' (coacheseye.com) and 'soccer meter' (www.soccermeter.com), allow for real-time performance analysis and immediate feedback. Carefully designed performance analysis can provide the player with objective feedback about their performance in competitive situations, such as response accuracy, response time, and win: loss ratios in specific situations. Practitioners are encouraged to consider performance statistics that may be indicative of high or low anticipation skill.

SUMMARY

We have outlined a number of tools and strategies that were used to assess and improve a professional tennis player's anticipatory response times at the net. These methods primarily focused upon training the player's visual search strategy to pick up advanced cues from more proximal information sources (e.g., shoulder and trunk). Guided-discovery methods of instruction and constraints-led approaches to practice were recommended to facilitate learning that is robust in the face of psychological pressure. While the methods presented are evidence-based, this reductionist approach to a specific aspect of anticipation does not allow informed speculation as to how various perceptual-cognitive skills inherent in anticipation training might overlap. Perceptual-cognitive skills such as advance-cue utilization, pattern recognition, and knowledge of situational probabilities interact dynamically so that a strength or weakness in one component will likely influence the other. In this regard, the training intervention outlined would likely be improved greatly by integrating practice methods to enhance pattern recognition and decision-making underlying situational probability accuracy.

FURTHER READING

Abernethy, B., Farrow, D., Gorman, A., & Mann, D. (2012) Anticipatory behavior and expert performance. In A. M. Williams & N. J. Hodges (Eds.), *Skill acquisition in sport: Research, theory and practice* (2nd ed., pp. 287–305). Abingdon: Routledge. Provides an overview of the importance of anticipation in sports.

Davids, K., Button, C., & Bennett, S. (2008). *Dynamics of skill acquisition. A constraints-led approach*. Champaign, IL: Human Kinetics. Explains the constraints-led approach to learning in detail.

Smeeton, N. J., Williams, A. M., Hodges, N. J. & Ward, P. (2005). The relative effectiveness of various instructional approaches in developing anticipation skill. *Journal of Experimental Psychology: Applied, 11*, 98–110. Compares different instructional approaches used to facilitate improvements in anticipation and their resistance to psychological stress.

Williams, A. M., Ford, P. R., Eccles, D. W., & Ward, P. (2011). Perceptual-cognitive expertise in sport and its acquisition: Implications for applied cognitive psychology. *Applied Cognitive Psychology, 25*, 432–442. Provides an applied account of the dynamic nature of perceptual-cognitive skills in sport.

REFERENCES

Abernethy, B., Farrow, D., Gorman, A., & Mann, D. (2012) Anticipatory behaviour and expert performance. In A. M.Williams & N. J. Hodges (Eds.), *Skill acquisition in sport: Research, theory and practice* (2nd ed., pp. 287–305). London: Routledge.

Abernethy, B., Gill, D. P., Parks, S. L., & Packer, S. T. (2001). Expertise and the perception of kinematic and situational probability information. *Perception, 30*, 233–252.

Abernethy, B., Schorer, J., Jackson, R. C., & Hagemann, N. (2012). Perceptual training methods compared: The relative efficacy of different approaches to enhancing sport-specific anticipation. *Journal of Experimental Psychology: Applied, 18*, (2), 143–153.

Abernethy, B., Woods, J. M., & Parks, S. (1999). Can the anticipatory skills of experts be learned by novices? *Research Quarterly for Exercise and Sport, 70*, 313–318.

Aglioti, S. M., Cesari, P., Romani, M., & Urgesi, C. (2008). Action anticipation and motor resonance in elite basketball players. *Nature Neuroscience, 11*, 1109–1116.

Anderson, D. I., Magill, R. A., & Sekiya, H. (1994). A reconsideration of the trials-delay of knowledge of results paradigm in motor skill learning. *Research Quarterly for Exercise and Sport, 65*, 286–290.

Bandura, A. (1997). *Self-efficacy: The exercise of control*. New York: W. H. Freeman.

Button, C., & Farrow, D. (2012). Working in the field (Southern Hemisphere). In A. M.Williams & N. J.Hodges (Eds.), *Skill acquisition in sport: Research, theory and practice* (2nd ed., pp. 367–380). London: Routledge.

Cañal-Bruland, R., van Ginneken, W. F., van der Meer, B. R., Williams, A. M. (2011). The effect of local kinematic changes on anticipation judgments. *Human Movement Science, 30* (3), 495–503.

Cañal-Bruland, R., & Williams, A. M. (2010). Movement recognition and prediction of movement effects in biological motion perception. *Experimental Psychology, 57*(4), 320–326.

Causer, J., Holmes, P. S., Smith, N. C., & Williams, A. M., (2011). Anxiety, movement kinematics, and visual attention in elite-level performers. *Emotion, 11*(3), 595–602.

Causer, J., Janelle, C., Vickers, J., & Williams, A. M. (2012). Perceptual expertise: What can be trained? In A. M.Williams & N. J.Hodges (Eds.), *Skill acquisition in sport: Research, theory and practice* (2nd ed., pp. 306–324). Abingdon: Routledge.

Carlson, R. A., & Yaure, R. G. (1990). Practice schedules and the use of component skills in problem solving. *Journal of Experimental Psychology: Learning, Memory, and Cognition, 16*, 484–496.

Chiviacowsky, S., Wulf, G., & Lewthwaite, R. (2012). Self-controlled learning: The importance of protecting perception of competence. *Frontiers in Psychology, 3*, 1–8.

Christina, R. W., Barresi, J. V., & Shaffner, P. (1990). The development of response selection accuracy in a football linebacker using video training. *Sport Psychologist, 4*, 11–17.

Coughlin, E. K., Williams, A. M., McRobert, A. P., & Ford, P. R. (2013). How experts practice: A novel test of deliberate practice theory. *Journal of Experimental Psychology: Learning, Memory, & Cognition, 40*(2), 449–458.

Cox, R. H., Martens, M. P., & Russell, W. D. (2003). Measuring anxiety in athletics: The Revised Competitive State Anxiety Inventory-2. *Journal of Sport & Exercise Psychology, 25*, 519–533.

Craig, C., & Watson, G. (2011). An affordance based approach to decision making in sport: Discussing a novel methodological framework. *Revista de Psicologia del Deporte, 20*, 689–708.

Crognier, L., & Féry, Y. (2005). Effect of tactical initiative on predicting passing shots in tennis. *Applied Cognitive Psychology, 19*, 1–13.

Davids, K., Button, C., & Bennett, S. (2008). *Dynamics of skill acquisition. A constraints-led approach*. Champaign, IL: Human Kinetics.

Ericsson, K. A., & Williams, A. M. (2007). Capturing naturally occurring superior performance in the laboratory: Translational research on expert performance. *Journal of Experimental Psychology: Applied, 13*, 115–123.

Farrow, D., & Abernethy, B. (2003). Do expertise and the degree of perception-action coupling affect natural anticipatory performance? *Perception, 32*, 1127–1139.

Farrow, D., Abernethy, B., & Jackson, R. C. (2005). Probing expert anticipation with the temporal occlusion paradigm: Experimental investigations of some methodological issues. *Motor Control, 9*, 332–351.

Ford, P. R., & Williams A. M. (2013). 'Game intelligence': anticipation and decision making. In A. M.Williams (Ed.), *Science and soccer III* (pp. 105–121). Abingdon: Routledge.

Ford, P. R., Yates, I., & Williams, A. M. (2010). An analysis of practice activities and instructional behaviours used by youth soccer coaches during practice: exploring the link between science and application. *Journal of Sports Science, 28*(5), 483–495.

Gillet, E., Leroy, D., Thouvarecq, R., & Stein, J. F. (2009). A notational analysis of elite tennis serve and serve-return strategies on slow surface. *Journal of Strength & Conditioning Research, 23*(2), 532–539.

Goulet, C., Bard, C., & Fleury, M. (1989). Expertise differences in preparing to return a tennis serve: A visual information processing approach. *Journal of Sport and Exercise Psychology, 11*, 382–398.

Guadagnoli, M. A., & Lee, T. D. (2004). Challenge point: A framework for conceptualizing the effects of various practice conditions in motor learning. *Journal of Motor Behavior, 36*, 212–224.

Hagemann, N., Strauss, B., & Cañal-Bruland, R. (2006). Training perceptual skill by orienting visual attention. *Journal of Sport & Exercise Psychology, 28*, 143–158.

Helsdingen, A. S., van Gog, T., & van Merrienboer, J. J. G. (2011a). The effects of practice schedule and critical thinking prompts on learning and transfer of a complex judgement task. *Journal of Education Psychology, 103*, 383–398.

Helsdingen, A. S., van Gog, T., & van Merrienboer, J. J. G. (2011b). The effects of practice schedule on learning a complex judgment task. *Learning and Instruction, 21*, 126–136.

Hodges, N. J., Edwards, C., Luttin, S., & Bowcock, (2011). Learning from the experts: Gaining insights into best practice during the acquisition of three novel motor skills. *Research Quarterly for Exercise & Sport, 82*, 178–187.

Huys, R., Cañal -Bruland, R., Hagemann, N., & Williams, A. M. (2009). The effects of occlusion neutralization, and deception of perceptual information on anticipation in tennis. *Journal of Motor Behavior, 41*, 158–171.

Jeannerod, M. (2001). Neural simulation of action: A unifying mechanism for motor cognition. *NeuroImage, 14*, 103–109.

Knoblich, G., & Flach, R. (2001). Predicting the effects of actions: Interactions of perception and action. *Psychological Science, 12*, 467–472.

Lee, T. D. (2012). Scheduling practice. In A. M.Williams & N. J.Hodges (Eds.), *Skill Acquisition in sport: Research, theory and practice,* (2nd ed., pp. 79–93). Abingdon: Routledge.

Le Runigo, C., Benguigui, N., & Bardy, B. G. (2010). Visuomotor delay, information-movement coupling, and expertise in ball sports. *Journal of Sports Sciences, 28*, 327–337.

Lewthwaite, R., & Wulf, G. (2010). Social-comparative feedback affects motor skill learning. *Quarterly Journal of Experimental Psychology, 63*, 738–749.

Lewthwaite, R., & Wulf, G. (2012). Motivation and skill learning. In A. M. Williams & N. J. Hodges (Eds.), *Skill acquisition in sport: Research, theory and practice* (2nd ed., pp. 173–191). Abingdon: Routledge.

Liao, C. M., & Masters, R. S. W. (2002). Self-focused attention and performancefailure under psychological stress. *Journal of Sport & Exercise Psychology,24*, 289–305.

Loffing, F., & Hagemann, N. (2014). On-court position influences skilled tennis players' anticipation of shot outcome. *Journal of Sport & Exercise Psychology, 36*, 14–26.

Low, J., Williams, A. M., McRobert, A. P., & Ford, P .R. (2013). The microstructure of practice activities engaged in by elite and recreational youth cricket players. *Journal of Sport Sciences, 31*(11), 1242–1250.

Magill, R. A., & Anderson, D. I. (2012). The roles and uses of augmented feedback in motor skill acquisition. In A. M.Williams & N. J. Hodges (Eds.), *Skill acquisition in sport: Research, theory and practice* (2nd ed., pp. 3–21). Abingdon: Routledge.

Masters, R. S. W. (2000). Theoretical aspects of implicit learning in sport. *International Journal of Sport Psychology, 31*, 530–541.

Masters, R. S. W., & Poolton, J. M. (2012). Implicit motor learning. In A. M. Williams & N. J. Hodges (Eds.), *Skill acquisition in sport: Research, theory and practice* (2nd ed., pp. 59–75). London: Routledge.

Maxwell, J. P., Masters, R. S. W., & Poolton, J. M. (2006). Performance breakdown in sport: The roles of reinvestment and verbal knowledge. *Research Quarterly for Exercise and Sport, 77*, 271–276.

Miles, H. C., Popa, S. R., Watt, S. J., Lawrence, G. P., & John, N. W. (2012). A review of virtual environments for training in ball sports. *Computers & Graphics, 36*, 714–726.

Müller, S., Abernethy, B., & Farrow, D. T. (2006). How do world-class cricket batsmen anticipate a bowler's intention? *Quarterly Journal of Experimental Psychology, 59*, 2162–2186.

Mulligan, D., & Hodges, N. J. (2014). Throwing in the dark: Improved prediction of action outcomes following motor training without vision of the action. *Psychological Research, 78*, 692–704.

Newell, K. M. (1986). Constraints on the development of coordination. In M. G. Wade & H. T. A. Whiting (Eds.), *Motor development in children: Aspects of coordination and control* (pp. 341–360). Dordrecht: Martinus Nijhoff.

Ng., J. Y. Y., Lonsdale., C., & Hodge., K. (2011). The Basic Needs Satisfaction in Sport Scale (BNSSS): Instrument development and initial validity evidence. *Psychology of Sport & Exercise. 12*(3), 257–264.

O'Donoghue, P. G., & Brown, E. J. (2008). The importance of service in Grand Slam singles tennis, *International Journal of Performance Analysis in Sport, 8*(3), 70–78.

O'Donoghue, P. G., & Ingram, B. (2001). A notational analysis of elite tennis strategy. *Journal of Sports Sciences, 19*, 107–115.

Petit, J. P., & Ripoll, H. (2008). Scene perceptions and decision making in sport simulation: A masked priming investigation. *International Journal of Sport Psychology, 39*(1), 1–19.

Roca, A., Ford, P. R., McRobert, A. P., & Williams, A. M. (2013). Perceptual-cognitive skills and their interaction as a function of task constraints in soccer. *Journal of Sport & Exercise Psychology, 35*, 144–155.

Sanli, E. A., Patterson, J. T., Bray, S. R., & Lee, T. D. (2013). Understanding self-controlled motor learning protocols through the self-determination theory. *Frontiers in Psychology, 3*, 1–17.

Savelsbergh, G. J., Haans, S. H., Kooijman, M. K., & van Kampen, P. M. (2010). A method to identify talent: Visual search and locomotion behavior in young football players. *Human Movement Science, 29*(5), 764–776.

Sherwood, D. E. (1988). Effect of bandwidth knowledge of results on movement consistency. *Perceptual and Motor Skills, 66*, 535–542.

Singer, R. N., Cauraugh, J. H., Chen, D., Steinberg, G. M., Frehlich, S. G., & Wang, L. (1994). Training mental quickness in beginning/intermediate tennis players. *The Sport Psychologist, 8*, 305–318.

Singer, R. N., Williams, A. M., Frehlich, S. G., Janelle, C. M., Radlo, S. J., & Barba, et al. (1998). New frontiers in visual search: An exploratory study in live tennis situations. *Research Quarterly for Exercise and Sport, 69*, 290–296.

Smeeton, N. J., Williams, A. M., Hodges, N. J., & Ward, P. (2005). The relative effectiveness of various instructional approaches in developing anticipation skill. *Journal of Experimental Psychology: Applied, 11*, 98–110.

Taylor, K., & Rohrer, D. (2010). The effects of interleaved practice. *Applied Cognitive Psychology, 24*, 837–848.

Triolet, C., Benguigui, N., Le Runigo. C., & Williams, A. M. (2013). Quantifying the nature of anticipation in professional tennis. *Journal of Sport Sciences, 31*(8), 820–830.

Urgesi, C., Savonitto, M. M., Fabbro, F., & Aglioti, S. M. (2012). Long- and short-term plastic modeling of action prediction abilities in volleyball. *Psychological Research, 76*, 542–560.

Vickers, J. N. (2007). *Perception, cognition and decision training: The quiet eye in action*. Champaign, IL. Human Kinetics.

Ward, P., & Williams, A. M. (2003). Perceptual and cognitive skill development in soccer: The multidimensional nature of expert performance. *Journal of Sport & Exercise Psychology, 25*, 93–111.

Ward, P., Williams, A. M., & Bennett, S. J. (2002). Visual search and biological motion perception in tennis. *Research Quarterly for Exercise and Sport, 73*, 107–112.

Williams, A. M. (2012). Sport expertise. In D. Lavallee, J.Kremer, A. P. Moran, & A. M., Williams (2012) *Sport psychology: Contemporary themes* (2nd ed., pp. 146–167). London: Palgrave
Williams, A. M., & Burwitz, L. (1993). Advance cue utilization in soccer. In T. Reilly, J. Clarys, & A. Stibe (Eds.), *Science and football II* (pp. 239–244). London: E. & F. N. Spon.
Williams, A. M., & Davids, K. (1995). Declarative knowledge in sport: A by-product of experience or a characteristic of expertise? *Journal of Sport & Exercise Psychology, 17*, 259–275.
Williams, A. M., & Davids, K. (1998). Visual search strategy, selective attention, and expertise in soccer. *Research Quarterly for Exercise and Sport, 69*(2), 11–128.
Williams, A. M., Davids, K., & Williams, J. G. (1999). *Visual perception and action in sport*. London: E. & F. N. Spon.
Williams, A. M., & Ericsson, K. A. (2005). Some considerations when applying the expert performance approach in sport. *Human Movement Science, 24*, 283–307.
Williams, A. M., & Ford, P. R. (2009). Promoting a skills-based agenda in Olympic sports: the role of skill-acquisition specialists. *Journal of Sports Science, 27*(13), 1381–1392.
Williams, A. M., Ford, P. R., Eccles, D. W., & Ward, P. (2011). Perceptual-cognitive expertise in sport and its acquisition: Implications for applied cognitive psychology. *Applied Cognitive Psychology, 25*, 432–442.
Williams, A. M., & Hodges, N .J. (2005). Practice, instruction and skill acquisition in soccer: Challenging tradition. *Journal of Sports Sciences, 23*, 637–650.
Williams, A. M., Hodges, N. J., North, J. S., & Barton, G. (2006). Perceiving patterns of play in dynamic sport tasks: Identifying the essential information underlying skilled performance. *Perception, 35*, 317–332.
Williams, A. M., Huys, R., Cañal-Bruland, R., & Hagemann, N. (2009). The dynamical information underpinning deception effects. *Human Movement Science, 28*, 362–370.
Williams, A. M., Vickers, J. N., & Rodriguez, S. T. (2002). The effects of anxiety on visual search, movement kinematics, and performance in table tennis: A test of Eysenck and Calvo's processing efficiency theory. *Journal of Sport & Exercise Psychology, 24*, 438–455.
Williams, A.M., & Ward, P. (2003). Perceptual expertise: Development in sport. *In* Expert performance in sports: Advances in research on sport expertise (pp. 219–249). Champaign, IL: Human Kinetics
Williams, A. M., & Ward, P. (2007). Anticipation and decision making: Exploring new horizons. In G. Tenenbaum & R. Eklund (Eds.), *Handbook of sport psychology* (3rd ed., pp. 203–223). Hoboken, NJ: John Wiley & Sons, Inc.
Williams, A.M., Ward, P., & Chapman, C. (2003). Training perceptual skill in field hockey: Is there transfer from the laboratory to the field? *Research Quarterly for Exercise and Sport, 74*, 98–103.
Wright, M. J., Bishop, D., Jackson, R., & Abernethy, B. (2010). Functional MRI reveals expert-novice differences during sport-related anticipation. *Neuroreport, 21*, 94–98.
Wulf, G., Chiviacowsky, S., & Lewthwaite, R. (2010). Normative feedback effects on the learning of a timing task. *Research Quarterly for Exercise and Sport, 81*, 425–431.
Yarrow, K., Brown, P., & Krakauer, J. W. (2009). Inside the brain of an elite athlete: The neural processes that support high achievement in sports. *Nature Neuroscience, 10*, 585–596.
Young, D. E., & Schmidt, R. A. (1992). Augmented feedback for enhanced skill acquisition. In G. E. Stelmach & J. Requin (Eds.), *Tutorials in motor behavior II* (pp. 677–693). North-Holland: Elsevier.

Part 4 Psychology of Physical Activity and Exercise

17 Promoting Physical Activity in Ireland: A Case Study of All Island All Active (AIAA)

GAVIN BRESLIN, FIONA CHAMBERS, AND DEIRDRE BRENNAN

LEARNING OBJECTIVES

AFTER READING THIS CHAPTER YOU SHOULD BE ABLE TO :

1. Develop knowledge of the benefits of physical activity for health.
2. Identify key stakeholders involved in promoting physical activity.
3. Highlight challenges faced when bringing academics, researchers, industry, policy-makers and practitioners together across two jurisdictions to promote physical activity.
4. Use a multi-theory approach to interrogate the development of the AIAA multi-sector cross-border body using (a) Bronfenbrenners' (1979) bioecological theory, (b) Sport and Exercise Pedagogy theory (Armour and Chambers, 2014) and (c) Design Thinking Theory (Pink, 2006).
5. Describe the first AIAA project – Sport For Life: All Island, a healthy lifestyle programme for 4,000 children from areas of social and financial disadvantage in Ireland.

AREAS TO CONSIDER WHEN READING THE CHAPTER:

1. Who holds responsibility for increasing physical activity levels at policy/practice/community level?
2. What are the challenges of developing a network of professionals to promote physical activity?
3. What is the best mechanism for managing multi-sector groups comprising academics, researchers, industry, policy-makers and physical activity practitioners who have a shared aim of increasing physical activity?

CLIENT AND BACKGROUND

Globally and locally, governments are taking physical inactivity more seriously through health promotion policies and interventions that promote lifelong physical activity. It is now widely accepted that physical activity engagement can offer a wide range of potential health benefits to individuals and communities, and lead to a reduction in government health care bills for aging populations (World Health Organization (WHO), 2010). Despite the many interventions which promote physical activity and an increased awareness of the benefits to health, many people are still not active enough to gain the benefits of exercise (Toronto Physical Activity Charter, 2010).

Description box **BOX 17.1**

TORONTO CHARTER – OUTLINING THE PHYSICAL INACTIVITY PROBLEM

Throughout the world, technology, urbanisation, increasingly sedentary work environments and automobile-focused community design have engineered much physical activity out of daily life. Busy lifestyles, competing priorities, changing family structures and lack of social connectedness may also be contributing to inactivity. Opportunities for physical activity continue to decline while the prevalence of sedentary lifestyles is increasing in most countries, resulting in major negative health, social and economic consequences.

(From Introduction to Toronto Charter for Physical Activity: Global Advocacy Council for Physical Activity, International Society for Physical Activity and Health)

In this chapter, we present the whole of Ireland as a case study (yes, this is a big challenge!) and outline how All Island All Active (AIAA), a new collaborative platform which facilitates cross-sector, multidisciplinary, top-down and bottom-up knowledge production in sport and physical activity, has emerged. AIAA aims to find new ways of effective engagement around physical activity promotion. The AIAA case study highlights this influence through (a) the use of the multi/interdisciplinary concept of Sport and Exercise Pedagogy (SEP), which is the underpinning philosophy of AIAA and (b) the Sport for Life: All Island project which presents a concrete example of how SEP works with psychological theory in action and, finally, (c) by analysing the formation of AIAA using both psychological theory and innovation theory we provide direction for psychologists who are maybe about to, or are currently engaging with, multidisciplinary teams in designing or delivering physical activity interventions.

The premise on which the AIAA platform was formed

Nerad (2010) highlights how globalization and increasing complexity of the twenty-first century places multiple challenges upon academic, business, and social institutions. It is clear that in spite of having a shared agenda to increasing physical activity levels and maintaining behaviour change, researchers and practitioners recognize the pressing need for the enactment of dynamic strategies to adapt such changing environments (Regan & Gold, 2010). AIAA was set up in Ireland, an island situated in the

North Atlantic Ocean on the western fringes of Europe. The island is separated politically into two jurisdictions: Northern Ireland in the north-east of the island and is part of the United Kingdom with an approximate population of 1.8 million people and the Republic of Ireland (the south) with a population of 4.6 million. Of the combined populations, few meet the physical activity guidelines for health.

Definition box **BOX 17.2**

Physical activity includes three elements: (i) skeletal muscle movement, which (ii) results in energy expenditure, and is (iii) positively correlated with physical fitness (Caspersen, Powell, & Christenson, 1985). Exercise is a sub-component of physical activity and in addition to the three components above, it also includes, 'planned, structured, and repetitive bodily movement', with the objective of maintaining and improving physical fitness (Caspersen et al., 1985, p. 127). Sport has been more difficult to define (Biddle & Mutrie, 2008) but is generally accepted to be a sub-component of physical activity that is rule-based, structured, and competitive (Rejeski & Brawley, 1988). The definition of physical activity adopted in this chapter is deliberately broad, encompassing informal exercise through to high intensity sporting training and competition.

According to these physical activity guidelines, which are the same in the north and south of Ireland, children should participate in 60 minutes of moderate to vigorous intensity physical activity each day of the week. For adults, 30 minutes of moderate intensity physical activity on at least five days a week, or 150 minutes of moderate intensity activity across the week are recommended. Despite these recommendations and the provision of educational programmes and public information campaigns, the Children's Sport Participation and Physical Activity (CSPPA, 2010) study found that three out of every four southern Irish adults and four out of five southern Irish children failed to engage in sufficient physical activity. Similarly, in Northern Ireland three out of four children failed to meet the guidelines (Breslin & Brennan, 2012) and two out of three Northern Irish adults failed to meet the guidelines (The Northern Ireland Sport and Physical Activity Survey, 2010). Similar inactivity figures have been shown in many countries globally (Kohl, et al; 2012). Some of these countries, of which Ireland is one, have indicated that the economic cost of low levels of engagement in physical activity is estimated to be between €150 – €300 per person per year (Cavill, Kahlmeier, & Racioppi, 2006), with a further estimate that over the next year a cost of between €945 m and €1.89 bn is likely, rising to between €9.45 bn and €18.9 bn by 2023 (estimate based on a combined island population of 6.4 m). These costs are mainly in the area of health, therefore prevention of poor health and recommending increases in physical activity are recommended.

To encourage an increase in physical activity levels, both governments in Ireland have developed separate national strategies that include physical activity, recreation, and sport promotion. In the Republic of Ireland, a national physical activity plan is in development, and an equivalent policy document, Sport Matters: The Northern Ireland Strategy for Sport and Recreation 2009–2019 was published. It is these frameworks and the views of academics, policy-makers, community and those involved in sport that AIAA draws upon to achieve increases in physical activity by 1% per year for the next 12 years.

Initial needs assessment

Prior to the organization of the initial AIAA networking platform meeting, the founders, Chambers and Brennan, conducted an initial needs assessment which focused on identifying who the interested parties would be in promoting physical activity and health. These are listed in Table 17.1. The discussion then turned to establishing the physical activity levels of the island's population (see Table 17.1) and charted attempts previously been made, both on the island and in the literature, to modify physical activity behaviour. As pointed out earlier, it was apparent that physical activity levels across the populations (in both jurisdictions) were below the recommended levels for health. This yielded the following insights, (a) inconsistent approaches, techniques, and styles of engagement by those stakeholders involved. For example, we viewed coaches delivering programmes that targeted large groups of the population versus university research institutes that had thoroughly designed research protocols for assessing impact but had lower numbers of people involved. (b) Lack of monitoring and assessment. Therefore, in the event that an intervention was effective in increasing physical activity there was no opportunity to understand how the intervention was successful, to replicate it, or disseminate the findings to others. (c) Research studies focused on either single or multidimensional approaches or did not have a theoretical approach underpinning the intervention, that is they were not explicitly based on psychological behaviour change theory or a combination of theories (e.g., Theory of Planned Behaviour, Ajzen, 1985, 1987; Social Cognitive Theory, Bandura, 1977; Self- Determination Theory, Deci & Ryan, 1985). It is the contention of AIAA that any intervention must have a robust theoretical framework and should comprise an evaluation component in order to measure impact. In addition, AIAA asserts that training professionals in behaviour change techniques, monitoring, and evaluation should be central to any intervention.

One mechanism of achieving changes in physical activity within communities, according to Armour and Chambers (2014), is to give consideration to 'Sport and Exercise Pedagogy' (SEP). SEP is defined as a sub-discipline that is located in the academic territory between education, sport, and

Table 17.1 *Members of AIAA represented at the meetings.*

AIAA has attracted various members who have all benefits to gain from making people more active, these include:

- Government departments
    - Transport, Tourism and Sport, Health, Culture and Leisure, Education
- Sports councils
    - Sport NI, Irish Sports Council
- Third-level education
- Federation of Irish Sports
- National governing nodies
- Coaching Ireland
- Special Olympics Ireland
- Industry, small medium enterprises (SMEs)
- Community sport and school physical education
- Exercise and fitness professionals
- Others who have a genuine interest in increasing physical activity levels throughout Ireland
- International centres for local and regional aevelopment
- Other non-sport/physical activity bodies.

exercise sciences. It is both multidisciplinary and interdisciplinary wherein it is proposed that SEP academics and perhaps exercise psychologists must be prepared to cross the traditional discipline and sub-discipline boundaries, including those between the natural and social sciences, and challenge traditional professional boundaries, such as those between teaching and coaching.

Definition box

BOX 17.3

Sport and Exercise Pedagogy (SEP) is defined as a sub-discipline that is located in the academic territory between education, sport, and exercise sciences. It is both multidisciplinary and interdisciplinary where SEP academics including exercise psychologists must be prepared to cross the traditional discipline and sub-discipline boundaries, including those between the natural and social sciences, and challenge traditional professional boundaries, such as those between teaching and coaching (Armour & Chambers, 2013).

Accordingly, we propose in this chapter that by adopting or being cognizant of SEP and the psychology of human development brings with it a focus on (a) the needs of diverse learners of all ages in a wide range of physical activity/sport settings, including schools, (b) the abilities of professional teachers, coaches, and instructors to meet those needs, and (c) the contexts in which relevant sport, exercise/health and physical education policy and knowledge are developed and delivered (Armour, 2011). As psychology practitioners it maybe more comfortable to apply our knowledge within our sub-disciplines (sport and exercise psychology, health psychology, educational psychology, organizational psychology, etc.) and not explore beyond these boundaries. However, we encourage a more exploratory connective approach across disciplines and sub-disciplines as a more productive approach to promoting physical activity behaviour change. As documented elsewhere it is easy to perceive the false barriers between disciplines in psychology, when many of the interventions are based on the same psychological theories (see Woods et al., 2014). Therefore, an approach of bridging relationships between disciplines has been fostered in AIAA through adopting positive psychology and SEP. Through this collaboration it was envisaged that efforts could be made to cross the boundaries between government, school, community, university and industry to work jointly by bringing representatives from each into a dynamic 'third space' (a term coined by Bhabha, 1990, 1994; Soja, 1996). Based on Armour and Chambers (2014) and their notion of 'third place', a hybrid model (see Figure 17.1) was developed that promotes integration across sectors and disciplines.

The model is conceptualized as a dynamic enabling platform where effective pedagogies in sport and physical activity across the life-course can be designed, implemented, and evaluated. It is with this *'third place'*, SEP and psychology of development that AIAA was formulated in bringing interested parties together as one for tackling physical inactivity levels. By coming together, positive engagement opportunities have emerged for increasing physical activity which include: the development of consortia for applying for intervention and research funding both nationally and internationally, the sharing of ideas and best practice across the country, the sharing of recent developments or engagement events held by interested parties, and, the increased awareness of the AIAA group to community and government.

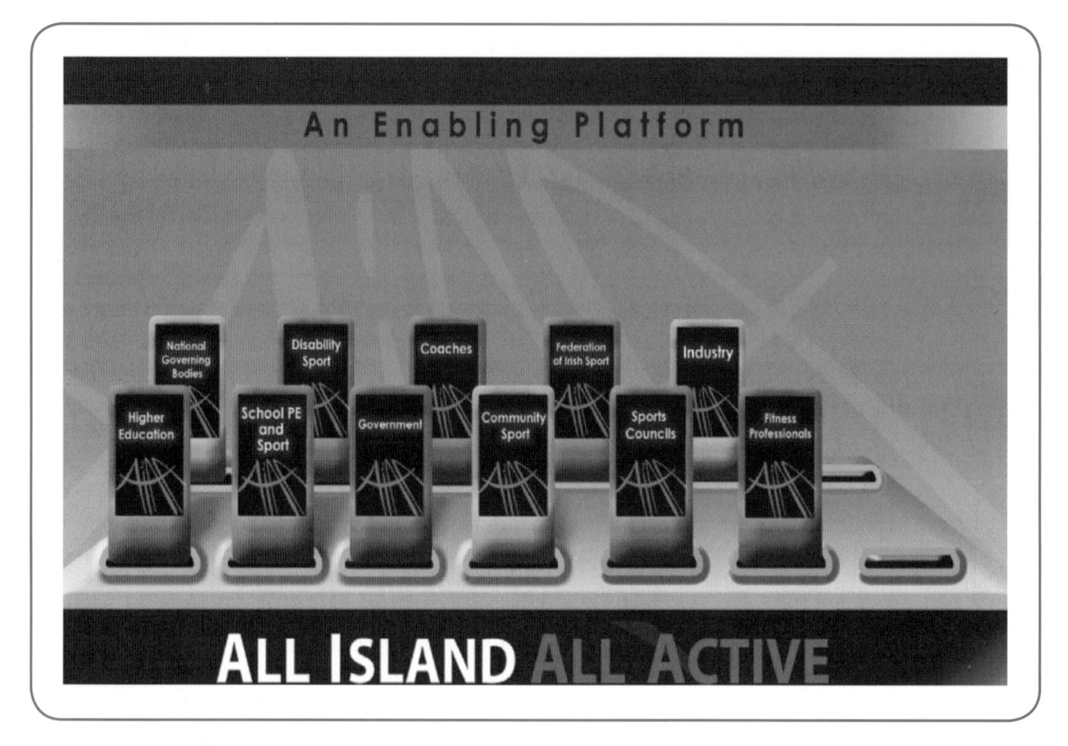

FIGURE 17.1 *Enabling platform using the docking station metaphor for project development, delivery and evaluation.*

Framework and intervention

The development of AIAA from November 2012 has been ongoing. AIAA has attracted various members who all have benefits to gain from making people more active (see Table 17.1).

The overall objective of AIAA is to contribute to sharing knowledge and expertise migration from both jurisdictions in increasing physical activity levels on the island of Ireland in line with physical activity guidelines outlined in the two respective National Physical Activity Plans.

The aim of AIAA is in the first instance to focus primarily on participant groups that are inactive for health, namely

- Older people
- Women and girls
- Disengaged young people
- Sedentary adults
- Adults and children suffering from a chronic condition
- Those recovering from illness/injury
- Those from a non-English speaking background – migrants and refugees
- Adults and children with a disability

As this list is essentially all those people in the population, it was important to refine it further to address physical inactivity in those most likely to be inactive. We now go on to discuss the formation of AIAA.

Theoretical basis underlying the formation of AIAA

To understand the milieu during the foundation and development of AIAA, Bronfenbrenner's (1979) bio-ecological model is relevant. It is particularly helpful as it provided a picture of the complex 'layers' from the environment, each having an effect on the individual's engagement (or otherwise) in physical activity, moving from individual level, to microsystem level, mesosystem, exosystem and macrosystem. As practitioners (psychologists) we may view our work to be client focused and we agree that this should be the case but also that by considering the bigger picture a more eclectic contextualized approach can be adopted. The bio-ecological model brought this additional component. Furthermore, the four stages of the ROSA Model (Chambers, 2015) and Social Cohesion Theory (Durkheim, 1933) were also considered. ROSA includes four key stages. The four stages traversed by members during the establishment of AIAA were **r**econnaissance, **o**pen consultation, **s**hared language, and **a**ctive negotiated meaning (Chambers, 2015):

Stage 1: reconnaissance

The process began with reconnaissance i.e. 'an inspection or exploration of the area or a preliminary survey to gain information' (Merriam-Webster Dictionary, 2011). At this stage an independent consultant was recruited to explore the role of AIAA and the use of the platform to engage stakeholders interested in promoting physical activity.

Stage 2: open consultation

The consultation process acknowledged the hierarchy of relationships on the AIAA platform and showed the benefits of partners having to listen to each other if they were to achieve the shared goal. Cooperative relationships between people or groups on the platform were raised as a process goal (see Field, 2005) as through effective collaboration, parties come to value each other's contribution, which can lead to parity of esteem between partners.

Stage 3: shared language

A common language between stakeholders was encouraged in relation to effective physical activity promotion amongst vulnerable groups (e.g., social and financial disadvantage). An important aspect of this process is the opportunity for stakeholders to share best practice and to jointly delineate AIAA codes of practice.

Stage 4: active negotiated meaning

This stage focused on partnership co-designing physical activity promotion programmes for vulnerable groups in society. An example of this was the Made to Move programme, the Community Health and Physical Activity Award, and Sport For LIFE: All Island programme underpinned by a shared philosophy of behaviour change.

At the heart of this process to developing some cohesion across the sectors was the need to find an agreed shared aim. This was agreed as:

> AIAA will use SEP and psychological knowledge exchange/development/research to support the increase in physical activity levels by 1% annually for the next 12 years (i.e. 12 in 12), with a particular focus on the most inactive groups (defined as social and financially marginalized groups/vulnerable citizens).[1]

[1]Based on WHO guidelines and the Institute of Public Health Community Profiling.

In spite of agreeing the 1% increase in physical activity, and who should lead AIAA quite early in the process, issues of parity across sectors and partners was clear. Armour and Chambers (2014) chronicled the development of AIAA, using Tuckman's (1965) sequence of four stages:

1. Forming (bringing interested parties in Northern Ireland and the Republic of Ireland together to tackle the problem of physical inactivity).
2. Storming (the fight to retain autonomy and leadership while working together to address physical inactivity).
3. Norming (the use of the docking station metaphor to increase parity of esteem and address autonomy issues); and
4. Performing (devising, implementing, and evaluating the Made to Move programme, Community Health and Physical Activity Award and Sport For LIFE: All Island).

In order to reveal a more nuanced account of the growth and development of AIAA through the ROSA stages, the work of Trubowitz (1986) was particularly helpful as he identifies eight phases which must be traversed in the formation of any new partnership. These include: (1) hostility and aggression, (2) lack of trust, (3) period of truce, (4) mixed approval, (5) acceptance, (6) regression, (7) renewal, and (8) continuing progress.

Trubowitz's (1986) phases align with the work of Amey and Brown (2004) who asserted that successful collaboration requires trust, mutual respect, shared vision time, open and frequent communication and flexibility, and time to develop and deliver on the agreed outcome (Doan, 1995; Krasnow, 1997). Williams (1997) viewed collaboration as an investment. He advocated a proactive stance to social cohesion which needed to be underpinned by four principal elements: (1) collaboration must be planned; (2) collaborative activities must have a shared vision; (3) collaborative activities must have a shared language, and; (4) collaboration is built on trust and understanding (p. 91). We also recognize that a proactive stance must consider that 'reciprocity is key and it must be addressed early and reviewed regularly' throughout the process (Trubowitz & Longo, 1997, p. 45).

The AIAA founders have used a design thinking approach (Pink, 2006) in attempting to address the problem of physical inactivity. Brown (2008) defines 'design thinking' as: 'a discipline that uses the designer's sensibility and methods to match people's needs with what is technologically feasible and what a viable business strategy can convert into customer value and market opportunity' (p. 86). While AIAA does not seek to make profit, it does desire to be financially stable such that it can remain viable and reach its societal goal. Design thinking adopts a user-centric approach beginning with 'empathy' such that products and services match real customer needs. In the case of AIAA, the customer is a person who finds it hard to begin to be physically active. This may be because of the person's socio-economic status, health issues, lack of education, lack of motivation, lack of time, living conditions or the environment, and so on. The process of developing the 'vehicle for behaviour change' involves the 'development of idea stages, applying an iterative process that forces them to move back and forth between inspiration, ideation and implementation' (Borja de Mozota & Peinado, 2013, p. 1). This attitude is characterized by empathy, integrative thinking, optimism, experimentalism, and collaboration that, while characteristic of designers, is not only available to them (Brown, 2008, p. 87). It is a process that employs abductive reasoning (Martin, 2007, p. 62). The founders of AIAA moved to a 'third logical mode' which Pierce (cited in Martin, 2007 p. 64) defined as being stimulated by 'wondering' which allowed them to 'infer possible new worlds' (Martin, 2007 p. 65) or opportunities. Hassi and Lakso (2011 cited in Peinado & Klose, 2011, p. 102) demonstrated a three-dimensional framework which captures the mindset of the 'design thinker' (see Table 17.2).

Table 17.2 *Mindset of the 'design thinker' (Hassi & Lakso, 2011, modified from Peinado & Kosta, 2011, p. 102).*

Practices	*Cognitive approaches*	*Mindset*
• Human centred approach • Thinking by doing • Visualizing • Combination of divergent and convergent approaches • Collaborative work	• Abductive reasoning • Reflective reframing • Holistic view • Integrative thinking	• Experimental and explorative • Ambiguity tolerant • Optimistic • Future oriented

Source: A. Peinado & S. Klose (2011). Design innovation: research – practice – strategy. Symposium proceedings. 1st International Symposium for Design Education Researchers. Cumulus Association/DRS. SIG on Design Pedagogy, Paris, France, pp. 97–111.

According to Borja de Mozota and Peinado (2013, p. 4) design thinkers have particular skills which enable them to create bespoke solutions/products for clients:

> Designers first identify and then solve problems in a learn by doing, highly experimental and iterative process ... This is possible because designers are trained in observation techniques, experimentation and the continuous testing of their ideas in what are often unstable contexts. Designers are risk-takers who learn how to manage uncertainty via prototyping based on observation and user-awareness and testing.

Through a three-step phased approach, a 1% annual increase in physical activity is the target for the next 12 years for the whole of Ireland. This will be achieved through the following mechanism:

Step 1: Inspire: ignite engagement in target groups using a Flagship Initiative known as the 'Made to Move Award' to initiate new learning and physical activity behaviour change.

Step 2: Deliver: the Made to Move Award will then be refined and implemented across the island through existing partnership networks (conglomerates of community groups, schools, sports clubs, churches, etc.) and progress towards AIAA's goal will be monitored using national monitoring surveys and a sub-sample of university-led research projects. This monitoring will include an assessment of physical activity, health, and wellbeing and from a societal perspective the cost-effectiveness of the intervention medium through to the longer term.

Step 3: Sustain: at the same time, AAIA will undertake an ongoing city based national programme of education, knowledge exchange, public engagement, community support and advocacy to raise the profile of lifelong learning experiences in physical activity.

AIAA impact

Since the establishment of AIAA, the first targeted physical activity programme started in 2014. The Sport For Life: All Island (SFL:AI) 12-week healthy lifestyle programme promotes physical activity and healthy eating in schools reaching 4,000 8 to 9 year olds from social and financial disadvantaged communities. The SFL:AI intervention programme is designed using social cognitive theory (Bandura, 1977). The programme was first delivered between 2009 and 2011 in Northern Ireland, and was then named Sport for Life (SFL). The findings from SFL (2009–2011) showed increases in light, moderate, and vigorous intensity physical activity as well as reductions in sedentary behaviour (Breslin & Brennan,

2012; Breslin et al., 2012). In this new project, the aim of the SFL:AI programme has been broadened to include the aim of increasing physical activity, improving healthy food choices, and increasing children's psychological wellbeing. Furthermore, a peer mentoring training tool with undergraduate students, across the whole of Ireland studying sport and exercise subjects was also piloted. SFL:AI is informed by psychological theory and comprises an evaluation component. It is intended that SFL:AI will: (a) provide skills to aspiring physical education teachers[2] from five higher education institutions across Ireland in the delivery of the physical activity programme, and; (b) provide training to undergraduate and postgraduate students in the evaluation of a school-based physical activity programme, and (c) validate a new mechanism of peer mentoring, tracking the learning relationship between primary teachers and students. At the time of writing this chapter, the programme has been delivered to over 4,000 children. Baseline data shows that physical activity levels for those children from lower socio-economic backgrounds is lower than other children in the population (Breslin et al, 2015). Further analysis is ongoing on the effect of the intervention on children and the effectiveness of peer mentoring.

REFLECTIONS

In this chapter we presented All Island All Active (AIAA), a new collaborative platform which facilitates cross-sectoral, multidisciplinary, top-down and bottom-up knowledge production in sport and physical activity. The aim of AIAA was to find new ways of effective engagement around physical activity promotion. The AIAA case study highlights this influence through the use of the multi/interdisciplinary concept of Sport and Exercise Pedagogy (SEP) with exercise psychology as a key component, which is the underpinning philosophy of AIAA. The Sport for Life: All Island project was outlined to show how SEP alongside psychological behaviour change theory works. Finally, by analysing the formation of AIAA using both psychological theory and innovation theory we provide direction for psychologists who may be are about to or are currently engaging with multidisciplinary teams in designing or delivering physical activity interventions. By conceptualizing AIAA as a 'third space', we were able to integrate psychological theory with theories from other disciplines in sport (Sport Coaching, Physical Education, Sports Development to name a few) and what arguably emerged through this process is a more eclectic approach to physical activity engagement and behaviour change. This chapter we believe presents exercise psychologists as more than what we traditionally view as the role of an exercise psychologist. It has moved the role of the exercise psychologist beyond one-to-one traditional consultations with an evaluation component to engendered collaborations around the notion of building relationships with government, learning about and with community groups through engagement. Put simply, it broadens our role as exercise psychologists to more than physical activity engagement or intervention but as mediators also.

The founders of AIAA have from the outset committed to and encouraged all participants to engage in reflective practice. This reflection has nurtured greater self-awareness, imagination, and creativity and dynamic modes of thinking and analysis (Schon, 1983). Indeed the AIAA platform is an open space which offers the possibility of transforming patterns and relationships within and between groups and organizations. This reflective practice has been a powerful tool in helping address positions of conflict, resistance, and power relations as well as points of synergy, commonality, and unity. One of AIAA's achievements has been bringing together a disparate group of professionals with

[2]University College Cork and Dublin City University has student Physical Education teachers, GMIT, IT Sligo and Ulster University students complete their primary degree in sport, exercise or outdoor pursuits before applying for PGCE.

an interest in public health for the common good of increasing physical activity. AIAA will need to remain responsive and flexible in order to successfully navigate these mutiple voices with a common goal of increasing physical activity.

AIAA is established at this point, albeit at an early stage of development. It has achieved much in a very short period of time as its raison d'être resonates with all those who have a vested interest in targeting physical inactivity on this island. The founders and many members of AIAA are design thinkers and as such are engaged in a constant iterative process, responding to and solving barriers to physical inactivity in a highly experimental fashion. More recently, as part of this critically reflective process, AIAA engaged a consultant to conduct 360 degree feedback on AIAA development and focus through engaging with each stakeholder. In this way, we manage the constant flux and uncertainty by constantly working with stakeholders to build an authentic model of best practice that is effective and sustainable and will result in increasing physical activity levels across the whole of Ireland.

FURTHER READING

Armour, K. M., & Chambers, F. C. (2014). 'Sport & Exercise Pedagogy'. The case for a new integrative subdiscipline in the field of Sport and Exercise Sciences/ Kinesiology/Human Movement Sciences. *Sport Education and Society* (Special Issue): 1–14. Further information is provided on Sport and Exercise Pedagogy (SEP). Tuckman's stage of group development are also applied to AIAA.

Breslin, G., & Brennan, D. (2012). A healthy lifestyle intervention delivered by aspiring physical education teachers to children from social disadvantage: Study protocol and preliminary findings. *Child Care in Practice, 18*(3), 1–19. This article outlines the design of a 12-week physical activity intervention for socially-disadvantaged children. The detail provided in the article will complement the experiences outlined in this chapter.

Peinado, A., & Klose, S. (2011). Design innovation: research – practice – strategy. Symposium proceedings (pp. 97–111). 1st International Symposium for Design Education Researchers. Cumulus Association/DRS. SIG on Design Pedagogy, Paris, France. This article will provide further information on the design innovation tools used to inspire the development of AIAA.

REFERENCES

Amey, M. J., & Brown, D. F. (2004). *Breaking out of the box: Interdisciplinary collaboration and faculty work*. Westport, CT: Greenwood Press/Information Age Publishing.

Ajzen, I. (1985). From intentions to actions: A theory of planned behavior. In J. Kuhl & J. Beckmann (Eds.), *Action-control: From cognition to behavior* (pp. 11–39). Heidelberg: Springer.

Ajzen, I. (1987). Attitudes, traits, and actions: Dispositional prediction of behavior in personality and social psychology. In L.Berkowitz (Ed.), *Advances in experimental social psychology*, Vol. 20 (pp. 1–63). New York: Academic Press.

Argyris, C., & Schon, D. A. (1974). *Theory in practice*. San Francisco: Jossey-Bass.

Armour, K. (Ed.) (2011). *Sport pedagogy: An introduction for teaching and coaching*. London: Prentice Hall

Armour, K., & Chambers, F. C. (2014). 'Sport and exercise pedagogy'. The case for a new integrative subdiscipline in the field of sport and exercise sciences/kinesiology/human movement sciences. *Sport Education and Society*, 1–14.

Bandura, A. (1977). *Social learning theory*. Englewood Cliffs, NJ: Prentice Hall.

Bhabha, H. K. (Ed.). (1990). *Nation and narration*. New York: Routledge.

Bhabha, H. K. (1994). *The location of culture*. New York: Routledge.

Borja de Mozota, B., & Peinado, A. (2013). New approaches to theory and research in art and design led educational programs – can 'Design Thinking' sparkle new answers to old problems? Annual Conference of the College of Art Association (CAA) in New York (February).

Breslin, G., & Brennan, D. (2012). A healthy lifestyle intervention delivered by aspiring physical education teachers to children from social disadvantage: Study protocol and preliminary findings. *Child Care in Practice*, *18*(3), 1–19.

Breslin, G., Brennan, D., Chambers, F., Woods, C., Smyth, P., & Hanna, D., et al. (2015). Preliminary findings from the Sport For Life: All island healthy lifestyle intervention for children aged 8–9 years (International Society for Behavioural Nutrition and Physical Activity, Edinburgh)

Breslin, G., Brennan, D., Rafferty, R., Gallagher, A., & Hanna, D. (2012). The effect of a healthy lifestyle programme on 8–9 year olds from social disadvantage. *Archives of Disease in Childhood*, *97*(7), 618–624.

Breslin, G., Gossrau-Breen, D., McCay, N., Gilmore, G., MacDonald, L., & Hanna, D. (2012). Physical activity, gender, weight status, and wellbeing in 9- to 11-year-old children: A cross-sectional survey. *Journal of Physical Activity and Health*, *9*, 394–401.

Bronfenbrenner, U. (1979). *The Ecology of Human Development: Experiments by Nature and Design*. Cambridge, MA: Harvard University Press. Retrieved from http://www.journals.elsevier.com/international-journal-of-psychophysiology/editorial-board/ology of human development

Brown, T. (2008). Design thinking. *Harvard Business Review*, June Issue, 86.

Caspersen, C. J., Powell, K. E., & Christenson, G. M. (1985). Physical activity, exercise and physical fitness: Definitions and distinctions for health-related research. *Public Health Reports*, 100, 126–131

Cavill, N., Kahlmeier, S., & Racioppi, F. (2006). Physical Activity for Health in Europe: Evidence for Action. World Health Organization.

Chambers, F .C. (Ed.). (2015). Mentoring pre-service teachers within a school-university partnership. In F. C. Chambers (Ed.), *Mentoring in sport coaching and physical education*. Abingdon: Routledge.

Deci, E. L., & Ryan, R. M. (1985). *Intrinsic motivation and self-determination in human behaviour*. New York: Plenum.

Doan, S. R. (1995). The collaborative model: The effective model for the increasing interdependence of organizations. ED 392 154. Retrived 16 January 2016 from http://files.eric.ed.gov/fulltext/ED392154.pdf.

Durkheim, E. (1933). *The division of labor in society*. Translated by George Simpson. New York: The Free Press.

Field, J. (2005). *Social capital and lifelong learning*. Bristol: Policy Press.

Kohl, H. W., Craig C. L., Lambert E. V., Inoue, S., Alkandari J. R., Leetongin, G., & Kahlmeier, S. (2012). *The pandemic of physical inactivity: Global action for public health*. Lancet Physical Activity Series Working Group. The Lancet, Early Online Publication, 18 July 2012. DOI:10.1016/S0140-6736(12)60898

Krasnow, M. (1997). *Learning to Listen Talk and Trust: Constructing collaboration*. AERA Chicago, 24–29 March.

Martin, R. L. (2007). *The opposable mind: How successful leaders win through integrative thinking*. Boston, MA: Harvard Business School.

Merriam-Webster Dictionary (2011). Reconnaissance. Merriam-Webster Online Dictionary. Retrieved 11 January 2016 from http://www.merriam-webster.com/dictionary/reconnaissance

Nerad, M. (2010). Globalization and the internationalization of graduate education: A macro and micro view. *Canadian Journal of Higher Education*, *40*, 1–12.

Peinado, A. D., & Klose, S. (2011). Design innovation: Research-practice-strategy, symposium proceedings: researching design education. First International Symposium for Design Education Researchers. Cumulus Association/DRS. SIG on Design Pedagogy Paris, France 18–21 May, 97–111.

Pink, D. H. (2006). *A whole new mind: Why right-brainers will rule the future*. New York: Riverhead.

Regan, J., & Gold, J. (2010). Think tanks with deliverables: How communities of practice helped LPL financial management growth and organizations' complexity. *Global Business and Organizational Excellence*, 29, 17–26.

Schon, D. A. 1983. *The reflective practitioner*. New York: Basic Books.

Soja, E. (1996). *Thirdspace: Journeys to Los Angeles and other real-and imagined places*. Oxford: Blackwell.

Tuckman, B.W. (1965). Developmental sequence in small groups. *Psychological Bulletin*, 63, 384–399.

Toronto Physical Activity Charter (2010). Final version 20 May. Retrieved 16 February 2015 from www.globalpa.org.uk.

Trubowitz, S. (1986). Stages in the development of school-college collaboration. *Educational Leadership*, *43*(5), 18–21.

Trubowitz, S., & Longo, P. (1997). *How it works – inside a school-college collaboration*. New York: Teachers College Press.

Williams, B. C. (1997). Challenges and opportunities for collaboration in teacher education programs. *Action in Teacher Education*, XIX(2), 89–96.

Woods, D., Breslin, G., Kremer, J., Cooke, Y., Corrie, S. & Clarke, A. (2014) Worlds apart sport psychology in the workplace. *Sport & Exercise Psychology Review*, *10*(3), 99–104.

18 Athlete Wellbeing

Abbe Brady

LEARNING OBJECTIVES

AFTER READING THIS CHAPTER YOU SHOULD BE ABLE TO:

1. Recognize the distinctions between wellbeing and ill-being.
2. Identify different dimensions of wellbeing and appreciate how these can be used to understand athlete wellbeing experiences and issues.
3. Develop a critical understanding of how a humanistic person-centred philosophy of practice supports athlete wellbeing by encouraging client-centredness, holistic athlete development and athlete empowerment.
4. Critically reflect upon the value of understanding athlete wellbeing to inform the discipline and practice of sport psychology.

AREAS TO CONSIDER WHEN READING THE CHAPTER:

1. Through examining everyday practices in high-performance (HP) sport and the sport science literature, what can we infer about beliefs relating to the relationship between athletic performance and athlete wellbeing?
2. Why is it important to consider multiple dimensions of athlete wellbeing?
3. How can an increased awareness of athlete wellbeing and techniques in positive psychology inform practice in applied sport psychology?

CLIENT AND BACKGROUND

Horse-racing is a highly popular spectator sport with a long history. The sport's attraction is manifold and includes the aesthetics of thoroughbred horses racing, the skills and guile of jockeys, the risk of danger for both horse and rider, the unpredictability of outcomes, and if gambling is involved, others can engage with the excitement of the race through anticipated financial gain. Behind the daily racing pages and television coverage, a large industry exists. Recent estimates state that in the UK there are thousands of racehorses and racehorse owners, hundreds of trainers and training yards, 900 amateur jockeys (evenly split between flat and jump events), 250 apprentice jockeys (again evenly spilt) and about 90 professional jump racing jockeys and 107 flat racing jockeys (McCrory, Turner, LeMasson, Bodere & Allemandou, 2006). Professional jockeys are very well known and highly respected within racing. In the UK and Ireland, racing and especially jump racing, is known for having the highest injury rates of any sport worldwide (Turner, McCrory, & Halley, 2002). Within sports medicine and sport science (including sport and exercise psychology), horse-racing has received most attention associated with injury, risk of injury, and nutritional and weight management strategies. Making the weight for races may mean jockeys reduce body weight by 4% and practices and policies around race weight management have received considerable attention (Dolan, Cullen, McGoldrick, & Warrington, 2013; Wilson, Durst, Morton, & Close, 2014). By contrast, limited attention has been given to the everyday lives and challenges faced by jockeys and this case study provides insight through the experience of one professional jockey.

Niall is a 24-year-old professional jockey. He had been very successful in his first few years as a professional but following several consecutive poor seasons and a major injury, he experienced depressed affect and low confidence. These were the reasons given by the doctor at the Professional Jockeys' Association (PJA) when speaking directly to the sport and exercise psychology consultant to explain why she had encouraged Niall to seek support.

As a child Niall's love of being around and working with horses was clear to his family and friends. As a young teenager the trainers and staff at the yard were impressed by his eagerness to help out. His dream was to become a jockey. Despite protestations from his parents and teachers, Niall frequently skipped school and when made to go to school (because he would be banned from the yard otherwise), he rarely paid much attention in class. By the time he was 15 years old, he was employed as a full-time stable hand and thoughts of achieving any qualifications at school were long forgotten. Niall was happy. His life revolved around the yard and that was everything he wanted. At 16 years of age, he was offered an apprenticeship as a jockey which meant more riding out with the racehorses, accommodation at the yard, and participating in amateur races. He worked six or seven days a week and Niall was proud to have been given the responsibility especially as he was younger than many of the other apprentices.

A typical day for Niall started with being at the stables by 5 am for the horses' morning training. Afternoons were spent travelling with horses to race meetings, preparing the horses, assisting professional jockeys, and occasionally entering amateur races. By the time the jockeys had returned to the yard, fed, and settled the horses, often the day's work typically didn't finish until 8 or 9 pm. Since his move to the yard, Niall only rarely paid visits to see his parents or his brothers and sisters, and he lost touch with his former friends. His life revolved around the yard.

Being much younger than all the other staff at the stables, Niall was careful to try to fit in as best as he could. He kept a low profile, worked hard, and kept himself to himself. Within a couple of years Niall was successfully racing regularly in amateur events where he achieved some of the highest accolades in the sport. With continued progress by the time he was 18 years old he was offered a contract. His contract as a second jockey allowed him to take rides for other trainers and through these opportunities he was sometimes able to ride in more prestigious events. His early success at some of the UK's premier festival events brought much more attention, more opportunities, and significant financial rewards. His agent Don took care of everything and phoned every day or two with a range of rides to choose from. Niall was busy doing something he had always dreamed of and was good at. His prospects were exciting and the financial rewards and sponsorship were keeping his accountant busy and his agent took care of his racing schedule. Everything was going well.

At a party with other professional young jockeys to celebrate the end of a national hunt event, the conversation turned to banter about which of the jockeys was most successful and they spoke about the money they'd been making, the cars and property they owned or were going to buy. It struck Niall that he'd just saved all his money and unlike the others, he was the only one who still lived at the yard and drove his first car (the one his parents had saved hard to buy him). In the following months, Niall bought his first property and bought a better car. Following a couple more good seasons, at 22 years of age and confident of continued success, he bought a second larger property and another better car. Niall started to spend more time with these jockeys and occasionally joined one or two of them in drinking heavily.

Life was busy and days though filled with early morning riding out and afternoon/evening racing. Niall had not had time for steady girlfriends until he met Sam, the sister of a fellow jockey. After a few months they were a couple and a year later Sam moved in with Niall.

A couple of years later when he was 24 years old and after a disappointing couple of seasons, Niall realized that his rankings were slipping. He wasn't always getting the best horses or as much choice of rides as before. He felt growing frustration that he had no idea whether or how he might become the first jockey for his trainer or for anyone else. He started to notice how everything about racing seemed much harder at this time and how his confidence and happiness was entirely dependent on wins, good placing, or ranking. He began to feel more anxious at race meetings and began to avoid or cut short post-race chats with the owners and trainers.

Over the last year, Niall's increasingly flat moods were noticed by Sam, but when she asked, he brushed them off as nothing. Every month or two Niall went along to the jockeys' socials typically held on the last day or two of big events. He noticed that the only time he felt free of worry was on these occasions after drinking too much.

In the spring at a top national hunt event Niall had a bad week with just a few good placings, no wins, and two falls. In his last race he fell and seriously broke his arm which doctors assured him would mean an end to that season. After several operations, he was going to be in rehabilitation for 4 to 5 months, missing the flat season and looking to return to jump racing in the autumn. During the early months he was largely housebound as he couldn't drive and soon felt out of touch with friends in racing and at the yard. Two weeks after the injury his accountant, who dealt with all financial matters, passed on news that Niall had a large tax bill, also that his mortgage payments would shortly increase, and all of this came just as his income was severely reduced. During the next few months Niall became progressively more concerned about his situation and especially his ability and future as a jockey. During a consultation with the doctor at the Professional Jockeys' Association (PJA), she suggested he see a sport and exercise psychologist.

INITIAL NEEDS ASSESSMENT

This case study used a framework for delivery that was aligned with principles from a humanistic approach focused on facilitating client-centred and holistic practice. This has fundamental implications for how initial needs assessment may be viewed and undertaken. Being client-centred requires recognition that the athlete's perceptual world is their reality and understanding his/her feelings, attitudes, and behaviour is best achieved by appreciating the internal perspective of the athlete from his/her point of view. Thus an important objective of this approach was to allow Niall to use his own ideas to articulate his internal world which Rogers (1965) referred to as the client's 'phenomenological field'. The first meeting was especially important for encouraging Niall to feel comfortable to be able to talk openly. An important objective of the first session related to gaining a sense of Niall's view of his situation and acknowledging the challenges and feelings he was experiencing.

One way that client-centredness is achieved is through the respective roles of the client and practitioner within sessions. I used a non-directive approach, meaning I did not follow a preordained sequence of procedures but was guided by the Niall's own account of the issues. During initial meetings and all other sessions, I was careful to avoid seeming to be 'identifying' or take a lead on focusing in on target problems or behaviours or using particular assessment techniques such as questionnaires, tests, or set questions. To do these things at all, but especially early on in the relationship, is highly incongruent with the principles of humanistic practice. Thus, the concept of an 'initial needs analysis' to inform subsequent intervention is a problematic notion and ironically could be counterproductive by disrupting the task of understanding Niall's view of his experience. Using standardized initial needs assessment could interfere with accessing the Niall's phenomenological field by creating a separate external view of what's really happening. This could introduce the image of me, the sport and exercise psychologist, as an authority figure using stock techniques which could reduce and depersonalize Niall's experiential account to a set of generalizable symptoms/factors. The consequent inequitable locus of power (with the consultant) and de-individuation of the client would be counter to the aims of and the growth of an internal locus of evaluation and empowerment for the client (McLeod, 1996). Standardized assessment could undermine other features central to effective relationships including, the importance of the client's contribution, collaboration, and sense of equity.

Having explained why standardized initial needs assessment is not appropriate in humanistic practice, the first meeting does serve distinct assessment related purposes for both the client and practitioner. It is a meeting where mutual decisions are made about whether to make a commitment to work together. Clients and especially those who are experiencing low wellbeing and/or the presence of ill-being may be especially vulnerable to not feeling empowered or appreciating the choices they have. Thus, it is especially important that the practitioner should encourage the client to consider whether s/he feels as though they could work with the practitioner by judging not only their credibility but also their interpersonal skills and humanity. The practitioner should also consider his/her personal reaction to the client and whether s/he foresees any personal barriers to establishing an accepting and congruent relationship with the client (Woolfe & Dryden, 1996). The latter requires the practitioner to trust their feelings about the client, the dyadic relationship potential and pay heed to identifying a need to refer the client.

Theoretical perspectives

Compared with other topics, athlete wellbeing has received limited attention in applied sport and exercise psychology to date and so this chapter draws from contemporary developments in the conceptualization of wellbeing emerging most recently through positive psychology (PP). Appreciating this lineage will help the reader locate the ideas and practices in the case study, some of which are not common within mainstream sport and exercise psychology.

There is now increasing consensus that wellbeing is distinct from merely the absence of illness or ill-being (Keyes, 2002; Seligman, 2008; Adie & Bartholomew, 2010) and as a separate state it warrants clear articulation. Albeit highly simplified, the continuum presented in Figure 18.1 can be useful for distinguishing the realm of PP focusing on optimal functioning and wellbeing compared with the corpus of psychological activity focusing on dysfunction.

Severe dysfunction Chronic ill-being	Mild dysfunction Low ill-being	Neutral	Moderate functioning Low wellbeing (*Languishing*)	Optimal function High wellbeing (*Flourishing*)
−10	−3	0	+3	+10

FIGURE 18.1 *A simplified continuum of functioning and wellbeing as a metaphor for locating the focus of positive psychology within applied psychology activities.*

Seligman and Csikszentmihalyi (2000) stated that applied psychology should do more than support a person's shift from minus 7 to minus 2 or zero. Addressing mainly the reduction of dysfunction and ill-being perpetuates what Hefferon and Boniwell (2011) refer to as the disease or medical model of psychology. Although it is undoubtedly vital to understand how to support clients in the reduction of dysfunction and distress, deficit reducing activities should not be viewed as those which automatically confer wellbeing because they are not focused on facilitating optimal states of feeling or functioning. An imperative for the discipline of PP was to develop an understanding of how to move people from minus 3 or plus 3 to plus 7 which required new knowledge and understanding about optimal psychological functioning and positive experiences, characteristics, and communities. A primary activity in PP to date, has been advancing this relatively new knowledge landscape and increasing understanding about the central concepts of wellbeing and flourishing.

Description box

BOX 18.1

Consensus about the meaning of wellbeing is most apparent at a broad level when it is described as the following: 'a positive and sustainable state that allows individuals, groups or nations to thrive and flourish' (Huppert, Baylis & Keverne, 2004, p. 1331). Flourishing is defined as: 'the experience of life going well. It is the combination of feeling good and functioning effectively' (Huppert & So, 2013, p. 838).

Associated with its use in everyday life, in science and its varied applications, wellbeing can mean quite different things to different people. Hence wellbeing can be a slippery concept to define.

A review of theoretical accounts of psychological wellbeing shows that there are many different ways of representing wellbeing and in most cases these are multidimensional (Ryff, 1989; Diener, 1984; Seligman, 2011; Keyes, 1998; Lundqvist, 2011; Mayoh & Jones, 2014). At an individual level, wellbeing is variously presented as involving one or more of a range of dimensions such as; subjective, psychological, physical, developmental, social and/or spiritual wellbeing.

Definition box **BOX 18.2**

This chapter adopts a broad definition of athlete wellbeing as, a multidimensional, positive, and sustainable state that allows the athlete to thrive and flourish.

Discussion box **BOX 18.3**

Do you agree, is athlete well-being especially relevant in high-performance sport if we believe that when an athlete is thriving (has high vitality and learning) and flourishing (has high levels of well-being and optimal functioning), s/he is more likely to be making progress towards realizing personal sporting goals?

A challenge faced by sport psychologists interested in athlete wellbeing is that whilst we intuitively know through our first-hand experience that athlete wellbeing is important in its own right and vital for sustained performance achievement in high-performance (HP) sport, actually we have little explicit research examining the topic or the wellbeing-performance relationship directly. This is a relationship that warrants enquiry. My own research and that of my research students has to date drawn heavily from findings across other contexts and disciplines. Increasing evidence in business, health sciences, and psychology demonstrates that people are successful across multiple life domains not only because success increases people's wellbeing but also because high wellbeing engenders success in many life domains (Fredrickson, 2004; Harter et al., 2003; Huppert, 2009; Huppert & So, 2013; Lyubomirsky et al., 2005; Seligman, 2008). Findings from cross-sectional, longitudinal and experimental studies repeatedly demonstrate how high levels of wellbeing are causally linked to positive outcomes such as productivity, performance, learning and personal development, personal resources, pro-social behaviour, constructive interpersonal relationships, good health and longevity. Governments around the world now recognize the importance of wellbeing for individual and societal thriving, and many have adopted measures of wellbeing as a key social indicator within national and European population surveys (Huppert & So, 2013). One justification for promoting athlete wellbeing and flourishing is associated with its potential to elicit myriad benefits for the person as well as his/her performance.

Activity box **BOX 18.4**

How would you investigate the wellbeing performance relationship? What benefits and issues could you foresee associated with monitoring HP athlete well-being as a social indicator for the effectiveness of HP sport? What criteria and what methods would you propose to use in such monitoring?

The lifestyles experienced by HP and professional athletes present many opportunities for, and obstacles to, wellbeing and flourishing. It has been argued that conforming to particular cultural practices in the pursuit of performance success in sport can compromise wellbeing and induce ill-being (Beamish & Ritchie, 2006; Miller & Kerr, 2002, Theberge, 2008). Lundqvist and Sandin (2014) acknowledge that a key challenge for the elite athlete is to 'protect and stimulate his or her well-being in the highly demanding and performance-oriented elite context'. Understanding athletes' (and others') wellbeing and also how cultural practices in high-performance/professional sport impacts upon wellbeing are important foci for future research on the grounds of ethical, legal, and also performance enhancement imperatives (Aquilina, 2013; Henry, 2013; Price et al., 2010).

Activity box

BOX 18.5

How could cultural practices in HP/professional sport impact upon athletes', coaches' and others' well-being? What are the ethical, legal, and performance enhancement imperatives for supporting HP athletes' well-being?

Sport and exercise psychologists play an important role in supporting athletes to appreciate the value of their personal wellbeing for health and achievement of sport and other life goals.

Thus an imperative for sport psychologists is to recognize the relevance and importance of athlete wellbeing and how this may inform their professional practice. Knowledge about wellbeing and one's philosophy of practice will undoubtedly influence awareness and ideas about the value of wellbeing for clients and its relevance within applied practice. Not all sport and exercise psychologists agree about the role of wellbeing within applied practice in elite sport and a range of critical real world issues emerge when the topic is debated (Brady & Maynard, 2010; Martindale, Collins, & Richards, 2014).

Discussion box

BOX 18.6

What issues, challenges and/or benefits do you envisage associated with supporting athlete wellbeing as an explicit focus of applied sport psychology support? Consider this question from the different perspectives of the practitioner, the athlete, the coach and/or other sport scientists.

Though different theoretical perspectives have developed in relation to wellbeing, consistent across all perspectives is the understanding that wellbeing is complex and multifaceted. Originating from ancient philosophy, two broad approaches to wellbeing have dominated contemporary research and these are referred to as the hedonic and eudaimonic traditions (Ryan & Deci, 2001). Hedonic and eudaimonic approaches to wellbeing are more commonly represented in psychology by the respective concepts of Subjective Wellbeing (SWB, Diener, 1984) and Psychological Wellbeing (PWB, Ryff, 1989). Keyes and Annas (2009) provide a helpful way of distinguishing between hedonic and eudaimonic accounts of wellbeing as respectively focusing on symptoms and feelings, and on functioning. SWB is the person's subjective evaluation of his or her life (Diener, 1984) measured by the relative balance of high positive and low negative affect states as well as the cognitive evaluation of life satisfaction (Diener & Suh, 1997). SWB has received considerably more empirical research attention than PWB and ease of measurement is certainly a contributory factor.

Eudaimonic theories such as PWB are seen as articulating the process of wellbeing via psychological needs fulfilment and functioning (Biswas-Diener, Kashdan, & King, 2009; Deci & Ryan, 2008). The most commonly represented form of eudaimonic wellbeing is that associated with the work of Ryff (1989) who introduced six interrelated dimensions of PWB; autonomy, environmental mastery, personal growth, positive relationships, purpose in life and self-acceptance. Keyes (1998) proposed that Social Wellbeing (SocWB) is an important aspect of eudaimonic wellbeing and presented five dimensions to capture how individuals were functioning well in their social world. These dimensions assess individuals' positive sense of the following: belongingness (via social integration), his/her value to society (via social contribution), interest and meaningfulness of the social world (via social coherence), potential for positive development within society (via social actualization), and acknowledgement and acceptance of other people (via social acceptance).

Though eudaimonic and hedonic traditions of wellbeing research have long been in opposition, recent developments in wellbeing theory have included integrated models of wellbeing in recognition of the distinct but closely related nature of both hedonic and eudaimonic traditions (see Keyes, 2002; Lundqvist, 2011; Page & Vella-Brodrick, 2009; Seligman, 2011). To be high in either eudaimonic or hedonic wellbeing but low in the other type of wellbeing, does not confer the same benefits (Keyes & Annas, 2009). Feeling good about life (high hedonic wellbeing) and functioning well (high eudaimonic wellbeing) is when the state of flourishing is most likely to be achieved. Flourishing among athletes is viewed as an individualized notion of optimal wellbeing (Ashfield, McKenna, & Backhouse, 2012) and our profession has only recently begun to consider its significance. Thus, in order to better support clients, sport and exercise psychologists are encouraged to critically consider how advancing theory in wellbeing can help us to understand people's lived experience of optimal wellbeing.

One integrated model of wellbeing has been presented specifically for sport. This model represents a significant development in seeking how to advance research in athlete wellbeing and especially in high-performance sport. As well as including components of SWB, PWB, and SocWB, Lundqvist (2011) further develops her model by adding another sport-contextualized version of each wellbeing component for the purpose of capturing both global and sport-specific experiences of wellbeing. This is an important development for facilitating understanding and supporting engagement with wellbeing in sport psychology.

Lundqvist's (2011) sport-specific domains of wellbeing are direct translations of SWB, PWB and SocWB as noted below.

- Subjective wellbeing in sport (SWB-S) refers to sport satisfaction and sport-related affect).
- Psychological wellbeing in sport (PWB-S) refers to self-acceptance as an athlete, positive relationships with coach and teammates, autonomy in sport practice, sport environmental mastery, purpose in sport, and personal growth as an athlete.
- Social wellbeing in sport (SocWB-S) refers to social acceptance in sport and social actualization through sport, social contribution to sport, social coherence in sport and social integration in sport.

FRAMEWORK AND INTERVENTION

Happiness and a person's pursuit of it, are viewed as important themes within humanistic approaches (Walker, 2010) which reinforces the saliency of this approach for understanding and supporting athlete wellbeing and flourishing. The humanistic approach encompasses a range of theories and these share many goals that in turn inform applied practice. Drawing mainly upon tenets associated with client-centeredness, empowerment, and holistic practice (Friesen & Orlick, 2010), support provision was informed by principles associated with achieving wellbeing via developing the whole person to be self-determining, self-actualizing, and fully-functioning.

Though recognized as important and yet sometimes underrepresented in sport and exercise psychology (Tod & Andersen, 2012), in many humanistic approaches, the client-practitioner relationship is considered to be the central vehicle for supporting positive change (Rogers, 1959). I sought to create an effective relationship that offered Niall a safe place to share aspects of his internal world through the core conditions of empathy, acceptance, and congruence. In sessions I sought to achieve this through being fully present, actively listening, seeking clarification, and reflecting his thoughts and feelings.

The consultancy lasted over a period of 15 weeks with initial meetings occurring weekly and extending to fortnightly and monthly as Niall successfully returned to training and racing. Over the course of the consultancy we met for eight formal sessions each lasting between 90–120 minutes. During this time, Niall demonstrated considerable shifts in his openness, reflexivity, self-awareness, mindfulness, self-compassion, and responsibility which in turn, facilitated the therapeutic alliance. These outcomes were achieved because the client-practitioner relationship helped Niall to become aware of his freedom to be open and express thoughts and feelings. Through doing so, Niall moved towards the wholeness and integration associated with the inherent actualizing tendency to develop capacities to maintain or enhance functioning and autonomy (Rogers, 1959).

To support the achievement of client-centredness and autonomy, certain features emerged in most/all sessions:

- At the start of sessions (from Session 2), Niall reviewed his thoughts on the last session and in the interim period. This provided insight into what was salient for Niall.
- Often the initial focus for sessions emerged out of the opening review and often also developed into other separate topics. In some instances, we agreed in a former meeting, to come back to discussing a topic. Examples included ways of viewing achievement in sport, and benefits of diary keeping (Niall had never kept a diary).
- At the end of each session, Niall considered what for him had been interesting and/or helpful to consider and why. This helped me gain a sense of what Niall found meaningful or useful from the session.
- Between session tasks (initiated after Session 3) were discussed as being helpful for: reinforcing ideas from sessions, raising awareness of thinking and behaviour, and also, helping Niall regain a sense of structured time as he prepared to go back to racing after three months where he felt days 'had merged into a blur'.

In seeking to understand Niall's world as he experienced it, most support, and especially that early on was non-directive. The proportion of non-directive and directive support I typically use within sessions is dependent on the self-awareness of the client and the clarity with which s/he describes his/her needs for support. Where deemed appropriate and used very carefully to preserve client autonomy, directive activity was characterized by infusing support provision with appropriately translated and evidence-based insights from sport and exercise psychology (about injury and return to sport, sport-life balance, autonomy, and framing achievement) and positive psychology (about wellbeing, thriving, learning, and PPIs).

Exploring Niall's view on a topic and gaining a sense of the edge of his awareness (the boundary of his phenomenological field) was sometimes a cue for carefully introducing a topic that might be helpful for extending his awareness and depth of reflection. Here I intentionally presented an idea related closely in some way to what Niall was referring to and one such area was that of wellbeing. In Session 2, when Niall was referring again (as he had in the first session) to how he used to be 'carefree and happy go lucky' and his main aim was to return to this state, we discussed what these terms meant for him and how he could achieve this goal. After a careful exploration and at a point where no new information was emerging, I first expanded on wellbeing by agreeing it was when we feel good (as Niall had identified) and I suggested it could also be viewed as when we function well. When prompted Niall offered some ideas about what functioning well in sport and life meant to him by mentioning, the importance of keeping fit, being healthy, being talented and hardworking, being successful in his career, feeling settled, and having a loving and supportive partner. So we agreed that there were quite a few aspects to his wellbeing.

To help expand our discussion, in the next session, I introduced the PERMA acronym (Seligman, 2011) as just one way of thinking about wellbeing. I thought it aligned well with Niall's account and by comparison with existing theory, it would help to make wellbeing seem more accessible as a concept by acting as a simple memorable mnemonic for integrating areas worth paying attention to. PERMA is an integrated model of wellbeing (Seligman, 2011) composed of five dimensions essential for wellbeing including: positive emotions, engagement, relationships, meaning, and accomplishments. Throughout the first two sessions, Niall's prior reference to wellbeing concepts relied mainly on talking about two areas only – his former performance accomplishments and his latter lack of them, and similarly, his previous happy self as a jockey and his more recent unhappy self. As well as being quite limited to performance-contingent views of these two concepts (achievement and positive emotions), the other PERMA dimensions of engagement, meaning, and relationships in sport had comparatively relatively little place in his unprompted accounts to that point.

The explicit use of PERMA was extremely useful for allowing Niall to consider expanding his previously, mainly hedonic account of wellbeing (presence of positive emotions, being carefree, and the absence of worry and negative states). It also served as a conceptual beacon at times by inviting Niall to consider a broader view of his situation and what that might look like and feel like for him. The process of choosing to consider alternative perspectives about his situation, helped Niall to recognize patterns in his behaviour which increased his reflexivity and self-awareness.

Findings from SWB demonstrate the powerful impact of elevating positive emotion for a range of outcomes aligned to PWB. There is growing evidence supporting the effectiveness of positive psychology interventions (PPIs) for reducing depressed and negative affect as well as enhancing positive affect (Cohn & Fredrickson, 2010; Seligman et al., 2005). Importantly, enhanced SWB is positively associated and causally related to the development of personal resources and interpersonal skills associated with successful outcomes (Lyubomirsky, King, & Diener, 2005). Many mechanisms have been proposed to explain the cumulative ways in which SWB has been casually linked with success and enhanced performance. These processes have considerable relevance to sport and include: broadened thinking, optimism and congruent goal generation; positive social interactions and relationship forging; improved physical and mental health; and developing effective problem solving, coping strategies, and resilience (Ashby, Isen, & Turken, 1999; Fredrickson, 2005; Huppert, 2006; Isen & Reeve, 2005; Lyubomirsky et al., 2005).

For its range of potential benefits, and only when it was natural to do so, I carefully introduced particular ideas about enhancing positive emotions and the value of doing so. An example of a time this occurred was in our second session. Niall was explaining how tough it had been for him to be at home, alone, unable to drive or train and how losing fitness was upsetting him. Though he'd tried to cheer himself up in different ways, he soon became unhappy again. Whilst people naturally use strategies to elevate happiness, the strategy's effects may not always be particularly long-lasting, as Niall had found. Niall had mainly relied on quite discrete and often passive strategies (purchasing something online, watching a film, and playing a game on his XBox). Evidence shows that activities requiring ongoing engagement and adaptation offer greater potential for adaptation to enhance sustainable changes in wellbeing (Kennon, Boehm, & Lyubomirsky, 2013). As a result, I introduced the idea of increasing SWB via 'activities that may help us feel better for longer'. I mentioned several PPIs I thought might be especially meaningful for Niall such as expressing gratitude, benefit finding, and acts of kindness. Niall was especially interested in benefit finding and doing so through the exercise 'three good things' (Seligman et al., 2005).

The mode of benefit finding activities such as 'three good things' can vary considerably. Niall chose to identify his three good things each evening before going to bed. He found a place to be still and quiet for five minutes to help him intentionally think as his mode of engaging with the task (he preferred thinking to writing or talking modes). Findings show that this PPI is especially effective in the short term but loses effectiveness with time (Seligman et al., 2005). Niall initially undertook the task for six days (between sessions) but later said, he often went back to this activity over the next few months, because he found it so uplifting and positive-state inducing. Niall's autonomous use of this PPI supports not only its value to him but his own constructive adaptation. Without formally planning to do so in sessions, Niall explained how because of 'the three good things' activity, he decided to be more appreciative and grateful for things at home and Sam had already remarked on 'the new man' in her life. Niall mentioned that he hadn't noticed that they were not getting along before but now he realized that they were getting on much better than they had for a while.

Another PPI activity Niall was keen to undertake (after Session 4) and this time via a written mode, was considering his best possible future self. Research shows that this activity is effective at increasing SWB (King, 2008; Seligman et al., 2005) including with athletes (Brady & Hughes, 2013). While early research findings often reported not using a time frame for this, personal experience in sport, has led me to invite the athlete or coach to think about one or possibly two useful time frames for this task. Niall wanted to consider his best self in three years' time. It was clear when Niall returned in the following session, he had invested considerable time thinking about his best self and planning what to write. I also learnt that these three pages of writing were the most Niall had written in any one time since he'd been at school ten years before. He said he felt the task was important but also hard to complete because he rarely thought very far ahead. It raised the point that he tends to think on a one or two week basis as this was a race planning timeframe adopted by his jockey colleagues and agents. The issues of organization, and career management and guidance also emerged from this exercise.

A goal throughout this approach to consultancy is to actively encourage the athlete towards congruence and self-actualization through revealing his/her real self, and the consultant needs to acknowledge and value the athlete's efforts to do so (Hill, 2001). Niall moved onto an entirely deeper level of engagement and reflection in the latter stages of the consultation period. He came to consider that sometimes, his pursuit of quick-fix positive emotions (the drink and some gambling) or sublimation of distress and anxiety (having to look mentally tough [*sic*], not talking to anyone in racing about worries) was due to coming to focus almost entirely on performance outcome and his public ratings as a successful jockey as key sources of wellbeing and validation. Niall realized that working hard to maintain the image of a successful and carefree jockey whilst suppressing his feelings of worry, fear, and confusion about his ranking was taking its toll on his mental state and making him unhappy. Niall said when he sustained the injury, it was a relief to have something tangible to explain his lack of performance. He realized that he had lost perspective and had paid too little attention to what it was in racing he found so engaging and satisfying. He became more aware that he had shifted focus from learning and growing as a jockey and as a person to thinking almost entirely about demonstrating his calibre as a champion jockey. Niall came to see he was displaying some attitudes and behaviours associated with a fixed mindset (Dweck, 2006). Niall realized that although he had been seriously injured before, he had not experienced the emotional toll as he had this time. The last time he had a serious injury with a number of months away from racing was when as an apprentice jockey. Then he had lived with friends in digs by the yard and had remained connected with life and events there. So he had maintained positive relationships and meaning through engagement in some daily routines and felt achievement through rehabilitation and progressive reintegration with life at the yard. This time the impact of his injury had been different and his awareness of the differences generated consideration around issues of loss of relationships, routines, social support, and social connectedness.

The use of structured wellbeing interventions in sessions was not predetermined or introduced associated with an earlier global categorization of Niall's needs though a formal needs analysis. Where a specific intervention was introduced, this occurred in response to within-session events and the potential interventions were discussed openly and reviewed for how they would or would not suit Niall or how they could be adapted to suit him. Thus, Niall and I discussed directly what Sheldon and Lyubomirsky (2004) referred to as 'person-fit' considerations about wellbeing interventions. In order to elicit independent problem solving and greater awareness of knowledge in action (Schon, 1983), I actively encouraged Niall to draw upon his or others' behaviours, qualities, and personal strengths to propose his own facilitative strategies or consider how techniques or strategies may or may not suit him. The introduction of formal techniques or interventions was always sensitively introduced and stimulated by within-session events, rather than prior planning on my part.

We used many techniques across and between sessions and these included narrative storytelling, reframing, reimagining, gestalt positioning (to view his situation and aspects of it using new perspectives), identifying and using strengths, extracting inspiration from role-models (especially those who have experienced career hurdles), expressing gratitude, acknowledging career achievements beyond winning, savouring special moments (a light mindfulness), three good things, best future self, intentional staged reflection (to support increased self-awareness, reflexivity, sense-making and a learning attitude), seeking information and sources of guidance (e.g., contacting a S&C professional), communicating constructively and seeking support (especially from trainers and owners), multi-level goal-setting and also diary keeping (part of being more independent).

REFLECTIONS

Though no psychometric scales or objective measures were used to monitor the support provision, as will be explained below, this support was considered effective in addressing Niall's concerns and enhancing his wellbeing. Rogers (1959) identified a number of changes he expected clients to experience as a result of successful humanistic support. Expected changes include how the person comes to see him/herself differently, accept the person they are and their feelings more fully, be more confident and self-directing, be more like the person they would like to be, be more flexible and less rigid in their perceptions, adopt more realistic goals, behave in a more mature manner, be more accepting of others, and become more open to the evidence (both within and outside of the self). My observations and Niall's own ongoing accounts served as helpful indicators that he showed substantial movement towards each of the characteristics outlined above, and in so doing he experienced enhanced functioning and wellbeing.

Person-centred support elicited enhanced Niall's wellbeing both in the short term as well as in the medium term and these outcomes occurred alongside the development of a number of interrelated and productive personal qualities, behaviours, and strategies. Using Lundqvist's model of global and sport-specific levels of wellbeing is helpful to capture one aspect of a holistic view of wellbeing, namely that which combines the performer's life in and outside sport. In Niall's case, I noted the interrelated changes between hedonic and eudaimonic wellbeing at global and sport-specific levels. Particularly notable areas of heightened wellbeing included: global SWB (via increased positive affect and satisfaction with life generally), global PWB (via enhanced autonomy, personal growth, and environmental mastery) and sport-specific PWB. Increased sport-specific PWB was most noticeable via increases in the dimensions of self-acceptance as an athlete, autonomy in sport practice, positive relations with others in sport, personal growth as an athlete, and sport-specific environmental mastery. The latter was associated not with performance directly, but through being more effective in self-management as a professional jockey. Because Niall's needs directed the focus and relevance of support within every session, it also supported the generation of ongoing social validity for processes adopted via considerations of person-fit (Sheldon & Lyubomirsky, 2004).

When initially engaging with a humanistic methodology, I came to realize that sometimes clients (especially young ones) thought we had not done much 'real' sport and exercise psychology (i.e., MST) as mostly 'we'd just chatted'. So, a valuable lesson I've learnt is to help signpost experiential and developmental processes involved to help the client see the journey they have made. So for example, to help Niall see how he was engaging in new ideas and seeing things in new ways, I invited him to recount main themes of particular meaning to him at the end of sessions and to start the following session with his reflections during the interim period. Niall's recounting also allowed me to gain an insight to what Niall was noticing and the way he was making sense of things, which Moon (1999, 2004) suggests will in turn guide a person's deeper learning and future sense-making.

In our final session which was couched as, for the purposes of catching up and evaluating our work together, we directly addressed the effectiveness of the support for Niall. It had been almost a month since we had previously met for a formal session which was six weeks after he had returned to racing. An obvious concern in this face-to-face review and evaluation would be the likelihood of the client feeling intimidated or awkward about expressing anything other than a glowing report by succumbing to social desirability bias. During our evaluation session, as noted in the latter few sessions, Niall became more effective at communicating his feelings and needs, which allowed us to communicate more critically and frankly about his progress, and how he and I might adapt what we were doing. Hence, my role evolved considerably with Niall's development. For example, without prompting in the latter sessions, Niall displayed greater self-initiated meta-communication, namely examining feelings, intentions, and understandings associated with his own responses (Woolfe & Dryden, 1996). He voluntarily offered alternative explanations and contrasted his behaviours with those that he felt were ideal or problematic. He sought and engaged in more complex and multifaceted explanations which Woolfe and Dryden (1996) identify as an outcome of a person moving towards greater self-awareness and an acknowledgement of the pervasiveness of meta-perspectives in everyday life. As well as encouraging Niall to compare his evolving views with earlier less developed ones, I occasionally drew attention to some of these process developments which served to highlight milestones in the therapeutic alliance.

In many ways Niall and I been negotiating and evaluating our progress together in an ongoing manner, so evaluating the support formally as a focus for the final session was not an alien experience. Thus, I was confident that if I retained an appropriate level of authenticity in how I framed the importance of knowing what had worked well and how I could have supported him more effectively, in attempting to help me, Niall would offer up ideas rather than refrain. While Niall noted that he found the support effective for both sport and life, he raised an interesting point about his role in the process. He considered that for the earlier sessions, he hadn't really appreciated that he would have to be as active in the process as he was. He'd hoped at the start, that I would provide him with quick-fix solutions and pep talks so that he could return to racing as his former self. This early behaviour is consistent with Rogers' (1958) seven-stage model of client progress. In the initial stage the client is having limited self-awareness or ability to articulate his/her situation and a limited desire for change. Niall later saw that engaging in sessions as he did, encouraged him to take more responsibility, think more critically, and be more independent and that these were important developments for him. This realization shows considerable affinity with the fifth and sixth stages of the client progress model. In these stages the client shows increasing responsibility via ownership of his/her feelings and behaviours and engages with the processes of self-acceptance, congruence, growth, and self-discovery (Rogers, 1958).

The seventh stage of Roger's client progress model is characterized by the client not needing the help of the consultant as they are now a more adaptive and growing person, in touch with their changing feelings and have a basic trust in their own inner processes (Rogers, 1958; Klein, Mathieu-Coughlan, & Kiesler, 1986). Though I felt at times Niall showed glimpses of features in this stage, I also became aware through our review session that he had not pursued some of the important goals he had set himself such as contacting a jockey coach or planning to speak more openly about his situation with the trainer. Ideally, I think that there may have been a need to see Niall for longer after he had returned to racing, as many of his challenges were not associated purely with return to sport post injury. I think both he and I, underestimated the support he may have needed to complete some of the more these challenging interpersonal tasks, especially once he'd slipped back into the hectic schedule of racing. In hindsight, to address these goals, I considered that Niall could have benefited from developing further in sport-specific domains of PWB (especially via positive relationships with his coach/trainer and also in personal growth as an athlete) and SocWB in sport via social acceptance in sport (what ambitious jockeys need to do to get on) and social coherence in sport (acknowledging the way things work in the sport).

My evaluation of consultancy was drawn from three main sources; the final evaluation session with Niall, my personal reflections and the reflections of others both during and after the formal support. I gained insights about Niall's developments from the S&C coach and the doctor who continued to work with Niall throughout the period. Both shared their personal observations about his general behaviour as happier, more composed, and communicative and they noted qualities such as optimism, confidence, and resilience. These qualities are central features of a concept referred to as positive psychological capital (PPC) which has been shown to be positively related to wellbeing (Avey, Luthans, Smith, & Palmer, 2010). Based on findings in other contexts, PPC has considerable potential to be a valuable concept within both applied support and future research enquiry into athlete wellbeing.

My reflections were staged, occurring at times during sessions (though I often 'parked' these) and after each session when I summarized key observations and developments. Also, reflections occurred as unplanned insights between sessions, when intentionally or not, I was prompted to recall or consider an aspect of Niall's experience or behaviour. The writing of this chapter has also elicited considerable insights several years later. Niall and I covered an expanse of themes largely determined by him taking stock of his career so far and making sense of the complex, developmentally-rooted and multi-layered situation he experienced whilst addressing his initial goal to be happy again. It has been a considerable challenge to decide what to include/exclude in this chapter and to what depth. This case study reinforces the value of wellbeing as a meaningful personal heuristic that helps athletes and those working with them, address authentic and complex challenges by embracing a holistic approach to support.

In this case study an implicit approach to support wellbeing existed through the use of a humanistic methodology. Wellbeing also emerged as an explicit objective in response to Niall's own stated goals to be happy as his reasons for seeking support and this was reinforced through the use of positive psychology and PPIs . It is essential to allow clients ample time to explore their own ideas about wellbeing before offering ideas to help the client develop their understanding. In this case study it was only after two sessions with no further development in his account of wellbeing (mainly hedonic) that I decided to introduce the idea of PERMA. Had Niall asked me directly beforehand to explain what I meant by wellbeing, I would have had to be careful to invite his ideas first and then only give a little information that does not discredit his account in any way. It is essential to avoid being seduced by a desire to help as soon as possible and falling into the trap of setting up a transmissional encounter whereby the client tells the consultant his problems and/or goals and the consultant gives him the answers! This is disempowering for the client and is made worse still if the consultant attempts to solve the client's 'problem' or challenge quickly. A key to successfully adopting a humanistic approach is having the patience to support clients to experience awareness, autonomy, moments of actualization and wellbeing at their own pace and in a way that makes sense to them.

FURTHER READING

Hefferon, K., & Boniwell, I. (2011). *Positive psychology: Theory, research and applications*. Maidenhead: McGraw-Hill. A good text for providing a critical synthesis of positive psychology research and development in the field to date.

Seligman, M. E. P., Steen, T., Park, N., & Peterson, C. (2005). Positive psychology progress: Empirical validation of interventions. *American Psychologist, 60*(5), 410–421. This paper provides; a good introduction to several PPIs, application considerations, and it analyses PPI effectiveness for enhancing WB.

REFERENCES

Adie, J. W., & Bartholomew, K. J. (2010). The well- and ill-being of participants in competitive sport settings: A review of motivational determinants. In C.Mohiyeddini (Ed.), *Advances in the psychology of sports and exercise* (pp. 109–140). Hauppauge, NY: Nova Science Publishers.

Aquilina, D. (2013). A study of the relationship between elite athletes' educational development and sporting performance. *International Journal of the History of Sport, 30*(4), 374–392.

Ashby, F. G., Isen, A. M., & Turken, A. U. (1999). A neuro-psychological theory of positive affect and its influence on cognition. *Psychological Review, 106*(3), 529–550.

Ashfield, A., McKenna, J., & Backhouse, S. (2012). The athlete's experience of flourishing. *Qualitative Methods in Psychology, 14*, 4–13.

Avey, J. B., Luthans, F., Smith, R. M., & Palmer, N. F. (2010). Impact of positive psychological capital on employee well-being over time. *Journal of Occupational Health Psychology, 15*(1), 17–28.

Beamish, R., & Ritchie, I. (2006). *Fastest, highest, strongest: a critique of high performance sport*. Abingdon: Routledge.

Biswas-Diener, R., Kashdan, T. B., & King, L. A. (2009). Two traditions of happiness research, not two distinct types of happiness. *The Journal of Positive Psychology, 4*(3), 208–221.

Brady, A., & Hughes, S. (2013). Exploring the impact of a best future-self intervention on the well-being of early career sport coaches: The mediating role of mindset. Oral presentation British Psychological Society, Division of Sport & Exercise Annual Conference, Manchester, December.

Brady, A., & Maynard, I. (2010). At an elite level the role of a sport psychologist is entirely about performance enhancement: A debate. *Sport and Exercise Psychology Review, 6*(1), 59–66.

Cohn, M. A., & Fredrickson, B. L. (2010). In search of durable positive psychology interventions: Predictors and consequences of long-term positive behavior change. *Journal of Positive Psychology, 5*(5), 355–366.

Deci, E. L., & Ryan, R. M. (2008). Facilitating optimal motivation and psychological well-being across life's domains. *Canadian Psychology, 49*, 14-23

Diener, E. (1984). Subjective well-being. *Psychological Bulletin, 95*, 542–575.

Diener, E., & Suh, E. M. (1997). Measuring quality of life: Economic, social and subjective indicators. *Social Indicators Research, 40*(1–2), 189–216.

Dolan, E., Cullen, S., McGoldrick, A., & Warrington, G. D. (2013). The impact of making weight on physiological and cognitive processes in elite jockeys. *International Journal of Sport Nutrition and Exercise Metabolism, 23*(4), 399–408.

Dweck, C.S. (2006). *Mindset*. New York: Random House

Frederickson, B. L. (2005) The broaden-and-build theory of positive emotions. In *The Science of Well-Being* (eds F. A. Huppert, N. Baylis & B. Keverne), pp. 217–240. Oxford University Press.

Friesen, A., & Orlick, T. (2010). A qualitative analysis of holistic sport psychology consultants' professional philosophies. *The Sport Psychologist, 24*(2), 227–244.

Hefferon, K., & Boniwell, I. (2011). *Positive psychology: theory, research and applications*. Maidenhead: McGraw-Hill

Henry, I. (2013). Athlete development, athlete rights and athlete welfare: A European Union perspective. *International Journal of the History of Sport, 30*(4), 356–368.

Hill, K. L. (2001). *Frameworks for Sport Psychologist: Enhancing Sport Performance*. Champaign, IL: Human Kinetics

Huppert, F. A. (2006). Positive emotions and cognition: Developmental, neuroscience and health perspectives. In J. P.Forgas (Ed.), *Hearts and minds: Affective influences on social cognition and behavior* (pp. 235–252), New York: Psychology Press.

Huppert, F. A., & So, T. T. C. (2013). Flourishing across Europe: Application of a new conceptual framework for defining well-being. *Social Indicators Research, 110*(3), 837–861.

Isen, A. M., & Reeve, J. (2005). The influence of positive affect on intrinsic and extrinsic motivation: Facilitating enjoyment of play, responsible work behavior, and self-control. *Motivation and Emotion, 29*(4), 297–325.

Kennon, M., Boehm, J. K., & Lyubomirsky, S. (2013). Variety is the spice of happiness. In S. A. David, I. Boniwell, & A. Conley Ayers (Eds.). *The Oxford handbook of happiness* (pp. 901–914). New York: Oxford University Press.

Keyes, C. L. M. (1998). Social well-being. *Social Psychology Quarterly, 61*(2), 121–140.

Keyes, C. L. M. (2002). The mental health continuum: From languishing to flourishing in life. *Journal of Health and Behavior Research, 43*, 207–222.

Keyes, C. L. M., & Annas, J. (2009). Feeling good and functioning well: Distinctive concept in ancient philosophy and contemporary science. *The Journal of Positive Psychology, 4*(3), 197–201.

King, L. A. (2008). Interventions for Enhancing SWB: The pursuit of happiness. In R. J. Larsen and M. Eid (Eds.), *The science of subjective well-being* (pp. 431–448). New York: The Guildford Press.

Klein, M. H., Mathieu-Coughlan, P., & Kiesler, D. J. (1986). The experiencing scales. In L. S. Greenberg & W. M. Pinsof (Eds.), *The psychotherapeutic process: A research handbook* (pp. 21–71). New York: Guilford Press,

Lundqvist, C. (2011). Well-being in competitive sports- the feel-good factor? A review of conceptual considerations of well-being. *International Review of Sport and Exercise Psychology, 4*(2), 109–127.

Lundqvist, C., & Sandin, F. (2014). Well-being in elite sport. Dimensions of hedonic and eudaimonic well-being among elite orienteers. *The Sport Psychologist, 28*(3), 245–254.

Lyubomirsky, S., King, L., & Diener, E. (2005). The benefits of frequent positive affect: Does happiness lead to success? *Psychological Bulletin, 131*(6), 803–855.

Martindale, A., Collins, D., Richards, H. (2014). Is elite sport good for you? *Sport and Exercise Psychology Review, 10*(3), 68–76.

Mayoh, J., & Jones, I. (2014). Making well-being an experiential possibility: The role of sport. *Qualitative Research in Sport, Exercise and Health, 7*(2), 235–252.

McCrory, P., Turner, M., LeMasson, B., Bodere, C., & Allemandou, A. (2006). An analysis of injuries resulting from professional horse racing in France during 1991–2001: A comparison with injuries resulting from professional horse racing in Great Britain during 1992–2001. *British Journal of Sports Medicine. 40*, 614–618.

McLeod, J. (1996). The humanistic paradigm. In R. Woolfe & W. Dryden (Eds.), *The handbook of counselling psychology* (pp. 133–155). London: Sage Publications.

Miller, P. S., & Kerr, G. (2002). Conceptualising excellence: Past, present and future. *Journal of Applied Sport Psychology, 14*, 140–153.

Moon, J. A. (1999). *Reflection in learning and professional development: Theory and practice*. London: Kogan Page.

Moon, J. A. (2004). *A handbook of reflective and experiential learning: Theory and practice*. London: Routledge Falmer.

Page, K. M., & Vella-Brodrick, D. A. (2009). The 'what', 'Why' and 'how' of employee well-being: A new model. *Social Indicators Research, 90*(3), 441–458.

Price, N., Morrison, N., & Arnold, S. (2010). Life out of the limelight: Understanding the non-sporting pursuits of elite athletes. *The International Journal of Sport and Society. 1*(3), 69–79.

Rogers, C. R. (1958). A process conception of psychotherapy. *American Psychologist, 13*, 142–149.

Rogers, C. R. (1959). A theory of therapy, personality and interpersonal relationships, as developed in the client-centered framework. In S.Koch (Ed.), *Psychology: A study of science: Vol. 3. Formulations of the person and the social context* (pp. 184–256). New York: McGraw-Hill.

Rogers, C. R. (1965). Some questions and challenges facing a humanistic psychology. *Journal of Humanistic Psychology, 5*, 1–5.

Ryan, R. M., & Deci, E. L. (2001). On happiness and human potentials: A review of research on hedonic and eudaimonic well-being. *Annual Review of Psychology, 52*, 141–166.

Ryff, C. D. (1989). Happiness is everything, or is it? Explorations on the meaning of psychological well-being. *Journal of Personality and Social Psychology, 57*, 1069–1081.

Schon, D. A. (1983). *The reflective practitioner: How professionals think in action*. London: Temple Smith.

Seligman, M. E. P. (2008). Positive health. *Applied Psychology: An International Review, 57*, 3–18.

Seligman, M. E. P. (2011). *Flourish: A new understanding of happiness and well-being*. London: Nicholas Brealey Publishing.

Seligman, M. E. P., & Csikszentmihalyi, M. (2000). Positive psychology. *American Psychologist, 55*, 5–14.

Seligman, M. E. P., Steen, T., Park, N., & Peterson, C. (2005). Positive psychology progress: Empirical validation of interventions. *American Psychologist, 60*(5), 410–421.

Sheldon, K. M., & Lyubomirsky, S. (2004). Achieving sustainable new happiness: Prospects, practices, and prescriptions. In A. Linley & S. Joseph (Eds.). *Positive psychology in practice* (pp. 127–145). Hoboken, NJ: John Wiley & Sons, Inc.

Theberge, N. (2008). 'Just a normal part of what I do': Elite athletes' accounts of the relationship between health and sport. *Sociology of Sport Journal, 25*(2), 206–222.

Tod, D., & Andersen, M. B. (2012). Practitioner-client relationships in applied sport psychology practice. In S.Hanton & S. D.Mellalieu (Eds.), *Professional practice in sport psychology: A review* (pp. 272–306). Abingdon: Routledge.

Turner, M., McCrory, P., & Halley, W. (2002). Injuries in professional horse Racing in Great Britain and the Republic of Ireland during 1992–2000. *British Journal of Sports Medicine, 36*, 403–409.

Walker, B. (2010). The humanistic/person-centred theoretical model. In S. J. Hanrahan & M. B. Andersen, (Eds.), (*Routledge handbook of applied sport psychology* (pp. 123–130). Abingdon: Routledge.

Wilson, G., Durst, B., Morton, J. P., & Close G. L. (2014). Weight-making strategies in professional jockeys: Implications for physical and mental health and well-being. *Sports Medicine, 44*, 785–796.

Woolfe, R., & Dryden, W. (Eds.). (1996). *The handbook of counselling psychology*. London: Sage.

19 Physical Activity and Self-concept: A Humanistic Intervention

SUSAN O'NEILL AND JOHN KREMER

LEARNING OBJECTIVES

AFTER READING THIS CHAPTER YOU SHOULD BE ABLE TO:

1. Critically evaluate the significant role that self-concept plays in encouraging and sustaining physical activity.
2. Critically appraise the central role that gender plays in defining both self-concept and motives for exercise.
3. Compare and contrast the diverse literature addressing participation motivation and physical activity.
4. Assess how qualitative techniques can help interpret individual experiences and motives, and underlying meanings attached to exercise behaviour.
5. Construct a systematic yet adaptive one-to-one intervention programme based on idiographic/qualitative principles.

AREAS TO CONSIDER WHEN READING THE CHAPTER:

1. How self-concept, and specifically your gender, may influence your attitude to physical activity.
2. The individual nature of the exercise experience – why do you exercise and what do you think about when you do?
3. The variety of interpretive responses that may be given to seemingly similar situations.

CLIENT AND BACKGROUND

Jenny was a 45-year-old married woman living in Belfast Northern Ireland with two children aged 15 and 18 at the time of the intervention. She worked part-time as a clerical officer and was from a white socio-economic middle-class background. She wished to start an exercise programme as she was concerned about her weight. Jenny felt it was only recently that she had noticed putting on weight and this was causing her unhappiness as she was worried about her appearance. A friend had made a casual comment about her weight gain and this was the primary reason she had decided to take action.

Jenny admitted that she had little interest in physical activity in the past but at the same time actively encouraged her two children to take part in school sports and after school physical activities, stating that she was, 'more inclined to want the children to be better at sport than I ever was'. As a mother, she regularly chaperoned her two children to sporting events. In particular, her daughter was a member of a local swimming club and Jenny often watched her train but was never inclined to take part. Twice in the past she had attended an introductory gym class as she thought she 'should' be doing something but didn't keep it up, revealing that when she was thinner she lacked any real commitment. She also said she never really enjoyed exercise experiences in the past and found them too painful and challenging, especially as she had never been 'sporty' and hated physical education at school.

More recently, Jenny decided that exercise could help her achieve her weight-loss goal and had a particular weight target in mind (see later). Although she was also concerned about her health, she was not experiencing ill-health at the time of the intervention. Jenny had recently attended a well-woman clinic at her local surgery and had her blood pressure, cholesterol level, and weight checked. Again, reference was made to her weight gain by the nurse who recommended some diet changes and beginning an exercise programme. Jenny was only vaguely aware that there were recommended physical activity guidelines, stating that she thought she should be exercising maybe three times per week. Jenny contacted me through a friend who had taken part in a previous research project on women exercisers that I had conducted at the local leisure centre.

Definition box **BOX 19.1**

Physical activity includes three elements: (i) skeletal muscle movement, that (ii) results in energy expenditure, and is (iii) positively correlated with physical fitness. (Caspersen, Powell, & Christenson, 1985).

Research reveals that being overweight and obese is now a worldwide epidemic. The most recent fact-sheet from the World Health Organization (WHO, 2014) reports an estimated 1.4 billion adults as overweight, with 200 million men and 300 million women classed as obese. In America, 34.9% of adults over the age of 20 were reportedly obese (Ogden, Carroll, Kit, & Flegal, 2014). This is mirrored in the UK, with around 24% of men and 26% of women obese, and 41% of men and 33% of women overweight (National Health Service (NHS, 2013). It is estimated that around 3.4 million adults die each year as a result of being overweight or obese. Obesity and being overweight are also linked to cardiovascular diseases, diabetes, musculoskeletal disorders, and a number of cancers (WHO, 2014). The direct cause of obesity has been attributed to an energy imbalance, where more energy is taken in through food and drink than expended (Department of Health, Social Services, and Public Safety for Northern Ireland (DHSSPSNI), 2012). One of the ways to prevent obesity is by engaging in regular physical activity (WHO, 2014). In addition, research indicates that regular exercise protects against various somatic complaints including heart disease, diabetes, and osteoporosis (Biddle & Mutrie, 2008; Biddle, Fox, & Boutcher, 2000; Hillsdon & Thorogood, 1996). Moreover, with regards to the psychological effects of exercise, there is now a wealth of research highlighting the positive psychological benefits attaching to healthy and appropriate exercise (Ekkekakis & Backhouse, 2009).

Not surprisingly, physical activity guidelines have now been issued by bodies including the United States government, the UK Chief Medical Officers, and WHO (2014) aimed at achieving or maintaining health benefits. Each advocates 150 minutes of moderate intensity activity a week for adults, based on a flexible approach that includes at least 30 minutes a day, five times per week and which may be achieved in bouts of at least ten minutes (DHSSPS, 2011; US Department of Health & Human Services, 2008).

Disappointingly, despite the reported benefits of physical activity and the advertised recommendations, only around 20% of the adult American population exercise sufficiently to benefit their health. Men exercise more regularly than women (24% and 17% respectively), with activity rates decreasing across the lifespan (Centers for Disease Control and Prevention (CDC), 2013). In the UK, 39% of men and 29% of women met the recommended levels of physical activity participation (NHS, 2013).

The motives that were outlined by Jenny for exercise participation are far from unique. Research has reported that exercising to lose weight and improve appearance have long been recognized as primary motives for exercise participation among women (Tiggemann & Williamson, 2000). More generally, body dissatisfaction remains prevalent among women in western society where it is often considered a normative experience (Rodin, Silberstein, & Striegel-Moore, 1984). In a recent Channel 4 television series, responses to a scale devised specifically for the programme (the 'Body Confidence Test') revealed that 54% of women 'rarely feel proud of their appearance', while 70.2% reported that they felt pressurized to conform to the ideal body from the media (Diedrichs, Paraskeva, & Rumsey, 2011, p. 896).

This pressure to conform to the thin-beauty ideal (Stice, 1994) has both psychological and physical consequences. The cultural emphasis on slenderness is so powerful that simply viewing photographs (including media images) of physically attractive women with idealized body images can lead to diminished self-evaluations of attractiveness, lowered self-esteem, increased anger, anxiety, lowered moods, eating disorder symptoms, increased body shame, appearance anxiety, decreased flow states, and insensitivity to body cues and approval of cosmetic surgery (e.g. Birkeland et al., 2005; Brown, Meadows, & Elder, 2007; Durkin, Paxton, & Sorbello, 2007; Grabe, Ward, & Hyde, 2008; Hamilton, Mintz, & Kashubeck-West, 2007; Harper & Tiggemann, 2008).

The focus in western society on the female body and outward appearance, as opposed to internal characteristics and abilities, has been argued to result in a process known as self-objectification whereby girls and women internalize society's view of the body as a sexualized object to be looked at and evaluated (Fredrickson & Roberts, 1997). Self-Objectification Theory proposes that women tend to adopt ideas about their bodies as held by others with important psychological consequences.

While issues attached to appearance and body dissatisfaction have traditionally been linked with women and girls, a more recent literature has emerged in relation to young men and in particular body dysmorphic disorder (BDD) (Bjornsson, Didie, & Phillips, 2010). BDD often manifests itself as 'muscle dysmorphia', or a pathological preoccupation with muscularity. Men with muscle dysmorphia feel that they look 'puny' or 'small' (Pope et al., 2005). In its extreme form the condition can be associated with obsessive compulsive symptoms linked to excessive workouts and meticulous diets, and in some cases can extend to substance abuse including anabolic steroids (see Pope, Phillips, & Olivardia, 2000). The condition is particularly prevalent among gym users including weightlifters and bodybuilders (Choi, Pope, & Olivardia, 2002; Hildebrandt, Schlundt, Langenbucher, & Chung, 2006).

Self-concept is one of the oldest constructs in the social sciences. William James proposed a multiplicity of selves in terms of the social 'me' where 'a man has as many social selves as there are individuals who recognise him' (1890, 1892, p. 294). Cooley (1902) further elaborated on the idea that others were important in defining the self when he proposed the concept of the 'looking glass self', arguing that the concept of self, developed by imagining what significant others thought of 'me', and then incorporated these attitudes into the self. George Herbert Mead (1934) further suggested that it is not what others actually think of us that matters but what we perceive they are thinking. Accordingly, learning one's identity occurs through a process of taking the role of significant others towards the self, then adopting their perspectives to your own. Like James and Cooley, Mead (1934) argued that the self, 'is essentially a social structure, and it arises in social experience' (p. 140).

To this day the self continues to be identified as a core construct in social psychology, with the self implicated in a person's decision-making, motivation, and behaviour (Hagger & Chatzisarantis, 2005), as well as central to a person's psychological well-being (Craven & Marsh, 2008). This contemporary literature contains a multitude of terms, often used interchangeably, to define the self and including self-concept, self-esteem, self-regard, self-perceptions, self-image, and self-description (Hagger & Chatzisarantis, 2005). A broad definition of the self-concept is, 'the totality of the individual's thoughts and feelings having reference to himself [*sic*] as an object' (Rosenberg, 1979, p. 7). Gordon and Gergen (1968) define self-concept as a, 'person's subjective cognitions and evaluations of himself' (p. 3), and suggests that the underlying assumption behind self-concept research is that people behave in ways that support their self-conceptions. Within this literature, gender is recognized universally as particularly salient to a person's self-concept, influencing 'how we think of ourselves and others, how we relate to others, and how social life is organised at all levels' (Roth & Basow, 2004, p. 263).

The term gender refers to the meanings given within a society about what it means to be female and male (Golden, 2008). In western culture, gender roles, namely those behaviours and characteristics that are considered to be typically male and female, are a core element of socialization, and have a profound influence on subsequent behaviours (Basow, 2008). A variety of sources are identified as shaping these behaviours through childhood, such as parents, siblings, school, peers, and the media (Etaugh & Bridges, 2010). For example, from birth, boys and girls are socialized differently by parents, with differences in clothing, toys, and room furnishings (Basow, 2008). Boys are played with more roughly than girls by both mothers and fathers (Bronstein, 2006). In schools, teachers' pay more attention to boys than girls, with boys receiving more praise, corrections, assistance, and constructive criticisms (see meta-analysis of empirical studies conducted by Jones & Dindia, 2004). Peers exert a powerful influence on gender-appropriate behaviour with rewards of acceptance, while inappropriate behaviours result in teasing and rejection (Rubin, Bukowski, & Parker, 2006). Furthermore, children who watch more television are more likely to possess a greater awareness of gender stereotypes (Ward, 2007).

During conversations with Jenny, it became apparent that her sense of identity did not include reference to 'being sporty'. She hated physical education at school, and still did not enjoy sport or exercising generally. Jenny may not be alone in this regard. It has been reported that 'exercise is not inherently enjoyable for most people, and is prompted by both external pressures, such as media campaigns and interpersonal influence, and by internal goals such as health concerns or guilt' (Lutz, Karoly, & Okun, 2008, p. 562). This negativity towards exercise may have its roots in early childhood. Certainly, gender is argued to be particularly influential in how both males and females are socialized in the context of physical activity. Boys continue to receive more encouragement, support, and opportunities to participate in physical activity from significant others such as parents and peers (Messner, 1988) than girls (Hall, 2008). As a consequence of reduced opportunities and declining interest through adolescence, girls develop less confidence in their physical abilities than do boys and men (e.g. Corbin, Landers, Feltz, & Senior, 1983). Leaper and Brown (2008) examined perceptions of sexism among 600 adolescent girls aged between 12 and 18 years old in both educational and physical activity contexts – 76% of girls were reportedly ridiculed about their athletic abilities and sports involvement. The main sources of athletic sexism came from close male friends or brothers (45%) and other male peers (54%). However, these were closely followed by close female friends or sisters (31%), other girls (38%), fathers (30%), other family members (31%), teachers and coaches (28%), mothers (25%), and neighbours (21%). On the other hand, physical activity, and in particular sport, is argued to be an arena for men to display their 'masculine' characteristics, and thus is viewed as a more 'natural' domain for men (e.g. Anderson, 2005; Light & Wedgwood, 2012; Messner, 1988, 2002), while for women physical activity is not central to their feminine identity formation (Choi, 2000).

The masculine social construction of physical activity, the cultural pressure attaching to the ideal body image (thin, sexy, toned, and fit), the media's promotion of physical activity as a means to achieve this ideal (Wiseman, Gray, Mosimann, & Ahrens, 1992), alongside other messages that suggest that this image is unattainable for the majority of women (Etaugh & Bridges, 2010), and even less so through exercise (Bagozzi & Edwards, 2000; Hill, 2005), appears to present physical activity as a socially constructed dilemma for women (O'Neill,2013). Add to this the research which shows that participating in physical activity for appearance reasons may not be conducive to promoting self-worth (Wilson & Rodgers, 2002), may have psychological costs (Eccles & Wigfield, 2002), may result in lower motivation (Deci & Ryan, 1985; Fredrickson & Roberts, 1997), and is not associated with physical activity adherence (Segar, Eccles, & Richardson, 2011), it is not surprising to learn that, as outlined earlier, few women in the UK are engaging in sufficient physical activity to benefit their health (NHS, 2013), with these trends mirrored in the United States (CDC, 2013).

INITIAL NEEDS ASSESSMENT

An initial in-depth interview with Jenny was undertaken, based on Grounded Theory (Charmaz, 2006; Corbin & Strauss, 2008; Glaser & Strauss, 1967) and adopting a humanistic approach (Hill, 2001; Rogers, 1980) to aid understanding of the client's personal circumstances (see later in Framework and Intervention sections). The schedule of questions is outlined below, although the precise content was modified by the flow of exchange between Jenny and me (first author):

1. Tell me about your past exercise experiences?
2. What type of exercise did you do?
3. How did you feel when you exercised?
4. What do you think prevented you from continuing with exercise in the past?
5. Can you describe any positive experiences you have had with exercise in the past?
6. Tell me about why you want to begin an exercise programme now?

The use of a series of general open-ended questions was designed to elicit a more in-depth understanding of Jenny's exercise history, the obstacles, both personal and structural, which stood in her way in the past and may be likely to stand in her way in the future, and what motives underpinned her desire to begin exercising today. An unstructured interview enables the interviewee to focus on issues that are salient and important to them (Corbin & Morse, 2003). Further probing questioning was guided by Jenny's responses and my knowledge of the physical activity and psychological literature and focused on areas such as past physical activity history, why the motive of weight loss was important, and so on. The quality of these types of interactions is dependent upon the role of the interviewer. It was also important to create an environment that was collaborative in nature (Morrow, 2007), with the client actively involved in the process (Rich, 2000).

Jenny began by outlining her earlier exercise experiences starting with school and home:

Me: If you would like to tell me about your exercise history Jenny, when you started, etc., and we will take it from there. Is that OK?

Jenny: OK. Well, ah, I was never particularly interested in sport at school and part of it I think was just a location thing because um, I lived in the country and a lot of the afterschool sports, you know, involved getting a bus home, etc. and there was no real enthusiasm or history of sports in our family. I didn't come from a sporting background and I wasn't particularly good at it and I didn't have very good co-ordination and I think I was also taught by teachers who had no real interest, you know. My PE teacher I can still vividly see, immaculately dressed in her short skirt and her hair in a sort of like a French roll and she just used to sit on the radiator and you just were told to do things and you were never really taught the skills and I just was clumsy and not good, and I think actually it probably affected my confidence so I never really participated at lot, you know, right through school student days … I think an awful lot of it really was a lack of encouragement and the fact that you just didn't have the confidence to be doing anything very good and I think that just stays with you, you know, there's nobody there to sort of coach or involve you or if you were playing sports maybe with parents.

It appeared from this opening statement that Jenny had less than positive early experiences of engaging in learning or performing sport. As a result, it appeared that she had little confidence in her physical abilities, a common story for many girls (Choi, 2000).

Jenny mentioned that she had attempted to exercise on two occasions in the past, the first when she attended aerobics classes and the second in a local gym. I asked her about these:

Me: The first time you went to aerobics, did you enjoy it? Tell me about that experience.

Jenny: Yes, I liked the aerobics because … I do like music, …I liked the routine, you know, of going sort of once a week and the challenge of it and also sort of the fact that there was variety in the exercise and um, I suppose it's like everything else, if the instructor was good you were a bit more motivated to continue going and the music was good and I think the exercise to music helps as well.

This part of the conversation highlighted some positive experiences for Jenny and proved invaluable when designing the intervention. Jenny also mentioned that she had exercised in a local health club for a while and I asked her what type of activities she participated in and how she felt about this type of exercising:

Jenny: Well I would usually do … cardio, … the treadmill, the cross trainer, … I hate the bicycle, don't do the bicycle, then they had a tread-climber at the gym which was quite good and that would be the main sort of cardio and then I would have done, oh the rowing machine.

However, Jenny did not appear to like this type of exercise regimen:

Jenny: I get bored in the gym, I must say, you know, I like it when I get a new programme, I'm fine and I get going and I get in a routine but then I find if you're not doing that about three times a week regularly then, you know, the momentum sort of goes.

Me: When you say that after a while you got bored and then you were given a new programme and it re-motivated you again, what sorts of changes to the programmes were made?

Jenny: Sometimes it was slightly different machines … each trainer might have told you, say it was the cross trainer, they might have given you a different programme that you may not have been aware of was on the machine or I found that perhaps the last programme I got worked a bit better because it was shorter periods on each of the machines for the cardio … there was a little bit more variety in that … I mean I never really break into much of a sweat at the gym … I don't really push myself beyond what they say to do and I don't go beyond or set myself targets other than what they do … sometimes I found it difficult I must admit, if I was tired to do the whole programme, … I probably cheated a bit on it at times … I didn't maybe do all that I was supposed to do … When I came out, I found that … I used to think, oh I have to try and get up those stairs out (to leave the fitness club). So I was probably quite relieved when I finished it but I suppose I came back, you know, sort of bouncing, … I was in good form when I came out and you felt good, … very positive about it. Yes definitely. I wasn't disheartened or anything like that or I didn't feel I must really just do this, you know, because otherwise I wouldn't be going.

Despite this last statement, something was not working for Jenny; she had stopped going to the gym. When I asked why, she admitted that she was just not enjoying the experience so it was hard to motivate herself. I also wanted to know why, despite these past experiences, Jenny now wanted to begin exercising again. What were her present motives? Jenny stated that:

> I was always very slim when I was a young girl and once I got married I had two children thirteen months apart, so I never saw seven and a half stone again.

She had accepted that this weight was not achievable for her now but wished to attain a weight of just under 10 stone. She said that following the birth of her children she had managed to maintain her 10 stone weight target until recently and was now 11.5 stone. When I asked why losing weight was important to her, Jenny replied:

> You do kind of compare yourself and think, ah, I'm a lot bigger than my friends, … and you kind of think, right I'll have to do something about it, … I don't want to be the odd one out, I want to lose weight and kind of fit in with everyone … I mean really doesn't everybody exercise to, nobody wants to be obese. I mean I certainly don't want to be fat or fatter.

The above excerpts provide some understanding of Jenny's past physical activity experiences and present motives for wanting to begin another exercise programme. Understanding of meaning is now recognized as being central to the exercise experience (Biddle & Mutrie, 2008). Researchers now acknowledge that exercise should be viewed as a personal, subjective experience, and have also expressed surprise that the meaning or cognitive appraisals of physical activity have not been more fully examined. According to Berger and Tobar (2007), 'there is a relative lack of information, however, within the exercise psychology literature about what exercise means to the participant. This is surprising because personal meaning reflects the heart of the exercise experience' (p. 612).

Within the sub-discipline of Health Psychology, qualitative methods of inquiry have revealed that people exercise for a multitude of reasons. For example, Graham, Kremer, and Wheeler's (2008) research into the effects of exercise on psychological well-being among individuals with chronic illnesses such as stroke, cancer, diabetes, and arthritis revealed a range of meanings from feeling fitter despite physical impairments, reclaiming athletic identity, sense of connection with 'similar others', and enhancement of self-image. Priest (2007), examining the effects of walking outdoors in a group exercise with people from a mental health day facility, also found a range of meanings given to this experience, from reducing stress, a feeling of belonging, being able to connect with others, a sense of achievement, feeling 'normal' when usually feeling different due to illness (physical or psychological), feeling closer to what is more natural, 'being me', and feeling safe. Likewise, a further qualitative study that examined the effects of exercise on older adults found a decrease in loneliness, improvements in sleep patterns, social life, sex life, and self-confidence (Emery & Blumenthal, 1990).

Graham's et al.'s (2008) research led them to state that, 'exercise experiences are determined by complex mechanisms and the exercise/psychological well-being (PWB)/affect relationship is far from linear or simplistically dose-dependent' (p. 456). My own PhD research also supported the supposition that the exercise experience is a complex psychosocial process, and that subjective well-being centred on the ability to mediate a specific and favourable self-perception (O'Neill, 2013). In short, cognitive appraisals of the exercise experience have been under researched but are now recognized as critically important in developing understanding of physical activity adherence (Ekkekakis, 2003, 2005).

By training, many psychologists and sport scientists would initially be drawn to a method of accurately quantifying self-concept in an exercise context. Indeed, there are a number of reliable and validated questionnaires that measure aspects of the physical self-concept within this context. A multidimensional, hierarchical model of physical self-concept has been developed by Fox and Corbin (1989) and Fox (1997), with four subdomains that include sports competence, physical conditioning, body attractiveness, and physical strength. The Physical Self-Perception Profile was typically used to measure these aspects of the self-concept. Marsh (1997) extended this work to include 11 subscales, namely strength, body fat, activity, endurance, sports competence, co-ordination, health, appearance, flexibility, global physical and global self-concept. The Physical Self-Description Questionnaire (Marsh et al., 1994) is now acknowledged as the leading physical self-concept instrument for use with adolescents and adults (Byrne, 1996), and in sport and exercise psychology, this multidimensional view of the physical self-concept is now largely accepted (Fox & Corbin, 1989; Marsh, 1997, 2002).

The development of these questionnaires reflects the dominance of quantitative methods of inquiry within sport and exercise research. These approaches typically examine aggregate data (i.e. nomothetic data) but not specific data points (i.e. idiographic data) and while they may tell us about 'norms' or trends, they say little about the individual or the meaning attached to the behaviour (i.e. hermeneutics). This sentiment was articulated clearly by Van Landuyt, Ekkekakis, Hall, and Petruzzello (2000) when referring to exercise-affect research. They argued that these nomothetic approaches can show trends across populations but 'provide poor accounts of the diversity encountered in real-life responses' (p. 228). So while psychometric questionnaires may indicate what aspect of the physical self-concept is important to a client, they simply describe the 'what' but not the 'why' it is important or has meaning to the individual (see Roberts, 2001).

Activity box — BOX 19.2

Next time you participate in physical activity, reflect on:

1. What you are thinking before you begin physical activity?
2. How you were feeling and what you were thinking during physical activity?
3. How you felt and what your thoughts focused on after physical activity?
4. Why did you select the specific type of activity you participated in?

Not surprisingly, there has been a recent recognition that qualitative methods may help provide 'different kinds of evidence' within the physical activity field of research (Biddle & Mutrie, 2008, p. xiv). Carless and Faulkner (2003) suggest that qualitative methods are ideal for providing a more in-depth understanding of the exercise / well-being phenomenon from the perspective of lived-experiences that are unique to the exerciser. Understanding the subjective states of the individual using an idiographic approach is suggested to be crucial to aid adoption and long-term maintenance of a healthy lifestyle that incorporates physical activity (Rejeski, 1992).

As noted from conversations with Jenny, and also highlighted in recent research (O'Neill, 2013), a questionnaire would have simply have identified that some women exercised to lose weight or to maintain their already 'ideal' weight and size. However, more in-depth analysis of Jenny's, and the women in O'Neill's (2013), conversations revealed that there were different 'motives' linked to the weight-loss goal. For Jenny, her motives were to 'fit in' and not be the 'odd one out', and to avoid what she perceived to be negative comments from her friends and her nurse. In O'Neill (2013), the primary meanings given by the women to exercise were related to descriptions of salient self-perceptions that appeared to represent the 'what' (content) was being mediated (i.e., weight loss). However, explicit, and sometimes implicit, in the findings were the 'why' (the motives) they were being mediated. The majority of these motives appeared to be related to others in some way, especially in terms of how the women would perceive how others may view them. For example, for the women who reported weight loss as their main reason for exercising, it was the meaning or motive of weight loss that differentiated them. Anne did not want to suffer any more taunts. Carol wanted to be able to play with her children, did not want to embarrass them when they were older, and did not want her friends to talk about her in terms of the weight she had gained. Weight loss to Frances meant that she was the same as her peers and therefore would feel more confident around them. For Heather, weight loss meant she would be admired by both men and women. For Jean, weight loss meant she would be more attractive to the opposite sex. Laura received support from her husband for her weight loss and fitness efforts, and this support defined her relationship with him (O'Neill, 2013).

Therefore, taking into account the lessons from this literature and previous research, rather than turning to an 'off the shelf' questionnaire, an initial needs assessment involved an in-depth one-to-one interview with Jenny. This type of interview provided me with an understanding of the meaning Jenny attached to her experiences by acknowledging how complex these processes are and recognizing the multifaceted nature of such personal phenomena (Morrow, 2007). As mentioned earlier, while western scientific psychological tradition has typically focused on what is known as a reductionist approach, whereby attempts are made to reduce complex phenomena to a few quantifiable variables (Gough & McFadden, 2001), more recent research tries to understand individual motives at a more holistic, integrative, contextual, and personal level.

FRAMEWORK AND INTERVENTION

Framework

In considering a framework within which an intervention occurs, it is important to be aware that sport and exercise psychologists have the opportunity to draw on a wide range of approaches which in combination can best serve the needs of the client (e.g., Rich, 2000). This is known as adopting an eclectic approach, and Rich argues that being eclectic is necessary in order to best equip the practitioner with 'tools' that are responsive to the wide range of needs as presented by a wide range of clients.

A number of approaches identified within applied sport and exercise psychology includes behavioural, psychodynamic, humanistic, cognitive, social, biological, social constructionist, and neuropsychology and all focus on different perspectives operating at varying levels of explanation. As you become knowledgeable about these approaches you will inevitably be drawn to some and not others and as such, you may decide to adopt one or several approaches, thus being more eclectic in how you work with your clients (Jarvis, 2000).

Key future research box **BOX 19.3**

See Jarvis (2000) for an overview of a variety of psychological approaches used in applied sport settings, along with case study examples of how they work in practice.

Influencing your decision as to the type of framework you choose is what is known as your epistemological position. Epistemology simply refers to how you view reality. Modern, positivist, empiricist perspectives view the world as an objective reality that is waiting to be discovered. It is believed that through experiment and observation, the objective 'truth' will be revealed. The methodology favoured is quantitative in nature (Gergen, 2001). This type of inquiry has dominated psychology in general but has been criticized for its reductionist approach (Ryan, 2006). In other words, it is well suited to looking at the wood as a collective entity but not necessarily as adept at studying each of the trees within the wood.

An alternative approach to studying human beings evolved slowly during the twentieth century in opposition to the western tradition of positivism and empiricism, and is known collectively as social constructionism (Burr, 1995).

Discussion point box **BOX 19.4**

For a discussion on the historical developments and importance of epistemologies within scientific inquiry see Creswell (2007) or Denzin and Lincoln's (2005) handbook.

While there are many different approaches within social constructionism, Burr argues that they all share some underlying assumptions. In summary, they challenge the view that the world is objective; they argue that understanding the world needs to take account of history and culture; and they recognize that knowledge of the world is sustained through social processes and interactions between people. As such, language is viewed as key to understanding the social world,

> Language provides the basis for all our thought – language and thought are inseparable. Language provides and constructs our experiences of ourselves and each other (Burr, 1995, p. 44).

This approach recognizes that a person cannot be understood independently but needs to take a person's culture and history into account. Therefore, 'psychology, within this framework, becomes the study of a socially constructed being' (Burr, 1995, p. 111). This approach has important implications for sport and exercise. As discussed earlier, the self is best conceptualized as multifaceted and while gender is acknowledged as salient, other constructs also form part of the self-concept (e.g., race, ethnicity, sexual orientation, disability, socio-economic status, religion, etc.). Unfortunately, it appears that socio-cultural factors have received little attention in the sport and exercise psychology literature (Ram, Starek, & Johnson, 2004). In addition, it appears that much of sport and exercise psychology knowledge was developed from observations and practice involving only one section of society, namely young, collegiate, white, middle-class, fit, male athletes, and ignoring many others (e.g. women, athletes of colour, the LGB community, people with disabilities, and the older population (Schinke & Hanrahan, 2009).

Rather than rehearsing the problems of the past, Sue (2006) argues that it is time to move forward by recognizing non-conscious biases and becoming fully aware of one's own beliefs, values and biases; to develop knowledge of others' worldviews, cultures, and expectations; and thereby to develop interventions that are culturally relevant and sensitive.

To achieve this goal, it is important to adopt the current epistemological position. One potential and popular approach within the social constructionist framework is known as Grounded Theory, developed by Glaser and Strauss (1967) as a systematic procedure for collecting and analysing qualitative data. This method has relevance within a client/practitioner relationship as it has the potential to: (a) understand meaning given to people's personal, subjective experiences; and (b) is able to examine the complex and multifaceted nature of human phenomena at both an individual, person level while appreciating that people act within a larger background that includes socio-cultural influences (Corbin & Strauss, 2008).

Another popular idiographic framework is the humanistic approach which emphasizes 'personal meanings assigned to experience' (Hill, 2001, p. 122). Similar to social constructionism, there is no single accepted humanistic theory but all share some underlying principles such as a celebration of the individual, a focus on the development of the whole person, and a belief that a person develops through self-actualization to achieve the highest levels of 'personal attainment and accomplishment' (Hill, 2001, p. 108). It encourages the development of the self-concept, intrinsic motivation, and personal responsibility (Sherrill, 1998) through individualized instruction that incorporates client choice (Rich, 2000). The client is held in high regard through a display of empathy, genuineness, and non-judgemental caring from the practitioner. Active listening, acceptance, and co-operative goal setting are also characteristics of the humanistic approach.

Humanistic Theory became popular in the 1950s mainly through the work of Maslow (1954; Self-actualization Theory) and Carl Rogers (1980; Fully Functioning Self-theory). By using this approach, it is anticipated that the client will develop a more positive self-concept so s/he will become more intrinsically motivated. Research has shown that the more internalized a goal and intrinsically motivated a person is, the more likely it is that s/he will engage in exercise, and sustain engagement in the longer term (Lutz et al., 2008).

While many psychologists may side with a specific approach, others argue that all traditions operating in combination are valuable in advancing our understanding of the complexity of human experience. This support for the development and use of various approaches in psychological research is argued to encourage more of a focus on, 'linking theory to societal action ... (and) exploring the theory/action relationship more fully' (Gergen & Zielkeb, 2006, p. 304) in order to contribute to our understanding and, more importantly, to apply psychology to benefit humankind.

The approach taken with Jenny was a combination of social constructionism, specifically Grounded Theory, and a humanistic approach. As already discussed, the social constructionist approach was applied in order to understand a self that is influenced by culture and history, while appreciating an active self-in-action who was able to interpret her own experiences. The humanistic approach equips the practitioner with the skills to be able to actively listen to the client's needs with empathy and genuine understanding, while guiding and supporting the client to develop her own goals. As mentioned, quantitative research has attempted to examine individual variables that influence physical activity uptake and adherence. This knowledge was also used when appropriate to both guide the intervention process and to educate Jenny so that she could make informed decisions.

Intervention

By asking probing questions during interviews, you can use your knowledge of the physical activity literature and previous experiences of consultancy to search for consistent trends or patterns, and thereby solutions. These patterns may typically be anchored in the social realm. For example, the initial interview revealed that Jenny adopted gender norms in relation to body appearance, specifically weight and size, exhibiting body dissatisfaction and creating psychological ill-being, recognized as a normative experience for women in western society. In addition, Jenny's socialization within the physical activity context had not been a positive one which led to a lack of confidence in her physical abilities. Further influences identified where Jenny's concern about what others would think of her and her desire to 'fit in' with her peers in terms of her appearance. This supports the self-objectification theory that proposes the adoption of the 'others' view about how her body should look. Although socialization processes are argued to occur outside conscious awareness (Coole, 1995; Forgas, 1981; Markus, Kitayama, & Heiman, 1996; Mead, 1934), Jenny was still active in interpreting her personal experiences and giving them meaning, implying an element of subjectivity. In this case, she was unhappy and did not feel good about herself, motivating her to contact me.

After developing an understanding of Jenny's motives for exercise participation, the first part of the intervention consisted of educating/informing Jenny as to what the research says in relation to the motives underpinning this behaviour among women in general. In collaboration with Jenny, a personalized fitness programme was then developed. In addition to the first interview, a further seven consultations, outlined later, were conducted.

Jenny's 'education' was based on the extant psychological literature. From a social constructionist perspective, it appears that exercise represents a dilemma for women as it is not promoted or perceived as central to feminine identity on the one hand (O'Neill, 2013), yet it is promoted both by health professionals and the media as a way to lose weight and improve health on the other (Segar et al., 2011). As mentioned, women have been socialized to believe that the thin-beauty ideal will be achieved through adoption of this behaviour. However, there has been a shift in the focus and promotion of exercise from body appearance and health (argued to promote feelings of compliance rather than autonomy due to these cultural expectations and pressure) (McQuail, 2005; Rodin et al., 1984; Wray, 2007), to enhancing aspects of daily living (Segar et al., 2011). By expanding the meanings of exercise beyond appearance and health, there may be the potential to increase participation and adherence among female exercisers, including Jenny. Indeed, a recent successful intervention encouraged women to change motives away from culturally prescribed goals to 'lose weight' or 'exercise as medicine' to focusing on enjoyment and pleasure (Segar, Jayaratne, Hanlon, & Richardson, 2002). I asked Jenny to focus on these throughout the exercise intervention. I also explained to Jenny that her earlier socialization experiences with physical activity was a normative experience for lots of women but that exercise encompassed an enormous diversity of activities that could appeal in different ways to a range of different abilities. Therefore, she could find activities that she could connect with and enjoy.

Brown suggests that self-enhancement or the desire to feel good about the self is a dominant self-goal (1998). Certainly within the exercise context, more recent research on the intensity/affect relationship has taken a, 'paradigmatic shift from a prescription-based to a preference-based model of exercise promotion' that has the potential to increase both pleasure and adherence to exercise programs (Ekkekakis, Parfitt, & Petruzzello, 2011, p. 662). In Jenny's case, this involved developing an exercise regimen based around the following principles:

Self-paced. Self-paced exercise is related to higher levels of enjoyment among exercisers (Ekkekakis & Lind, 2006; Parfitt, Rose, & Burgess, 2006). In addition, it appears that self-paced exercise will be self-regulated to an intensity that results in positive affective responses (Ekkekakis, Backhouse, Gray, & Lind, 2008; Ekkekakis & Petruzzello, 2000). Encouragingly, people who self-select their exercise intensity appear to select an intensity that approaches but does not exceed their venentilator threshold (V.T. is the transition from aerobic to anaerobic metabolism and exceeding this has been reported to produce a substantial shift towards negative affect) (e.g., Ekkekakis, Lind, & Joens-Matre, 2006; Rose & Parfitt, 2007).

This principle was evident when Jenny discussed her earlier exercise experiences when she talked about not pushing herself beyond other's prescribed targets and not doing 'all that I was supposed to do'. I therefore encouraged Jenny to self-regulate her exercise intensity so that she was experiencing pleasure (Ekkekakis & Lind, 2006; Parfitt et al., 2006). As cognitive appraisals are recognized as important below the V.T. threshold, each consultation that followed her first five weekly exercise sessions focused on how she was interpreting the intensity experience and the meanings she was giving to them. Jenny created her own self-talk around this, telling herself that she was exercising for enjoyment and this proved to be a very effective strategy for her personally.

Self-choice. Exercisers display higher levels of positive affective responses when they choose their own type of exercise (Daley & Maynard, 2003; Parfitt & Gledhill, 2004). Based on my own research, preferred choice of activity was dependent upon subjective interpretation of the activity in terms of its potential to mediate a favourable self-perception. Therefore, Jenny was encouraged to initially sample a range of exercise activities in order to facilitate a positive evaluation as to the type of activity preferred. From the initial interview, it was clear that Jenny enjoyed exercising to music, aerobic-type classes, and she liked variety. To build on this, I acquired a list of the classes available at her local leisure centre (40 were available each week). In collaboration with Jenny, we drew up a list of classes she would like to sample and set a five-week time frame. Jenny committed to participating in physical activity three times per week. The first week she attended step and body tone classes, both aerobics and Zumba in the second week, Yoga and Body Combat in the third week, and legs, bums, and tums in the fourth week. I also suggested that Jenny incorporate some weight training into her programme in weeks four and five. One session per week would also be in the gym and Jenny chose her own equipment – rowing machine, stepper, and treadmill. I suggested she create music for an iPod to help motivate her during these sessions. Her daughter helped her with this.

Self-selection. The components of frequency and duration have received much less attention in research compared to intensity and type of exercise, but my own research supported the view that self-selection of all the exercise components was an important condition to exercise progression, adherence, and well-being. In this study, self-prescribing was crucial to the subjective interpretation of the experience as mediating a more favourable self-perception (O'Neill, 2013). Initially, Jenny wished to exercise three times per week. In terms of duration, she was happy that the classes were for one hour. Weight training was set at 30 minutes, while her time in the gym was 45 minutes (15 minutes per machine).

Enjoyment. A recent successful intervention in the United States also encouraged women to choose pleasure-based activities that increased positive responses to exercise and successful adherence (Segar et al., 2002). By encouraging Jenny to sample a wide range of activities, an assessment with regards enjoyment would be ongoing.

Meanings. A range of meanings can be generated through participation in exercise. I discussed with Jenny the meanings that other people have reported in order to provide her with a broader view of how exercise can aid feeling good about the self beyond traditional beauty and medicine motives. I asked Jenny to keep a diary of her experiences. The use of a diary as a way of capturing personal experiences is popular within qualitative research (Iida, Shrout, Laurenceau, & Bolger, 2012). Two broad categories are used, time-based and event-based (Bolger, Davis, & Rafaeli, 2003). Jenny was encouraged to use an event-based diary to record her experiences following each exercise session. Jenny was asked to record her own meanings of why exercise made her feel good, when and why it created negative experiences, perceived barriers to participation, and any other information she deemed relevant.

Timescale. This was discussed with Jenny and there were eight consultations in total. The first was the initial interview, and the second was to discuss an action plan. One consultation took place each week following five weeks of exercise. The final was week 12.

Each week we discussed the content of Jenny's diary in order to understand the meanings she was giving to her experiences. The humanistic method was applied in order to collaboratively look to strengthen positive and overcome negative experiences. Central to humanistic philosophy is client choice and autonomy. A goal setting principle known as SMART (Specific, Measurable, Action-orientated, Realistic and Timely) (Lavallee, Kremer, Moran, & Williams, 2004), viewed as a motivational tool within physical activity (Hagger & Chatzisarantis, 2005), was used to focus our conversations on specific goals.

Jenny reported enjoying the aerobics and step classes. As identified in the initial interview, she very much enjoyed exercising to music. In addition, she reported that she really enjoyed the Body Combat class as it was, 'very good mentally because it pumps the adrenalin, it really gets the blues away, mentally it is fantastic'. She reported that she was surprised she liked the weight training, stating that, 'I quite I suppose enjoyed the weights because it was slower and all the movements were slower and you didn't have that sort of you know, pumping some of them you like better than others and some of them are easier than others'. In addition, Jenny revealed that her mother had suffered from osteoporosis and liked the weights because, 'my mother had osteoporosis... quite badly. She had two artificial hips and numerous things and um, I know weight-bearing exercise is good'. Finally, Jenny reported that training in the gym was more enjoyable now that she could choose her own machines and her choice of music. Overall, the variety of activities appealed to her and kept her motivated; boredom had not been an issue. She did not enjoy Yoga because, 'I am a bit hyper sometimes and I used to lie in the relaxation bit just thinking about all the things I had to do, so it was a bit counter-productive (laughs). When you were supposed to be concentrating on the candle or the flickering flame etc. you know, or lying down, I used to sort of think about other things, so I got a bit impatient with it.'

Following a consultation in week 12, Jenny reported exercising four times per week; she had self-selected the frequency of exercise sessions. It was also clear that Jenny had learnt to self-regulate her intensity levels, while her choice of activities proved motivational for her. Overall Jenny reported feeling good about herself because she was taking positive action in terms of exercising and also enjoying the experience for the first time. She admitted that her main motive was still weight loss and appearance but she showed more appreciation of why these were important to her (and women in general) from a socio-cultural perspective, admitting that the motive no longer affected her psychological well-being to the same degree as she had other reasons to feel good through exercise.

REFLECTIONS

This intervention was novel as it was based on a preference-based rather than prescription-based model of exercise participation. This recent move towards a preference-based model has been supported in previous studies (Ekkekakis et al., 2011; O'Neill, 2013).

Central to the success of the intervention was the appreciation of the cognitive appraisals or meanings that Jenny gave to her exercise experiences. Ekkekakis (2003, 2005) suggests that these appraisals will show variability as they are shaped by personal experience. Hence, it must be understood that subjectivity will play a key feature of the intervention's efficacy.

Typically, subjectivity has been ignored in psychology as it has been inaccessible due to the type of scientific inquiry typically endorsed, namely those based on quantitative methods. Using the methods suggested in this intervention provided the opportunity to access Jenny's subjective experiences and provide insight into her internal mental processes. It was also vital to appreciate that within a social context (in this case the exercise context), Jenny had numerous options available to choose from, and only she could explain how and why she made specific choices and under what conditions.

This awareness and understanding of the subjectivity of human nature is crucial in the monitoring and evaluation process. Ultimately, it was Jenny who was active in interpreting her exercise experiences. In cooperation with Jenny, there was an ongoing evaluation of both the positive and negative outcomes of this experience. The aim of this monitoring and evaluation was to help Jenny develop strategies to progress towards achieving more enjoyment and fulfilment in undertaking exercise. Jenny's diary, as well as our conversations, provided some insight into her own monitoring and evaluative processes. While the diary was not completed after every physical activity, its use proved to be invaluable in uncovering Jenny's feelings, thoughts and actions as a running record in 'real-time', rather than attempting to reflect back. Ultimately, and in the humanistic tradition, Jenny was encouraged to set her own standards and make her own choices, moving towards feelings of autonomy and self-acceptance and hence improvements in psychological well-being followed (Ryan & Deci, 2000).

A practice known as reflexivity or reflection is considered to be a 'hallmark of excellent qualitative research' (Sandelowski & Barroso, 2002, p. 222). It is recognized by many as a crucial element in the process as it involves the continuous practice of reflection by a researcher on his or her values, beliefs, and behaviour, and their influence on the participants' responses and the interpretation of the data (Parahoo, 2006; Primeau, 2003). In terms of the interaction with Jenny, it was important to be aware of how my own beliefs and values may impact on the client/practitioner relationship. Central to the humanistic approach was empowering Jenny to make her own choices and not have the practitioner's imposed upon her. Additionally, this self-awareness facilitated the empathy, genuineness, and non-judgemental style argued to promote the co-operative environment necessary to aid a successful client/practitioner relationship.

There are several other ways in which an intervention could have been delivered to Jenny. One of which is to use a battery of questionnaires and physical measurements for profiling self-concept. Physical Self-Description Questionnaire (Marsh et al., 1994) may have initially been used to measure aspects of Jenny's physical self-concept (strength, body fat, activity, endurance, sports competence, co-ordination, health, appearance, flexibility, global physical and global self-concept). A Body Mass Index (BMI) would have provided an objective baseline measure that could then be reassessed at the end of the intervention and used as an objective measure of success of the intervention. The Feeling Scale (FS) (Hardy & Rejeski, 1989), a self-report measure of affective responses (pleasure-displeasure), would have provided a scale to assess Jenny's reactions during exercise. The physical activity consultation method (Loughlan & Mutrie, 1995), based on the trans-theoretical model of behaviour change that has proved successful within the physical activity context (Marshall & Biddle, 2001), is another approach that could have been used. This method suggests that people move through stages (pre-contemplation, contemplation, preparation, action, and maintenance). One-to-one, person-centred interviews are a central feature of the physical activity consultation method, with an emphasis on guiding clients as opposed to directing them. The aim is to provide encouragement to help a client develop her/his own motivations and take responsibility for their behaviour. It is argued that this approach may be delivered with minimal training on the part of the practitioner (Kirk, Barnett, & Mutrie, 2007).

The intervention outlined in this chapter requires in-depth knowledge of the physical activity literature in terms of motives and barriers to participation, insight and appreciation of the socio-cultural influences on an individual's cognitions about the self and physical activity; an understanding that subjectivity and personal meaning play a crucial role in physical activity adoption and maintenance; and training and experience in the specific methodologies selected. However, as mentioned earlier, an eclectic approach can best assist a practitioner in serving the needs of a client (Rich, 2000). While this intervention focused on using a qualitative, idiographic approach, combining many of the above objective measures has the potential to strengthen any intervention. For example, measuring changes in the self-concept using the Physical Self-Description Questionnaire (Marsh et al., 1994) pre- and post-intervention may have subsequently highlighted other perceived improvements (such as health, strength, etc.) that broaden the positive meanings Jenny may give to her exercise experiences. The physical activity consultation would have helped identify Jenny's stage of behaviour change, while providing useful guidelines for facilitating the one-to-one conversations with her.

SUMMARY

A skilled and knowledgeable practitioner's role is to guide and support a client through the various stages and processes involved in physical activity. Understanding the complexity of the physical activity experience from a social, historical, and an individual perspective enables a more comprehensive understanding of a person's reason(s) for participation (or not). While quantitative approaches are typically used in interventions, this discussion has attempted to highlight an alternative method: qualitative, humanistic, and idiographic. The discussion has also attempted to show how a combined approach can further strengthen any intervention. Ultimately, all practitioners need to acknowledge that subjectivity will play a key role in physical activity adoption and adherence.

As demonstrated in this study, tackling exercise behaviours at an individual belief and attitude level ignores the role played by socio-cultural norms. Beliefs and attitudes need to be reconstructed at a societal level, as well as an individual level. The challenge for sport and exercise psychologists, along with others involved in the promotion of physical activity, is to aid this transformation both at an individual and at a societal level. A new discourse for physical activity is needed which could follow the lines that were used with Jenny for example education, self-exploration, self-reflection, an appreciation of a self-in-action, and client-practitioner collaboration. There is now a responsibility to promote physical activity beyond health and beauty behaviours, and in a way that embraces all sections of the population, without labels or judgements.

FURTHER READING

Choi, P. Y. L. (2000). *Femininity and the physically active woman*. London: Routledge. This book provides a comprehensive examination of women's experiences from a critical feminist and gendered perspective. It looks at the social construction of physical activity and gender and how they interact to reduce female participation.

Schinke, R. J., & Hanrahan, S. J. (Eds.). (2009). *Cultural sport psychology*. Champaign, IL: Human Kinetics. This textbook provides a description of how cultural factors such as gender, religion, and so on, play a role in contributing, positively or negatively, to sporting performance and an athlete's well-being. Although specifically focused on sport, the insight it provides is potentially transferable into the exercise context.

REFERENCES

Anderson, E. (2005). *In the game: Gay athletes and the cult of masculinity*. Albany, NY: State University of New York.

Bagozzi, R. P., & Edwards, E. A. (2000). Goal-striving and the implementation of goal intentions in the regulation of body weight. *Psychology and Health*, *15*(2), 255–270.

Basow, S. A. (2008). Gender socialisation, or how long away has baby come? In J. C. Chrisler, C. Golden, & P. D. Rozee (Eds.), *Lectures on the psychology of women* (pp. 80–95). New York: McGraw-Hill.

Berger, B. G., & Tobar, D. A. (2007). Physical activity and quality of life: Key considerations. In G. Tenenbaum & R. C. Eklund (Eds.), *Handbook of sport psychology* (3rd ed., pp. 598– 620). Hoboken, NJ: John Wiley & Sons, Inc.

Biddle, S. J. H., Fox, K. R., & Boutcher, S. H. (Eds.). (2000). *Physical activity and psychological well-being*. London: Routledge.

Biddle, S. J. H., & Mutrie, N. (2008). *Psychology of physical activity: Determinants, well-being and intervention* (2nd ed.). Abingdon: Routledge.

Birkeland, R., Thompson, J., Herbozo, S., Roehrig, M., Cafri, G., & van den Berg, P. (2005). Media exposure, mood, and body image dissatisfaction: An experimental test of person versus product priming. *Body Image*, *2*, 53–61.

Bjornsson, A. S., Didie, E. R., & Phillips, K. A. (2010). Body dysmorphic disorder. *Dialogues in Clinical Neuroscience*, *12*(2), 221–232.

Bolger, N., Davis, A., & Rafaeli, E. (2003). Diary methods: Capturing life as it is lived. *Annual Review of Psychology*, *54*, 579–616.

Bronstein, P. (2006). The family environment: Where gender role socialisation begins. In J. Worell & C. D. Goodheart (Eds.), *Handbook of girls and women's psychological health: Gender and well-being across the lifespan* (pp. 262–271). New York: Oxford University Press.

Brown, J. (1998). *The self.* New York: McGraw Hill.

Brown, J. S., Meadows, S. O., & Elder, G. H., Jnr. (2007). Race-ethnic inequality and psychological distress: Depressive symptoms from adolescence to young adulthood. *Development Psychology*, *43*, 1295–1311.

Burr, V. (1995). *An introduction to social constructionism*. London: Routledge.

Byrne, B. M. (1996). *Measuring self-concept across the life span: Issues and instrumentation*. Washington, DC: American Psychological Association.

Carless, D., & Faulkner, G. (2003). Physical activity and mental health. In J. McKenna & C. Riddoch (Eds.), *Perspectives on health and exercise* (pp. 61–82). Basingstoke: Palgrave Macmillan.

Centers for Disease Control and Prevention (CDC) (2013). *National Centre for Health Statistics: Health United States, 2013*. Retrieved 7 July 2014 from http://www.cdc.gov/nchs/data/hus/hus13.pdf#068.

Charmaz, K. (2006). *Constructing grounded theory: A practical guide through qualitative analysis*. Thousand Oaks, CA: Sage.

Choi, P. Y. L. (2000). *Femininity and the physically active woman*. London: Routledge.

Choi, P. Y. L., Pope, H. G., Jr., & Olivardia, R. (2002). Muscle dysmorphia: A new syndrome in weightlifters. *British Journal of Sports Medicine*, *36*(5), 375–376.

Coole, D. (1995). The gendered self. In D.Bakhurst & C.Sypnowich (Eds.), *The social self* (pp. 123–139). London: Sage.

Cooley, C. H. (1902). *Human nature and the social order.* New York: Schocken Books.

Corbin, C. B., Landers, D. M., Feltz, D. L., & Senior, K. (1983). Sex differences in performance estimates: Female lack of self-confidence versus male boastfulness. *Research Quarterly for Exercise and Sport*, *54*, 407–410.

Corbin, J. M., & Morse, J. (2003). The unstructured interview: Issues of reciprocity and risks when dealing with sensitive topics. *Qualitative Inquiry*, *9*(3), 335–354.

Corbin, J. M., & Strauss, A. L. (2008). *Basics of qualitative research* (3rd ed.). London: Sage.

Craven, R., & Marsh, H. W. (2008). The centrality of the self-concept construct for psychological wellbeing and unlocking human potential: Implications for child and educational psychologists. *Education and Child Psychology*, *25*, 104–118.

Creswell, J. W. (2007). *Qualitative inquiry and research design: Choosing among five approaches*. Thousand Oaks, CA: Sage.

Daley, A. J., & Maynard, I. W. (2003). Preferred exercise mode and affective responses in physically active adults. *Psychology of Sport and Exercise*, *4*, 347–356.

Deci, E. L., & Ryan, R. M. (1985). *Intrinsic motivation and self-determination in human behaviour.* New York: Plenum Press.

Department of Health, Social Services, and Public Safety (DHSSPS) (2011). *Physical activity guidelines for adults (19–64 years): Factsheet 4*. Retrieved 7 July 2014 from https://www.gov.uk/government/uploads/system/uploads/attachment_data/file/213740/dh_12814

Department of Health, Social Services, and Public Safety for Northern Ireland (DHSSPSNI) (2012). *A fitter future for all: Framework for preventing and addressing overweight and obesity in Northern Ireland 2012–2022*. Retrieved 7 July 2014 from http://www.dhsspni.gov.uk/framework-preventing-addressing-overweight-obesity-ni-2012-2022.pdf.

Diedrichs, P., Paraskeva, N., & Rumsey, N. (2011). *Channel 4 online Body Confidence Test: Preliminary report.* Bristol: Centre for Appearance Research.

Durkin, S. J., Paxton, S. J., & Sorbello, M. (2007). An integrative model of the impact of exposure to idealised female images on adolescent girls' body dissatisfaction. *Journal of Applied Social Psychology, 37*, 1092–1117.

Eccles, J. S., & Wigfield, A. (2002). Motivational beliefs, values and goals. *Annual Review of Psychology, 53*, 109–132.

Ekkekakis, P. (2003). Pleasure and displeasure from the body: Perspectives from exercise. *Cognition and Emotion, 17*(2), 213–239.

Ekkekakis, P. (2005). The study of affective responses to acute exercise: The dual-mode model. In R.Stelter & K. K.Roessler (Eds.), *New approaches to sport and exercise psychology* (pp. 119–146). Oxford: Meyer & Meyer Sport.

Ekkekakis, P., & Backhouse, S. H. (2009). Exercise and psychological well-being. In R. Maughan (Ed.), *Olympic textbook of science in sport* (pp. 251–271). Hoboken, NJ: John Wiley & Sons, Inc.

Ekkekakis, P., Backhouse, S. H., Gray, C., & Lind, E. (2008). Walking is popular among adults but is it pleasant? A framework for clarifying the link between walking and affect as illustrated in two studies. *Psychology of Sport and Exercise, 9*, 246–264.

Ekkekakis, P., & Lind, E. (2006). Exercise does not feel the same when you are overweight: The impact of self-selected and imposed intensity on affect and exertion. *International Journal of Obesity, 30*(4), 652–660.

Ekkekakis, P., Lind, E., & Joens-Matre, R. R. (2006). Can self-reported preference for exercise intensity predict physiologically defined self-selected exercise intensity? *Research Quarterly for Exercise and Sport, 77*(1), 81–90.

Ekkekakis, P., Parfitt, G., & Petruzzello, S. J. (2011). The pleasure and displeasure people feel when they exercise at different intensities: Decennial update and progress toward a tripartite rationale for exercise intensity prescription. *Sports Medicine, 41*(8), 641–671.

Ekkekakis, P., & Petruzzello, S. J. (2000). Analysis of the affect measurement conundrum in exercise psychology: I. Fundamental Issues. *Psychology of Sport and Exercise, 1*(2), 71–88.

Emery, C. F., & Blumenthal, J. A. (1990). Perceived change among participants in an exercise program for older adults. *The Gerontologist, 30*, 516–521.

Etaugh, C. A., & Bridges, J. S. (2010). Women's lives: *A psychological exploration* (2nd ed.). Boston, MA: Pearson Education, Inc.

Forgas, J. P. (1981). Epilogue: Everyday understanding and social cognition. In J. P. Forgas (Ed.), *Social cognition: Perspectives on everyday understanding* (pp. 259–272). London: Academic.

Fox, K. R. (1997). The physical self and processes in self-esteem development. In K. R. Fox (Ed.), *The physical self: From motivation to well-being* (pp. 111–139). Champaign, IL: Human Kinetics.

Fox, K. R., & Corbin, C. B. (1989). The physical self-perception profile: Development and preliminary validation. *Journal of Sport and Exercise Psychology, 11*, 408–430.

Fredrickson, B. L., & Roberts, T. (1997). Objectification theory: Toward understanding women's lived experiences and mental health risks. *Psychology of Women Quarterly, 21*, 173–206.

Gergen, K. J. (2001). Psychological science in a postmodern context. *American Psychologist, 56*(10), 803–813.

Gergen, K. J., & Zielkeb, B. (2006). Theory in action. *Theory and Psychology, 16*(3), 299–309.

Glaser, B., & Strauss, A. (1967). *The discovery of grounded theory.* Chicago: Aldine.

Golden, C. (2008). The intersexed and the transgendered: Rethinking sex/gender. In J. C. Chrisler, C. Golden, & P. D.Rozee (Eds.), *Lectures on the psychology of women* (pp. 136–152). New York: McGraw-Hill.

Gordon, C., & Gergen, K. J. (Eds.). (1968). *The self in social interaction, (Vol. 1): Classic and contemporary perspectives.* New York: John Wiley & Sons, Inc.

Gough, B., & McFadden, M. (2001). *Critical social psychology: An introduction.* Basingstoke: Palgrave.

Grabe, S., Ward, L. M., & Hyde, J. S. (2008). The role of the media in body image concerns among women: A meta-analysis of experiential and correlational studies. *Psychological Bulletin, 134*, 460–476.

Graham, R., Kremer, J., & Wheeler, G. (2008). Physical exercise and psychological well-being among people with chronic illness and disability: A grounded approach. *Journal of Health Psychology, 13*(4), 447–458.

Hagger, M., & Chatzisarantis, N. (2005). *The social psychology of exercise and sport.Maidenhead*: Open University Press.

Hall, D. M. (2008). Feminist perspectives on the personal and political aspects of mothering. In J. C. Chrisler, C. Golden, & P. D. Rozee (Eds.), *Lectures on the psychology of women* (pp. 58–79). New York: McGraw-Hill.

Hamilton, E. A., Mintz, L., & Kashubeck-West, S. (2007). Predictors of media effects on body dissatisfaction in European Amercian women. *Sex Roles, 56*, 397–402.

Hardy, C. J., & Rejeski, W. J. (1989). Not what, but how one feels: The measurement of affect during exercise. *Journal of Sport and Exercise Psychology, 11*(3), 304–317.

Harper, B., & Tiggemann, M. (2008). The effect of thin ideal media images on women's self-objectification, mood, and body image. *Sex Roles, 58*, 649–657.

Hildebrandt, T., Schlundt, D., Langenbucher, J., & Chung, T. (2006). Presence of muscle dysmorphia symptomology among male weightlifters. *Comprehensive Psychiatry, 47*(2), 127–135.

Hill, J. O. (2005). Role of physical activity in preventing and treating obesity. *Journal of Applied Physiology, 99*, 765–770.

Hill, K. L. (2001). *Frameworks for sport psychologists: Enhancing sport performance.* Leeds: Human Kinetics.

Hillsdon, M., & Thorogood, M. (1996). A systematic review of physical activity promotion strategies. *British Journal of Sports Medicine, 30*, 84–89.

Iida, M., Shrout, P. E., Laurenceau, J. P., & Bolger, N. (2012). Using diary methods in psychological research. In H. Cooper, P. M. Camic, D. L. Long, & A. T. Panter (Eds.), *APA handbook of research methods in psychology Vol. 1: Foundations, planning measures and psychometrics* (pp. 277–305). Washington, DC: American Psychological Association.

James, W. (1890). *Principles of psychology (Vol. 1).* New York: Holt.

James, W. (1892). *Psychology.* New York: Holt.

Jarvis, M. (2000). *Theoretical approaches in psychology.* London: Routledge.

Jones, S. M., & Dindia, K. (2004). A meta-analytic perspective on sex equity in the classroom. *Review of Educational Research, 74*, 443–471.

Kirk, A. F., Barnett, J., & Mutrie, N. (2007). Physical activity consultation for people with Type 2 diabetes. Evidence and guidelines. *Diabetic Medicine, 24*, 809–816.

Lavallee, D., Kremer, J., Moran, P., & Williams, M. (2004). *Sport psychology: Contemporary themes.* Basingstoke: Palgrave Macmillan.

Leaper, C., & Brown, C. S. (2008). Perceived experiences with sexism among adolescent girls. *Child Development, 79*, 685–704.

Light, R. L., & Wedgwood, N. (2012). Revisiting 'sport and the maintenance of masculine hegemony'. *Asia-Pacific Journal of Health, Sport and Physical Education, 3*(3), 181–183.

Loughlan, C. & Mutrie, N. (1995). Conducting and exercise consultation: Guidelines for health professionals. *Journal of the Institute of Health Education, 33*, 78–82.

Lutz, R., Karoly, P., & Okun, M. (2008). The why and the how of exercise goal pursuit: Self-determination, goal process cognition, and exercise participation. *Psychology of Sport and Exercise, 9*, 559–575.

Markus, H. R., Kitayama, S., & Heiman, R. J. (1996). Culture and basic psychological principles. In T. T. Higgins & A. W. Kruglanski (Eds.), *Social psychology: Handbook of basic principles.* New York: The Guildford Press.

Marsh, H. W. (1997). The measurement of physical self-concept: A construct validation approach. In K. Fox (Ed.), *The physical self-concept: From motivation to well-being* (pp. 27–58). Champaign, IL: Human Kinetics.

Marsh, H. W. (2002). A multidimensional physical self-concept: A construct validity approach to theory, measurement, and research. *Psychology: The Journal of the Hellenic Psychological Society, 9*, 459–493.

Marsh, H. W., Richards, G. E., Johnson, S., Roche, L., et al. (1994). Physical self-description questionnaire: Psychometric properties and multitrait-multimethod analysis of relations to existing instruments. *Journal of Sport and Exercise Psychology, 16*(3), 270–305.

Marshall, S. J. & Biddle, S. J. H. (2001). The trans-theoretical model of behaviour change. A meta-analysis of applications to physical activity and exercise. *Annals of Behavioural Medicine, 23*, 229–246.

Maslow, A. (1954). *Motivation and personality* (1st ed.). New York: Harper & Row.

McQuail, D. (2005). *McQuail's mass communication theory* (5th ed.). London: Sage.

Mead, G. H. (1934). *Mind, self and society.* Chicago: University Press of Chicago.

Messner, M. A. (1988). Sports and male domination: The female athlete as contested ideological terrain. *Sociology of Sport Journal, 5*(3), 197–211.

Messner, M. A. (2002). *Taking the field: Women, men and sports.* Minneapolis, MN: University of Minnesota Press.

Morrow, S. L. (2007). Qualitative research in counselling psychology: Conceptual foundations. *The Counselling Psychologist, 35*(2), 209–235.

National Health Service (2013). The information centre for health and social care: Statistics on obesity, physical activity and diet. Retrieved 1 July 2014 from http://www.hscic.gov.uk/catalogue/PUB10364/obes-phys-acti-eng-2013-rep.pdf.

Ogden, C. L., Carroll, M. D., Kit, B. K., & Flegal, K. M. (2014). Prevalence of childhood and adult obesity in the United States, 2011–2012. *The Journal of the American Medical Association, 311*(8), 806–814.

O'Neill, S. (2013). *Self-perceptions and well-being of women exercisers: A grounded theory approach* (Unpublished PhD thesis, Queen's University, Belfast.

Parahoo K. (Ed.). (2006). *Nursing research: Principles, processes and issues* (2nd ed.). Basingstoke: Palgrave Macmillan.

Parfitt, G., & Gledhill, C. (2004). The effect of choice of exercise mode on psychological responses. *Psychology of Sport and Exercise, 5*, 111–117.

Parfitt, G., Rose., E. A., & Burgess, W. M. (2006). The psychological and physiological responses of sedentary individuals to prescribed and preferred intensity exercise. *British Journal of Health Psychology, 11* (Pt. 1), 39–53.

Pope, C. G., Pope, H. G., Menard, W., Fay, C., Olivardia, R., & Phillips, K. A. (2005). Clinical features of muscle dysmorphia among males with body dysmorphic disorder. *Body Image, 2*(4), 395–400.

Pope, H. G., Phillips, K. A., & Olivardia, R. (2000). *The Adonis Complex: The secret crisis of male body obsession*. New York: Free Press.

Priest, P. (2007). The healing balm effect: Using a walking group to feel better. *Journal of Health Psychology, 12*, 36–52.

Primeau, L. A. (2003). Reflections on self in qualitative research: Stories of family. *American Journal of Occupational Therapy, 57*, 9–16.

Ram, N., Starek, J., & Johnson, J. (2004). Race, ethnicity, and sexual orientation: Still a void in sport and exercise psychology. *Journal of Sport and Exercise Psychology, 26*, 250–268.

Rejeski, W. J. (1992). Motivation for exercise behaviour: A critique of theoretical directions. In G. C. Roberts (Ed.), *Motivation in sport and exercise* (pp. 129–158). Chicago, IL: Human Kinetics.

Rich, S. M. (2000). Instructional strategies for adapted physical education. In J. P. Winnick (Ed.), *Adapted physical education and sport* (pp. 75–92). Champaign, IL: Human Kinetics.

Roberts, G. C. (Ed.). (2001). *Advances in motivation in sport and exercise.* Champaign, IL: Human Kinetics Publishers, Inc.

Rodin, J., Silberstein, L., & Striegel-Moore, R. (1984). Women and weight: A normative discontent. *Nebraska Symposium on Motivation, 32*, 267–307.

Rogers, C. (1980). *A way of being.* New York: Houghton Mifflin.

Rose, E. A., & Parfitt, G. (2007). A quantitative analysis and qualitative explanation of the individual differences in affective responses to prescribed and self-selected exercise intensities. *Journal of Sport and Exercise Psychology, 29*, 281–309.

Rosenberg, M. (1979). *Conceiving the self.* New York: Basic Books, Inc.

Roth, A. R., & Basow, S. A. (2004). Femininity, sports, and feminism: Developing a theory of physical liberation. *Journal of Sport and Social Issues, 28*(3), 245–265.

Rubin, K. H., Bukowski, W. M., & Parker, J. G. (2006). Peer interactions, relationships, and groups. In W. Damon, R. M. Lerner, & N. Eisenberg (Eds.), *Handbook of child psychology: Vol. 3. Social, emotional, and personality development* (6th ed., pp. 571–645). Hoboken, NJ: John Wiley & Sons, Inc.

Ryan, A. B. (2006). Methodology: Analysing qualitative data and writing up your findings. In M. Antonesa, H. Fallon, A. B. Ryan, A. Ryan, T. Walsh, & L Borys (Eds.), *Researching and writing your thesis: A guide for postgraduate students* (pp. 12–26). Maynooth, Ireland: Adult and Community Education.

Ryan, R. M., & Deci, E. L. (2000). Self-determination theory and the facilitation of intrinsic motivation, social development, and well-being. *American Psychologist, 55*, 68–78.

Sandelowski, M., & Barroso, J. (2002). Reading qualitative studies. *International Journal of Qualitative Methods, 1*(1), Article 5. Retrieved 1 March 2012 from http://www.ualberta.ca/~iiqm/backissues/1_1Final/html/sandeleng.html.

Schinke, R. J., & Hanrahan, S. J. (Eds.). (2009). *Cultural sport psychology.* Champaign, IL: Human Kinetics.

Segar, M. L., Eccles, J. S., & Richardson, C. (2011). Rebranding exercise: Closing the gap between values and behaviour. *International Journal of Behavioural Nutrition and Physical Activity, 8*(94), 1–14.

Segar, M. L., Jayaratne, T., Hanlon, J., & Richardson, C. (2002). Fitting fitness into women's lives: Effects of a gender-tailored physical activity intervention. *Women's Health Issues, 12*, 338–349.

Sherrill, C. (1998). *Adapted physical activity, recreation and sport: Crossdisciplinary and lifespan.* Boston: WCB/McGraw-Hill.

Stice, E. (1994). A review of the evidence for a socio-cultural model of bulimia nervosa and an exploration of the mechanisms of action. *Clinical Psychology Review, 14*, 633–661.

Sue, S. (2006). Cultural competency: From philosophy to research and practice. *Journal of Community Psychology, 34*, 237–245.

Tiggemann, M., & Williamson, S. (2000). The effect of exercise on body satisfaction and self-esteem as a function of gender and age. *Sex Roles, 43*, 119–127.

U.S. Department of Health and Human Services (2008). *2008 Physical Activity Guidelines for Americans.* Atlanta, GA: U.S. Department of Health and Human Services, Centers for Disease Control and Prevention. Retrieved 2 August 2014 from http://www.health.gov/paguidelines/pdf/paguide.pdf.

Van Landuyt, L. M., Ekkekakis, P., Hall, E. E., & Petruzzello, S. J. (2000). Throwing the mountains into the lakes: On the perils of nomothetic conceptions of the exercise-affect relationship. *Journal of Sport and Exercise Psychology, 22*, 208–234.

Ward, L. M. (2007). A longitudinal study of media use and gender role beliefs among Black and White 6th graders. In L. M. Ward (Chair), *Television role in the gender and sexual socialisation of Black adolescents.* Paper symposium conducted at the meeting of the Society for Research in Child Development, Boston.

Wilson, P. M., & Rodgers, W. M. (2002). The relationship between exercise motives and physical self-esteem in female exercise participants: An application of self-determination theory. *Journal of Applied Biobehavioural Research, 7*, 30–43.

Wiseman, M. A., Gray, J. J., Mosimann, J. E., & Ahrens, A. H. (1992). Cultural expectations of thinness in women: An update. *International Journal of Eating Disorders, 11*, 85–89.

World Health Organisation (2014). Obesity and overweight: Fact sheet No. 311. Retrieved 1 July 2014, from http://www.who.int/mediacentre/factsheets/fs311/en/.

Wray, S. (2007). Health, exercise and well-being: The experiences of midlife women from diverse ethnic backgrounds. *Social Theory and Health, 5*, 126–144.

20 Developing a School-based Physical Activity Protocol for Those with Intellectual Disabilities

Ben Lee Fitzpatrick, Gavin Breslin, and Laurence Taggart

LEARNING OBJECTIVES

AFTER READING THIS CHAPTER YOU SHOULD BE ABLE TO:

1. Describe a physical activity and fitness protocol designed for those with intellectual disability.
2. Describe the main theoretical approaches to psychological interventions for those with intellectual disability.
3. Consider the various issues that may be presented during assessment of physical activity and fitness that practitioners may have to respond to.
4. Consider the perceptions of physical education for those with intellectual disability.

AREAS TO CONSIDER WHEN READING THE CHAPTER:

1. How a sport and exercise psychologist may design an intervention promoting physical activity to those with intellectual disabilities.
2. How you might deal with the sequencing of sessions when assessing physical activity and fitness with those with intellectual disability.
3. What it must be like for those with intellectual disability taking part in physical education classes.

CLIENT AND BACKGROUND

This case study concerns a group of adolescents who have been diagnosed with a mild to moderate intellectual disability (ID). ID is a disability characterized by significant limitations in both intellectual functioning and in adaptive behaviour, which covers many everyday social and practical skills and originates before the age of 18. We detail a group of young people who were identified from one school in Northern Ireland where special education is delivered to approximately 200 students from the age of 4 to 18 years. There were ten males and nine females in the group aged 15 to 18 years. One member of the group had Down Syndrome and the others had an undetermined cause of their ID. Within the group only one person was meeting the physical activity guidelines for health.

For people with ID, engaging in physical activity, exercise, and sport can provide physical, psychological, and social benefits. People with ID are known to have a higher prevalence of experiencing cardiovascular disease, hypertension, obesity, Type 2 diabetes and mental health difficulties (Taggart & Cousins, 2014). All of these conditions can, in some way, be prevented or alleviated by taking part in regular physical activity and exercise. As a preventative measure against some of the conditions listed above, the World Health Organization (WHO, 2012) recommended that adolescents between the ages of 13 and 19 years should take part in 60 minutes of moderate to vigorous intensity physical activity (MVPA) per day to decrease the likelihood of becoming obese and cut the risk of developing coronary heart disease and Type 2 diabetes. Despite this recommendation, the most recent report of MVPA in young people in the UK found only 33% of boys and 21% of girls met the government guidelines (British Heart Foundation, 2013).

Adolescents with ID are two or three times more likely to be obese than their non-ID peers (Rimmer, Yamaki, Davis Lowry, Wang, & Vogel., 2010). Also, adolescents with ID demonstrated up to 3.7 times lower levels of physical activity than their non-ID peers (Emerson & Glover, 2010). The positive relationship between physical activity and physical fitness in the non-ID adolescent is well documented (Lotan, Isakov, Kessel, & Merrick, 2004; Pahkala, Hernelahti, Heinonen, Raittinen, Hakanen, Lagström, Viikari, Rönnemaa, Raitakari, & Simell, 2013). This is no different for those with ID (Stanish & Temple, 2012), except that those with ID have been found to be significantly less physically fit than their non-ID peers (Lotan et al., 2004; Chow, Frey, Cheung, & Louie 2005; Oriel, George. & Blatt, 2008).

There are well-established barriers that people with ID face when trying to access sport and leisure services. These range from a lack of support, lack of tailored services, the absence of support for inclusive physical activity programmes and the stigma and other psychological obstacles that people with ID face on an almost daily basis. However, the right to participate in exercise, sport, and physical activity is enshrined within the United Nations Convention on the Rights of People with Disabilities (2006) Article 30.5. This legally binding international policy addresses the rights of people with disabilities with regard to sport. In particular it requires that children and adolescents with disabilities be included in physical education (PE) within the school system to the fullest extent possible and enjoy equal access to play. This legislation marks a step away from the historic framing of disability as a medically defined social welfare issue and towards a rights-based approach in support of inclusion (Nanverkis, Cousins, Válková, & MacIntyre, 2014).

For the majority of young people, sport and exercise is first introduced through physical education in school. Although the 2006 UN convention identified the population of people with disabilities as having the right to have equality of rights when it comes to sport and exercise, people with ID remain at particular risk of falling behind their peers when it comes to PE. Traditionally, young people with ID have been provided with their education in special education schools where curriculums are often tailored to particular groups or individuals which is dependent on their cognitive ability (Coates & Vickerman, 2010). Although there are some obvious advantages of receiving such a tailored programme, many special education schools remain focused on social education lessons that include teaching young people about their personal care and welfare, cooking, communication, and basic reading, writing, and arithmetic skills. Although vitally important, it can be purported that these areas of learning are often given precedence over PE and games. For one teacher in the special education school who was contacted during the preparation of this case study, PE plays 'second fiddle' to other subjects and was a constant source of frustration and 'a major barrier in promoting the physical health of the children I see every day'.

Within mainstream education (non-special education schools) PE is becoming increasingly recognized as a key worthwhile part of the curriculum. This has been acknowledged within the UK by a recent report conducted by the Office for Standards in Education (Ofsted, 2012) where, from the 230 schools inspected, three-quarters demonstrated teaching practices and PE lesson planning that were 'good' or 'outstanding'. While the same Ofsted Report acknowledged an improvement in PE practices in special education schools for students with ID, there were only seven such schools included in their report across England and Wales. Arguably this low number of visits by Ofsted (2012) to special education schools to assess the delivery of PE did not reflect the recommendations of the Every Child Matters document (ECM; Department of Education, 2005). ECM strongly advocated the inclusion and monitoring of PE in special education schools, and indeed for every child with a disability. Although ECM suggested that there is a change in focus and attitude in a favourable sense towards PE, there is qualitative evidence suggesting that for those children and adolescents with disabilities there is a tangible sense of anxiety associated with PE lessons. This is illustrated in an article from Fitzgerald and Stride (2012) who captured the thoughts of adolescents with physical disability on participation in PE. The adolescent remarks were quite profound as evidenced by the following comment:

> As I move into the sports hall eyes start staring. I feel like I'm in the middle of a big pride of lions, like the ones I saw on last night's programme, circling me, eyes staring intensely at me and only me. This isn't a friendly place to be, not for me. (p. 287)

There is an implication within the few lines of this testament that there is a major psychological element to taking part in PE for young people with disabilities. Arguably, when you consider PE within the world of education, you think about the physical health benefits and perhaps not so much what the psychological effects of participation are. Of course it is well documented that physical activity and exercise can enhance psychological factors such as self-efficacy (Lackaye, Margalit, Ziv, & Ziman, 2006) and self-determination (Hutzler & Korsensky, 2010), but is this the case for young people who have a disability who do not enjoy PE and refuse to take part for fear of how it will make them feel. Although the aforementioned article from Fitzgerald and Stride (2012) contains just a small number of stories such as the one we quote above, they capture the anxiety and trepidation associated with PE that many young people with disabilities face. To address these issues this chapter will present a case study that describes the methods of adopting a novel protocol to enhance participation in an exercise to test the fitness of adolescents with ID in schools during PE lessons.

INITIAL NEEDS ASSESSMENT

The school we go on to describe was included within a longitudinal research project which investigated the levels of physical activity, physical fitness, and psycho-social wellbeing of adolescents with ID. The present initial needs assessment was conducted by the first author and took place during the first introductory session with the adolescents in the school.

Attitude and reflections on PE experiences from the group

During this introductory session, the first author facilitated a focus group and recorded detailed notes regarding the attitudes and experiences the ID group had of taking part in PE. Real names of participants have been replaced by pseudonyms to protect confidentiality. Reflections made by some members of the group echoed findings from existing research carried out in non-ID adolescent cohorts of feeling embarrassed and anxious about taking part in PE class (Dwyer, Allison, Goldenberg, Fein, Yoshida, & Boutilier, 2005; Dwyer, Chulak, Maitland, Allison, Lysy, & Faulkner et al., 2012). One female member of the group commented: 'I felt like I was being watched and laughed at... the boys are better than us' (Chloe (Pseud.)). This was a reflection echoed by many of the group members and especially among the females. When asked what part of PE they didn't like another replied:

> 'It's too rough... I can't keep up with the boys.... I prefer other lessons in school' (Helen)

In contrast, one of the male members of the group said: 'I like PE. Especially football – we don't do it enough ... I would do PE all day' (James). This apparent difference in attitude towards taking part in PE between males and females is not a new phenomenon and has been reported elsewhere (Dwyer et al., 2005). Furthermore, the comments made by Chloe and Helen illustrate the reluctance to participate in activity that may be deemed as competitive. This had a direct effect on their attitude towards PE and they reported that they would often 'forget their PE kit on purpose!'

During the initial needs assessment process the participants in the ID group completed the self-report physical activity questionnaire (IPAQ-SF, Booth, Ainsworth, Pratt, Ekelund, Yngve, Sallis, & Oja, 2003). The results of these questionnaires, illustrated that the apparent reluctance to take part in physical activity and exercise was not altogether exclusive to school time. The male members of the group were reported to be taking part in some physical activity after school such as playing soccer, swimming, or weight training. All but one of the female participants recorded little or no physical activity after school. When asked for further explanation on why they did not partake in exercise the female members of the group stated that they were not enjoying exercise or that there was nothing for them to do or nowhere for them to go during the PE session.

Reflection from teachers

In addition to the thoughts and experiences of the ID group of students towards PE, the teacher who had responsibility for delivering PE in the special school was also asked to provide some reflections on the physical activity levels and the delivery of PE.

Teacher A was asked for his thoughts on the physical activity and fitness levels of the group and how he thought things might be improved:

> There is a difference between some of the more physically able and confident boys in taking part in PE ... we try to encourage participation in PE and after school clubs but often we have kids come in without kit or no-one to lift (pick up the children) after school.

The teacher was asked what prevented or made students with disabilities uncomfortable with exercise and taking part in PE:

> A lot of children associate PE with being competitive sport ... especially girls. The boys who play more sports get more out of PE ... You can see kids getting worried about it (PE) and their confidence drops which is so important in these kids (young people with ID).

When asked if the teacher felt there was enough curriculum time devoted to PE he replied: 'No. But teachers would tell you the same in mainstream schools. It's so important for these kids though as they are already disadvantaged.'

And regarding the issue of the lack of enjoyment associated with taking part in PE within this marginalized group of people the teacher commented:

> I don't think anyone can enjoy something they are uncomfortable with. Students who don't enjoy PE are the students who don't enjoy that competitive element. It's not for everyone ... But it should be ... Unfortunately we don't get the opportunity to change the mind-set (of the young people).

There is a recurring theme emerging here between the ID students and their teacher with regard to a certain level of anxiety associated with taking part in physical activity, exercise, and PE. This is displayed by students being unwilling to participate in PE lessons or physical activity outside school. This can perhaps be due to the lack of opportunities for PE teachers to teach these young people about the benefits of physical activity and not having enough time to provide lesson plans that include activities that avoid feelings of competiveness and anxiety. Therefore it was considered important to establish what skill levels those with ID have when it comes to PE.

Initial assessment of PE skills

An initial assessment of PE skills was carried out to establish if the group of participants within this case study would be able to complete a fitness test protocol. This protocol was designed to incorporate key fitness test components from various tests that had previously been employed to measure fitness levels in people with and without ID. Such fitness assessment tests included the Eurofit Battery Test (Salaun & Berthouze-Aranda, 2012) and the Presidential Fitness Test (PFT, Oriel, George, & Blatt, 2008). The critique of these established fitness tests when using them in vulnerable populations such as the one described here, are that they are 'clinical' in their format and there is no element of fun or enjoyment to encourage maximum participation and motivation to complete each element of the test. The fitness test protocol used in our case study, included elements that measured cardiovascular endurance, muscular endurance, flexibility and speed and co-ordination. These elements were incorporated into a circuit training session that also included elements of fun games and tasks to enhance participation and enjoyment (see Figure 20.1).

In order to provide an initial assessment of the skills required to complete the tasks, the first author demonstrated each 'station' of the circuit training activity. Particular attention was given to the stations that were being measured as part of the fitness test. Cardiovascular endurance was measured by a shuttle run, muscular endurance by a sit-up test, flexibility by a sit and reach test and speed and co-ordination by a short task-based speed activity. During the demonstration of these tasks it became evident that the majority of young people with ID had not completed these 'simple' gym tasks on previous occasions. On observation it was clear that many of the fundamental motor skills (e.g., agility, balance, co-ordination, and speed) involved in these tasks were not as easily performed when compared to participants in the study from the mainstream schools. This was most evident during the speed and co-ordination test (see Figure 20.2.).

This test required each participant to pick up and place down cones at designated points while running at speed. On observing this particular task it became apparent that many of the participants in the ID group stopped at each point to pick up and place a cone. In contrast, the preferred, more efficient method which was initially demonstrated to them was to pick up the cone and move towards the next target in one fluid motion. When this test was administered in mainstream schools, the young people without ID performed significantly quicker as they were able to adopt the correct motor skill to perform the task.

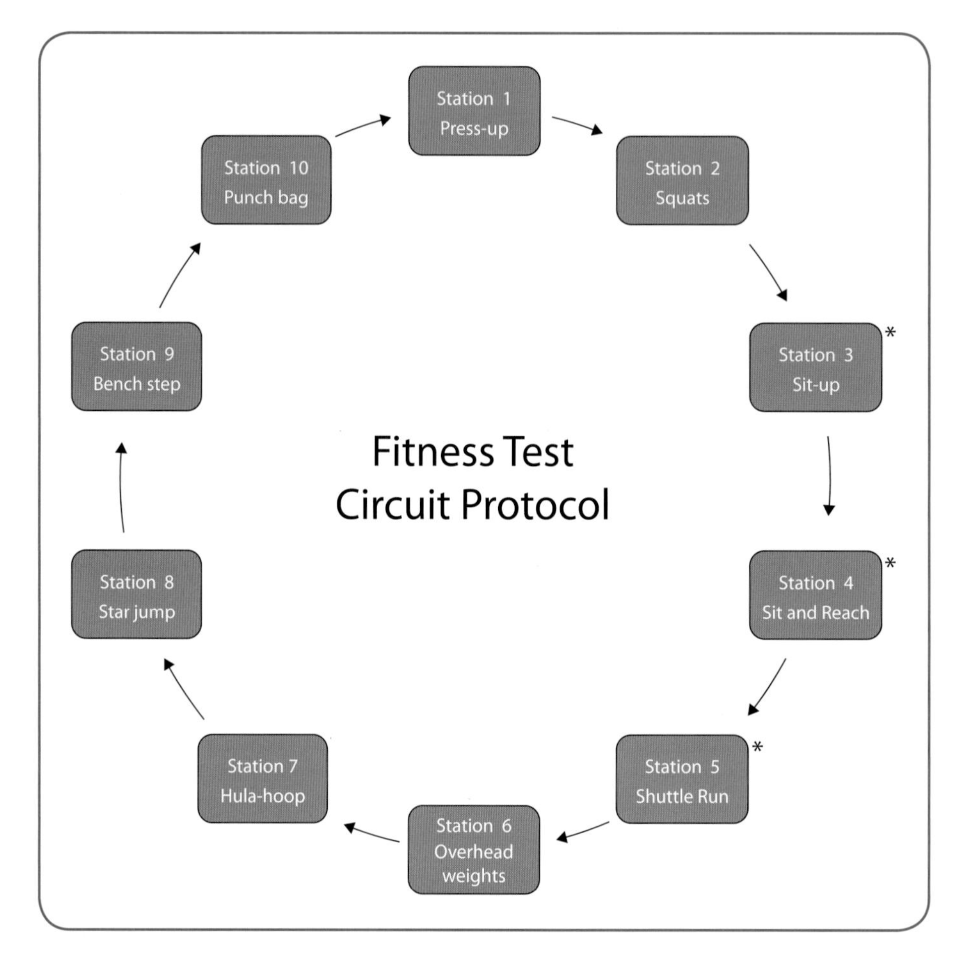

FIGURE 20.1 *Circuit training layout of the fitness test protocol.*

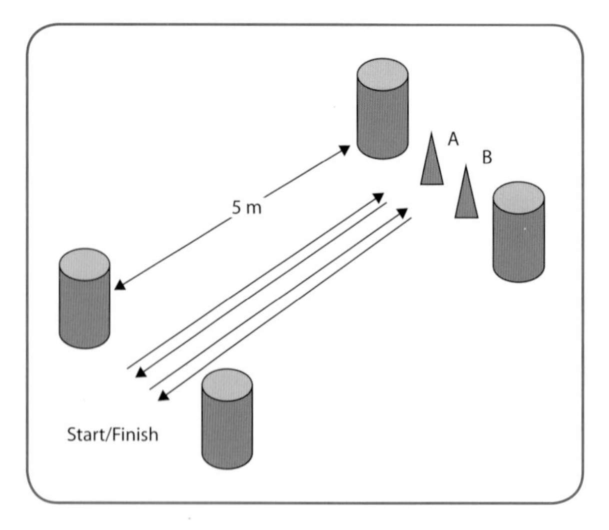

FIGURE 20.2 *Speed and co-ordination test*

This apparent difference in motor skill competence can perhaps be assigned to the lack of PE taught in school and therefore a lack of physical practice in such activities. A lower level of motor skill competence in young people with ID has been reported previously (Hartman, Houwen, Scherder, & Visscher., 2010; Westendorp, Houwen, Hartman, & Visscher, 2011; Chiviacowsky, Wulf, & Ávila, 2013; Capio, Poolton, Sit, Eguia, & Masters 2013). A study by Westendorp et al. (2011) examining gross motor skill function and participation in physical activity reported that children with mild-moderate ID (n = 156) have significantly poorer gross motor skills than their non-ID peers (n = 255). Furthermore, Westendorp et al. demonstrated that there was a significant positive relationship between motor skill function and participation in physical activity. A recommendation from Westendorp and colleagues was previously highlighted following the findings from Hartman et al. (2010) who found that early and prolonged interventions boosted motor development in children with ID. This is essential for future adoption and compliance of a physically active lifestyle.

Taken collectively the initial assessment conducted in the current case study illustrated the tangible need for enhanced participation levels in PE as reported in the literature. This is supported by the students' and teachers views' outlined earlier.

FRAMEWORK AND INTERVENTION

Two key theoretical approaches have informed this protocol to test the fitness of young people with ID. They are Self-efficacy Theory (Bandura, 1997) and Self-determination Theory (Deci & Ryan, 1985).

Self-efficacy Theory

Self-efficacy refers to beliefs in one's capabilities to organize and execute the courses of action required to produce given attainments (Bandura, 1997). There is evidence that demonstrates compared to their non-ID peers, adolescents with ID have lower levels of self-efficacy (Frederickson & Jacobs, 2001; Lackaye, Margalit, Ziv, & Ziman, 2006). For example, Lackaye et al. (2006) compared a group of adolescents with ID (n = 123) with a non-ID group (n = 123). Following completion of questionnaires in this cross-sectional study, the authors reported that the ID group presented a lower level of social, emotional, and academic self-efficacy. The authors argued that this was a worrying finding for an already vulnerable population and that further research should be conducted to find ways to encourage the enhancement of self-efficacy in this population and thus improve their psychological health and future opportunities. Furthermore, following a meta-analysis which found that effective interventions can enhance self-efficacy, Elbaum and Vaughn (2003) surmised that self-efficacy is a critical indicator for future wellbeing of people with ID. Moreover, the authors suggested that the tendency for young people with ID to fail to achieve personal goals such as securing paid employment, attending higher education, and being able to live independently, can in part be attributed to low self-efficacy.

Self-efficacy can affect an individual's ability to cope with the demands of maturing through adolescence and therefore influences the type of activities and social environments they engage in (Steinberg, 2008). Those adolescents with higher self-efficacy can reap the benefits with increased social status and functioning (Bandura, 1997). Therefore as physical activity facilitates higher levels of self-efficacy (Hepler & Chase, 2008; Heazlewood & Burke 2011), the importance of increasing participation in physical activity is all the more important. Given that the present ID group have had limited opportunities to take part in physical activity and PE, the self-efficacy levels of the group may therefore be compromised. It is important therefore that when the opportunity does arise to take an active part in PE or any form of physical activity, young people with ID are provided with lessons that promote inclusion and integration that will enhance belief in their physical activity capabilities. This promotion of inclusion was central to the design of the protocol we describe in this chapter.

Self-determination Theory

According to Deci and Ryan (1985) Self-determination Theory describes an individual's internal motivation to participate, learn, and to experience behaviours and outcomes (Wehmeyer & Schwartz, 1997). Self-determination is founded on the concept that humans are motivated by accomplishing three psychological needs of autonomy, competence, and relatedness (Deci & Ryan, 1985).

Definition/description box — BOX 20.1

SELF-DETERMINATION THEORY CONSTRUCTS

Autonomy
If a person has autonomy in choosing the activity themselves, versus someone choosing on their behalf they will be more intrinsically motivated to perform the activity.

Competence
If a person has a positive self-perception of their competence, and feels that they have mastered the performance of a goal-directed behaviour (e.g., successfully completing a drill during a PE lesson), they will be more inclined to be motivated to repeat that behaviour.

Relatedness
The construct of relatedness refers to the extent physical activity provides a feeling of connection with others within an activity context, for example a social connection to the teacher or classmates whilst participating.

When these three components are met, self-determined behaviour is said to occur. Having self-determined behaviour is important as studies in the field of sport and exercise show that more self-determined individuals report a greater feeling of acceptance within a group and a higher level of enjoyment in sport pursuits (Murcia, de San Romain, Galindo, Alonso, & González-Cutre, 2008). Arguably within the field of physical activity promotion, young people with ID are at a disadvantage with regard to achieving more self-determined behaviours because of the lack of opportunity to participate in PE and/or the perceived anxiety associated with participating in physical activity.

Following a systematic literature review investigating the correlates of physical activity in persons with ID, Hutzler and Korsensky (2010) concluded that heightened motivation to take part in physical activity facilitated improvements in perceived wellbeing, physical fitness, elevated skill level, and mediated the perception of self-efficacy and social competence. Outside the field of physical activity, higher levels of self-determination in adolescents with ID have been found to facilitate more 'positive adult outcomes' such as securing paid employment and earning a higher rate of pay (Wehmeyer & Schwartz, 1997). However, the notion of self-determined behaviour developing autonomy, competence, and relatedness is a vital one, especially in adolescents with ID who are particularly vulnerable. It is therefore important that self-determined focused interventions or programmes are sought for people with ID.

Although we have described two separate theories that have informed the protocol, both theories are linked. This linking relationship is described by Nouwen, Ford, Balan, Twisk, Ruggiero, & White (2011) who surmise that the common factor between self-efficacy and self-determination is the notion of perceived competence. Perceived competence is the belief in one's ability which is an integral role of self-efficacy. Nouwen and colleagues also found that the participants in their study who had higher levels of perceived self-competence were also more autonomous in choosing to lead healthy lifestyles. This close relationship between the theories was further demonstrated by Sweet, Fortier, Guerin, Tulloch, Sigal, Kenny, and Reid (2009) who recruited university students (n = 225) to compare results from individual self-efficacy and self-determination questionnaires and a questionnaire that integrated the two theories to establish if there was a difference in predicting physical activity behaviour. This study used the results of the individual self-efficacy and self-determination questionnaires to guide the design of an integrated questionnaire. The results confirmed the close relationship of the two theoretical approaches by demonstrating significant correlations between individual and integrated approaches in predicting physical activity levels.

BENEFITS OF PARTICIPATING IN PE

Reducing the psychological stress of 'competing' in PE through promoting inclusion and enjoyment may change the feelings and the relationship that young people with ID have with physical activity and exercise. In a qualitative study, Coates and Vickerman (2010) identified that PE in special education schools was popular with students when there was a 'games' element as opposed to a win/lose element. This games element prompted one participant in the Coates and Vickerman (2010) study to comment:

> The benefit of PE is that you're not all rubbing it in other people's faces and you're just having a go and working together as a team. (p. 1522)

This reflection demonstrated that when delivered in an appropriate way, PE can be inclusive and enjoyable. This is important if we are to encourage young people of all abilities to take part in and reap the rewards of more active lifestyles. Perhaps therefore PE is not the barrier as such but it is more the format of traditional PE lessons where there is a winner and a loser (Coates & Vickerman, 2010). It is apparent from the evidence presented in the earlier section that for young people with ID the design of physical activity intervention needs to be inclusive, enjoyable, and to a certain extent should avoid a win or lose scenario. This approach would foster a sense of interaction and solidarity which has also been observed by Stanish and Temple (2012). They described a 15-week peer-guided exercise programme where adolescents with ID were supported by their non-ID peers to participate in the team up for fitness programme in a familiar community setting. Following the successful completion of this programme Stanish and Temple (2012) stated:

> Exercise interventions for youth with intellectual disabilities are typically conducted under highly controlled conditions with less emphasis on creating the physical and social circumstances to support enhanced engagement. (p. 320)

This observation by Stanish and Temple (2012) succinctly describes a major issue with interventions that are designed for people with ID. In particular this statement can be applied to the methods which will now be discussed that have been used to assess the fitness of young people with ID.

In this following section we will provide a detailed description of the fitness test protocol which was used to achieve these aims but also how the protocol can act as a means of accurately testing the fitness levels of young people with ID. When used in subsequent research, this protocol can be used as a tool to assist in informing future research. This is important because being able to gauge the levels of fitness in vulnerable populations compared with their peers will help health workers identify and understand the similarities or disparity that exists between them.

Measuring fitness in adolescents with ID

The fitness level of adolescents with ID has been assessed in previous research (Oriel et al. 2008; Elmahgoub, Van de Velde, Peersman, Cambier, & Calders, 2012; Salaun & Berthouze-Aranda, 2012). From this research, there are a number of limitations that can be identified. A major limitation is that existing studies do not demonstrate a consistent method of measuring physical fitness and methods are often inappropriate for the vulnerable group of people we are concerned with. For example, the Eurofit test which was employed by Salaun and Berthouze-Aranda (2012) contained elements that could not be completed by a number of the ID participants despite the investigators making the recommended adaptations for the population of people with ID. Clearly, by setting tasks that cannot be achieved does not promote improvement in self-efficacy or indeed the for self-determination to take place. A further limitation, is the sense that testing physical fitness using formal, clinical environments is inappropriate for young people with ID. This clinical approach was adopted by Elmahgoub et al. (2012) who used a six-minute walking test to compare its reliability to the gold standard VO_2 max protocol to test physical fitness. One of the aims of the Elmahgoub et al. (2012) study was to ascertain if the walking protocol could replace the VO_2 max test to measure fitness levels in this population. The results from the two methods demonstrated a significant positive correlation in fitness level scores indicating that the walking test would be a reliable alternative. However, the six-minute walking test that they used asked the participants to walk up and down a school corridor for six minutes while the distance they walked in that time was monitored. One could question the validity and transferability of such a test as arguably such a protocol cannot reflect overall fitness that is required to complete many day-to-day tasks. In contrast the Hong Kong fitness assessment that was adopted by Frey and Chow (2006) suggested a more rounded multicomponent/activity fitness test. This test involved both cardiorespiratory and muscular endurance components in a similar fashion to the Eurofit test (Salaun & Berthouze-Aranda, 2012) and the Presidential Fitness Test that was used by Oriel et al. (2008) but had fewer tests which were shorter in duration. These shorter duration tests were first advocated by Johnson and Lavay (1989) when physical fitness testing in people with ID was first identified as being significantly underrepresented in existing literature. These points were considered when designing the fitness test protocol and therefore the following components were included into the protocol to measure key markers of physical fitness as informed by the Eurofit test and the Presidential Fitness Test. The four components that were included in the fitness test were; cardiovascular endurance, muscular endurance, flexibility, speed, and co-ordination. Adopting shorter components to test fitness (as per the Eurofit), than those required by more clinical tests (PFT) may promote higher levels of self-efficacy as the tests are more accessible and easier to complete. Furthermore, within our protocol the participants are taking part as a group which promotes self -determination through enhancing relatedness which Deci & Ryan (2000) described as a sense of community that is felt by the individual.

Measuring cardiovascular endurance

Cardiovascular endurance was measured using a shuttle run protocol which has been used previously in research relating to measuring fitness levels within this age group (Frey & Chow, 2006). The shuttle run protocol involved a ten-metre track measured between two points identified by two taped white lines. Each participant was instructed to run between the two lines as many times as possible over the course of 60 seconds. For the purpose of clarification each shuttle run was counted when a part of the participant's body touched the white line. The first author physically demonstrated an acceptable completed shuttle run using both his foot and outstretched hand to touch the line. The shuttle runs were counted by either a teacher or a classroom assistant during the circuit training protocol. Only fully completed shuttle runs were included in the final count. Once completed, the participants recorded the number of completed shuttle runs onto a fitness test score sheet.

Measuring muscular endurance

Muscular endurance was measured using a sit-up protocol. The primary rationale for using a sit-up protocol to test muscular endurance was because it was assumed that performing a sit-up would be a familiar exercise for school children to perform. However, as the initial assessment demonstrated this was not evident within the school included in this case study. Therefore the first author demonstrated the required method of completing a sit-up in the protocol before the testing took place. In this case the participants with ID were instructed to bend their legs at approximately 90 degrees with the feet flat on the floor and instructed to place the hands behind their head.

A sit-up was deemed to be complete when the participant's elbow touched the top of the participant's knee. To assist with the correct performance of the sit-up the feet were either secured by the lead investigator or a classroom assistant / teacher. During testing the participants were asked to complete as many sit-ups as they could in a one-minute period. The number of correctly completed sit-ups was then recorded onto the fitness test score sheet.

Measuring flexibility

Flexibility was measured using a sit and reach test that has been previously used in measuring flexibility in investigations within this age group of participants (Salaun & Berthouze-Aranda, 2012). The sit and reach test measures hamstring flexibility using a sit and reach box that incorporates a measuring gauge along the top of the apparatus. Sitting on the floor and with their legs in a straight position, the participants were asked to reach as far along the top of the box as they could. They were asked to perform this movement in a smooth fluid motion as opposed to an explosive 'jerk' along the measuring gauge. At the furthest point of the participants' reach they were asked to hold their position for two seconds. The score was then recorded on the fitness test proforma. Each participant attempted the test three times and the average was carried forward as the test result. Following a demonstration all participants were allowed a practice attempt to ensure the correct technique was adopted.

Measuring speed and co-ordination

Speed and co-ordination were measured using a simple, novel test that was designed by the first author to measure the ability to perform a basic co-ordination task while running at speed. A five-metre track was set up between two points indicated by white taped lines (see Figure 20.2). The participants were asked to sprint at full speed between the two points performing a total of four shuttle runs. Two small cones (objects A and B in Figure 20.2) were placed on the taped line opposite the start / finish line. The investigator started the test with '3, 2, 1, GO' and the participant was instructed to run and pick up the first cone (A) and return to the start / finish line where they would *place* the cone down on the white tape. They would then return to lift the second cone (B) before sprinting through the start / finish line where the test would end. The participants were instructed not to place the second cone on the white line but run straight through the finish line. A test would be re-run if there was a false start and / or if the first cone was not placed exactly on the white line. Recording of this test required a stopwatch and the result then recorded on the fitness test sheet. As with all other aspects of the fitness test, the first author demonstrated the speed and co-ordination test for the participants.

Circuit training

The fitness test components described above were incorporated into the circuit training session. The fitness testing took place within the gymnasium of the school that was participating in this case study. The circuit was split into ten 'stations' and at each station was a different exercise activity. Each station had an A4 sheet of laminated card with a written title of the activity to be performed at that station along with a pictorial representation of the activity. The components of the circuit session that were to be included in the fitness test were adjacent to each other to allow the first author to easily monitor that these tasks were being performed correctly. Before the participants began, the first author walked round the circuit with the participants to demonstrate the activity at each station. Participants were given time to practise at each station and ask questions.

Creating the right atmosphere

Before the fitness test protocol began the first author led a warm-up session which consisted of stretching exercises and games to allow the participants to feel comfortable in the environment. Music was played in the school gymnasium throughout the session for motivational purposes and water was provided for hydration.

Results from the pilot study

A pilot study was conducted to test the suitability of the protocol with those with ID. The fitness test results of a group of adolescents with ID (n = 16) were compared to a group of adolescents without ID (n = 16). The compliance rate of both cohorts was 100%. In all components of the protocol the non-ID group performed significantly better than their ID peers (see Table 20.1).

As discussed earlier, from previous research the lower fitness levels of non-ID adolescents are to be expected (Salaun & Berthouze-Aranda, 2012). However, in addition to being able to measure the fitness levels of this group of adolescents, the purpose of the protocol was to maximize compliance to the exercise. A subsequent focus group discussion following the completion of the pilot study confirmed that the participants were happy to participate, in particular there were:

Table 20.1 *Pilot study scores for those with and without ID performing the fitness test.*

	Shuttle run *(Number completed)*	***Sit-up*** *(Number completed)*	***Sit & reach*** *(Centimetres)*	***Speed / coordination*** *(Seconds)*
Adolescents with ID (n = 16)	27.50 *(27)*	18.00 *(27)*	10.5 *(25)*	9.71 *(5.79)*
Adolescents non-ID (n = 16)	36.43 *(7.35)**	27.00 *(13)***	16.0 *(9)**	*7.21(2.34)***

Values are median scores (range). Significant differences: * $p < 0.05$, ** $p < 0.01$

- No reports of feeling embarrassed by taking part in exercise with others, and
- None of the participants was worried or concerned about performing the tests following explanations of what was to be involved.

One of the participants commented before the test began: 'Looking forward to doing something different' (Helen). And following the test: 'I enjoyed the different parts...but I needed help to show me how to do some of the exercises' (David). Further experiences from the group are detailed later in the chapter.

REFLECTIONS

In this chapter we described a protocol that assessed the level of fitness of people with ID. This intervention was designed to address two issues. The first issue was the perceived lack of enjoyment and the associated anxiety when taking part in physical activity that some members of the group with disabilities that were involved in this case study reported. This led to a lack of participation in physical activity and PE. Second, we have referred to the lack of data available that can accurately report the levels of physical fitness in this vulnerable group of young people. To tackle both of these issues we presented a fitness test protocol that not only encourages full participation in an enjoyable physical activity but also allows researchers to gain valuable information on the fitness levels of young people with ID. This is achieved through incorporating both fun elements along with measurable fitness outcome components into our fitness test protocol.

We now turn to a discussion on how the protocol was delivered, the compliance to the activities involved in the circuit training, and reflections from the participants themselves on their experiences. The protocol was delivered during 'free time' that was normally allotted to students to use as a break from their daily lessons. This time, according to the participants, was normally used for 'surfing the internet' or 'hanging about with others on the course'. This period of school time was used so as not to cause disruption from other lessons and to avoid upsetting some members of the group whose daily school routine was vitally important to them.

Ensuring compliance to the fitness test

A number of methods were used to enhance and measure the compliance to the fitness test session.

1) Preparatory session

Before the fitness test the participants met the first author who provided an explanation, context and a rationale for conducting the fitness test. This session allowed the participants to ask questions and raise any concerns they had regarding the session. The majority of concerns raised related to the anxiety of being laughed at by their peers when undertaking the activity. These fears were allayed by explaining that all participants would be taking part in exercise at the same time as each other and therefore they would be involved in their own particular task of the circuit training session.

2) Fitness test proforma

During the fitness testing each participant was given a fitness test proforma that was used to record the results of each of the test components. This allowed the research team not only to be able to record the results but also as a means for the first author to check that each component was being performed correctly. The fitness test proforma was printed on A4 paper and the participants were asked to carry the sheet around with them throughout the session. On reflection it might have been more advantageous to keep a log of participants and their results at each of the fitness test component stations. During the session many of the participants would forget to take the sheet around with them and time between activities was taken for finding their fitness sheet as opposed to recovering and preparing for the next physical activity task. The fitness sheet particularly upset one participant who asked:

> What's fun about carrying round a sheet of paper?!(David)

On the other hand the first author observed that the fitness proforma, for some participants, acted as a visual prompt or motivating factor that allowed them to receive instant feedback from their efforts after completing each fitness test. This feedback feeds into the competence construct of Self-determination Theory where positive feedback satisfies an innate need of perceived competence (Deci & Ryan, 2000). Those who desired to do so were able to share their results with their peers which added an extra motivational factor to perform. Arguably, the fitness sheet also performed as an external focus of attention which was found to be a useful tool in this field of research. Work by Chiviacowsky et al. (2013) has demonstrated how an external focus of attention can enhance motor skill performance and learning in children with ID. Within their study Chiviacowsky et al. (2013) compared two groups of children with ID to perform tasks similar to those incorporated into our protocol, and found that those who were asked to focus on external factors when performing physical tasks, outperformed those who were asked to focus on internal factors such as their own physical movements.

3) Providing verbal cues to promote motivation to participate

Within Johnson and Lavay's (1989) guidelines for fitness testing for children with ID they explained the importance of verbal encouragement and praise to motivate the participants. This again has links with self-efficacy where verbal persuasion through external factors (such as verbal encouragement) or internal factors such as self-talk can enhance self-efficacious behaviour (Bandura, 1997) Providing verbal motivational cues was regarded to be particularly important considering the remarks provided by participants within the first section of this chapter where many participants admitted a lack of motivation to participate in exercise. Johnson and Lavay (1989) also recommended the combination of visual and verbal cues to the participants to assist in their full participation. Earlier in the chapter we have described how visual cues were provided by way of the physical demonstrations carried out by first author. Verbal cues were provided during the participation of the fitness test through the first author or a classroom assistant or teacher counting out loud the number of completed shuttle runs or sit-ups. This simple intervention provided the participant with immediate feedback indicating when they had performed a complete component of the exercise but it also provided motivation to better their friends' scores as they were able to communicate their achievements with each other throughout the session. Johnson's and Lavay's (1989) guidelines recommended that verbal counting was administered at a desired cadence or tempo while each student performed a sit-up. This recommendation was not adhered to as providing a regular tempo would have affected the performance of each participant. On reflection the verbal cues provided a valuable intervention to the participant.

Compliance to the fitness test

For this case study all participants completed all components of the fitness test protocol. We assigned this level of compliance to our protocol directly addressing the issues that had been identified through examining the existing literature and were perceived to be barriers to this vulnerable population to taking part in physical activity. Reflections from the participants themselves confirmed this suggestion in their comments following a subsequent visit by the first author to their school. Referring to the circuit training element of performing different exercises one participant remarked: 'I enjoyed the different games in the lesson' (Chloe). This was certainly something that the first author observed when leading the session. Elements such as the dancing station and the 'punch-bag' station were especially popular. The male participants especially enjoyed the 'free weight' components of the circuit training session. 'I enjoy the weights ... I would like to do more of that at a gym' (David).

This comment by David is particularly encouraging as it would appear that the protocol we delivered fostered some desire in him to further pursue the idea of going to a gym and taking part in more physical activity pursuits. 'It was fun. I liked the different parts to it ... I enjoy that kind of PE' (Helen). Although all participants completed all the elements of the fitness test some remained sceptical about their participation in physical activity: 'It was OK. I prefer the free time where I can hang out with my friends' (Rachel). Although Rachel's comment was not as positive as some of her classmates, further encouragement for the research team came from the fact that this intervention was delivered in 'free time' during school hours and therefore attendance at the session was not compulsory. This was made clear by the first author at the initial meeting with the group but all members of the group, including Rachel chose to participate in the fitness test protocol.

What would you do differently?

This chapter has described the theory, design, and piloting of a novel protocol to measure the physical fitness and encourage participation of young people with ID. Given the large positive relationship between physical fitness and health outcomes this protocol provides health researchers, PE teachers, and physical activity coaches with a new protocol to collect information about this vulnerable group. This protocol has application as it was designed through responding to flaws in previous literature to boost participation and through the use of a theoretical underpinning which is a new approach in the field of ID. The positive response of those who took part in the piloting of the protocol assures the acceptability of its use within the field of physical activity research. This is further enhanced by the 100% compliance rate in completing the protocol, albeit, with a relatively small number of participants.

Following the design of any protocol or intervention for vulnerable people, there are ways in which their development can be improved. In this case if we were to alter our approach to the protocol development, we would have engaged with participating individuals prior to the conception of the protocol to ask that they not only share their experiences about PE but also include them in the design of the protocol itself. This practice would have further related our method to self-determination theory through the participants being more autonomous in the design of the protocol. Meaning that, although a number of flaws and issues with previous physical fitness and activity exercises were considered during the design process, consulting with the target audience earlier would have allowed us to assess their ability to perform the tests and to some extent avoid the shortcoming issue of the comment relating to poor motor skill competence. There are also possible implications for self-efficacy here as the participants would have been assured that they would be able to perform the tasks asked of them. However, altering the test components too much may have raised question marks over the reliability of the test and the ability to use the protocol in other populations to compare different cohorts.

Finally, we recommend that when researchers, coaches, or teachers adopt this protocol or design new ones they should allow enough time to consult with participants about their ability to perform all tasks and build in time for extra practice and familiarization with the exercise. We also recommend that the process of designing physical activity programmes be based on a theoretical framework which can underpin the aims and objectives of the activity. This would enable coaches, teachers, and researchers to measure the effectiveness of their own given physical activity programme that in turn will further develop activities for vulnerable groups such as this one.

FURTHER READING

Coates, J., & Vickerman, P. (2010). Empowering children with special educational needs to speak up: Experiences of inclusive physical education. *Disability & Rehabilitation, 32*(18), 1517–1526. This article provides a background of the issues that young people with disabilities face associated with taking part in physical activity. The narrative of young people who were interviewed adds a powerful element that will enhance understanding of the issues vulnerable people face.

Stanish, H. I., & Temple, V. A. (2012). Efficacy of a peer-guided exercise programme for adolescents with intellectual disability. *Journal of Applied Research in Intellectual Disability, 25*(4), 319–328. Following a peer-guided programme for young people with ID, this article makes recommendations for furthering opportunities for this vulnerable group to take part in physical activity.

Taggart, L., & Cousins, W. (2013). Health promotion for people with intellectual and developmental disabilities. Maidenhead: McGraw-Hill Education. This book provides a comprehensive overview of the issues, difficulties, and barriers to health people with ID face on a daily basis. Chapters incorporate physical activity and health promotion in schools.

REFERENCES

Bandura, A. (1997). The anatomy of stages of change. *American Journal of Health Promotion, 12*, 8–10.

Booth, M. L., Ainsworth, B. E., Pratt, M.., Ekelund, U., Yngve, A., & Sallis, J. F. et al. (2003). International physical activity questionnaire: 12-country reliability and validity. *Medical Science in Sports and Exercise, 19*(5), 1381–1395.

British Heart Foundation (2013). *Children and young people statistics 2013*. Oxford; University of Oxford.

Capio, C. M., Poolton, J. M., Sit, C. H. P., Eguia, K. F., & Masters, R. S. W. (2013). Reduction of errors during practice facilitates fundamental movement skill learning in children with intellectual disabilities. *Journal of Intellectual Disability Research, 57* (4), 295–305.

Chiviacowsky, S., Wulf, G., & Ávila, L.T.G. (2013). An external focus of attention enhances motor learning in children with intellectual disabilities. *Journal of Intellectual Disability Research, 57*(7), 627–634.

Chow, B., Frey, G. C., Cheung, S., & Louie, L. (2005). An examination of health-related physical fitness levels in Hong Kong youth with intellectual disability. *Journal of Exercise Science and Fitness, 3*(1), 9–16.

Coates, J., & Vickerman, P. (2010). Empowering children with special educational needs to speak up: Experiences of inclusive physical education. *Disability & Rehabilitation, 32*(18), 1517–1526.

Deci, E. L., & Ryan, R. M. (1985) *Intrinsic motivation and self-determination in human behaviour*. New York: Plenum.

Deci, E. L., & Ryan, R. M. (2000). The 'what' and 'why' of goal pursuits: Human needs and the self-determination of behaviour. *Psychological Inquiry, 11*, 319–338.

Dwyer, J. J., Allison, K. R., Goldenberg, E. R., Fein, A. J., Yoshida, K. K., & Boutilier, M. A. (2005). Adolescent girls' perceived barriers to participation in physical activity. *Adolescence, 41*, 161, 75–89.

Dwyer, J. J., Chulak, T., Maitland, S., Allison, K. R., Lysy, D. C., & Faulkner, G. E. et al. (2012). Adolescents' self-efficacy to overcome barriers to physical activity scale. *Research Quarterly for Exercise and Sport, 83*(4), 513–521.

Elbaum, B., & Vaughn, S. (2003). For which students with learning disabilities are self-concept interventions effective? *Journal of Learning Disabilities, 36*(2), 101–108.

Elmahgoub, S. S., Van de Velde, A., Peersman, W., Cambier, D., & Calders, P. (2012). Reproducibility, validity and predictors of six-minute walk test in overweight and obese adolescents with intellectual disability. *Disability and Rehabilitation, 34*(10), 846–851.

Emerson, E., & Glover, G. (2010). *Health checks for people with learning disabilities. improving health and lives: learning disabilities observatory.* London: Department of Health.

Fitzgerald, H., & Stride, A. (2012). Stories about physical education from young people with disabilities. *International Journal of Disability, Development and Education, 59*(3), 283–293.

Frederickson, N., & Jacobs, S. (2001). Controllability attributions for academic performance and the perceived scholastic competence, global self-worth and achievement of children with dyslexia. *School Psychology International, 22*(4), 401–416.

Frey, G. C., & Chow, B. (2006). Relationship between BMI, physical fitness and motor skills in youth with mild intellectual disabilities. *International Journal of Obesity, 30*, 861–867.

Hartman, E., Houwen, S., Scherder, E., & Visscher, C. (2010). On the relationship between motor performance and executive functioning in children with intellectual disabilities. *Journal of Intellectual Disability Research, 54*(5), 468–477.

Heazlewood, I., & Burke, S. (2011). Self-efficacy and its relationship to selected sport psychological constructs in the prediction of performance in ironman triathlon. *Journal of Human Sport & Exercise, 6*(2), 328–350.

Hepler, T. J., & Chase, M. A. (2008) Relationship between decision-making self-efficacy, task self-efficacy and the performance of a sport skill. *Journal of Sports Sciences, 26*(6), 603–610.

Hutzler, Y., & Korsensky, O. (2010). Motivational correlates of physical activity in persons with an intellectual disability: A systematic literature review. *Journal of Intellectual Disability Research, 54*(9), 767–786.

Johnson, R. E., & Lavay, B. (1989). Fitness testing for children with special needs: An alternative approach. *Journal of Physical Education, Recreation & Dance, 60*(6), 50–53.

Lackaye, T., Margalit, M., Ziv, O., & Ziman, T. (2006). Comparisons of self-efficacy, mood, effort and hope between students with learning disabilities and their non-LD matched peers. *Learning Disabilities Research and Practice, 21*(2), 111–121.

Lotan, M., Isakov, E., Kessel, S., & Merrick, J. (2004). Physical fitness and functional ability of children with intellectual disability: Effects of a short-term daily treadmill intervention. *The Scientific World, 4*, 449–457.

Murcia, J. A. M., de San Romain, M. L., Galindo, C. M., Alonso, N., & González-cutre, D. (2008). Peers' influence on exercise enjoyment: A self-determination theory approach. *Journal of Sports Science and Medicine, 7*, 23–31.

Nankervis, K., Cousins, W., Válková, H., & Macintyre, T. (2014). Physical activity, exercise, and sport. *Health Promotion for People with Intellectual and Developmental Disabilities* (pp. 174–182). Maidenhead: McGraw-Hill/ Open University Press.

Nouwen, A., Ford, T., Balan, A. T., Twisk, J., Ruggiero, L., & White, D. (2011). Longitudinal motivational predictors of dietary self-care and diabetes control in adults with newly diagnosed type 2 diabetes mellitus. *Health Psychology, 30*(6), 771.

Ofsted (2012). *Beyond 2012, Outstanding physical education for all.* Manchester: Ofsted.

Oriel, K. N., George, C. L. & Blatt, P. J. (2008). The impact of a community based exercise program in children and adolescents with disabilities: A pilot study. *Physical Disabilities: Education and Related Services, 27*(1), 5–20.

Pahkala, K., Hernelahti, M., Heinonen, O. J., Raittinen, P., Hakanen, M., & Lagström, H., et al. (2013). Body mass index, fitness and physical activity from childhood through adolescence. *British Journal of Sports Medicine, 47*, 71–77.

Parliament. House of Commons. Education, & Skills Committee. (2005). *Every child matters.* (Vol. 2). London: The Stationery Office.

Rimmer, J. H., Yamaki, K., Davis Lowry, B. M., Wang, E., & Vogel. L. C. (2010). Obesity and obesity related secondary conditions in adolescents with intellectual/developmental disabilities. *Journal of Intellectual Disability Research 54*(9), 787–794.

Salaun, L., & Berthouze-Aranda, S. E. (2012). Physical fitness and fatness in adolescents with intellectual disabilities. *Journal of Applied Research in Intellectual Disabilities, 25*(3), 231–239.

Stanish, H. I., & Temple, V. A. (2012). Efficacy of a peer-guided exercise programme for adolescents with intellectual disability. *Journal of Applied Research in Intellectual Disability, 25*(4), 319–328.

Steinberg, L. (2008). A social neuroscience perspective on adolescent risk-taking. *Developmental Review, 28*(1), 78–106.

Sweet, S. N., Fortier, M. S., Guerin, E., Tulloch, H., Sigal, R. J., & Kenny, G. P., et al. (2009). Understanding physical activity in adults with type 2 diabetes after completing an exercise intervention trial: A mediation model of self-efficacy and autonomous motivation. *Psychology, Health & Medicine, 14*(4), 419–429.

Taggart, L., & Cousins, W. (Eds.) (2014). *Health promotion for people with intellectual disabilities*. Maidenhead: Open University Press/McGraw-Hill.

United Nations Convention on the Rights of Persons with Disabilities (2006). Retrieved November 2014 from http://www.un.org/disabilities/convention/conventionfull.shtml.

Wehmeyer, M., & Schwartz M. (1997). Self-determination and positive adult outcomes: A follow-up study of youth with mental retardation or learning disabilities. *Exceptional Children, 63*(2), 245–255.

Westendorp, M., Houwen, S., Hartman, E., & Visscher, C. (2011). Are gross motor skills and sports participation related in children with intellectual disabilities? *Research in Developmental Disabilities, 32*(3), 1147–1153.

World Health Organization (WHO) (2012). World Health Statistics 2012. World Health Organisation.

21 Exercise and Body Image

Ruth Lowry

LEARNING OBJECTIVES

AFTER READING THIS CHAPTER YOU SHOULD BE ABLE TO:

1. Critically evaluate the main theoretical approaches to psychological interventions for clients with body-image concerns.
2. Demonstrate understanding of the methods and techniques presented to extend previous knowledge and apply to working with clients who have body-image concerns.
3. Consider the various psychological issues that may be presented during the consultation process that practitioners may have to respond to.

AREAS TO CONSIDER WHEN READING THE CHAPTER:

1. How a sport and exercise psychologist might approach body image with a client.
2. How you might deal with the sequencing of sessions to explore the reframing of body-image concerns.
3. What body image and exercise issues are outside the boundaries of expertise of a sport and exercise psychologist.

CLIENT AND BACKGROUND

The case study described in this chapter is a hypothetical client called 'Tara'. The information presented regarding the intervention is therefore the approach that the author would take with a client presenting with such issues.

Tara is a 35-year-old female, married mother of a five-year-old daughter who works full-time in a middle management position within the civil service. She regards herself as a regular exerciser completing three gym sessions per week of 30 to 40 minutes (excluding the warm up and cool down), at a moderate intensity, using mainly cardiovascular equipment. As part of her daily commute to work, she walks approximately 20 minutes (at a brisk pace) from the train station to her workplace and the same on her return. She is 5 feet 7 inches and weighs approximately 14 stone 1lb (BMI = 30.8 which is in the obese category). She has been a member of her local fitness club for seven years. However, in recent months her resolve to exercise has waned and she describes exercise now as an effort. She was a competitive netball player during her years in education, representing her school and university at inter mural and national competitions. In the early years after graduation she moved several times for work reasons and attributes this as a barrier to remaining involved in competitive sport.

Missing the camaraderie of team sport and training sessions, she joined gyms but does admit to feeling isolated and increasingly awkward around other club members. During her university years, Tara describes her physique as being muscular and lean that required little effort to maintain but in the years that have followed she has struggled with her weight and muscle tone. She put on what she regards as excessive weight (approximately three stone) in the early years after university which she attributed to long hours at work (office based), not taking care of her diet or alcohol intake and doing little physical activity in her spare time. When Tara decided she needed to do something to address her weight she restricted her calorie intake and did intense cardiovascular based exercise for an hour most days of the week. This method she says led to quick weight loss which she found gratifying and so increased the amount of exercise and restricted her food intake further. Tara admits that she did little research into how to approach her weight loss, as she didn't want to disclose to others that she had weight problems. After experiencing 'dizzy spells' at work and feeling a lack of control emotionally, Tara eased back from her restrictive diet and exercise routine, at her lowest weight, nine years ago, she was 7 stone and 8 pounds (BMI = 16.6, underweight classification). This was around the time she met her husband and this relationship occupied more of her time. Since her marriage her weight has gradually crept up but she has not tried to diet to the same extent as before saying that family life and work get in the way. She also does not want to become a cliché of a woman in her thirties and forties who is known as 'the dieter'. At present Tara feels that whilst she is never going to be the size she was, her current dress size of 14, 'is as good as it will get' in terms of her overall size. She expresses that her anxieties now lie in how her body changed after losing weight, followed by the birth of her daughter who is now five years old and the latest weight gain. Tara feels as if she has little control in terms of the muscle tone and places where her body is changing. She feels as if she is losing a feminine shape and does not 'feel comfortable in her own skin'. Whilst she indicates that she is happy with the other areas of her life, she does feel that her body concerns are increasingly harder to hide from her husband and those close to her. Tara says she is reluctant to speak to her husband, family, or friends about her concerns as they will simply tell her she should be happy with the way she is. She thinks that having body-image problems, when she is 'just a bit overweight' will be regarded as a trivial issue by others. She finds that exercising at the fitness centre is eroding what confidence she has. Tara is also concerned that her own issues may be passed on to her daughter and is concerned about the way her daughter speaks about weight.

DEFINING BODY IMAGE

Body image refers to how individuals think, feel, and consequently behave in relation to their body shape and features that constitute physical appearance (Bulik, 2012). When working with clients there is a need to understand the multiplicity of issues that might be revealed during consultation. A common misconception is that body image concerns diminish with age. However, as Veale, Willson, and Clarke (2009) indicate, if a woman's self-worth has been based on appearance it is doubtful that this will change as she ages. Whilst there is consistent research evidence that exercise has a positive influence on body image (Campbell & Hausenblas, 2009; Hausenblas & Fallon, 2006), it is not unusual to find exercisers with body-image concerns. An assumption is that as fitness improves, body image will also change positively but this is not necessarily the case. It is more probable that the perception of meaningful change in body shape, strength, and fitness is more strongly correlated than image, therefore any assessment should seek to clarify the exerciser's body shape goals before developing an intervention (Martin Ginis & Bassett, 2011).

INITIAL NEEDS ASSESSMENT

Burns and Nolen-Hoeksema (1991) suggested that the strongest predictor of an effective outcome is the quality of client engagement. Relationships are reciprocal encounters, therefore it is necessary to consider the role a client will play as well as that of the sport and exercise psychologist. Therefore the aim of conducting the initial needs assessment is not simply to diagnose but more importantly to communicate the approach adopted and to establish rapport and trust with the client. Bordin (1979) regarded the therapeutic relationship as a 'working alliance' whereby the client and practitioner agree on the goals, tasks, and bonds (based on trust and commitment). It is this working alliance that will be central to the effectiveness of the intervention and without the establishment of mutual respect and value whatever approach is employed is unlikely to enable positive change in the client. This initial meeting and needs assessment might last between one and a half and two hours to enable the time and space needed without feeling pressured to hurry through the various agenda items.

The initial needs assessment or formulation would be conducted through the use of semi-structured interviewing. Bruch and Prioglio (2006) argue that a *symptom-technique matching* approach to psychological intervention is rather superficial and by using the scientist-practitioner model (Kennedy & Llewelyn, 2001) of formulation, the relative complexity of the case can be fully explored. Given that Tara's case presented affective, behavioural, and cognitive (ABC) components, it was necessary to consider multiple hypotheses and prioritize these to form an effective intervention. Whilst Cash (2008) recommends the multi-dimensional assessment of body-image components to provide a comprehensive understanding of body-image concerns (for a list of validated measures see http://www.body-images.com/assessments/), I am reluctant to formally use multiple psychometric measures at this early stage when establishing rapport with a client and also where there is ambiguity regarding the precise nature of the issues that may emerge (Harwood, 2009). Rather I prefer to explore topics such as body-image evaluations (satisfaction-dissatisfaction), cognitions, emotions, self-concept investment, quality of life, coping strategies and exercise behaviour through semi-structured interviewing, elaboration, and clarification probes (Patton, 2002). It should be noted that diet was a factor with this particular case, an area not included in the competencies of a sport and exercise psychologist, and so Tara was encouraged to seek the support of a suitably trained dietitian.

My initial discussion with Tara was to establish why she had decided to seek assistance from a psychologist to gain a clear understanding of what goals she had and thereby gauge how achievable these were. During this discussion, I asked her if she had any past experience of psychological support and/or what her impressions of psychological support were. With this particular topic it is important to clarify if she is primarily seeking support to change her body (weight-loss strategies) or her mind (acceptance of her current body appearance). Without this clarification of her desires and my approach, there is the possibility that the two are incompatible and she disengages from the intervention. After this, I clarified my position and hers by explaining that she should regard herself as an active agent in a collaborative process rather than the passive recipient of my help. I encouraged Tara to ask questions and seek clarity of the terminology I used. Exploring areas in an open-ended way assisted Tara in comprehending her situation and thereby creating a climate of supportive enquiry during the intervention. Without warmth, empathy, and unconditional regard, during this process I would be unable to foster a climate where Tara would be 'willing to reveal personally significant material, [or] to carry out frightening and difficult new behaviours and to feel safe' (Westbrook, Kennerley, & Kirk, 2011, p. 32). Through the use of open-ended questions during the initial interview, the aims were to seek greater understanding of the following areas: (a) what problems she had experienced, (b) if these problems are mainly psychological, behavioural, social, or a combination, (c) what she regarded as the reasons for the development of these problems, and (d) what issues Tara attributed as responsible for the maintenance of these problems (refer to Bruch & Prioglio, 2006). By listening carefully for I was able to gather any expressions of irrational beliefs (Ellis, 1962, 1993), contradictory beliefs (cognitive dissonance, Festinger, 1962), ambivalence, and readiness to change (Miller & Rollnick, 2002).

This line of questioning during the initial meeting was to establish her interpretation of the circumstances surrounding her physical appearance. To gain more detail I used closed, probing questions that established the type, severity, frequency, duration, and context of her thoughts, emotions, and behaviours (Morrison, 2014). By using these questions I was able to build a comprehensive picture of how Tara views the circumstances surrounding her weight status, namely, the antecedents, behaviours, and consequences.

The final stage of the initial needs assessment was to return to the original opening question asked. I rephrased this by asking Tara what she hoped to gain as a result of seeking psychological assistance. By asking her to restate this I was able to identify if Tara's original goals had changed, become more detailed, or changed in terms of priority. Whilst she had initially considered that the purpose of seeking assistance was to provide strategies to plan her immediate weight-loss goals and increase her physical activity levels (in the hope this would make her happier about her appearance) by the end of this initial session she expressed her willingness to engage in a mind to body approach and seek to understand more fully her negative views about her physical appearance.

Findings of the needs assessment

A calculation of Tara's current levels of physical activity would suggest that she is participating in sufficient planned leisure exercise and active commuting to meet the current UK government recommendations of 150 moderately intense minutes of physical activity for physical health benefits (Department of Health (DOH), 2011). If her perception of 'brisk' is at a moderate level, Tara's active commuting to and from work is sufficient to achieve the 150 minutes (200 minutes completed, in blocks greater than ten minutes). For this reason I would regard her as an active individual. My concern for her health status is that she should minimize the amount of time spent

Definition/description box

BOX 21.1

EXAMPLES OF OPEN-ENDED QUESTIONS USED

Question: Tell me about the issues you have been experiencing.
Rationale: Used to establish why the client decided to seek assistance at this stage in her life and gain a more comprehensive picture of what she considered to be the main issues of concern.
Listening out for: Comments regarding what component(s) of body image concerned her and how these cognitions or emotions affect her quality of life, relationships and general psychological wellbeing.

Question: What do you believe are the underlying problems?
Rationale: Used to explore how complex and interwoven the client believed the issues to be. For example, did she believe that her body image concerns were triggered by particular contexts (such as the gym) or are they more pervasive?
Listening out for: What initially the client was willing to articulate as the underlying reasons. This will provide me with an early indication of what she was comfortable to discuss and what areas might cause resistance later in the intervention process. These disclosed areas provided insight into what is expressed as a priority for Tara and therefore what aspects of the issue she is willing to address first.

Question: Can you explain to me what you think may have led to these problems developing?
Rationale: Used to establish how the client rationalized what had happened to her over the years with regard to her exercise involvement, changes in weight and attitudes towards her body.
Listening out for: By asking this question the aim was to understand what Tara's working hypotheses were regarding the causal attributions made between the factors identified. By reflecting back to the previous questions, areas of contradiction and ambivalence in her thought processes were identified.

Something for the reader to try: Now for the next question, can consider what you should be listening out for and why as a psychologist?
Question: What aspects of your life do you think continue to thwart your best efforts to change?
Rationale: Used to explore the barriers and facilitators of past attempts to change and her current situation to establish her patterns of thinking and the extent of her repertoire of coping strategies Tara had employed and whether these are adaptive or maladaptive.

Activity: Now consider what additional open-ended questions you could ask Tara at this initial stage and the rationale and listening points are for these questions.

sitting at work and at home and that she incorporates muscle strengthening exercises into her exercise routine (in keeping with the wider DOH, 2011 recommendations). Her previous strategy to lose weight might have been successful in terms of reaching a target weight. However by restricting her diet and exercising intensely this is not an approach to endorse for the future. The UK National Health Service Choices (2012) currently suggests that weight loss of 0.5 to 1 kg (1 to 2 pounds) per week is appropriate for adults. Given her previous self-directed attempts at calorie restriction, I would advise Tara to speak with a dietitian to understand her energy intake and see if there are areas that might help to explain her gradual weight gain and how weight loss might be best achieved. Her current level of physical activity would not be sufficient to achieve loss of the weight regained over recent years and to move from her current BMI group of obese to normal (between a BMI of 18.5 to 24.9 or a weight of 8 stone 6 pounds to 11 stone 6 pounds; NHS Choices,

2014). Those who have lost weight need to engage in as much as 60 to 90 minutes of activity per day to maintain weight loss in the absence of reductions of energy intake (DOH, 2011; Schoeller, Shay, & Kushner, 1997).

Another issue related to Tara's case is her reported diminishing enthusiasm for exercise. Using the Self-determination Theory (Deci & Ryan, 1985, 2000), it could be argued that Tara is not intrinsically motivated towards her current exercise routine but rather views exercise as a regulated behaviour. It may be that this regulation is resulting in less effort during exercise sessions which means there is less return (body shape improvement) on the investment of time. It may also be the case that Tara is experiencing a lack of need fulfilment in her current exercise in comparison to her exercise past (relatedness of netball team, competence of seeing success in terms of body shape changes or competition). Two elements of Tara's case to note that may present difficulties during the consultation process are the strategies to control body shape in the past and her reluctance to share the issue with others.

FRAMEWORK AND INTERVENTION

As stated in the previous section, approaches to intervening with clients who present with body-image concerns tend to be divided into two groups, those that seek to change the body and those that seek to change the mind. In addition there is a recent increase in the need to consider prevention strategies for young people in particular (Cash & Smolak, 2011). Body Image is not a one-dimensional construct but rather a multifaceted and complex issue that can often challenge the individual's self-concept and identity. Fox (2000) explains, 'The physical self has occupied a unique position in the self-system because the body, through its appearance, attributes and abilities provides the substantive interface between the individual and the world' (p. 230). Therefore it is plausible that issues other than just body-related concerns will also need to be addressed. An example of this complexity is the link made between body weight, body image, and wellbeing, whilst achieving and maintaining a 'healthy weight' status is associated with certain health benefits. It is not a precursor to body acceptance or to psychological wellbeing. The present intervention is based on a cognitive-behavioural approach.

Behaviourism suggests that an individual's learnt actions can be understood by the rewards and reinforcements available, the schedule of reinforcement, and the client's repertoire of previous responses in similar contexts (McLeod, 2008). The cognitive principle suggests that the client's emotional and behavioural responses to an event are largely influenced by their cognitions (beliefs, interpretations). When cognitions are 'crooked' they will result in maladaptive behaviour and emotions (Ellis, 1962). In a meta-analysis of published body-image treatments, Jarry and Berardi (2004) concluded that the majority of interventions with non-clinical populations (for example clients did not have a clinical eating disorder) have been underpinned by cognitive-behavioural principles and have had long-term success. An eight-step cognitive-behavioural intervention was developed for Tara based on Cash (2008) and colleagues. This approach was developed in the 1980s and since then has been evaluated as an effective minimal strategy for the reduction of body-image disturbance without weight loss (Cash & Hrabosky, 2003; Cash & Lavallee, 1997). The approach has similarities to other cognitive-behavioural interventions, namely cognitive dissonance (Stice, Shaw, Black Becker, & Rohde, 2008), mindfulness (Crane, 2009) and acceptance and commitment therapy (Hayes, Strosahl, & Wilson, 2011).

Definition/description box

BOX 21.2

BRIEF OUTLINE OF THE EIGHT-STEP SELF-DIRECTED PROGRAMME FOR BODY IMAGE CONCERNS (CASH, 2008)

- Step 1 – Self-discovery
  - Exploring strengths and weaknesses in relation to body image.
- Step 2 – Origins of negative body image
  - Exploring the underlying causes of negative associations with the body.
- Step 3 – Mindfulness and acceptance
  - Exploring the day-to-day experiences using self-monitoring.
- Step 4 – Private body talk
  - Addressing dissonance in self-talk to alter dysfunctional schemas and the potential influence on wider wellbeing and self-concept.
- Step 5 – Modifying mental mistakes
  - Continuing to explore own body self-talk and the associated thought patterns.
- Step 6 – Body-image avoidance
  - Addressing the avoidant behaviours engaged in to cope with negative thoughts and emotions. During this time attention will be given specifically to physical activity involvement.
- Step 7 – Body-image rituals
  - Addressing negative body image rituals such as appearance checking or camouflaging.
- Step 8 – Being kind to your body
  - Positive body image experiences including reaffirming involvement in physical activity.

(Cash, T. F. (2008). *The body image workbook: An 8-step program for learning to like your looks* (2nd Ed.) Oakland, CA: New Harbinger Publications)

The approach set out in this section is a description of the Cash (2008), eight-step cognitive-behavioural approach, but this has been modified and whilst it was conducted over eight sessions these do not map directly to Cash's approach. In the description below, I specify when and why I have deviated from Cash's steps (e.g., Steps 7 and 8 were combined into one; Session 7 described here took the form of a review of Tara's available social support which was not part of Cash's approach). My reasons for adapting and deviating from Cash's approach was an ongoing response to the issues raised during the consultation as well as my own reading and training regarding body-image interventions. The contents of each session are outlined below.

Session 1 – self-discovery

Cash (2008) recommends conducting a comprehensive body-image audit which provides a useful overview of various dimensions of body image including body areas of concern, frequency of negative body-image thoughts, situations that may cause anxiety in relation to appearance evaluations, the relative importance of physical appearance to self, coping strategies when facing appearance related challenges or threats, and body-image quality of life. Using these methods with Tara allowed her the space to complete these with little interruption to ensure that she has the time to reflect on the various dimensions. Rather than giving these as tasks to complete in her own time (after the initial needs assessment), these were completed during the first session so I could provide support and clarification whilst she completed them.

Definition/description box **BOX 21.3**

BODY IMAGE QUESTIONNAIRES USED (PROVIDED IN FULL IN CASH, 2008)

Body-image areas evaluation: Ten body image areas are listed and the individuals are asked to rate their level of satisfaction on a - point scale (very dissatisfied to very satisfied). This will indicate what specific areas are of concern to the individual.

Body-image cognitions: Individuals are presented with a 20-item list of thoughts concerning their body and are asked to indicate how frequently they experience such thoughts in the last month (rarely/never, once every several days or daily). These thoughts include 'I can't stand my appearance anymore', 'I wish I was better looking' and "I wish I looked like someone else.'

Body-image distress: This 20-item measure examines the situations an individual might experience that causes them distress (mirror, social gatherings, shopping for clothes and watching TV). Again individuals are asked to indicate how frequently in the last month they have experienced distress.

Appearance importance: This is a true or false list of 12 beliefs regarding the importance of physical appearance. Beliefs include, 'If I like how I look on a given day, it's easy to feel happy about other things' and 'My physical appearance has a big influence on my life.'

Body image coping: Individuals use various strategies to cope with poor body image. Twenty-nine coping strategies are listed which reflect: appearance fixing (I think about what I should do to change my looks), experiential avoidance (I avoid looking at myself in mirrors), and positive rational acceptance (I remind myself that I feel better after a while). Individuals are asked to indicate if these strategies are most like them or mostly not like them.

Body image quality of life: This assesses how body image affects various aspects of life (my relationships with friends, my day-to-day emotions, my ability to control my weight). Containing 19 items, the client is asked if these areas have a negative, positive, or no effect on their life.

Each of the tests is scored and the total score is then coded into an acceptance, risky, or problem zone thereby providing a comprehensive picture of what aspects of body image are of particular concern.

(Cash, T. F. (2008). *The body image workbook: An 8-step program* for learning to like your looks (2nd Ed.) Oakland, CA: New Harbinger Publications.

Once Tara had completed the various elements and her responses were scored, I compiled them into a summary profile which was coded into three zones, scores indicative of body-image acceptance, risk, and problems. By using this method it was visible what areas Tara indicated to be causing her the most concern and therefore what we needed to pay particular attention to. I asked Tara to examine the body-image profile and talk through what her impressions of the findings were. For example, I asked if this confirmed her previously-held views or if anything surprised her. After the initial first response of pointing out the 'danger', problem areas (see Table 21.1), I asked her not just to focus on problem zones of the profile but also to consider areas within these evaluations that were of particular concern. This process revealed a few areas that were worth considering for future meetings.

Table 21.1 *Summary of Tara's body image profile results.*

Body-image test scores	*Acceptance zone*	*Risky zone*	*Problem zone*
	Body image zones		
Body-image evaluation __4__ + __4__ = __8__	0 1	2 3 4 5	6 7 **8** 9 10 11 12 13 14 15 16 17 18 19 20
Body-image thoughts __15__ + __10__ = __30__	0 1 2 3 4 5	6 7 8 9 10 11 12 13 14 15 16 17	18 19 20 21 22 23 24 25 26 27 28 29 **30** 31 32 33 34 35 36 37 38 39 40
Body-image distress __14__ + __12__ = __26__	0 1 2 3 4 5	6 7 8 9 10 11 12 13 14 15 16 17	18 19 20 21 22 23 24 25 **26** 27 28 29 30 31 32 33 34 35 36 37 38 39 40
Appearance importance	0 1 2	3 4 5 6	7 8 **9** 10 11 12
Body-image coping			
Appearance fixing	0 1 2	3 4 5 6	7 **8** 9 10
Experiential avoidance	0 1	2 3 4 **5**	6 7 8
Positive rational acceptance	11 10 9 8 7	6 5 **4** 3	2 1 0
Body-image quality of life			
Negative impact	0 1	2 3 4 5 6 7	8 9 10 11 12 13 **14** 15 16 17 18 19
Positive impact	19 18	17 16 15 14 13 12	11 10 9 8 7 6 **5** 4 3 2 1 0

In a number of the questionnaires it was evident that Tara avoided looking at her appearance in mirrors and situations where this might occur were avoided (such as shops, gyms). Her ratings suggested that she did not evaluate or think of her body in relation to others but that she feared the evaluation of her own body by others. The body areas of particular concern were the mid- and lower torso.

At the end of the session, I gave Tara a blank journal and asked her to consider this as a means of journaling her thoughts, emotions, and behaviours (considering some of the issues identified through the Body Image Profile) over the time we would be meeting. I emphasized that in addition to tasks and exercises that I would be giving her she could use the journal to record her own thoughts and observations that she may want to discuss in future sessions. Finally to progress forward I asked Tara to consider what goals she could set for herself in each of the areas assessed and to write these down in her journal. These were phrased as 'I need to…'. One example of a goal set was, 'I need to … stop thinking about the body I had as a teen, that was a different time and I need to work with what I've got now.'

Session 2 – origins of negative body image

The aim was to explore the origins and development of her body-image concerns and how this might have influenced her thoughts, emotions, and behaviours (including her exercise history). For this session I deviated from Cash's workbook and employed a more visual technique of a timeline. To aid her memory and reduce cognitive defences such as resistance (Walker, 1982), I asked Tara to bring along photographs of herself at various points in her life where she had been positive or negative about her appearance (Berman, 1993). These photographs were combined with the use of a lifeline or timeline (Gramling & Carr, 2004). I used a large landscape noticeboard and an assortment of coloured markers. Drawing a horizontal timeline along the bottom of the board, I indicated key age milestones that she had disclosed in previous sessions (early childhood, late childhood, adolescence, university years, early adulthood, dating, marriage, pregnancy, motherhood and present day). I then asked Tara to post the pictures she had brought along on the timeline (above the timeline). The remainder of the board was then divided into layers of influencing factors (personality, physical body changes, other people, and the wider world). Integrated models of the exercise and health literature such as the ecological model (Evans, Roy, Geiger, Werner, & Burnett, 2008), the biopsychosocial model (Rodgers, Paxton, & McLean, 2013) or social cognitive theory (Dzewaltowski, Noble, & Shaw, 1990) would argue that the influences on the individual's body image are as complex as the elements of body image discussed previously. By using a mixture of personal photographs and a timeline rather than just interviewing in the intervention it allows me to see how much self-reflection Tara has and will engage in to explore the antecedents of her current circumstances as well as continuing to build an effective therapeutic alliance (Berends, 2011).

Researchers would indicate that underlying psychological variables such as self-esteem (Grilo, Wilfley, Brownell, & Rodin, 1994), self-worth (Verplanken &Tangelder, 2011), and self-presentational perfectionism (Cummings & Duda, 2012) might emerge during the consultation process as they are significantly correlated with body image. In terms of physical changes, I wanted to see how Tara related to changes in her body shape at key time points such as puberty, her athlete body during the university years, her deconditioned body post university, her weight loss, her weight gain during pregnancy, after the birth, and her current status. In the initial case presented, I mentioned Tara's reluctance to share her concerns with others. For this reason it was important for me to establish what role others in her social network had and currently play in reinforcing her thoughts about appearance. It is apparent, that a plethora of authors (e.g., Bergstrom, & Neighbors, 2006; Cash & Smolak, 2011; Martin Ginis, Bassett-Gunter, & Conlin, 2012; Strahan, Wilson, Cressman, & Buote, 2006; Tiggemann, 2004; Yamamiya, Cash, Melnyk, Posavac, & Posavac, 2005) also seek to understand the wider social-environmental influences on body image. I wanted to establish if Tara had or did attribute her body-image concerns to the influence of media or her cultural upbringing including the subcultures of the workplace and gym.

During the timeline exercise, Tara began to talk more freely and fully about her concerns. She was able to talk without the need for many prompts from me and found it easier to talk whilst occupied in the activity of chronicling her story. It became clear that Tara's concerns were often expressed as her perceptions of what others thought about and attributed her appearance to (husband, family, friends, and gym users). When I asked if these attitudes and 'blame' had been expressed to her formally, she indicated that they had not but she 'just knew what they were thinking' and did not 'want to hear it first-hand'.

Session 3 – mindfulness and acceptance

The purpose of the third session was to raise Tara's self-monitoring skills, to assist her in becoming more aware of, and to record, the antecedents, behaviours and consequences of body-image experiences. Cash (2008) outlines a mindfulness exercise in body awareness but at this stage I used guided deep breathing and Jacobson's (1938) Progressive Muscular Relaxation (PMR) script to guide Tara in a body to mind awareness and relaxation. This decision was based on my greater experience with PMR in comparison to the use of mindfulness.

Next I asked Tara to complete a guided mirror exposure exercise (Delinsky & Wilson, 2006). She was asked to stand in front of a full length mirror and spend a few minutes scanning her body from head to toe, with the emphasis placed upon not focusing on particular 'problem' areas but to look at all areas (front, side, and back). To guide this process we worked systematically from head to toe, I prompted her area of gaze by using phrases like 'what does your hair look like', 'what do your shoulders look like'. She was then asked to describe what she saw (size, shape, and symmetry) rather than making evaluation or judgemental statements. Tara was asked to simply state feelings but to then move to another area. Tara was reminded to describe her physical appearance in neutral, objective, and precise terms rather than negative, emotive language such as 'I'm fat', 'invisible' to avoid negative judgemental thoughts (Moreno-Domínguez, Rodríguez-Ruiz, Fernández-Santaellab, Jansenc, & Tuschen-Caffier, 2012). After the exercise was complete, I debriefed her about the experience. It had caused some degree of slight anxiety but she did not feel distressed and reported that as she concentrated on each area she felt in more control of her emotions. During the debrief we discussed how this method of examining her body differed from her normal practice and she recognized that her normal mode is very emotive and critical, rarely focusing on what she likes but more often what she does not like to see. The techniques of mirror exposure and neutral descriptions are forms of cognitive restructuring and have been successfully employed with individuals who have body-image concerns either with or without an eating disorder (Moreno-Domínguez et al., 2012).

As homework between this and the next session, Tara was asked to integrate the use of the PMR into her daily routine. She was also asked to repeat the mirror exposure task daily but wearing different outfits (work clothes, evening outfit, gym clothes, and underwear, etc.) and to record her experiences, feelings, and learning from each session in her journal. We would then revisit this in the next session. In keeping with Cash's (2008) approach, Tara was also asked to record her negative body-image episodes using a series of prompts:

- A – activator(s) – what triggered your negative feelings about your appearance?
- B – belief(s) – what is going on in your mind, how did you interpret this event?
- C – consequences – what is emotional consequence of these thoughts?
    - T – type of emotions experienced
    - I – intensity of the emotions (scale from 0 'not intense at all' to 10 'extremely intense')
    - D – duration of the emotions before they subsided (minutes, hours)
    - E – effects on your subsequent behaviour

Session 4 – private body talk

The purpose of this session was to address Tara's internal dialogue or negative self-talk by exploring the cognitive schemas associated with body image that Tara had and employed to interpret her reality (Cash, 2008). To start this session we examined together some common image schemas (e.g., women who have a thin body shape are healthy and happy) and explored the research literature that highlights the lack of supporting evidence. On a worksheet (refer to Box 21.4) Tara was presented with negative schemas that reflected her most problematic thoughts from the first session starting with the phrase 'When I assume that ...'. At this point she was prompted to write down what she focused on, how this made her think and feel. Finally, I then asked Tara to write down ways of challenging these comments with a new internal voice. The use of cognitive restructuring and Socratic questioning is regarded as an effective way in which to collaboratively problem solve (Hofmann & Asmundson, 2008).

Definition/description box **BOX 21.4**

APPEARANCE ASSUMPTION

When I assume that ...
'The only way I can accept my appearance would be to change my appearance.'

- This makes me focus on...
  - *my weight, exercise routine and dieting.*
- And I think ...
  - *if I was slimmer I would be happier and more successful.*
- And I feel ...
  - *if I don't change something I'll never be content.*
- My internal voice argues with this appearance assumption ...
  - *The last time I was not happy with my appearance I dieted and exercised to lose weight, I did, whilst feeling happy initially, this didn't last long. Whatever weight I was I wanted to be slimmer.*

Is my appearance really the main thing that makes me feel unhappy? What do I really need to concentrate on?

After completing the reframing exercise for the various appearance assumptions, Tara was encouraged to read these aloud and to rephrase if necessary so that the means of expression was her own. She was then encouraged to read these new internal voice statements for a few minutes every day and also to use these statements to challenge the body-image conversations had with others. The process encourages greater acceptance from Tara by taking ownership for the rephrased statements and has been found to be effective in treating body-image related disorders (Hartmann, Thomas, Greenberg, Rosenfield & Wilhelm, 2014).

Session 5 – modifying mental mistakes

The objective for the fifth session was to reflect further on her negative body talk by using cognitive restructuring tasks. By exploring Tara's existing body-image thoughts and consequences from her ongoing journal, I sought with her greater detail as to the triggering events that often preceded negative body cognitions and then seek to assist her in articulating and documenting alternative internal dialogues. The gym environment was identified as one such triggering environment which led to thoughts of critical, negative scrutiny from other members and therefore a lack of companionship at the gym. By asking Tara to describe the circumstances in greater detail than she had documented, it enabled greater explanation of the facts of the situation and the possible areas where she may have misattributed the actions of others. After this, Tara was asked if she had ever initiated a conversation with another member of the gym which led to a discussion of reciprocity and steps she was willing to try on her next gym visit.

To build on Tara's journaling structure provided in Session 3 (activators, beliefs and consequences), as homework she was encouraged to incorporate the content of this session. She was asked to record her restructured *dialogues* for negative cognitions encountered and then to record the emotional and behavioural *effects* of these restructured cognitions.

Session 6 – body-image avoidance

In this session I explored the avoidant behaviours Tara engaged in to reduce negative feelings of anxiety, embarrassment, or self-consciousness. During previous sessions it has become apparent that

Tara avoids situations where she views her body and social circumstances where she thinks others are doing so. Individuals with social physique anxiety tend to avoid social situations where their bodies will be scrutinized and unfortunately due to the social nature of exercise this may result in withdrawal from exercise settings (Crawford & Eklund, 1994; Leary, 1992). To explore the situations where Tara engages in avoidant behaviour, I asked her to write down (a) behaviours she adopts to avoid scrutiny from others (such as always wearing make-up, wearing dark colours), (b) places she avoids (swimming pools, communal changing rooms), and (c) people she avoids (certain family members, people she regards as more attractive). I then asked Tara to indicate the frequency by which she employs these tactics (occasionally, often, frequently). This revealed that she continues to feel uncomfortable in public places where others may view her, when in these situations she feels anxious and ashamed. At the gym she avoids changing in front of others. She chooses to buy clothes online and has found excuses not to socialize in the evening with friends where she would have to 'dress up'.

Cash (2008) recommends the use of the PACE (prepare, act, cope, and enjoy) acronym to structure a coping strategy for these situations. I asked her to consider what she will do to overcome her old behaviour: what situation and when she will act on this before the next session; what negative thoughts and feelings does she think this situation will elicit and how will she cope; and finally how will she reward herself after successfully executing her plan. We worked through examples of her anxieties over changing at the gym. Tara agreed to try changing into her gym kit at the gym (rather than arriving at the gym in her kit), she felt that this situation would be more manageable than changing after the session. To cope with her emotions she would practise the relaxation and breathing techniques learnt in session three. To reward these gains in approaching her fears she chose to download songs for her workouts.

Session 7 – personal social network

Tara had indicated that she enjoyed the camaraderie of training during her competitive sporting career as a younger adult but as she has got older has struggled with maintaining her exercise motivation and not having someone to exercise with. She has also indicated a reluctance to discuss her weight and body-image concerns with others. These circumstances suggested that it was important to address who Tara had in her life that she could rely on for different forms of support, namely emotional, esteem and tangible (Wills & Shinar, 2000) as she sought to change her behaviour. In this session I wanted to explore Tara's connections with individuals close to her. The purpose was for Tara to articulate her understanding of her social network and therefore gain a picture of the relationships she has that could be utilized as a supportive resource as well as understanding those relationships that have hindered her in the past in terms of enabling positive behaviour change. Researchers have become increasingly aware of the significant role other people play in enabling or thwarting behaviour change (Sluzki, 2010).

To do this I asked Tara to consider those individuals she was closest to, writing each name down on a small post-it label (these can be substituted for pebbles, buttons, or other more tactile objects depending on the appropriateness to the client). Once she named all those she had a significant relationship with I asked her to place them onto a blank piece of paper and categorize into the social groups that these people form (family, friends, neighbours, co-workers, and others). Once Tara was content that she has represented her network accurately we then explored the meaning of these individuals to her and her exercise involvement and concerns about her physical appearance. I explored with Tara who did and continues to provide what type of support to her and who provided sources of resistance or created anxiety in relation to the exercise and body image. I then encouraged her to explore how people act as a means of providing different types of support, what areas she perceives as being currently deficient, and how she may source this support in future. This approach is based upon the theory of symbolic interactionism where her personal social network may assist in understanding how Tara interprets exercise and body-image concerns and how the network may assist in her accessing a new construction of her circumstances (Heaney & Israel, 2008).

From this session it was clear that Tara led a very secretive life regarding her concerns over physical appearance. By conducting the mapping exercise she expressed that by not discussing these matters with those she was close to, she felt that perhaps she was responsible for creating a barrier where such discussions were then taboo. This was something she wanted to change, initially with her husband and then perhaps with a close work colleague who was open about her own body image issues.

Session 8 – being kind to your body

In this last session we returned back to the issue of appearance behaviours previously explored in the sixth session. Together we examined Tara's checking and fixing rituals concerning her appearance. Through discussion, it became clear that her compulsions to check and subsequently fix her appearance were triggered in various exercise environments where she felt 'exposed' and under scrutiny from people who did not know her. Other trigger situations she had identified were when she was having her photo taken and special events when she had to 'dress up for the occasion'. These appearance rituals appeared to result in behaviours such as pulling at her clothing, changing her outfit many times before leaving the house, quick glances in mirrors and reflective surfaces and hiding or refusing to have her photo taken or asking for photos to be deleted. We then discussed strategies to overcome these rituals and she indicated that she would try to delay and restrict her use of such rituals. Using Cash's (2008) PACE acronym introduced in Session 6, Tara was asked to record each of the rituals she would attempt to control providing details of her preparation, action, coping, and enjoyment (reward for success).

In this last session with Tara, it was important to explore how she intended to continue to monitor and develop. Whilst it was clear that Tara had and continued to exercise for the health benefits, she still felt as if she was missing an element. As indicated in Self-determination Theory (Deci & Ryan, 2000), whilst Tara may derive autonomy need fulfilment from her exercise programme there was little evidence of competence or relatedness need fulfilment. We discussed other activities that she could try outside and inside the gym environment that might meet these needs. She had not previously considered exercising with her daughter or husband but would explore with her husband family activities. She also indicated a desire to start dancing classes with her husband. To complete the session, I asked Tara to express how she felt her approach to her physical appearance had changed and to formally document this alongside her goals discussed in the session. Tara was familiar with the SMART technique and therefore happy to quantify and time date the goals set.

REFLECTIONS

As stated at the start of this chapter, the case of Tara is a hypothetical one and given this I will outline the process of evaluation and monitoring I would conduct with such a client.

Evaluation

To evaluate the effectiveness of an intervention I would seek ongoing informal feedback from Tara thereby allowing time for natural discussion with her during the intervention. The purpose of these discussions would be to explore what she felt was working (leading to a change in cognition, emotions, and behaviour) and what areas were proving more difficult. Whilst this informal feedback is limited in terms of objective measurement, it is important in terms of maintaining the practitioner-client working alliance (Bordin, 1979). Through these discussions Tara's perceptions of the appropriateness of, and willingness to, participate in the psychological intervention would be assessed. To evaluate the effectiveness of the intervention a more formal evaluation would take place in a follow-up session. I would ask Tara to complete the body-image concerns questionnaires conducted during Session 1. This would permit me to explore what areas of body image had moved from being in a problem to risky zone or risky to an acceptance zone. This would enable Tara to see what progress she has made during the intervention and what areas she would still need to be aware as potential risky and problem areas.

Monitoring

With any intentional behaviour change there is the likelihood of relapse. The Transtheoretical Model (Prochaska & DiClemente, 1983; Prochaska, DiClemente, & Norcross, 1992) suggests that until individuals have reached the maintenance stage of change there is a high probability of relapse to an earlier stage which can take between six months and five years to achieve. I would encourage Tara to continue monitoring her exercise behaviour and negative self-talk through the continued use of the journal provided. This would ensure that the occasional lapses (which can be accommodated) do not spiral into relapse. One issue would be to identify situations which are likely to cause the client anxiety. These situations are likely to be very specific and therefore it is best to discuss and plan for these events with the client. After the completion of the eight sessions, contact was maintained with the client remotely via email and phone calls to ensure that periodic monitoring of her progress could be made and the opportunity for further follow-up sessions could be offered.

Reflective practice

By adopting a cognitive-behavioural approach, the client can be viewed as the passive receiver of directed therapeutic education (akin to a teacher-pupil or coach-athlete relationship). This view could be construed as passive. However this fails to account for the active role the client plays during the intervention (Meichenbaum, 1994). I do believe that the approach is an inherently interpersonal approach that grants the psychologist the latitude to work creatively and flexibly with the client. There is a potential imbalance of status and power within this therapeutic working alliance between psychologist and client, and this may not suit all clients. I was aware that by adopting a cognitive-behavioural approach to the intervention that this would result in a very structured approach with an expectation of *homework* to be completed between sessions by the client. Whilst it has been documented that the client's intellectual and motivational capacity play an important mediating role in the success of such an approach (Sheldon, 2010), I felt that this style would suit Tara's situation. In the initial discussions it was clear that she internalized a lot of her concerns and did not freely express these to other individuals. As an adult in graduate-level employment, the approach did not appear to be demanding beyond her capabilities. Some of the activities completed in sessions were adapted to give a more visual means of exploring issues. Using the technique of a timeline and photographs to explore changes in body image, allows me to guide more than instruct the client to explore their own thoughts and emotions regarding their appearance. Prins (2013) stated that ' a photograph often culminates in a deep recognition that helps a client consciously re-inhabit that aspect of their self and reclaim and re-integrate it back into their personality' (p. 31). The role of myself as the practitioner is to facilitate and prompt the client in their recall.

As a practitioner, I recommended the use of a journal for the client and I also made written notes after each session, not just to document my notes on the session but also to commit my own thoughts to a permanent record for future reference. Smith (1985) refers to the relative permanence of writing that permits the writer to return back to the product of their thoughts allowing them to ruminate and consider meaning. In keeping notes my objective is to become more self-aware of potential inherent biases or theoretical standpoints that could potentially impact on my interactions with the client and conclusions made. In a similar way, I also wish to examine potential biases that may exist in terms of my own personal experiences of the issues experienced by the client as well as gender, cultural, and racial expectations (Bager-Charleson, 2010). By documenting the sessions the ability to reflect and learn from each session is also facilitated. Using the ACT SMART model of reflective practice (Roffey-Barentsen & Malthouse, 2009) the aim is to *acknowledge* (observe and record), *consider*, and *connect* (make sense of and provide meaning to), *transform* into practice (working with the meaning) before creating an action plan using traditional goal setting criteria namely *specific, measurable, achievable, realistic* and *time bound*.

Two issues worthy of further discussion are the boundaries of professional practice and the similarities between client and practitioner. As indicated in the description of the client, when dealing with psychological issues of physical appearance, diet and more specifically, diet restriction may come to the fore. The Health and Care Professions' Council's (2010) standards of proficiency for practising psychologists recommend that the psychologist acts in the best interest of the client at all times and therefore, 'understand the need to respect, and so far as possible uphold, the rights, dignity, values and autonomy of every service user including their role in the diagnostic and therapeutic process and in maintaining health and wellbeing' (p. 6). It is not within the skill competencies of an exercise psychologist to comment or intervene with the client's diet and therefore strong encouragement is needed to refer the client to a suitably qualified practitioner if one has not been sought thus far. The second issue that can facilitate or inhibit the effectiveness of the intervention is one of similarity to the client. Noffsinger, Pellegrini, and Burnell (1983) found that first impressions were, 'frequently and strongly affected by attitudes which the perceiver had developed toward another person whom he associated with the stimulus person' (p. 188). It is possible that the effectiveness of the intervention may be attributable to the degree to which the client identifies with the practitioner. In this situation, the effectiveness of myself as a practitioner may rest in how closely the client identifies with me in terms of my background (factors such as age, gender, socio-economic status, ethnicity and education). Whilst in this case there is close compatibility between myself and the client, this might not always be the case and therefore careful documentation of sessions would enable me to reflect on how this may or may not impact on the effectiveness of my practice.

Considering how I might have worked differently with a client such as Tara and exploring strategies for future work, I would have liked to observe Tara in the gym environment to assess some of the issues and to perhaps conduct a brief intervention in situ. Ravizza (1998) discussed the need for sport psychologists to spend time with the client to establish rapport and to strengthen the client-practitioner relationship, a process described by Andersen (2000) as *just being there*. I would argue that the same issue applies to the exercise psychologist. Where possible I would ask the client to consider allowing me to observe high-risk situations which result in negative self-talk to address these intrusive thoughts as they occur by exploring the origins and alternatives. By witnessing these triggering events first-hand it would have provided context and personal meaning during more the structured one-to-one sessions thereby encouraging an atmosphere of collaboration rather than instruction. Given more time with Tara it would have been better to explore some of the issues raised in more detail and I am aware that by following the approach of Cash (2008) that I may have been ambitious in the amount of information covered in the time frame available. I would have liked more time to ensure that Tara consolidated the skills and techniques taught before moving forward.

Alternative approaches

The approach adopted by Cash (2008) has developed from CBT and now incorporates elements of Mindfulness and Acceptance and Commitment Therapy. The CBT approach has been found to be effective in treating a range of populations who suffer from body-image issues including non-clinical (Rosen, Salzberg, & Srebnik, 1989), obesity (Ramirez & Rosen, 2001), eating disorders (Bhatnagar, Wisniewski, Solomon & Heinberg, 2013) and body dysmorphic disorder (Neziroglu & Yaryura-Tobias, 1993) individuals. Other approaches have been documented and evaluated. For example, Wade, George and Atkinson (2009) found evidence for the effectiveness of cognitive dissonance (counter attitudinal thinking) and acceptance (acknowledging thoughts) approaches at improving appearance satisfaction of female college students. Mindfulness has also been found effective to decrease the 'likelihood of impulsive, destructive behaviours and increased insight about the complexity of the body image experience' (Stewart, 2004, p. 788). Whichever technique is used it is clear that gender must be taken into consideration. Whilst the client described is female and so corresponds to the majority of the literature, men can also present with BID but their experiences of and willingness to engage in treatment may be very different (Burlew & Shurts, 2013).

SUMMARY

The aim of this chapter was to provide some insights into the complexities and challenges faced when working with a client who has body-image concerns. The concept is multifaceted and therefore the intervention should be so. I chose to follow a CBT approach developed by Thomas Cash that combines psychoeducational and self-monitoring strategies. Whilst clients may initially come to discuss weight-loss strategies it was important to establish and raise her awareness regarding where her body dissatisfaction came from. By mapping the nature of her body-image concerns we were then able to explore change and more adaptive thoughts and coping strategies. As certain issues came to the fore such as anxiety relating to looking in mirrors and distancing herself from social relationships, I chose to deviate from Cash's steps to explore these areas in greater depth.

I hope through the chapter to have outlined a number of considerations that practitioners may need to consider when dealing with such clients and provided guidance as to further sources of information.

FURTHER READING

Bulik, C. M. (2012). The woman in the mirror: How to stop confusing what you look like with who you are. London: Bloomsbury. This book provides a very useful insight into the developmental origins of female body-image issues. It provides a useful guide as to how to separate self-esteem concerns from body esteem, exploring cues and triggers such as negative self-talk. A number of strategies are offered. A supporting website contains links to further resources and worksheets cited in the book (http://womaninthemirrorbook.com).

Cash, T. F., & Smolak, L. (Eds.) (2011). *Body image: A handbook of science, practice and prevention* (2nd ed., pp. 378–386). New York: The Guilford Press. This book is a very useful source of information of research evidence relating to body image. The short chapters give useful overviews of areas such as developmental, individual, and cultural differences in body image as well as associated clinical issues and interventions.

Morgan, J. F. (2008). *The invisible man: A self-help guide for men with eating disorders, compulsive exercise and bigorexia.* London: Routledge. The literature in this area is very female focused but increasingly it is recognized that men also experience body-image issues that may result in over exercising. This book provides a self-help guide to assist men, dealing with specific male issues with the support of research. It contains reference to the cultural demands on men and boys and how the body is perceived before offering an evidence-based cognitive-behavioural approach to treatment.

Sandoz. E., & DuFrene, T. (2013). *Living with your body and other things you hate: How to let go of your struggle with body image using acceptance and commitment therapy.* Oakland, CA: New Harbinger Publications, Inc. This self-help manual is written from the ACT perspective and therefore would suit those coming from a dialectical behaviour therapy or mindfulness-based cognitive therapy background.

Veale, D., Willson, R., & Clarke, A. (2009). *Overcoming body image problems including body dysmorphic disorder: A self-help guide using cognitive behavioral techniques.* London: Robinson This book is part of a series of self-help guides for people with a range of mental health concerns (other related titles include, weight problems, eating disorders, self-esteem and social anxiety). The book is written by practising UK, CBT clinicians. It includes a number of useful examples of specific issues such as skin picking, disfigurement, and cosmetic surgery.

REFERENCES

Andersen, M. J. (2000). *Doing sport psychology.* Champaign, IL: Human Kinetics.

Bager-Charleson, S. (2010). *Reflective practice in counselling and psychotherapy.* Exeter: Learning Matters.

Berends, L. (2011). Embracing the visual: Using timelines with in-depth interviews on substance use and treatment. *The Qualitative Report, 16,* 1–9. Retrieved 9 December 2015 from http://www.nova.edu/ssss/QR/QR16-1/berends.pdf

Bergstrom, R. L., & Neighbors, C. (2006). Body image disturbance and the social norms approach: An integrative review of the literature. *Journal of Social and Clinical Psychology, 25,* 975–1000.

Berman, L. (1993). *Beyond the smile: The therapeutic use of the photograph.* London: Routledge.

Bhatnagar, K. A. C., Wisniewski, L., Solomon, M., & Heinberg, L (2013). Effectiveness and feasibility of a cognitive-behavioral group intervention for body image disturbance in women with eating disorders. *Journal of Clinical Psychology, 69,* 1–13.

Bordin, E. (1979). The generalizability of the psychoanalytic concept of the working alliance. *Psychotherapy: Theory, Research and Practice, 16,* 252–260.

Bruch, M., & Prioglio, A. (2006). The case formulation procedure. In A. V., Nikcčevicć , A. R., Kuczmierczyk, & M.Bruch (Ed.) *Formulation and treatment in clinical health psychology* (pp. 1–18). Abingdon: Routledge.

Bulik, C. M. (2012). *The woman in the mirror: How to stop confusing what you look like with who you are.* London: Bloomsbury.

Burlew, L. D., & Shurts, W. M. (2013). Men and body image: Current issues and counseling implications. *Journal of Counseling & Development, 91,* 428–435.

Burns, D., & Nolen-Hoeksema, S. (1991). Coping styles, homework compliance, and the effectiveness of cognitive behavioural therapy. *Journal of Consulting and Clinical Psychology, 59,* 305–311.

Campbell, A., & Hausenblas, H. A. (2009). Effects of exercise interventions on body image: A meta-analysis. *Journal of Health Psychology, 14,* 780–793.

Cash, T. F. (2008). *The body image workbook: An 8-step program for learning to like your looks* (2nd ed.) Oakland, CA: New Harbinger Publications.

Cash, T. F., & Hrabosky, J. (2003). The effects of psychoeducation and self-monitoring in a cognitive-behavioral program for body-image improvement. *Eating Disorders, 11,* 255–270.

Cash, T. F., & Lavallee, D. M. (1997). Cognitive-behavioral body-image therapy: Extended evidence of the efficacy of a self-directed program. *Journal of Rational-Emotive and Cognitive-Behavior Therapy, 15,* 281–294.

Cash, T. F., & Smolak, L. (2011). Understanding body images: Historical and contemporary perspectives. In T. F. Cash & L. Smolak (Eds.), *Body image: A handbook of science, practice, and prevention* (pp. 3–11). New York: Guilford Press.

Crane, R. (2009). *Mindfulness-based cognitive therapy: Distinctive features (CBT distinctive features)*. New York: Routledge.

Crawford, S., & Eklund, R. C. (1994). Social physique anxiety, reasons for exercise, and attitudes toward exercise settings. *Journal of Sport & Exercise Psychology, 16*, 70–82.

Cummings, J., & Duda, J. L. (2012). Profiles of perfectionism, body-related concerns, and indicators of psychological health in vocational dance students: An investigation of the 2 × 2 model of perfectionism. *Psychology of Sport & Exercise, 13*, 729–738.

Deci, E. L., & Ryan, R. M. (1985). *Intrinsic motivation and self-determination in human behavior*. New York: Plenum.

Deci, E. L., & Ryan, R. M. (2000). The 'what' and 'why' of goal pursuits: Human needs and the self-determination of behavior. *Psychological Inquiry, 11*, 227–268.

Delinsky, S. S., & Wilson, G. T. (2006). Mirror exposure for the treatment of body image disturbance. *International Journal of Eating Disorders, 39*, 108–116. DOI: 10.1002/eat.20207.

Department of Health. (2011). Start active, stay active: A report on physical activity from the four home countries' chief medical officers. Retrieved 9 December 2015 from https://www.gov.uk/government/uploads/system/uploads/ attachment_data/file/216370/dh_128210.pdf

Dzewaltowski, D. A., Noble, J. M., & Shaw, J. M. (1990). Physical activity participation: Social cognitive theory versus the theories of reasoned action and planned behavior. *Journal of Sport and Exercise Psychology, 12*, 388–405.

Ellis, A. (1962) *Reason and emotion in psychotherapy*. Secaucus, NJ: Citadel.

Ellis, A. (1993). Reflections on rational-emotive therapy. *Journal of Consulting and Clinical Psychology*, 61, 199–201.

Evans, R. R., Roy, J., Geiger, B. F., Werner, K. A., & Burnett, D. (2008). Ecological strategies to promote healthy body image among children. *Journal of School Health, 78*, 359–367.

Festinger, L. (1962). Cognitive dissonance. *Scientific American, 207*, 93–107. DOI: 10.1038/scientificamerican1062–93.

Fox, K. R. (2000). Self-esteem, self-perceptions and exercise. *International Journal of Sport Psychology, 31*(2), 228–240.

Gramling, L. F., & Carr, R. L. (2004). Lifelines: A life history methodology. *Nursing Research, 53*, 207–210.

Grilo, C. M., Wilfley, D. E., Brownell, K. D., & Rodin, J. (1994). Teasing, body image, and self-esteem in a clinical sample of obese women. *Addictive Behaviors, 19*, 443–450.

Hartmann, A. S., Thomas, J. J., Greenberg, J. L., Rosenfield, E. H., & Wilhelm, S. (2014). Accept, distract, or reframe? An exploratory experimental comparison of strategies for coping with intrusive body image thoughts in anorexia nervosa and body dysmorphic disorder. *Psychiatry Research*. DOI: 10.1016/j.psychres.2014.11.031.

Harwood, C. G. (2009) Enhancing self-efficacy in professional tennis: Intensive work for life on the tour. In B. Hemmings & T. Holder (Eds.), *Applied sport psychology: A case-based approach* (pp. 7–32). Chichester: Wiley.

Hausenblas, H. A., & Fallon, E. A. (2006). Exercise and body image: A meta-analysis. *Psychology & Health, 21*, 33–47.

Hayes, S. C., Strosahl, K. D., & Wilson, K. G. (2011). *Acceptance and commitment therapy: The process and practice of mindful change* (2nd ed.). New York: Guilford Press.

Health & Care Professions Council (2010). Standards of proficiency: Practitioner psychologists. Retrieved 9 December 2015 from http://www.hcpc-uk.org/publications/standards/index.asp?id=198

Heaney, C. A., & Israel, B. A. (2008). Social networks and social support. In K.Glanz, B. K. Rimer, & K. Viswanath (Eds.), *Health Behavior and Health Education: Theory, Research and Practice* (4th ed.) (pp. 189–201). San Francisco: Jossey-Bass.

Hofmann, S. G., & Asmundson, G. J. (2008). Acceptance and mindfulness-based therapy: New wave or old hat? *Clinical Psychology Review, 28*, 1–16.

Jacobson, E. (1938). *Progressive relaxation*. Chicago: University of Chicago Press.

Jarry, J., & Berardi, K. (2004). Characteristics and effectiveness of stand-alone body image treatments: a review of the empirical literature. *Body Image, 1*, 319–333.

Kennedy, P., & Llewelyn, S. (2001). Does the future belong to the scientist-practitioner? *The Psychologist, 2*, 74–78.

Leary, M. J. (1992). Self-presentation processes in exercise and sport. *Journal of Sport and Exercise Psychology, 14*, 339–351.

Martin Ginis, K. A., & Bassett, R. C. (2011). Exercise and changes in body image. In T. F. Cash & L. Smolak (Eds.) *Body image: A handbook of Science, practice and prevention* (2nd ed., pp. 378–386). New York: The Guilford Press.

Martin Ginis, K. A., Bassett, R. C., & Conlin, C. (2012). Body image and exercise. In E. O.Acevedo (Ed.), *The Oxford handbook of exercise psychology* (pp. 55–75). Oxford: Oxford University Press.

McLeod, J. (2008). *Introduction to counselling* (Ed. D. Langdridge). Maidenhead, Milton Keynes: The Open University Press, The Open University.

Meichenbaum, D. (1994) *A clinical handbook practical therapist manual for assessing and treating adults with post-traumatic stress disorder*. Ontario: Institute Press.

Miller, W. R., & Rollnick, S. (2002). *Motivational interviewing: Preparing people for change* (2nd ed.). New York: Guilford Press.

Moreno-Domínguez, S., Rodríguez-Ruiz, S., Fernández-Santaella, M.C., Jansen A., & Tuschen-Caffier, B. (2012). Pure versus guided mirror exposure to reduce body dissatisfaction: a preliminary study with university women. *Body Image, 9*, 285–288.

Morrison, J. (2014). *The first interview* (4th ed.). New York: Guilford Press.

National Health Service Choices (5 December 2012). Getting started on the NHS weight loss plan. Retrieved 9 December 2015 from http://www.nhs.uk/Livewell/weight-loss-guide/Pages/losing-weight-getting-started.aspx

National Health Service Choices (2014). BMI healthy weight calculator. Retrieved 9 December 2015 from http://www.nhs.uk/Tools/Pages/Healthyweightcalculator.aspx?Tag=

Neziroglu, F. A., & Yaryura-Tobias, J. A. (1993). Exposure, response prevention, and cognitive therapy in the treatment of body dysmorphic disorder. *Behavior Therapy, 24*, 431–438.

Noffsinger, E. B., Pellegrini, R. J., & Burnell, G. M. (1983). The effect of associated persons upon the formation and modification of first impressions. *The Journal of Social Psychology, 120*, 183–195.

Patton, M. Q. (2002). *Qualitative research and evaluation methods* (3rd ed.). Thousand Oaks, CA: Sage.

Prins (2013). Photographs in therapy. *Therapy Today, 24*(2). Retrieved 15 January 2016 from http://www.therapy-today.net/article/show/3602/photographs-in-therapy/

Prochaska, J. O., & DiClemente, C. C. (1983). Stages and processes of self-change of smoking: Toward an integrative model of change. *Journal of Consulting and Clinical Psychology, 51*, 390–395.

Prochaska, J. O., DiClemente, C. C., & Norcross, J. C. (1992). In search of how people change: Applications to addictive behavior. *American Psychologist, 47*, 1102–1114.

Ramirez, E. M., & Rosen, J. C. (2001). A comparison of weight control and weight control plus body image therapy for obese men and women. *Journal of Consulting and Clinical Psychology, 69*, 440–446.

Ravizza, K. (1998). Gaining entry with athletic personnel for season-long consulting. *The Sport Psychologist, 2*, 243–254.

Rodgers, R. F., Paxton, S. J., & McLean, S. A. (2013). A biopsychosocial model of body image concerns and disordered eating in early adolescent girls. *Journal of Youth and Adolescence, 43*, 814–823,

Roffey-Barentsen, J., & Malthouse, R. (2009) *Reflective practice in the lifelong learning sector*. Exeter: Learning Matters.

Rosen, J. C., Salzberg, E., & Srebnik, D. (1989). Cognitive behavior therapy for negative body image. *Behavior Therapy*, 20, 393–404.

Schoeller, D. A., Shay, K., & Kushner, R. F. (1997). How much physical activity is needed to minimize weight gain in previously obese women? *American Journal of Clinical Nutrition, 66*, 551–556.

Sheldon, B. (2010). *Cognitive behavioural therapy: Research, practice & philosophy*. London: Routledge.

Sluzki, C. E. (2010). Personal social networks and health: Conceptual and clinical implications of their reciprocal impact. *Families, Systems & Health, 28*, 1–18.

Smith, F. (1985). *Writing and the write*. London: Heinemann.

Stewart, T. M. (2004). Light on body image treatment: Acceptance through mindfulness. *Behavior Modification, 28*, 783–811.

Stice, E., Shaw, H., Black Becker, C., & Rohde, P. (2008). Dissonance-based interventions for the prevention of eating disorders: Using persuasion principles to promote health. *Preventive Science, 9*, 114–128.

Strahan, E. J., Wilson, A. E., Cressman, K. E., & Buote, V. M. (2006). Comparing to perfection: How cultural norms for appearance affect social comparisons and self-image. *Body Image, 3*, 211–227.

Tiggemann, M. (2004). Body image across the adult life span: Stability and change. *Body Image, 1*, 29–41.

Veale, D., Willson, R., & Clarke, A. (2009). *Overcoming body image problems including body dysmorphic disorder: A self-help guide using cognitive behavioral techniques*. London: Robinson.

Verplanken B., & Tangelder Y. (2011). No body is perfect: The significance of habitual negative thinking about appearance for body dissatisfaction, eating disorder propensity, self-esteem and snacking. *Psychological Health, 26*, 685–701.

Wade, T., George, S. M., & Atkinson, M. (2009). A randomized controlled trial of brief interventions for body dissatisfaction. *Journal of Consulting and Clinical Psychology, 77*, 845–854.

Walker, J. (1982). The photograph as a catalyst in therapy. *Canadian Journal of Psychiatry, 27*, 450–454.

Westbrook, D., Kennerley, H., & Kirk, J. (2011). *An introduction to cognitive behaviour therapy: Skills and applications* (2nd ed.). London: Sage.

Wills, T. A., & Shinar, O. (2000). Measuring perceived and received social support. In S. Cohen., L. G. Underwood., & B. H.Gottlieb (Eds.), *Social support measurement and intervention: A guide for health and social scientists* (pp. 86–135). Oxford: Oxford University Press.

Yamamiya, Y., Cash, T. F., Melnyk, S. E., Posavac, H. D., & Posavac, S. S. (2005). Women's exposure to thin-and-beautiful media images: Body image effects of media-ideal internalization and impact-reduction interventions. *Body Image, 2*, 74–80.

22 Physical Activities to Improve Children's Health (PATCH): Implementing a School-Based Intervention for Children

Gavin Breslin, Conor Cunningham, and Marie H. Murphy

LEARNING OBJECTIVES

AFTER READING THE CHAPTER YOU SHOULD BE ABLE TO:

1. Develop knowledge of the physical activity guidelines for children and young people.
2. Understand the links between health and wellbeing and children's physical inactivity.
3. Critically evaluate theories of behaviour change.
4. Develop knowledge of how to apply a theory of behaviour change to a physical activity intervention for children.
5. Have a critical understanding of the challenges when delivering 'real world' health interventions in a school setting.

AREAS TO CONSIDER WHEN READING THE CHAPTER:

1. What volume and intensity of physical activity should children participate in to gain health and wellbeing benefits?
2. What are the challenges of developing and implementing a school-based physical activity intervention and what should be evaluated in such a programme to show effectiveness?
3. Why is adapting a theory of behaviour change important when designing an intervention to change health behaviour?

CLIENT AND BACKGROUND

In this chapter we describe factors important for designing, implementing, and evaluating school-based interventions aimed at increasing physical activity or reducing sedentary behaviour among children in order to improve health. We describe the levels of physical activity being achieved by children living in Northern Ireland in a school setting and provide evidence as to why taking part in physical activity has health benefits. We then outline how we conducted a needs assessment to design the 'Physical Activities to Improve Children's Health' (PATCH) programme content. We also consider the various psychological theories/models and associated behaviour-change techniques that underpin physical activity interventions, the practical issues to be considered when implementing such interventions, the measurement tools used to evaluate intervention outcomes and finally provide a critical reflection on our approach with the intention of providing direction to practitioners and researchers involved in, or about to embark on designing a physical activity intervention for children in a school setting.

Research evidence has shown regular physical activity to have positive effects on the health and psychological wellbeing of children (Janssen & LeBlanc, 2010) including depression (Motl, Birnbaum, Kubik & Dishman, 2004), global self-esteem (Parfitt & Eston, 2005; Breslin, Brennan, Rafferty, Gallagher & Hanna, 2012a), vigour and physical self-worth (Cheung et al., 2008; Raustorp, Stahle, Gudasic, Kinnunen & Mattsson, 2005). However, many children are not active enough to accrue these benefits. For example, as few as 24% of 9- to 11-year-old children in Northern Ireland achieved the recommended level of 60 minutes of moderate to vigorous physical activity (MVPA) per day (Breslin et al., 2012a). More recently, a study investigating adherence to physical activity guidelines among 7-to 8-year-old children across the UK, found that children in Northern Ireland were least likely to meet the recommended daily MVPA guideline (43%) (Griffiths, Cortina-Borja, Sera, Pouliou, Geraci, Rich, Cole, Law, Joshi, Ness, Jebb & Dezateux, 2013). Therefore there is a need for interventions to target children's inactivity levels.

A total of 99 children (boys = 51, girls = 48) with a mean age of 10.5 ± (0.5) years from three primary schools in Belfast, Northern Ireland took part in the PATCH 12-week intervention programme between February and May 2012 (Cunningham, Breslin, Boddy, Stratton, Nevill, & Murphy, under review). Before the intervention only 12% of the children were sufficiently active to meet physical activity guidelines for health (Department of Health, 2011). At baseline, the mean daily MVPA of participants measured objectively using an accelerometer was 41.9 (± 14.5) minutes; 39.2 (± 13.3) for boys and 44.5 (± 15.3) minutes for girls. The aim of PATCH was to increase physical activity and was developed as part of a programme of research conducted by the Centre for Physical Activity and Health Research (CPAHR) based at Ulster University, Northern Ireland. The multidisciplinary team included a sport and exercise psychologist (GB), physical education teacher/PhD student (CC), and an exercise physiologist (MM). This multidisciplinary approach brought with it benefits when determining the children's needs in terms of behaviour change and health assessment, both of which will be discussed later in the chapter.

Physical activity and health

Strong scientific evidence confirms that regular participation in physical activity in childhood is associated with enhanced health in both childhood and in later adult life (Department of Health, 2011). Physically active children demonstrate lower rates of metabolic syndrome, obesity, diabetes, hypertension, hypercholesterolemia, and depression than their inactive peers (Hsu, Belcher, Ventura,

Byrd-Williams, Weigensberg, & Davis, et al., 2011; Jiménez-Pavón, Kelly, & Reilly; 2010, Janssen & LeBlanc, 2010). In a recent national survey in Northern Ireland, it was shown that children who met the recommended level of MVPA for health showed higher scores in psychological wellbeing than children who did not (Breslin et al., 2012a). Active children reported more satisfaction and comfort with their lives, felt more resilient, and had a higher perception of their own achievement levels. The same children also reported higher scores in global self-esteem, social acceptance, and positive relationships with peers. Despite these benefits, few children meet the recommended level of physical activity. Moreover the physical activity habits that are formed in childhood and adolescence may track into adulthood (Cleland, Timperio, Salmon, Hume, Telford, & Crawford, 2011; Telama, Yang, Viikari, Välimäki, Wanne, & Raitakari, 2005; Trudeau, Laurencelle, & Shephard, 2004), therefore, active children may be more likely to become active adults, which will in turn lead to more long-term health benefits (Telama, 2009).

Most national and international physical activity guidelines recommend that children and young people aged between 5 and 18 years should engage in at least 60 minutes per day of moderate to vigorous-intensity physical activity, with vigorous-intensity activities incorporated at least three times per week (Department of Health, 2011; Department of Health Australia, 2008; Australian Government, Department of Health, 2014; Tremblay, Warburton, Janssen, Paterson, Latimer, & Rhodes et al., 2011; World Health Organization, 2010). Despite the established importance of childhood physical activity to health and the public health guidelines on the quantity and intensity of physical activity required for children to gain health benefits, levels of inactivity in children are at an all-time high. Cross sectional design research studies consistently report that significant proportions of children in developed countries do not meet current physical activity recommendations (Griffiths et al., 2013; Fakhouri, Hughes, Burt, Song, Fulton, & Ogden, 2014; Colley, Garriguet, Janssen, Wong, Saunders, & Carson et al., 2011; Department of Health Australia, 2008; Currie, Zanotti, Morgan, Currie, deLooze, & Roberts et al., 2012). Evidence also suggests that activity levels in childhood decline through adolescence and that marked differences are evident between genders with fewer girls getting sufficient levels of physical activity for optimal health (Dumith, Gigante, Domingues, & Kohl, 2011; Griffiths et al., 2013).

In addition to the low proportions of children meeting guidelines for physical activity, there is increasing evidence that high levels of sedentary behaviour may have a detrimental impact on children's health. Sedentary behaviours are characterized by a sitting or reclining posture with energy expenditure in the range of 1.0 to 1.5 METs, where 1 MET is the energy expenditure at rest. High levels of sedentary behaviour are now recognized as a health risk even for those who meet current physical activity guidelines. Physical activity and sedentary behaviours are considered to be independent from each other (British Heart Foundation, National Centre, Sedentary Behaviour Evidence Briefing, 2011) in that children can be both physically active (i.e., play, physical education, sport) and spend prolonged periods of time engaged in sedentary behaviours (sitting whilst playing video games, watching television, using mobile devices or whilst at school in the classroom). The recent physical activity guidelines in the UK suggest that children and young people should minimize the amount of time spent sitting for extended periods of time (Department of Health, 2011). In other countries, such as Canada, sedentary behaviour guidelines have been made more specific recommending that children aged between 5 to 11 years limit recreational screen time to no more than 2 hours per day and limit motorized transport, extended sitting, and time spent indoors throughout the day (www.csep.ca/guidelines). Schools have been identified as a setting for the promotion of physical activity in childhood (WHO, 2004), and well-designed theory-based interventions also have the potential to change patterns of sedentary behaviour (Breslin et al., 2012a). In the next section, we discuss the design and delivery of the PATCH intervention that was developed to provide primary school children with both the knowledge of the benefits of being physically active, but also the opportunity to be active during the school day.

INITIAL NEEDS ASSESSMENT

Before an initial needs assessment was conducted the team discussed the potential benefits of conducting the assessment and what form this should take. We discussed the methods, the use of a survey, individual interviews, focus groups and with whom these would be conducted; the parent, teacher, school principal, and/or with the children. It became apparent from discussions that a 'one size fits all approach' does not work in terms of intervening to change children's physical activity behaviour. Therefore following ethical approval from Ulster University's Research Ethics Committee we conducted an initial needs assessment involving interviews with the school teachers (n = 6), then focus groups with the children (n = 3) to ascertain what they would like included in an intervention to increase physical activity (see examples included in text boxes below). By gathering motivational and preference information, it was felt that when the programme was finally designed, children and teachers could feel a sense of ownership of the programme content. Ease of delivery without the need for substantial training or costly resources, enjoyment for the children and linked to the educational curriculum were the priorities expressed by the teachers. The children wanted to perform activities that were enjoyable and fun and could be performed with friends in class or in the playground. Taking this information and adopting the National Institute of Health and Clinical Excellence (NICE) 2009 guidelines that physical activity interventions should be multicomponent and holistic, the PATCH intervention was created, and the school setting chosen.

Definition/description box **BOX 22.1**

EXAMPLES OF WHAT TEACHERS WANT IN A PHYSICAL ACTIVITY INTERVENTION

'Something simple to get kids moving, maybe a chart of exercises?'

'Something quick and easy to deliver during the day'.

Definition/description box **BOX 22.2**

EXAMPLES OF WHAT CHILDREN WANT IN A PHYSICAL ACTIVITY INTERVENTION

'I'd like to do dancing activities'.

'Something fun where we get to move around'.

Why school-based interventions?

In most developed countries daily attendance at school is compulsory from age 4–6 through to 16–18 (with the exception of home-schooled children), therefore the school setting allows physical activity behaviour-change interventions to be applied uniformly to all children regardless of age, ethnicity, gender, and socio-economic status (Naylor, Macdonald, Warburton, Reed & McKay, 2006). Previous interventions to promote physical activity in a school setting have included active transport (walking and cycling) to and from school (Chillon, Evenson, Vaughn, & Ward, 2011), curriculum physical education provision (Cale & Harris, 2006), classroom-based physical activity breaks (Kriemler, Zahner, Schindler, Meyer, Hartmann, & Hebestreit et al., 2010), break-, lunch-, and physical activity, the provision of playground markings (Stratton & Mullan, 2005), provision of equipment to encourage activity (Jago & Baranowski, 2004), after-school sports and physical activity sessions (Pate & O'Neill, 2008), educational components designed to increase knowledge and understanding of the health benefits of activity (Gortmaker, Peterson, Wiecha, Sobol, Dixit, Fox, & Laird, 1999), physical activity homework assignments (Kriemler et al., 2010) often including parental and family involvement (Jurg, Kremers, Candel, Van der Wal, & De Meij, 2006), and finally alterations to technology within the school that would lead to behaviour change (Lanningham-Foster, Foster, McCrady, Manohar, Jensen, & Mitre et al., 2008).

Schools in particular, have been identified as the primary institutions with responsibility for promoting physical activity in youth (WHO, 2004), and are ideal settings for providing opportunities for children to be active (WHO, 2004). Schools have the potential to become the central element in a community that ensures students participate in the recommended amount of time engaged in physical activity (Pate, Davis, Robinson, Stone, & McKenzie, 2006) and develop healthy behaviours that track into adulthood (NICE, 2009). Physical Education (PE) is one way to encourage activity in school and develop fitness in childhood, and for many children PE will be their only preparation for an active lifestyle. Schools in Northern Ireland, as with the rest of the UK, are 'encouraged' to provide pupils with at least 2 hours of high quality PE per week (Department of Culture, Arts &Leisure (DCAL), 2009). However, there are no statutory requirements for schools to devote specific amounts of time to PE (Office for Standards in Education, Children's Services, & Skills (OFSTED), 2013). As a result, increasing pressures on schools to find more time for academic subjects (Tremblay, Inman, & Willms, 2000), and increasing demands on teachers to attain high standards for pupils in standard attainment tests (SATs) have led to the erosion of time for PE in schools (Weiler, Allardyce, Whyte, & Stamatakis, 2013; Tremblay et al., 2000). The Northern Ireland Strategy for Sport and Physical Recreation 2009–2019 'Sport Matters' (DCAL, 2009) outlines, as part of the key steps for success, to 'pursue' a target for 2 hours of PE *per week* for children of compulsory school age. However it has been reported that as few as 17% of primary (Sport NI, 2009) and 9% of post-primary (Sport NI, 2010) pupils take part in less than ≥ 2 hours of PE per week. As already outlined above, the current UK guidelines for physical activity recommend that children spend more time taking part in physical activity than engaged in sedentary behaviours (DOH, 2011). However, research shows that school-age boys and girls spend on average 7–8 hours per day being sedentary, primarily 'sitting' in compulsory academic lessons at school (Craig, Mindell, & Hirani, 2009). Attempts therefore should be made to change this behaviour and in doing so select an appropriate theory / model of behaviour change on which to develop and evaluate any intervention.

Choosing a suitable theory of health behaviour change to guide the intervention

Many behaviour-change theories have been used in the design of school-based physical activity interventions. To name a few, these include: the Theory of Planned Behaviour (TPB; Ajzen, 1985, 1987); the Theory of Competence Motivation (Harter, 1985); Self-determination Theory (Deci & Ryan, 1985); and Social Cognitive Theory (Bandura, 1977). Each theory proposes a process by which the target behaviour is controlled; it is these factors that dictate the techniques that researchers use when attempting to change physical activity behaviour. Below is a brief description and critical evaluation of each theory and a rationale for the one chosen in the design of the PATCH Programme.

According to Ajzen (1985, 1987) the TPB is a theory of volitional (conscious) behaviour change, were behaviour is primarily influenced by what intentions can determine the behaviour. Intentions are defined as 'indications of how hard people are willing to try, of how much of an effort they are planning to exert, in order to perform the behaviour' (Ajzen, 1991, p. 181). Consequently, the greater the intention, the more likely the behaviour will be performed. Intention is influenced by three factors: attitude towards the behaviour (a person's positive or negative evaluation of participating in physical activity behaviour), subjective-norm (the social pressure to perform or not perform the behaviour), and perceived behavioural control (an individual's perception of the ease or difficulty of being active). The TPB has been used successfully to predict changes in physical activity (Hagger, Chatzisarantis, Biddle, & Orbell, 2001; Rhodes, Macdonald, & McKay, 2006), and has predicted active school commuting in children (Murtagh, Rowe, McMinn, & Nelson, 2012).

Harter's (1987) Theory of Competence Motivation is based on the premise that if a child has a positive self-perception and believes that he/she has mastered the performance of a given behaviour, they will be more inclined to be motivated to repeat that behaviour. For example, if a child is shown successfully how to jump, kick or catch a ball by inducing positive feedback from adults and peers, the child will be more likely to have a positive self-perception and be motivated to repeat the behaviour. Alternatively, if low self-perceptions or feelings of incompetence are present when performing the skill, the behaviour will be less likely to be repeated, in an effort to avoid fear of failure and criticism from peers (Crocker et al., 2000). By deciding to avoid moderate or vigorous motor activities or games that may lead to perceptions of failure or criticism from others, children with low self-perception will reduce their opportunity to participate in play and sporting activities. According to Harter (1987), efforts should therefore be made to provide children with opportunities to learn and practise motor skills, including fundamental movement skills (agility co-ordination and balance), in a supportive instructional environment, wherein competency in performing the skills is actively encouraged and steps are taken to maximize the opportunities for perceived success. The result should be an increase in children's motor competence and self-perception, which may increase the future likelihood of participation in physical activity that includes sport, play, and games. Harter's competency-based framework has been applied to a national physical literacy programme for children in Northern Ireland that aims to increase physical activity though the development of perceived and actual competency of performing fundamental movement skills (Breslin et al., 2012b; Haughey, Breslin, Toole, & McKee, 2013; McKee, Breslin, Haughey, & Donnelly, 2013).

Self-determination Theory (SDT; Deci & Ryan, 1985) is a theory of human motivation, concerning people's inherent growth tendencies and their innate psychological needs. It is concerned with the *motivation* behind the *choices that people make without any external influence and interference*. SDT focuses on the degree to which an individual's behaviour is self-motivated. According to SDT physical activity is more likely to occur when greater choice of activities are offered and the person feels central to deciding what they would like to do. Three constructs central to self-determination are (a) competence, (b) autonomy, and (c) relatedness. Deci and Ryan (1985) showed that higher feelings of competence in being able to perform a task will lead to higher intrinsic motivation and a greater likelihood to perform a behaviour. This view is also consistent with Harter's (1987) Theory of Competence Motivation. If a person has a positive self-perception, and feels that they have mastered the performance of a goal-directed behaviour (e.g., successfully completing a drill during a PE lesson), they will be more inclined to be motivated to repeat that behaviour. Similarly, if a child has a high perceived behavioural control, as outlined in the TPB, they will likely have a higher intention to behave in a certain way. If a person has autonomy in choosing the activity themselves, versus someone choosing on their behalf they will be more intrinsically motivated. Therefore by asking children to choose an activity to perform at break time, or to contribute to the development of the PATCH Programme, the physical activity behaviour will be more likely to be sustained. The construct of relatedness refers to the extent physical activity provides a feeling of connection with others within an activity context, for example a social connection to the teacher or classmates whilst participating. Guay and colleagues (2001) assessed teachers' provision of autonomous support with children aged 11–12 years by measuring children's motivations towards attending school and their perceived competence during a one-year period. They showed that as teachers' levels of autonomous support increased, children's perceived competence also increased as did their intrinsic motivation to attend. It is predicted that as the teacher provides more autonomous support with regard to physical activity, children will become more motivated and active as a result.

Despite the various theoretical frameworks available, it appears that effective programmes have integrated elements of Bandura's (1986) Social Cognitive Theory (SCT) into their interventions (Salmon, Booth, & Phongsavan, 2007; Gorely, Nevill, & Morris, 2009; Harrison, Burns, McGuinness, Heslin, & Murphy, 2006; Breslin et al., 2012a). Social Cognitive Theory is a learning theory based on the idea that people learn by observing others. Observational learning is defined as the process whereby an observer views the behaviour of another and adapts their behaviour as a result of the interaction (Williams, Davids, & Williams, 1999). The behaviour that is performed is perceived to be the optimal movement solution to accomplishing a specific task goal (Hodges, Hayes, Breslin, & Williams, 2005; Sidaway & Hand, 1993). It has been suggested that a model (a person performing the action) is powerful for displaying complex human movement patterns to improve performance (Gould & Roberts, 1982). Modelling is amongst the most frequently used instruction techniques to enhance motor skill acquisition (Gould, Hodge, Peterson, & Giannini, 1989; Weinberg & Jackson, 1990). According to Bandura (1971), observing a human movement will result in the formation of a 'cognitive representation' for that action. The cognitive representation then acts as a reference during subsequent performances of the action, where the learner compares each individual performance with this representation to reduce errors in movement (also see Carroll & Bandura, 1982). Bandura (1965) emphasized that physical performance or practice was not always necessary for observational learning to occur. He claimed that verbal or visual imagery of the model's action mediated observers' responses, allowing a learner to acquire a given behaviour prior to the behaviour being physically practised. This gave rise to what Bandura termed 'no-trial learning'. At the time, Bandura's approach showed a marked transition away from repeated reinforcement associated with behaviourist accounts of modelling, with explanations for this phenomenon now based on the formation of internal representations of a model's action. In the case of promoting physical activity in the PATCH Programme, the model was the teacher, parent, or other children. To encourage the modelling process, the 12 week PATCH intervention made modelling explicit, in addition to supporting modelling with other enablers and reinforcers.

SCT was used to design the PATCH Programme. Successful school-based physical activity interventions have tended to adopt elements of Bandura's Social Cognitive Theory (SCT) (Bandura, 1986) (Gorely, Nevill, Morris, Stensel, & Nevill, 2009; Breslin et al., 2012a; Breslin & Brennan, 2012). Common techniques used in SCT based interventions emphasize the concepts of modelling (e.g., copying teachers, parents, or siblings on how to be active), self-monitoring (e.g., increase awareness as to how they spend their leisure time), goal-setting (e.g., setting goals and awarding points to be active), problem-solving (e.g., overcoming barriers to increasing activity) and social support (e.g., parents support child to be active). The content of the PATCH intervention and how it constructively aligns to SCT is discussed later.

Interestingly, Abraham and Michie (2008) have produced a taxonomy of 26 techniques which can be used to change health-related behaviours. All of the theories described above draw upon combinations of the techniques outlined in this taxonomy. It is useful for those approaching a school-based intervention to consider the range of techniques available and be able to describe those selected consistently using the Behaviour Change Taxonomy (BCT). For example, the PATCH intervention used several techniques to change behaviour: BCT No. 10 Self-monitoring of behaviour – children in the intervention arm of the research were encouraged to record their physical activity in a daily diary in addition to their physical activity being measured by accelerometry; BCT No. 15 Prompts/cues – teachers and pupils were encourage to decorate noticeboards within the classroom with reminders of the physical activity guidelines and examples of intervention activities which they enjoyed.

Recruitment of schools to the PATCH intervention

For the PATCH Study, we were able to draw upon the good contacts Ulster University have with local schools. We present below some recommendations that should be taken into account when recruiting schools to a physical activity intervention. First, the choice of school may be dictated by the nature of the research. For example, if the research is focused on altering physical activity in socially-disadvantaged children then researchers may want to find ways of classifying schools or children according to a reliable measure of deprivation or social class. We have used the proportion of children receiving free school meals, the postcode or location of the school, or the individual postcode of children attending a school as an index of socio-economic class status (Breslin & Brennan, 2012), with other researchers using deprivation indexes or parents' occupation, employment status of income as a measure (Fairclough, Hackett, Davies, & Gobbi, 2013). Schools can be categorized by many other variables such as geographic location (urban versus rural), school size, single-sex or co-educational, state or privately funded, faith or non-faith based, and so on. Based on these, researchers need to consider how the school type selected can help/hinder them in terms of addressing their specific research question (e.g., comparison of active transport between urban and rural school children) or allow/prevent their findings being applied across the population (e.g., findings in more affluent areas of a town or city being applied to those from socially-disadvantaged areas or schools and vice versa).

Once decisions about recruiting schools are made and researchers are certain that the schools they have selected represent the population to which they wish to apply their findings, they should seek approval from the school principal. This will often require the research to be considered by the schools senior management team or board of governors. If possible, researchers should meet with these key decision makers to outline the purpose of the intervention, the associated research aims, and answer any questions. In our experience interventions to promote physical activity are generally welcomed, as most principals are aware of the importance of physical activity to health. Although a letter to the school principal is often the starting point for contact between the researcher and the school, the researcher should be aware that schools receive many requests to participate in a range of initiatives and need to make decisions based upon their assessment of the suitability of the project for their particular setting, the timing of the project, and the potential benefit for their children.

Accessing schools with whom you have not already worked can be challenging. For this reason researchers often use 'convenience sampling' where schools are chosen because of their accessibility, proximity to the researcher, or having established a relationship or worked with them previously. This is the approach we took to recruit for PATCH. While the principal, senior management, board of governors, and education board are the gatekeepers for school-based research, physical activity interventions targeted at individual children (as opposed to a change in the curriculum delivered), at least in the UK, require parental consent and assent from each child participating in the intervention. This requirement mainly comes from research ethics governance.

Ethical considerations in physical activity research with children

In most countries including the UK and Ireland all research with human participants requires ethical approval. If based at a university the process will vary by institution but usually involves a peer review of the proposed study to ensure that the research is robust and is likely to address the research questions proposed. The review by a committee aims to consider the ethical issues that may arise from the proposed study, and a cost/benefit analysis is conducted to assess whether the burden that participation in the research places upon participants is justifiable given the potential knowledge that will be gained by undertaking the research. For school-based intervention research ethics committees need to be assured that the intervention and the associated research to be carried out is not likely to cause any harm to children who participate. When developing a programme, researchers and practitioners should consider the amount of time that their intervention and any measurement is likely to take, how this might impact on the delivery of the existing curriculum and what will happen in terms of alternative activities for children who do not wish, or whose parents do not wish them to participate. Informed consent is an important part of any research study and requires getting permission from participants before conducting the research. As the name suggests, consent should be requested after participants have been made fully aware of the purpose of the study. When working with children, informed consent can only be given by the parent or guardian and so often a description of the intervention and research is provided, in lay language, to each parent whose child is being invited to take part. Parents are then given an opportunity to seek clarification on any issue before agreeing whether or not that their child can participate. Usually this information is sent to parents via the school who will know which adult has parental responsibility for the child in cases where this responsibility is not shared between two parents.

Once a parent/guardian has given their consent, assent is sought from the child. Even if the parent has given consent, a child should have an opportunity to agree or decline to participate. In order to gain informed assent from a child, information about the intervention and the associated research needs to be presented in an age-appropriate manner. Often this is done by simplified child-friendly information sheets supplemented by the researcher answering any questions the children may have. It is important that each child is made aware that they can refuse to take part in the study and that they are free to withdraw from the study at any time. It goes without saying that the confidentiality, anonymity, and storage of the data reflecting the children's personal scores on any measurements or tests used are dealt with carefully.

Ensuring the fidelity of the PATCH intervention

The PATCH intervention was delivered in a number of classes within a school and indeed across several schools. Often, interventions are delivered by teachers (as was PATCH) or other school staff and day-to-day contact with researchers is minimal. Although such interventions are more likely to ensure sustainability than those in which the intervention is delivered by a researcher, they present significant challenges. For research purposes, it is important to ensure that the key components of the intervention are delivered in a similar manner across the classes and schools so that any pooling of data from children who have received the intervention can be justified. Intervention fidelity has been described as 'strategies that monitor and enhance the accuracy and consistency of an intervention to ensure it is implemented as planned and that each component is delivered in a comparable manner to all study participants over time' (Smith, Daunic, & Taylor, 2007, p. 121). Therefore practitioner and researchers need to ensure that the intervention is implemented as intended and any changes to this implementation are carefully noted. Some practical examples of how fidelity can be achieved include: recording sessions (audio/video), observing sessions (researcher, teacher, or independent person), using diaries or logs to note what was done or what was happening in school on a given day, providing standardized information packs, presentation content, or resources including teaching plans. In the PATCH intervention, teachers received both initial and ongoing training in the use of PATCH intervention components. They were also provided with classroom resources (e.g. a wall chart on which children recorded their 'favourite' daily classroom-based exercises) and were encouraged to keep a weekly diary to record the delivery of intervention components. It was planned that this would increase intervention fidelity. By checking that the intervention has been delivered the researcher can be more confident that any changes observed following an intervention can be attributed to the intervention, limiting the effects from confounding variables. A detailed written description of how the intervention should be implemented, training for those deliverers, and regular contact with the researcher may enhance the fidelity of intervention research and helps to ensure that the intervention is delivered as designed.

Evaluating the PATCH intervention: what was measured?

To monitor the effects of the PATCH intervention a quantitative approach was adopted with a 2 (groups) × 3 (measurement time points) mixed research design. Classes within schools were randomly assigned to either a PATCH intervention or control group (no programme). The inclusion of the control group allowed any changes in physical activity that may result from the PATCH intervention to be determined.

Physical activity was measured objectively with tri-axial accelerometers (ActiGraph GT3X, MTI Health Services, Pensacola, FL, United States), which were distributed to participants in school, and worn on the right hip for seven consecutive days using a 5-second epoch of data collection. An accelerometer is a mechanical device that assesses the amount and intensity of physical activity. Using an accelerometer overcomes any bias or shortcomings of self-report measures. The minimum wear-time for inclusion in data analysis was 10 hours of registered time for ≥3 days (Mattocks, Ness, Leary, Tilling, Blair, & Shield et al., 2008). Sustained ≥20-minute periods of consecutive zero counts were removed from the analysis of daily wear-time (Catellier, Hannan, Murray, Addy, Conway, & Yang et al., 2005). As large individual differences exist in counts at different activity intensities (Rowlands, 2007), data were analysed using individually calibrated thresholds. These thresholds were generated from accelerometer data collected during a pre-intervention treadmill protocol to VO_2peak. A threshold of 100 counts per minute (Trueth, Schmitz, Catellier, McMurray, Almeida, Going, & Norma et al., 2004) was implemented to denote sedentary time in the analysis. For each valid day, minutes of sedentary time, light physical activity, moderate physical activity, and vigorous physical activity were calculated for each individual. In addition, a filter was applied to the physical activity data to enable 'school-time' physical activity variables to be calculated for each participant. Furthermore anthropometric measurements of height and weight were collected and children completed a questionnaire.

Pilot testing

Pilot testing was useful in determining the logistics of the fieldwork, and in scheduling the chronological order of questionnaire completion, anthropometric measurements taken, followed by physical activity measurement. We are focusing only on the physical activity measurement in this chapter, but other measures were also taken at the time of the intervention. Prior to physical activity measurement, participants were fitted with accelerometers during school-based presentations. General information on how to wear the monitor was given during this session. In addition, participants were also given an ActiGraph information and resource pack. This pack provided information about physical activity monitoring for parents/guardians and contained additional resources for participants (e.g., a poster and diary) to promote adherence to wear-time criteria. The physical activity breaks component of the intervention were also practised with the intervention group for suitability, understanding, engagement, and to confirm that the physical activities were at least moderate-vigorous intensity.

Consultation with the teachers, school principal, as well as the parents during the pilot phase also led to a protocol being put in place on how to approach teachers and school principals to take part. This was considered important as it increased the level of 'buy in' to the programme. The consultation led to a short presentation being delivered at a parent-teacher evening to inform teachers and parents of the project aims and what was entailed in terms of the content of the programme and the research element.

FRAMEWORK AND INTERVENTION

A cognitive behavioural approach was taken to the design of the intervention, specifically, the PATCH intervention was based on SCT (Bandura,1977). PATCH provided primary school children with both the knowledge of the benefits of physical activity and the opportunity to be active during the school day (see Figure 22.5 for a flow of participants through the study). The intervention was teacher-led, and aimed to increase daily physical activity by incorporating classroom-based physical activity bouts throughout the course of the school day, an approach that has been used effectively in a number of school-based interventions (Donnelly, Greene, Gibson, Smith, Washburn, & Sullivan, 2009; Naylor et al., 2006; Jurg et al., 2006; Caballero, Clay, Davis, Ethelbah, Rock, & Lohman, 2003). In addition to the daily physical activity breaks, intervention teachers delivered a weekly theory-based lesson on the key themes of, 'exercise and activity', 'reducing screen time and sedentary behaviour', and 'healthy eating and nutrition'. This 'knowledge' component of the intervention was designed to complement, and integrate into, the Northern Ireland Key Stage 2 Personal Development and Mutual Understanding (PDMU) curriculum. Integrating multiple components of the PATCH intervention within the Northern Ireland school curriculum and using teachers to deliver the intervention, made the intervention both sustainable and low-cost. The PATCH intervention also aimed to increase overall daily MVPA with the inclusion of 'physical activity at home' as families are important mediators of physical activity behaviour outside the school (Salmon et al., 2007). The findings of several reviews recommend including a family component to increase the effectiveness of physical activity interventions with children (Dobbins et al., 2013; Kriemler, Meyer, Martin, Van Sluijs, Andersen, & Martin, 2011). Therefore PATCH involved daily physical activity 'homework' and monthly parental newsletters to inform parents/guardians of the benefits of physical activity for children's health. An example from Abraham and Michie's (2008) taxonomy of BCTs which was relevant to the content of this intervention component is, BCT No. 36 'instruction on how to perform a behaviour'. For example, intervention participants and their parents/guardians were provided with information on the current physical activity guidelines, describing the amount and type of physical activity that is recommended for children in this age group.

A range of SCT components incorporated into the design of the PATCH intervention included: modelling positive healthy behaviours to encourage learning (observing teachers, parents and siblings perform physical activity), providing opportunities to learn, rehearse, and practise activities at school and at home, and self-monitoring of physical activity behaviour by providing feedback (e.g., looking at how they can be active at home, Figure 22.1). In addition, opportunities to problem solve, wherein children learn ways to overcome barriers to being active indoors and outdoors despite constraints such as the weather or lack of facilities or equipment was included. Setting physical activity goals that were attainable, measurable, and rewarded positively when achieved were also used. Furthermore, classroom and homework-based activities were tailored to include a physical activity component. Both classroom-based work and homework were provided to show children how and where they could be active with their families.

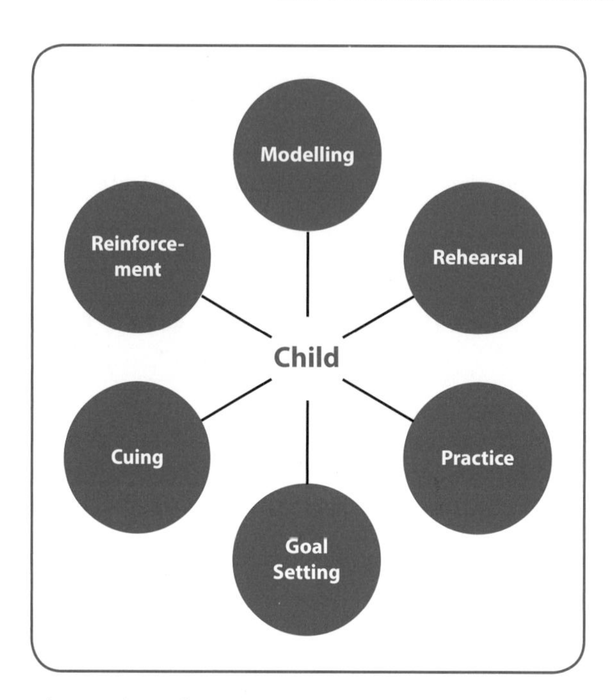

FIGURE 22.1 *Outlining the matching of SCT components with the PATCH intervention.*

The activity break was teacher-led, and aimed to increase daily MVPA by incorporating classroom-based physical activity bouts throughout the course of the school day. The delivery of physical activity breaks was designed to be flexible and have minimal impact on the academic component of the normal school day. As such, the goal of this component was to increase school-based physical activity by a minimum of 30 minutes. Physical activity bouts were delivered prior to, and after natural breaks in the school day (e.g., 10 minutes in the morning before academic classes began, 5 minutes prior to break time, 5 minutes prior to lunch and after lunch, and 5 minutes before the end of the school day). It was important that this component would not increase teacher preparation time and be enjoyable for the teacher as well as the children. Therefore, to facilitate teachers they received multimedia resources (a PowerPoint presentation with video demonstrations of activities) to support the delivery of the activity session.

Figure 22.2 a consists of an excerpt taken from the intervention teacher's physical activity resource booklet (which accompanied the interactive whiteboard PowerPoint and video package). The physical activity resource booklet was used by teachers to direct exercises in school environments where an interactive whiteboard was not available (e.g., school assembly hall). The booklets include names, a description, and a photo of each activity. All 60 activities in the booklet were designed to be suitable for safe use within the classroom environment. The screen capture (Figure 22.2 b) shows the content of the physical activity resource booklet in PowerPoint format. The PowerPoint package was designed to be displayed on the interactive whiteboard and each slide contained a video demonstration of the activity being performed. Intervention class teachers were free to choose the number and order of activities used during physical activity breaks. Appropriate musical accompaniment was available in intervention classrooms to enhance pupils' enjoyment of the activity breaks (for a review see Karageorghis and Priest, 2012). Teachers received two 40-minute training sessions on the delivery of both the PATCH curriculum components and the use of multimedia resources prior to the commencement of the intervention with their class. One session involved in-class demonstrations of the

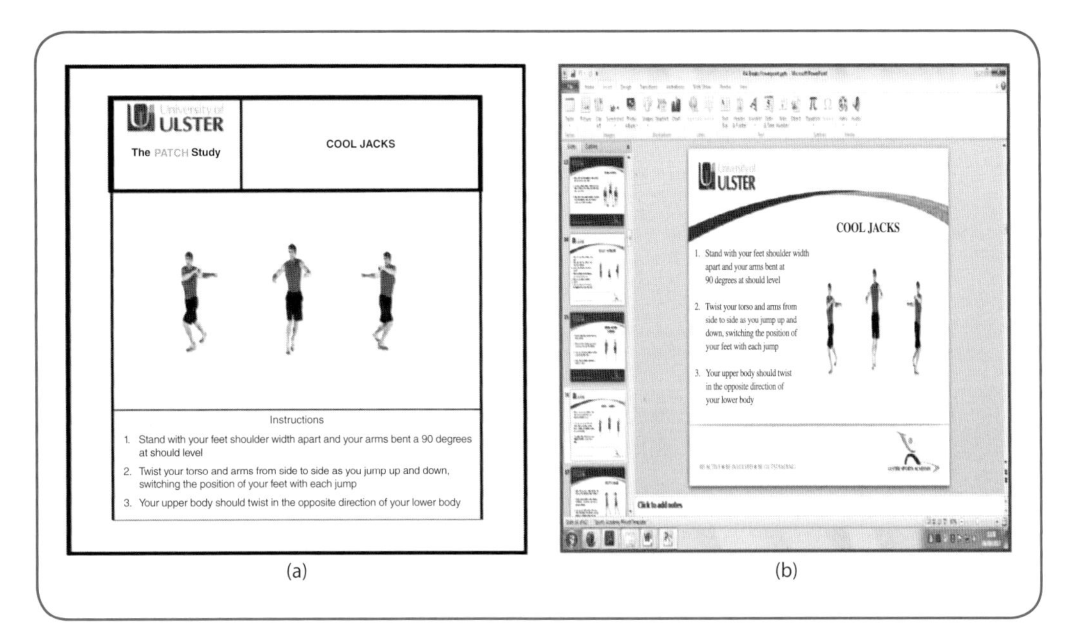

FIGURE 22.2 (a) *Example of physical activity break taken from the intervention teacher's physical activity resource booklet.*

FIGURE 22.2 (b) *Example of physical activity break taken from the interactive whiteboard PowerPoint and video demonstration package.*

set-up and delivery of interactive whiteboard activities and the second session discussed the rationale, development and delivery of the PATCH curriculum. Training on the delivery of both new and updated resources was ongoing during the intervention.

Daily physical activity at home messages aimed to get pupils active with a minimum requirement of 10 minutes of physical activity. This component was designed to minimize the amount of time spent in sedentary behaviour at home and outside school. The rationale for this extra-curricular component of the intervention was to increase overall daily physical activity by establishing a positive link between the daily school-based intervention activities and the home environment. Whereas the weekly PDMU lesson provided pupils with the knowledge of the benefits of physical activity, reducing sedentary behaviour and healthy nutrition, the school-based physical activities provided pupils with practical examples of activities that could be carried out at home or outside school.

During the course of the intervention, monthly newsletters (three in total over the course of the 12-week intervention) were delivered to parents and guardians on the key themes of, 'exercise and activity', 'reducing screen time and sedentary behaviour', and 'healthy eating and nutrition'. The rationale for this component of the intervention was to establish a positive link between the school and home environment by informing parents of the content of school-based intervention lessons and activities. Parents and guardians play an important role in encouraging children to be physically active (Brockman, Jago, Fox, Thompson, Cartwright, & Page, 2009) and usually have primary responsibility for their children's participation in physical activity (Giles-Corti, Kelty, Zubrick, & Villanueva, 2009; for a review see, Beets, Cardinal, & Alderman, 2010). For example, Newsletter 1 reflected the content of pupil's lessons on the theme of 'exercise and activity' and provided parents with information on current physical activity guidelines, the benefits of physical activity in youth, and advice on how parents and guardians could help their children to be active. Figure 22.2 c displays an example of a parent or guardian newsletter.

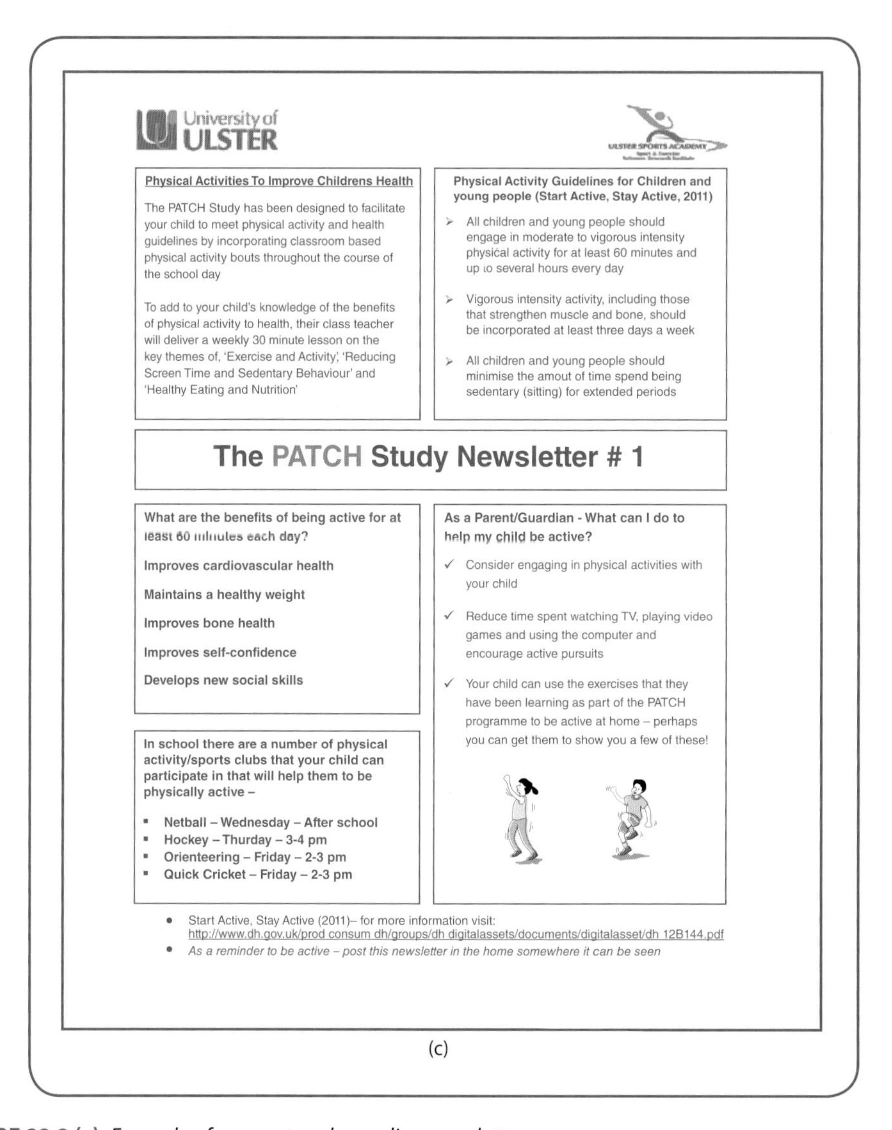

University of ULSTER

ULSTER SPORTS ACADEMY

Physical Activities To Improve Childrens Health

The PATCH Study has been designed to facilitate your child to meet physical activity and health guidelines by incorporating classroom based physical activity bouts throughout the course of the school day

To add to your child's knowledge of the benefits of physical activity to health, their class teacher will deliver a weekly 30 minute lesson on the key themes of, 'Exercise and Activity', 'Reducing Screen Time and Sedentary Behaviour' and 'Healthy Eating and Nutrition'

Physical Activity Guidelines for Children and young people (Start Active, Stay Active, 2011)

- All children and young people should engage in moderate to vigorous intensity physical activity for at least 60 minutes and up to several hours every day
- Vigorous intensity activity, including those that strengthen muscle and bone, should be incorporated at least three days a week
- All children and young people should minimise the amout of time spend being sedentary (sitting) for extended periods

The PATCH Study Newsletter # 1

What are the benefits of being active for at least 60 minutes each day?

Improves cardiovascular health

Maintains a healthy weight

Improves bone health

Improves self-confidence

Develops new social skills

In school there are a number of physical activity/sports clubs that your child can participate in that will help them to be physically active –

- **Netball – Wednesday – After school**
- **Hockey – Thurday – 3-4 pm**
- **Orienteering – Friday – 2-3 pm**
- **Quick Cricket – Friday – 2-3 pm**

As a Parent/Guardian - What can I do to help my child be active?

✓ Consider engaging in physical activities with your child

✓ Reduce time spent watching TV, playing video games and using the computer and encourage active pursuits

✓ Your child can use the exercises that they have been learning as part of the PATCH programme to be active at home – perhaps you can get them to show you a few of these!

- Start Active, Stay Active (2011)– for more information visit: http://www.dh.gov.uk/prod consum dh/groups/dh digitalassets/documents/digitalasset/dh 12B144.pdf
- *As a reminder to be active – post this newsletter in the home somewhere it can be seen*

(c)

FIGURE 22.2 (c) *Example of a parent and guardian newsletter.*

Key findings

The PATCH intervention resulted in significant increases in school time moderate to vigorous physical activity and school-time vigorous physical activity and also significantly increased total daily moderate to vigorous physical activity and total daily physical activity (by 14 $\pm$ (14) minutes and 27 $\pm$ (23) minutes respectively), compared to decreases of 4 $\pm$ (13) minutes of daily MVPA and 6 $\pm$ (34) minutes of total daily PA in the control group (pre- to mid-intervention). These findings are consistent with the results of a number of previous school-based PA interventions (Gorely et al., 2009; Kriemler et al., 2010; Breslin et al., 2012a) and provide support for the utility of school-based interventions in increasing daily physical activity in primary school children in the UK. There were no changes in weight or BMI as a result of the intervention.

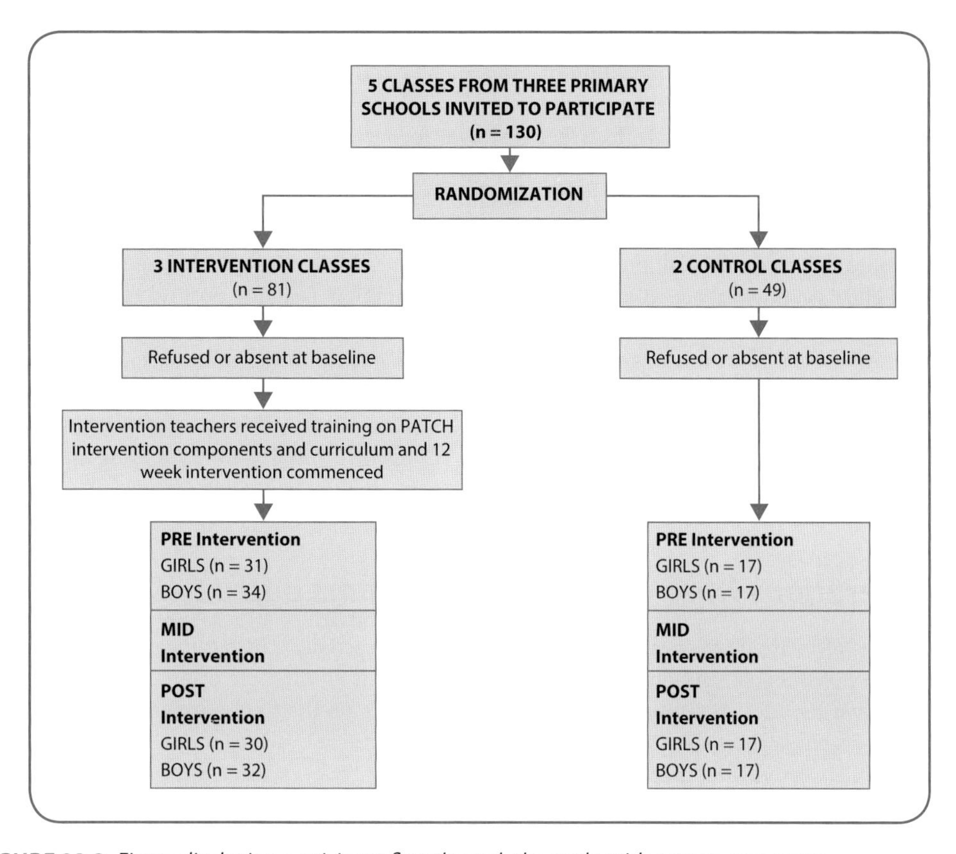

FIGURE 22.3 *Figure displaying participant flow through the study, with outcome measures.*

REFLECTIONS

Lessons learnt

The PATCH intervention was designed to have minimal impact on teacher preparation and academic time as well as being enjoyable for teachers and pupils. Research suggests that 'enjoyment' of physical activity is an important mediator of physical activity in school-based physical activity interventions (Salmon et al., 2007) and that children prefer fun, non-competitive activities, and opportunities to explore a range of physical activities (Coulter & Woods, 2011). Interventions should aim to enhance 'enjoyment' in order to maintain and increase children's physical activity (Ferrer-Caja & Weiss, 2000). To meet these objectives, class teachers received training on the content and delivery of school-based intervention components prior to the intervention and the content of intervention components was developed and enhanced through consultation with the intervention teachers during the programme. Integrating the multiple components of the PATCH intervention within the existing NI curriculum and using class teachers to deliver the intervention was a sustainable, low-cost approach that could be reproduced effectively in primary schools throughout Northern Ireland.

The PATCH intervention provided all children in intervention classes with additional structured and compulsory activity, including those who might have dropped out if given a free choice, and regardless of whether they consented to undergo study measurements. The inclusion of all children in a class also avoided any stigmatization of overweight and unfit children, and gave all children an equal chance to benefit from this type of physical activity intervention.

On reflection, despite positive effects being shown for increasing physical activity in the school environment, practitioners may need to include more vigorous-intensity physical activity (to increase total energy expenditure) and extend the duration of intervention (e.g., one academic year) to see substantial and sustained changes in physical activity levels. Repeatedly exposing participants to key health promotion messages and intervention activities over a longer period of time may result in a sustained effect on physical activity (Gorely et al., 2011) and may facilitate positive changes in body composition (e.g., development of lean mass and a reduction in adiposity). Continually reinforcing healthy lifestyle behaviours related to energy expenditure (e.g., promoting physical activity, encouraging healthy eating, and reducing sedentary behaviour) may encourage sustained changes in behaviour and increase the effectiveness of the intervention to attenuate increases in adiposity over time (Bacon & Aphramour, 2011). Utilising a 'whole-school' model of health promotion and adopting a combined physical activity and diet strategy may also help to prevent children becoming overweight/ or obese in the long term.

Considerations when assessing programme outcomes

A wide range of methods are available for measuring physical activity which can generally be divided into objective, self-report, and observational. Accelerometry is an example of an objective measure and has shown the most promise for providing accurate data on the frequency, intensity, duration, and pattern of physical activity. Accelerometers, of which there are various models, are small waist, wrist, or ankle worn devices which record movement in one, two, or three axes. They can be programmed to collect data every second or few seconds or minute for periods of up to seven days or more (Cain, Conway, Adams, Husak, & Sallis, 2013). Although expensive, these devices can be reused and over time are likely to decrease in cost and represent a useful tool for the objective measurement of physical activity in school-based interventions and for comparison across interventions. The advent of smart-phone and wearable technologies looks set to revolutionize the cost of objective monitoring of physical activity; therefore future interventions may benefit from less expensive wearable devices to monitor physical activity.

Multicomponent interventions (like PATCH) which include a variety of techniques to enhance physical activity have the potential to reach more children by broadening the types of physical activity on offer (Kriemler et al., 2011). Although recent NICE guidelines (NICE, 2009), several studies (Magnusson et al., 2011; deMeij et al., 2011; Kriemler et al., 2010; Donnelly et al., 2009; Gorely et al., 2009; Salmon et al., 2007; Naylor et al., 2006; Caballero et al., 2003; Jurg et al., 2006) and recent reviews (Dobbins et al., 2013; Kriemler et al., 2011) have suggested that school-based interventions should adopt a multicomponent design, such designs are problematic when attempting to identify which of the individual components of the intervention contribute most to the promotion of physical activity behaviour change. This view is supported in a review of 44 studies that included 36,593 children and adolescents which evaluated the impact of school-based interventions on increasing physical activity. The authors concluded that no two effective school-based programmes had the same combination of intervention components (Dobbins et al., 2013).

In the PATCH intervention teachers received both initial and ongoing training in the use of PATCH intervention components. They were also provided with classroom resources (e.g., a wall chart on which children recorded their 'favourite' daily classroom-based exercises) and were encouraged to keep a weekly diary to record the delivery of intervention components. It was envisaged that these resources would increase intervention fidelity. However, a potential limitation was that physical activity feedback was not provided to pupils or teachers during the intervention. Without accurate objective feedback it may have been difficult for teachers to gauge the appropriate intensity of classroom-based physical activity and may have resulted in pupils engaging in more light-intensity activities. Future studies should include specific measures to assess the intensity of classroom-based physical activity; perhaps by using the validated time-moment sampling procedure 'System for Observation of Fitness Instruction Time' (SOFIT; McKenzie, Sallis, & Nader, 1991).

In summary, the short-term results of the PATCH Study are encouraging and highlight the utility of multicomponent interventions that are theoretically based to promote healthy behaviours in school-age children. However, further research is required in order to establish how to transfer short- into long-term behaviour change with the potential for meaningful health outcomes in adulthood.

FURTHER READING

Breslin, G., & Brennan, D. (2012). A healthy lifestyle intervention delivered by aspiring physical education teachers to children from social disadvantage: Study protocol and preliminary findings. *Child Care in Practice, 18*(3), 1–19. This article outlines the design of a 12-week physical activity intervention for children from social disadvantage. The detail provided in the article will complement the experiences outlined in the present chapter.

Breslin, G., & McCay, N. (2012). Perceived control over physical and mental wellbeing: The effects of gender, age and social class. *Journal of Health Psychology,* 18(1), 38–45. This article outlines a cross sectional survey of physical activity and wellbeing in children. The measures used in the article may have relevance to those interested in the assessment of wellbeing and quality of life in children.

DiClemente, R. J., Salazar, L. F., & Crosby, R. A. (2013). *Health behaviour theory for public health. Principles, foundations, and applications.* Burlington, MA: Jones and Bartlett. This book provides further detail on using Social Cognitive Theory in the design of health behaviour-change interventions.

McMinn, D., Rowe, D., Murtagh, S., Nelson, N., Ivan, C., & Almir, A., et al. (2014). Psychosocial factors related to children's active school travel: A comparison of two European regions. *International Journal of Exercise Science, 7*(1), 75–86. This article applies the theory of planned behaviour to predict children's active travel across a sample of children from several countries in Europe. The article is of interest to those developing an active school travel initiative for schools.

REFERENCES

Abraham, C., & Michie, S. (2008). A taxonomy of behavior change techniques used in interventions. *Health Psychology, 27*(3), 379–387.

Ajzen, I. (1985). From intentions to actions: A theory of planned behavior. In J. Kuhl & J. Beckmann (Eds.), *Action-control: From cognition to behavior* (pp. 11–39). Heidelberg: Springer.

Ajzen, I. (1987). Attitudes, traits, and actions: Dispositional prediction of behavior in personality and social psychology. In L. Berkowitz (Ed.), *Advances in experimental social psychology* (Vol. 20, pp. 1–63). New York: Academic Press.

Ajzen, I. (1991). The theory of planned behavior. *Organizational behavior and human decision processes, 50*, 179–211.

Australian Government, Department of Health (2014). Australia's physical activity and sedentary behaviour guidelines for children *(5–12 years)*. Department of Health and Ageing: Canberra

Bacon, L., & Aphramour, L. (2011). Weight science: Evaluating the evidence for a paradigm shift. Nutrition Journal, *10*(9).

Bandura, A. (1965). Vicarious processes: A case of no-trial learning. In L. Berkowitz (Ed.), *Advances in experimental social psychology* (Vol. 2, pp. 1–55). New York: Academic Press.

Bandura, A. (1971). Analysis of modelling processes. In A. Bandura (Ed.), *Psychological modeling: Conflicting theories* (pp. 1–62). Chicago: Adline-Atherton.

Bandura, A. (1977). *Social learning theory*. Englewood Cliffs, NJ: Prentice Hall. Bandura, A. (1986). *Social foundations of thought and action: A social cognitive theory*. Englewood Cliffs, NJ: Prentice- Hall, Inc.

Beets, M. W., Cardinal, B. J., & Alderman, B. L. (2010). Parental social support and the physical activity-related behaviors of youth: A review. *Health Education and Behavior*, *37*(5), 621–644.

Biddle, S. J. H., Pearson, N., Ross, G. M., & Braithwaite, R. (2010). Tracking of sedentary behaviours of young people: *A systematic review. Preventative Medicine*, *51*, 345–351.

Breslin, G., & Brennan, D. (2012). A healthy lifestyle intervention delivered by aspiring PE teachers to children from social disadvantage: Study protocol and preliminary findings. *Child Care and Practice*, *18*(3), 1–19.

Breslin, G., Brennan, D., Rafferty, R., Gallagher, A., & Hanna, D. (2012a). The effect of a healthy lifestyle programme on 8–9 year olds from social disadvantage. *Archives of Disease in Childhood*, *97*, 618–624.

Breslin, G., Murphy, M. H., Dempster, M., Delaney, B., & McKee, D. (2012b). The effect of teachers trained in a fundamental movement skills programme on children's self-perceptions and motor competence. *European Journal of Physical Education Review*, *18*(1), 114–126.

British Heart Foundation (2011). Sedentary behaviour: Evidence Briefing.

Brockman, R., Jago, R., Fox, K. R., Thompson, J. L., Cartwright, K., & Page, A. S. (2009). 'Get off the sofa and go and play': Family and socioeconomic influences on the physical activity of 10–11 year old children. *BioMed Central Public Health*, *21*, 253.

Brown, H., Hume, C., Pearson, N., & Salmon, J. (2013). A systematic review of intervention effects on potential mediators of children's physical activity. *BMC Public Health*, *13*, 165–175.

Caballero, B., Clay, T., Davis, S. M., Ethelbah, B., Rock, B. H., Lohman, T. (2003). Pathways: A school-based, randomized controlled trial for the prevention of obesity in American Indian school children. *American Journal of Clinical Nutrition*, *78*, 1030–1038.

Cain, K. L., Conway, T. L., Adams, M. A., Husak, L. E., & Sallis, J. F. (2013). Comparison of older and newer generations of ActiGraph accelerometers with the normal filter and the low frequency extension. *International Journal of Behavioural Nutrition and Physical Activity*, 10(51).

Cale, L., & Harris, J. (2006). School-based physical activity interventions: Effectiveness, trends, issues, implications and recommendations for practice. Sport, *Education and Society*, *11*, 401–420.

Carroll, W. R., & Bandura, A. (1982). The role of visual monitoring in observational learning of action patterns: Making the unobservable observable. *Journal of Motor Behavior*, *14*, 153–167.

Catellier, D. J., Hannan, P. J., Murray, D. M., Addy, C. L., Conway, T. L., & Yang, S., et al. (2005). Inputation of missing data when measuring activity by accelerometry. *Medicine and Science in Sports and Exercise*, *37*, S555–S562.

Cheung, S. Y., Mak, J. Y., & Chan, J. (2008). Children's physical activity participation and psychological wellbeing. *Research Quarterly for Exercise and Sport*, 79 (Suppl.1), A30.

Chillon, P., Evenson, K. R., Vaughn, A., & Ward, D. (2011). A systematic review of interventions for promoting active transportation to school. *International Journal of Behavioral Nutrition and Physical Activity*, 8(10).

Cleland, V., Timperio, A., Salmon, J., Hume, C., Telford, A., & Crawford, D. (2011). A longitudinal study of the family physical activity environment and physical activity among youth. *American Journal of Health Promotion*, *25*, 159–167.

Cole, T. J., Bellizzi, M. C., Flegal, K. M., & Dietz, W. H. (2000). Establishing a standard definition for child overweight and obesity worldwide: International survey. *British Medical Journal*, *320*, 1240–1243.

Colley, R. C., Garriguet, D., Janssen, I., Craig, C. L., Clarke, J., & Tremblay, M. S. (2011). Physical activity of Canadian children and youth: Accelerometer results from the 2007 to 2009 Canadian health measures survey. *Health Reports*, *22*(1), 15–23.

Colley, R. C., Garriguet, D., Janssen, I., Wong, S. L., & Saunders, T. J. (2013). The association between accelerometer-measured patterns of sedentary time and health risk in children and youth: Results from the Canadian Health Measures Survey. *BMC Public Health*, *7*(13), 200–209.

Coulter, M., & Woods, C. B. (2011). An exploration of children's perceptions and enjoyment of school-based physical activity and physical education. *Journal of Physical Activity and Health*, *8*, 645–654.

Craig, R., Mindell, J., & Hirani, V. (2009). *Health survey for England: Physical activity and fitness* (Chapter 6, Accelerometry in children, 160–173). Leeds: Health and Social Care Information Centre.

Crocker, P. R. E., Eklund, R. C., & Kowalski, K. C. (2000) Children's physical activity and physical self-perceptions. Journal of Sports Science, *18*, 383–394.

Cunningham, C., Breslin, G., Boddy, L., Stratton, G., Nevill, A. & Murphy, M. H. (under review). *A multicomponent intervention to increase physical activity levels in primary school children:* The PATCH Study.

Deci, E. L., & Ryan, R. M. (1985). *Intrinsic Motivation and Self Determination in Human Behaviour.* New York: Plenum.

deMeij, J. S., Chinapaw, M. J., & van Stralen, M. M. (2011). Effectiveness of JUMP- in, a Dutch primary school-based community intervention aimed at the promotion of physical activity. *British Journal of Sports Medicine, 45*, 1052–1057.

Department of Culture Arts and Leisure (DCAL) (2009). The Northern Ireland Strategy For Sport And Physical Recreation 2009–2019. Northern Ireland.

Department of Health (2011). Start active, stay active: A report on physical activity for health from the four home countries' chief medical officers.

Department of Health Australia (2008). 2007 Australian national children's nutrition and physical activity survey. Main findings. Department of Health and Ageing, Australian Food and Grocery Council, Department of Agriculture, Fisheries and Forestry. Australian Government.

Dobbins, M., De Corby, K., & Robeson, P. (2009). School-based physical activity programs for promoting physical activity and fitness in children and adolescents aged 6–18. *Cochrane Database Systematic Reviews*, 1.

Dobbins, M., Husson, H., DeCorby, K., & LaRocca, R. L. (2013). School-based physical activity programs for promoting physical activity and fitness in children and adolescents aged 6 to 18. Cochrane Database of *Systematic Reviews*, 2.

Donnelly, J. E., Greene, J. L., Gibson, C. A., Smith, B. K., Washburn, R. A., & Sullivan, D. K. (2009). Physical activity across the curriculum (PAAC): A randomized controlled trial to promote physical activity and diminish overweight and obesity in elementary school children. *Preventive Medicine, 49*, 336–341.

Dumith, S. C., Gigante, D. P., Domingues, M. R., & Kohl, H. W. (2011). Physical activity change during adolescence: A systematic review and a pooled analysis. *International Journal of Epidemiology, 40*, 685–698.

Fairclough, S. J., Hackett, A. F., Davies, I. G., & Gobbi, R. (2013). Promoting healthy weight in primary school children through physical activity and nutrition education: A pragmatic evaluation of the CHANGE! Randomised intervention study. *BMC Public Health, 13*, 626–640.

Fakhouri, T. H. I., Hughes, J. P., Burt, V. L., Song, M., Fulton, J. E. & Ogden, C. L. (2014). *Physical activity in U.S. youth aged 12–15 years*, 2012 (NCHS Data Brief No. 141). Hyattsville, MD: National Center for Health Statistics.

Ferrer-Caja, E. & Weiss, M. R. (2000). Predictors of intrinsic motivation among adolescent students in physical education. *Research Quarterly for Exercise and Sport, 71*, 267–279.

Giles-Corti, B., Kelty, S. F., Zubrick, S. R., & Villanueva, K. P. (2009). Encouraging walking for transport and physical activity in children and adolescents: How important is the built environment? *Sports Medicine, 39*, 995–1009.

Gorely, T., Morris, J. G., Musson, H., Brown, S., Nevill, A., & Nevill, M. E. (2011). Physical activity and body composition outcomes of the GreatFun2Run intervention at 20 month follow-up. *International Journal of Behavioral Nutrition and Physical Activity*, 8, 74.

Gorely, T., Nevill, M. E., & Morris, J. G. (2009). Effect of a school-based intervention to promote healthy lifestyles in 7–11 year old children. *International Journal of Behavioural Nutrition and Physical Activity*, 6(5).

Gortmaker, S., Peterson, K., Wiecha, J., Sobol, A., Dixit, S., & Fox, M., et al. (1999). Reducing obesity via a school based interdisciplinary intervention among youth (Planet Health). *Archives of Pediatrics and Adolescent Medicine, 153*, 409–417.

Gould, D., Hodge, K., Peterson, K., & Giannini, J. (1989). An exploratory examination of strategies used by elite coaches to enhance self-efficacy in athletes. Journal of Sport *& Exercise Psychology, 11*, 128–140.

Gould, D., & Roberts, G. C. (1982). Modelling and motor skill acquisition. *Quest, 33*, 214–230.

Griffiths, L. J., Cortina- Borja, M., & Sera, F. (2013). How active are our children? Findings from the Millennium Cohort Study. *BMJ Open*, 3, e002893.

Guay, F., Boggiano, A. K., & Vallerand, R. J. (2001). Autonomy support, intrinsic motivation, and perceived competence: Conceptual and empirical linkages. *Personality and Social Psychology Bulletin, 27*, 643–650.

Hagger, M., Chatzisarantis, N., Biddle, S., & Orbell, S. (2001). Antecedents of children's physical activity intentions and behavior: Predictive validity and longitudinal effects. *Psychology and Health, 16*, 391–407.

Harris, K. C., Kuramoto, L. K., Schulzer, M., & Retallack, J. E. (2009). Effect of school-based physical activity interventions on body mass index in children: a meta-analysis. *Canadian Medical Association Journal, 180*, 719–726.

Harrison, M., Burns, C. F., McGuinness, M., Heslin, J., & Murphy, N. M. (2006). Influence of a health education intervention on physical activity and screen time in primary school children: 'Switch Off–Get Active'. *Journal of Science and Medicine, 9*(5), 288–294.

Harter, S. (1985). Manual for the *self-perception profile for children*. Denver, CO: University of Denver.

Harter, S. (1987). The determinants and meditational role of global self-worth in children. In N. Eisenberg (Ed.), *Contemporary issues in developmental psychology* (pp. 219–242). New York: John Wiley & Sons, Inc.

Haughey, T., Breslin, G., Toole, S., & McKee, M. (2013). Developing physical literacy through coach education A Northern Ireland perspective. *Journal of Sport Science and Physical Education, 65*, 253–257.

Hodges, N. J., Hayes, S., Breslin, G., & Williams, A. M. (2005). An evaluation of the minimal constraining information during movement observation and reproduction. *Acta Psychologica, 119*(3), 264.

Hsu, Y. W., Belcher, B. R., Ventura, E. E., Byrd-Williams, C. E., Weigensberg, M. J., & Davis, J. N., et al. (2011). Physical activity, sedentary behavior, and the metabolic syndrome in minority youth. *Medicine and Science in Sports and Exercise, 43*(12), 2307–2313.

Jago, R., & Baranowski, T. (2004). Non-curricular approaches for increasing physical activity in youth: A review. *Preventative Medicine, 39*, 157–163.

Janssen, I., & LeBlanc, A. G. (2010). Systematic review of the health benefits of physical activity and fitness in school-aged children and youth. *International Journal of Behavioural Nutrition and Physical Activity*, 7, 40.

Jiménez-Pavón, D., Kelly, J., & Reilly, J. J. (2010). Associations between objectively measured habitual physical activity and adiposity in children and adolescents: Systematic review. *International Journal of Paediatric Obesity 5*(1), 3–18.

Jurg, M. E., Kremers, S. P. J., Candel, M. J. J. M., Wal, M. F. van der, & Meij, J. S. B. de (2006). A controlled trial of a school-based environmental intervention to improve physical activity in Dutch children: JUMP-in, kids in motion. *Health Promotion International, 21*(4), 320–330.

Karageorghis, C. I., & Priest, D. L., (2012). Music in the exercise domain: A review and synthesis (Part II). *International Review of Sport and Exercise Psychology*, 5(1), 67–84.

Kriemler, S., Meyer, U., Martin, E., van Sluijs, E. M., Andersen, L. B., & Martin, B. W. (2011). Effect of school-based interventions on physical activity and fitness in children and adolescents: A review of reviews and systematic update. *British Journal of Sports Medicine, 45*, 923.

Kriemler, S., Zahner, L., Schindler, C., Meyer, U., Hartmann, T., & Hebestreit, H. et al. (2010). Effect of school based physical activity programme (KISS) on fitness and adiposity in primary schoolchildren: Cluster randomised controlled trial. *British Medical Journal*, 340, 785.

Lanningham-Foster, L., Foster, R. C., McCrady, S. K., Manohar, C., Jensen, T. B., & Mitre, N. G., et al. (2008). Changing the school environment to increase physical activity in children. *Obesity, 16*, 1849–1853.

Magnusson, K. T., Sigurgeirsson, I., Sveinsson, T., & Johannsson, E. (2011). Assessment of a two-year school based physical activity intervention among 7–9-year-old children. *International Journal of Behavioural Nutrition and Physical Activity, 8*, 138.

Mattocks, C., Ness, A., Leary, S., Tilling, K., Blair, S., & Shield, J., et al. (2008). Use of accelerometers in a large field-based study of children: Protocols, design issues, and effects on precision. *Journal of Physical Activity and Health, 5*, S98–S111.

McKee, M., Breslin, G., Haughey, T., & Donnelly, P. (2013). Research assessing physical literacy in Northern Ireland. *Journal of Sport Science and Physical Education, 65*, 284–289.

McKenzie, T. L., Sallis, J. F., & Nader, P. R. (1991). SOFIT: System for observing fitness instruction time. *Journal of Teaching in Physical Education, 11*, 195–205.

McMinn, D., Rowe, D., Murtagh, S., Nelson, N., Ivan, C., & Almir, A., et al. (2014). Psychosocial factors related to children's active school travel: A comparison of two European regions. *International Journal of Exercise Science, 7*(1), 75–86.

Motl, R. W., Birnbaum, A. S., Kubik, M. Y., & Dishman, R. K. (2004). Naturally occurring changes in physical activity are inversely related to depressive symptoms during early adolescence. *Psychosomatic Medicine, 66*(3), 336–342.

Murtagh, S., Rowe, D. A., McMinn, D., & Nelson, N. M. (2012). Predicting active school travel: The role of planned behavior and habit strength. *International Journal of Behavioral Nutrition and Physical Activity, 9*, 65.

National Institute for Health and Clinical Excellence (NICE) (2009). *Promoting physical activity, active play and sport for pre-school and school-age children and young people in family, pre-school, school and community settings*. London: National Institute for Health and Clinical Excellence.

Naylor, P. J., Macdonald, H. M., & Warburton, D. E. (2008). An active school model to promote physical activity in elementary schools: Action schools! *BC. British Journal of Sports Medicine, 42*, 338–343.

Naylor, P. J., Macdonald, H. M., Zebedee, J. A., Reed, K. E., & McKay, H. A. (2006). Lessons learned from Action Schools! BC – an 'active school' model to promote physical activity in elementary schools. *Journal of Science & Medicine in Sport, 9*, 413–423.

Parfitt, G., & Eston, R. G. (2005). The relationship between children's habitual activity level and psychological well-being. *Acta Paediatrica, 94*(12), 1791–1797.

Pate, R. R., Davis, M. G., Robinson, T. N., Stone, E. J., McKenzie, T. L., & Young, J. C. (2006). Collaboration with the councils on cardiovascular disease in the young and on nutrition, physical activity, and metabolism (Physical Activity Committee) in schools: A scientific statement from the American Heart Association council promoting physical activity in children and youth: A leadership role for cardiovascular nursing. *Circulation, 114*, 1214–1224.

Pate, R. R., & O'Neill, J. R. (2008). After-school interventions to increase physical activity among youth. *British Journal of Sports Medicine, 43*, 14–18.

Raustorp, A., Stahle, A., Gudasic, H., Kinnunen, A., & Mattsson, E. (2005). Physical activity and self-perception in school children assessed with the Children and Youth – Physical Self-Perception Profile. *Scandinavian Journal of Medicine & Science in Sports, 15*(2), 126–134.

Rhodes, R. E., Macdonald, H. M., & McKay, H. A. (2006). Predicting physical activity intention and behaviour among children in a longitudinal sample. *Social Science and Medicine, 62*(12), 3146–3156.

Rowlands, R. V. (2007). Accelerometer assessment of physical activity in children: An update. *Pediatric Exercise Science, 19*, 252–266.

Salmon, J., Booth, M. L., & Phongsavan, P. (2007). Promoting physical activity participation among children and adolescents. *Epidemiology Reviews, 29*, 144–159.

Sidaway, B., & Hand, M. J. (1993). Frequency of modelling effects on the acquisition and retention of a motor skill. *Research Quarterly for Exercise and Sport, 64*, 122–125.

Smith, S. W., Daunic, A. P., & Taylor, G. G. (2007). Treatment fidelity in applied educational research. Expanding the adoption and application of measures to ensure evidence-based practice. *Education and Treatment of Children, 30*(4), 121–134.

Sport Northern Ireland (2009). A baseline survey of timetabled PE in primary schools in Northern Ireland.

Stratton, G., & Mullan, E. (2005). The effect of multicolor playground markings on children's physical activity levels during recess. *Preventive Medicine, 41*, 828–833.

Telama, R. (2009). Tracking of physical activity from childhood to adulthood: A review. *The European Journal of Obesity, 3*, 187–195.

Telama, R., Yang, X., Viikari, J., Välimäki, I., Wanne, O., & Raitakari, O. (2005). Physical activity from childhood to adulthood: A 21-year tracking study. *American Journal of Preventative Medicine, 28*, 267–273.

Tremblay, M. S., Inman, J. W., & Willms, J. D. (2000). The relationship between physical activity, self-esteem, and academic achievement in 12-year-old children. *Pediatric Exercise Science, 12*, 312–324.

Tremblay, M. S., LeBlanc, A. G., Janssen, I., Kho, M. E., Hicks, A., Murumets, K., Colley, R. C., & Duggan, M. (2011). Canadian sedentary behaviour guidelines for children and youth. *Applied Physiology, Nutrition and Metabolism, 36*, 59–71.

Treuth, M. S., Schmitz, K., Catellier, D. J., McMurray, R. G., Murray, D. M., & Almeida, et al. (2004). Defining accelerometer thresholds for activity intensities in adolescent girls. *Medicine and Science in Sports and Exercise, 36*, 1259–1266.

Trudeau, F., Laurencelle, L., & Shephard, R. J. (2004). Tracking of physical activity from childhood to adulthood. *Medicine and Science in Sport and Exercise, 36*, 1937–1943.

van Sluijs, E. M., McMinn, A. M., & Griffin, S. J. (2007). Effectiveness of interventions to promote physical activity in children and adolescents: Systematic review of controlled trials. *British Medical Journal, 335*, 703.

Weiler, R., Allardyce, S., Whyte, G. P., & Stamatakis, E. (2014). Is the lack of physical activity strategy for children complicit mass child neglect? *British Journal of Sports Medicine*, *48*(13), 1010–1013, published online first 9 December 2013.

Weinberg, R., & Jackson, A. (1990). Building self-efficacy in tennis players: A coach's perspective, *Journal of Applied Sport Psychology*, *2*, 164–174.

World Health Organization (2004). *Global strategy on diet, physical activity and health*. Geneva: World Health Organization.

World Health Organization (2010). *Global recommendations on physical activity for health*. Geneva: World Health Organization.

Williams, A. M., Davids, K., & Williams, J. (1999). *Visual perception and action in sport*. London: E. & F. N. Spon.

23 Contemporary Lifestyle Interventions for Public Health – Potential Roles for Professional Sports Clubs

Colin Baker, Elizabeth Loughren, Diane Crone, Adam Tutton and Peter Aitken

LEARNING OBJECTIVES

AFTER READING THIS CHAPTER YOU SHOULD BE ABLE TO:

1. Understand the public-health problem of low population physical activity and its impact on health and wellbeing in a community.
2. Critically appraise the role and function of sports clubs in the promotion of healthy lifestyle messages and interventions.
3. Critique the emergence of social media and 'applications' in health-enhancing interventions in the community.
4. Demonstrate a sound appreciation of the complexity of participation in physical activity and healthy lifestyle behaviours using a social determinants health model and pathway framework for delivery.
5. Understand the potential challenges of delivering 'real-world' health interventions.

AREAS TO CONSIDER WHEN READING THE CHAPTER:

1. What does the evidence say about the public-health challenges facing the developed world and how might these be addressed?
2. What are the challenges of developing and implementing a health-promotion intervention that is capable of demonstrating long-term positive health outcomes in a variety of populations?
3. What is the place of mobile technology in health-promotion interventions now and in the future?

CLIENT AND BACKGROUND

Globally, non-communicable diseases including heart disease and stroke are the leading causes of death and many of these are attributable to lifestyle factors including physical inactivity and excess body weight (WHO, 2008a). These issues have been increasing in severity so that more than one-third of Americans and Australians are obese (i.e., people with a BMI of 30kg/m^2 or over) and dramatic increases in obesity are taking place in developing countries such as China and Mexico (Centres for Disease Control (CDC), 2014; National Heart Foundation of Australia, 2012; Popkin, Adair, & Ng, 2012). Closer to home, among the 19 European Union member states it is the UK that ranks particularly poorly in terms of the number of obese men (22.1%) and women (23.9%) (Eurostat, 2011) and it is predicted that 60% of adult men and 50% of adult women will be classified as obese by 2050 (Information Centre for Health and Social Care, 2014). Obesity is not just costly to personal health, being associated with increased risk of developing Type 2 diabetes, cardiovascular disease, and cancer, but also places a significant and costly burden on the UK's health services; the costs attributable to overweight and obesity are projected to reach £9.7 bn per year by 2050 (Public Health England, 2013).

Regular physical activity (defined by Caspersen, Powell, & Christenson (1985), as any bodily movement produced by skeletal muscles that results in energy expenditure) has beneficial effects for population health including protection from serious illness such as cardiovascular disease (CVD) which easily exceed the effectiveness of drugs or other medical treatments (Department of Health, 2009a). It is recommended that all adults should aim to be active daily, engaging in moderate-intensity physical activity for at least 150 minutes per week including activities that improve muscle strength on at least two days a week (Department of Health, 2011). However, in keeping with a global trend in developed nations the UK population is failing to do enough physical activity for health, with 26% of women and 19% of men being classed as inactive in 2012. (Information Centre for Health and Social Care, 2014). At a global level it is estimated that 31% of the world's population is failing to undertake the minimum recommended physical activity (Hallal, Andersen, Bull, Guthold, & Haskell, et al., 2012) while less than half of all adult Americans meet recommended guidelines and 35% of adults in European countries seldom do any form of regular physical activity (CDC, 2014; Eurostat, 2011). Such is the extent of the problem that the World Health Organization has established a series of strategies that seek to minimize and control the spread of non-communicable diseases that prioritize the health of all people and tackle growing inequities in health worldwide whereby those who experience deprivation face poorer health outcomes than those in less deprived areas (WHO, 2008b).

The UK's population is in danger of becoming less physically active than is beneficial for health and dangerously overweight. Yet, never before has access to such a wealth of knowledge, information, and support to healthy lifestyle choices been so widespread via websites, forums, newsletters, and mobile device applications (apps) that have the potential to support individuals' health and fitness goals. Further, perhaps now more than at any time in history there is in place a plethora of public and private services designed specifically to help individuals adopt and maintain healthy lifestyle behaviours. Seated within this paradox is the uncomfortable fact that while the health risks associated with obesity and physical inactivity are borne by the individual, it is society that bears the costs, whether direct, namely treatment, or indirect, namely premature mortality and disability (Lee et al., 2012; Trogdon, Finkelstein, Hylands, Dellea, & Kamal-Bahl, 2008). Consistent with strategies outlined by the World Health Organization that promote innovative and multi-faceted responses from organizations across society (WHO, 2011); there has been an increasing focus in the UK on strategies that seek to use sport and physical-activity programmes as a means of promoting health through closer links with local authorities, primary-care trusts (PCTs), and sporting organizations (Department of Health,

2009b; WHO, 2011). These approaches are supported by the new Health and Social Care Act (2012) which emphasizes the importance of collaboration between a diverse range of local organizations in order to help prevent disease and improve population health and wellbeing (Department of Health, 2012). Problematically, while it is understood that physical activity is beneficial for health it is less well understood how practitioners can ensure that people from all sectors of society are able to reap the rewards of regular participation wherever they live and whatever their circumstances. Hence, scholars and health practitioners seeking to promote population physical activity are challenged by a lack of evidence concerning the effectiveness of community physical-activity interventions (Baker, Francis, Soares, Weightman, & Foster, 2011) and the use of sport settings for health promotion (Donaldson & Finch, 2012). Developing and implementing sport and physical-activity programmes as a means of promoting health is challenging at all levels particularly at the community level where the majority of programmes take place. In this respect the need for innovative health-promotion programmes to improve the health of local adults in Bristol, a large city in the south west of the UK, is no different from any other town or city within the EU.

The client – Bristol Rovers Community Trust

Bristol Rovers Community Trust (BRCT) is a charity that is financially independent of Bristol Rovers Football Club. BRCT has four main strands of work including providing sport, social inclusion, health and education projects throughout Bristol and South Gloucestershire to a variety of people and ages. Having been a registered charity since 2001, BRCT is reliant upon external funding streams in order to achieve its objectives. Using the power of football and the brand of Bristol Rovers Football Club to achieve its objectives, BRCT aims to provide projects for as many sectors of the community as possible to give people the opportunity of enhancing and improving their life choices. A principal objective is to help benefit the communities throughout Bristol and South Gloucestershire by promoting participation in health and education projects. These projects seek to improve health and wellbeing throughout the region and reduce health and social inequalities within the community. This presents a significant challenge given the huge diversity within Bristol's population and the range of factors that need to be understood and accommodated if the organization is to achieve all its goals.

As a football club Bristol Rovers FC is located to the north of Bristol city centre. With an estimated population of 441,300 people, Bristol is the largest city in the south west and one of the eight 'Core Cities' in England with a culturally diverse population. While there are areas of affluence there are striking contrasts with areas of high deprivation. Deprivation is something that relates to people's roles and relationships, membership, and social contacts (Townsend, 1987). The Marmot Review (2010) identified that the lower a person's social position, the worse his or her health is likely to be and that risk factors for ill health such as obesity, are associated with social and economic deprivation across all age ranges. Of the 252 Lower Super Output Areas (geographical areas typically containing a population of around 1,500 people used to assess population data) in the City of Bristol, 32 are among the most deprived 10% nationally and home to approximately 59,000 people. Based on the Indices of Multiple Deprivation (IMD), two areas represent the worst in the country in terms of education deprivation for children and young people and of the ten most deprived wards, seven are located in the north of the city with three of the wards located within approximately one mile of the Bristol Rovers Memorial Stadium including Lockleaze, Southmead, and Ashley. These three wards are among the 10% most deprived communities in England and experience high rates of unemployment with between 23.4% and 29.2% of the population having claimed unemployment benefit for 12 months or more (Bristol City Council, 2012). Hence, it is clear that deprivation extends across many people's lives in Bristol and is likely to significantly impact health.

Description box **BOX 23.1**

INDICES OF MULTIPLE DEPRIVATION (IMD)

Deprivation is considered to be a multi-dimensional problem, encompassing a range of domains such as financial, health, education, public services, and crime. The indices of multiple deprivation (IMD) assesses indicators of deprivation that can be combined to calculate a measure of multiple deprivation experienced by people living in a specific area. IMD can be used to rank specific geographic areas in England according to their relative level of deprivation.

Bristol's status as a large urban centre also contrasts dramatically with the rest of the south west region which is relatively rural and affluent. For example, there have been significant increases in Bristol's Black and ethnic-minority population from 8.2% (in 2001) to 16% (in 2011) and it is recognized that life for many Black and ethnic-minority communities can be more difficult than for the majority population as evidenced by the incidence of mental health problems and emergency hospital admissions. A significant proportion of men and women are classified as overweight and obese 55.4% and 44.5% respectively, with deprived neighbourhoods having highest levels of obesity and it is known that physical-activity levels are generally lower among Black and minority ethnic groups (Bristol City Council, 2011a). These data suggest that health-promotion programmes must be keenly attuned to the needs and preferences of the target population and recognize the challenges, and opportunities, that are posed by the contexts in which people live. This provides a stark challenge within a city that has a history of developing health initiatives but where only 12% of adults are estimated to be regularly physically active and less than one-third eating healthily (APHO and Department of Health, 2010). Historically, local interventions have struggled to engage a wide variety of participants, particularly men. Results from a NHS Bristol weight-management scheme show that only 12% of participants have been men, even less in the three nearest deprived wards to the Memorial Stadium.

INITIAL NEEDS ASSESSMENT

Historically, there has been a lack of evidence concerning interventions implemented through sporting organizations for promoting healthy behaviour change (Priest, Armstrong, Doyle, & Waters, 2008). An emerging trend for developing health-promotion programmes within football clubs might be taken as an indication that this deficiency is beginning to be addressed in the UK. Early research in this area has demonstrated the potential in both engaging men and producing positive health outcomes (Brady, Murdoch, & McKay, 2010; Witty & White, 2010) but it is evident that more research is needed to ensure that intervention programmes are effective at securing positive health and behaviour outcomes (Biddle, Brehm, Verheijden, & Hopman-Rock, 2012). More recently, football clubs have been located at the centre of health-intervention programmes notably Premier League Health (PLH), Fit Fans, and Football Fans in Training (FFIT) which have targeted weight loss as key outcomes with a dual focus on educating participants about the benefits of healthy eating and regular physical activity. Secondary outcomes have included lifestyle modifications including alcohol consumption, resting blood pressure, and mental well-being. In addition, the recently launched Europe-wide EuroFIT programme seeks to tap into football fans' loyalty and attachment to their clubs to promote engagement of inactive men in tailored lifestyle programmes supported by professional football clubs and public-health experts. Using sports clubs as a resource for behaviour change offers an innovative way of adopting a more nuanced approach towards men's health promotion which emphasizes positive aspects of masculinity, something which Smith and Robertson (2008) highlight has traditionally been associated with negative health behaviour traits.

Early evidence concerning the use of elite football clubs as a setting for men's health-promotion programmes show promising results. An evaluation of Premier League Health (PLH), a £1.63m three-year men's healthy lifestyle promotion programme delivered by health trainers, managers, and health professionals and 16 Premier League football clubs (White, Zwolinsky, Pringle, McKenna, Daly-Smith, & Robertson et al., 2012), recognized that club branding, consultation with target participants and strong support networks, including workplaces, voluntary and charitable organizations, and local businesses were critical for success. It was also found that informal approaches that allowed flexibility in attendance and activity type was important for encouraging engagement as was minimizing the over-use of health messages. Interestingly, the majority of participants in the programme perceived that their health was good or very good despite a large proportion displaying at least one negative health behaviour, a failure to meet recommended physical-activity levels, and a general lack of consumption of fresh fruit and vegetables. The evaluation by White et al. (2012) suggests that innovative approaches which use sports clubs as settings for health-promotion programmes can help participants to make one or more positive changes to their health although it was more effective at eliciting short term (i.e., less than 12 weeks) than long-term lifestyle behaviour changes which the authors note was partly due to a relatively low response rate for the follow-up questionnaires conducted at 12 weeks post- completion of the programme.

Importantly, there are clear parallels between Bristol Rovers FC and the PLH programme where it was noted that that young men, particularly those from socio-economically deprived backgrounds, have a high clustering of lifestyle-related health risk factors, and that football stadiums are often located in or close to socially-deprived areas and have community development programmes (Robertson, Zwolinsky, Pringle, McKenna, Daly-Smith, & White 2013). The potential of club-based approaches to effect positive changes in health within specific populations has recently been demonstrated within the FFIT programme, a group-based 12-week free weight-management programme including physical activity and healthy eating components (Gray, Hunt, Mutrie, Anderson, Leishman, & Dalgarno, L., 2013), has shown promising results where it was found that men who participated lost more than nine times as much weight as men who had not completed the programme. A particular strength of this programme is that a pragmatic randomized controlled trial was adopted in order to assess the impact of the intervention on the 747 male participants (aged 35—65 years with a body-mass index (BMI) of 28 kg/m^2), thus helping to control for the influence of between and within the group differences and providing clearer evidence as to the effects of the intervention (Hunt, McCann, Gray, Mutrie, & Wyke, 2014).

The evidence to date suggests that targeting structured health interventions at male participants within sports-club settings has the potential not only to support populations who traditionally struggle to engage with health-promotion interventions but also to effect positive health outcomes in individuals with no reported health problems, at least in the short term (Hunt et al., 2014; Pringle, Zwolinsky, McKenna, Daly-Smith, Robertson, & White, 2013a; White et al., 2012). This is an important finding given that men tend to have a poorer knowledge of health than women and are reluctant to engage in preventive healthcare services (European Commission, 2011). Three key questions that arise from the evidence to date concern the potential of sports-club settings to engage women in health-promotion interventions, the use of these settings for fans of other sports (e.g., rugby union, rugby league, and cricket), and the feasibility of developing fan-focused health-promotion interventions outside top-flight football leagues. Indeed, excluding the Premiership, data for the 2012–2013 football season indicate that average match attendances ranged between 4,420 (League 2) and 17,558 (Championship) which suggests a very large potential target audience for club-based health-promotion programmes. It is apparent that group-based components that foster team spirit appear to be effective at increasing physical activity in men but that interventions need to run long term in order to help sustain participation, behaviour changes, and health outcomes (George, Kolt, Duncan, Caperchione, Mummery, & Vandelanotte et al., 2012). Furthermore, research into weight-management services suggests that a one-size-fits-all approach is unrealistic and it is important to take into account the motivators and barriers experienced by different population groups (McCarthy & Richardson, 2011; Rowe & Basi, 2010). Hence, while research within the field of sports clubs as settings for health promotion is beginning to yield useful data for practitioners and academics there are many more questions to be addressed.

Description box **BOX 23.2**

NEEDS ANALYSIS

A needs analysis allows researchers and practitioners to obtain data that helps to develop an understanding of the nature and background of target populations, understand their needs and preferences, what they want from an intervention, and how this should work in practice.

In order to help develop evidence concerning how to begin to design and implement a health-promotion programme with Bristol Rovers Community Trust, the University of Gloucestershire undertook a project to investigate sports fans' perceptions, attitudes, and opinions of sports clubs as settings for a hypothetical health-promotion programme, and to identify aspects of health-promotion programmes that sports fans perceived as important and how these should be delivered. Initiated in May 2013, and completed the following December, the project adopted a mixed-methods design involving quantitative and qualitative techniques in order to maximize the scope for data collection and analysis.

Description box **BOX 23.3**

QUALITATIVE VS. QUANTITATIVE RESEARCH

Qualitative researchers seek to develop an in-depth understanding of social phenomena and the underlying meanings and patterns of relationships via data collection and analysis techniques that focus on the lived experiences of people.

Quantitative research seeks to develop and verify theories and hypotheses relating to phenomena using statistical, mathematical, and numerical data collection and analysis techniques. These techniques purport to reduce bias and increase the relevance of results at a larger population level than results from qualitative research.

Mixed-methods approaches are distinguished from other research by the integration of quantitative and qualitative components (O'Cathain, Murphy, & Nicholl, 2008) and have been promoted as useful research responses to complex social issues (Greene & Caracelli, 1997). Following Bryman (2006), the principal reason for the research approach was that of completeness, that is the use of more than one method (i.e., interview data and survey data) within a single piece of research would provide a more sophisticated response to the research problem and would allow for greater insight into fans' perceptions and experiences. The aim was to receive feedback from 250 sports fans from across England. Purposive sampling (i.e., selecting participants based on their perceived relevance to the needs of the research) and opportunistic sampling (i.e., recruiting participants as and when opportunities arise) was used in order to establish a broad sample which included adult sports fans from range of locations and sport types (including football, rugby union, rugby league, cricket, and horse racing). The criterion for inclusion was adult sports fans (18 years and older). The original proposed target population was adjusted to include males *and* females following expert feedback from NHS funding managers who questioned the rationale of focusing only on male participants. Including male *and* female sport fans also allowed us to maximize response rates and to filter respondents by type, namely physical inactivity level, and whether male or female, at the point of data analysis.

Description box **BOX 23.4**

MIXED-METHODS APPROACHES

Mixed-methods approaches are characterized by the integration of quantitative and qualitative research components and have been promoted as useful research responses to complexity in social problems. It is the integration of data that distinguishes mixed methods from mono-method research.

Findings

The project demonstrated that the majority of respondents (males n = 72%) were rugby union (40.7%) or football (30.2%) fans. Most were not season ticket holders (63%) and attended between two and four matches per month. Similar to the evaluation by White et al. (2012), the majority of respondents rated their health as average (35.7%) or good (35.7%) although 18.2% of females and 13.9% of males indicated that they did have some sort of health concern. Interestingly, there was a high perception of 'good' (39.8%) and 'better than good' (46.8%) health knowledge and 39% stated indicated being active for 30 minutes per day for up to three days a week although in light of existing evidence in this area it is likely that many participants are not likely to meet current physical-activity recommendations (Pringle et al., 2013a). It was clear that friends (89.5%), family (84.9%), and facilities (e.g., parks, leisure centres) (80.6%) were perceived as key resources for helping to lead a healthy lifestyle over and above general practitioners (GPs). In terms of the content of the hypothetical health-promotion programme, physical activity was the highest-rated subject fans wanted included (98.6%) followed by health checks (87%) and dietary advice (81.7%). Interestingly, we found that differences between genders were not necessarily as expected. Only a small proportion of female respondents preferred women-only classes while it was clear that both males and females agreed strongly that inter-team competition, namely the use of a league approach within the programme to encourage participants to undertake more activities, would provide a source of motivation. The findings also indicated that respondents felt support from players and or sport professionals would attract them to the programme (92.4%) and that they would like the programme offered on weekday evenings

(87%), while perceived barriers to participating included too little time (77.1%) and work commitments (73.7%) reflecting issues identified by Gray et al. (2013) as reasons for non-completion.

It was noted that 84% of respondents owned a smartphone or smart technology (e.g., iPad), 79.1% stating that they used apps on a daily basis, and 82.7% indicating that apps could help them be healthy by providing a means of recording achievements during the programme (e.g., attendance, activities completed, and as a resource for dietary advice). Small differences were observed between genders, with females tending to agree more that apps could help provide motivation for sustaining involvement in a healthy lifestyle intervention, and assist with monitoring physical activity, recording achievements, and weight management. The majority of males and females agreed that apps in general could help them lead healthier lifestyles. It is probable that the most effective type of app is one that can provide a simple means of supporting individuals to engage with behaviour changes over the long term (Azar, Lesser, Laing, Stephens, Aurora, & Burke, et al., 2012) although there is little evidence at present concerning what features and in what contexts apps are most effective. Dennison, Morrison, Conway, & Yardley, (2013) suggest a relationship between the appeal and usefulness of apps and a user's level of motivation to change lifestyle behaviours. Hence, it is likely that apps alone are likely to prompt meaningful behaviour changes without a pre-existing level of motivation to do so, something that enrolment in a structured healthy lifestyle programme might be able to instil. However, this qualitative study involved only a very small sample of young adults and it is not possible to generalize these across contrasting population groups. Indeed, by employing a median split in respondents' ages (35.5 years old) it was possible to see that much fewer over-35 year olds (64.1%) than under-35 year olds (96.1%) owned smart technology capable of supporting apps, and fewer agreed (67.1% vs. 91.3%) that mobile technology applications (apps) could help them lead healthier lifestyles.

The findings of the project suggest that apps have the potential to augment healthy lifestyle programmes by providing a means of communication with participants, reinforcement of key messages, and recording achievements in a way that fits well with participants' normal social media habits. Heath, Parra, Sarmiento, Andersen, Owen, and Goenka et al. (2012) also highlight that decision prompts, namely signs placed near escalators that encourage people to use the stairs instead are important for promoting changes in physical-activity behaviour. In the same vein, apps might provide a tool for communicating prompts, such as using the stairs more often, that nudge participants in to looking for alternative and more positive health behaviours. However, as a word of caution it is also clear that apps and other technologies for example, internet-based approaches, should not necessarily be relied upon as sole features of health-intervention programmes that involve a diverse range of participants because factors including weight status and location, that is urban or rural are likely to influence participants' preferences for delivery (Short, Vandelanotte, & Duncan, 2014). Instead, technological approaches should represent just one component of a multi-stranded intervention.

FRAMEWORK AND INTERVENTION

In response to the initial needs analysis and a range of inputs from health professionals and the BRCT, a pilot healthy lifestyles programme entitled 'Fans4Life' was developed. Located within a settings-based approach to health promotion, Fans4Life recognizes the wider social, environmental, cultural, and economic factors affecting health behaviour (Marks, Murray, Evans, Willig, Woodall, & Sykes, 2005). In response, it provides support across a range of health behaviours that recognize the complexity of issues affecting an individual's health. Settings-based health promotion commonly employs complementary and multidisciplinary approaches that help to understand factors influencing people's health status beyond a conventional focus on morbidity and mortality (Green & Tones, 2010).

Description box **BOX 23.5**

MULTIDISCIPLINARY APPROACHES

Considering what is required to support behaviour change at a broader strategic level helps to ensure health promotion interventions will be effective and last long term. These involve collaboration between relevant organizations and agencies whose work impacts the topic of focus e.g., men's health to identify appropriate resources, models of delivery, and expertise.

This brings into focus the wider context in which people live their lives and the diverse range of social, political, and economic factors impacting health. Settings-based health-promotion approaches are closely aligned with the Social Determinants of Health model (SDH), a model championed by the World Health Organization (2008c) that provides researchers and practitioners with a tool with which to begin to unravel the complexity of factors affecting people's health including structural factors, for example gender, income, and education which are responsible for creating stratification and social class divisions, and intermediary factors such as biological factors and material circumstances, which together are responsible for an individual's health status (Figure 23.1). The Social Determinants of Health model helps us to develop an awareness of a community's ecology in which an individual is located and thus to develop 'culturally sensitive' (Butterfoss & Kegler, 2002: p. 162) interventions that conceptualize multiple levels of influence at the organizational, community, public policy, individual, and interpersonal level (Kegler, Crosby, & Diclemente, 2002; McLeroy, Norton, Kegler, Burdine, & Sumaya, 2003).

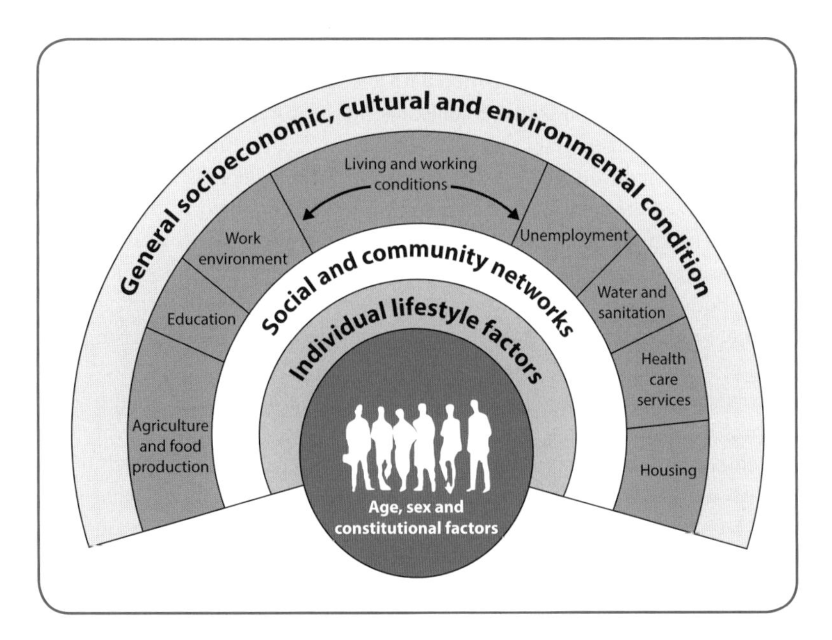

FIGURE 23.1 *Social determinant of health model.*

Source: Dahlgren, G. & Whitehead, M. (1991). *Policies and strategies to promote social equity in health.* Stockholm: Institute for Future Studies.

The intervention

The Fans4Life healthy lifestyles programme aims to improve the health and wellbeing of sedentary football fans at risk of poor health via a 12-week health education and exercise programme. A modified physical-activity care pathway (PACP) was adopted in order to provide a structured approach to the management of participant progress within the programme. This also provided a means of evaluating the programme in order to ascertain which areas worked well and which required improving. Physical-activity care pathways support changes in health behaviour by providing a clear structure in which goal setting, written resources and follow-up support are provided in order to maximize opportunities for individuals to increase their physical-activity levels. These have been promoted as a useful means of delivering real-world health programmes in applied settings, principally because they provide a degree of flexibility so that health programmes that can be adapted to local circumstances (Department of Health, 2009a, b, c) and thus provide a cost-effective means of increasing physical activity in the general population (NICE, 2006, Heath et al., 2012).

The primary target outcomes for the Fans4Life pilot are weight loss, increased participation in physical activity, and improved wellbeing. Substantial weight loss is often difficult to achieve (O'Donovan, Blazevich, Boreham, Cooper, Crank, & Ekelund, et al., 2010) particularly given the relatively short duration of the pilot programme. Indeed, Hunt et al. (2014) looked for only a 5% weight-loss difference between the intervention group and the comparison group within the FFIT programme over a 12-month period. As such, additional primary outcomes include improved levels of physical activity and healthy lifestyle behaviour in lieu of weight loss in the short term, overall weight loss being more likely to be observed during the follow-up periods. Combining physical activity with modest reductions in energy intake (approximately 500 to 700 kilocalories per day) through healthier eating and smaller portion sizes provides a means of maximizing the influence of physical activity on weight loss (Jakicic & Rogers, 2013). Consequently, the dual focus on these key behaviours was understood to provide a realistic means of establishing small changes in participant behaviour through an increased understanding of, and exposure to, positive lifestyle habits including physical activity and eating more healthy foods. Longer term, physical activity tied with a weight-loss plan will provide participants with a stable approach to weight loss that is sustainable beyond the duration of the programme. A number of secondary outcomes were also established including changes in positive lifestyle behaviours including smoking cessation and reduced alcohol consumption. These reflected a holistic approach to health promotion that recognized the relevance of tackling multiple determinants of poor health. A key difference in the present programme was the target audience whereby PACPs were originally developed for a clinical population, namely patients assessed by a GP, whilst Fans4Life focuses specifically on sports fans and anybody in Bristol's general population who might benefit from participating.

Following the Let's Get Moving physical-activity care pathway, the Fans4Life programme recruited participants for three independent 12-week consecutive programme offerings. A core advisory group was developed to shape the project. This included input from local public-health and obesity advisors, a mental health and wellbeing expert, a physical-activity deliverer, an evaluation and health programme developer, the local city council and NHS, and directors from the club and community trust. The partners worked together to establish an evidence-based pathway that was informed by best practice and linked to services and physical-activity opportunities in the wider community. The pathway involved five key stages (Figure 23.2). First, patients, or participants in the case of Fans4Life, were recruited into the pathway. Second, at the screening stage, participants' lifestyles were reviewed to assess their current physical-activity levels and whether they would consider undertaking more physical activity as part of a structured programme. Fans4Life included additional assessments including mental wellbeing, lifestyle behaviours (e.g. smoking habits, and measures of blood pressure and body-mass index (BMI)). The third stage involved the intervention whereby participants had a number

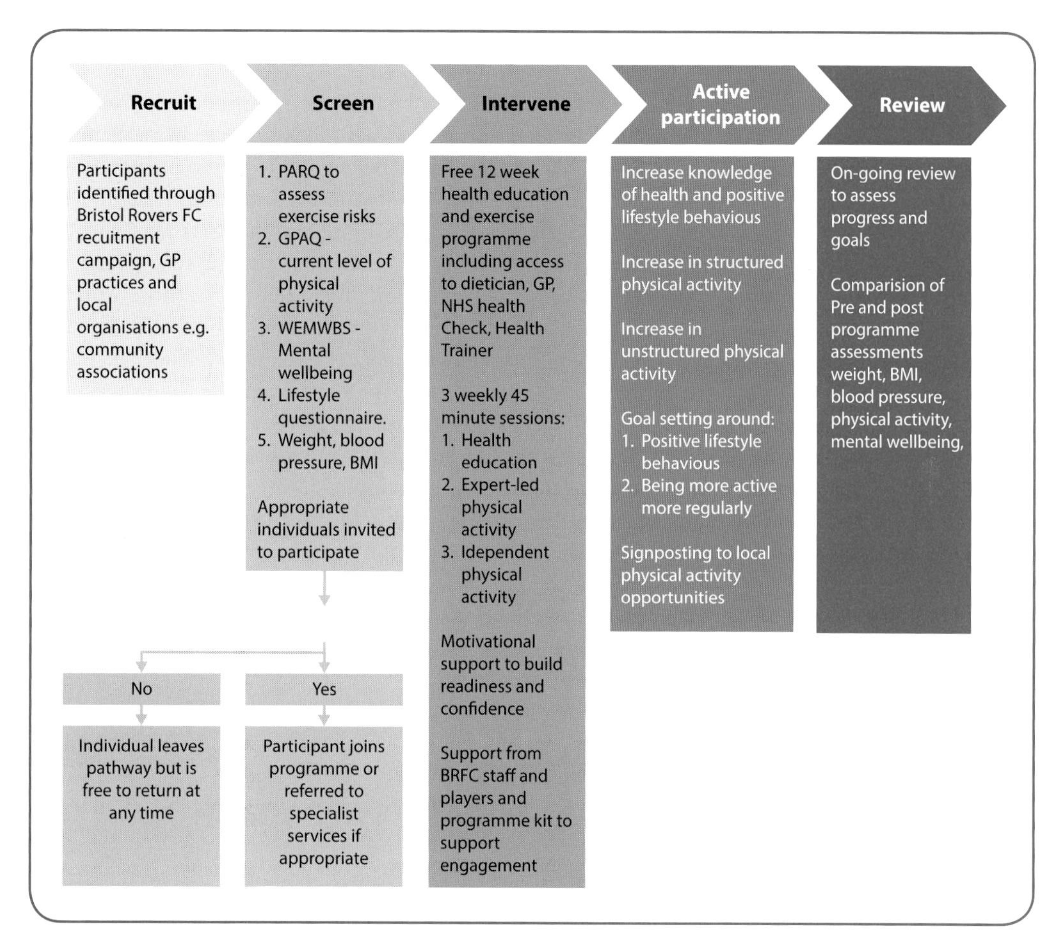

FIGURE 23.2 *Fans4Life programme pathway*

Source: Adapted from: Department of Health (2009c). *Let's get moving. A physical activity care pathway.* London: HMSO.

of options including becoming more physically active on their own or with support, to undertake motivational interviewing techniques for assistance, or to leave the programme.

The structure and format of Fans4Life provided participants with a 12-week programme of structured and unstructured physical activity together with health education supported by a range of expert practitioners including a GP, Health Trainers, and Bristol Rovers FC club staff. Participants established physical-activity goals during the active participation stage of physical-activity care pathway via one-to-one motivational interviews and increased their unstructured such as walking, and structured for example, group-based or specialist classes depending on individual health status. Fans4Life provided signposting to local physical-activity opportunities as additional support for participant goals in order to help them identify local opportunities to be more active. This was premised on the notion that adherence to health interventions is notoriously challenging. Hence, creating a socially inclusive atmosphere, gender-specific health information, expert support, flexible approaches to participation and a variety of physical-activity opportunities (Gray et al., 2013; Pringle et al., 2013a; Robertson et al., 2013) was recognized as an important means of supporting participant adherence. Finally, the review stage helped participants to assess progress, make sense of future physical-activity opportunities available to them, and to support long-term increases in motivation and confidence to be physically active. These are outlined in more detail below.

Recruitment

In collaboration with BRCT, Fans4Life created a recruitment strategy in order to identify potential participants for the programme. Informal approaches to recruitment for example, word of mouth and club-related activities for example, match-day programmes have provided an important means of engaging with potential programme participants (Pringle, Zwolinsky, Smith, Robertson, McKenna, & White, 2011; Pringle et al., 2013a;). While the principal target was sports fans with low levels of physical activity (i.e., not meeting minimum recommendations) it was recognized that the programme also needed to appeal to a range of participants including men, those in socio-economically disadvantaged circumstances, and ethnic-minority populations who are understood to be less likely to engage with physical-activity interventions (Waters, Galichet, Owen, & Eakin, 2011). Consequently, the proposed recruitment approach was one that promotes the programme to a wide range of people irrespective of their background or existing physical-activity levels whilst being cognizant of individual and cultural factors that potentially influence their willingness to engage in the programme. While this approach contrasts that adopted in other sports-club settings for example, Football Fans in Training (Hunt et al., 2014) which focused on men only, it reflects directly the data acquired from the needs analysis which did not make a clear case for using a gender-sensitized approach.

Description box **BOX 23.6**

STAKEHOLDER/COLLABORATIVE APPROACH

Collaboration is a way of working that involves multiple organizations and agencies with common interests, or stakeholders, working together toward a shared objective. This involves pooling of financial and other types of resources to produce added value that would not be available through the efforts of a single organization alone.

The first element of the strategy used marketing and events to publicize the programme to Bristol Rovers football fans. As with other club-based health-intervention programmes (Hunt et al., 2014) The Fans4Life programme was promoted via the Bristol Rovers FC and BRCT websites, posters around the club, match-day programmes, information on ticket stubs, club newsletters, and online supporter forums. Flyers were also distributed to fans on match days and public announcements promoting the programme were made at half time. Social media was also employed via tweets from Bristol Rovers FC players promoting the programme to fans. The second element of the strategy used local media including radio and newspapers to advertise the project to the wider Bristol population. Finally, events including a chance to meet Bristol Rovers FC players and staff and the hosting of match-day NHS health checks were used as a means of attracting people to the Bristol Rovers ground in order to promote the programme and to discuss how they might benefit from participation. Participants signed up via an online application form available via a dedicated Fans4Life website that was returned to a designated administrator who then made contact to arrange completion of programme screening forms.

Screening

Prior to starting the programme all participants were screened via a Physical Activity Readiness Questionnaire (PAR-Q) to ascertain who may need to seek a GP's permission for health reasons. While not necessarily ruling out the possibility that participants may experience adverse health events during the programme (Hunt et al., 2014), this ensured that risks to participants' were minimized and only those appropriate to receive the intervention participated. A Global Physical Activity Questionnaire (GPAQ) which can be effective in reflecting increased physical-activity levels (Herrmann, Heumann, Ananian, & Ainsworth, 2013) was used to record participants' existing physical-activity levels prior to beginning the programme. In addition, the participants' mental health status was assessed using the Warwick-Edinburgh Mental Wellbeing Scale (WEMWBS) which has been proven to accurately measure aspects of mental health and wellbeing including happiness and feelings of fulfilment (Clarke, Friede, Putz, Ashdown, Martin, & Blakeet al., 2011). Additional information concerning participants' lifestyle behaviour such as food consumption, alcohol, and smoking was obtained via a lifestyle questionnaire as with other programmes in this area for example, the Premier League Health Programme (Robertson et al., 2013). These allowed practitioners to establish a picture of participants' health and provided a means of tracking changes over time as participants progress through the pathway. Collecting data of this kind is common both within PACPs (Bull & Milton, 2010) and within health-promoting sports-club settings (Hunt et al., 2014; Pringle et al., 2013b; Robertson et al., 2013). Key participant data including demographic information and the types of physical activity and lifestyle goals set was recorded in individual participant booklets to facilitate the evaluation of the programme overall.

Intervene

Physical-activity care pathways similar to those used in Fans4Life combine goal setting, written resources, and follow-up support to maximize opportunities for individuals to increase their physical-activity levels. Recognizing that it is important to focus on only a limited number of physical-activity goals rather than multiple physical activities (Baker et al., 2013), Fans4Life encouraged participants to set a single physical-activity goal that was meaningful, realistic, and achievable. This was achieved via a motivational approach based on the principles of motivational interviewing. Motivational interviewing is a behaviour change technique commonly used in primary-care settings to strengthen motivation for change by enhancing an individual's intrinsic motivation At its core are three principles including collaboration with the participant to establish a supportive relationship, evocation, namely the assumption that the participant has within them the resources and motivation needed to make changes, and autonomy whereby participant changes and actions are reinforced via support from staff (Miller & Rollnick, 2002). Similar motivational support also helped participants to make positive lifestyle changes for example, diet as they became ready to change. While motivational interviewing techniques might be useful for encouraging long-term changes in CVD risks, particularly in people who already have a high number of CVD risk factors (Hardcastle, Taylor, Bailey, Harley, & Hagger, 2013), more evidence is required concerning its effectiveness and in what circumstances it elicits positive lifestyle modification. Fans4Life recognized that motivational support based on the principles of motivational interviewing held promise for achieving behaviour change in physical activity, dietary, and alcohol behaviours and was consistent with recommendations (Morton, Beauchamp, Prothero, Joyce, Saunders, & Spencer-Bowdage, et al., 2014). The programme used objective measures to assess participant outcomes, for example number of goals achieved so that the role of motivational interviewing approaches was understood. As such, the Fans4Life programme provided a key learning opportunity in the use and potential effectiveness of a support structure that was informed by the guiding principles of motivational interviewing within a multi-faceted health-promotion intervention that helped inform the development of the programme in the future.

Following the SDH logic of using multidisciplinary approaches to address complex health behaviours, support from a range of health and exercise professionals including a GP, Health Trainers, a dietitian and fitness instructors were embedded in the programme that provided complimentary skills and expertise to ensure that best practice was applied throughout all aspects of the programme whilst ensuring that health messages were simple and given in a way that was intelligible to all participants (Bartholomew et al., 2011). This complimented a friendly, supportive, and safe environment that promoted trust and camaraderie between participants as had been successfully achieved in similar club-based health programmes (Gray et al., 2013; Robertson et al., 2013). In addition to physical activity the educational sessions covered topics including healthy eating and food preparation, alcohol and its effect on the body, diabetes, heart health, smoking cessation, stress and its impact on the body, well-being and mental health. Recognition of participant attendance and commitment was demonstrated by recognition in match-day programmes, Fans4Life and BRFC websites showing progress, and by providing participants with a Fans4Life sports kit including a t-shirt, water bottle, and track-suit bottoms. Post completion, participants were provided with a family ticket for a home Bristol Rovers FC game. Participants were also able to nominate one of their peers as the 'Person of the Match' in order to highlight the particular efforts or achievements of those that had made significant progress.

Active participation

The purpose of this stage was to provide participants with the opportunity to engage with structured and unstructured physical activity and to begin to enact lifestyle changes in pursuit of goals established around being more physically active and adopting a more healthy diet. Fans4Life provided participants with three sessions per week for a 12-week period in order to help establish new routines and to embed learning and new behaviours within daily routines. Existing research in this area shows that 12-week intervention programmes have the potential to positively impact physical-activity levels (NICE, 2006) and healthier eating for example, the consumption of fresh fruit and vegetable (Pringle et al., 2013a). Importantly, this also helps practitioners to define the format and timing of the intervention so that each component of the programme can be managed effectively and that those funding the programme are able to ensure accountability for delivery and outcomes.

The Fans4Life project adopted an expanded format of the Let's Get Moving PACP and includes weekly structured and unstructured physical activity combined with a variety of education sessions on healthy eating, food preparation, mental health, and stress. Throughout this period participants maintained a personal diary of their experiences and were signposted to additional services through the NHS, such as smoking cessation programmes, exercise referral schemes, health checks, or a meeting with a health trainer or nutritionist to maximize opportunities to acquire knowledge concerning how to lead a healthier life by making small changes in daily habits. Participants with more complex health needs requiring more intensive weight-management support were referred to the Specialist Adult Weight-Management Service so that they could be provided with essential support for up to six months outside the programme. Participants were also be signposted to local leisure centres and swimming pools, neighbouring exercise facilities, and sports centres to provide opportunities for family and friends to join together for physical activities.

Review

The review stage helped participants to engage in a reflexive exercise that allowed them to review their progress and identify their own needs and preferences concerning how to maintain healthier lifestyles long term. The participant diaries provided a key resource in this respect, allowing participants to look back at their concerns and achievements over the 12-week period. Consistent with recommendations (Department of Health, 2009c), participant progress was reviewed at completion of the programme and at three, six, and 12 months. This provided evidence concerning participant progress against the primary and secondary outcomes and also provided a means of reviewing the efficacy of the Fans4Life programme as an intervention within a specific and novel setting. Assessing the relative success of interventions is hampered when process evaluations do not take place (Biddle et al., 2012). To ensure the relative successes and weakness of the programme were understood, participant data for the whole cohort was reviewed for each stage of the programme and at the same follow-up periods as above. Qualitative research was also be undertaken to explore the attitudes, opinions, and experiences of those participants who did, and did not, complete the programme. This helped explore participant experiences of the programme, whether expectations were met and general feedback regarding the programme format and processes and in doing so established evidence with which to inform the development of the Fans4Life programme and other similar health-intervention approaches. Conducted by the University of Gloucestershire, a programme evaluation report was supplied to the local Health and Wellbeing Board and Clinical Commissioning group with a view to investigating the potential of commissioning similar programmes in other sports clubs across the city. This had the potential to influence the development of similar programmes further afield using a modified PACP approach.

REFLECTIONS

Sports clubs as health-promoting settings represent an emerging area for health promotion and potentially provide an exciting and novel way of engaging sports fans and the wider population in programmes that promote health-enhancing behaviour. Early evidence from this field suggests that setting-based approaches using football clubs can engage those who fail to meet physical-activity recommendations (Pringle et al., 2013a) and help participants lose a significant amount of weight (Hunt et al., 2014) within an environment that promotes sociability rather than focusing purely on health (Robertson et al., 2013). While current programmes have focused specifically on male participants, emphasizing their potential disinclination for physical activity, high prevalence of obesity and challenges in engaging them in health-promotion strategies it is likely that sports clubs as health-promoting settings may offer a unique way of engaging men and women with diverse backgrounds in health-promotion programmes. This is particularly important given that football stadiums are often located near or within socially-deprived areas and have community development programmes embedded within their organization (Robertson et al., 2013), as with Bristol Rovers FC, thus lending themselves as a potentially powerful resource in tackling population health issues at a local level.

Fans4Life represents a real-world applied health-promotion intervention. As such, it is subject to a number of constraints including funding, staff capacity, and availability, personal commitments and broader social, economic, and political factors that are likely to influence its implementation at every stage. In response, the PACP approach provides a structure for progression, monitoring, and evaluation that will help to anticipate or offset some of these challenges. This brings into focus the importance of developing a pilot programme that is informed by existing research in this area but at the same time sensitized to the local context. Piloting is an important part of developing interventions that can be replicated by others in different settings and provides evidence concerning the feasibility of running the intervention processes as intended (Medical Research Council (MRC), 2008). It is anticipated that this approach will provide space for the development of a larger programme in the future that is oriented towards Bristol's population. However, it is recognized that these factors also present a number of practical and methodological limitations that are likely to influence any intervention of this type. For example, if funding, staff resources, and availability of built facilities were all unlimited Fans4Life could run across an entire football season or operate independently of this entirely. This would provide a much longer period over which to assess the efficacy of the programme in producing improvements in health, that is its impact on wider metabolic conditions including diabetes, and the effectiveness of longer (i.e., 12 months) versus short term (i.e., 12 weeks) intervention programmes. Hitherto, it is not known what the effect of sport club-based programmes run over much longer periods such as one year would have on participant motivation, retention within the programme pathway, and impacts on participants and their families, programme staff and local health services. As such, longer-term programmes would have the potential to address the knowledge gap in terms of how to develop the theoretical and methodological underpinnings of programmes in sport settings (Donaldson & Finch, 2012). This is critical for establishing data on these aspects and would help to provide researchers and practitioners with a greater depth of knowledge concerning how to use sports clubs as settings for health promotion and how these can be linked, and integrated, with wider local health services.

A further limitation of the present Fans4Life project is the lack of resources to develop mobile technology that is designed specifically to support PACP interventions of this type. A wide range of diverse proprietary apps have been developed that purport to support people to lead healthier lifestyles and evidence suggests that technology can benefit participants striving for a number of physical-activity and weight-loss goals if supported by education (Stephens & Allen, 2013). Apps can add a novel and fun component to an intervention that provides a means of recording and sharing progress towards goals (Vickey et al., 2012) but more evidence is needed concerning which aspects of the technology prove effective at supporting behaviour change and how use changes over time (Carter, Burley, Nykjaer, & Cade, 2013; Stephens and Allen, 2013). The needs analysis conducted by the Fans4Life team showed that mobile technology provided a potential source of support for all participants who owned smartphones but that there were likely to be differences in how this was used based on gender and age. As such, consideration should be given to the equity of interventions that rely on technology as a principal form of support where not all participants own smartphones and where usage varies between and within intervention cohorts. These things considered, were sufficient resources available, the Fans4Life team would divert funding and attention to the development of technology that was accessible for all participants which would complement the pathway, and its component stages, rather than providing the main resource for long-term behaviour change.

Fans4Life as with many other health-intervention programmes faces the challenge of how to keep the participants engaged in continuing with the newly learnt lifestyle or exercise habits once a structured programme is complete. Many times participants have a tendency of falling back to old habits when not attending a programme on a routine basis. When developing the intervention consideration needs to take into account of how to make the programme a true lifestyle behaviour change approach that builds in long-term sustainable features. This could include how to incorporate friends, family, or co-workers in the change process. For instance, passing on healthy cooking and dining options or food portion sizes to a spouse or partner could stress that eating a better balanced and nutritional meal could aid weight loss. Additionally, giving the participants opportunities to identify facilities in their neighbourhood that are convenient to use (e.g., local gym, swimming pool), providing maps of walking routes or cycle lanes, and suitable local events, such a family fun days, and options that are enticing may help to reinforce new lifestyle habits. Finally, providing further health or medical resources for those who may wish to quit smoking, attend a weight-management programme, or learn more about stress and mental health may provide a full range of support that reinforces positive health behaviour in the long term.

FURTHER READING

Brownson, R. C., Baker, E. A., Leet, T. L., Gillespie K. N., & True, W. R. (2010). *Evidence based public health* (2nd ed.). Oxford: Oxford University Press. The authors critique the effectiveness of intervention approaches and provide practical guidance on how to choose, carry out, and evaluate evidence-based programmes and policies in public-health settings.

Green, J., & Tones, K. (2010). *Health promotion planning and strategies* (2nd ed.). London: Sage. This book outlines models for defining health promotion and the factors involved in planning health-promotion programmes. Providing a critical appraisal of health promotion the authors focus on creating individual choices, advocacy for social change, and the role of evaluation in health-promotion programmes.

Hunt, K., McCann, C., Gray, C .M., Mutrie, N., & Wyke, S. (2013). 'You've got to walk before you can run': Positive evaluations of a walking programme as part of a gender sensitized, weight-management programme delivered to men through professional football clubs. *Health Psychology*, *32*(1), 57–65. This paper reports on a randomized controlled trial of a health intervention for male football fans from 13 Scottish professional football clubs. The authors show that programmes in sports-club settings can help a large proportion of men to lose a clinically important amount of weight.

Robertson, S., Zwolinsky, S., Pringle, A., McKenna, J., Daly-Smith, A., & White, A. (2013). 'It is fun, fitness and football really': A process evaluation of a football-based health intervention for men. *Qualitative Research in Sport, Exercise and Health*, *5*(3). Football in particular has emerged as a field that has utility for engaging men in community-health initiatives. This paper presents secondary analysis of data collected during the evaluation of the Premier League Health (PLH) programme and highlights factors critical to programme success.

REFERENCES

APHO and Department of Health (2010). *Health Profile Bristol 2010*. Retrieved 9 December 2015 from: http://www.apho.org.uk/resource/view.aspx?RID=92174

Azar, K. M. J., Lesser, L. I., Laing, B. Y., Stephens, J., Aurora, M. S., & Burke, L. E., et al. (2013). Mobile applications for weight management theory-based content analysis. *American Journal of Preventive Medicine*, *45*(5), 583–589.

Baker, C., Crone, D., Gidlow, C., Loughren, E., James, D., & Mahmood, T. (2013). Looking at the feasibility of using a physical activity pathway with children in school. *British Journal of School Nursing*, *8*(7), 338–345.

Baker, P. R. A., Francis, D. P., Soares, J., Weightman, A. L., & Foster, C. (2011). Community wide interventions for increasing physical activity. *Cochrane Database Systematic Reviews*, *13*(4).

Bartholomew, L. K., Parcel, G. S., Kok, G., Gottlieb, N. H., & Fernandez, M. E. (2011). *Planning health promotion programs: An intervention mapping approach* (3rd ed.). San Francisco: Jossey Bass.

Biddle, S. J. H., Brehm, W., Verheijden, M., & Hopman-Rock, M. (2012). Population physical activity behaviour change: A review for the European College of Sport Science. *European Journal of Sport Science*, *12*(4), 367–383.

Brady, A. J. B., Murdoch, P. C., McKay, D. L., & McKay, G. (2010). Sustained benefits of a health project for middle-aged football supporters, at Glasgow Celtic and Glasgow Rangers Football Clubs. *European Heart Journal*, *31*, 2966 2968.

Bristol City Council (2011a). *Active Bristol Physical Activity Strategy 2011–2016*. Bristol: Bristol City Council. Retrieved 9 December 2015 from https://www.bristol.gov.uk/sites/default/files/documents/health_and_adult_care/health_and_medical_advice/Bristol's%20Physical%20Activity%20Strategy.pdf.

Bristol City Council (2011b). *Physical activity in Bristol facts and figures about who does what*. Bristol: Bristol City Council. Retrieved 9 December 2015 from: http://www.bristol.gov.uk/sites/default/files/documents/health_and_adult_care/health_and_medical_advice/Active%20Bristol%20Fact%20Sheet.pdf.

Bristol City Council (2012). *Number of unemployed claimants by ward in Bristol – April 2012*. Bristol: Bristol City Council. Retrieved 9 December 2015 from http://www.bristol.gov.uk/sites/default/files/documents/council_and_democracy/statistics_and_census_information/Unemployed%20claimants%20by%20ward%20(April%202012).pdf.

Bryman, A. (2006). Integrating quantitative and qualitative research: How is it done? *Qualitative Research, 6*, 97–113.

Bull, F., & Milton, K. (2010). A process evaluation of a 'physical activity pathway' in the primary care setting. *BMC Public Health, 10*, 463–470.

Butterfoss, F. D., & Kegler, M. C. (2002). Towards a comprehensive understanding of community coalitions moving from practice to theory. In R. J.Diclemente, R. A.Crosby, & M. C.Kegle (Eds.), *Emerging theories in health promotion practice and research strategies for improving public health* (pp. 159–193). San Francisco: Jossey Bass.

Caspersen, C. J., Powell, K. E., & Christenson, G.M. (1985). Physical activity, exercise, and physical fitness: Definitions and distinctions for health-related research. *Public Health Reports, 100*(2), 126–131.

Carter, M. C., Burley, V. J., Nykjaer, C., & Cade, J. E. (2013). Adherence to a smartphone application for weight loss compared to website and paper diary: Pilot randomized controlled trial. *Journal of Medical Internet Research*, 15, e32.

Centers for Disease Control (2014). Facts about physical activity. Retrieved 9 December 2015 from http://www.cdc.gov/physicalactivity/data/facts.html

Clarke, A., Friede, T., Putz, R., Ashdown, J., Martin, S., & Blake, A. et al. (2011). Warwick-Edinburgh Mental Well-being Scale (WEMWBS): Validated for teenage school students in England and Scotland: A mixed methods assessment. *BMC Public Health, 11*, 487. Retrieved 9 December 2015 from http://www.biomedcentral.com/1471-2458/11/487

Dennison, L., Morrison, L., Conway, G., & Yardley, L. (2013). Opportunities and challenges for smartphone applications in supporting health behaviour change: Qualitative study. *Journal of Medical Internet Research, 15*(4). Retrieved 9 December 2015 from http://www.ncbi.nlm.nih.gov/pmc/articles/PMC3636318/.

Department of Health (2009a) *On the state of public health: Annual Report of the Chief Medical Officer 2009*. London: HMSO

Department of Health (2009b). *Be active, be healthy: A plan for getting the nation moving*. London: HMSO.

Department of Health (2009c). *Let's get moving. A physical activity care pathway*. London: HMSO.

Department of Health (2011). *UK physical activity guidelines*. London: HMSO.

Department of Health (2012). *Health and Social Care Act 2012 factsheet A1: Overview of the Act*. London: HMSO. Retrieved 9 December 2015 from http://www.legislation.gov.uk/ukpga/2012/7/contents/enacted.

Donaldson, A., & Finch, C. F. (2012). Sport as a setting for promoting health. *British Journal of Sports Medicine, 46*, 4–5.

European Commission (2011). *The state of men's health in Europe*. Brussels: European Commission. Retrieved from http://ec.europa.eu/health/population_groups/docs/men_health_report_en.pdf

Eurostat (2011). *European Health Interview Survey*. Brussels: European Commission. Retrieved 9 December 2015 from http://epp.eurostat.ec.europa.eu/cache/ITY_PUBLIC/3-24112011-BP/EN/3-24112011-BP-EN.PDF

Football League, The (2013). *Football League Attendance Report – Season 2012/13*. Preston: The Football League.

George, E. S., Kolt, G. S., Duncan, M. J., Caperchione, C. M., Mummery, W. M., &Vandelanotte, C. et al. (2012). A review of the effectiveness of physical activity interventions for adult males. *Sports Medicine, 42*(2), 281–300.

Gray, C. M., Hunt, K., Mutrie, N., Anderson, A. S., Leishman, J., & Dalgarno, L. (2013). Football fans in training: The development and optimization of an intervention delivered through professional sports clubs to help men lose weight, become more active and adopt healthier eating habits. *BMC Public Health, 19*, 232. Retrieved 9 December 2015 from http://www.biomedcentral.com/1471-2458/13/232

Green, J., & Tones, K. (2010). *Health promotion: Planning and strategies* (2nd ed.). London: Sage.

Greene, J. C., & Caracelli, V. J. (1997). Defining and describing the paradigm issue in mixed-method evaluation. *New Directions in Evaluation, 74*, 5–18.

Hallal, P. C., Andersen, L. B., Bull, F.C., Guthold, R., & Haskell, W. (2012). Global physical activity levels: surveillance progress, pitfalls, and prospects. *The Lancet*, 380, 247–257.

Hardcastle, S. J., Taylor, A. H., Bailey, M. P., Harley, R. A., & Hagger, M. S. (2013). Effectiveness of a motivational interviewing intervention on weight loss, physical activity and cardiovascular disease risk factors: a randomised controlled trial with a 12-month post-intervention follow-up. *International Journal of Behavioral Nutrition and Physical Activity, 10*, 40. Retrieved 9 December from http://www.ijbnpa.org/content/10/1/40.

Heath, G. W., Parra, D. C., Sarmiento, O. L., Andersen, L. B., Owen, N., & Goenka, S., et al. (2012). Evidence-based intervention in physical activity: Lessons from around the world. *The Lancet, 380*, 272–281.

Herrmann, S. D., Heumann, K. J., Der Ananian, C. A., & Ainsworth, B. E. (2013). Validity and reliability of the Global Physical Activity Questionnaire (GPAQ). *Measurement in Physical Education and Exercise Science, 17*, 221–235.

Hunt, K., McCann, C., Gray, C. M., Mutrie, N., & Wyke, S. (2013). 'You've got to walk before you can run': positive evaluations of a walking programme as part of a gender sensitized, weight-management program delivered to men through professional football clubs. *Health Psychology, 32*(1), 57–65.

Information Centre for Health and Social Care (2014). *Statistics on obesity, physical activity and diet – England, 2014*. Leeds: Information Centre for Health and Social Care. Retrieved 9 December 2015 from http://www.hscic.gov.uk/catalogue/PUB13648/Obes-phys-acti-diet-eng-2014-rep.pdf.

Jakicic, J. M., & Rogers, R. J. (2013). The importance of physical activity for losing weight, maintaining weight, and preventing weight gain. *President's Council on Fitness, Sports and Nutrition, 14*(2). Retrieved 9 December 2015 from:https://www.presidentschallenge.org/informed/digest/docs/201306digest.pdf.

Kegler, M .C., Crosby, R .A., & Diclemente, R. J. (2002). Reflections on emerging theories in health promotion practice. In R. J.Diclemente, R. A. Crosby, & M. C.Kegler (Eds.), *Emerging theories in health promotion practice and research strategies for improving public health* (pp. 386–395). San Francisco: Jossey-Bass.

Lee, I. M., Shiroma, E. J., Lobelo, F., Puska, P., Blair, S. N., & Katmarzyk, P. T. (2012). Effect of physical inactivity on major non-communicable diseases worldwide: An analysis of burden of disease and life expectancy. *The Lancet, 380*, 219–229.

Marks, D. F., Murray, M., Evans, B., Willig, C., Woodall, C., & Sykes, C. (2005). *Health psychology theory research and practice* (2nd ed.). London: Sage

Marmot Review, The (2010). *Fair society, healthy lives*. London: The Marmot Review.

McCarthy, M., & Richardson, N. (2011). *Report on best practice approaches to tailoring lifestyle interventions for obese men in the primary care setting*. Carlow: Centre for Men's Health, Institute of Technology.

McLeroy, K. R. Norton, B. L., Kegler, M. C., Burdine, J. N., & Sumaya, C. V. (2003). Community-Based Interventions. *American Journal of Public Health, 93*(4), 529–533.

Medical Research Council (2008). *Developing and evaluating complex interventions: New guidance*. London: Medical Research Council.

Miller, W. R., & Rollnick, S. (2002). *Motivational interviewing: Preparing people for change* (2nd ed.). New York: The Guilford Press.

Morton, K., Beauchamp, M., Prothero, A, Joyce, L., Saunders, L., & Spencer-Bowdage, S., et al. (2014). The effectiveness of motivational interviewing for health behaviour change in primary care settings: a systematic review. *Health Psychology Review*, 1–33.

National Heart Foundation of Australia (2012). *Overweight and obesity statistics*. Sydney: National Heart Foundation of Australia. Retrieved 9 December 2015 from http://www.heartfoundation.org.au/SiteCollectionDocuments/Factsheet-Overweight-and-obesity.pdf.

NICE (2006). *Four commonly used methods to increase physical activity: Brief interventions in primary care, exercise referral schemes, pedometers and community-based exercise programmes for walking and cycling*. London: NICE. Retrieved 9 December 2015 from http://www.nice.org.uk/PH2.

O'Cathain, A., Murphy, E., & Nicholl, J. (2008). The quality of mixed methods research studies in health services. *Journal of Health Services Research and Policy, 13*(2), 92–98.

O'Donovan, G., Blazevich, A. J., Boreham, C., Cooper, A. R., Crank, H., & Ekelund, U., et al. (2010). The ABC of physical activity for health: A consensus statement from the British Association of Sport and Exercise Sciences. *Journal of Sports Sciences, 28*(6), 573–591.

Popkin, B. M., Adair, L. S., & Ng, S. W. (2012). Global nutrition transition and the pandemic of obesity in developing countries. *Nutrition Reviews, 70*(1), 3–21.

Priest, N., Armstrong, R., Doyle, J., & Waters, E. (2008). Policy interventions implemented through sporting organisations for promoting healthy behaviour change. *Cochrane Database of Systematic Reviews, 16*(3), CD004809.

Pringle, A., Zwolinsky, S., McKenna, J., Daly-Smith, A., Robertson, S. & White, A. (2013a). Effect of a national programme of men's health delivered in English Premier League football clubs. *Public Health, 127*(1), 18–26.

Pringle, A., Zwolinsky, S., McKenna, J., Daly-Smith, A., Robertson, S., & White, A. (2013b). Delivering men's health interventions in English Premier League football clubs: Key design characteristics. *Public Health, 127*(8), 716–726.

Pringle, A., Zwolinsky, S., Smith, A., Robertson, S., McKenna, J., & White, A. (2011). The pre-adoption demographic and health profiles of men participating in a programme of men's health delivered in English Premier League football clubs. *Public Health, 125*(7), 411–416.

Public Health England (2013). *About obesity.* London: Public Health England. Retrieved 9 December 2015 from http://www.noo.org.uk/NOO_about_obesity.

Robertson, S., Zwolinsky, S., Pringle, A., McKenna, J., Daly-Smith, A., & White, A. (2013). It is fun, fitness and football really': A process evaluation of a football-based health intervention for men. *Qualitative Research in Sport, Exercise and Health, 5*(3), 419–439.

Rowe, B., & Basi, J. K. T. (2010) *Maximising the uptake of weight management services.* London: Department of Health.

Short, C. E., Vandelanotte, C., & Duncan, M. J. (2014). Individual characteristics associated with physical activity intervention delivery mode preferences among adults. *International Journal of Behavioral Nutrition and Physical Activity, 11*(1), 25.

Smith, J. A., & Robertson, S. (2008). Men's health promotion: A new frontier in Australia and the UK? *Health Promotion International, 23*(3), 283–289.

Stephens, J., & Allen, J. (2013). Mobile phone interventions to increases physical activity and reduce weight: A systematic review. *Journal of Cardiovascular Nursing, 28*(4), 320–329.

Townsend, P. (1987). *Deprivation. Journal of Social Policy, 16*(2), 125–146.

Trogdon, J. G., Finkelstein, E. A., Hylands, T., Dellea, P. S., & Kamal-Bahl, S. J. (2008). Indirect costs of obesity: A review of the current literature. *Obesity Reviews, 9*(5), 489–500.

Vickey, T., Breslin, J., & Williams, A. (2012). Fitness – there's an app for that: Review of mobile fitness apps. *The International Journal of Sport and Society, 3*, 109–127.

Waters, L. A., Galichet, B., Owen, N., & Eakin, E. (2011). Who participates in physical activity intervention trials? *Journal of Physical Activity and Health, 8*, 85–103.

White, A., Zwolinsky, S., Pringle, A., McKenna, J., Daly-Smith, A., & Robertson, S., et al. (2012). *Premier league health: A national programme of men's health promotion delivered in/by professional football clubs, final report 2012.* Leeds: Centre for Men's Health & Centre for Active Lifestyles, Leeds Metropolitan University.

WHO (World Health Organization). (2008a). *WHO global strategy on diet, physical activity and health: A framework to monitor and evaluate implementation.* Geneva: WHO. Retrieved 9 December 2015 from http://www.who.int/dietphysicalactivity/M&E-ENG-09.pdf.

WHO (World Health Organization). (2008b). *2008–2013 Action plan for the global strategy for the prevention and control of noncommunicable diseases.* Geneva: WHO. Retrieved from http://www.who.int/nmh/publications/9789241597418/en/.

WHO (2011). *Promoting sport and enhancing health in European Union countries: A policy content analysis to support action.* Geneva: WHO. Retrieved 9 December 2015 from http://www.euro.who.int/__data/assets/pdf_file/0006/147237/e95168.pdf

Witty, K., & White, A. (2010). Tackling men's health: Implementation of a male health service in a rugby stadium setting. *Community Practice, 84*, 29–32.

24 Exercise Dependence

DAVE SMITH, BRUCE D. HALE, AND CHRISTINE SELBY

LEARNING OBJECTIVES

AFTER READING THIS CHAPTER YOU SHOULD BE ABLE TO:

1. Understand how the concept of exercise dependence is related to weight lifting and endurance competitions and introduce various psychological problems (muscle dysmorphia, eating disorders, steroid use) that often accompany this disorder.
2. Try to differentiate how exercise dependence differs from exercise commitment in weight lifters and elite athletes.
3. Familiarize researchers and clinicians with the preferred exercise dependence questionnaires available, compare the behaviours being measured, and the validity and reliability of them, and explore different components of the construct.
4. Present various counselling, treatment, and therapies used to counter the negative medical and psychological consequences of exercise dependence in weight lifters and endurance athletes.

AREAS TO CONSIDER WHEN READING THE CHAPTER:

1. Are there potential differences in abnormal behaviours between weight lifters who may suffer from primary exercise dependence and endurance athletes who may suffer from secondary exercise dependence?
2. Which questionnaires are appropriate for measuring exercise dependence/muscle dysmorphia in weight lifters and endurance athletes? Similarly, which questionnaires might be appropriate for measuring clinical issues such as obsessive-compulsive behaviours, and eating disorder behaviours?
3. What are the psychological clinical approaches currently used to treat exercise dependence and muscle dysmorphia, eating disorders, and obsessive-compulsive disorders?

HYPOTHETICAL CLIENTS AND BACKGROUND

Though all medical practitioners agree that regular exercise should be an important part of a healthy lifestyle, some individuals develop an obsessive approach to it that can be damaging physiologically, psychologically, and socially. The addictive qualities of exercise have been known to researchers for 40 years since the work of Baekeland (1970). Many researchers in this topic refer to this excessive exercise behaviour as 'exercise dependence'. Recent research has suggested that about 3–13% of adult exercisers may suffer from symptoms of exercise dependence (Allegre, Souville, Therme, & Griffiths, 2006; Hausenblas & Symons Downs, 2002; Terry, Szabo, & Griffiths, 2004).

Definition box **BOX 24.1**

Exercise dependence (ED) has been defined as 'a craving for leisure time physical activity that results in uncontrollable excessive exercise behaviour and that manifests in physiological symptoms (e.g., tolerance, withdrawal) and/or psychological symptoms (e.g., anxiety, depression)'. (Hausenblas & Symons Downs, 2002, p. 90).

Exercise dependence has been measured reliably and validly by the Exercise Dependence Scale (EDS; Symons Downs, Hausenblas, & Nigg, 2004). This scale was constructed based on DSM-IV criteria for substance dependence (American Psychiatric Association, 1994) and the questionnaire validation process produced seven scales: Tolerance, Withdrawal Effects, Continuance, Lack of Control, Reductions in Other Activities, Time, and Intention.

Morgan (1979) initially concluded that excessive exercise seemed to be a form of 'negative addiction' where exercisers showed the following symptoms: exercised when vocationally, socially, and medically contraindicated, needed daily exercise in order to cope, said they could not live without running or exercise, and experienced withdrawal symptoms without exercise. In the last decade, exercise psychologists, clinical psychologists, and psychiatrists have been debating what term should be used to accurately describe these symptoms and under which category of psychological disorders this problem should be listed. For example, in the literature dealing with anaerobic exercise dependence in weight lifters, some have concluded that the behaviours are part of an obsessive-compulsive disorder diagnosis (e.g., Pope, Phillips, & Olivardia, 2000), while others suggest that the symptoms appear to be part of a body dysmorphia or body-image disorder diagnosis (e.g., Lantz, Rhea, & Mayhew, 2001; McCreary & Sasse, 2000), and still others have sought to differentiate it from a type of primary eating disorder (e.g., Hausenblas & Symons Downs, 2002).

More recently Berczik et al. (2012) have argued forcefully that excessive exercise is a type of behavioural addiction. They believe that exercise dependence should be more appropriately labelled as exercise addiction because it includes both dependence and compulsion aspects. In addition, they speculate that the six common symptoms of addiction (salience, mood modification, tolerance, withdrawal symptoms, personal conflict, and relapse) have been already measured by numerous scales in the EDS, Bodybuilding Dependence Scale (BDS; Smith, Hale, & Collins, 1998), Exercise Dependence Questionnaire (Ogden, Veale, & Summers, 1997), and the Exercise Addiction Inventory (EAI; Terry, et al., 2004).

Exercise dependence has been measured in both aerobic (primarily runners) and anaerobic (primarily bodybuilders) athletes in past studies. Most early measures were unidimensional, involved interviews, lacked proper psychometric validation, focused on aerobic activity (running), and lacked any theoretical basis (Hausenblas & Symons Downs, 2002). Later studies (Smith et al., 1998; Hurst, Hale, & Smith, 2000) measured anaerobic exercise dependence in weight lifters using validated, multidimensional questionnaires (e.g., BDS).

Many studies suggested that there might be different psychological motivations of ED in men and women. Whereas most women may yearn to be thin and muscular (Thompson, Heinberg, Altabe, & Tantleff-Dunn, 1999), men in western societies in the last three decades are showing increasing scores in drive for muscularity (e.g., McCreary & Sasse's [2000] Drive for Muscularity Scale). Some young men (and a few women) become heavily involved in weight lifting, sometimes either becoming power lifters (strength-gain goals) or bodybuilders (muscular-hypertrophy goals). Some weight lifters may develop muscle dysmorphia (MD), view themselves as too thin, and feel pressure to gain muscle size and/or strength even though they may actually be quite large and muscular (Lantz, et al., 2001; Olivardia, 2001).

Definition box **BOX 24.2**

Muscle dysmorphia is thought to be an obsessive-compulsive body image disorder where individuals perceive their body is not muscular enough (Lantz et al., 2001). Components include: body image distortion/dissatisfaction, dietary constraints, pharmacological aids, dietary supplements, exercise dependence, physique concealment, and low self-esteem, and are measured by the Muscle Dysmorphia Inventory (MDI) created by Rhea, Lantz, and Cornelius (2004).

Activity box **BOX 24.3**

Which antecedents are the most powerful predictors of later exercise dependence symptoms in weight lifters and endurance athletes?

Hypothetical Client – Daniel: a bodybuilder

Daniel is a 35-year-old competitive bodybuilder who presents himself to a sport/exercise psychology consultant, ostensibly with performance enhancement issues (frustration at 'staleness' and lack of progress with his training of late), but also displaying severe symptoms of both primary exercise dependence and muscle dysmorphia. The roots of these issues stretch back to Daniel's mid-teens, when he was overweight and sedentary with a poor body image, but a high drive for muscularity. At this age he had become acutely aware of the male muscularity ideal present in the media, and felt that his overweight physique did not measure up. He began at this point to worry about his attractiveness to the opposite sex. At 18 Daniel began sixth-form-college and started to lift three times per week in the college gym, initially with the purpose of keeping fit. He liked the positive effects the training had on his physique and began to associate socially with some of the gym's hardcore lifters. Once he finished college, keen to continue lifting, he joined a gym; at this point he began to display behaviour patterns clearly associated with exercise dependence and muscle dysmorphia. Dissatisfied with his lifting progress, he became involved with a lifting support group at the gym and increased his training time to three hours per day and while using a wide array of bodybuilding supplements. His social life now revolved entirely around the gym, and his girlfriend complained constantly that his training had become all-consuming. As his physique improved, he began to enter local bodybuilding contests.

Eventually, Daniel became more and more frustrated as his physique refused to grow past a certain point. Since improving his physique further would need more training, and this was incompatible with the demands of a full-time job and a normal social life, he gave up his lucrative employment and his girlfriend to spend 4–6 hours daily training with a group of hardcore lifters. To make ends meet, he started working part-time at the gym and also began to take anabolic steroids, purchased from one of his lifter friends. He began to enter regional and national bodybuilding contests, and at this point his life revolved solely around the gym and contest preparation. He increased his use of steroids, performing complex cycles of various combinations of drugs, dieted rigorously, sticking rigidly to a high protein, very low-fat diet, and made very extensive use of bodybuilding supplements. He won his first national contest and earned money from a photo shoot with a bodybuilding magazine and a minor acting role as a bodybuilder in a movie.

Despite this apparent success in bodybuilding, Daniel was profoundly unhappy. He was worried about the possible health ramifications of his drug use, having already suffered side-effects such as headaches, acne, and gynecomastia. However, terrified of losing muscle size, he felt unable to stop. He began to miss having a normal social life and a well-paid job, and despite his competition success was still very unhappy with his physique, thinking of himself as small and puny when in fact he was large and muscular. Outside contests he would conceal his physique with baggy clothing, worried about how others would judge it. He was terrified of losing his muscular 'suit of armour' as he called it and thought that easing up on any component of his bodybuilding lifestyle would cause this. However, his physical and mental exhaustion were making him feel burned out.

Daniel's feelings of physique inadequacy and consequent drive for muscularity are part of a well-documented trend for males to report increasing levels of body dissatisfaction (Leone, Sedory, & Gray, 2005; Phillips & Drummond, 2001) and to engage in pathological behaviours to achieve the cultural ideal of a muscular physique (Grieve, 2007). In addition, Daniel's obsessive adherence to a very strict diet and extensive use of nutritional supplements have been noted by Pope et al. (2000), who found that dysmorphic weightlifters differed from non-dysmorphic weightlifters in their eating attitudes and drug use. Daniel's apparent compulsive exercise behaviour illustrates the key symptoms of exercise dependence described in the literature (e. g., Hausenblas & Symons Downs, 2002). For example, such individuals almost always grossly overtrain even when suffering from injuries or 'flu'. Also, they often place such an inordinate emphasis on their training that other important areas of their life, such as work or family, suffer (Chan & Grossman, 1988; Sachs & Pargman, 1979; Morgan, 1979; Thaxton, 1982; Veale, 1995).

Hypothetical Client – Victoria: a triathlete

Victoria has been running all her life. She remembers being very active as a child and constantly running with her younger brothers. She was a thin, spindly child, who succeeded regularly in outrunning boys several years older. In secondary school she began to train and run competitively on the girls' track and cross-country teams. When she was 14 her body began to change; she began to develop 'womanly curves' and added more body fat. She began to control the amount of calories she would eat daily, rarely ate three decent meals a day, and rarely allowed herself sweets. When Victoria looked in the mirror, she began to worry that her extra weight was making her less competitive and fatter than the female long-distance runners that she had seen in the Olympics on television. But she continued to excel in both sports, regularly winning the mile run in track and 3K in cross-country meets. Her coach pushed her to continue training hard and win more events so she could get a track scholarship to college.

She did earn a scholarship to a prestigious university to run both track and cross-country for varsity competition. Her coach was a 'win-at-all-costs' mentor, who believed that more training (above 100 miles a week) and a regimented diet were critical to success. The coach weighed her once a week on Fridays before competition, and if she was a pound or two overweight, she was told to cut back on her eating and exercise more. Secretly, Victoria began to go to the sauna with a rubber shirt on to dramatically lose weight on Fridays. Once she had competed successfully on Saturday, she would go out with teammates and splurge on pizza, eating almost a whole pizza herself. Once back in the hall of residence, she began to feel guilty and began sticking a finger down her throat to vomit. This routine continued for four years of college and she remained thin and competitive, but not happy with her over-eating and problem in making weight.

In the summers she began swimming and cycling to stay in shape. She was a superb cyclist and a decent swimmer, and decided to enter a local triathlon. Incredibly she won the event several minutes faster than many of her experienced competitors. She was hooked on triathlon and spent the summers racing every weekend. She upped her training from 2 to 4 hours daily and began winning every regional race, but she was still unhappy with her curvy figure and how other serious competitors might perceive it. In her senior year she was approached by a national triathlon team coach and asked if she would like to become a professional. Aged 23 she found herself living at the national training centre. Her life revolved around 4–6 hours of training a day, a highly regimented diet, specialized training on swimming and cycling techniques, and little social life. Her coach was even more critical of her weight, and she had to weigh in three times a week. If she was overweight, she had to put in extra workout time. Secretly she continued to purge after big meals or skipped meals altogether before weigh-ins. For six years she trained hard as a professional triathlete and competed successfully for her country in the Olympics. Her strict diet and training had paid dividends, but she still was not winning often enough for her coach and she still thought she was carrying extra weight.

When she was 30 she married another runner but continued to compete professionally. When she was 32 she began to develop shin splint problems that ultimately were diagnosed as a stress fracture caused by incessant pounding and a poor diet. The doctor forced her to take a month off, but she continued to ride her bike and swim regularly for 2–3 hours per day. She entered a triathlon soon afterward, but struggled in the running part with terrific pain. She put this down to lack of sufficient training, putting on several pounds, and insufficient healing. She decided to further restrict her diet, take more supplements and vitamins, and secretly continued to purge. Her husband was unaware of her bulimic behaviours and her low body image. She continued with non-weight-bearing training and increased her daily workouts to 4–6 hours a day.

She entered another triathlon a month later and felt she could succeed, but half-way through the Iron Man marathon, the pain in her shin became unbearable. She stopped, hoped it would subside, and started running again, but the pain returned with even more intensity. She tried walking and then limping home, but finally in tears she collapsed 6 miles from the end of the marathon. She felt it was the end of the world, the end of her career. She was depressed, full of self-hate at her failure, and didn't like the way her body looked after the doctor forced her to stop all exercise while she wore a walking cast.

Freimuth, Moniz, and Kim (2011) suggest that Victoria's life has progressed in four stages from recreational exercise as a child to full-blown exercise addiction as a professional triathlete. Victoria's life is dominated by the negative consequences of her addiction: long-term impairments to her health and daily functioning, loss of critical relationships, low self-esteem and body image, and depression.

Activity box **BOX 24.4**

How does exercise dependence differ from exercise commitment in elite athletes?

INITIAL NEEDS ASSESSMENT

Daniel

The initial needs assessment with Daniel consisted of a triangulated approach combining a clinical interview, observation, and questionnaires. In the interview the sport/exercise consultant explored his exercise history, drug use, supplement use, eating and training behaviours and his social and work life, using the theoretical frameworks provided by Lantz et al. (2001) for the study of muscle dysmorphia, and that of Smith et al. (1998) for the study of bodybuilding dependence. Lantz et al.'s (2001) work indicates that people with MD exhibit specific behavioural and psychological characteristics that can be divided into two categories: nutrition and physique concerns. Nutrition is comprised of behaviours concerned with pharmacological use, supplement use, and dietary behaviour. The model suggests that muscle dysmorphic persons are more likely to engage in these nutritional behaviours in pursuit of enhancing muscular, well-defined physiques than non-dysmorphic individuals. Physique Concerns, the second category associated with the psycho-behavioural model of MD, is characterized by concerns surrounding body size or symmetry, physique protection (behaviours designed to avoid having the body viewed by others), and exercise dependence.

Exercise dependence in bodybuilders, according the findings of Smith et al. (1998), appears to have three distinct subcomponents: social dependence, training dependence, and mastery dependence. Social dependence reflects the need to be in the bodybuilding social environment. Another subscale (training dependence) seems to reflect the need to engage in regular weight training. The third subscale (mastery dependence) appears to measure the need to exert control over training schedules.

In the interview the consultant explored all of these issues. Any of these factors alone would not constitute a diagnosis of MD, but several behaviours considered in concert would appear to be symptomatic of muscle dysmorphia.

To enable comparison of Daniel's self-perceptions and the perceptions of others regarding his behaviour, the consultant then interviewed Daniel's training partner, his trainer, and close family members. The information gained from the interviews was then supplemented by observation of Daniel in both the training environment (e.g., spending time observing his behaviour in the gym) and also eating, to determine whether his behaviours fit with the models of muscle dysmorphia and exercise dependence mentioned previously. With regard to eating behaviours, these were also to be observed to determine whether Daniel exhibited any signs of an eating disorder, and thus whether the observed exercise dependence was 'primary' (i.e., there is no evidence of an eating disorder), or 'secondary' (part of an eating disorder).

The final part of this triangulated needs analysis involved Daniel completing a number of self-report questionnaires aimed at assessing the extent to which he displayed symptoms of muscle dysmorphia, exercise dependence, and highly restrictive eating patterns. The consultant used theoretically-based, well-validated measures. In this case he used the Exercise Dependence Scale (EDS; Hausenblas & Symons Downs, 2002), which is based on the seven criteria for substance dependence identified in DSM-IV (4th edition, American Psychiatric Association, 1994), and has a scoring logarithm that allows computation of a total score to categorize clients as 'exercise dependent', 'non-dependent symptomatic', or 'non-dependent asymptomatic'. Consultants could alternatively have used Terry et al. (2004) Exercise Addiction Inventory (EAI). This latter scale consists of one item for each of the seven dependence criteria and purports to be able to accurately identify people at risk for exercise addiction.

Because neither scale was constructed specifically to measure exercise dependence in an anaerobic setting (i.e., weight training), the consultant also administered the Bodybuilding Dependence Scale (BDS; Smith et al., 1998), a three-factor, nine-item Likert-scored scale (scores range from 5–35 for Social Dependence, 3–21 for Training Dependence, and 2–14 for Mastery Dependence) aimed at measuring the three components of bodybuilding dependence. This has been well-validated by Hurst, Hale, Smith, and Collins (2000) and Smith and Hale (2004, 2005).

To measure muscle dysmorphia, the Muscle Dysmorphia Inventory (MDI; Rhea, et al., 2004) was used. This is based upon Lantz et al.'s (2001) psycho-behavioural model of muscle dysmorphia (scoring ranges from 4–24 for Diet, Supplement, and exercise dependence subscales, 6–36 for the Physique Protection subscale, 5–30 for the Size / Symmetry subscale, and 3–18 for the Pharmacology subscale) and has been shown to be psychometrically sound (Rhea et al., 2004). Unfortunately, neither the Muscle Dysmorphia Inventory nor the Bodybuilding Dependence Scale offers available norm-referenced standards (cut-off scores) for a clinical population, but the authors suggest that higher scores indicate more symptomatic behaviour of ED and MD, respectively.

Activity box

BOX 24.5

Are common exercise dependence questionnaires measuring the same behaviours or different components of the construct? Are they valid? Are they reliable?

Can these questionnaires be used to predict exercise dependence and muscle dysmorphia in later weight-lifting behaviours? Can clinicians and practitioners use these questionnaires with confidence to measure the potential for exercise dependence?

To examine the possibility of Daniel having an eating disorder the Eating Disorders Inventory-2 (EDI-2; Garner, 1991) was administered. Hausenblas and Symons Downs (2002) have used the subscale to categorize participants scoring above '14' as having a possible eating disorder and demonstrating signs of 'secondary exercise dependence'.

In addition to these well-validated measures, Daniel also completed a self-report seven-day exercise history (7-Day Physical Activity Recall Questionnaire; PAR; Sallis & Saelens, 2000) to determine whether his exercise behaviours met the usual criteria for exercise dependence (exercising every day (or multiple times per day) for more than 1 hour per session at approximately the same time and place at the gym; Smith & Hale, 2011). Although elite and highly committed athletes may also follow this routine, questioning may reveal a dependent person who has no or few long-term competitive goals and feels he / she must undergo this tightly controlled regimen to keep at bay feelings of low self-esteem and poor body image. In addition, these individuals suffer an abnormal amount of overuse injuries resulting from this excessive workout programme. They experience negative affect if they miss an exercise session for any reason. With exercise dependence, the need to exercise controls the exerciser, not vice versa. Scores on these questionnaires indicated potential muscle dysmorphia and exercise dependence, with analysis of the EDS scores resulting in a classification of 'exercise dependent' using Hausenblas and Symons Downs' (2002) criteria, near-maximum scores on all MDI and BDS subscales, and the PAR indicating multiple daily exercise sessions totalling 4–6 hours per day. Daniel's EDI-2 score of 12 did not quite meet Hausenblas and Symons Down's criterion for indicating an eating disorder and secondary exercise dependence, but it was high enough to warrant concern regarding his eating patterns.

Victoria

Victoria's initial assessment came as a result of her husband's insistence that she go to the doctor at the training centre to have him examine her for her continued depression and refusal to accept the diagnosis of a seriously dysfunctional stress fracture. The physician at the centre immediately noticed her lethargic, down demeanour and put it down to her injury. But when she refused to give up training for the next three months, he became concerned. After viewing her X-ray of her stress fracture, he had her undertake an osteoporosis test which proved positive for osteopenia. Finally he noticed the signs of acid burns on her fingers and that her weight had continued to drop even after she had ceased training. He decided that she needed to see the licensed sport psychologist at the centre to further discuss her state of mind. She reluctantly agreed to see him.

On her first session with the sport psychologist, who was a clinical psychologist by training, he listened to her discuss her down moods, loss of energy and emotions, and pessimistic attitude towards the lack of competition in the future. But like the physician, he also noticed the tell-tale acid burns on the tips of her fingers and the canker sore she had developed on her mouth.

The sport psychologist also used a triangulated method of diagnosis with Victoria. For his clinical interview, he interviewed Victoria about her athletic history, her injury history, her diet, her social and married life, and her state of mind prior to and after her stress fracture. He noticed that she seemed overly dedicated to training and competition, seemed to have her whole identity immersed in triathlon, and often exercised while she was hurt or sick. Since he could no longer observe her actual training and exercising, he talked to her coach, fellow triathletes, and husband about her training attitudes and regimen. They reported that she seemed driven to exercise, never took time off from training, continuously focused on increasing her training regimen, was very judgmental about herself based on her performance, and didn't seem to have a social life outside competition and training. Her husband also said that she ate irregular meals, and often after a large meal she disappeared into the bathroom for long periods. The sport psychologist had her complete the Exercise Dependence Scale (Hausenblas & Symons Downs, 2002), the 7-Day Physical Activity Recall Questionnaire (Sallis & Saelens, 2000) for a typical training week, and the Drive for Thinness (DFT) Scale of the Eating Disorder Inventory-2 (Garner, 1991). When all three scores were calculated at extremely high levels, he concluded that she might be suffering from a potential eating disorder that was compounded by her addictive need to exercise many hours a day. Research (Freimuth et al., 2011) shows that 39-48% of people suffering from eating disorders also have exercise dependence. He knew that he did not have the proper training to deal with eating disorders, so he made a referral to his local friend who was a clinical psychologist who specialized in treating eating disorders.

Definition box **BOX 24.6**

Primary exercise dependence: an individual who shows all the behaviours and symptoms of exercise dependence (Hausenblaus & Symons Downs, 2002) without any apparent eating disorder. Daniel may fall under this category.

Secondary exercise dependence: An individual with an eating disorder where exercise dependence may be one of the behaviours used to maintain weight loss in addition to strict dieting. Victoria may fall under this category.

FRAMEWORK AND INTERVENTION

Both Daniel and Victoria displayed symptoms consistent with one or more psychiatric disorders. Due to the nature of their symptoms and the sport context in which they exist, it was important for both Daniel and Victoria to be evaluated by a licensed mental health practitioner who also had training in sport. Given Victoria's eating-related symptomology, it was especially important that she was referred to a practitioner who also had specific training in identifying and treating eating disorders.

Both athletes required an interdisciplinary treatment approach which is recommended for all patients grappling with eating disorders and related concerns (American Psychiatric Association, 2006). In addition to ongoing mental health treatment, both athletes worked closely with a licensed medical professional, a registered dietitian, and a psychiatrist who prescribed and monitored medication. This interdisciplinary treatment team regularly consulted with one another in order to co-ordinate care. Regular consultation ensured that all treatment providers had the same data with which to work, and where discrepancies existed they were clarified with the patient. It was also important for one treatment provider to 'take point' on the case in terms of directing treatment. Initially, the medical professional on the team directed care to ensure medical stability for both patients. Thereafter, the professional with the most experience working with the primary psychiatric diagnosis was considered the team leader which in both cases was the treating psychologist.

When the patient's physical health is compromised it is best for the medical professional to direct care; however, when medical issues are stabilized and the mental health concerns can be more cogently attended to, it will likely be best for the mental health professional to direct care. One caveat to this is when a complex disorder such as an eating disorder or body dysmorphia are present. If it is determined that one or both of these diagnoses are appropriate, the individual with the most knowledge and experience with treating these disorders should direct the patient's care. For example, a highly skilled general practitioner physician may be untrained in terms of medical complications with eating disorders. Therefore, it may be appropriate to defer to the eating disorder expert, regardless of their discipline, in the treatment team in terms of which medical tests should be conducted and what constitutes normal results (Tyson, 2010).

In addition to getting a treatment team in place, it was also important to identify other important or influential individuals in the patient's lives particularly in the context of sport. Thompson and Sherman (2010) recommend that a 'sport management team' is also assembled. They have recommended the importance of including this type of team when working with athletes with eating disorders and related concerns for more than 25 years (Thompson, 1987). They note that individuals on this team (e.g., coaches, athletic trainers, and sport psychologists who are not providing treatment) can be invaluable for providing information to the treatment team about how the athlete is doing. Thompson and Sherman (2010) also noted that the sport management team should be managed by one of the health-care providers in the treatment team which also includes the health-care provider indicating in what ways the members of the sport management team can be an asset in helping the athlete recover.

Finally, family members involved in the treatment process were encouraged to seek some form of support for themselves. Getting one's own support while supporting someone with a psychiatric illness can result in one's own reduction in distress and sense of feeling burdened (Hibbs, Rhind, Leppanen, & Treasure, 2014). Thus, support team members were provided with book titles, online resources, and information about local support groups.

Daniel's intervention

Upon further assessment it was determined that Daniel's symptoms were consistent with a diagnosis of body dysmorphic disorder (BDD). Muscle dysmorphia is not a specific diagnosis as such, but is a form of body dysmorphia, and is included as a diagnostic specifier in the Diagnostic and Statistical Manual of Mental Disorders, 5th edition (DSM-5; American Psychiatric Association, 2013). The diagnosis of BDD is supported when a patient is preoccupied with a perceived physical flaw or deformity which is not noticeable by others. In Daniel's case he was highly focused on the size and shape of his muscles. He perceived that they were not large enough, when in fact, others indicated that they were. During the course of treatment he also revealed that he perceived his muscles to be significantly asymmetrical. This, too, was something that others did not see either at all or to the degree that he did. The diagnosis of BDD was further warranted by the level of distress Daniel experienced regarding his physique and the lengths he has gone to pursue muscular perfection at the cost of his relationships and his job. In addition to BDD, a co-occurring diagnosis of depression was also identified which is the most common co-occurring disorder (Phillips et al., 2010).

As noted above, effective treatment for Daniel required attention to his mental health, his physical health, and his dietary intake. His attending physician was able to determine that Daniel was not, at the time of treatment, experiencing negative effects of steroid use coupled with his restrictive diet. His registered dietitian, however, helped Daniel reconnect with what his body needed in order to perform not only its vital functions, but also what was needed to maintain muscle mass since that was a significant concern of Daniel's. Daniel entered treatment with erroneous assumptions and misinformation about what he actually needed to eat and/or avoid in order to obtain the results he desired. Daniel's dietitian had a well-developed understanding of sport nutrition as well as body dysmorphic disorder and was able to help him consume what he needed in order to be healthy and to sustain a reasonable amount of muscle mass. Finally, Daniel's psychiatrist monitored his psychotropic medications. The FDA has not yet approved medications for the treatment of body dysmorphic disorder; however, selective serotonin reuptake-inhibitors (SSRIs) have limited evidence that they may be effective in alleviating some symptoms of BDD (Ipser, Sander, & Stein, 2009). Because Daniel is also coping with depressive symptoms the SSRI may also help to alleviate those symptoms. The use of medication to reduce the intensity of Daniel's symptoms had the effect of allowing him to engage more fully in psychotherapy.

Throughout the course of psychotherapy, Daniel struggled significantly with letting go of the idea that his body needed to be perfect. Thus, an important part of his treatment was to address his misperception of what his body looks like. Cognitive-Behavioural Therapy (CBT) is often useful in helping patients identify the specific thoughts they have about themselves including when these thoughts occur, how negative the thoughts are, and what emotions are associated with the thoughts (Jarry & Cash, 2011). Daniel, for example, had thoughts not only about how 'bad' he believed his body looked but also consistent negative thoughts about his overall self-worth. It was common for Daniel to report that because he could not get rid of his body's flaws he was a 'failure' and that he 'was not good enough' until he could grow his muscles and make them perfectly symmetrical. Identifying these patterns and themes in Daniel's thoughts helped help him learn about not only what he thinks about himself and how that contributed to him feeling anxious much of the time, but it also allowed him the opportunity to attack his negative thinking and make positive changes. Prior to Daniel developing this type of cognitive awareness he was unable to acknowledge let alone change his negative thinking.

Daniel also benefited from motivational interviewing (Miller & Rollnick, 2002). Motivational Interviewing is essentially an approach that recognizes the patient's own goals and drives to help them make changes that align with what they want for themselves and their life. It can be particularly effective for those who are ambivalent about making any changes which was the case with Daniel. Although Daniel's primary sources of motivation were muscle- and competition-related, he did state that he was interested in having a long-term romantic relationship in his life again adding that he had regret about ending his previous relationship in order to devote more time to his bodybuilding. Work around these issues focused on putting his bodybuilding goals in context and help him identify what he has had to give up in his life in order to pursue muscle perfection at all costs.

Finally, although not always desired by the patient nor necessary for effective treatment, Daniel benefited from psychodynamic psychotherapy. The benefit of pursuing this form of treatment is not only for 'insight' into the problem but also to help the patient identify when he is heading down a similar path and knowing how he got there (Parker, 2010). Through this type of insight-oriented work Daniel became aware of how his pursuit of muscle perfection was connected to early childhood experiences. He noted that while growing up he was consistently picked on for being 'small' and 'puny.' He also recalled that his elder brother picked on him for these reasons as well. As a result, Daniel developed an overwhelming sense of shame about his body. Daniel remembered that when he was introduced to weight lifting in middle-school gym class he was determined to transform his body and ensure that no one would ever think he was puny again. Despite bulking up he still regularly dressed in baggy clothing to hide what he perceived to be an inadequate body. Having this awareness helped Daniel further put his excessive pursuit in perspective. He was able to contemplate whether the goal of making sure no one ever thought he was small again was more important than having a partner with whom he might one day have a family.

When patients are able to recognize familiar behaviour patterns (e.g., pursuit of perfection, avoidance of shame, focusing on a singular pursuit at the expense of other interests) and why they are so powerfully drawn to them, they have the opportunity to prevent destructive behaviour patterns and make healthier choices. Without this degree of understanding it is much easier to 'rationalize' why old, destructive behaviours are in fact good and healthy.

Victoria's intervention

Victoria's case was as complicated as Daniel's; however, she was engaged in behaviours that were potentially much more lethal. Based on Victoria's symptoms, a feeding and eating disorder (DSM-5) diagnosis was warranted. Eating disorders themselves have one of the highest mortality rates of any psychiatric illness primarily explained by anorexia nervosa (Neumärker, 2000). As noted in the initial assessment prior to referral Victoria's weight has continued to drop and was at 100 pounds which is approximately 15% below her ideal weight. A diagnosis of anorexia nervosa, purging type was rendered due to Victoria's steadily dropping weight, fear of gaining weight, and her regular use of self-induced vomiting as a method to manipulate her weight. Victoria's low weight in combination with excessive exercising and regular self-induced vomiting can lead to numerous serious or lethal physical complications including complications with cardiorespiratory, gastrointestinal, endocrine, and neuropsychiatric functioning (Academy for Eating Disorders, 2012). Having a medical professional on the treatment team who is well-versed in the treatment of athletes as well as eating disorders can be illustrated by the importance of being able to distinguish between a low heart rate (bradycardia) as a result of athletic participation or as a result of malnutrition (Thompson & Sherman, 2010). Additionally, the cessation of one's menstrual cycle is often viewed by those in the sporting culture as a marker of commitment by the female athlete to their training programme. Amenorrhea has a direct impact on bone health and if left uncorrected can lead to osteoporosis (American College of Sports Medicine, 2011). In the world of sport participation low energy availability, menstrual abnormalities, and decreased bone density is referred to as the Female Athlete Triad (initially conceptualized by Yeager, Agostini, Nativ, & Drinkwater, 1993) and there is evidence that Victoria is experiencing all three. Regardless, the presence of any one of these three elements warrants an assessment of the other two.

Victoria was referred to a physician trained in the assessment and treatment of eating disorders to evaluate her medical stability. Ongoing medical evaluation and monitoring was indicated in order to prevent irreversible medical issues including loss of bone density, heart damage, gastrointestinal issues, dental damage, and so on. Victoria has already been diagnosed with osteopenia (precursor to osteoporosis) and has shown signs of regular self-induced purging. Results of Victoria's blood work, however, which included the recommended tests for thyroid functioning, complete blood count, serum metabolic profile, electrolytes and enzymes, and electrocardiogram (Academy for Eating Disorders, 2012) were, at this point, negative. Since negative findings in this regard are not unusual for those with anorexia nervosa who do not use purging type behaviours (Brown, Mehler, & Harris, 2000) it is highly likely that Victoria's future tests will reveal evidence of pathological functioning, thus it was particularly important for her to routinely have blood work done.

An additional consideration in Victoria's treatment was determining the appropriate level of care she needed in order to be both physically and psychologically healthy. Although Victoria's weight was significantly below what would be healthy for her given her sex, age, and height, the normal medical findings and her reported willingness to engage in treatment suggested that outpatient therapy was appropriate. Victoria's treatment team consisting of her physician, psychologist, psychiatrist, and registered dietitian conferenced regularly (i.e., every other week or weekly as needed). Regular contact among treatment providers allowed them to comprehensively monitor her progress. Initially, Victoria was required to at least maintain her weight and continue to abstain from exercise until her stress fractures were completely healed. Once healed she was severely restricted in the amount and intensity of exercise. She was then expected to start slowly gaining weight. Without adherence to these initial treatment goals Victoria would have been admitted either to an inpatient facility or a residential treatment centre.

Admittance to an inpatient facility specializing in the treatment of eating disorders would have been indicated should Victoria's medical stability have been in question which would have included such things as low values for heart rate, glucose and/or potassium, electrolyte imbalance, compromised renal and/or cardiovascular functioning, and poor social support (American Psychiatric Association, 2006). Should Victoria have required inpatient care managing the 'refeeding' process would have been a point of focus in her medical recovery. Improperly refeeding someone who is severely underweight can lead to 'refeeding syndrome' (Academy for Eating Disorders, 2012), which can result in issues such as catastrophic problems with cardiovascular and/or respiratory function and potentially death. By contrast, placement in a residential treatment centre would have been appropriate for Victoria should she have been medically stable (e.g., no need for IV fluids or tube feedings, nor required lab tests more than once daily (American Psychiatric Association, 2006)) but unable to enact necessary recovery based behaviours (e.g., follow exercise prescription, eat appropriately as identified by the registered dietitian).

Victoria, however, was able to adhere to treatment recommendations and showed slow but steady progress. Her most significant struggle was in reducing the amount and intensity of her exercise. She was concerned not only about what would happen to her weight if she was unable to ramp up her exercise regimen, but also about what she feared would happen to her performance level. Thus, an important part of psychological treatment was to help Victoria address her erroneous thoughts and fears about weight gain and performance (Thompson & Sherman, 2010).

Although the prescription to abstain from weight-bearing exercise was indicated due to Victoria's stress fractures, it was also warranted based on her weight being too low (based on her age, gender, height, weight history, and activity level) and restrictive food intake. This was, of course, devastating for Victoria and led to an exacerbation of depressive symptoms. Based on the eating disorder diagnosis alone, the directive to cease all activity is not always clear cut – this is particularly true for athletes and regular exercisers (Madison & Ruma, 2003; Sherman & Thompson, 2001). Researchers have found that engaging in regular physical activity can improve overall quality of life (Penedo & Dahn, 2005) and reduce psychiatric symptoms including those related to anxiety (DeBoer, Power, Utschig, Otto, & Smits, 2012). Moreover, someone for whom physical activity is a part of their identity (e.g., a triathlete) not being 'allowed' to engage in physical activity can be a contributing factor in the development, or exacerbation of, a depressive or anxiety-based syndrome. Thus, when Victoria's fracture eventually healed to the point that someone without an eating disorder would be cleared to re-engage in physical activity, additional medical (e.g., negative blood work) and psychological markers (e.g., ability to reframe her exercise to become a part of her life rather than being her life) were evaluated to determine if, or to what degree, she was able to resume physical activity. Once cleared Victoria's activity level in terms of duration, type of activity, and intensity was monitored so that she did not re-engage in over-exercising. Her primary source of support (i.e., her husband) was instrumental in helping to ensure the treatment team received accurate information with respect to Victoria's physical activity.

Relearning how to eat appropriately was necessary alongside relearning how to exercise appropriately. Although Victoria was well-versed in the nutritional content of most foods (e.g., calories, fat content, fibre content) she no longer knew what a normal meal looked like nor how much she needed to consume in order to keep her vital systems working and to fuel her high level of training. A registered dietitian with training and experience in working with individuals with eating disorders (and who has knowledge of treating athletes) was critical in helping Victoria manage reintroducing foods she had eliminated from her diet as well as increasing her overall caloric intake. This process was severely distressing for Victoria which is not uncommon. Fears about gaining weight, a presumed decline in athletic performance, and potential rejection by others for 'getting fat' were intensified for Victoria early in the treatment process. When these fears surfaced the registered dietitian was able to communicate this to the treatment team so Victoria's concerns could be adequately addressed by the treating mental health professional in order to help Victoria effectively manage these reactions.

Victoria continued to struggle with fears not only about losing training time, because her training was severely restricted, but also with getting healthy which for Victoria translated into weight gain and to her meant that she wouldn't be able to perform at the same level. It is important to note that although Victoria initially noticed an improvement in performance prior to her referral for treatment and which seemed to coincide with the eating disorder behaviours. She also experienced inevitable performance decline and injury (Thompson & Sherman, 2010). Her body simply no longer had what it needed to perform at its peak level and to repair itself because it was not being properly fuelled and it had depleted the nutritional stores that did exist. Victoria also experienced intense fears about gaining weight and becoming fat. This was particularly an issue early on in the treatment process as her body adjusted to having more fuel available. Initial weight gain is disproportionately fat and tends to be deposited in the abdominal area (Pagliato, Corradi, Gentile, & Testolin, 2000; Scalfi et al., 2002) while she was re-nourishing her body. Her body therefore 'held on to' as much fuel as possible since it had been in a starved or semi-starved state for so long. As a result Victoria experienced bloating, especially in the abdominal area. Part of treatment, therefore, involved not only helping her to cope with this experience, but also providing education around what is happening with her body and the fact that the initial changes are temporary.

What would not be temporary, of course, would be the inevitable weight gain necessary for her overall health. This was the most significant treatment obstacle even after eating disorder behaviours were significantly diminished. Body-image issues are often one of the last concerns to extinguish – and for some, may persist even after they have recovered from their eating disorder (Eshkevari, Rieger, Longo, Haggard, & Treasure, 2014). Reminders of the weight gain will be experienced in terms of how one's clothes fit, how the body feels when it moves, how the individual looks in the mirror and photographs, and comments that others may make about how they look. When treating these concerns a combination of both supportive psychotherapy (McIntosh et al., 2006; Stiles-Shields et al., 2013), for the purpose of empathizing with the difficulty of living with a body that looks and feels different, especially in the context of a weight obsessed culture, and Cognitive-Behavioural Therapy to help manage negative thoughts and feelings that surround the change in physique can be beneficial

(Cash & Hrabosky, 2003). This combination of approaches is also helpful as the patient navigates the coinciding changes in their food intake.

Identifying the antecedents of Victoria's restricting and purging behaviours was helpful. It is common for there to be a pattern to the circumstances that led up to the desire to restrict and/or to purge. It is not always easy for patients to identify what immediately precedes these behaviours. The focus of this part of treatment should be on the patient's thoughts. Usually the predicting variable is not so much a specific type of event or experience, but the thoughts and feelings the patient experiences about these situations. For Victoria, the themes revolved around fears of being rejected. She was able to determine that prior to a binge-purge episode or an intense run she felt rejected by someone important in her life. If her coach constructively criticized her she felt like she was not good enough for him and thus felt rejected. A similar pattern emerged in her relationship with her husband. She noticed that whenever they got into a fight she would either go on a punishing run or overeat to the point of needing to vomit to relieve the physical discomfort. Once these patterns were identified Victoria was able to begin the work of determining whether or not her coach or husband were actually rejecting her. She usually knew the answer was that they were not; however, if she was unsure, she learnt how to ask for reassurance in an assertive, direct way. This type of psychodynamic work (see Winston, 2012 for discussion of treatment recommendations and a brief review of evidence base in use of this approach with eating disorders) was useful for Victoria and might also aid in identifying other themes and concerns such as perfectionism, desire for control, history of trauma, lack of a sense of identity apart from athletics and/or the eating disorder, and difficulties in interpersonal relationships.

Finally, psycho-education specifically with Victoria's coaches was indicated. Both the National Collegiate Athletic Association (2009) and the International Olympic Committee (2006) have crafted statements regarding eating disorders and athletes addressing the role coaches should play in issues related to eating concerns. Both organizations recognize the need for the athlete's health and wellbeing to supersede athletic participation, and that coaches should not comment on nor monitor an athlete's weight. Coaches who conduct weigh-ins and advise whether or not an athlete should gain or lose weight may put athletes at risk for medical issues and may contribute to the development of an eating disorder.

Future prognosis

Both Daniel and Victoria have the potential to recover from their unhealthy pursuits and live happy and healthy lives. Their engagement in their respective sports at a competitive level does not have to end but will have to be approached with a perspective much different from what they each currently have. Because both Daniel and Victoria have been dealing with some aspect of their current concerns for many years (more than a decade), they may require longer-term treatment in comparison to those whose concerns are identified within months or a just few years of when they began. Regardless, a positive outcome for both athletes will require a co-ordinated and collaborative interdisciplinary treatment team that has regular contact with one another. It will also require a well-educated support team which may include friends, family, teammates, coaches, and athletic trainers. Of course, both Daniel and Victoria will have to engage in their respective treatment processes in order to get healthy; however, they may not be fully 'on board' with the treatment and recommendations made especially if their activity is restricted. That simply means that any initial component of treatment will focus on helping each of them see what their unhealthy pursuit of their sport has cost them and what it will continue to cost them should they continue with their current approach.

REFLECTIONS

Weight training participants, endurance athletes, health-care specialists, sport and exercise psychologists, clinical and counselling psychologists, and psychiatrists need to become more aware of the potential dangers of exercise dependence and eating disorders and should have access to educational information about the causes, consequences, and symptoms of each disorder. Like other addictive and compulsive behaviours, if people know the warning signals and outward symptoms (e.g., highly regulated workout regimens, unhealthy eating patterns or pervasive withdrawal responses, regular compulsive thoughts and words about exercise, etc.), often participants can change their own behaviours or external helpers can recommend things that will help avoid the short- and long-term deleterious effects of these disorders. Helpers in the athletic and exercise realms, such as coaches and personal trainers, should be educated about such behaviours and unhealthy attitudes and have intervention or referral strategies available for their local clientele. Bodybuilders and endurance athletes also need to be self-aware, monitoring their own thoughts and behaviours. Alarm bells should ring if they have an obsessive-compulsive personality, suffer from low body image and self-esteem, had prior problems with an eating disorder, have a history of obesity as a child, or have a family history of obsessive-compulsive disorders or eating disorders. If their daily train of thought is dominated by thoughts of exercising and they cannot seem to control and limit their workout motivation, they are likely to be at risk for exercise dependence or muscle dysmorphia. Self-awareness may help keep exercisers from transforming from committed, healthy patterns into dependent, unhealthy behaviours.

Behavioural strategies can be very useful in avoiding or limiting the early onset of exercise dependence or muscle dysmorphia. Berger, Pargman, and Weinberg's (2007) list of strategies, which we regard as very sensible suggestions, include: keeping exercise workouts brief and not too frequent (limited to three or four times per week for 30–60 minutes), alternating hard and easy training days to avoid overuse injuries, finding a workout partner who is not obsessed with exercise, scheduling regular rest days, setting realistic short- and long-term goals, and when injured making sure of full recovery before restarting.

We would also add that moderation should be a goal in exercisers' activity schedules with a cross-training component added to their regimen that avoids the same repetitive, high intensity anaerobic or aerobic workout to control compulsive addictive behaviours and limit physiological and psychological damage. Modeling of other non-compulsive behaviours by trainers and coaches can also help lifters to realize that other workout or coping strategies are available. Exercisers should learn self-monitoring skills for their work out behaviours, practise coping strategies to help deal with stress, and develop behaviours to help them improve relationships and foster interests outside the gym.

Serious exercise dependence, muscle dysmorphia, and eating disorder behaviours warrant serious clinical and psychiatric interventions. While weight lifters may not suffer from the early life-threatening damage that many anorexics or bulimics do, the continuous damage caused by years of excessive exercise, overuse of legal and illegal ergogenic aids, poor diet, and social and psychological isolation is also very unhealthy and can lead to a premature demise. When exercise or psychological helpers notice clients with potentially damaging behaviours, attitudes, and cognitions, they need to encourage these lifters to seek professional counselling or make a referral for these individuals. In this chapter, since we are both exercise/sport psychology consultants and a licensed clinical psychologist, we have based our suggested interventions primarily on both Cognitive-Behavioural and Supportive Psychotherapeutic Models. We believe that disorders such as primary and secondary exercise dependence and muscle dysmorphia require a team approach to treatment since specialized skills are needed from many areas. For both Daniel and Victoria, referrals should be made to specially-trained nutritionists, professional coaches and trainers, sport and exercise psychologists, physicians, clinical and counselling psychologists, and psychiatrists.

For initial evaluation, a triangulated method of assessment is necessary to accurately measure and diagnose unhealthy attitudes towards exercise and eating, excessive exercise behaviours, and related psychological disorders. For Daniel's body dysmorphia, this would involve an interview exploring his exercise history, drug use, supplement use, eating and training behaviours, observation of training regimen and practices, coaches, and workout partners, and extensive use of valid self-report questionnaires such as the EDS, EAI, MDI, BDS for exercise dependence and other questionnaires such as the EDI-2 and PAR to investigate eating and exercise habits. For Victoria, since an eating disorder was suspected, the EDI-2, a clinically-structured interview questionnaire, and other psychological inventories for depression and obsessive-compulsive disorders may be appropriate for diagnosis in addition to the specific exercise dependence questionnaires suggested for Daniel. Psychologists, coaches, family, and training partners should also observe Victoria's exercise and eating habits. Shorter questionnaires (e.g., EAI, DFT, BDS) could be administered regularly to Daniel and Victoria to closely monitor behaviours and evaluate the effectiveness of psychological interventions over time, though it should be noted that the sensitivity to these measures to short-term changes has yet to be tested. Recently a study by Heaney, Ginty, Carroll, and Phillips (2011) showed that exercise dependent participants displayed a blunted cardiovascular and cortisol reaction to stress, similar to those seen in alcohol and smoking dependence; this finding may offer a more accurate, objective measurement of exercise dependence that could be monitored throughout diagnosis and intervention phases with patients.

As exercise psychology consultants and clinical psychologists, our specialized expertise and training would limit the interventions that individually we would undertake with both Daniel and Victoria. We must operate within our competencies and refer to sport and clinical specialists when the client needs another specialized intervention. It would be our professional responsibility to refer both individuals to physicians, licensed clinical or counselling psychologists, eating disorder specialists, or psychiatrists since both are suspected of having serious psychological disorders. As the first two authors are exercise psychology consultants, our role would be to help gather information for further diagnosis by observation and questionnaires, undertake limited exercise-behavioural interventions, and make the proper referrals to knowledgeable, expert clinicians like the clinical psychologist third author.

In this chapter we have presented hypothetical interventions by psychological professionals for both Daniel and Victoria based on several psychological approaches. We realize that other professionals might base their intervention programme on a diagnosis of an obsessive-compulsive disorder, body dysmorphic disorder, or addictive behaviour model that may utilize a different set of questionnaires, observational procedures, and behaviour change strategies that differ from the approach we have selected. Because exercise dependence is not specifically included under new DSM-5 criteria, it is difficult to recommend a specific treatment approach. Freimuth et al. (2011) stated that most treatment programmes to date are based on cognitive-behavioural principles utilized in behavioural addiction management, but other treatments may be effective when early diagnosis occurs. For example, Dunn, Deroo, and Rivara (2001) have shown that motivational interviewing, a technique for increasing motivation to change, has been successful in creating positive behaviour change in individuals with chemical or behavioural dependence. We suggest that professionals dealing with exercise dependence become familiar with a variety of intervention approaches that may work differently for individuals with primary vs. secondary exercise dependence and muscle dysmorphia. In particular, for the diagnosis of primary vs. secondary exercise dependence, we suggest that practitioners become aware of differing diagnostic criteria summarized by Adams (2009) in the first table of his review article. In addition, while Daniel's hypothetical treatment programme may be successfully undertaken in an outpatient clinic, it may be necessary to treat Victoria's potentially life-threatening eating disorder in a full-time, live-in clinical setting. Furthermore, Adams (2009) offered a decision-making tree for diagnosing and treating exercise dependence which may offer guidance to those not familiar with potential exercise dependence disorders.

Since we lack the qualifications to dispense medications that may help in these intervention programmes, we are reluctant to advise usage or point to specific drug intervention regimens. For example, like Pope et al. (2000) have documented, some psychiatrists might prescribe serotonin-reuptake or dopamine–reuptake inhibitors to limit the effects of diagnosed OCD behaviours and enhance mood for Daniel's hypothesized intervention. In addition, anti-depressant medications might be part of the intervention programme that Victoria receives. Further research is necessary to see if these drugs specifically relieve the varied symptoms of primary and secondary exercise dependence.

Dependent and addictive behaviours may be difficult to totally eliminate, but with proper help, they can be controlled. The first step is awareness and education in both participant and helper. Although many professionals may believe that exercise dependence is of minor concern in the face of the obesity / sedentary epidemic of the last 30 years, it is a behavioural disorder that can have serious consequences for over-committed exercisers. It is our hope that this information will reduce its prevalence and lead to more effective interventions in the future.

Key future research box

BOX 24.7

1. Test various models (e.g., Jacob's (1986) psychobiological addictions model, Thomson & Blanton's (1987) physiological model of exercise dependence) to see which seems to predict resulting exercise dependence behaviours more accurately.
2. Questions about validity and reliability of ED measures still remain (e.g., are the EDS and EDQ measuring gender-biased components of exercise dependence in differing constructs?).
3. More progress needs to be undertaken on accurately describing the prevalence of exercise dependence in weight lifters and other related syndromes (e.g., muscle dysmorphia, eating disorders).
4. The use of drugs and anabolic steroids as potential influences on exercise dependence and the relationship of eating disorders to ED need to be more fully examined from both theoretical and treatment perspectives.
5. Research needs to be undertaken on the success of various therapeutic approaches (e.g., cognitive-behavioural, drug supplemented, motivational interviewing, etc.) on both primary and secondary exercise dependence.

FURTHER READING

Adams, J. (2009). Understanding exercise dependence. *Journal of Contemporary Psychotherapy*, 39, 231–240. The author provides a basic conceptual basis for exercise dependence, reviews some theoretical explanations, and provides lists of diagnostic criteria and treatment steps.

Berczik, K., Szabo, A., Griffiths, M. D., Kurimay, T., Kun, B., Urban, R., & Demetrovics, Z. (2012). Exercise addiction: Symptoms, diagnosis, epidemiology, and etiology. *Substance Use and Misuse*, 47, 403–417. The authors present a strong argument that exercise dependence is really just another form of exercise addiction with a strong review of current knowledge.

Hale, B. D., & Smith, D. (2012). Bodybuilding. In T. Cash (Ed.), *Encyclopedia of body image and human performance* (pp. 63–77). Oxford: Elsevier. In this chapter the authors review the history of research, possible symptoms and causes, and possible interventions of exercise dependence and muscle dysmorphia in bodybuilders.

Smith, D., & Hale, B. D. (2011). Exercise dependence. In D. Lavallee & D. Tod (Eds.), *The psychology of strength training and conditioning* (pp. 126–147). London: Routledge. The authors examine the concept of exercise dependence from an applied perspective as it relates to weight lifting and offer case studies of bodybuilders.

Thompson, R. A., & Sherman, R. T. (2010). *Eating disorders in sport.* New York: Routledge. The authors discuss the clinical elements of eating disorders including how this class of disorders manifests in sport, and how to identify and intervene with athletes who may have an eating disorder.

REFERENCES

Academy for Eating Disorders. (2012). *Eating disorders: Critical points for early recognition and medical risk management in the care of individuals with eating disorders.* Deerfield, IL: Academy for Eating Disorders.

Adams, J. (2009). Understanding exercise dependence. *Journal of Contemporary Psychotherapy, 39,* 231–240.

Allegre, B., Souville, M., Therme, P., & Griffiths, M. (2006). Definitions and measures of exercise dependence. *Addiction Research and Theory, 14,* 631–646.

American College of Sports Medicine. (2011). *The female athlete triad.* Indianapolis, IN: American College of Sports Medicine.

American Psychiatric Association. (1994). *Diagnostic and statistical manual of mental disorders* (4th ed.). Washington, DC: American Psychiatric Association.

American Psychiatric Association. (2006). *Practice guideline for the treatment of patients with eating disorders* (2nd ed.). Washington, DC: American Psychiatric Association.

American Psychiatric Association. (2013). *Diagnostic and statistical manual of mental disorders* (5th ed.). Washington, DC: American Psychiatric Association.

Baekeland, F. (1970). Exercise deprivation: Sleep and psychological reactions. *Archives of General Psychiatry, 22,* 365–369.

Berczik, K., Szabo, A., Griffiths, M. D., Kurimay, T., Kun, B., & Urban, R., et al. (2012). Exercise addiction: Symptoms, diagnosis, epidemiology, and etiology. *Substance Use and Misuse, 47,* 403–417.

Berger, B., Pargman, D., & Weinberg, R. (2007). *Foundations of exercise psychology* (4th ed.). Morgantown, WV: Fitness Institute Technology.

Brown, J. M., Mehler, P. S., & Harris, R. H. (2000). Medical complications occurring in adolescents with anorexia nervosa. *Western Journal of Medicine, 172,* 189–193.

Cash, T. F., & Hrabosky, J. I. (2003). The effects of psychoeducation and self-monitoring in a cognitive-behavoral program for body-image improvement. *Eating Disorders: The Journal of Treatment & Prevention, 11,* 255–270.

Chan, C. S., & Grossman, H. Y. (1988). Psychological effects of running loss on consistent runners. *Perceptual and Motor Skills, 66,* 875–883.

DeBoer, L. B., Powers, M. B., Utschig, A. C., Otto, M. W., & Smits, J. A. (2012). Exploring exercise as an avenue for the treatment of anxiety disorders. *Expert Review of Neurotherapeutics, 12,* 1011–1022.

Dunn, C., Deroo, L., & Rivara, F. P. (2001). The use of brief interventions adapted from motivational interviewing across behavioural domains: A systematic review. *Addiction, 96,* 1725–1742.

Eshkevari, E., Rieger, E., Longo, M., Haggard, P., & Treasure, J. (2014). Persistent body image disturbance following recovery from eating disorders. *International Journal of Eating Disorders, 4,* 400–409.

Freimuth, M., Moniz, S., & Kim, S. R. (2011). Clarifying exercise addiction: Differential diagnosis, co-occurring disorders, and phases of addiction. *International Journal of Environmental Research and Public Health, 8,* 4069–4081.

Garner, D. M. (1991). *Eating Disorders Inventory-2: Professional manual*. Odessa, FL: Psychological Assessment Resources, Inc.

Grieve, F. G. (2007). A conceptual model of factors contributing towards muscle dysmorphia. *Eating Disorders, 15*, 63–80.

Hausenblas, H., & Symons Downs, D. (2002). How much is too much? The development and validation of the Exercise Dependence Scale. *Psychology and Health, 17*, 387–404.

Heaney, J., Ginty, A., Carroll, D., & Phillips, A. (2011). Preliminary evidence that exercise dependence is associated with blunted cardiac and cortisol reactions to acute psychological stress. *International Journal of Psychophysiology, 79*(2), 323–329.

Hibbs, R., Rhind, C., Leppanen, J., & Treasure, J. (2014). Interventions for caregivers of someone with an eating disorder: A meta-analysis. *International Journal of Eating Disorders, 48*, 349–361.

Hurst, R., Hale, B. D., & Smith, D. (2000). Exercise dependence in bodybuilders and weight lifters. *British Journal of Sports Medicine, 11*, 319–325.

Hurst, R., Hale, B.D., Smith, D. & Collins, D. (2000). Exercise dependence, social physique anxiety, and social support in experienced and inexperienced bodybuilders and weightlifters. *British Journal of Sports Medicine, 34*, 431-435.

International Olympic Committee Medical Commission Working Group on Women in Sport. (2006). *Position stand on the female athlete triad*. Retrieved 9 December 2015 from http://www.olympic.org/documents/reports/en/en_report_917.pdf.

Ipser, J. C., Sander, C., & Stein, D.J. (2009). Pharmacotherapy and psychotherapy for body dysmorphic disorder. *The Cochrane Database of Systematic Reviews, 1*, CD005332

Jarry, J. L., & Cash, T. F. (2011). Cognitive-behavioral approaches to body image change. In T. F. Cash & L. Smolak (Eds.), *Body image: A handbook of science, practice, and prevention* (2nd ed., pp. 415–423). New York: Guilford.

Lantz, C. D., Rhea, D. J., & Mayhew, J. L. (2001). The drive for size: A psycho-behavioral model of muscle dysmorphia. *International Sport Journal, 5*, 71–85.

Leone, J. E., Sedory, E. J., & Gray, K. A. (2005). Recognition and treatment of muscle dysmorphia and related body image disorders. *Journal of Athletic Training, 40*(4), 352–359.

Madison, J. K., & Ruma, S. L. (2003). Exercise and athletic involvement as moderators of severity in adolescents with eating disorders. *Journal of Applied Sport Psychology, 15*, 213–222.

McCreary, D. R., & Sasse, D. K. (2000). An exploration of the drive for muscularity in adolescent boys and girls. *Journal of American College Health, 48*, 297–304.

McIntosh, V. V. W., Jordan, J., Luty, S. E., Carter, F. A., McKenzie, J. M., Bulik, C.M., & Joyce, P. R. (2006). Specialist supportive clinical management for anorexia nervosa. *International Journal of Eating Disorders, 39*, 625–632.

Miller, W. R., & Rollnick, S. (2002). *Motivational interviewing: Preparing people for change* (2nd ed.). New York: Guilford.

Morgan, W. P. (1979). Negative addiction in runners. *The Physician and Sports Medicine, 7*, 57–77.

National Collegiate Athletic Association. (2009). *Nutrition and performance resources*. Retrieved 9 December 2015 from http://www.ncaa.org/health-and-safety/nutrition-and-performance/nutrition-and-performance-resources.

Neumärker, K. J. (2000). Mortality rates and causes of death. *European Eating Disorders Review, 8*, 181–187.

Ogden, J., Veale, D., & Summers, Z. (1997). The development and validation of the Exercise Dependence Questionnaire. *Addiction Research, 5*(4), 343–356.

Olivardia, F. (2001). Mirror, mirror, on the wall, who's the largest of them all? The features and phenomenology of muscle dysmorphia. *Harvard Review of Psychiatry, 9*, 254–259.

Pagliato, E., Corradi, E., Gentile, M.G., & Testolin, G. (2000). Changes in body composition and resting energy expenditure in anorectic patients after a weight gain of fifteen percent. *Annals of the New York Academy of Sciences, 904*, 617–620.

Parker, R. (2010). Critical looks: The psychodynamics of body hatred. In G.Heuer (Ed.), *Sacral revolutions: Reflecting on the work of Andrew Samuels – Cutting edges in psychoanalysis and Jungian analysis*. New York: Routledge.

Penedo, G. J., & Dahn, J. R. (2005). Exercise and well-being: A review of mental and physical health benefits associated with physical activity. *Current Opinion in Psychiatry, 18*, 189–193.

Phillips, J. M., & Drummond, M. J. N. (2001). An investigation into the body image perception, body satisfaction and exercise expectations of male fitness leaders: Implications for professional practice. *Leisure Studies, 20*, 95–105.

Phillips, K. A., Stein, D. J., Rauch, S. L., Hollander, E., Fallon, B. A., & Barsky, A., et al. (2010). Should an obsessive-compulsive spectrum grouping of disorders be included in DSM-V? *Depression and Anxiety, 27*, 528–555.

Pope, H. G., Phillips, K. A., & Olivardia, R. (2000). *The Adonis complex: The secret crisis of male body obsession*. New York: Free Press.

Rhea, D. J., Lantz, C. D., & Cornelius, A. E. (2004). Development of the Muscle Dysmorphia Inventory (MDI). *The Journal of Sports Medicine and Physical Fitness, 44*, 428–435.

Sachs, M., & Pargman, D. (1979). Commitment and dependence upon regular running. Paper presented at the annual meeting of the American Alliance for Health, *Physical Education and Recreation*. New Orleans, LA.

Sallis, J. F., & Saelens, B. E. (2000). Assessment of physical activity by self-report: Status, limitations, and future directions. *Research Quarterly for Exercise and Sport, 71* (Supplement): S1–S14.

Scalfi, L., Polito, A., Bianchi, L., Marra, M., Caldara, A., & Nicolai, E., et al. (2002). Body composition changes in patients with anorexia nervosa after complete weight recovery. *European Journal of Clinical Nutrition, 56*, 15–20.

Sherman, R. T., & Thompson, R. A. (2001). Athletes and disordered eating: Four major issues for the professional psychologist. *Professional Psychology: Research and Practice, 32*, 27–33.

Smith, D., & Hale, B. D. (2004). Validity and factor structure of the Bodybuilding Dependence Scale. *British Journal of Sports Medicine, 38*, 177–181.

Smith, D., & Hale, B. D. (2005). Exercise dependence in bodybuilding: Antecedents and reliability of measurement. *Journal of Sports Medicine and Physical Fitness, 45*, 401–408.

Smith, D., & Hale, B. (2011). Exercise dependence. In D. Tod & D.Lavallee (Eds.), *The psychology of strength and conditioning* (pp. 126–147). Champaign, IL: Human Kinetics.

Smith, D. K., Hale, B. D., & Collins, D. J. (1998). Measurement of exercise dependence in bodybuilders. *Journal of Sport Medicine and Physical Fitness, 38*, 66–74.

Stiles-Shields, C., Touyz, S., Hay, P., Lacey, H., Crosby, R. D., & Rieger, E., et al. (2013). Therapeutic alliance in two treatments for adults with severe and enduring anorexia nervosa. *International Journal of Eating Disorders*, 46, 783–789.

Symons Downs, D., Hausenblas, H., & Nigg, C.R. (2004). Factorial validity and psychometric examination of the Exercise Dependence Scale-Revised. *Measurement in Physical Education and Exercise Science, 8*, 183–201.

Terry, A., Szabo, A., & Griffiths, M. (2004). The Exercise Addiction Inventory: A new brief screening tool. *Addiction Research and Theory, 12*, 489–499.

Thaxton, L. (1982). Physiological and psychological effects of short-term exercise addiction on habitual runners. *Journal of Sport Psychology, 4*, 73–80.

Thompson, J. K., Heinberg, L. J., Altabe, M. N., & Tantleff-Dunn, S. (1999). *Exacting beauty: Theory, assessment and treatment of body image disturbance*. Washington, DC: American Psychological Association.

Thompson, R. A. (1987). Management of the athlete with an eating disorder: Implications for the sport management team. *The Sport Psychologist, 1*, 114–126.

Thompson, R. A., & Sherman, R. T. (2010). *Eating disorders in sport*. New York: Routledge.

Tyson, E. P. (2010). Medical assessment of eating disorders. In M. Maine, B. H.McGilley, & D. W. Bunnell (Eds.), *Treatment of eating disorders: Bridging the research-practice gap* (pp. 89–110). New York: Academic Press.

Veale, D. (1995). Does exercise dependence really exist? In J. Annett, B.Cripps, & H. Steinberg (Eds.), *Exercise addiction: Motivation for participation in sport and exercise* (pp. 1–5). Leicester: British Psychological Society.

Winston, T. (2012). Psychodynamic approaches to eating disorders. In J. Fox & K. Gross (Eds.) *Eating and its disorders* (pp. 244–259). Oxford: Wiley-Blackwell.

Yeager, K. K., Agostini, R., Nativ, A., & Drinkwater, B. (1993). The female athlete triad: Disordered eating, amenorrhea, and osteoporosis. *Medicine & Science in Sports & Exercise, 25*, 775–777.

25 Long-term Behaviour Change Through an Exercise Intervention During Breast Cancer Treatment

ANNA CAMPBELL AND KATE HEFFERON

LEARNING OBJECTIVES

AFTER READING THIS CHAPTER YOU SHOULD BE ABLE TO:

1. Understand the reasons why physical activity during cancer survivorship is important.
2. Summarize the physical and psychological benefits of physical activity during and after cancer treatment.
3. Critically evaluate behaviour-change frameworks for interventions aimed at increasing physical activity levels in cancer survivors.
4. Understand and apply the use of group and individual consultations as a tool for behaviour change.
5. Comprehend the use of assessment tools for the analysis of physiological and psychological changes due to an exercise intervention.
6. Outline key issues concerning the setting for a physical activity intervention for breast cancer patients.

AREAS TO CONSIDER WHEN READING THE CHAPTER:

1. As a practitioner, how might you approach assessing the psychological effects of an exercise intervention with a cancer survivor?
2. What barriers or obstacles might prevent a cancer survivor from engaging in regular physical activity?
3. What strategies might you adopt to encourage sustained engagement in regular physical activity of a cancer survivor?

CLIENT AND BACKGROUND

Breast cancer is one of the most common cancers in the UK with 49,936 new cases diagnosed in 2011 (CRUK, 2014). Better detection methods and improved cancer treatments have increased the number of breast cancer survivors with an expected five-year survival rate from 52% in the 1970s to 85% during 2005–2009 (CRUK, 2014). However, as a result of surgery and adjuvant anticancer treatments, a significant number of treatment-related symptoms and side effects that impact on quality of life have been recorded.

Description box — BOX 25.1

How is breast cancer treated? Women diagnosed with breast cancer will have a combination of treatments such as surgery, chemotherapy, radiotherapy, hormone therapy, and targeted biological therapy. It is impossible to generalize about breast cancer treatment because different factors influence the treatment regime such as the type of cancer, the size of the tumour, the pathology of the tumour, menopausal status, and whether the cancer cells have receptors for particular cancer drugs.

Breast cancer surgery may result in limited range of movement around the shoulder and arm, nerve pain and numbness, lymphoedema and low perceptions of body image (Shimozuma, Ganz, Petersen, & Hirji, 1999). Potential side effects of chemotherapy and radiotherapy include pain, arthralgia, peripheral neuropathy, fatigue, nausea, and vomiting, weight gain, myelosuppresion, skin rashes, and skin toxicity (Shapiro & Recht, 2001). Some symptoms, such as cancer related fatigue (CRF), are chronic and can be predictive for functioning limitations and overall quality of life (QoL), years after cancer treatment (Arndt, Stegmaier, Ziegler, & Brenner, 2006). Other side effects of treatment such as lymphoedema, osteoporosis, and cardiotoxicity can appear years after cancer diagnosis and treatment. In addition, it has been shown that psychological symptoms of anxiety and depression are significantly elevated after cancer treatments (Mitchell et al., 2011).

Over the past 20 years, a considerable body of research has emerged on the positive effects of physical activity on the physical and psychological health and wellbeing of cancer survivors and its potential to alleviate the burden of symptoms and optimize the health of the cancer survivor (Speck, Courneya, Mâsse, Duval, & Schmitz, 2010). Recent Cochrane reviews have shown that physical activity interventions after cancer treatment significantly increase quality of life (Mishra et al., 2012) and reduce fatigue (Cramp & Byron-Daniel, 2012). Engaging in physical activity has also been found to reduce the risk or lessen the effect of several treatment side effects such as lymphoedema (Kwan, Cohn, Armer, Stewart, & Cormier, 2011) weight gain (Demark-Wahnefried et al., 2012), bone and heart problems (Scott et al., 2013; Winters-Stone, Schwartz, & Nail, 2010) and co-morbid illnesses (Fong et al., 2012). In addition, epidemiological studies have consistently suggested that after breast cancer diagnosis, regular physical activity may reduce the risk of breast cancer recurrence or death by approximately 30% (Ibrahim & Al-Homaidh, 2011).

To date, no negative effects of being active have been reported in the literature. The majority of exercise interventions published have been moderate intensity (typically 50–70% of maximum performance). However, one RCT examined the effects of a high-intensity multimodal exercise programme over six weeks compared with usual care in cancer patients receiving chemotherapy (Adamsen et al., 2009). The intervention was a combination of aerobic exercise on stationary bicycles (85–95% of maximum heart rate), and resistance exercises (70–100% of one repetition maximum) on three days a week. The intervention was safely completed by participants and led to improvements in aerobic capacity, muscular function, fatigue, and psychological wellbeing. A set of guidelines relating to safety considerations for cancer survivors have been published in the ACSM's Guidelines for Exercise Testing and Prescription (Pescatello, 2014). These recommendations, with reference to screening and participation eligibility are deliberately conservative and mostly applicable within a clinical setting rather than most community-based settings. To date, no community-based standardized recommendations have been published.

With increasing numbers of people living with and beyond a breast cancer diagnosis, and many survivors experiencing chronic and late appearing side effects that affect their quality of life, the evidence cited above provides a strong rationale for the incorporation of a physical activity programme into a cancer care pathway. The main aim of an exercise intervention should be to assist cancer survivors to remain or become more active during treatment and to ensure that they maintain this behaviour change in the long term.

Activity box — BOX 25.2

What other chronic conditions are usually provided with an exercise-based rehabilitation programme and how effective are these programmes?

Despite the evidence cited above, a study looking at behaviour changes after a cancer diagnosis (Blanchard et al., 2003) found that nearly 46% of smokers quit smoking, 47% improved their dietary habits, but 30.1% exercised less; in fact, twice as many adults decreased the amount of physical activity they did after cancer diagnosis than increased the amount. These findings were in accordance with previous research, which showed that physical activity levels significantly declined in breast cancer survivors from pre-diagnosis to during treatment and did not reach pre-diagnosis levels after treatment (Courneya & Friedenreich, 1997). A study by the American Cancer Society on survivors' health-related behaviour changes after a cancer diagnosis found that those whose physical health was most compromised by cancer treatments had less energy and motivation and increased levels of depression, leading to a negative behaviour change (e.g., less time exercising and getting involved in social/recreational activities). It is postulated that this is a bi-directional relationship where negative behaviour changes also results in poorer health status (Hawkins, Smith, Luhua, Berkowitz, & Stein, 2010). A more recent study of over 9,000 American cancer survivors showed that only 37.1% of breast cancer survivors were meeting the physical activity recommendations (Blanchard, Courneya, & Stein, 2008) significantly lower than that reported for the general population globally (69%) and in the Americas (57%)(Hallal et al., 2012). Studies on the prevalence of regular physical activity suggest that starting a physical activity programme during or after a chronic illness, such as cancer, appears to be a significant challenge. The motivation to be physically active is a complex process involving internal and external factors, which affect thoughts, feeling, and actions around exercise and physical activity. In this chapter we provide a case study of a theory-based intervention, which aimed to change the physical activity behaviour of breast cancer patients during cancer treatment and to ensure that adherence to this change was maintained in the long term. Overall, this chapter presents an amalgamation of several published results from quantitative, qualitative, and longitudinal perspectives.

The intervention (defined as the original study) described in this chapter was the first randomized controlled trial (RCT) exercise study conducted during breast cancer treatment in the UK. The primary research question, informed by the results of our pilot study in 2005 (Campbell, Mutrie, White, McGuire, & Kearney, 2005) was to find out if a pragmatic community-based group exercise intervention could decrease fatigue levels and improve quality of life, physical functioning, and mood.

The second research question, which is pertinent to this chapter from an applied physical activity psychology perspective, was to find out if there were any sustained benefits of the intervention at six months, 18 months and five years post-intervention. This chapter will contain the strategies incorporated in the exercise intervention to help the study participants become independent exercisers; an analysis of the views on exercise adherence between the women who received the behaviour change and exercise intervention to those who did not; and a discussion on which parts of the intervention and assessments worked and which parts that could have been performed differently and/or more effectively.

RECRUITMENT AND ASSESSMENT

Recruitment strategy and selection of participants

With considerable evidence showing the benefits of physical activity during cancer treatment, we decided that any woman being treated for early-stage breast cancer and attending outpatient chemotherapy and radiotherapy clinics at three National Health Service (NHS) hospital sites in Glasgow would be eligible to participate in the study. Prior to the start of recruitment to the study, three dedicated clinical recruiters were trained to provide the appropriate information on the study to all eligible women (Campbell, White, & Mutrie, 2005). It was our experience that the involvement of dedicated health professionals trained in brief intervention practices and named as the 'study champions' significantly increased the number of women willing to join the study. Women were invited to join the study around the time of their second or third chemotherapy cycles or during second to third weeks of radiotherapy treatment. This ensured that cancer treatments had been established with no particular problems noted such as wound healing complications, thrombocytopenia, anaemia, fever, or active infection (Wolin, Schwartz, Matthews, Courneya, & Schmitz, 2012). Study exclusion criteria focused on co-morbidities such as unstable cardiac, hypertensive, or respiratory disease and because this was a research clinical trial, women already participating in regular exercise (obtained from self-report seven-day recall questionnaire) or with cognitive dysfunction were also excluded.

The recruiters approached 1,144 women over a 12-month recruitment period and 313 agreed to attend pre-screening. The reasons for declining to participate in the study are outlined in Table 25.1.

Table 25.1 *Recorded reasons why women declined to participate in the exercise study.*

The reasons why 831 women declined to participate were:

- transport problems (425)
- not interested/not a priority (79)
- other health problems (63)
- already exercising (59)
- work conflicts (50)
- other explanations (primarily too old, too tired, looking after close relatives etc., 155)

The main barrier – transport problems – is explained by the fact that the Oncology Centre in Glasgow provides treatment for women from all parts of the west coast of Scotland and therefore for the majority of breast cancer patients, travelling up to 100 miles to attend an exercise class, was not feasible. Apart from transport, the main barriers to participation were comparable to those reported elsewhere (i.e., lack of priority, self-discipline, procrastination, other health problems and fatigue) (Rogers, Courneya, Shah, Dunnington, & Hopkins-Price, 2007).

Key future research box **BOX 25.3**

The major reported barrier of transport and travel to a venue to take part in the exercise programme suggests that future interventions should offer home-based interventions for those women unable to travel to specific cancer exercise classes. More research needs to be undertaken on the uptake and efficacy of home based exercise interventions with cancer patients.

The women agreeing to participate in the study were, on average, aged just over 50 years (range = 29–75) and slightly overweight according to BMI [27.4 (+/−5.6)]. Their self-reported physical activity levels were similar to other sedentary populations and the recorded baseline 12-minute walk test levels was comparable to breast cancer patients during cancer treatment in other studies (Mock et al., 2005). A major success of this study was that we recruited an equal spread of women from socio-economic deprivation and affluence, from a variety of localities across Glasgow and women with a variety of occupational backgrounds. We believe this is due to the employment and training of the clinical recruiter/ 'study champion' who ensured there was no selection bias and that every woman was approached and invited to the study.

Of the 313 women who applied to participate, 203 women took part in the original study. The 203 participants were randomly allocated into one of two groups: The exercise intervention group (n = 101) or the control usual care group (n = 102). Out of 203 in the original study, 148 agreed to be contacted at 18 months and participate in the first follow-up study. One hundred and fourteen attended this follow up (58 in the intervention group and 56 in the control group). Sixty months later, all women who had agreed to be contacted were re-invited to participate in the five-year follow up and 87 participants were assessed at this stage: 44 originally allocated to the exercise intervention and 43 originally allocated to the control group.

Assessments undertaken

The outcomes assessed at baseline in the original study and again at each further time point were chosen for a number of reasons. First, we chose to measure physical and psychological outcomes that had been reported as major side effects of treatment (e.g., cardiovascular deconditioning and depression) and outcomes that had some evidence base of positive changes with exercise interventions (e.g., quality of life). Second, we used tools that were validated and reliable and had been used in previous studies including the pilot study (Campbell, et al., 2005) allowing us to compare our results with population norms and other cancer exercise intervention studies such as Segal's RCT on the effects of self-directed or supervised exercise on quality of life during breast cancer treatment (Segal et al., 2001).

The following quantitative assessments were undertaken:

1. *Quality of life (QoL)* was measured by the **F**unctional **A**ssessment of **C**ancer **T**herapy – **G**eneral (FACT-G) questionnaire (Cella et al., 1993). The FACT-G (Version 4) is a 27-item compilation of general questions divided into four primary QoL domains: Physical Wellbeing, Social/Family Wellbeing, Emotional Wellbeing, and Functional Wellbeing. It is considered appropriate for use with patients with any form of cancer. Subscales have been developed to address relevant disease, treatment, or condition-related issues. In this study we also used the breast cancer specific subscale which when added to the FACT-G score is described as FACT-B (Brady et al., 1997), likewise the **F**atigue subscale added to FACT-G results in FACT-F (Yellen, Cella, Webster, Blendowski, & Kaplan, 1997), and the Endocrine Symptoms subscale when added to FACT-G gives the FACT ES score (Fallowfield, Leaity, Howell, Benson, & Cella, 1999). This allowed us to assess the physical, psychological, social, emotional, breast cancer specific, hormonal and fatigue aspects of their quality of life and monitor if the exercise intervention was able to positively affect any of these scores.
2. *Depression* was measured with **B**eck **D**epression **I**nventory (BDI; Beck, Steer, & Brown, 1996): This is one of the most common questionnaires used for assessment of depression in exercise studies. The most up-to-date version includes the DSM-IV criteria. Clinical depression on the BDI is defined as a score of 16 or above but this questionnaire is often also used to monitor the relationship between exercise and the non-clinical population with mild to moderate symptoms. The participants in the original study had an average baseline score of 12.5, which suggest low mood/mild depression.
3. *Mood* was monitored with **P**ositive **a**nd **N**egative **A**ffect **S**cale (PANAS; Watson, Clark, & Tellegen, 1988): This consists of two ten-item affect scales assessing positive affect (e.g., excited, enthusiastic, and inspired) and negative affect (e.g., distressed, hostile, and irritable). It is a general scale not specific to physical activity and has good psychometric properties. Again, the PANAS is widely used in physical activity studies, thus the results can be compared against other research findings.
4. *Body Mass Index* (BMI): BMI is a measure based on an individual's mass and height and is used in a wide variety of contexts as a simple method to assess how much an individual's body weight departs from what is normal or desirable for a person of his or her height.
5. *Physical activity level:* **S**cottish **P**hysical **A**ctivity **Q**uestionnaire (SPAQ; Lowther, Mutrie, Loughlan, & McFarlane, 1999) is a self-report seven-day physical activity recall questionnaire which has been shown to be reliable and to hold strong concurrent validity and also criterion validity.
6. *Cardiorespiratory fitness* (McGavin, Gupta, & McHardy, 1976): The 12-minute walk test is a timed walk test over a 12-minute interval which has been used to help evaluate patients with a number of chronic diseases, including cancer. The distance covered is used as a measure of cardiorespiratory fitness and improvements in distance walked within the test interval is attributed to improvement in cardiac output, ventilation, or muscular conditioning.
7. *Shoulder mobility* (Halverstadt & Leonard, 2000): Breast cancer surgery and radiotherapy to the armpit can affect the range of movement and strength in the arm and/or shoulder. This may affect one's ability to do everyday activities, such as household chores. This questionnaire provided a very pragmatic way of monitoring shoulder internal rotation, flexion, and extension before and after the exercise intervention.

At three time-points, the qualitative evaluations were conducted at the same time as the collection of the quantitative information: that is, the end of the 12-week intervention, the six-month follow up, and at the 5-year follow up. Additional qualitative data was gathered one-year post intervention and additional quantitative data at 18-month follow up. For the first round of data collection, we chose focus groups as the best method of data collection because we felt it was important to re-create the group environment into which the participants had been exposed (Emslie et al., 2007). Focus groups are a method of data collection used in qualitative research to elicit the personal understandings and views of the participants in a group environment (Howitt & Cramer, 2007). Focus groups usually consist of between four to eight people and are led by a knowledgeable moderator. It has been argued that focus groups are more naturalistic than one-to one interviews (Fine & Gordon, 1989) and allow for interactions between the researcher, participants, and among themselves.

Due to these identified methodological benefits, focus groups were conducted at the end of the original study (Emslie et al., 2007) with both the RCT exercise and control groups and two further semi-structured focus groups on intervention participation: one focus group contained those identified as high attendees (70%+) and the other with those identified as low attendees (<70%). The six-month follow up consisted of four focus groups: the exercise intervention and the control group further separated into regular versus non-regular exercisers (>30 min on +5 days week versus <30 min). The semi-structured schedule focused on the experiences (both positive and negative) of participation in the trial, the perceived barriers or facilitators to exercise, their family and friends' reactions, and their own changes to identity. Overall, 36 women participated in all focus groups (average five per group; range = 3–6). The sample ranged across a variety of ages, marital, parental and social status as well as treatment types.

At the one-year follow up, participants were also invited to take part in a one-to-one semi-structured interview on their experience of post-traumatic growth (PTG) and the role of the intervention in facilitating PTG. PTG posits that following traumatic events (such as the diagnosis of cancer), changes may arise that propel an individual to a higher level of functioning than that which existed before the event occurred (Linley & Joseph, 2004). Areas of reported positive change include: *perceived changes in self* (e.g., feeling stronger in the self, more authentic); *improved relationships* (e.g., stronger bonds with family and friends, including fellow trauma survivors); *changed life philosophy with increased existential awareness* (e.g., increased understanding of vulnerability of life); *changed priorities* (e.g., less emphasis on material items, changed goals) and *enhanced spiritual beliefs* (e.g., closer to a higher power) (Calhoun, Cann, & Tedeschi, 2010). Although PTG has been found to occur within 40–70% of traumas, it is important to recognize that it is not universal. Furthermore, all five domains do not need to be present; an individual may only experience a change in one or two of these domains. Finally, PTG can co-exist with distress (Joseph, Murphy, & Regel, 2012).

The researchers chose the methodology of interpretative phenomenological analysis (IPA; Smith, Flowers, & Larkin, 2009) as it uses small samples sizes (n=10) and was deemed the most appropriate to understand the lived experiences of this under-researched phenomenon with this unique participant pool (Hefferon & Gil-Rodriguez, 2011; Smith et al., 2009). IPA is unique to other methodologies as it harnesses the researcher and their interpretations of the data (double hermeneutic) to produce a rich and detailed account of the analysis.

At the five-year follow up, participants were invited to participate in a brief structured interview on their experience of exercise adherence over the past five years. This method of data collection was chosen due to the very large sample size and the limited time available in the follow-up sessions (15 minutes). In these situations, structured interviews can help researchers gain access to a large amount of researcher-led data (Howitt & Cramer, 2007). Eighty-three of the 87 returning participants chose to participate (four declined due to lack of time). This study was the first to assess long-term activity participation within breast cancer populations using qualitative methodologies (Hefferon, Murphy, McLeod, Mutrie, & Campbell, 2013). Due to the limited depth of data produced from employing a structured interview technique, the data set was subjected to inductive thematic analysis (TA) to assess the long-term barriers to implementation (Braun & Clarke, 2006). Thematic analysis is a popular analytic technique that can be used with large and varied samples. TA tends to demand less intensive engagement and produce less in-depth data than other methodologies (e.g., IPA), however, TA is a flexible and respected methodology for coding data sets such as the one produced (Braun & Clarke, 2013). Furthermore, as the data set was quite large, we chose to re-analyse the accounts using abbreviated grounded theory (Charmaz, 2008) in order to assess the key motivators and facilitators of exercise adherence over the five-year gap. AGT identified a model of long-term exercise adherence and motivators for this specific population (Murphy, Hefferon, McLeod, Mutrie, & Campbell, Charmaz, submitted). Lastly, in addition to the aforementioned five-year follow-up qualitative studies, the large data set (n=83) was subjected to a further thematic analysis (Braun & Clarke, 2006) to assess the serendipitous expression of post-traumatic growth as well as the role of physical activity / the body in the facilitation of this phenomenon. This, again, was the first study to assess long-term experiences of post-traumatic growth and the links to activity participation within breast cancer populations using qualitative methodologies (Hefferon et al., 2013).

FRAMEWORK AND INTERVENTION

The researchers used the Medical Research Council (MRC) framework for complex interventions (Craig et al., 2008) because we believed that measuring the effects of a community-based group exercise intervention on physiological and psychological outcomes and long-term adherence to a physical activity lifestyle was indeed complex. One of the key questions in evaluating a complex intervention is about practical effectiveness – whether the intervention works in everyday practice. Therefore it was important to understand the whole range of effects: how they varied among recipients of the intervention, between sites, over time, and so on, and the causes of that variation. To gain as much information as possible from this study, the researchers used a pragmatic research paradigm (Creswell & Clark, 2007) thereby employing the benefits of both quantitative and qualitative inquiry. The utilization of multi-methods guaranteed a more holistic understanding of the exercise experience from diagnosis and treatment through to the survivor phase (five years later) (Flick, 2007). The quantitative approach employed a post-positivist paradigm utilizing a longitudinal repeated measures design, assessing the participants' changes within several measurement tools over time and in comparison to each other (intervention versus control). The qualitative research component employed an interpretivist / constructionist approach utilizing several methodologies (e.g., ethnographic meta-synthesis, interpretative phenomenological analysis, thematic analysis, abbreviated grounded theory) and methods of data collection (e.g., one-to-one interviews, focus groups) at differing time-points. Ultimately, the qualitative research shifted emphasis from the nomothetic (group) to idiographic (the individual) depending on the question posed.

The following section provides more details on the intervention (who, what, where, when, and why) delivered to the experimental group in the study as well as the overarching theoretical framework we employed when working with our breast cancer patients.

Behaviour-change framework

It was decided to use a cognitive behavioural approach as the overarching theoretical framework since the key objective of this research was retention to the exercise programme and long-term lifestyle change. The research therefore aimed to address factors around delivery that would maximize adherence to the programme and determine long-term success. In adopting a cognitive framework, our planned investigations were to explore these influences both in terms of what facilitates or prevents participation in physical activity. This framework guided the weekly consultation/ discussion sessions, which followed each exercise class.

A number of theoretical models have been used to explain physical activity engagement and to inform practice. For example, the Health Belief Model (Becker et al., 1977) proposes that health behaviour change is related to the potential to protect against disease. The Theory of Reasoned Action (TRA; Fishbein & Ajzen, 1975) and the Theory of Planned Behaviour (TPB; Ajzen, 1991) both examine a person's intention to perform or not perform a behaviour. Based on the evidence and guidelines (Kirk, Barnett, & Mutrie, 2007), we decided to provide a physical activity group consultation grounded on the Trans-theoretical Model of behaviour change (TTM). The TTM was originally used to understand the cessation of negative health behaviours (Prochaska & DiClemente, 1984; Prochaska, Norcross, Fowler, Follick, & Abrams, 1992; Prochaska & Velicer, 1996; Prochaska et al., 1994) and has been applied successfully within physical activity settings (Marcus, Eaton, Rossi, & Harlow, 1994). The term trans-theoretical is used to describe the framework that encompasses both the 'when' and the 'how' of behaviour change including the processes of change and moderators of change such as decisional balance and self-efficacy. A meta-analysis in 2001 looking at the application of the TTM to physical activity in the general population provided strong support for the use of this model (Marshall & Biddle, 2001).

The TTM assumes that there are five stages which individuals potentially go through when changing behaviour (Marcus & Simkin, 1994). The five stages include:

1) Pre-contemplation: this stage represents when an individual is not currently physically active (at a level specified) and is not even contemplating engaging at that point in time or in the near future.
2) Contemplation: the individual is also not engaging in the specified level of physical activity but has contemplated the idea of starting to engage in such behaviours in the future.
3) Preparation: the individual has made some attempts to become more active but is not undertaking the behaviour on a regular basis.
4) Action: the individual has only recently started to engage in the desired level of activity (e.g., government recommendations of 30 minutes five times a week of moderate-intensity physical activity).
5) Maintenance: the individual continues their exercise regime and meets the criteria for being physically active for more than six months.
6) Relapse: this stage is sometimes also included although little data are available in physical activity. This is a regressive movement back to either contemplation or pre-contemplation.

While progressing through these stages, an individual engages in ten different cognitive and behavioural processes of change (e.g., self-evaluation, contingency management) that are important in the adoption and maintenance of the new behaviour. For example, research in adoption of an exercise regimen suggests that cognitive processes of change (e.g., setting realistic goals) should be encouraged with those currently in pre-contemplative or contemplative stage while behavioural processes (e.g., putting prompts to remind the person to exercise at home or work) are more beneficial in the more advanced stages of motivational readiness (Marshall & Biddle, 2001). The model is cyclical in nature and individuals will move forward or regress across the stages depending on their current situation (e.g., negotiating injury). The reason this model can be valuable is that it enables the health promoter to better target interventions to individuals (and societies) depending on where in the cycle the individuals may currently sit (Biddle & Mutrie, 2008).

Using a consultation approach for increasing physical activity

Loughlan and Mutrie (1995) provided guidelines for the development of a person-centred exercise consultation approach based on TTM to increasing physical activity levels. This format has been successfully used for the promotion of physical activity in people with Type 2 diabetes (Kirk et al., 2007). The consultation is semi-structured using a guiding style rather than a directing style and ultimately the client decides if, when and how to change their behaviour (Rollnick et al., 2005). The person guiding the consultation is encouraged to have the excellent communication and reflective listening skills (Miller & Rollnick, 2002).

The content of the consultation is largely determined by the individual's personal motivational status and needs but would also include stage-specific strategies depending on their TTM stage. For example, precontemplators would be provided with information or advice on risks of inactivity and benefits of activity whereas consultations with clients in contemplation or preparation stage would focus on enhancing motivation, overcoming barriers, and developing a realistic activity plan with achievable goals. With cancer survivors, it appears that exercise consultations are most successful when key psychosocial determinants of change, such as self-efficacy, are affected (Bennett, Lyons, Winters-Stone, Nail, & Scherer, 2007).

Exercise intervention. Substantial evidence from efficacy RCTs supports the integration of exercise during treatment for breast cancer (McNeely et al., 2006). However, calls have been made by patients, clinicians, funders, and policy-makers for more pragmatic trials in order to simplify the likely benefits, harms, and costs to be expected when implementing the intervention in a real-world situation (Zwarenstein et al., 2008). We therefore sought to provide a pragmatic exercise intervention that had the ability to translate into everyday practice. All women in our study received their usual adjuvant breast cancer care treatment (which varied from visits to the hospital five times a week for radiotherapy treatment to a visit to the hospital for a cycle of chemotherapy once every three weeks). The women randomized to the exercise intervention were also invited to attend a supervised group exercise programme twice weekly for 12 weeks. Each week 14 exercise classes, run by specifically trained cancer exercise specialists, took place in eight locations throughout Glasgow. All venues were accessible by public transport and timetabled at various times in the day and evening. The exercise intervention was based on the exercise prescription guidelines for cancer patients and survivors available at that time (Courneya, Mackey, & McKenzie, 2002). The classes consisted of a five-to-ten- minute warm up, 30 minutes of moderate-intensity exercise (which included walking, cycling, low-level aerobics and resistance training or a circuit consisting of specifically tailored exercises) and a 10–15 minute cool down and relaxation period. The exercise class lasted around 45–55 minutes in total. Women were monitored throughout the class to ensure that they were exercising at a moderate intensity (Rate of Perceived Exertion (RPE) 11–14). The aims of the exercise session were to improve their cardiorespiratory, muscular, and flexibility fitness and at the same time to provide an environment in which the women felt safe, confident, and had fun. After each class, a ten- to 20-minutes group discussion (see details below) was held to promote behaviour change and encourage the women to become independent exercisers by the end of the 12-week programme.

Group behaviour-change intervention. Each week, for six weeks, a specific theme was addressed during the group discussion and supported with specifically constructed handout materials (see examples in Box 25.3). These themes, guided by the TTM described previously, addressed the health benefits from exercise, enhancing self-efficacy, overcoming barriers, achieving a supportive environment, setting goals and finding activity options in the community (see Table 25.2).

Table 25.2 *Group behaviour change weekly tutorial.*

Title of handout	*Description of handout*	*Component of TTM*	*PA group consultation strategy*
Why exercise? What's in it for me?	Provide evidence on benefits of physical activity and risks of inactivity	Decisional balance Consciousness raising Dramatic relief	Discussion of the benefits of being more active during cancer treatment – based on evidence and encouraging anecdotal and personal experiences.
How much should I exercise?	Description of current physical activity recommendations for cancer survivors	Consciousness raising Self re-evaluation	Discussion of frequency, intensity, type and time (FITT) components of exercise prescription and examples to help personalize to suit each individual. Think about current physical activity status.
What are the pros and cons of exercising?	Decisional balance table	Decisional balance Environmental re-evaluation	Sharing of personal benefits and barriers to exercising and a discussion of ways to overcome or work round barriers that may stop one getting the benefits one deserves. Exploring the social and environmental benefits of PA
Who will support me?	Table in which to list who will support the client to keep active	Helping relationships	Discussion on who, how, and when all friends, family and health professionals can support the client to become/stay active
Setting goals	Listing SMART* activity goals: short term (<2 weeks), intermediate (3 months) and long-term goals (9 months)	Self liberation Self efficacy Reinforcement management	Planning short-term and long-term activity commitments. Thinking of realistic and achievable activity opportunities which would lead to success, enjoyment, and achievement. Rewarding successful attempts.
What next?	Provision of leaflets signposting to local physical activity opportunities	Social liberation Stimulus control	Increasing awareness of potential physical activity opportunities. Looking at situations that may cause one to stop exercising and how to prevent relapse.

*SMART = specific, measurable, achievable, relevant, time bound

The six-week block was repeated on a rolling basis allowing all participants to participate in the discussion on the same themes twice. This enabled women on the repeat session to share experiences and advice with women discussing the topic for the first time. The group sessions were well received and this educational component of the class was repeatedly mentioned as one of the group dynamic benefits along with the actual physical activity itself (Emslie et al., 2007; Hefferon, Grealy, & Mutrie, 2008).

Individual behaviour-change intervention. At the end of the study, the women were assisted in constructing an individual exercise programme tailored to suit each person's needs to encourage them to move on to exercising independently. This took place in the form of a person-centred exercise consultation (lasting approximately 30 minutes, see Table 25.3) based on the TTM model and following the steps described by Loughlan and Mutrie (1995).

Table 25.3 *Exercise consultation format.*

Physical activity history	Complete SPAQ and use this as prompt to discuss recent past and distant past activities especially those activities they used to enjoy
Decisional balance	Personal pros and cons to exercising and ways to reduce the cons
Social support	Who can and will support them
Goal setting	SMART goals
Relapse	How to prevent relapse in different scenarios – after illness, holiday, bad weather, etc.
Local opportunities	Discuss local activities and signpost to relevant ones such as local swimming pool timetable

During the consultation, and in discussion with the consultant, the participant wrote down their answers on the consultation sheet.

Control group allocation (usual care plus monitoring). The control group in the original study received usual care from the health-care team and completed the questionnaires and walking test at baseline, three months, six months, 18 months and five years post-intervention. After randomization, this group received a two-page leaflet entitled 'Exercise after cancer diagnosis' which provided safe guidelines for exercising. They did not receive the group exercise intervention or the discussion groups. At the end of the original study period (after six-month follow up) they were assisted by the senior researcher in constructing their own personalized exercise plan (exercise consultation) and invited to join the GP referral scheme, which is extensively available within Glasgow.

Overall study findings

End of original intervention and one-year follow up. Detailed analysis of the results of the RCT are reported elsewhere (Mutrie et al., 2007). Briefly, Figure 25.1 shows that significant intervention effects were observed at the end of the 12-week intervention period and also at the six-month follow up for metres walked in 12 minutes, minutes of moderate intensity activity reported in a week (SPAQ), shoulder mobility, breast cancer specific quality of life (FACT-B subscale) and positive mood (PANAS positive).

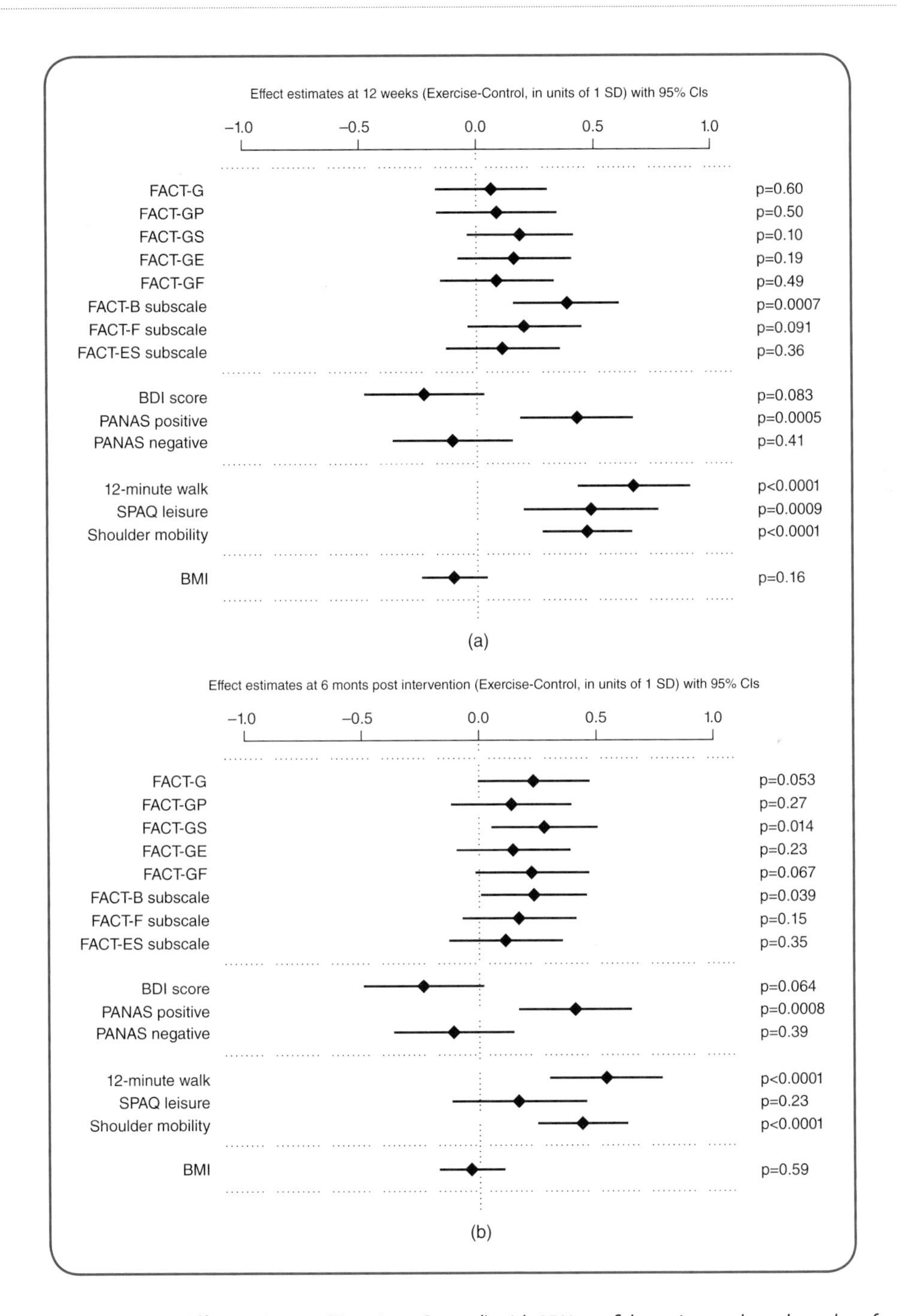

FIGURE 25.1 *Effect estimates (Exercise – Control) with 95% confidence intervals and p-values for outcome variables at (a) the 12 week assessment, and (b) the 6 month follow-up assessment, expressed in units of one standard deviation (SD) of the outcome distributions, based on mixed effects models adjusting for baseline values, study site, therapy at baseline and age.*

Source: Mutrie, N., Campbell, A. M., Whyte, F., McConnachie, A., Emslie, C., Lee, L., Kearney, N., Walker, A., & Ritchie, D. (2007). Benefits of supervised group exercise programme for women being treated for early-stage breast cancer: Pragmatic randomised controlled trial. *British Medical Journal, 334*(7592), 517.

Thus, the intervention appeared to provide short- and medium-term positive physical and psychological benefits to the participants. Attendance at the group exercise classes appeared to be difficult for some women, with only around 40% of the women in the study managing to attend at least 70% of the exercise sessions.

The qualitative results at the end of the original intervention and at the six and 12- month follow ups found that overall, the participants were very pleased with the intervention and reported the importance of the classes being led by specifically trained and knowledgeable exercise specialists. They also highlighted the importance of the group support and dynamic in a space where they did not need to explain themselves nor felt out of place, as well as participating in a productive activity rather than a passive group setting focusing and ruminating on the illness (Emslie et al., 2007 for the full report). The one-to-one interviews using IPA also highlighted the imperative role of physical activity and strengthening/reconnecting to the body as a key component in their journey of post-traumatic growth (see Hefferon et al., 2008 for the full report). More specifically, the women reported that the class provided a safe environment where they could seek professional guidance and a positive support system as well as engage in new positive health behaviours. The women even reported feeling stronger psychologically through the rebuilding of their physical selves via exercise (somatopsychic principle) and this new connection to their corporeal self was seen as a positive outcome of the intervention.

18-month and five-year follow up. There were no differences in the proportion of women randomized to the control or exercise group that responded at either 18-month or five-year time-points (Mutrie et al., 2012). Those who participated in the follow up at five years were, at baseline, three years older and 5 kg lighter on average and were faster walkers (i.e., probably fitter); and were slightly less depressed and with less negative mood than those who did not participate at the five-year time point. Women in work prior to diagnosis and those that were less deprived were more likely to participate at the five-year time point than those who were housewives or more deprived.

Quantitative findings at the five-year follow up found significant differences between the intervention and the control group for the recall of the amount of leisure time physical activity over the past week using SPAQ and also for PANAS positive mood with the intervention group reporting significantly higher activity and more positive mood. At five years, the intervention group achieved on average around 200 minutes of physical activity per week more than the control group.

Interestingly, for several of the outcomes there was a larger difference between the exercise groups at five years than at 18 months, with significant differences for the SPAQ leisure time activity and PANAS positive score. Even for the rest of the outcomes, for which there was no significant difference at five years, the exercise group were consistently observed to do better than the control group throughout the entire five-year follow-up period.

The three qualitative studies found exciting insights into the barriers and motivators of exercise adherence as well as experiences of PTG at the five-year follow up. The first thematic analysis which focused on the perceived barriers to sustained exercise engagement reported three main themes and several subthemes including: psychological barriers (lack of motivation, fears, dislike of gym, not being the 'sporty type'), physical barriers (the ageing process, cancer treatment and other physical co-morbidities, fatigue and weight gain) and contextual and environmental barriers (employment, traditional female care-giving roles, proximity or access to facilities, and seasonal weather). This analysis also noted persistent differences in physical activity engagement between the two original allocation groups as outlined in Table 25.4 (Hefferon et al., 2013).

In summary, both the qualitative and quantitative findings (Mutrie et al., 2012) found that even after five years, those within the original intervention group were still more active and engaged in structured exercise, and expressed more accounts of post-traumatic growth, than the original control group. From these study results, we purport that physical activity should be strongly encouraged during this crucial time period (cancer treatment) as it can enable individuals to regain some sense of normality, control over their body, and harness the somatopsychic principle (Hefferon et al., 2013).

Table 25.4 *Notable differences in physical activity engagement between original intervention and control group five-years post cancer diagnosis.*

Intervention group	*Control group*
More aware of importance of exercise to health and wellbeing	Understood importance but not to same extent as intervention group
More knowledgeable in how to exercise safely	Felt lost as to how to start exercising safely
More self-assured in engagement in different types of activity (weights, classes)	Discussed lower levels of self-efficacy
Integrated exercise into lifestyle	More likely to be at 'contemplative' stage of change
More likely to be 'gym goers' (44% vs. 2.5%)	More likely to be 'walkers' (44% control vs. 22% intervention)

REFLECTIONS

Successes of the design and study

We believe that one of the critical components for the success of the study was the use of clinical health professional 'champions'. These health professionals were trained before the start of the study to initiate a conversation about physical activity with all eligible women during their breast cancer outpatient visit and, if a woman was interested, to refer them to the study (Campbell et al., 2005). Therefore if planning a clinical research study or implementing a physical activity programme, we would suggest that the preparation of a clear referral pathway and the training of specific recruiters in brief interventions skills could significantly improve the number of cancer patients and clients to the study or programme.

The effectiveness of the original intervention was assessed using various evaluation tools. For example, the study employed subjective self-report measurement tools on wellbeing including: FACT – a quality of life questionnaire, Beck Depression Inventory, Positive and Negative Affect Scale and SPAQ – a seven-day recall of physical activity. Potential physiological changes due to the intervention were assessed via objective measures including: 12-minute walk test, shoulder mobility test, and Body Mass Index. Anecdotally from our intervention, and in more recent exercise interventions during cancer treatment (Speck et al., 2010), positive effects have also been observed on muscular strength and endurance, balance, and flexibility. Therefore future studies should continue to assess effectiveness with subjective assessments (e.g., quality of life) and objective assessments (e.g., pedometers or accelerometers) but also include other measurements of exercise benefits such as improvements in strength and balance. Recent literature has also highlighted the strong influence of self-efficacy on PA behaviour change among cancer survivors. In a recent study of women with breast cancer, self-efficacy completely mediated the relationship between behavioural processes and physical activity (Loprinzi & Cardinal, 2013) and in another study of older breast and prostate cancer survivors, a change in self-efficacy for PA predicted level of PA adherence at the two-year follow up (Mosher et al., 2013).

When implementing evidence-based programmes for cancer survivors 'in the real world', there has to be a compromise between measuring the effectiveness of the programme and ensuring that this does not become a time- and resource-consuming burden on the client and/or the instructor. Depending on who or why this information is required, we believe that a subjective or ideally an objective measure of changes in physical activity levels and a questionnaire on quality of life and on self-efficacy should suffice. Other questionnaires and assessments could be bolted onto the standard assessment, depending on the cancer population, any specific side effects of cancer treatment the programme is trying to address (e.g., fatigue), and if necessary, information required by commissioners to prove that the implementation has been successful.

In our study, the group circuit intervention was well received. It was based on a community-based cardiac rehabilitation circuit class incorporating a ten-minute warm up followed by a variety of cardiovascular and resistance exercise stations – with three options varying in intensity at each station and working to the beat of enjoyable appropriate music. The fact that it was in a 'normal setting' out of a clinical or hospital environment and that the teacher was a cancer exercise specialist was very important. Participants valued the solidarity, friendship, empathy, acceptance and information that they gained from others in the group exercise classes. These benefits may appear to have much in common with the experiences reported by people who attend cancer support groups. However our qualitative results (Emslie et al., 2007) suggest that many of the women did not like the idea of support groups.

> I certainly preferred the exercise class (to support group) ... I get bored listening to myself far less anybody else! Just want to get away from it ... I mean there is something else in life as well (as cancer). (R3, FG3, p. 832)

> I wouldn't have been interested in just sitting round a table talking about cancer, I'm sorry, you know, that's really the last thing you want to do. I mean ... we did, talk about it quite a lot because we were right in the middle of it (treatment) ... But it was kind of alongside of what you were doing (exercise), it wasn't the main focus of why you got together. (R4, FG1, p. 833)

A recent evaluation of a community-based group exercise programme in Seattle for cancers survivors of mixed diagnoses and ages, provided by YMCA qualified fitness instructors, was shown to be safe and effective in providing physiological and psychosocial benefits (Rajotte, Yi, Baker, Gregerson, Leiserowitz, & Syrjala, 2012). In the UK a national occupational standards awarding body (Skills Active) now ensures that all training providers teaching how to design, adapt, or review programmes for cancer patients must be registered. Training providers such as CanRehab (www.canrehab.co.uk) (Campbell, 2014) provide such training for both fitness instructors and health professionals. This assists in the creation of workable referral pathways from the clinic to safe and effective community-based programmes.

Since the publication of the study results in 2007, community-based programmes to encourage cancer survivors to become more active have become more prevalent throughout the UK. Initiatives such as MoveMore Scotland circuit classes use the same exercise format as in our study and where possible, clinical champions such as clinical nurse specialists or physiotherapists help to refer patients to the programmes. (https://www.macmillan.org.uk/Aboutus/Healthandsocialcareprofessionals/Newsandupdates/MacVoice/Spring2014/MoveMore.aspx).

Areas for improvements and future research

Despite the success of this pragmatic research endeavour, there are several areas that, with hindsight, could have been expanded or enhanced. This last section will review these, with suggestions for future research.

In terms of further understanding the complexities of the participant pool, it would have been beneficial to learn more about those who declined to take part in the study – such as sociodemographic status, age, employment status, marital status, BMI, PA levels prior to diagnosis. There is a gap in the literature on the predictors and determinants to non-participation to exercise interventions with this population and obtaining this type of information would be of benefit for future researchers.

Logistically, we observed that the main barrier to participating in the intervention was travel. In a mail survey of breast cancer survivors living in rural areas in North America, 31% of the women stated that they would prefer a home-based programme as opposed to a gym based one (Rogers, Markwell, Courneya, McAuley, & Verhulst, 2009). Problems with transport, coupled with the fact that group exercise is not everyone's preference, suggests that future exercise programmes should also offer a home-based option. At an initial assessment and consultation, women unable or unwilling to travel to the group exercise classes or living in rural environments could be provided with an individualized home-based programme using behaviour-change prompt tools such as a cancer specific exercise DVD, diary, and pedometer. A number of small studies demonstrate physical and psychological benefits from home-based exercise programmes with breast cancer survivors (Matthews et al., 2007; Baruth, Wilcox, Der Ananian, & Heiney, Matthews et al., in press; Vincent et al., 2013) and recent studies are looking at web-based interventions that could potentially be translated into eHealth recommendations for cancer survivors (Kuijpers, Groen, Aaronson, & van Harten, 2013). From a research perspective, the inclusion of a home-based exercise group in the RCT would have permitted the separation and analysis of the impact of the social environment (group effect) on the observed positive psychological changes.

This series of studies was the first to link post-traumatic growth and physical activity within cancer populations (Hefferon et al., 2008). However, the majority of research into this connection has thus far been exploratory in nature. Ideally, it would have been advantageous to include some quantitative measurement tools (e.g. Post-traumatic Growth Inventory; Tedeschi & Calhoun, 1996) at baseline and all follow-up sessions to assess the extent of PTG across the participants, and over time, in addition to the qualitative work that was conducted (Hefferon et al., 2008). This longitudinal PTG quantitative component could have also been cross-referenced with objective markers (e.g., 12-minute test) to show objective positive health behaviour changes following breast cancer diagnosis. Additionally, it would have been advantageous to collect focus-group data at various time-points beyond the first data collection as these group sessions would have complemented the more idiographic data collected. Furthermore, the qualitative research found that there was a strong perceived benefit to participating in the group-based activity environment, with evidence of positive role modelling, social support, and information seeking within the women's narratives. Indeed, the social elements of the classes were arguably equally alluded to as key elements in the effectiveness of the intervention. Understanding the social context and the role of social support in physical activity engagement during and after cancer care is an important area for future research (Barber, 2012).

Activity box

BOX 25.4

How would you assess the role of social support when trying to determine the effectiveness of an exercise intervention?

Another exciting area for inquiry would be to follow up the qualitative research findings, which raised important connections between the body and wellbeing. Similar to the works of Frank (2002) and Merleau-Ponty (1962) the participants experienced an increased corporeal awareness following their diagnosis and reported negotiating difficult changes to their body throughout the survivorship period. It would be advantageous to include a more targeted inquiry into this dynamic relationship between the body and the self during the path to recovery and beyond.

Finally, as we did not anticipate the long-term positive effect of the exercise intervention on the participants, we did not specifically address this in the five-year follow-up interviews. The findings suggest that the cancer treatment window is important in promoting education and sustained activity engagement and shows promise for future research (Demark-Wahnefried, Aziz, Rowland, & Pinto, 2005). Isolating this window and probing into the perceived connections would add to the understanding of activity adherence over the survivorship period.

FURTHER READING

Campbell, A., Stevinson, C., & Crank, H. (2012) The BASES expert statement on exercise and cancer survivorship. *Journal of Sports Science, 30*, 949–952. A concise overview of the role of exercise in cancer survivorship written for the British Association of Sport and Exercise Sciences.

Demark-Wahnefried, W., Aziz, N. M., Rowland, J. H., & Pinto, B. M. (2005). Riding the crest of the teachable moment: Promoting long-term health after the diagnosis of cancer. *Journal of Clinical Oncology, 23*(24), 5814–5830. This paper is a landmark addition to the scientific understanding of positive health behaviour changes following the diagnosis of cancer.

Joseph, S. (2011). *What doesn't kill us: The new psychology of posttraumatic growth.* New York: Basic Books. This book is an accessible, comprehensive review of the area of post-traumatic growth written by leading UK clinician and researcher, Professor Stephen Joseph.

Prochaska, J. O., Velicer, W. F., Rossi, J. S., Goldstein, M. G., Marcus, B. H., & Rakowski, W., et al. (1994). Stages of change and decisional balance for 12 problem behaviours. *Health Psychology, 13*(1), 39–46. This is an early paper assessing the applicability of the Trans-theoretical Model across 12 different 'problem' behaviours and the pattern of changes in decisional balance.

Rock, C. L., Doyle, C., Demark-Wahnefried, W., Meyerhardt, J., Courneya, K. S., & Schwartz, A. L., et al. (2012). Nutrition and physical activity guidelines for cancer survivors. *Cancer Journal for Clinicians, 62*, 243–274. A comprehensive discussion of issues relating to physical activity following cancer diagnosis provided by the American Cancer Society.

REFERENCES

Adamsen, L., Quist, M., Andersen, C., Moller, T., Herrstedt, J., & Kronborg, D., et al. (2009). Effect of a multimodal high-intensity exercise intervention in cancer patients undergoing chemotherapy: Randomised controlled trial. *British Medical Journal, 339*, b3410.

Ajzen, I. (1991). The theory of planned behavior. *Organizational Behavior and Human Decision Processes, 50*, 179–211.

Arndt, V., Stegmaier, C., Ziegler, H., & Brenner, H. (2006). A population-based study of the impact of specific symptoms on quality of life in women with breast cancer 1 year after diagnosis. *Cancer, 107*(10), 2496–2503.

Barber, F. D. (2012). Social support and physical activity engagement by cancer survivors. *Clinical Journal of Oncology Nursing, 16*(3), E84–98.

Baruth, M., Wilcox, S., Der Ananian, C., & Heiney, S. (in press). Effects of home-based walking on quality of life and fatigue outcomes in early stage breast cancer survivors: A 12-week pilot study. *Journal of Physical Activity and Health,, 12*, S110–S118.

Beck, A. T., Steer, R. A., & Brown, G.K. (1996). *Manual for the Beck Depression Inventory-2*: San Antonio, TX: Psychological Corporation.

Becker, M. H., Haefner, D. P., Kasl, S. V., Kirscht, J. P., Maiman, L. A., & Rosenstock, I.M. (1977). Selected psychosocial models and correlates of individual health-related behaviors. *Medical Care, 15*, 27–46.

Bennett, J. A., Lyons, K. S., Winters-Stone, K., Nail, L. M., & Scherer, J. (2007). Motivational interviewing to increase physical activity in long-term cancer survivors: A randomized controlled trial. *Nursing Research, 56*(1), 18–27.

Biddle, S. J., & Mutrie, N. (2008). *Psychology of physical activity: Determinants, well-being and interventions* (2nd ed.). London: Routledge.

Blanchard, C. M., Courneya, K. S., & Stein, K. (2008). Cancer survivors' adherence to lifestyle behavior recommendations and associations with health-related quality of life: Results from the American Cancer Society.s SCS-II. *Journal of Clinical Oncology, 26*(13), 2198–2204.

Blanchard, C. M., Denniston, M. M., Baker, F., Ainsworth, S. R., Courneya, K. S., & Hann, D. M., et al. (2003). Do adults change their lifestyle behaviors after a cancer diagnosis? *American Journal of Health Behaviour, 27*(3), 246–256.

Brady, M. J., Cella, D. F., Mo, F., Bonomi, A. E., Tulsky, D. S., & Lloyd, S. R., et al. (1997). Reliability and validity of the Functional Assessment of Cancer Therapy: Breast quality-of-life instrument. *Journal of Clinical Oncology, 15*(3), 974–986.

Braun, V., & Clarke, V. (2006). Using thematic analysis in psychology. *Qualitative Research in Psychology, 3*(2), 77–101.

Braun, V., & Clarke, V. (2013). *Successful qualitative research: A practical guide for beginners*: Thousand Oaks, CA: Sage.

Calhoun, L. G., Cann, A., & Tedeschi, R. G. (2010). The Posttraumatic Growth Model: Sociocultural considerations. In T.Weiss & R.Berger (Eds.), *Posttraumatic growth and culturally competent practice* (pp. 1–14). Hoboken, NJ: John Wiley & Sons, Inc.

Campbell, A. (2014). *Cancer rehabilitation*. Retrieved 10 October 2014 from http://canrehab.co.uk/.

Campbell, A., Mutrie, N., White, F., McGuire, F., & Kearney, N. (2005). A pilot study of a supervised group exercise programme as a rehabilitation treatment for women with breast cancer receiving adjuvant treatment. *European Journal of Oncology Nursing, 9*(1), 56–63.

Campbell, A., Stevinson, C., & Crank, H. (2012). The BASES expert statement on exercise and cancer survivorship. *Journal of Sport Science, 30*(9), 949–952.

Campbell, A., Whyte, F., & Mutrie, N. (2005). Training of clinical recruiters to improve recruitment to an exercise intervention during breast cancer treatment. *Clinical Effectiveness in Nursing, 9*(3–4), 211–213.

Cella, D. F., Tulsky, D. S., Gray, G., Sarafian, B., Linn, E., & Bonomi A., et al. (1993). The Functional Assessment of Cancer Therapy scale: Development and validation of the general measure. *Journal of Clinical Oncology, 11*(3), 570–579.

Charmaz, K. (2008). Constructionism and the grounded theory method. In J. A. Holstein & J. F. Gubrium (Eds.), *Handbook of constructionist research* (pp. 397–412). New York: Guilford Press.

Courneya, K. S., & Friedenreich, C. M. (1997). Relationship between exercise during treatment and current quality of life among survivors of breast cancer. *Journal of Psychosocial Oncology, 15*(3–4), 35–57.

Courneya, K. S., Mackey J. R., & McKenzie, D. C. (2002). Exercise for breast cancer survivors: Research evidence and clinical guidelines. *The Physician and Sportsmedicine, 30*(8), 33–42.

Craig, P., Dieppe, P., Macintyre, S., Michie, S., Nazareth, I., & Pettigrew, M. (2008). Research methods and reporting: Developing and evaluating complex interventions: The new Medical Research Council guidance. *British Medical Journal, 337*(1655).

Cramp, F., & Byron-Daniel, J. (2012). Exercise for the management of cancer-related fatigue in adults. *Cochrane Database of Systematic Reviews* (11), Art. No.: CD006145. DOI: 006110.001002/14651858.CD14006145.pub14651853.

Creswell, J. W., & Plano Clark, V. L. (2007). *Designing and conducting mixed methods research*. Thousand Oaks, CA: Sage.

CRUK. (2014). Retrieved April 2014 from http://www.cancerresearchuk.org/cancer-info/cancerstats/incidence/commoncancers/.

Demark-Wahnefried, W., Aziz, N. M., Rowland, J. H., & Pinto, B. M. (2005). Riding the crest of the teachable moment: Promoting long-term health after the diagnosis of cancer. *Journal of Clinical Oncology, 23*(24), 5814–5830.

Demark-Wahnefried, W., Morey, M. C., Sloane, R., Snyder, D. C., Miller, P .E., & Hartman, T. J., et al. (2012). Reach out to enhance wellness home-based diet-exercise intervention promotes reproducible and sustainable long-term improvements in health behaviors, body weight, and physical functioning in older, overweight/obese cancer survivors. *Journal of Clinical Oncology, 30*(19), 2354–2361.

Emslie, C., Whyte, F., Campbell, A., Mutrie, N., Lee, L., & Ritchie, D., et al. (2007). 'I wouldn't have been interested in just sitting round a table talking about cancer': Exploring the experiences of women with breast cancer in a group exercise trial. *Health Education Research, 22*(6), 827–838.

Fallowfield, L., Leaity, S., Howell, A., Benson, S., & Cella, D. (1999). Assessment of quality of life in women undergoing hormonal therapy for breast cancer: Validation of an endocrine symptom subscale for the FACT-B. *Breast Cancer Research and Treatment, 55*, 189–199.

Fine, M., & Gordon, S. (1989). Feminist transformations of/despite psychology. In M.Crawford & M.Gentry (Eds.), *Gender and thought: Psychological perspectives* (pp. 146–174). New York: Springer.

Fishbein, M., & Ajzen, I. (1975). *Belief, attitude, intention and behaviour: An introduction to theory and research*. Reading, MA: Addison-Wesley.

Flick, U. (2007). *Designing qualitative research*. Thousand Oaks, CA: Sage.

Fong, D. Y. T., Ho, J. W. C., Hui, B. P. H., Lee, A. M., Macfarlane, D. J., & Leung, S. S. K., et al. (2012). Physical activity for cancer survivors: Meta-analysis of randomised controlled trials. *British Medical Journal, 344*(7844), 1–14.

Frank, A. W. (2002). *At the will of the body: Reflections on illness*. Boston, MA: Houghton Mifflin Harcourt.

Hallal, P. C., Andersen, L. B., Bull, F. C., Guthold, R., Haskell, W., & Ekelund, U. (2012). Global physical activity levels: Surveillance progress, pitfalls, and prospects. *The Lancet, 380*(9838), 247–257.

Halverstadt, A., & Leonard, A. (2000). *Essential exercises for breast cancer survivors*. Boston, MA: Harvard Common Press.

Hawkins, N. A., Smith, T. Z., Luhua, R. J., Berkowitz, Z., & Stein, K. D. (2010). Health-related behavior change after cancer: Results of the American Cancer Society's studies of cancer survivors (SCS). *Journal of Cancer Survivorship, 4*(1), 20–32.

Hefferon, K., & Gil-Rodriguez, E. (2011). Interpretative phenomenological analysis. *Psychologist, 24*(10), 756–759.

Hefferon, K., Grealy, M., & Mutrie, N. (2008). The perceived influence of an exercise class intervention on the process and outcomes of post-traumatic growth. *Mental Health and Physical Activity, 1*(1), 32–39.

Hefferon, K., Murphy, H., McLeod, J., Mutrie, N., & Campbell, A. (2013). Understanding barriers to exercise implementation 5-year post-breast cancer diagnosis: A large-scale qualitative study. *Health Education Research, 28*(5), 843–856.

Howitt, D., & Cramer, D. (2007). *Introduction to research methods in psychology*. New York: Pearson Education.

Ibrahim, E. M., & Al-Homaidh, A. (2011). Physical activity and survival after breast cancer diagnosis: Meta-analysis of published studies. *Medical Oncology, 28*, 753–765.

Joseph, S., Murphy, D., & Regel, S. (2012). An affective–cognitive processing model of post-traumatic growth. *Clinical Psychology & Psychotherapy, 19*(4), 316–325.

Kirk, A. F., Barnett, J., & Mutrie, N. (2007). Physical activity consultation for people with Type 2 diabetes: Evidence and guidelines. *Diabetic Medicine, 24*(8), 809–816.

Kuijpers, W., Groen, W. G., Aaronson, N. K., & van Harten, W. H. (2013). A systematic review of web-based interventions for patient empowerment and physical activity in chronic diseases: Relevance for cancer survivors. *Journal of Medical Internet Research, 15*(2), e37.

Kwan, M. L., Cohn, J. C., Armer, J. M., Stewart, B. R., & Cormier, J. N. (2011). Exercise in patients with lymphedema: A systematic review of the contemporary literature. *Journal of Cancer Survivorship, 5*(4), 320–336.

Linley, P. A., & Joseph, S. (2004). Positive change following trauma and adversity: A review. *Journal of Traumatic Stress, 17*(1), 11–21.

Loprinzi, P. D., & Cardinal, B. J. (2013). Self-efficacy mediates the relationship between behavioral processes of change and physical activity in older breast cancer survivors. *Breast Cancer, 20*(1), 47–52.

Loughlan, C., & Mutrie, N. (1995). Conducting an exercise consultation: Guidelines for health professionals. *Journal of the Institute of Health Education, 33*(3), 78–82.

Lowther, M., Mutrie, N., Loughlan, C., & McFarlane, C. (1999). Development of a Scottish physical activity questionnaire: A tool for use in physical activity interventions. *British Journal of Sports Medicine, 33*, 244–249.

Marcus, B. H., Eaton, C. A., Rossi J. S., & Harlow, L. L. (1994). Self-efficacy, decision-making, and stages of change: An integrative model of physical exercise. *Journal of Applied Social Psychology, 24*, 489–508.

Marcus, B. H, & Simkin, L. (1994). The transtheoretical model: Applications to exercise behaviour. *Medicine & Science in Sports & Exercise, 26*(11), 1400–1404.

Marshall, S. J., & Biddle, S. J. (2001). The transtheoretical model of behavior change: A meta-analysis of applications to physical activity and exercise. *Annals of Behavioural Medicine, 23*(4), 229–246.

Matthews, C. E., Wilcox, S., Hanby, C. L., Der Ananian, C., Heiney, S.P., & Gebretsadik, T. et al. (2007). Evaluation of a 12-week home-based walking intervention for breast cancer survivors. *Supportive Care in Cancer, 15*(2), 203–211.

McGavin, C. R., Gupta, S. P., & McHardy, G. J. R. (1976). Twelve-minute walking test for assessing disability in chronic bronchitis. *British Medical Journal, 1*, 822–823.

McNeely, M. L., Campbell, K. L., Rowe, B. H., Klassen, T. P., Mackey, J. R., & Courneya, K. S. (2006). Effects of exercise on breast cancer patients and survivors: A systematic review and meta-analysis. *Canadian Medical Association Journal, 175*(1), 34–41.

Merleau-Ponty, M. (1962). *Phenomenology of perception*. London: Routledge.

Miller, W. R., & Rollnick, S. (2002). *Motivational interviewing: Preparing people for change* (2nd ed.). New York: Guilford Press.

Mishra, S. I., Scherer, R. W., Geigle, P. M, Berlanstein, D. R., Topaloglu, O., & Gotay, C. C., et al. (2012). Exercise interventions on health-related quality of life for cancer survivors. *Cochrane Database of Systematic Reviews* (8), Art. No.: CD007566. DOI:007510.001002/14651858.CD14007566.pub14651852.

Mitchell, A., Chan, M., Bhatti, H., Halton, M., Grassi, L., & Johansen, C., et al. (2011). Prevalence of depression, anxiety, and adjustment disorder in oncological, haematological, and palliative-care settings: A meta-analysis of 94 interview-based studies. *The Lancet Oncology, 12*(2), 160–174.

Mock, V., Frangakis, C., Davidson, N. E., Ropka, M. E., Pickett, M., & Poniatowski B., et al. (2005). Exercise manages fatigue during breast cancer treatment: A randomized controlled trial. *Psycho-oncology, 14*, 464–477.

Mosher, C. E., Lipkus, I., Sloane, R., Snyder, D. C., Lobach, D. F., & Demark-Wahnefried, W. (2013). Long-term outcomes of the FRESH START trial: Exploring the role of self-efficacy in cancer survivors' maintenance of dietary practices and physical activity. *Psychooncology, 22*(4), 876–885.

Murphy, H., Hefferon, K., McLeod, J., Mutrie, N., & Campbell, A. (submitted). 'I feel alive when I exercise. That's the difference, I feel alive!' Embedding exercise into everyday life: the five-year breast cancer diagnosis follow-up. *Health Education Research*.

Mutrie, N., Campbell, A., Barry, S., Hefferon, K., McConnachie, A., and Ritchie, D., et al. (2012). Five-year follow-up of participants in a randomised controlled trial showing benefits from exercise for breast cancer survivors during adjuvant treatment. Are there lasting effects? *Journal of Cancer Survivorship, 6*(4), 420–430.

Mutrie, N., Campbell, A. M., Whyte, F., McConnachie, A., Emslie, C., & Lee, L., et al. (2007). Benefits of supervised group exercise programme for women being treated for early stage breast cancer: Pragmatic randomised controlled trial. *British Medical Journal, 334*(7592), 517.

Pescatello, L. (2014). *ACSM's guidelines for exercise testing and prescription* (Vol. 9). Philadelphia: Wolters Kluwer/Lippincott Williams & Wilkins Health.

Prochaska, J. O., & DiClemente, C. C. (1984). Self change processes, self efficacy and decisional balance across five stages of smoking cessation. *Progress in Clinical and Biological Research, 156*, 131–140.

Prochaska, J. O., Norcross, J. C., Fowler, J. L., Follick, M. J., & Abrams, D. B. (1992). Attendance and outcome in work site weight control program – processess and stages of change as process and predictor variables. *Addictive Behaviors, 17*(1), 35–45.

Prochaska, J. O., & Velicer, W. F. (1996). Addiction versus stages of change models in predicting smoking cessation – on models, methods and premature conclusions – Comment. *Addiction, 91*(9), 1281–1283.

Prochaska, J. O., Velicer, W. F., Rossi, J. S., Goldstein, M. G., Marcus, B. H., & Rakowski, W., et al. (1994). Stages of change and decisional balance for 12 problem behaviors. *Health Psychology, 13*(1), 39–46.

Rajotte, E. J., Yi, J. C., Baker, K. S., Gregerson, L., Leiserowitz, A., & Syrjala, K. L. (2012). Community-based exercise program effectiveness and safety for cancer survivors. *Journal of Cancer Survivorship, 6*(2), 219–228.

Rogers, L. Q., Courneya, K. S., Shah, P., Dunnington, G., & Hopkins-Price, P. (2007). Exercise stage of change, barriers, expectations, values and preferences among breast cancer patients during treatment: A pilot study. *European Journal of Cancer Care, 16*(1), 55–66.

Rogers, L. Q., Markwell, S. J., Courneya, K. S., McAuley, E., & Verhulst, S. (2009). Exercise preference patterns, resources, and environment among rural breast cancer survivors. *Journal of Rural Health, 25*(4), 388–391.

Rollnick, S., Butler, C. C., McCambridge, J., Kinnersley, P., Elwyn, G., & Resnicow, K. (2005). Consultations about changing behaviour. *British Medical Journal, 331*(7522), 961–963.

Scott, J. M., Lakoski, S., Mackey, J. R., Douglas, P. S., Haykowsky, M. J., & Jones, L. W. (2013). The potential role of aerobic exercise to modulate cardiotoxicity of molecularly targeted cancer therapeutics. *The Oncologist, 18*(2), 221–231.

Segal, R., Evans, W., Johnson, D., Smith, J., Colletta, S., & Gayton, J., et al. (2001). Structured exercise improves physical functioning in women with stages I and II breast cancer: Results of a randomized controlled trial. *Journal of Clinical Oncology, 19*(3), 657–665.

Shapiro, C. L., & Recht, A. (2001). Side effects of adjuvant treatment of breast cancer. *New England Journal of Medicine, 344*, 1997–2008.

Shimozuma, K., Ganz, P. A, Petersen, L., & Hirji, K. (1999). Quality of life in the first year after breast cancer surgery: Rehabilitation needs and patterns of recovery. *Breast Cancer Research and Treatment, 56*(1), 45–57.

Smith, J. A, Flowers, P., & Larkin, M. (2009). *Interpretative phenomenological analysis: Theory, method and research*. Thousand Oaks, CA: Sage.

Speck, R. M., Courneya, K. S., Mâsse, L., Duval, S., & Schmitz, K. H. (2010). An update of controlled physical activity trials in cancer survivors: A systematic review and meta-analysis. *Journal of Cancer Survivorship, 4*(2), 87–100.

Tedeschi, R. G., & Calhoun, L. G. (1996). The Posttraumatic Growth Inventory: Measuring the positive legacy of trauma. *Journal of Traumatic Stress, 9*(3), 455–471.

Vincent, F., Labourey, J. L., Leobon, S., Antonini, M. T., Lavau-Denes, S., & Tubiana-Mathieu, N. (2013). Effects of a home-based walking training program on cardiorespiratory fitness in breast cancer patients receiving adjuvant chemotherapy: A pilot study. *European Journal of Physical Rehabilitation Medicine, 49*(3), 319–329.

Watson, D., Clark, L. A., & Tellegen, A. (1988). Development and validation of brief measures of positive and negative effect: The PANAS scales. *Journal of Personality and Social Psychology, 54*(6), 1063–1070.

Winters-Stone, K., Schwartz, A., & Nail, L. (2010). A review of exercise interventions to improve bone health in adult cancer survivors. *Journal of Cancer Survivorship, 4*(3), 187–201.

Wolin, K. Y., Schwartz, A. L., Matthews, C. E., Courneya, K. S., & Schmitz, K. H. (2012). Implementing the exercise guidelines for cancer survivors. *Journal of Supportive Oncology, 10*(5), 171–177.

Yellen, S. B., Cella, D. F., Webster, K., Blendowski, C., & Kaplan, E. (1997). Measuring fatigue and other anemia-related symptoms with the Functional Assessment of Cancer Therapy (FACT) measurement system. *Journal of Pain and Symptom Management, 13*(2), 63–74.

Zwarenstein, M., Treweek, S., Gagnier, J. J., Altman, D. G., Tunis, S., & Haynes, B., et al. (2008). Improving the reporting of pragmatic trials: An extension of the CONSORT statement. *British Medical Journal, 337*, a2390.

Index

Page numbers with an *f* or *t* suffix refer to figures and tables.